NIGHT THOUGHTS

The Surreal Life of the Poet
David Gascoyne

BY ROBERT FRASER

OXFORD
UNIVERSITY PRESS

OXFORD
UNIVERSITY PRESS

Great Clarendon Street, Oxford OX2 6DP

Oxford University Press is a department of the University of Oxford.
It furthers the University's objective of excellence in research, scholarship,
and education by publishing worldwide in

Oxford New York

Auckland Cape Town Dar es Salaam Hong Kong Karachi
Kuala Lumpur Madrid Melbourne Mexico City Nairobi
New Delhi Shanghai Taipei Toronto

With offices in

Argentina Austria Brazil Chile Czech Republic France Greece
Guatemala Hungary Italy Japan Poland Portugal Singapore
South Korea Switzerland Thailand Turkey Ukraine Vietnam

Oxford is a registered trade mark of Oxford University Press
in the UK and in certain other countries

Published in the United States
by Oxford University Press Inc., New York

© Robert Fraser 2012

The moral rights of the author have been asserted
Database right Oxford University Press (maker)

First published 2012 by Oxford University Press

British Library Cataloguing in Publication Data

Data available

Library of Congress Cataloging in Publication Data

Data available

Typeset by SPI Publisher Services, Pondicherry, India
Printed in Great Britain
on acid-free paper by
MPG Books Group, Bodmin and King's Lynn

ISBN 978–0–19–955814–8

1 3 5 7 9 10 8 6 4 2

Acknowledgements

Throughout the writing of this book I have enjoyed the full support both of David Gascoyne's literary executor Stephen Stuart-Smith of the Enitharmon Press and of the poet's widow and personal executor, the late Judy Gascoyne. I am deeply grateful to both of them for the time and material that they put at my disposal, their permission to quote, their generosity of spirit, and the enthusiasm with which they both followed my halting progress. Judy died in June 2010, and it is a cause of some sadness to me that I will not be able to place a copy of this book in her hands. Without her cheerfulness and determination the story it has to tell in its closing chapters would have been almost inconceivably different. My debt to her is both incalculable and, I fear, now unpayable.

Nobody who undertakes any writing, critical or biographical, about this particular subject can remain ignorant for long of how much is owed to the most accomplished and diligent of all Gascoyne scholars. Dr Roger Scott has devoted the better part of two decades to pursuing all sorts of related trails, tracking down and frequently transcribing notebooks, drafts, and other written material across the world, and in several instances seeing this work into print for the very first time. Roger not only shared his copious knowledge with me but valiantly answered all sorts of nagging and inconvenient questions, especially at proof stage. I am also deeply grateful to Christine Jordis, the French translator of David's journals, who on three separate occasions spared precious hours from her busy professional schedule in Paris, made available to me Gascoyne's letters to her over a thirty-year period, and proved an invaluable source of information on the re-establishment of his presence and reputation in France from 1979 onwards. I would also like to thank Professor Michel Remy of the University of Nice who met me early on in my preparations and helped contextualize Gascoyne's youthful writing within the shifting frame of the Surrealist movement, Continental and British.

It was the poet Andrew McNeillie who in his then capacity as commissioning editor for literature at the Oxford University Press first manifested a desire to publish this biography, and then took the steps to make this possible. I warmly thank him, the Delegates of the Press, and his successors Jacqueline Baker and Ariane Petit for their commitment, their attention to detail, and their moral and professional encouragement over three years. During the second year of preparation the Beinecke Manuscript and Rare Book Collection at Yale elected me to a Jackson Brothers Fellowship to spend one month in New Haven accessing their extensive Gascoyne holdings. Frank M. Turner, its director, made this possible; during my enjoyable stay and since, Naomi Saito was scrupulous in her attention to my research needs, and I received prompt assistance from Kevin Repp, who arranged and chaired my talks at the Beinecke, and from Susan Klein, Laurie Klein, Leah Jehan, Moira Fitzgerald, Kathryn James, Anne Marie Menta, and Rebecca Martz. The Open University put funds at my disposal enabling me to visit Aix-en-Provence, and defrayed the cost of the colour illustrations. I am further indebted to the staff of several other libraries and archives for their attention and support: to the curators and desk staff of the British Library in London, the Bibliothèque Nationale in Paris, the Gabrielle Kieller Collection of the Scottish National Gallery of Art in Edinburgh, the Wren Library at Trinity College, Cambridge, the library of the Faculté des Lettres, Université de Provence, Les Archives Municipales d'Aix-en-Provence, the Berg Collection at New York Public Library, the McFarlin Library at the University of Tulsa in Oklahoma; the Wellcome Library, University of London; the London Metropolitan Archives; the National Art Library, Victoria and Albert Museum, London; the Library of the Open University, the archives of Oxford University Press (and especially my old friend Martin Maw), of Tate Britain, Westminster University, Salisbury Cathedral School, Bedales School, Gonville and Caius College, Cambridge, the Royal Literary Fund, and, through the agency of Henrik Lundback, the Danish Resistance Museum in Copenhagen.

I am grateful to Brian Keeble, Literary Executor for the Estate of Kathleen Raine, for permission to quote from her writings, published and unpublished, and to Curtis Brown and the literary estate of Lawrence Durrell for permission to quote in full Durrell's poem 'Journal', which is dedicated to Gascoyne. I am further grateful to Lucian Freud and his agent Diana Rawston for permission to reproduce Plates 15 and 16 in high-quality reproductions by the photographer John Riddy, to the Tate Modern for Plate 11, to Tony Penrose and the Roland Penrose Estate for Plate 12, and to the Estate of Graham Sutherland for the woodcuts and lithographs assembled in Plate 18.

From almost the very beginning Marcus Williamson, administrator of the Gascoyne website, together with his partner in life Corella, have entered into this project with an alacrity and intelligence that I found heartening, ferreting out places, references, and links, serving as hosts, guides, and drivers in the South of France and Cornwall, and on one occasion scouting wooded slopes in search of an elusive Gascoyne residence. Several other individuals, both in France and in England, also proved unstinting, either in their provision of material or in the sharing of insights and advice. Among them I wish especially to thank Dannie Abse, Professor Roger Ackling, Jean Ackling, Jamie Andrews, Dennis Archer, Liz Baird, Sebastian Barker, Hilary Barker, Colin Benford, Philippa Bernard, Sandra Boselli, Victoria Braybrooke, Alan Brownjohn, Alastair Brotchie, Angela Buckland, Richard Burns, Simon Callow, Michel Carassou, Dr Sandra O'Connell, Diane de Margerie, Michèle Duclos, Professor John Edwards, Robin Ford, Romona Fotiade, Simon Frost, Kate Griffin, Anne Goossens, Lucie Guillevic, Eileen Gunn, Eleanor Harding, Dr Brian Hinton MBE, Professor Hermione Lee, Peter Janson-Smith, the late Dr David Kelley, Dr Jean Khalfa, Jenny Lewis, Grevil Lindop, Professor David MacKitterick, Professor Jean-Yves Masson, Julian Nangle, Sue Oldershaw, Tony Penrose, Lee Plumley, Jeremy Reed, John Riddy, Stephen Romer, Bettina Shaw-Lawrence, Julia Shaw-Lawrence, André Luck, Pierre Oster, Clive Sinclair, Iain Sinclair, Peter L. Smith, Jane Snaider, Professor Jon Stallworthy, Ron Stocker, Salah Stétié, Liz Taylor, Professor Norman Vance, Ruth Valentine, and Dr Guy Williams.

My wife Catherine accompanied me on several expeditions, and proved an indispensable source of astute questions during several interviews. During the writing process my son Benjo supplied unflustered technical backup. Rowena Anketell was admirably sensitive and meticulous in her attention to the copy-editing, as was Douglas Matthews FRSL in his to the Index. Last and far from least, my brother-in-law Dr Peter Birkett of Columbia University's Medical Faculty provided accommodation during several American forays, professional information of much relevance to my theme, and most of the solutions during our weekly recreational assaults on the *TLS* crossword.

Contents

NIGHT THREE: 1964–2001

List of Plates

Sources and Abbreviations

For much of his life David Gascoyne was a conscientious, if inconsistent, steward of his own early editions, manuscripts, letters, journals and drafts. But he was also a magnanimous man who tended to lend books and papers to people, and then forget to whom he had lent them. He was also fairly peripatetic in his early years, and had a tendency to leave caches of papers in odd places, and with a variety of acquaintances in different countries. As a result the Gascoyne archive was at one time exceptionally widespread, to the extent that its originator suspected it of being unrecoverable. Happily, there had been some consistencies. Shortly after the war, when staying with his friend Robin Waterfield in the Edgware Road, Gascoyne had entrusted several boxes of material to his friend's care. He had also abandoned quite a lot of manuscripts in America during his stay there in 1951–2. During the late fifties, while living in France, he had ditched other bundles in Aix or Paris. When Waterfield returned to Britain on leave from Isfahan in 1966 he arranged for the material in his possession to be assessed for value; with the help of a grant from the Arts Council it was then acquired by the British Library and became the nucleus of their important Gascoyne collection. About the same time Alan Clodd arrived on the scene as David's protector, agent, friend, and eventual publisher. Clodd saw to it that the surviving papers were classified and others restored, and in his capacity as agent sold large quantities of manuscripts, ephemera, and pictures to international libraries to help keep David financially afloat. Other items serendipitously turned up. As a result, large batches of Gascoyne's papers, artwork, and recordings were acquired from 1975 by the Beinecke Rare Book and Manuscript Library at Yale, who at present hold more Gascoyniana than any other library in the world, and the McFarline Library at Tulsa. In the 1990s much of this material was accessed by Roger Scott, who edited selected items for publication, mostly by Enitharmon, which had already issued the miraculously rediscovered journals, and had in the meantime been inherited by Stephen Stuart-Smith, who remained Gascoyne's publisher until the poet's death in 2001, and has continued to issue much that is of interest since. At Judy Gascoyne's death, which occurred when this book was already well advanced, Enitharmon inherited one final trove of papers from the marital home, and generously allowed me access to it as my work went through its revision stage.

The fullest guide to Gascoyne's printed output up until his sixty-ninth year, whether in separate volumes, anthologies, or periodicals, remains Colin T. Benford's *David Gascoyne: A Bibliography of His Works (1929–1985)* (Ryde: The Heritage Press, 1986). Colin has since continued his work in longhand, and gracefully allowed me to make full use of the resulting listings. I have, however, chosen to restrict citations to essential sources in the belief that banked-up notes at the bottom of the page look unattractive and unwelcoming. Certain compendia or single works by Gascoyne are referred to repeatedly, in which cases I have economized by adopting abbreviated titles in the footnotes.

Collected Journals	*Collected Journals 1936–42*, introd. Kathleen Raine (London: Skoob Books, 1991).
Collected Poems (1965)	*Collected Poems*, ed. and introd. Robin Skelton (London: Oxford University Press, 1965).
Collected Poems (1988)	*New and Collected Poems* (London: Oxford University Press, 1988).
Collected Verse Translations	*Collected Verse Translations*, ed. Alan Clodd and Robin Skelton (London: Oxford University Press, 1970).
Journal 1936–1937	*Journal 1936–1937* with *Death of An Explorer* and *Leon Chestov* (London: Enitharmon, 1980).
Journal 1937–1939	*Paris Journal 1937–1939*, pref. Lawrence Durrell (London: Enitharmon, 1978).
Poems 1937–1942	*Poems 1937–1942* (London: Editions Poetry London, 1943).
Selected Poems	*Selected Poems* (London: Enitharmon, 1994).
Selected Prose	*Selected Prose 1934–1996*, ed. Roger Scott, introd. Kathleen Raine (London: Enitharmon, 1998).
Selected Verse Translations	*Selected Verse Translations*, ed. Alan Clodd and Robin Skelton, introd. Roger Scott (London: Enitharmon, 1996).

Short Survey	*A Short Survey of Surrealism* (London: Enitharmon, 2000).

For other printed sources, whether by Gascoyne or not, the publisher and the place and year of publication are given in each case alongside the first citation within a given chapter. Unless otherwise indicated, the translations offered are by the author. For repeatedly cited archival collections and sound recordings, the following abbreviations have been used:

Beinecke	Beinecke Rare Books and Manuscript Library, Yale University, David Gascoyne Collection Gen. MSS 529, 24 Boxes, 395 files.
Berg	Berg Collection, New York Public Library.
BL Add.	Additional Manuscripts, Department of Manuscripts, British Library.
BL Lives	British Library Sound Archive, National Life Story Collection, Lives of the Artists, C 466/03, David Gascoyne's interviewed by Mel Gooding, 6 tapes numbered F1380-F1385, recorded Northwood, I-O-W, 9-10 Mar. 1991.
Enitharmon Papers	Material collected from Northwood subsequent to Judy Gascoyne's death, since lodged in the British Library's Department of Manuscripts as Deposit 10670 uncatalogued, and as yet uncatalogued.
JOT	Julian Otto Trevelyan papers in the Wren Library, Trinity College, Cambridge.
LMA	London Metropolitan Archives.
OUP	Archives of the Oxford University Press.
RLF	The archives of the Royal Literary Fund.
TGA	Tate Gallery Archive 9326/1/39, Meraud Guevara Collection.
Tulsa	Department of Special Collections and University Archives, McFarline Library, University of Tulsa at Oklahoma, David Emery Gascoyne Papers, 1985-2001.
Waterfield Papers BL	Papers of Robert and Sophie Waterfield, lodged in the British Library's Department of Manuscripts as Deposit 10511, and as yet uncatalogued.

I have for the most part avoided cross-referring to parallel sources except where the duplication seemed significant. The author of *A Short Survey of Surrealism* lived a long life: economy in its documentation, however, seemed a lesson this study should learn from that seminal text.

Epigraph

So Hölderlin's soul went travelling. And from its travels it brought back great splendours and deep anguishes. It went far away and lived in various times, among the gods and among men. It took note of what it saw and was possessed of the great desire to say nothing that was not true. Formerly, the poet had thought the soul sufficed to render what he had seen; but now the soul knows that the world is there, and that one must listen for a long while, and that in the great silence of ourselves it is scarcely granted us to render the voices that come to us from every side and the images that pass by when one flies over the lands below. But sometimes the sounds and the images escape him and become confused, or rather it does not know how to render them exactly as they were and without mixing something of its own with them. It is in these moments that it feels a deep distress because it is afraid of losing the images and no longer hearing the sounds from the moment it is no longer sure of being able to fix them.

Therefore it goes on long voyages and tries to say what it sees; but never did it find itself so alone. For those who stay at home remain in themselves, and a great solitude unites all men. But those who travel far and hear voices unheard by the others, do not know community. They know that they are not understood. Nor at the same time can they keep silence; for one must speak of what one has seen. The voices demand it and one cannot disobey them.

David Gascoyne's translation of Bernard Groethuysen,
'Avant-Propos' to *Poèmes de la Folie de Hölderlin*, a French
translation from the German by Pierre Jean Jouve
and Pierre Klossowski (1930), 17–18.

Consequently I rejoice, having to construct something
Upon which to rejoice ...

T. S. Eliot, 'Ash Wednesday', 1930.

e 'l pensamento in sogno trasmutai.

Dante, *Purgatorio*, xviii. 145.

Twilight

Two Deaths

On the gentle counter-escarpment of the Mont-Sainte-Geneviève, round the corner from the bustle of the Rue Mouffetard, lies one of the most tranquil and, in more senses than one, elevated streets in Paris. In the seventeenth century, when the Rue Rollin was known as the Rue Neuve-Saint-Etienne, two of the most distinguished thinkers in all of France were counted among its residents. In the 1640s René Descartes spent the Parisian interludes of his prolonged employment in the Netherlands in a house now numbered 14, towards the street's western end, and in the 1660s Blaise Pascal lodged in a dwelling towards the eastern end, leaving his posthumously published *Pensées* unfinished at his death there in August 1662. From 'cogito ergo sum' to 'le silence éternel de ces espaces infinis m'effraie', this narrow and sloping byway—ignored by most tourists and unknown to many otherwise well-informed Parisians—encompasses much of the history of immediate pre-Enlightenment European thought.

In the nineteenth century the soon-to-be renamed alley lost its last few houses to make way for the long grind of the Rue Monge below, towards which two steep flights of steps now descend. Nowadays the Rue Rollin is a hard-to-find impasse, its red and grey cobbles running between restored houses with wall-bracketed lamps and balconies bearing geraniums in pots. The most obvious change, however, is among the more recent, since at its eastern extremity, in front of what was Pascal's house and at the summit of the steps, a ring of kerbstones around a water sluice has been renamed 'La Place Benjamin Fondane'. Two signs in the municipality's regulation blue explain this as an act of homage to 'Benjamin Fondane 1898–1944, Poet and Philosopher, Deported, Assassinated in Auschwitz'. Outside number 6, a broad-fronted house with a scroll-framed entrance, a marble slab further explains that Fondane—a Romanian exile, film-maker, and writer in several genres—lived there between 15 April 1932 and 7 March 1944, and from there was sent to his death. It goes on to quote these lines from his prose poem 'Sur les fleuves de Babylon':

> 'Remember only that I was innocent and, like you fellow mortals of my time, possessed like yours a face marked by anger, pity and by joy.'[1]

In the bleak winter nights of 1937, a very tall, very lean, and somewhat introspective English poet made his way each week towards this house from his garret room off the Rue Saint-Jacques. David Gascoyne had a growing reputation in England and France as a champion and proponent of the Surrealist movement, about which he had recently published a trenchant little book. Already he had sketched out—in French as it happened—the first manifesto of the English Surrealist movement behind which he was one of the prime movers, just as he had provided a key element in the organization of the International Surrealist Exhibition in London the following year. Yet Gascoyne was already disillusioned with the politics and ideology of the movement, and he knew that Fondane, a one-time Dadaist who had broken with André Breton, was similarly disenchanted. In search of new insights and a fresh direction, he believed Fondane, with whom he had been corresponding for some months, could help him find them. He had, of course, no intimation then of Fondane's eventual fate. Yet seventy years later, when I started work on this book, I was well aware that the arrest and gassing of this protean central European intellectual, a man who had always worn his Jewishness quite lightly, was to come in later years to wound my subject's spirit deeply, and to inform his understanding.

Gascoyne was to lose several close associates during the war, many under cruel circumstances. At least one other loss, as I rapidly ascertained, had encumbered him more than he usually dared say. Bent von Müllen had been almost exactly David's own age, a student and seeker from the affluent coastal town of Skodsborg in Denmark. They had met in Paris shortly after Gascoyne's first encounter with Fondane, had enjoyed a brief but—for Gascoyne at least—fairly intense love affair, and then von Müllen had returned home. Gascoyne had lost touch with him during the confusions of the war years, and shortly before the Armistice he had written to his family

---

1. From 'Sur les fleuves de Babylon', prose preface to Benjamin Fondane, *L'Exode* (Paris: Sernet, 1965), 13–16.

address in an attempt to resume contact. He had received a brief letter from Bent's mother informing him that, a few months previously and in the last few months of the Nazi occupation, her son had been hanged—together with his father and several neighbours—in retaliation for the murder of a senior member of the local Gestapo. Gascoyne wrote nothing about this harsh discovery at the time, yet in June 1964, when he was lying in a suburban Parisian psychiatric hospital after the first of his serious mental breakdowns, he was to portray himself spiritually as a widow: 'The fears which so much conditioned the subconscious of my youth', he then surmised, 'had a perfectly real origin. After all, the most beloved friend of my life was hanged by the Nazis as a hostage (so was his father).'[2]

It was some time before the dreadful details of the deaths of two men who had once been so close to him were to become generally known. Fondane at least seems always to have had a strong feeling of foreboding. In June 1939, some months before the German invasion, he had alarmed his Argentinian fellow writer Victoria Ocampo by entrusting to her care some of his most precious typescripts—transcripts of conversations with his mentor, the exiled Russian philosopher Léon Chestov—telling her that he doubted he would survive to see them through the press. In August 1940 he had been interned in a prisoner-of-war camp then, escaping, had lived in virtual hiding in his Rue Rollin apartment for several months until, losing patience with his isolation, he had begun to flaunt himself in the streets. Someone, possibly the concierge, had then denounced him and he had been taken away to the military camp at Drancy, and thence to Poland. Two years later André Montagne, a fellow prisoner who had escaped execution and survived the rigours of the camp, told of his last days.

Fondane had arrived in the camp under his birth name of Weschler in the late spring of 1944, and was almost immediately put to hard labour building stone terraces. Within weeks his delicate constitution had succumbed, and in September he was admitted to the infirmary. 'I remember vividly', Montagne later wrote, 'how he processed between the rows of beds, paying visits to French friends who had been admitted like himself, a rough coverlet thrown across his back above his threadbare shirt (he had not managed to procure himself a proper gown).' It was, Montagne felt, as if Fondane was still holding court in some private Parisian salon: he even wrote a poem for the younger man's birthday, scrawled on greasy margarine wrapping, all that he had.

---

2. 'My First Post-Apocalyptic Notebook', 1964, Tulsa, Section B (Notebooks) 2.3, Entry for 15 May.

Towards the end of the month, judged restored, he was returned to hard labour. But the advancing Russian army was now within 130 kilometres of Auschwitz, and the commandant determined to exterminate those prisoners deemed too weak for a forced march. On Saturday morning, 30 September, they were rounded up in Block Ten. 'We knew that they were going to be gassed. Fondane knew it too.' The following Monday afternoon, 2 October, in tipping rain, the lorries arrived to collect them. There were 700 to be transported that day. 'I saw Fondane emerge from the block, pass right in front of the SS, button the collar of his vest to protect himself against the cold and wet, then climb into the truck.' The laden vehicles groaned towards Birkenau. 'Two hours later, our comrades were dead.'[3]

Gascoyne had already published a poem in honour of his mentor; in 1948, after news of the execution got through, he retitled it 'I.M. Benjamin Fondane.'[4] In later years he would pay several further tributes, though the open space in front of the house in the Rue Rollin, where David had often walked, was not named after his friend until 2006, five years after Gascoyne's own natural death. Much of this I already knew, but von Müllen's fate continued to puzzle me: Gascoyne had not talked of it until 1991, and the details seemed hazy (the letter from Bent's mother, for example, had long since disappeared). In 2008, one year into the biography, I decided to learn more, and wrote through a friend to the Danish Resistance Museum in Copenhagen. There was a long pause, and then I received a very precise, very terrible answer.

Like Gascoyne, though unbeknown to him, von Müllen had opted during the war years to sign on as an actor with a touring theatre group. In December 1944 the company had been performing a Christmas show at the Royal Theatre in Odense, when news came through that Hardvig Larsen, a Danish member of the pro-Nazi security forces, had just been eliminated by the so-called 'Peter Group', the active terrorist cell of the national resistance movement. In Copenhagen the Gestapo high command decided on punitive action: they sent a telex though to their branch office in Kolding, some ninety kilometres to the west of Odense, and ordered a retaliatory killing. As the Reich crumbled around them, the local Nazi authorities were becoming increasingly jumpy and desperate: victims were now being selected on

---

3. André Montagne, 'Les Derniers Jours de Benjamin Fondane mort d'un des nôtres', *Non-Lieu*, 2 (Special Fondane Number, ed. Michel Carassou; 1978), 65–6; repr. from *Les Lettres françaises*, 26 Apr. 1946, 5.
4. David Gascoyne, 'I.M. Benjamin Fondane', *Poems 1937–1942* (Poetry London Editions, 3rd impression, 1948), 13–14. Neither previous impression carries the 'I.M.'.

grounds of national prominence rather than any connection with a given incident. Among von Müllen's troupe was the matinee idol Arne von David, sufficiently recognizable to target, and sufficiently celebrated to serve as an example. On the morning of 29 December three of the collaborators from Kolding drove across to Odense and set up temporary headquarters in the local agricultural college. Learning that the leading man was not in town that day, they decided to exterminate another member of the company, and in the early evening, as soon as the box office opened, Nedermann Hansen walked over to the theatre to buy a programme, in which von Müllen's photograph was clearly displayed. When the performance ended at 9 o'clock, the revenge squad were waiting at the stage door. As each member of the company left the building they requested an ID card. When Bent appeared chatting with one male and two female colleagues, he was instantly spotted. Bothildsen Nielsen asked him for his card, and as soon as it was produced, he shot him directly through the head. The actresses ran screaming, and Nielsen discharged his remaining ammunition into von Müllen's neck and brain, and left him bleeding on the ground. The three officers then walked briskly back through the Royal Gardens, and caught a bus back to the college.

These facts were not published until 2004, and it is just as well that Gascoyne was then past reading them.[5] Quite why his own version of his lover's death was circumstantially at variance—though symbolically surely much the same—I do not know. Perhaps he had misremembered the contents of Fru von Müllen's letter, written, read, and probably destroyed some fifty years before, merging in his mind collateral details. Or perhaps she had attempted to spare his raw feelings by offering him a less dreadful, potentially a more sublime, picture of the truth. Or perhaps—just perhaps—she was herself not fully aware of the gruesome nature of her son's death. The personal and historical burden implied by the passing of two such intimates—revered teacher and heart's desire—mown down within four months of one another when the German menace was fast crumbling in Europe, remains nonetheless unassailable.

When I began this biography I had no inkling of these facts, though the names of both Fondane and von Müllen were well known to me. Gascoyne in old age was a tactful and courteous presence, generous and precise in his recollections when asked, but reluctant to reveal his deeper feelings, the clues to which lay in piles of old journals, and in his poems. He was easy to

5. Frank Bøgh, *Peter-Gruppen: tysk terror i Danmark* (Hellerup: Documentas 2004), 184.

warm to. For me personally furthermore, there were points of affinity. I had already written a biography of his lifelong friend George Barker, a poet so different in temperament, whose gusto for life—and markedly contrasted private life—had invariably, Gascoyne soon told me, cheered him up. I had also enough in common with my subject to approach his life with some understanding. Both us had grown up on the banks of the Thames, both had sung in the choirs of one of the great southern cathedrals, an experience which for both of us had proved lasting in its influence. Both of us were drawn towards France and French literature in our twenties, and both had at different times lived in the same Paris street: la Rue de la Bûcherie, a quaint thoroughfare twisting along the *quais* of the Left Bank in two sections divided by the gardens of that former mortuary chapel, the church of Saint-Julien-le-Pauvre.

True, there were aspects of Gascoyne's existence I could not claim to share: his extreme mental refinement, for example, his deep-rooted poetic vocation or his tortuous sexuality. As time went on however, and as I talked to his many friends and read through his journals and papers, I felt myself more and more drawn towards him as a subject: his unvarying modesty, his integrity, his humour, his reluctance to take emotional advantage of others: all of these inspired my warmth and interest. In April 1995, while preparing my book about Barker, I travelled with my family to the Isle of Wight and interviewed him as the rain tipped down outside his house. Often he had deflected my questions and spoken instead of his own past in great unwinding parentheses. Intent as I then was on another book, I found these verbal excursions distracting at the time, and occasionally cut off his flow. Listening back to the resulting tapes recently on my ageing cassette player, I was struck by how frequently his digressions answered the very questions I would now wish to put to him in my very different capacity as his own biographer. But, just as he was getting to the vital point of information, I had impatiently chipped in. Seldom can a biographer have cursed himself so roundly.

In the end I chose to present my account as a series of nights, a pattern suggesting dreaming and, with it, the subliminal approach of Surrealism that—whatever his later misgivings about certain dogmatic aspects of the movement—had always remained an aspect of Gascoyne's attitude. The arrangement will remind some of the successive nights of William Blake's *The Four Zoas* and, beyond that, of Edward Young's *Night Thoughts*, the late eighteenth-century meditative poem that—absorbed it is true through a rather misleading French prose translation—had influenced the founders of

Surrealism, featuring in André Breton's First Surrealist Manifesto as 'Surrealist from cover to cover'. For all of these reasons Gascoyne adopted Young's phrase as the title of one of his own most satisfying works, justification enough I thought for applying it to a life that retained throughout all its fascinating phases a certain oneiric quality. The tragic facts outlined above may help place this private night journey in context, though they can of course fully account neither for a poet's tribulations nor for his temperament, least of all for his art.

NIGHT
ONE

1916–1939

I

Among Women

Along the Firth the grey shapes moved slowly in the cold morning light. As she held him up to the low windowsill with one arm, the boy's mother pointed with the forefinger of her other hand, and he strained to see. He had been woken early for this. It was chilly in the step-fronted, whitewashed cottage, the equinoctial winds of November were blowing hard and, out on the roof, slates had rattled all night.[1] He heard the words 'German' and 'fleet'. The shapes slid onwards. The show was over. The war was over. Gingerly, Winifred Isobel Gascoyne lowered him to the floor.

Mother and son had come up by train to join the boy's father Leslie Gascoyne who had been stationed for months out at Kinghorn on the northern shore of the Firth, guarding the big guns positioned there to dissuade the German ships from bombarding Edinburgh. Now the ships were spoils of war, escorted in twos and threes towards Orkney. The victorious allies could not agree what to do with them. Nor would they until, in impatient defiance, Admiral Reuter gave the order for the hatches to be opened so the battleships and destroyers could settle to the bed of Gutter Sound. It would be Midsummer's Day 1919 when this happened. By then the 2-year-old and his mother would be back in Harrow in a narrow, high-gabled house near the railway station. For almost three years they had lived together there among a small community of women ruled with some firmness by the boy's godmother, Win's mentor, former teacher, and employer: the redoubtable, stubbornly Germanophile, determinedly unmarried Florence Mole.

Florence too was a battleship of sorts, though built more like a tug. Around her, younger women scurried like dutiful cruisers. Born in Middlesex in 1860, she had trained in the Froebel teaching method in

1. David Gascoyne, *Eyes At The Back of the Head,* autobiographical MS, Dec. 1987, Beinecke, Box 5, Folder 61.

Thuringia and returned to practise it in London schools. Until the outbreak of war this spirited educator had governed her academic establishment for young ladies, and had done so since the reign of Queen Victoria.
By the accession of Edward VII she had already installed herself at Warrant
House, Peterborough Road on a steep slope leading up to the more famous
Harrow public school (and benefiting from its swanky address at 'Harrow-
on-the-Hill'). It was both school and a home, and Florence shared it with
nine female boarders. In the 1901 Census she is entered as headmistress and
head of this exclusively female household: assistants, servants, and pupils:
Louisa the maid; Ethel Beavis (36), single schoolmistress; Marion Harper
(24), single governess; Florence Hammond (18), also a single governess;
Ethel Hill (15), pupil; Dorothy Rodgers (13), pupil, Barbara Parington (13),
pupil, and Olga Gwenings (11), boarder. Among them already, also 11, there
was little Win herself.

Win had been there since she was 8, and it was the only stable home she
had ever known. She had scant recollection of her own mother, a musician
and actress who had once sung the part of Trilby in the wings during the
stage adaptation of George du Maurier's novel, employed because the actress
hired to play opposite Herbert Beerbohm Tree's Svengali was tone-deaf.
Nor had she much better recollection of her sister, less still of their father
Samuel Emery, an unsuccessful actor who had absconded in Huddersfield
in 1896 six years after her birth. Not that his behaviour had been at all surprising. The Emery family were all employed in the theatre, and several of
the men had proved bolters. Her paternal grandfather, also Samuel, for
example, had gone on tour to Australia in 1878 and returned only to die.
Five years later her uncle Edward had married Florence Farr, actress, feminist, performer on the psaltery, and intimate of W. B. Yeats. In 1893 he had
gone on tour to America and not returned (the couple had divorced in
1895).[2] The Emery women were used to picking up the pieces. Thus Win
had been rescued and adopted by the aunt after whom she was named: her
father's sister Winifred, austerely beautiful and, after Ellen Terry, perhaps the
most celebrated actress in England.

Emerys of both sexes had graced the stage since the late eighteenth century, when Mr and Mrs Mackle Emery had appeared at the Haymarket
Theatre. One of their sons, John, Win's great-grandfather, had appeared with

---

2. Pamela Maud, *Worlds Away*, Foreword by Dame Sybil Thorndike (London: John Baker, 1964),
   26; *Oxford Dictionary of National Biography*, 'Florence Farr'.

Charles Kemble, whom he liked to outwit on stage. On the night her elusive grandfather had been born, they had been playing opposite one another
in Sheridan's *Pizarro*, in which Kemble was Rolla, and John Emery a senti-
nel, whom he is made to ask, 'Have you a wife?' 'I have,' replied John Emery.
'Children?' asked Kemble. 'I had two this morning,' Emery had replied.
'I have three now.'[3] In recognition of this anecdote or not, performing plays
by Sheridan had been a family tradition ever since.

Loftily conscious of this family past, Aunt Winifred was a long-time
member of the Lyceum Company: she had appeared opposite Henry Irving
as Annette in *The Bells*, and as Nerissa in *The Merchant of Venice*. In two successive tours of America she had served as Terry's understudy. In 1888 at the
Savoy Chapel she had married Cyril Maude, a character actor specializing
in costume parts: Mr Hardcastle in Goldsmith's *She Stoops to Conquer* (spectacles worn low down on nose; pearl-buttoned waistcoat; buckled shoes;
spats); Bob Acres in Sheridan's *The Rivals* (riding crop; high boots; frock
coat); or Colonel Cazenove in Sydney Grundy's determinedly anti-feminist
The New Woman (turned-up whiskers; top hat; raffish umbrella).[4] Thenceforth, the couple frequently played as a twosome, again specializing in
Sheridan and Goldsmith. They were especially successful as Sir Peter and
Lady Teazle in *A School for Scandal*. Soon their names were riding through
the West End together on the sides of omnibuses. When Win was 2, Aunt
Winifred had enjoyed at the St James's Theatre the greatest acclaim she
would ever know as the first ever Lady Windemere.

But as she and Cyril began raising children of their own—two daughters
and a son—it became obvious there would be scant room for Win either in
their Kensington home or their seaside residence at Bexhill. In any case,
Maude's thoughts were turned less towards his niece than towards what he
loved to call 'that loveliest sound an actor ever hears: applause'.[5] In the year
of Win's legal adoption, he felt established enough to take out a ten-year
contract as joint manager with Frederick Harrison of the Haymarket. In the
history of the theatre he wrote several years later, he evokes the financial
anxieties of that year: 'To this hour they haunt me in my dreams—the

3. Cyril Maude, *The Haymarket Theatre, Some Notes and Reminiscences*, ed. Ralph Maude (London:
   Grant Richards, 1903), 85–8.
4. Cyril Maude, *Parts I Have Played 1893–1908: A Photographic and Descriptive Essay* (London: Abbey
   Press, 1909).
5. Cyril Maude and Charles Hanson Towne, *The Actor in Room 931* (New York: J. H. Sears,
   1926), 6.

worries, the anxieties, the fears, and the thousand and one little hitches inseparable from this business of ours.' The deal had been clinched after a hearty lunch in the vale of Harrow at Grim's Dyke, the mock Tudor mansion belonging to Cyril's 'old friend' W. S. Gilbert, librettist to Sir Arthur Sullivan.[6] After the lunch Maude's predecessor as manager, Squire Bancroft, had taken him for a leisurely walk in the spacious gardens, mooting plans and smoking cigars as they strolled round the artificial lake sunk into the lawns, surrounded by chestnut trees amid which Gilbert's pet lemurs sometimes lurked. Cyril had also had a heart-to-heart with his wife. Responsibilities were mounting: Win would soon have to go. Two years later, in 1898, they had found her a boarding place at Florence Mole's school, close enough to Grim's Dyke for their friend Gilbert to keep a watchful eye on her. Win had been with Florence ever since, as pupil, colleague, and now as companion and friend.

It was a house of fraught, precocious passions. Florence was forthright, opinionated, and boisterous. To her more devoted pupils she was known as 'Lolly'. She raced up and down the stairs, banging doors; she quarrelled with the maids. A freethinker and latterly a Unitarian, an avid and critical theatregoer, she cultivated advanced opinions and dressed loudly in un-schoolmistressy mauve. One by one she took her pupils under her wing, indoctrinated them, nurtured, and moulded them. She was difficult, psychologically, to resist.

As time went on her family-cum-academy grew. She took on a devoted deputy, a Mrs Godwin, with whom she was 'very intimate', and moved the school northwards to a larger if less salubrious building named 'Burnside' at 76 Welldon Crescent, a secluded road closer to Harrow town centre, where she continued collecting and educating her waifs and strays. Typically they were middle-class orphans, or daughters of dispersed or broken homes. In 1902 she adopted the latest of these: a diminutive and intelligent 17-year-old with the complicated name of Rebbie Feuer Wright who, since the death of her parents in the Fen country, had been lodging in the house of a piano teacher in Ipswich. Rebbie was musical, a voracious reader, gregarious, and clinging with her closest associates. She was probably taken on as what Florence liked to call a 'pupil teacher', an ambiguous status implying that she had some pedagogic responsibility and could be regarded as a governess or schoolmistress in training. She soon acquired a litany of nicknames:

6. Maude, *Haymarket Theatre*, 191–2, 228.

'Ginger' (though her hair was beige), 'Tiny' since she stood at five feet noth-ing. Tiny was smooth-faced, intense, pretty in a demurely intellectual way, with just a shadow of down on her upper lip. She was also prone to the most devastating crushes on other women. Soon she became the younger Win's closest, most devoted companion: at first to her delight, then to her embar-rassment, ultimately to her alarm. She would have an irresistible and lasting influence on Win's first son, who would later call her 'my first and dearest friend'.[7] It was also to be his opinion that Tiny was in love, hopelessly in love, with his mother.[8]

When Win reached the official leaving age of 14, there seemed to be nothing to do but stay on in one capacity or another. In any case, matters in the Maude–Emery household had been proving ever more difficult. In 1905, Cyril's tenure at the Haymarket over, he took out a lease on the Avenue Theatre to the south of Trafalgar Square, which he immediately started to remodel. On 5 December that year the high roof of the adjoining Charing Cross station collapsed, taking the theatre, and much of Maude's investment, with it. Assistance from her aunt and uncle now out of the ques-tion, Win remained in Florence's genteel community, becoming teacher and governess to the younger girls. In 1909 Florence, nearing 50, decided to step down from day-to-day running of the school. She asked the 23-year-old, unqualified, Tiny to take over, assisted by 18-year-old Win, who, benefiting from her family's skill at enunciation, was specializing in teaching elocution. That, however, was as far as thespian influence would go. About this time young Win had asked her aunt whether there would be any chance of her entering the family profession. Unwilling to encourage someone for whom, should failure result, she would be responsible, Winifred encouraged the more practicable plan of her becoming a schoolmistress.

Florence continued to live in the house and retained the lease. With this proviso, Tiny and Win took over. They were inexperienced, and prone to mishaps. If at a loss, they organized expeditions out to Pinner, where Gilbert was always at home to them at Grim's Dyke. Now in his late seventies, Gilbert took a delight in entertaining teachers and pupils there when they were in need of a break, during bank holidays or at weekends. In the sum-mer months they had free run of his freshwater lake in the garden, where he liked to see them frolic about, even sometimes to bathe with them.

7. David Gascoyne, Afterword to *Collected Journals*, 372–3.
8. BL Lives, F1380, Side B.

Not all of the guests, however, were able to swim. Shortly after Tiny and Win took over at the school, the student body was joined by two upper-crust though impecunious sisters. Sybil and Ruby Preece were the daughters of an army officer and, during his absences on duty, lived with their mother in a flat in South Kensington from which, during terms, they were boarded out at the refined academy in Harrow. They were a couple of years apart in age and by 1911 the younger Ruby was a tall, leggy insecure 17-year-old with challenging eyes and winning ways. On Whit Monday of that year, which fell on 29 May, Win decided to take advantage of Gilbert's generosity and escort Ruby to Grim's Dyke. It was an unseasonably fresh late spring day, but despite the temperature Gilbert, invariably in attendance on these occasions, suggested they all take a dip. He donned his one-piece swimming suit and they their ladylike, unrevealing costumes, and all three lowered themselves into the lake. But its bed at that time of year was soft with rushes underfoot and after several minutes, Ruby felt herself sinking. She called out 'Oh, Sir William, I am out of my depth, I'm out of my depth!' Win attempted to wade over to rescue her, but Gilbert was closer. He swam across calling, 'It's not very deep; don't splash; you'll be alright.'

With that Ruby Preece placed her hand on his shoulder, and both of them slumped beneath the surface. When she re-emerged, there was no sign of Gilbert, whose inert form came up a few seconds later. His appearance was such that the gardeners were called, who managed to row him ashore. Lady Gilbert was alerted and then two doctors who, after vainly attempting artificial respiration for about an hour, confirmed that Gilbert had suffered a cardiac arrest. The librettist of *HMS Pinafore* had expired in his very own pond.[9]

That evening various headlines across the billboards of the West End announced that Sir W. S. Gilbert had ended his days at home in the company of Winifred Emery. These did little to alleviate the suspicions of suburban commuters concerning the private morals of the theatrical profession. Nor did Aunt Winifred take kindly to the exposure, even if all ambiguity was laid to rest two days later when Win and Ruby were called to give evidence at the Inquest, held at Grim's Dyke under the chief coroner for Middlesex. Ruby related her version of events, then Win was called to the stand:

9. *The Times*, 30 May 1911, p. 11; Jane W. Stedman, *W. S. Gilbert: A Classic Victorian and His Theatre* (Oxford: Oxford University Press, 1996), 392; BL Lives, F1380, Side A.

Miss Winifred Emery, who gave the same address as Miss Preece, said she was bathing with Sir William at the time of his death. Miss Preece got into difficulties and called to Sir William for help, and he at once swam to her. The witness tried to get to them, but could not. She could see Miss Preece splashing about, and then Sir William disappeared.

THE CORONER, – So he really lost his life in endeavouring to save Miss
                    Preece?

MISS EMERY, – I think so.[10]

Then Win returned to her seat sobbing. The same day she wrote contritely to Lady Gilbert, 'I cannot tell you how terribly, terribly sorry I am. I do not feel that you can ever forgive me. If it had not been for me, it would never have happened.'[11]

At the inquest Ruby requested her name be suppressed; the coroner refused. But it was far from the end of her unfortunate effect on great men. A year later she changed her name to 'Patricia Price', and went to study painting at the Slade Institute, where she met a more talented painter, Dorothy Hepworth. Together in 1927 they would settle in the riverside village of Cookham in Berkshire. When financially out of their depth, they again sought male assistance, this time from the local celebrity painter, the already married Stanley Spencer. Disguising from him the nature of her relationship with Hepworth, she inveigled him into divorcing his wife and marrying her before expelling him from his family home, taking up residence there with Dorothy. She refused all marital relations with her husband. In several of Spencer's later canvases she appears in sullenly voluptuous folds of flesh, her frustrated and bespectacled spouse beside her, an epitome of despondent longing.

Back at the school, shortly after the accident, another of Win's charges, Dorothy Gascoyne, introduced her to her 26-year-old brother Leslie, who was training as a cashier at the headquarters of the Midland Bank in Pall Mall. Photographs taken at the time show a solid-looking young man soberly dressed. Aunt Winifred found him dull, but he was at the polar extreme from all those feckless Emery men. His father, born in the Mile End Road in the East End, had migrated westwards for most of his life: after working in West Ham and Lewisham, he had eventually become an accountant in a local firm in Hammersmith, providing his second son with a social background that

10. *The Times*, 1 June 1911, 6.
11. Winifred Emery to Lady Gilbert, 31 May 1911, BL Add. 49341.

appears to belong in the pages of that Edwardian classic of suburban life: *The Diary of a Nobody*. For Win this very stability and ordinariness were surely part of his attraction. Deprived of a normal family life by the irresponsibility of her own father—a fact ever present in her mind, even when her aunt and protectress did not drive it in—Win saw in this shy, self-deprecating wage-slave a provider who would not let her down. Such a view of him was how-ever skin-deep, as was his ordinariness. As events would prove, Leslie Noel Gascoyne was in reality a highly strung, at times morbidly sensitive person with weak lungs and eyesight, who, though deeply conscientious—or almost certainly because so—found the responsibilities of his lower middle-class profession irksome, at times even oppressive. A minor alleviating fact, was that his paternal family were remotely related to the aristocratic Cecils, whom, however, they had assuredly never met. (The literary scholar Lord David Cecil, who bore the middle name Gascoyne, was a distant cousin.) In vain did Win plead these redeeming characteristics to her aunt. In vain did she stress her ability to open out, enliven, and thus redeem this irreproachable servant to lower middle-class drudgery. Aunt Winifred would never relent and lend her approval to her ward hitching herself to a bank clerk, and a trainee cashier at that.

The couple were both agnostics, but in her role as Win's effectual guard-ian Florence seems to have insisted on a church wedding. On 23 April 1912, eleven months after the tragic accident at Grim's Dyke, the couple were married at St George's church, Headstone in the parish of Hatch End. Florence signed as a witness of Win's side, and Leslie's widowed mother on his. Neither Maude nor Aunt Winifred was present. There was little money, so the newly married couple moved straight in with Florence and the other women at the schoolhouse at Welldon Crescent, from where Leslie commuted daily to Pall Mall. When war was declared two years later, he promptly volunteered. Since his health was poor, he was not deemed fit for service on the Western Front. He was sent up to Kinghorn to help guard the Firth of Forth.

In wartime conditions it was going to be difficult to maintain the school, so it was now closed and, when Florence retired to a high-gabled house at 59 Gayton Road, about a mile from where she had first established her acad-emy, Win went with her, writing to Leslie in Scotland when she could. There were infrequent leaves south of the border, and on occasions Win went up to join him. For the rest of the time she stayed put in north London with Florence. Soon, the inseparably devoted Rebbie joined them.

It was into this well-established single sex household that the poet David
Emery Gascoyne was born during his father's absence on 10 October 1916.
He was named David after *David Copperfield*, a novel of which his parents
were both fond, and Emery after his mother's family, perhaps in an attempt
to win them over. For his first two years his father was next to invisible. The
male role in the home was taken by the still sociable, still dominant Florence
Mole, who at his christening in 1912 had taken on the role of godmother.
There is little doubt about this, and for the rest of his life Gascoyne's unconscious mind, in which he placed perhaps too much trust, insistently informed
him so. His conscious mind in turn would inform successive analysts that
this had been the case: 'Analysis coming alone nicely: unearthed a lot about
Harrow and Florence Mole this morning' runs a not untypical entry after
meeting his French analyst in October 1938.[12] In his eighties he was still
persuading readers that this early and eccentric domestic set-up offered the
best key to his temperament. 'I was a spoilt child,' he declared in the year
2000. 'But the love which was lavished on me was not so much a mother's
as a godmother's. This woman, who was once my mother's schoolmistress
and who died when I was fifteen, had an extremely powerful, dominating
and masculine personality; during my childhood I think she must have
played the mother role even more than my own mother.'[13]

Florence was the mainstay of his childhood, as she had once been of his
mother's. She provided the stability behind the changes of circumstance and
address, the emotional stability that he needed. In practice throughout the
years of his infancy, David's childcare seems to have been shared out almost
equally between Florence, Win, and Tiny, now a constant presence in the
house. More than the others, it seems to have been Tiny—a frustrated artist
and a loner—who most stimulated his imagination. She occupied a large
front bedroom with a bay window, and it was in her bed that the young
David spent the early hours of each morning as she read to him. In his novel
Opening Day, which is dedicated to his mother, she appears as the Aunt, Sue
Cotteram. 'He used', reads one passage, 'to get up early in the morning and
creep into her bed where she would feed him with biscuits from the bright-
coloured tin by her bedside and read stories to him of Riki-tiki-tavi and
Mowgli from Kipling's *Jungle Book*.'[14] In the longer term, an emotional and

12. *Journal 1937–1939*, 75.
13. David Gascoyne, *April*, ed. Roger Scott (London: Enitharmon, 2000), 112.
14. David Gascoyne, *Opening Day* (London: Cobden-Sanderson, 1933), 29.

practical dependence on forceful middle-aged women became a pattern that would remain constant in him throughout his life. Long after Florence's death in 1931, when physically in the vicinity of her grave, he had to always resist the temptation to visit it. She stomped assertively through his dreams. Throughout his young manhood and his middle and old age, whatever his hormones told him, he would be emotionally drawn to, and dependent on, strong and capable women, drifting from one to another and, between times, seemingly almost lost.

In 1918, shortly after Win and David's last short stay in Kinghorn, Leslie was demobbed and returned to his job in London. Four winters in Scotland had done little to help his weak respiration. Soon after his demobilization, and on doctor's advice, his employers decided to move him out of London, and early in 1919 he and his small family were transferred to Bournemouth, then as now the mildest seaside resort in England. It was the first time they had enjoyed a home of their own, and the first time for seventeen years that Win had not lived under Florence's roof. They were given a flat near the station, then a large house on Branksome Chine at the west end of town, from where mother and child could take afternoon trips towards Studland Bay, and longer weekend expeditions to Corfe Castle and beyond, often with Tiny, when she came to visit. Win taught elocution to suitable young women, just as she had in Harrow, and she even had a regular radio programme reading poetry, employing her inherited family skills on the sound waves and in productions for the Bournemouth Amateur Dramatic Society. Leslie's working duties were light, and the journey each day not irksome. It was an idyll of sorts that lingered in David's memory as a paradise of togetherness and happiness. His parents were relieved to be under the same roof, relieved that the war was over. His bond with his mother grew ever closer.

In snaps taken at the time, the intimacy and trust between Win and David are palpable. In his early manhood, thoughts of early childhood were associated in his mind with the slow movements of Bartók's Second and Third Piano Concertos: 'night, the open air, mysterious joy, adventure, and something we had forgotten, a certainty. . .'[15] One of his persistent memories was of holding onto Win's hand on 11 November 1919, the first Remembrance Day, as they stood together at the back door of their Bournemouth house

15. BL Add. 71704 H, fo. 23.

listening to the unaccountable hush during the two minutes' silence.[16] Another was of waking early one May morning three years later to watch the dawn rise. In his imagination, and in a poem he wrote many years afterwards about the fitfulness of inspiration, the clouds opened like flowers around the beckoning sun.[17]

16. 'November in Devon', *Collected Poems* (1988), 228–9.
17. 'Prelude to a New Fin-de-Siècle', *Collected Poems* (1988), 221–2.

2

'The Earl of Salisbury's Pavanne'

After Leslie had cut his teeth as assistant manager in Bournemouth for two years, he was moved to the more important branch of the Midland in Salisbury. At first the Gascoynes were given a thatched cottage to the west of the city. While there, in the renewed flu outbreak of 1920, Win and David both came down with the bug: 'We were', he later recalled, 'seriously ill and had to stay in bed for weeks on end.'[1] When they looked out of the front windows, they saw processions of mourners laying their dead to rest beneath the yew trees in the nearby cemetery. After that, the family was moved to a cottage at the southern end of the cathedral close, beyond the Harnham Gate. Each week Win took the train back to Bournemouth where she was still involved in radio work and elocution teaching. On her return she read simplified Dickens to her son before he slept. As soon as he was old enough to read for himself, he was taken up the gentle rise of Milford Hill to the Godolphin School, a girls' college with a mixed kindergarten.

Damp in winter, sometimes airless in summer, permeated by streams above and below ground, the cathedral precincts seemed to them a world apart, and to David a place enchanted. To their right, as the Gascoynes walked out of their low front door, rose the thirteenth-century cathedral with its dramatically blended early English architecture, its grey-green limestone arches dressed in black Purbeck marble, its soaring spire of almost unbelievable solidity yet lightness. To their left lay the water meadows where the rivers Avon and Nadder join, and beyond that the broad Harnham Road and the village of Bemerton, where in the 1630s George Herbert had been

---

1. BL Lives, F1380, Side A.

incumbent at the church of St Andrew. From the flint stone rectory he would stroll across to evensong in the cathedral on Sunday evenings, passing as he did so beneath the Harnham Gate.

To a growing infant, much of this history was mystical, yet it sank into his mind permanently. Like Florence Mole, her ghost never to be laid, Salisbury, the city and its historic church, became the stuff of his dreams. Thirty years later, his night thoughts were still entangled with them, as they would be into old age. Here he is in October 1951:

> I dreamed of the Cathedral at Salisbury last night—of how in its proportions is preserved some knowledge and reminder of the ancient nobility and wisdom of Northern humanity—of justice and lovely aspiration. But passing the West front it seemed that more recent second-rate carvings had replaced the old figures; and then an irreverent and incongruous Army jeep or tank rattled past us as though it had right of way there too. Then we came to the field that used to be our playing field when I was at school, and in it all the grass had grown tall and wild again; and a little further on I saw the path turned aside into the field, and there were new waterways made there, broader than the little stream that used to run along the border of the field, and there were (pentagonal?) walls put up and it was newly converted into a sort of public garden or promenade. I pointed towards the Harnham Gate and said: 'Look, there where I used to live when I was six years old, in front of my parents' cottage, there is now a broad stream of water as though from a mill-stream'. And I went on round to where the games pavilion used to be and Canon Myers' house, and there the path sloped down towards the new waterway, and there I found my enemies, who boldly had the impudence to make their lying suggestions even to my face, and I would have struck them, but they slid away evasively and I awoke.[2]

It is a dream of perfection and degeneration. It is also a Surrealist collage and, as so often in dreams, the memories came out jumbled, merging different phases of his experience, before guttering into paranoia. The water meadows have been transposed inside the close, and the peace of the early 1920s is rent by the memory of war. Around such juxtapositions would a poet's temperament turn.

But in 1920 when the Gascoynes arrived, the cathedral possessed a slightly alien charm. Beyond the cloisters and the great west front was the choir school in Wren Hall from whose entrance every morning a crocodile of boys of varying sizes dressed in dark cloaks, Eton collars, and blue

2. BL Add. 71704 L, fo. 13. Canon Myers was the precentor and *custos puerorum*, responsible for intoning the versicles at cathedral services.

mortar boards walked across Choristers' Green to their practice room near the Bishop's Palace. They repeated this routine, by the more direct route to and from the cathedral cloisters, for evensong late each afternoon. To outsiders—and religiously speaking David's parents were emphatically that—the parade appeared exotic, like the booming of the great Willis organ after matins on Sundays. At much the same period, the quaintness of the musical foundation as observed by outsiders was captured by another child resident of the close:

> When we were younger than the choristers we admired them very much—at least I did. To meet them in their Eton suits, ham-frills, and mortar-boards, marching briskly in procession to a Cathedral service always ranked as a spectacle. If they had had a band, it would have been better still of course. 'Right, left, right, left', said the Bishop's Boy. With the purposefulness of a train, the, small, dark crocodile swung out of the sunshine into the shadow of a porch which gulped the whole lot up.[3]

The bishop's boy was the head chorister. On the enthronement of each new bishop it was his duty publicly to welcome him with an enconium in Latin. In the Middle Ages his predecessor had put on his mitre and preached from the pulpit in the nave, lording it over the cathedral, its chapter, its canons and vicars choral each year from St Nicholas's Day on 6 December until the Holy Innocents' Day on 28 December. These prerogatives had been laid down in ancient statutes by Roger de Mortival in 1319. The legend of the boy bishop was still a powerful element in the folklore of the place. 'He is even', a folklorist had recently written, 'said to have enjoyed the right of disposing of such prebends as happened to fall vacant during the days of his episcopacy. But the pranks of the boy bishop were not confined to the church. Arrayed in full canonicals he was led about with songs and dances from house to house, blessing the grinning people and collecting money in return for his benedictions.'[4]

Initially at least, the cathedral and its traditions signified little to David's freethinking parents, much though they would come to mean to him.

---

3. Geraldine Symons, *Children in the Close* (London: T. S. Batsford, 1959), 28.

4. J. G. Frazer, *The Scapegoat* (London: Macmillan, 1913), 338. For further background to the choral foundation, see Dora H. Robertson, *Sarum Close: A History of the Life and Education of the Cathedral Choristers for 700 Years* (London: Jonathan Cape, 1938) and Peter L. Smith, *900 Years of Song: A Concise History of the Cathedral School, Salisbury, 1091–1991* (Salisbury: Salisbury Cathedral School, 1991).

Instead, Leslie and Win threw themselves into theatricals. A year into their stay they attempted to recreate one of her aunt's and uncle's successes by appearing as Sir Peter and Lady Teazle in a performance of *The School for Scandal* for the Salisbury Amateur Dramatic Society. Their costumes were modelled on Winifred's and Cyril's, and David watched from the stalls. At 5 he was roped into the performances. 'We did a sort of potted version of *As You Like It* in the open air', he later told an enquirer, 'and I was a page and my mother was Rosalind.'[5] Less outgoing than either of them, and occasionally morose, Leslie was Jaques.

The following year the Gascoynes had twin sons, John and Tony, christened in the cathedral on 18 September 1922.[6] From now on Win's attention on was divided, the exclusive affection seen in early photos with David a thing of the past. Leslie too had more demands on his energy and time. Now 36, with two assistant posts behind him, he was considered ready for a branch of his own. So when David was 6, and his brothers not yet fully weaned, the family decamped once more, ten miles down the Avon to Fordingbridge in the New Forest, a town much favoured by artists. For Leslie it was a professional challenge; for David it proved a sort of interlude. For all their religious views, or rather lack of them, Leslie and Win had been seduced by what they had seen of the choir school in Salisbury and of the education provided for the boys who boarded there, which had the further advantage of being subsidized by the cathedral chapter. So, after some elementary vocal training at the parish church in Fordingbridge, David was taken by Win back for the day to Salisbury where he had lunch with the kindly headmaster, Canon Robertson, and attended a voice trial in the tiny medieval song school attached to the house of the organist and master of the choristers, Dr Walter Alcock. After a few ear tests and singing a specimen verse from a hymn, he was accepted as a probationer.

Thus, aged 8, David joined the daily procession of dark cloaked and frill-collared boys marching across the close. The regime, he soon found, was regimented, but in the most gentle sort of a way. The school was tiny: forty pupils with three resident masters, a visiting teacher, and the matron, who happened to be the headmaster's wife. All lessons were taken in a high-windowed, whitewashed, and oak-panelled schoolroom designed by a pupil

5. BL Lives, F1380, Side A.
6. Baptismal certificate for John Win Gascoyne, Beinecke, Folder 16, File 355.

of Sir Christopher Wren in 1717. There were only two classes, which sat back to back. The more senior faced a dais where the headmaster was enthroned beneath a ticking clock, above which hung an honours board with a cross, surrounded by framed photos of old boys slain in the late conflict. The more junior faced the opposite end where an assistant master, or sometimes Mrs Robertson, quietly worked. She and the canon lived next door at Braybrooke House, divided from the school internally by his study and externally by a low wall, up which hollyhocks grew in summer.

The human closeness was palpable since there were only two dormitories, one for senior boys above the schoolroom, the other for juniors to the west of it in a small extension next to the sickbay. The atmosphere was paternalistic, caring, and inspired by Broad Church principles. The Robertsons were well aware that these children were away from home for most of the year: not only through the long terms but throughout the extended 'choir times' during the Christmas, Easter, and summer holidays. Until his voice broke at 14, David would not see Win, Leslie, or his brothers for more than eight weeks a year.

It soon became clear that he was no scholar in the conventional sense of the word. Maths did not come easily to him, nor did Latin, with which he struggled. English, as one might expect, was a source of refreshment. Encouraged by Win, he had started to read quite widely. At 9 he began to learn the piano (many boys, in fact, studied two or more instruments). Above all there was the singing, under Alcock's stern though not unsympathetic eye.

David was lucky to have arrived at a time when the sung services in the cathedral were under the direction of one of the country's most accomplished church musicians. Alcock was an expert and sensitive organist, as his recordings of works by J. S. Bach, Félix Guilmant, Edwin Lemare, and his own modest compositions still testify. He also enjoys the distinction of being the only organist to have played at the coronation of three successive British kings: Edward VII in 1902, George V in 1911, and George VI in 1937. From the choir he coaxed what were for the time high standards, employing a mixture of firmness, humour, and guarded concern. Morning practices were held in the low-roofed medieval song room overlooking his garden. Around its walls was evidence of his offduty enthusiasms: a telescope and a photograph of a miniature steam engine that he had built for the choristers and was still sometimes taken into the garden for their use on fine days. In the middle of the room was the grand piano, around which the boys stood in pairs wearing ruffs, reading music from shared, high desks. The bishop's boy at the time was Clive Jenkinson who, when himself an organist of repute, later recalled that

> Choristers went through a little door in the garden and entered the school from a garden door. It was cool in summer and bitterly cold in winter. Dr Alcock would come in at the grand piano with his back to a somewhat unenthusiastic fire. I remember him as a being perfectly dressed, very often in dove-grey suits with a huge white collar. Practises consisted of a series of scales and then a run through the known services [settings of the morning and evening canticles] and anthems and, always at the end, tackling something new. He would forgive and understand failure to get a difficult interval correctly when sight reading, but was coldly furious with any boy who went down instead of up, or vice-versa.[7]

Alcock had the perfect recipe for inconvenient colds. If a child started sniffing or singing hoarsely, he would request the sufferer to stand next to him at the piano, sucking a gracefully offered cough sweet. The taste of this was so peculiarly nauseating, and the smell so acridly pervasive, that the ailment seldom recurred. A disciplinarian over small matters, Alcock maintained an unrelenting war with the minor cathedral clergy, whom he considered unpardonably warm-hearted and lenient. Slackness he did not condone. The result in the song school was an atmosphere of awe and mild trepidation. In the cathedral, it was splendour.

Few cathedral choristers ever get over the sound of their own voice bouncing off the vaulted roof of a great historic building, the intensity of cadences as they fade away into ancient walls, the stained glass reflected on flagstones, the muffled candlelight. Nor could a potential poet fail to respond to the words of the King James Bible, of Coverdale's English psalms sung to Anglican chant, or Cranmer's liturgy. In Gascoyne's novel *Opening Day*, written when he was 17, the narrator distils this combination of aural and visual appeal, colouring the music as he goes:

> Every service was to him a wonder. At Evensong, when a subdued and vernal light penetrated the very ancient windows, bathing the tombs in beauty, they sang long and dramatic anthems by Stainer and Sullivan, or passages from *Elijah* and *The Messiah*, with lengthy passages of recitation for bass and

7. 'From the Recollections of Clive R. Jenkinson', booklet accompanying disc 1 of 'Salisbury Cathedral Choir and Organ Recordings 1927–1965' (Salisbury Cathedral, 2002). SCS276501, pp. 5–6.

impassioned choruses about the Daughter of Sion and the Redeemed of the Lord and They that sow in tears. The organ made the stone floor richly inlaid with mosaic, to rumble, and the violet stretch of air between the high, carved choir-stalls to quiver. At length the Archdeacon reached the word 'evermore' and the choir said 'Amen' and waited in silence for a moment until the organ began to fill the still, chill stretches of emptiness with deep, purple notes, warm, like velvet, like chastened orchids, when the choir, wine-cassocked and white, rose from their places and wound slowly out through the gilded and heavily-detailed gates to their quiet vestries.[8]

We can attest to the effects of these settings by Handel or Sullivan, since a recording exists of Gascoyne and his fellow choristers singing both. In July 1928 Alcock arranged for the sound engineers of His Master's Voice to record the choir on two sides of a 78 rpm disc. It is the first recording ever made by Salisbury choir, among the first of any English cathedral, and, of course, the first recording of Gascoyne's voice.[9] The first side is taken up by an abridged version of 'He shall feel his flock like a shepherd' from *Messiah*, wispily and ethereally sung in unison by the trebles, including the 12-year-old Gascoyne, against Alcock's cooing organ accompaniment. The second features an a cappella rendition by the whole ensemble of 'Yea, though I walk through the valley of the shadow of death', by Alcock's former teacher, Arthur Sullivan. The selection was evidently made with a view to the consoling potential of Christian music for a sentimental mass market: both texts involve sheep going astray, and the reassuring presence of shepherds. Among the boy choristers are some of the most distinguished English musicians of that generation: the future composer Geoffrey Bush and Bernard Rose, later *Informator Choristarum* at Magdalen College, Oxford. In such company, Gascoyne was used to performing well.

As a group they were constantly together. Cohesion was encouraged by rugby or cricket on the sports field to the south of the cloisters, and fortunately for David there were regular plays, especially out of term when the choristers were still in residence but lessons were light. These were directed by Dora Robertson, who in a later generation would not have remained satisfied with life as a headmaster's wife; at the time she was immersed, with the assistance of one of the canons, Christopher Wordsworth (a great-nephew of the poet), in writing an impressively scholarly history of the

---

8. David Gascoyne, *Opening Day* (London: Cobden-Sanderson, 1933), 45.
9. 'Salisbury Cathedral Choir and Organ Archive Recordings 1927–1965', disc 1 SCS276501, tracks 4 and 5.

choral foundation. To begin with, David was on the short side, with clear eyes and a bright complexion, and was invariably chosen to play female roles. He made quite an eye-catching wench. In January 1926, when he was 9½, Dora cast him as Phoebe Lollipop, the 'belle of the village' in her post-Christmas entertainment: a mock seventeenth-century intrigue called *At Ye Sign of Ye Sugar Heart*. She kitted him out in a wig that prickled, a mop cap, laced collar, linen apron, and full broad-striped skirts. In this fetching outfit he danced a hornpipe with Charles II, played by 12-year-old Stephen Clissold, in later life a distinguished diplomat and expert on Yugoslavian affairs. After he had sung a fetching song about a turtle dove, they performed a slow and stately pavanne to the music of William Byrd's 'The Earl of Salisbury', with Alcock at the piano. The sensation of dancing evidently sank in. Six years later he would imagine a fire-lit room opening to reveal a surreal vista, a royal pageant through which his body still swayed:

> We will dance a slow pavanne
> down a dark alley of cypresses.
> We will let our brocades trail through the dewy grass.
> We will let laughter and low lute-notes float across the lake.
> In this antique but newly discovered paradise
> we shall meet apes and parrots.
> The light shall be subdued.[10]

Despite her regal dalliance, in the final act, Phoebe marries a sailor of her own class. 'As Phoebe', Mrs Robertson was later able to report, 'David Gascoyne was a complete success. In voice, gesture and expression he was a faultless girl, and must be given credit for a performance of all-round merit.'[11]

The following June saw the seven hundredth anniversary of the granting of the Royal Charter to the city by Henry III, and the town council requested a pageant from the city's schools. Since the choir school, thought to date from 1314, was the oldest, it put on the grandest show. Clissold played the boy bishop, and other classmates were dressed as dignitaries associated with the foundation across the centuries. A long procession formed on the lawns of the close. At its tail was the school crest, impersonated by 10-year-old David Gascoyne. The crest was a lily. To imitate this becoming flower, David wore a costume of which Great-Aunt Winifred would have been proud:

10. David Gascoyne, 'Transformation Scene', *Roman Balcony and Other Poems* (London: Lincoln Williams, 1932), 31.
11. Dora Robertson, 'The Choristers' Amateur Theatricals', *St Osmond's Magazine* (Dec. 1926), 10–14.

THE SCHOOL CREST

White tights, blue pointed mediaeval shoes, a tunic of pale blue satin, very
beautifully painted by the Rev. Leonard Packer, with the School Crest of lilies
and a scroll 'Domine dilexi decorum domus tuae' [Lord, respect the beauty of
Thine house].

   Tight silver tissue sleeves, a cherubim's wig of massed fair curls; in the hand a
white staff to which was attached a sheaf of Madonna Lilies from the garden.[12]

Canon Robertson then took a photograph of the crest-bearer in petal-
like pose before the flower beds around his back lawn, looking like some
latter-day Oscar Wilde.[13]

Naturally Win attended these occasions and, since they normally occurred
towards the end of choir time, she then bore David back to Fordingbridge
where he re-encountered growing twin brothers and an increasingly stressed
father. Authority and responsibility had not come naturally to Leslie. In the
late 1920s the world of finance was increasingly precarious, and even in
rural Hampshire the effects could be felt. Fortunately his branch had one or
two clients of exemplary affluence. In his second year there, the painter
Augustus John moved into the town, where he set up a studio and opened
an account with the Midland. He was very welcome but, as Mr Gascoyne
meekly announced to his impressed family, he would no more consider
visiting the painter than flying.

Opposite the house lived the local GP, John Rake, a keen amateur artist.
His son, also John Rake, was a close acquaintance of William Coldstream,
also the son of a doctor, and currently a student at the Slade. As he got older,
they lent Gascoyne books and, when up in London, began to escort him to
art galleries. As the attractions of Hampshire wore off, London visits were
becoming more frequent. Win was still deeply attached to Florence and
Tiny. In any case, as David's cultural awareness grew, there was simply more
for them to do. By 1928 Florence moved yet again: to Crediton Road in
West Hampstead, where she became a member of the thriving Unitarian
community in Hoop Lane, Golders Green. She took Win and David along
there one weekend to show off the new church building erected that year.
It was a Byzantine-style edifice in red brick, its apse spanned by a semicircular
mural by the rising artist and designer Ivon Hitchens: originally painted in
1919 as a war memorial, and his first known work.

---

12. 'The City 1227; The School 1314', *St Osmond's Magazine* (Dec. 1927), 9–16.
13. Salisbury School Archives, Robertson collection.

Though Win was still not reconciled with the Emery clan, Florence made up for it by treating them to shows. Increasingly David went along without Win, his bond with his godmother deepening with every passing year. She took him to the Golders Green Hippodrome for pantomimes and *Treasure Island* and *Lilac Time*, and to the Palladium or the Coliseum to see Pavlova dance. The sight of the two of them together was becoming increasingly incongruous since Florence was now stooping slightly, while for David the Cecil genes had kicked in just before his twelfth birthday, sending him to over six feet in his short trousers. He was not entirely comfortable with this.

Other troubles loomed. In October 1927, just after he had arrived back in Salisbury for the Christmas term, there was alarming news from home. One of Leslie's customers, a local ironmonger, had over-borrowed on his account to see him through the economic downturn. Alarmed at the size of his overdraft, which Leslie had underwritten, the client had committed suicide. A few days later, Leslie went missing from work. He was discovered in the New Forest, his car nose-deep in a ditch. He was wandering the forest paths, apparently with little awareness of how he had come there, or even who he was.

Leslie was given temporary leave and, after consulting with its doctors, the Midland decided the pressures of being a manager were too onerous for someone with his fragile temperament and underlying poor health. He was relieved of his post, and sent back to work in a less demanding clerical capacity in the Head Office in London. The handsome house in Fordingbridge was given up, and his salary appreciably dropped. Luckily David's fees were met by the cathedral chapter until his voice broke, but with two more sons to educate, Leslie found the transition hard to take, and not a little humbling. Accommodation too was a problem, since Florence was never going to open her doors once more to a family of five. So the bank found them one of three pokey flats above their branch at 402 Richmond Road, East Twickenham. When David returned home after Christmas, it was no longer to a pleasant bedroom at the top of a spacious house overlooking greenery in a leafy country town. It was to a bedroom not much higher than himself next to the tiny living room, overlooking drab shops and the ceaseless grind of traffic. The only redeeming feature was that, if one strained one's neck hard to the right, one could catch a sideways view of Richmond Bridge. Even that served to remind the Gascoynes just how far they had sunk in the social scale: beyond lay the sumptuous squares and terraces of Richmond on the Surrey bank.

A group photograph taken by Canon Robertson in his front garden late the following spring is revealing. Sixteen choristers sit along the low wall dividing his house from the school, with eager faces, ruffs in place, and brightly polished shoes. Amongst them are several names later famous in English music: Geoffrey Bush and Bernard Rose. Most have their hands crossed as they stare into the camera on what was obviously a sunny and flower-crowned afternoon. These are little boys, though talented little boys, and they look contented and well cared for. There is one exception. David Gascoyne is third from the left, a good few inches taller than any of his companions. Gone is the cute little chap who played Phoebe Lollipop. His feet dangle awkwardly down the wall. His arms are crossed, tightly and self-consciously, and his face is stern and unsmiling. He looks disconcerted and, for the first time in any of his photographs, just a little depressed.

The music too had turned dark. Alcock had decided that the choir was now fit to take on a concert-scale work. Edward Elgar sometimes came across from his home in the Malvern Hills to attend evensong. In the March following the HMV recording they planned a performance of *The Dream of Gerontius* with Alcock conducting the London Symphony Orchestra, the Salisbury Musical Society, the Southampton Philharmonic Society, and the cathedral choir. Elgar was in the audience. The work is a setting of Newman's poem of death and confrontation with the Divine. Despite the Anglican setting, this was Roman Catholic music by the greatest living English Catholic composer, setting a meditative, allegorical text by a cardinal and leader of the revived nineteenth-century English Catholic Church. Gascoyne sometimes spoke of that performance on Wednesday, 13 March 1929 as one of the most moving experiences of his life. At its climax, Gerontius encounters the divine love, evoked by a crash of percussion. As Gerontius, the tenor Steuart Wilson sang the chastened soul's response:

> Take me away, and in the lowest deep
> There let me be,
> And there in hope the lone night-watches keep,
> Told out for me.
> There, motionless and happy in my pain
> Lone, not forlorn,
> There will I sing my sad perpetual strain,
> Until the morn,
> There will I sing, and soothe my stricken breast,
> Which ne'er can cease
> To throb, and pine, and languish, till possest

Of its Sole Peace.
There will I sing my absent Lord and Love: –
Take me away …

This was the year in which Gascoyne started writing poetry. He had yet to come into contact with any modern verse, the best the schoolroom in Wren Hall was able to provide being extracts from Christina Rossetti or the Georgians. The four pieces he wrote that autumn possess Georgian echoes, and a sub-Georgian form. There are also hints of Blake's *Songs of Innocence and Experience*, but the most discernible single influence is probably Newman's. All are poems of exclusion. In one an angel arrives at Heaven's Gate too late to be let in, and dissolves into shameful tears. Another is a dialogue between two of the flowers in Canon Robertson's garden: a rose that is free to blow about, and a stock that is condemned to stand unmoving (one thinks of grim and stiff-looking Gascoyne in that recent photograph, surrounded by his roseate fellows). The last is a study of the young poet standing alone outside on a windy October evening, as the lawns of the close are strafed by the great cathedral bell:

> I took a breath of the sharp clear air
> The Autumn tang was rich and rare
> 'A clanging peal breaks forth from the spire
> Offering the stars its musical fire
> The lawns of the Close, dim white outspread
> Are as a mist on the sea' I said.
> 'This Autumn is but a stage
> A step, on my house of pilgrimage.'[14]

At 13 he was now so tall that one new boy mistook him for a master.[15] Gangling and plunged into silent thought, he was ready to move on. In September 1929 the conscientious and amiable Canon Robertson retired from the headship. His replacement, the Revd K. G. Sandberg, was a different proposition altogether: a martinet determined to raise the academic level of the school. He also possessed an implicit faith in the wisdom of military men, one of whom—the parent of a junior boy—was soon counselling him on the beneficial effects of muscular Christianity. Sandberg installed a draconian regime: no gloves to be worn on even the most bitter of winter days, rugby

14. 'Four of Several Poems Written by David Gascoyne (Chorister), September 1929', *St Osmond's Magazine* (Dec. 1929), 18.
15. Interview with Peter Janson-Smith, 31 Jan. 2008.

to be played even when the pitch was hard. As soon as January 1930 was over, and there was even the slightest discernible softening in the weather, swimming was resumed in the icy waters of the Avon. New boys were taught to swim by the simple expedient of flinging them from the bank.

Gascoyne endured all of this for a couple of terms before he began to notice some difficulty in reaching the high notes at evensong. Soon his voice started to lurch about, even when speaking. His days as a chorister were over. With that, his prospects were uncertain since, as Sandberg brusquely informed his parents, there was no point in entering this pensive but unstudious poet for a scholarship at one of the public schools, however minor. Leslie in any case could never have afforded the fees, even if David had struggled through the Common Entrance Examination, entitling him to a paying place.

By the summer term plans for his future were still insecure. The idyll was over, and he was as yet unsure what would follow it. One evening in July 1930, during his last term, he leant out of the window of the senior dormitory above the schoolroom. It was a balmy night, and several old boys who had returned for the annual festival reunion were singing catches out on the lawns of the close, smoking in the mild moonlit air. In *Opening Day* the protagonist Leon stands apart, listening:

> The limes cast shadows thicker than darkness in front of the school, swimming in warm air. Through the open door that opened on to the court-yard, under the small window on the sill of which stood a plaster bust of Handel, flowed a smoke-stained cascade of light, yellow, brilliant. Outside in the warm night, beyond the reach of the courtyard, voices were uniting and creeping quietly over all the objects near. The notes of the part-song climbed up in a string through the faintly clattering lime leaves and upon reaching the empty stretches of the air above the top of the trees, descended and followed one another in a close chase over the warm grass. People in coats stood grouped together listening underneath the limes. The concert was over. That was why there were clouds of tobacco smoke floating in the yellow light of the almost empty schoolroom. Leon stood with his hands in his pockets, alone, in the thick lime-tree shadows. The subdued notes of the last part-song mingled with the tobacco smoke and a dog's bark and whispered conversation and the creak of the gate (that swung white for a moment in the gloom) and mounted slowly in a tepid stream of sound through the trees, through the broad expanses of the air of this summer night towards the spire. Somebody swung a hand-lamp. Somebody came crunching along the road that led through the Close. Somebody said: 'We had better go in now'. That was the end of the Summer Term.[16]

It was his last memory of Salisbury.

16. David Gascoyne, *Opening Day*, 46–7.

But the following term, when he was far away, a disturbance was heard in the close. The military parent who had been advising Sandberg on the moral welfare of his charges had discovered that there was more to the new regime than stoically swimming in icy waters. It included the caning of younger boys in the study of the headmaster, who in the process sometimes permitted his non-beating hand to stray. Among the victims had been the son of the colonel, who appeared one morning at the front door of Wren Hall when lessons were in progress, carrying a horsewhip. He passed rapidly between the rows of desks and entered the headmaster's study without knocking. The boys heard the fall of the whip and the cries, which went on for several minutes.[17] Trusting 10-year-old Geoffrey Bush, who had rather enjoyed the more taxing lessons, was at a loss to understand when a few days later it was announced that, after so short tenure of office, the new headmaster would also be leaving.

17. Interview with Peter Janson-Smith, 31 Jan. 2008.

3

'Rolling and Unrolling'

Then Leslie and Win took a questionable decision. Strapped for cash, with three children to support on Leslie's diminished salary, unable to afford the fees at one of the boarding public schools Salisbury boys usually went on to, they opted for a makeshift solution. Since Richmond station—a penny bus ride across the bridge—was on the direct railway line into Waterloo Leslie used every weekday, they decided David should commute to a day school in central London. The inappropriate institution they chose for him was the Polytechnic Secondary School at 309 Upper Regent Street.

In Portland Place, opposite the side entrance to Broadcasting House, stands a memorial designed by Sir George Frampton in 1906 that has much to tell us about the nature and purpose of the academy to which David was now being sent. On a white marble plinth are three figures in bronze. Two are of adolescents of around 14 or 15, Gascoyne's own age in 1930. The younger is standing in shorts and holds a football under his left arm whilst his right is held trustingly across the shoulders of a seated middle-aged dignitary with high forehead and neat, sleeked-back hair: a man goat-bearded and suited, who reads from an open book. The man's right hand is lifted in appreciation or admonition, and his left knee is clasped by an older youth who rests on his haunches gazing adoringly up at him. In his right hand the senior pupil carries a slighter volume, which is closed. A name in capitals beneath the lip of the plinth identifies the object of all this veneration: the polytechnic's backer and saviour, in effect its founder, Quintin Hogg (1845–1903). Taken together, the group epitomizes the charitable ambiance of late Victorian educational paternalism. It is a tribute to application, and to intellectual subservience. Never would David Gascoyne, who always preferred to learn for himself, make one of those passively grateful young students. Never would he crouch clasping a closed book whilst regarding with awe one who held the key to all acceptable knowledge.

Hogg was an old Etonian who had made a fortune in the West Indian sugar trade. In his own youth he had played in the amateur side called the Wanderers Football Club which in the professional era would become Wolverhampton Wanderers; in middle age his twin passions were association football (which had originated in Eton) and Christian philanthropy directed at those excluded from the great public schools. The Forster Education Act of 1870 had laid on elementary schooling in the three R's for everyone; later, in 1902, a further Education Act would provide the first-ever state-funded secondaries. In the meantime, however, there had been a gap which Hogg had attempted to fill, first by setting up a ragged school in the East End, then by taking over the almost defunct Polytechnic Institution founded by the engineer George Cayley on the Regent Street site in the late 1830s. Underwriting and expanding its operations, he had by the late 1880s added to it two secondary schools, one for boys and another for girls.

One reason for the setting-up of these schools had been that the Polytechnic proper only ran evening classes, and there was plenty of class-room space unused during mornings and afternoons. As Hogg saw it, his innovation exemplified the Aristotelian principle of *horror vacui:* 'They say that nature abhors a vacuum and I confess to having a strong dislike to see so many rooms at the Poly lying empty during the daytime, when there are so many useful purposes to which they may be put.'[1] The schools, his pride and joy, had opened on 1 January 1886, with divisions for professional, commercial, and industrial classes. The avowed object of the boys school was to prepare lower-class young men for entry into the clerical grades of the Civil Service, or for menial or junior managerial posts in industry. Since 1919 the headmaster had been P. Abbott, a robust and diligent mathematician, whose main claim to fame—and one of the reasons that he had landed the job in the first place—was that he had once played in goal for Arsenal when that team was in the amateur league. Occasionally Abbott would be spotted on Saturday afternoons at Arsenal matches, but in general he avoided his colleagues out of school hours, and went to some lengths to ensure his distance from the staff and boys even during the school day. Nobody had ever discovered his Christian name, and he was thus known throughout the Polytechnic School simply as 'P.A.'.

P.A. possessed a passion for statistics. Every speech day this latter-day Gradgrind would rise to his feet and read out the examination scores for

1. Quoted in I. C. B. Seamon, *The Quintin School 1886–1956* (London: Quintin School, 1957), 8.

the year, followed by the results of the annual sporting fixtures, then sit down without further comment. His behaviour was much the same at daily assemblies, held in the cinema next door. His notion of success was governed by figures, and a succession of quantified tests. Entry to the school was by examination for nineteen free places offered each year (for which in 1922, for example, there had been 320 candidates). The rest of the students were given part-bursaries, but a small number of full feeing places were offered at 13 or 14 to boys who had come through the private system. It was one of these places that Gascoyne was given in September 1930, when he was placed in the D or bottom stream of the Lower Fourth.[2] The low allocation suggests he had actually failed the entrance test, but P.A. sometimes took a risk on boys in this position provided their performance improved within two years. If it did not, they were asked to leave, in case their low marks compromised the average annual score in publicly marked exams.

Inspired by Florence Mole, Gascoyne asked to study German. It was not on the syllabus, so he continued with Latin, for which he had little ability. Otherwise, the standard of teaching was prosaic to say the least. Maths set the tone, so much so that, according to the school's historian, 'In some respects and for some boys, particularly for those to who, mathematics was not, as it was to the headmaster, a favourite subject, it could seem rather a soulless place.'[3] The French master was J. Stevenson who had 'an air of great haste, as if he was anxious to get back as soon as possible to his Surrey garden', assisted by the only francophone on the premises, a Monsieur Chevrollier, whose idea of his role was confined to 'indefatigably and self-lessly plugging away at French grammar through the years'. For an artistically inclined pupil, there were two bright spots: the art master P. J. Walford, and a Fabian-inclined English teacher called J. B. Coates, who alone seemed to have some conception of the movements in literature and culture sweeping the world beyond the Polytechnic's sooty mock Corinthian facade. His lessons, observes the school history, 'were but part of a life which found room for a Personalist Society in later years and in early years a Natural History Society on whose rambles senior boys divided the time between observation of redstarts and willow warblers and solemn discussions on the ideas of Wells and Shaw and Dostoyevsky and Samuel Butler, and were made

---

2. *The Quintinian*, 8/17 (Autumn 1930).
3. Seamon, *Quintin School*, 59.

aware of the intellectual currents of the time, of which for the most part the
School, like the Polytechnic, remained completely ignorant'.

After *The Dream of Gerontius*, after evensong in rosewood choir stalls, it
must all have been a shock. The sheer scope of it—720 pupils as opposed to
the 40 cherubs at Salisbury—was daunting, and the only skills rewarded
were those for which David had little gift. There was one consolation:
London itself. Excitedly, in his first term, Gascoyne sent back to the choir
school an evocation of the underground, and that moving wonder, an escalator with its motley human hoard: 'office men, chorus girls, tramps, engine
drivers, belles dames and shop women, all self-centred and entirely unconscious of those about them... But if CHRIST HIMSELF (with all reverence) were to pass over it, the escalator would still go on unconscious. Day
and night, never ceasing to rest any day of the week or any week of the year.
Alive, and yet unbounded by law, fate or God, it still continues.'[4] The description anticipates that of an escalator from the 'Megalometropolitan' section
of his radiophonic poem *Night Thoughts* by twenty-five years.

Every evening he could pick up the Bakerloo Line at nearby Oxford
Circus back to Waterloo. Luckily he sometimes walked: down Regent Street
to Oxford Circus, left along Oxford Street and then right down the Charing
Cross Road, past its many bookshops. On his left past Cambridge Circus
was Foyles with its acres of shining volumes, then a little further to the right
at the corner of Litchfield Street, No. 80: Zwemmer's. Its stock was diverse
and international: books in French and German, the latest periodicals from
Paris, and an art gallery upstairs. A few yards further on lay a row of flourishing antique book dealers, including A. H. Mayhew at No. 56, whose double
front with its stacks of al fresco shelves advertised 'Libraries Purchased'.
Further on towards Trafalgar Square he reached a narrow passageway to the
left running through to St Martin's Lane, lined to either side with antiquarian and exotic outlets. This was Cecil Court, Mecca of the London rare
book trade. On the southern side No. 17 was presided over by the loquacious
and informative David Low, described by Robin Waterfield, who later
worked for him, as 'generous, knowledgeable, creative, with a discreet flamboyance'.[5] Next door at Nos. 19 to 21 were—and still are—the broad-fronted,
capaciously cellared Watkins Books, established in 1892 to specialize in

4. 'The Escalator', *St Osmund's Magazine* (Oct. 1930), 15–16. Compare *Collected Poems* (1965),
   149.
5. James Fergusson, *Ahasuerus the Bookseller* (London: James Fergusson, 2008), 78.

mysticism and the occult. Gascoyne dawdled, he browsed, and inevitably, spending his meagre pocket money, he bought.

What Gascoyne found in such places was a lot more inviting than the humdrum academic fare doled out at the Polytechnic. Soon, instead of swotting irregular Latin verbs, he had his nose stuck into the two volumes of *Marius the Epicurean*, Pater's attractively decadent novel evoking the fading imperial Rome of the Antonine emperors. Instead of swotting dates, he was absorbing *The Decline of the West*, Oswald Spengler's fashionable survey of successive societies as they rise and fall, passing from vigorous culture to effete 'civilization'. The view toned in well with Pater's pessimism. Soon he was imagining himself as one of these same emperors outside a villa at sunset, in the poem 'Roman Balcony':

> FAR-OFF, palpitating tide!
> In the pale light I sit here,
> Sad with sin, gazing on the city,
> On the yellow waters of the distant Tiber,
> On a stone sphinx at the gate of my villa.
>
> A wild pipe-tune climbs through the cold air
> From the rain-beaten roses under the balcony,
> Like the vast, tumbling cloud that sweeps
> Whirling over the faded sky,
> Full of the shadow of death.[6]

If Rome had risen and fallen, so might London. Spengler had predicted as much, since according to his sweeping scheme Western culture was 'Faustian'. It had reached too far, progressing from medieval spirituality to the glories of the Renaissance, then retreated through the Enlightenment to degenerate industrialism. The downward curve set off memories of apocalyptic lessons from the Old Testament at Salisbury. Dedicating a longish poem to Spengler, Gascoyne voiced such concerns in 'The New Isaiah':

> A new Isaiah walks the City streets
> with burning coals of fire on his head
> who cries his warnings to the careless crowds
> who heed him not but arm themselves for wars,
> who whet their swords for one another's blood,
> who go a-whoring with their own inventions
> deaf to the cries of one who sees their fate:

---

6. David Gascoyne, *Roman Balcony and Other Poems* (London: Lincoln Williams, 1932), 7.

'As Rome fell, ye shall fall,
as falling ye are now.'[7]

When up in town, and not writing verses or rummaging among shelves, David frequented a childhood friend. Late in 1931, when he had just turned 15, Florence Mole died and was buried in Golders Green cemetery. Her death plunged Win into temporary bereavement, but it brought David a modest but in time quite useful legacy for which, in his Freudian days, he would become convinced he had symbolically murdered his godmother. There had been consequences too for the emotionally clinging Tiny. Stuck for a job or a home, she eventually found a position she loathed in the London branch of the bank Credito Italiano. She lived for the evenings when she could withdraw to her Bloomsbury flat at 45 Mecklenburg Street, overlooking Mecklenburg Square Gardens at the front, and Gray's Inn Road at the rear. The house belonged to Alida Klemantaski, estranged Polish-born wife of Harold Monro, the Georgian-style poet and anthologist who ran the celebrated Poetry Bookshop opposite the main gates of the British Museum. David took to calling on Tiny there at weekends or after school and, on one of his early visits, she introduced him to Alida.

It was a fortunate meeting. Alida had a fine reading voice, and for years she had run the weekly readings above Harold's Georgian-fronted shop.[8] Partly as a result, she existed at the epicentre of literary London, having met many of the leading writers of the day. The tide of gossip flooded upstairs to Tiny's flat where Alida would often call, confiding in her—and in David when present—concerning the increasingly obsessive behaviour of her bosom companion Vivienne Eliot, another estranged wife but of a more famous poet. Vivienne herself would drop round in the afternoons, lie on the carpet, and, looking up at the ceiling in studied despair, would complain—as Alida put it—of 'Tom's iniquities'.[9]

Soon Eliot emerged from this calumny or myth. Since Alida ran the Poetry Bookshop readings, to which she contributed herself, she began to take David and Tiny along. One January evening all three of them were present when Old Possum himself came round from the offices of Faber and Faber in Russell Square, stooping slightly to ease his height—for he was

---

7. Ibid. 77.
8. For her career and contribution, see Joy Grant, *Harold Monro and the Poetry Bookshop* (Berkeley and Los Angeles: University of California Press, 1967), 86–92.
9. BL Lives, F1380, Side B.

almost as tall as David—up the narrow stairwell from the ground floor towards the narrow room where the readings took place, on the top floor beneath the pediment and eves. Eliot had an intoxicatingly dry voice, but did not read his own work. Instead, seeing as it was New Year, he intoned Christina Rossetti's 'Old and New Year Ditties':

> Passing away, saith my Soul, passing away:
> With its burden of fear and hope, of labour and play,
> Hearken what the past does witness and say:
> Rust in thy gold, a moth is in thine array,
> A canker is in thy bud, thy leaf must decay.
> At midnight, at cockrow, at morning, one certain day,
> Lo, the bridegroom shall come and shall not delay:
> Watch thee and pray.
> Then I answer'd: yea.[10]

Since the museum was immediately opposite the shop, Alida gave David a letter of introduction to use the reading room there. Thus, aged 15, he spent the hours intended for school homework imbibing the mystical writings of Emanuel Swedenborg, from which he culled his own vision of doom in a sequence entitled 'Mirabilia'. In Arthur Symons's *The Symbolist Movement in Literature* he encountered the names Laforgue, Baudelaire, and, in the chapter on Gérard de Nerval, a discussion of the relationship between poetry and madness. Most revealing of all was the case of Arthur Rimbaud, from the biography of whom in the relevant chapter he discovered that the author of *Illuminations* had been a youth of about his own age.

Beyond the library itself there were the collections of the museum to explore. One day in the Japanese section he came across five tiny ivory figures in a glass case. They were *netsukés*, ornamental toggles used to secure pouches to the sash of a kimono. On the label they were attributed to the fourteenth-century Buddhist artist Hottara Sonja. Each told a story. Applying from Symons his new familiarity with Imagism, Gascoyne wrote a miniature verse around each:

> No larger than my finger-nail
> This little face so finely carved,
> More pink than the cherry in bloom

Finer than silk the tiny hairs
Smoothly over the forehead combed,
As delicate as spiders' thread.

What lovely landscapes do you see,
O tiny gazing Eastern eyes,
so constant in your ivory?[11]

He even tried out such interesting experiments on his uncomprehending
school. Thinking back to his infant years in Bournemouth, he composed
two seascapes in contrasted styles: the first in 'Traditional Form', the second
in 'Modernist Form'. The first was a conventional sestet of tetrameters
grouped in rhymed couplets:

BY THE SEA
TRADITIONAL FORM

The sea rolls to and from the land,
Leaving white patterns on the sand.
To watch the waves I wander here
Along the water's edge—I hear
The whole world crying out in sleep,
With voice of winds and waves that weep.

The second version owed something to a poet's innate adventurousness, a
little to e.e.cummings, but even more to numbers of the Paris-based magazine *transition* that he had been picking up at Zwemmer's and in which
Joyce had been trying out some fragments from his *Work in Progress* that
would emerge in May 1939 as *Finnegan's Wake*. In Gascoyne's teenage experiment, the undulations of the waves became a fluidity of language and
typography—eliding, splitting, and foaming.

BY THE SEA
MODERNIST FORM

(1)

the whiskey windwhite
                              waves spit in my
face they are so grey so stony cold the
                              waves
                    are grey stone walls the
sea is an old washerwomen wh

---

11. *Roman Balcony and Other Poems*, 27.

o (ooo) spitsand flings grey stones   atm
e (eee)

(2)

       bluer and blue   meeting
       bluer the sea rushes and
       retreats folding   (o) and
   ex   pan   ding   l   ike   a
       concertina

(3)

       lettuces are grow
       ing in the blue   c
            averns
            little f
            ish sw
            ish in
            and out of them

(4)

LOOK!

        it is the shark
        with the little   no
        selike   al
              umpo
        fsugar he jumps)
        out of the water) (sh-)…spl…ash…ashing
        us with spray likes
        ilver tea-leaves

(5)

     awave   touches
        aus Trali A
        and another
        r touches C
        hinajingl
        ing likech
        ains the   waves   join   am
                                  er
        (booo…o…ooom)   ic
                                a

   to Europe where the flags   fly
   but no wave touches Switzerland
   where the mountains, like taller
   waves only whiter reach for the

                               sky

(6)

the sea is an old washerwoman
forever folding and unfolding
her blue with cold enormous
arms
forever rolling and unrolling
her white froth with enormous
eyes.[12]

A few months later this literary double-experiment appeared in the pages of the school magazine. It found its editors at a complete loss, with so little appreciation of what they had received that they set a routine sports announcement following immediately on from the Modernist version of the poem, on the same page, and in the same lineation and spacing. 'School v. O.Q's Cricket Match, Chiswick, June 24th, at 2.30', however, owed nothing to the influence of James Joyce.

Gascoyne was in completely the wrong environment. He had strug-gled up to the Lower Fifth where, despite his intensive and variegated reading, his personal aversion to exams and to passive instruction was such that he still languished in the lower half of the bottom stream. In July 1932 P.A. called Leslie and Win up to his pokey lair at the Regent's Street site, from which he was seldom seen to emerge. They were, he told them, wasting their money on the formal education of this preco-ciously literate fifth former.[13] Though he had landed prizes in English and Music over the last year, P.A.'s advice to them was that they should withdraw him forthwith, since he would never pass the Matriculation Examination—the rough equivalent of today's GCSE—looming at the end of the following academic year. Even if he did so, he would drag down the general average to an embarrassing extent. Still less, in the eyes of this dull-eyed pedagogue, was Gascoyne a credible candidate for entry into the Sixth Form that P.A. was proud of having recently instituted, or for the Higher Certificate (the equivalent in today's terms of A levels) that would alone permit him entry into university. Thus it was that, three months shy of his sixteenth birthday, David Gascoyne completed his formal education.

12. *The Quintinian*, 24 (Spring 1933), 31–2.
13. BL Lives, F1380, Side A.

The severance was more of a judgement on the system than on him. In decades to come when asked by compilers of questionnaires or biographical dictionaries which university he attended, he would enter 'The Regent Street Polytechnic'. As a matter of fact he had abandoned secondary school at the point at which he ceased to believe it was contributing to his self-generated—if a little one-sided—intellectual development. The bitter—and sometimes proud—consciousness of this fact goes some way to explain the suspicion and disdain with which in early manhood and middle life Gascoyne tended to regard what he sometimes referred to as the 'Professoriat'. He was to become one of the best-read members of his generation, yet without a single certificate to his name, a state of affairs that was to contribute in no small measure to his subsequent financial insecurity. This background in turn helps explain the hunger with which, throughout the rest of his life, he turned to the self-imposed task of immersing himself in literature, art, music, philosophy, and theology from almost every European country. Formal educational achievement, as far as he was concerned, was for spiritless conformists. Ever afterwards, Gascoyne remained a shining example of that seldom-advertised phenomenon: the advantages of attending a bad school.

4

'Voiles'

Six months later Gascoyne's first volume of verse, *Roman Balcony and Other Poems*, appeared in print. He later claimed to have forgotten who had issued it.[1] In fact the publisher was Lincoln Williams, a firm in St Martin's Place that specialized for the most part in illustrated guides to male body-building. The frontispiece bore a pen-and-ink likeness of its author by Stuart A. Ray, son of an art master at the Polytechnic. It showed an angular and self-absorbed face, partly obscured by spectacles that caught the light, refracting it into a bundle of obtuse and refracted angles. One of the best, and later much anthologized, pieces in the book was entitled 'Prison', and it gave an irresistible impression of the stifling mental environment from which the young author had recently escaped:

> It is dark and stifling within this cupboard.
> I cannot open the door.
> In the faint light I see a Chinese mask
> That glares down upon me
> From one high corner.
>
> When I move, the walls move.
> They follow my movements like the moon...[2]

One does not need a lot of imagination either to trace one original of this particular cell to David's restricted bedroom in East Twickenham. Rather too low-ceilinged for his lofty frame, it was where he slept, wrote, and dreamed. Physical and social flight seemed necessary but difficult. He had fled school, but had yet to break free from the parental home or, except

1. Gascoyne in answers to publisher's questionnaire, 1965, OUP PB/ED/017417, Box 2353.
2. *Roman Balcony and Other Poems* (London: Lincoln Williams, 1932), 19. Quoted by Robin Skelton in the Introduction to *Collected Poems* (1965), pp. ix–x.

through his reading, from his English background. One of the main themes of the collection was the stranglehold of the familiar, and the desire to loosen its grip. Already, claustrophobia is a recognizable Gascoynian theme.

His parents exacerbated this sense, much though he loved them. Win was still keeping up with local newspapers from Bournemouth, posted on to her by friends. One day she read there a brief notice on an inquest into the death of a widow, proprietress of a run-down guesthouse on the front, who early one morning had run into her garden and across to the beach, then drowned herself in the sea. The incident had suggested a poignant item in David's book. In 'Seaside Tragedy' different parts of the distracted woman's mind speak in clashing, discordant voices:

> She went across the lawn
> Towards the sea [...]
> 'This is perfectly serious,
> perfectly serious (I mean it);
> Measures may have to be taken.
> Something ought to be stopped.
> This kind of thing ought not to be allowed.' [...]
> She saw the sea.
> She heard the barrel-organs
> Playing eternally
> At the bottom of the sea.
>
> She remembered,
> (As she approached the sea),
> The linoleum,
> And the artichokes,
> And the geyser.[3]

Less dramatically, David's own paths of escape lay through music, art, film, and above all and through reading, and in particular the radical texts obtainable through certain West End bookshops. Already, before leaving school, he had attended a course of evening lectures on contemporary film just round the corner from Waterloo Station, at Morley College, and he was now developing fairly advanced musical tastes.[4] The musical fare at Salisbury had been on the conservative side. In the cathedral they had sung no twentieth-century Continental music, and as far as British composers were concerned

---

3. *Roman Balcony*, 69–70.
4. BL Lives, F1380, Side B. The lecturer was the Scottish pioneer of documentary film John Grierson.

the most innovative composers on offer had been Elgar and John Ireland, both personal friends of Alcock's. Now David started acquiring gramophone recordings of the Second Viennese School, which introduced him to a world of atonal harmony equivalent in its daring to the poems and fiction that he was sampling from publications on offer at Zwemmer's. Alban Berg, whose opera *Wozzeck* to a libretto based on Georg Büchner, was to become well known to him, rapidly became a favourite. He started to develop his piano technique by acquiring the simpler volumes of *Mikrokosmos*, the graded method that Béla Bartók had been compiling since 1928 to introduce amateur and young musicians to the idioms of contemporary, and especially modal, music. As his competence increased, he tackled the easier Preludes of Debussy, which he had already heard the virtuoso Harriet Cohen—friend of Albert Einstein, mistress of the composer Arnold Bax, and Jewish activist—perform at the Wigmore Hall. He even tackled the serialist spareness of Arnold Schoenberg's *Sechs Kleine Klavierstücke*, Op. 9 of 1911, with their contrasted tempi and textures, one of the earliest works in which Schoenberg had broken with the grand Mahlerian tradition and championed a fresh starkness of structure.

In the bookshops he explored a world of answering literary inventiveness. It was in Harold Monro's Poetry Bookshop, for example, that he came across an issue of the intermittently issued magazine *Chapbook* edited by the leading British Imagist, Frank Stuart Flint. It championed Imagist techniques which had already seeped into 'By The Sea', and some items in *Roman Balcony*. For even more demanding fare he went down to Zwemmer's, which stocked *transition*. There too he discovered an intriguing number of the bilingual magazine *This Quarter*, edited from 8 Rue Delambre in Montparnasse by Edward W. Titus and financed by Titus's wife, the diminutive cosmetics millionairess Helena Rubinstein. It was the fifth issue—a Surrealist special—and it contained contributions by André Breton, Paul Eluard, and René Crevel, alongside artwork by Marcel Duchamp, Dalí, and others. It also included extracts from the movement's one-time house magazine *La Révolution surréaliste*; soon Gascoyne was taking its back numbers, then successive issues of its successor from 1929, *Le Surréalisme au service de la révolution*. Frustrated by the inept French with which he had been furnished at school, he was soon mugging the language up from dictionaries, the more eagerly so since Arthur Symons's book had encouraged him to read the great French poets of the nineteenth century. He soon acquired a copy of Baudelaire's *Fleurs du mal*, and read it enthusiastically whilst sitting in nearby Kew Gardens. It was followed by the Mercure de France edition of Rimbaud's *Illuminations* between bright yellow covers. Rimbaud's work spoke to him most astutely, written by an *enfant terrible* such as in 1933 David clearly liked to think of himself as being. The hallucinatory vision of *Illuminations*, a text that the Surrealists claimed as fount and inspiration, the swagger, verbal virtuosity, and defiance: all strongly appealed.

The Poetry Bookshop closed its doors that year since Monro himself had recently died, and in any case his star had long been sinking. As far as British poetry was concerned, a more exciting arena was now offered by a book-shop that had just opened at 4 Parton Street, a narrow and now demolished passageway near Red Lion Square, conveniently close to Tiny's flat. Unpromisingly signposted above its doorway as simply 'New Books', it was inefficiently if enthusiastically run by a kindly young man from Wiltshire called David Archer.

Archer is one of the unsung heroes of mid-twentieth-century British verse, his life uncharted by either biography or obituary; without him, how-ever, British poetry of the immediate pre-war period would look very dif-ferent.[5] Like many radicals of the thirties, he was the child of relative wealth, son of a retired major from the village of Castle Eaton in Wiltshire, where his family had owned substantial holdings of land since 1856. The male Archers had mostly been in the army, and David had duly been sent to Wellington College in Berkshire, a school established in the aftermath of the Crimean War to train recruits for nearby Sandhurst and the Woolwich academy. But the college was also a nursery for revolt among those—like the Romilly brothers and the poet Gavin Ewart—who failed to fit into its philistine, sporting ambience. At Cambridge, where he had opted for the aggressively modern subjects of economics and psychology, Archer had rubbed shoulders with a number of those who would later enjoy success as writers (the translator George Reavey was at the same college) graduating with a double third in 1928.[6] All of this had produced a leftward-leaning young man of slightly bumbling benevolence and eclectically radical tastes. Despite this essential attitude, Archer retained an inherited military posture, what one of his many protégés later called 'an awkward tensity of body, an almost Prussian stiffness', accentuated by the fact that he invariably carried

5. A rare exception to this general neglect is A. T. Tolley, *The Poetry of the Thirties* (London: Victor Gollancz, 1975), 222–30.
6. *Biographical History of Gonville and Cauis College* (Cambridge: Cambridge University Press, 1948), v. 295. Gonville and Caius College Cambridge Matriculation Book TUT/01/01/09.

some sort of reading matter under his left arm as if bearing a regimental baton. The reason was that this limb was withered, another fact that cannot have made life at the robustly sporty Wellington any easier. Archer was thin and tall, with arresting pale blue eyes. He had modish rather than firm convictions, and little ability for making money, or for paying—even for opening—his utility bills. His creativity was oblique, encouraging poets without himself being one (in fact he read little himself apart from detective stories, claiming that he could detect the smell of a true poet without needing to read him[7]) and fostering revolution in those around him without taking a stand on anything in particular. Unenergetically homosexual, he was diffident in manner, and had never—as long as anybody could remember—finished a spoken sentence, leaving the majority of his statements hanging beneficently in mid-air. Despite—or perhaps because of—his outer helplessness, he possessed a flair for making young male friends, to whom his loyalty and generosity proved unstinting. Luckily, as a result of the sale of much of the Castle Eaton estate in 1925, he had the use of a small fortune from his father, which he employed in renting this four-storey Bloomsbury building, in accommodating impoverished protégés rent-free on mattresses placed on its upper floors, and in purchasing for the downstairs shop the variegated but mostly radical reading matter he seldom seemed actually to sell. His shop was the closest London could come at the period to the gregarious and radical *librairies* of the Latin Quarter: part social club, part debating chamber, part dosshouse. It was a mess, but it was a glorious and fertile mess. A vivid impression of its abundant chaos and suffused ethos of urgency is given by Philip Toynbee, son of a famous Oxford historian, who first stepped into this hectic and heady muddle the following year:

> That shop! The archetype of all the 'People's Books', 'Worker's Bookshops', 'Popular Books' that I was to know in the next few years. The solemn red-backed classics of the Marx-Engels-Lenin Institute, the mauve and bright yellow pamphlets by Pollitt and Palme Dutt, the Soviet posters of moonlit Yalta and sunlit tractors—the whole marvellous atmosphere of conspiracy and purpose.[8]

Not only was Archer a facilitator of friendship: he also aspired to publish poetry, and encouraged editors to meet promising young authors on the premises. In the former capacity he was about to bring out *Thirty*

---

7. Interview with George Barker, Oct. 1981.
8. Philip Toynbee, *Friends Apart: A Memoir of Esmond Romilly and Jasper Ridley in the Thirties* (London: MacGibbon and Kee, 1954), 18.

Preliminary Poems by the 20-year-old poet George Barker, another habitué of this frenetically hospitable establishment who, like everybody else, was perpetually to be involved in the 'complicated epicycles of friendship and jealousy' that characterized the place.[9] Among those caught in its social coils were passionate politicos, fugitive undergraduates, and off-duty actors. T. E. Lawrence sometimes called round for tea. Michael Redgrave put in an occasional appearance, as did the young Alec Guinness. But the shop also attracted professional bibliophiles, including a 19-year-old assistant at Foyles, Robin Everard Waterfield. An enthusiast for arcana, Waterfield had dropped out of the medical training his Beccles-based doctor father had wished on him, and was now feeling his uncertain way towards a future as Anglican missionary and, later in life, a flamboyant, gruffly eccentric bookseller. Before long, Waterfield had become one of Gascoyne's closest—and spiritually most empathic—friends.

There was one further great advantage to participation in this atmosphere of subversive gregariousness, even for someone as essentially introverted as Gascoyne. Parton Street attracted editors in their droves, and many of the most innovative magazines of the period started life there. Among other enterprises, the shop housed the headquarters of the Promethean Society which combined high-minded Socialism of the Independent Labour Party variety with a commitment to bodily health and mental well-being; its official organ the *Twentieth Century* (in which Barker published several early essays and poems) appeared from the same address. For poets loath to be sucked into the prevailing and—so Parton Street aficionados tended to think—social exclusiveness of the Auden school, there was also *New Verse*. Early in 1933, both Gascoyne and Barker—who as yet knew one another slightly—severally encountered in Parton Street its editor Geoffrey Grigson, an assertive and cantankerous individual who was to have an enabling effect on both of their writing careers.

Grigson possessed authority alongside a temperamental and, in print at least, irrepressible rancour. The rancour was perhaps understandable: he had detested his various schools and Oxford, from which he had come down with a third in English. He had also lost three beloved brothers in the First World War, and was to lose the rest of his siblings in the Second. Bitterness slowly stole into him. In 1933, when he was still working during the week as literary editor of the *Morning Post*, he tended to hide it on first meeting, confining his

9. George Barker in *Coming to London* (London: John Lehmann, 1950), 52.

spleen to his journalism, which could be especially biting. Outwardly he was personable, striking Gascoyne as 'a man of great sensitivity, and a wonderful sense of Englishness, and very good taste in painting'.[10] His regular attendance at Archer's shop was motivated by a desire to recruit talent for his magazine. *New Verse* was in fact pretty catholic in its content. It featured members of the Auden school, up-and-coming stars, and Grigson's own bilious criticism.

Grigson clearly found Gascoyne promising but half-educated (which in one sense he was). He also clearly found him malleable, and was soon arranging to see him for what amounted to weekly tutorials at a tea-house opposite the offices of the *Morning Post* in Fleet Street.[11] Here the older man aired his pet loves and hates: there was, David soon found, a 'pet hate of the week', usually forgotten by the following session. As their intimacy grew, Grigson also invited him to the regular Sunday afternoon tea parties held in his smart house in Keats Grove, Hampstead hung with paintings by Ben Nicholson. It was here, among the scones and the literary chitchat, that David met for the first time many who were to become important to him in years to come: Herbert Read (a near neighbour of Grigson's), Norman Cameron, Charles Madge, Kathleen Raine. A good few years younger than the rest was Gavin Ewart, still a schoolboy at Wellington, his revulsion from which, though more satirically expressed, was as strong as Archer's had been. At 16, though, Gascoyne was the youngest of the lot. He was six foot three, he wore thick horn-rimmed glasses, he looked serious, and he was eager to learn. He talked. Slowly he achieved presence.

As yet, however, he was unsure where his omnivorous tastes and talents would lead him. Was it to be poetry or prose? Volume by volume he had been following *Pilgrimage*, Dorothy Richardson's thirteen-volume novel sequence around her own life told through the medium of a stream of consciousness or, as she somewhat misleadingly preferred to call it, 'interior monologue'. Intrigued, in May 1933 he embarked on an exercise of his own along similar lines, provisionally entitled *Study in the Third Person Singular*, in which one Leon Bristow stands in for himself, just as Miriam Henderson had stood in for Richardson. This hapless and introspective youth lives with an impossible father and his grumpy housekeeper in a modern semi in Cambridge Park, Twickenham, a new estate on the outskirts of historic Marble Hill House, a few streets to the south-east of the dingy block where

10. BL Lives, F1382, Side A.
11. Ibid.

David himself was still living with his family (and where, in the book, the boy's boon companion Ross is condemned to reside). He spends his days reading Rimbaud and Baudelaire, scouring *The Writers and Artists Year Book* for 1931, playing piano pieces by Debussy, Satie, Bartók, and Schoenberg, relishing his reproduction of Van Gogh's *Fishing Boats of Saintes-Maries*, and borrowing from the library the mystical novels of Arthur Machen. When fed up with these activities he takes the train into central London, where he visits his aunt Sue Cotteram in her Bloomsbury apartment at 45 Mecklenburg Street (Tiny's actual address). She offers him a room under her roof and, when he returns to announce this fact to his tyrannical dad, a tussle ensues, in which the father suffers a cardiac seizure and dies. The housekeeper malevolently contacts the police. At the very moment he thought that he had broken free, shades of the prison house close around the growing boy.

As in *David Copperfield*, the mother is dead, and this particular David dedicated the book to his own. Win was no fit object of resentment, and too much love was invested in her for her to appear on the page in any sort of fallible shape. The twins have been spirited away. Instead there is a sister stillborn at the time of the mother's death and in the year of the twins' births. Both the father—a 'pompous and indifferent' businessman quite unlike the mild mannered, tolerant Leslie—and the fictitious ogre of a housekeeper are figments of that Dalí-esque condition, paranoia. This state intensifies when the two of them announce their forthcoming marriage, partners in philistinism and hence the boy's foes. The hostility ditches the narrative structure—neither the dialogue nor the plot really convince. What distinguishes the work as a product of the poetic imagination is its evocation of a fluid and versatile consciousness, a pimply precocity ill at ease with itself and uncertain where to turn.

The keynote in this respect is sounded when Leon picks up his copy of Rimbaud's *Illuminations* and turns to the third poem in the mini-sequence 'Jeunesse', the prose poem 'At Twenty' ('Vingt Ans'):

> Les voix instructives exilées ... L'ingénuité physique amèrement rassise ... — Adagio—Ah! l'égoïsme infini de l'adolescence, l'optimisme studieux: que le monde était plein de fleurs cet été! Les airs et les formes mourant.[12]

---

12. 'Banished sophisticated voices! Resourceful vigour uncomfortably housed ... Adagio—Ah! the infinite egoism and studious optimism of adolescence: how abundant with flowers the world was that summer! The dying breezes and forms ...'. Quoted in David Gascoyne, *Opening Day* (London: Cobden-Sanderson, 1933), 56.

In Leon's—and almost certainly Gascoyne's own—case, the problem is one of being unruddered by his own versatility. His swollen capacity not simply to appreciate quite different spheres of art, thought, and life, but to cross-lace all of these sensations, produces in him a spontaneous variety of synaethesia that is sometimes barely under his control. The fructifying influence in this respect is less Richardson than John Cowper Powys, whose essay *In Defence of Sensuality* of 1930 had been an apologia for a life saturated in sensual appreciation of every kind, especially for the interpenetration of different modes of sensitivity: towards music, towards art, towards words. What is fullness in Cowper Powys, however, here becomes an intense sensibility of a potentially unbalancing kind. At one point when he is sitting at the piano, Leon opens up volume i of Debussy's *Etudes* and plays through no. 8, 'La Fille aux cheveux de lin' ('The Girl with the Flaxen Hair'), which reminds him of Eliot's *La Figlia Che Piange* and the hyancinth girl from 'The Burial of the Dead'. Then he turns back to no. 2, 'Voiles':

> Voiles: what did that mean? Veils? He had an idea that it meant ships' sails. A mist of early morning was rising from the sea. White wings, pale white, idly floating wings, were appearing in the translucence of the fine salt mist, of the misty veils that arose from the hazy, lazily tossing sea. Opaque, cerulean blue, aquamarine, turquoise, crystalline jade, becoming azure, pale emerald turned by some sea magic into sapphire, all shades of blue from ultramarine to indigo, mingling with grey, a kaleidoscope of blues, blue, blues, blue,—the sea drifting tossing, swimming, beneath the floating veils of mist pierced with lazy white wings that it created to cover itself with, for the sake of a passing whim. And out of this blue uncertainty, blue vagueness, blue obscurity, came slow and stately a fleet of boats…or ships…or yachts, white and spotless…or maybe many-coloured sails of fishing boats…lovely sails, drifting like the wings of the gulls…blue of sea and white of sails, blue, and white of wings of sails, sails, slow sails, sails…voiles…voiles—[13]

This is not only a very musical passage, infused with the dreamy impressionism of Debussy's original and as good an evocation of the tone poem *La Mer* as of the piano piece described. It is also very painterly, and verbally fluid in the manner of the richly associated chaos of Rimbaud's 'Parade' as set six years later by Britten in his song sequence of Rimbaud's poems.[14] Gascoyne

---

13. Ibid. 100–1.
14. *Les Illuminations* for solo voice and orchestra (1939). Gascoyne and Britten were very often drawn towards the same texts. See also the latter's *Hölderlin Fragments* (1958).

is benefiting from Debussy's own pun, since *une voile* is a veil, while *un voile* is a sail, and in the plural the word can mean either. The ambiguity is consonant with the slightly epicene air of the prose and the visualization (elsewhere Leon admires Beardsley), and with the whole tone scale in which Debussy's music is couched, major/minor since strictly speaking neither with intimations of both.

Much in his life was now enabling Gascoyne to leapfrog barriers, linguistic, generic, and personal. As soon as he had finished his novel he handed it to Tiny who took it to Alida Monro. Alida in turn ferried it to the firm of Cobden-Sanderson in Montague Street, who had published her husband's *Collected Poems* with a Preface by Eliot the previous year. The firm accepted it and came up with an advance on signature of the contract. Putting this together with the £100 legacy that he had received from Florence's estate, David had enough money to spend at least a month abroad. He had never before left England, and his initial thought was to pursue one of Florence's own affinities by taking a job that he had seen advertised as a tutor to a family in Germany.[15] The plan came to nothing.

That summer, however, in Archer's shop, he encountered the second of his Svengalis, a scholarly, sociable, and cosmopolitan 26-year-old, over on a brief visit from Paris. George Reavey is another figure of the thirties frequently left out of accounts as too versatile to fit into journalistic or academic generalization.[16] An Irishman who had been brought up in Russia, his affinities were extraordinarily diverse and rich. When the Russian Civil War had broken out, his Russian mother Sophie Turchenko had fled with him from Nizhni Novgorod to Belfast, where they had been joined by the boy's Irish father, an industrialist who specialized in the processing of flax. After moving to London, Reavey had been educated at the Sloane School and at Gonville and Caius College, Cambridge where he had studied history then English, associating with a group of forward-looking undergraduates around the formative magazine *Experiment*. It was there that he had met the undergraduate Archer, almost his exact contemporary.[17] Reavey fitted uneasily into the parochial patterns of English cultural life. A polyglot, fluent in French and Russian, he was a European to his fingertips, and an

15. BL Lives, F1381, Side A.
16. An exception is Sandra O'Connell, 'George Reavey (1907–1976), The Endless Chain: A Literary Biography' (Trinity College Dublin, PhD, 2005), a perceptively informed treatment of Reavey's life and work.
17. *History of Gonville and Caius*, v. 321.

occasional—though scarcely a major—poet. After quitting university he had persuaded his father to let him live in France, ostensively so that he could improve his languages further to gain entrance to the Indian Civil Service. After working discontentedly as a tutor in Fontainebleau for a year, he had settled in a Montparnasse studio with another former Cambridge student, the painter Julian Trevelyan. Reavey was hospitable and encouraging, and he enjoyed putting friends of different nationalities in touch with one another and their inner selves. When he learned that Gascoyne's Leipzig plans had fallen through, Reavey suggested Paris instead. Deep into Rimbaud and Baudelaire, his wanderlust fired by Mallarmé, David needed little persuading.

'Fuir! là-bas fuir!' ran one of Mallarmé's best-known lines. In early September Gascoyne's novel, renamed *Opening Day*, was published at 7*s.* 6*d.* in a handsome crown octavo edition. On p. 113 it conveyed its protagonist's suppressed wanderlust: 'Travel! He wanted to be away, to be in a different place, to be alone.' Later that month Gascoyne was on the move.

5

Et in Arcadia

'The answer to all of my yearning seemed inescapably Paris, and so without many regrets I packed my bags.'[1] This might well have been David Gascoyne speaking about himself in the late summer of 1933. In fact the memoirist is the artist Julian Trevelyan, scion of a family with deep Cambridge academic connections. Two years earlier Trevelyan had quit the university to try his hand as a painter in Montparnasse. He might be voicing the aspirations of a mini-generation. For very many intellectually and artistically adventurous young men in the mid-1930s—and nowhere more so than among Trevelyan and Reavey's contemporaries in Cambridge, with whom Gascoyne was soon in touch—the fittest response to the England of George V—with its economic depression, its fading imperialistic glory, its dull consensual politics—beckoned across the channel.

Here is Trevelyan evoking the impact on his circle of another friend and contemporary to whom Gascoyne would in time draw even closer. Humphrey Jennings would achieve distinction as a maker of documentary films, as well as a painter and to a lesser extent poet. In 1931, however, he had been an energetic and academically successful student at Pembroke College in Cambridge, for whom being up-to-date was a kind of lodestar. Up-to-date-ness spelled France:

> Humphrey's was a prodigious intelligence; he devoured books, and as a dialectician he seemed invincible. He introduced us all to contemporary French painting through the medium of the *Cahiers d'Art* and through the various books on Picasso. He was alive to the ever-changing value of 'contemporariness' in art, and the word *weltanchauung* was used much by us at the time. 'That picture of yours hasn't got 1931-ness,' he would say, and the least one could say about his work was that it always had *that*.[2]

1. Julian Trevelyan, *Indigo Days: The Art and the Memoirs of Julian Trevelyan* (London: Scolar Press, 1957/1996), 20.
2. Ibid. 17.

Of nobody was this truer than the lively group of students clustered around the student magazine *Experiment*. Among them was William Empson who had studied maths and English, excelling at both while writing carefully wrought, elliptical poems. Jacob Bronowski, 'Bruno' to his many friends, was a doctoral candidate in geometry whose intelligence embraced chess along with modern poetry and art, and who would later seize the national limelight as the author of the 1970s television series *The Ascent of Man*. Hugh Sykes Davies had taken successive parts of his degree in classics and English, and was now lecturing in the latter, while dabbling in Surrealist fiction.[3] When Trevelyan had abandoned his degree and taken the ferry to France in November 1931, he had joined Reavey, who had already been living there for two almost years and was helping prepare special issues of Titus's *This Quarter*. Together they had moved to the Villa Brune, an artists' community on the southern edge of Montparnasse consisting of eight Bauhaus-style units to one side of an acacia-lined cul-de-sac overlooking a railway cutting leading to the nearby Gare. Soon Bruno was writing to them from Cambridge, soliciting poems by Paul Eluard, prints by Max Ernst, and an essay by Georges Hugnet for the magazine. They were, he infomed his friends, 'Experiment's envoys in Paris', and could be relied on to supply such things.[4]

So David was hardly walking into the dark. At the very least he was assured of a welcome in Montparnasse from Reavey and Trevelyan. Their studio was too small to accommodate him as well, since they shared it with Reavey's dark-haired French girlfriend, Andrée Conte. But the poet Winifred Holmes had given Gascoyne the address of the Hôtel Jacob in the seventh arrondissement. It was an eighteenth-century building set round a courtyard in the Rue Jacob, a couple of streets to the north of the Boulevard Saint-Germain, in which expatriate writers often put up (including at different times Ernest Hemingway and Djuna Barnes).[5] One day in late September, taking Herbert Read's latest book *Art Now* to read on the ferry, he crossed from Newhaven to Dieppe and in the late afternoon arrived via Saint-Lazare at the modest-looking hotel. After unpacking, he explored the *quartier* on foot: the boulevard with its fashionable bustle, the Rue Danton, then westwards towards the Place de l'Odéon. Then, a little agog, east to the

3. Hugh Sykes Davies, *Petron* (London: J. M. Dent, 1935).
4. Jacob Bronowski to George Reavey and Julian Trevelyan, 5 Mar. 1932, JOT 2/3.
5. It is now the three-star Hôtel d'Angleterre. The Treaty of Paris that ended the American War of Independence was signed there in 1783.

Place Saint-Michel and across the Seine by the Pont Neuf. Arriving at the Place du Châtelet, he indulged in his first timid luxury: a cheap seat at the Théâtre Sarah Bernhardt to see Alexander Dumas's play *La Dame au camélias*, in which Bernhardt herself had once played the lead. In the entr'acte he had intended to celebrate his arrival as an *in situ* Parisian *littérateur* with a glass of that *fin de siècle* gut-rotter, absinthe. The barman took one look at him, and persuaded him to accept a Pernod instead.[6]

Reavey had furnished him with several introductions, and in the morning he set out to visit the radical bookstores of the quarter, Sylvia Beach's Shakespeare and Company and Adrienne Monnier's 'Maison des Amis du Livre' which faced one another across the Rue de l'Odéon. Beach's was already the more celebrated (he bought a volume of Wallace Stevens from her), but Monnier had been earlier in the field, and she stocked principally French books for French customers. Her shop also had a useful and well-stocked lending library. Shakespeare and Company by contrast concentrated on fare in English for the growing American—and to a smaller extent British—community, several of whom used to hang out there, including Hemingway and increasingly Gascoyne himself, who later told the art historian Mel Gooding:

> One day Sylvia Beach said to me 'Would you like to meet Hemingway… He is passing through on his way to Africa?' I went back in the afternoon and he was there, and she introduced him to me. He was very charming… But when I went back to the shop the following day I found [the stock] in an extraordinary state of disarray.[7]

The previous evening Beach had made the mistake of pointing out to Hemingway a recent issue of the journal *Life and Letters*. It contained a vitriolic attack on him by Wyndham Lewis entitled 'The Dumb Ox'. Hemingway had run amok and wrecked the shop.

Though Gascoyne's reading in French was already quite impressive, his spoken command of the language was still at the level of the not very attentive schoolboy he had recently been. He improved it by staying up into the small hours chatting to the night porter in the hotel's large foyer. (The porter was francophone but unfortunately British; ever after Gascoyne's soon-fluent French was invariably delivered in an egregiously flat 'onglé' accent.)

6. David Gascoyne, 'Notes and Sketch for Paris Sixty Years After: Paris in 1933', BL Add. 71704N (1983), fos. 77–8.

7. BL Lives, F1380, Side A.

He also availed himself briefly of the facilities of the Institut Britannique, then in the Rue Val de Grâce near the Luxembourg Gardens, where he took conversation classes with a Mademoiselle Lalay.[8]

When not thus occupied, he loped across the broad-pathed Montparnasse cemetery with its illustrious dead, and called in at Trevelyan and Reavey's cramped studio. Trevelyan was practising intaglio printmaking and working in a variety of other media, including goache, enamel, and the cork he acquired in a little shop near the Gare Montparnasse. His friendship with Reavey was fractious, since Trevelyan was by far the richer, if the younger, of the two. He was also keeping Reavey financially afloat with a series of loans he demanded should be repaid at a fixed rate of 200 francs a month—more than Reavey could afford—a situation not improved by the fact that Reavey was still living with his French girlfriend. Treveleyan had the distinct impression he was maintaining both of them: he probably was.[9]

It was the more soft-peddling Trevelyan who seems to have taken Gascoyne in hand. Both had an instinctive gentleness, and their temperaments seem to have been complementary. Both were quiet rebels. Trevelyan was in subdued reaction against the distinguished academicism of his family (the historian G. M. Trevelyan was his uncle), and he was very much a product of a liberal-minded, arts-orientated ambience of Bedales, the progressive co-educational boarding school in Hampshire to which he had been sent by his shuffling, diffident classicist and poet father, Bob Trevelyan. Photographs of the period show him as humorously shy, slightly uncoordinated, ill at ease with his lanky height (another characteristic that he shared with David). At Cambridge he had struggled with the tripos in literature. Happier with his hands, he was feeling his way forward from one graphic medium to another until at length he would settle on a style of etching recognizably his own, which he would later teach at the Chelsea College of Art. For his own part, David had struggled against the exam-fixation of his inappropriate secondary schooling; yet he was a word-addicted creature who could not rest until he had thought a position through and articulated it on paper in notebook after notebook of flowing, urgent prose. A quarter of a century later Trevelyan retained a clear recollection of Gascoyne's 'great beautiful eyes opening wider and wider when I showed him photographs of

<hr />

8. Now affiliated to the University of London and accommodated in the British Council's premises on the Rue de Constantine.
9. Their irritable exchanges on this issue can be followed in JOT 24.

paintings of Hieronymus Bosch for the first time'.[10] The reaction was scarcely surprising. As Ernst Gombrich later observed, in Bosch triptychs such as *Last Judgement* (later one of Gascoyne's own projected titles) 'we see horror piled on horror, fires and torments and all manner of fearful demons, half animal, half human and half machine...for perhaps the first and for perhaps the only time an artist had succeeded in giving concrete and tangible shape to the fears that haunted the Middle Ages'.[11] For artists of Trevelyan's generation however—and Gascoyne was viewing Bosch through his eyes—the hectic visions of the Netherlandish artist, with their copulating couples, impaled pallid bodies, and hybrid beasts, were closer to phantasmagoria than to allegory. Bosch appeared to be a sort of proto-Surrealist, his fantastical creatures less like gargoyles than premonitions of Max Ernst.

There was a visible continuity, as Gascoyne soon learned, between historic and modern art. At right angles to the Rue Jacob runs the Rue de Seine, where in 1924 Pierre Loeb had opened his Galerie Pierre specializing in early Surrealist painting. Here one morning Gascoyne found a window display of canvases almost as animated as those of Bosch. They were by the Catalan artist Joan Miró, whose crowded compositions against their blank backgrounds featured ovoid or amoebic forms with wavy tendrils, suggestive in their combination of the ingenious innards of a clockwork mechanism. Miró would never regard himself as a Surrealist proper even if André Breton, acknowledged leader of the movement in France, thought him the most Surrealist of all contemporary painters. There was a deceptive innocence about his work, emphasized that very July when the Ballets Russes de Monte Carlo had brought to Covent Garden the ballet *Jeux d'enfants* based on piano pieces by Bizet and set in a nursery, with a set and costumes all by Miró. As Geoffrey Grigson had then noted, the British public had as a consequence come to associate this gruff, uncompromising Spaniard with childishness. For Gascoyne, the attraction of his painting lay as much in its energy as its archetypal simplicity, 'as old as art itself, spontaneous, vivid and full of verve'.[12]

Paris, Gascoyne soon discovered, was as much a congeries of interconnected colonies as a city. As far as the anglophone expatriate community were concerned, the focus was Montparnasse with its twin centres of attraction, the Dôme and Coupole cafés, facing one another across the junction of the boulevards Montparnasse and Raspail. Here one met English and

10. *Indigo Days*, 71.
11. Ernst Gombrich, *The Story of Art* (London: Phaidon, 1956), 264.
12. BL Lives, F1381, Side A.

American residents of the city, or regular visitors like Cyril Connolly, whose acquaintance Gascoyne made that autumn. Connolly, who was yet to acquire the louche fame his editorship of *Horizon* insecurely brought him, had been dropping in on Montparnasse since 1928, in which year his characteristically desultory journal had conveyed the gaudy, disjointed atmosphere of the district: 'Tarts. Lights. Taxis. Chemists' bottles. *Et in Arcadia ego*. And did those feet, lights of the Dôme, noise, laughter, girls' faces, gardens of the Luxembourg in winter, bookstalls on the Seine, the Bois, the Bal Nègre, the Mosque, mediaeval map of Paris brothels drawn to Piscator's erection.'[13] Now 29, and still in search of a definitive role, Cyril was married to Jean Bakewell, a 23-year-old American of ambiguous sexuality with 'short dark hair, green eyes, and high cheekbones, olive skin and a rather oriental appearance, like a young man from Indo-China'. They were intermittently frustrated with one another, and he with himself, struggling as he was to complete his only novel *The Rock Pool*. Connolly's principal claim to the celebrity he craved would be a book which explained his continual failure to produce other books he was convinced that he had within him.[14] He seems to have taken to David immediately, sensing in him a spirit as restless, prone to self-examination and self-castigation as his own.

Between them, Trevelyan and Connolly gave David access to some of the most forward-looking circles in Paris. Trevelyan had been studying print-making and engraving with the English master craftsman Stanley William Hayter, whose atelier had recently moved to 17 Rue Campagne-Première, a mews-like passage with studio and workshop spaces to either side of it up from the Hôtel Istria (itself a meeting place of the early Surrealists), just to the north of the Boulevard Raspail. 'Atelier Dix-Sept' as it came to be known was a hive of contacts: Miró had studied there as a mature student alongside Julian, as had Ernst, Oskar Kokoschka, and, briefly, Picasso. Gascoyne was soon caught up in its whirl. Soon after his arrival Hayter flung a party in the ominously named Passage d'Enfer, a precinct down the street that bent backwards at right angles towards the boulevard. The shindig broke up when someone smashed one of the thick glass weights with which Hayter pressed his prints, whereupon his current mistress threw the company out into the street. They decamped to the Rue de l'Ombre behind the

---

13. Cyril Connolly, *Journal and Memoir*, ed. David Pryce-Jones (London: Collins, 1983), 204.
14. Cyril Connolly, *Enemies of Promise: A Criticism of Modern Literary Tendencies* (London: Routledge, 1938).

Dôme, where they carried on regardless.[15] Hayter took it all in his stride, just as he did the politics of the art world, which he regarded with scarcely veiled contempt. He was no respecter of persons or of cliques, and told Gascoyne to go and visit everybody, regardless of faction or 'school'.

There was, for example, vivacious 25-year-old Maria Helena Vieira da Silva—known as 'Bichot' or 'little doe' to her many friends—born in Lisbon in 1908. David called round at her studio where she was developing her own style of abstract expressionism. There was Ossip Zadkine, a 43-year-old sculptor from Cuba who was evolving his own Primitivist style and trying to put clear water between himself and the Cubists, with whom he now felt that he had associated too closely since his arrival in Paris shortly after the Great War. The most versatile—and certainly the liveliest conversationalist—was the Normandy-born polymath Jean Hélion, to whom Gascoyne had already had a letter of introduction by Grigson. Hélion migrated between genres and interests: he had written poetry, had studied chemistry to which he had been attracted by the geometric shapes revealed by crystallography. He had been lured into painting by Poussin's canvases in the Louvre and was currently an abstractionist, an approach he would in later life ditch in favour of a figurative art filled with primary colours. The great service he performed for Gascoyne was to open his eyes to Poussin, whose paintings were attracting more and more attention from British artists like John Piper and scholars such as Anthony Blunt. Poussin's elusive allegories in any case appealed to the aspect of Surrealist sensibility attracted by the equally evasive empty townscapes of de Chirico. Gascoyne took the hint and called in at the Louvre to see *Les Bergers d'Arcadie*, in which toga-clad peasants against a darkening sky struggle to construe an inscription on a tomb which reads 'Et in Arcadia Ego': 'even I was in Arcady'.

Manifestly the artistic activity of Paris transcended all -isms. A quality many of Hayter's former students shared was a suspicion of fixed declarations and immutable positions. Gascoyne would absorb this lesson well and, though various theories of art or politics would sometimes briefly detain him, would in later life invariably move on—like Hayter, like Trevelyan, like Vieira da Silva, Zadkine, or Hélion—towards self-defined goals that would frequently confound his lazier critics.

In other aspects of his life he was torn. Shortly after his arrival, Trevelyan introduced him to a younger schoolmate of his from Bedales. Sixteen

15. BL Lives, F1381, Side A.

months older than David, Kathleen Mary Silvia Hime, known to her chums as 'Kay', was from Farnham and had left school in the summer of the previous year. Nature had been kind to her, since she had the sort of blonde, clean-limbed prettiness associated with female models in period advertisements for Raleigh bikes. Kay dressed smartly in pencil-line skirts, and she wore her hair swept back in the manner of Gertude Lawrence in the Cole Porter musical *Nymph Errant* which she has already seen at the Adelphi Theatre in London three times.[16] There had been plenty to aspire to in Lawrence's role as Evangeline Edwards, a young English girl from a Swiss finishing school intent on hitching herself to a suitable mate. With her natural blonde hair and rangy limbs she reminded David of the Russian ballerina Tatiana Riabouchinska, who in that Ballets Russes de Monte Carlo production of *Jeux d'enfants* had danced the role of the Child, clad in an asexual 'unitard' designed by Miró. They started dating, and for weeks they met every evening at six in the Dôme or the Coupole, parading elegantly along the Boulevard Raspail, drawing admiring and envious glances from passers-by or drinkers out on the terrasses, his dapper Noël Coward to her chic Gertrude Lawrence.

At the end of each evening David would escort her chastely back to her pension out at Passy. It was very friendly, but essentially all show since, though David was in his own mind sufficiently 'in love' with Kay, he was never quite clear what to do about—or more precisely *to*—her. An incident in early October did little to reassure her. They were sitting over dinner in the Dôme when a 20-year-old American called Charles Henry Ford briefly entered. Ford was an openly bisexual poet and collagist from Brookhaven, Mississippi who had taken to spelling his middle name 'Henri' to avoid been mistaken for an automobile manufacturer. He was currently engaged in co-writing a daring study of contemporary manners entitled *The Young and the Evil*, somewhat indebted to the ongoing drafts by his friend and later mistress Djuna Barnes for her novel in progress, *Nightwood*. In the longer term he was cohabiting in a studio near Vaugigard with the Russian Surrealist painter Pavel Tchelitchev, and modelling for openly homoerotic works by his boyfriend such as *The Swimmers* of that year. If his sexual orientation was not obvious from his appearance, the reproduction of that work with its narcissistically exposed torsos in Read's *Art Now*, which David had by his hotel bedside, would have given a fair clue.

<hr />

16. Afterword to *Collected Journals*, 344–5.

Ford exchanged a few remarks with this handsome, compatible-looking heterosexual couple, and then left. A few seconds later, Gascoyne rose to his feet and followed him out into the night, abandoning his consort for the evening in nonplussed isolation at their table. A couple of hours later he returned, sat down again, and attempted to resume their conversation where he had left off. She was not impressed.[17]

Such dinners and other outings were exhausting Gascoyne's funds, so he now moved out of the Hôtel Jacob and into a cheaper and more convenient hotel round the corner from Beach's shop. Unsurprisingly in the light of his recent treatment of Kay, he celebrated his seventeenth birthday by eating all by himself at La Rotonde on the Champs-Elysées, a last extravagance before a more austere regime of expenditure. But his conversational French was now passable, allowing him gradually to forsake the safety net of the anglophone bohemians in the Montparnasse cafés. Through Henriette Gomez, an assistant at Loeb's gallery in the Rue de Seine, he was given an entrée to the affluent and influential art dealer Jeanne Boucher, whose shop was in Montparnasse. Through her in turn he managed an introduction to Ernst. It was his first exposure to the Surrealist inner circle.

Ernst was, Gascoyne thought, 'probably the best educated and widely read of all the Surrealist artists', and someone who brought together the visual and the literary aspects of the Movement.[18] A decade earlier he had shared a house in the southern suburb of Eaubonne with the poet Eugène Emile Paul Grindel, who published under the name Paul Eluard, and his then wife Gala, later to marry Salvador Dalí. Almost certainly he had shared Gala's favours and, during the year (1923–4) had covered the doors and walls of the establishment with murals featuring *trompe l'œils*, fake recesses, and fabulous animal designs. When their marriage had broken up in 1929 the Eluards had sold the house, but Paul had remained close to Ernst, with whom he continued to collaborate on projects, and whose early art works he enthusiastically acquired. Ernst was in any case a profoundly verbal and literary man. A survivor from the movement's Dadaist phase, he possessed an addiction to aural puns and in 1929 had published the first of his collage novels entitled *La Femme 100 têtes*, which implied as much a headless woman (*sans tête*) as a hundred-headed female. Gascoyne had already purchased an

17. Afterword to *Collected Journals*, 349.
18. 'Loplop and His Aviary: The Surrealist Visions of Max Ernst and May Ray', *Times Literary Supplement* (8 Mar. 1991), 14–15. *Selected Prose*, 436–45.

exemplaire of this literary-cum-graphic narrative at the Surrealist bookshop established in 1925 by José Corti at 6 Rue de Clichy. It contained prints and engravings (including one of William Blake's) cut from eighteenth- and nineteenth-century periodicals, brought together in arresting disharmony. The double entendres, the story, the sexiness, and the subdued violence all proved attractive to David. When he called on Ernst one November afternoon in his disorderly flat at the corner of 26 Rue des Plantes, just up the road from Trevelyan's studio, the rapport was immediate. Both men, for example, were products of local religious cultures, Ernst of his Catholic family back in Cologne, Gascoyne of his Anglican choir school. Ernst shared with him one of his first memories, of his painter father showing him a study he had done of a monk squatting in a beech-wood reading a book: the work was entitled 'Loneliness'. Then, 'with sardonic amusement not unmixed with pride', he pointed to a childhood portrait his father had made of him in 1896 as a 5-year-old boy Jesus. The iconic self-image in several of his paintings was a bird figure to which Ernst invariably referred as Loplop. Gascoyne came to think of this creature as a kind of mother superior in a sacred aviary. Perhaps in deference to this sacred personage, before he left Paris that winter, he purchased from Ernst a recent gouache of his—one of his many bird images—called *L'Oiseau en forêt* for 500 precious francs.

Arriving back in East Twickenham in the first week of December, his head full of 1933-ness and his trunk of papers, Gascoyne hung Ernst's gouache on the wall of his bedroom, a space smaller than ever.

6

Out of Bounds

If Gascoyne wished to be taken seriously as an English exponent of Surrealism, he had laid the foundations for this ambition in the months prior to his visit to France. Since July he had been cultivating a relationship with the *New English Weekly*, launched by the Yorkshire-born man of letters, amateur economist, and mystic Alfred Richard Orage in April 1932 as a successor to his influential, though limited circulation, periodical the *New Age* (1907–24). The *New Age* had published Hilaire Belloc, Eric Gill, Augustus John, and Pound. The new journal had begun by bringing out some early Dylan Thomas ('And Death Shall Have No Dominion'); in the years following Orage's death it would be the first to issue three of Eliot's *Four Quartets*. In September 1933, Orage accepted Gascoyne's 'Ten Proses', which included an evocation of the disorientating visual effects, the sinister and mysterious stillness, of the Surrealist precursor de Chirico, drawing on his *Enigma of Arrival* and other canvases: 'Beyond the immobile equestrian statue which has stood at the edge of the square for so long that nobody can remember whom it commemorates, the sea lies waiting for an hour when it shall overwhelm the dead and empty city. Roman soldiers wander and terrific horses gallop over the sands.'[1]

While he had been away, Grigson had brought out in *New Verse* a poem that would seal his reputation for ever. 'And the seventh dream is the dream of Isis' was a tumbling exercise in a disconnected, phantasmogoric vein that has impressed itself on some readers, not entirely to its author's satisfaction, as a definitive expression of the Surrealist mood and technique. It not difficult to see why:

---

1. *New English Weekly*, 14 Sept. 1933, 516.

today is the day when the streets are full of hearses
and when women cover their ring fingers with pieces of silk
when the doors fall off their hinges in ruined cathedrals
when hosts of white birds fly across the ocean from america
and make their nests in the trees of public gardens
the pavements of cities are covered with needles
the reservoirs are full of human hair
fumes of sulphur envelop the houses of ill-fame
out of which bloodred lilies appear.[2]

Just as soon as he was back in London again, Gascoyne appeared in Orage's paper once more as the author of 'Ten Surrealist Cameos' featuring a similar stream of unlikely and macabre connections, with an occasional disturbed ecclesiastic undertow: in the third section the poet falls in love with a pear tree, out of which emerges an enormous brown butterfly that 'circled four times round my head beating a little gong under its wings, and ended up by trampling heavily for more than an hour, on my eyelids, while I repeated the words "Dust to Dust, ashes to ashes"'.[3]

He resumed his visits to Parton Street, where several of the new arrivals were younger than him. Early one morning the front bell sounded, and Archer went downstairs in his frayed blue dressing gown to be met on the doorstep by a stocky, determined-looking youth who announced that he had come to meet a Communist rumoured to be staying in one of the rooms above the shop. Stammering as ever, leaving each sentence dangling, Archer told him the comrade he sought was not yet up, but that he was welcome to wait downstairs, where a assortment of subversive literature was on show:

> It was quite unlike any bookshop that I had ever seen. The floor was covered with stray copies of *The Daily Worker, Russia Today, Communist International* and other exciting literature of this sort, the table had an odd collection of pamphlets, together with a good supply of household linen. A table at the back was arranged like a waste-paper basket with every conceivable bit of scrap piled up on it.[4]

While they waited, the visitor told Archer that his name was Romilly. They had something in common too: both were Wellingtonians. The young

---

2. *New Verse*, 5 (Oct. 1933), 9–12; *Selected Poems*, 23–5.
3. *New English Weekly*, 30 Nov. 1933, 157–8.
4. Giles Romilly and Esmond Romilly, *Out of Bounds: The Education of Giles Romilly and Esmond Romilly* (London: Hamish Hamilton, 1935), 200–1.

visitor was still at the school, where he had founded a politically active cell affiliated to pacifisim—the ultimate Wellingtonian betrayal—and other advanced causes. At 15 Esmond Romilly already possessed the burly appearance and bulldog assurance of his maternal uncle, Winston Churchill. Many of his recent school holidays had been spent at Chartwell where Winston had regarded him with indulgent amusement. The rest of his time was devoted to undermining the public school system which, in common with his elder, more cautious brother Giles, he had come to regard as the source of much evil in English life, a prop of the Empire and bulwark of international Fascism. In May he arrived at Parton Street again, equally early in the day, and announced that he had run away from school by the first train that morning. Archer gave him a job looking after the shop at £1 a week, on which slender wage he set up the magazine *Out of Bounds* soliciting contributions from Harrow or Winchester, and building up a network of undercover agents in every cloister and dormitory he could reach. One of his schoolboy correspondents was from Rugby, where his adolescent discontent had found in the paper a sympathetic echo. Philip Toynbee interpreted this mood as political, though, as he was later to admit, the root cause was that he was a duffer at cricket and had thus forfeited the respect of a younger boy with whom he was sentimentally in love. In early June he too arrived at Parton Street, just as Esmond was about to go out on his rounds:

> A boy was leaving the shop as my taxi drew up in Parton Street, a short, square, dirty figure with a square white face and sweaty hair. 'I'm looking for Esmond Romilly', I said.
>
> 'Yes?'
>
> He was instantly, dramatically, on his guard, conspiratorial, prepared for violent aggression or ingenious deceit. I thrilled and trembled more hysterically than ever.
>
> 'I'm Toynbee,' I said, 'Toynbee of Rugby.'[5]

For weeks they were inseparable: 'I was Verlaine to his Rimbaud,' Toynbee later recalled, 'not certainly of poetry but of pure defiance.' Soon Archer had introduced Gascoyne to both of them and then to a tousle-haired, 20-year-old poet who had just rolled up from South Wales. Dylan Thomas had already sampled Gascoyne's Isis poem whilst staying with his parents in 5 Cwndonkin Drive, Swansea, reporting back to his Clapham-based girlfriend Pamela

---

5. Philip Toynbee, *Friends Apart: A Memoir of Esmond Romilly and Jasper Ridley in the Thirties* (London: MacGibbon and Kee, 1954), 18.

Hansford Johnson that 'there are more maggots in his brain than there are in mine ... May he teach the bats in his belfry better manners.'[6] He appeared at the shop, small, thin, and, as Barker later recalled, 'with a dirty wool scarf wound round himself like an old love affair, looking liker to a runaway schoolboy than Esmond Romilly, who really was one'.[7]

Of the new spate of misfits or refugees, however, the most instrumental in Gascoyne's development was to be a slender, hyperactive youth who was living unhappily with his mother and half-sister in Hampstead. Roger Roughton had recently quit Uppingham where he had been monstrously bullied for his artistic tastes and moral intensity. Archer took him under his wing and accompanied Gascoyne to see him and his family in January 1934. There was a piano in the flat on which David performed one of Erik Satie's *Gymnopédies*, impressing the far less musical Roughton. But there was much they could discuss, since Roughton was an energetic, fair-to-middling poet, and far more conscious of Surrealism as a fertilizing movement in painting and literature than anybody in London apart from Gascoyne himself. He was yet to succumb to the political faith that inspired so many of Archer's protégés, and for this reason Esmond had little time for him. But Roughton was restless, had organizational drive, and was as widely read in modern literature as anybody in Parton Street. Gascoyne and he also shared a love of Eliot, whose lines from *The Waste Land* about dull-eyed commuters crossing the river to their offices in the City every morning 'on the final stroke of nine', seemed to David the height of disenchanted urban modernism, all the more so since Leslie was one of these same commuters.

Apart from anything else, Eliot's poem is a first-rate description of the Thames in its tidal and seasonal moods. In February 1934 the two friends set off to explore the dingy warehouse-haunted terrain downstream evoked in 'The Burial of the Dead'. Today, Pond Maze Street is a smart thoroughfare on the southern side of the regenerated, multi-storey Guy's Hospital. In 1934 it was a dingy street lined by Regency houses that had seen better days. They found a gaslit top floor there for a few shillings a week, away from the prying eyes of their families. Since several of Gascoyne's English friends were over from Paris, they held a well-fuelled house-warming a few days after settling in:

6. Dylan Thomas to Pamela Hansford Johnson, 15 Oct. 1933, in *The Collected Letters of Dylan Thomas*, ed. Paul Ferris (London: J. M. Dent, 1985/2000), 45–6.
7. George Barker, *Coming to London* (London: Phoenix House, 1950), 55.

At the end of the week during which we moved into Great Maze Pond with our few bits and pieces of furniture, crockery and other indispensable domestic items, and hung the Ernst gouache of a *Oiseau en forêt* that I'd brought back with me from Paris over the living-room fire place, we threw a housewarming party. My mother came up from East Twickenham to bring sandwiches and sausage-rolls, then withdrew. Mrs Roughton made no appearance. During the evening, enough guests arrived to pack the little flat to overflowing. I think I can claim that for a pair of teenage hosts in the Thirties, we gave quite a distinguished party. Arthur Bliss the composer, a family friend of Roger's, had been invited, but perhaps got lost on the way. Cyril and Jeannie Connolly were there, and they brought with them Peter Quennell and his current adored one, the most beautiful woman present (he spent most of the evening on his knees gazing at her beseechingly, unless my memory deceives me). Julian Trevelyan was undoubtedly there: at a climactic moment his abundant hair caught fire from the gas-bracket which provided picturesquely primitive illumination, and blazed alarmingly for a hilarious moment. David Archer of Parton Street must have been there, as were David Abercrombie, one of the two sons of Lascelles Abercrombie the Georgian poet and George Reavey, both frequenters of his bookshop.[8]

On the surface at least the occasion was a marked success, though the relationship between the hosts was as fragile as their finances, as a comically embarrassing incident at the end of the evening confirmed. Roger and David's conversations had ranged across many subjects during the few weeks since they had met. They had, however, steered clear of sex, since their respective orientations in that respect were far from clear: to other people, to one another, or indeed to themselves. When the last guest had left the scene Roughton, who had drunk quite a lot during the evening, thought he might grope his way towards some kind of a resolution:

> When it was all over and everyone had gone home, Roger and I certainly did not go sober to bed. After the gas was extinguished, I was surprised to find Roger slipping between my sheets. This was not at all what I had expected of him, nor had I given him reason to suppose otherwise. I believe that the party had generated a certain atmosphere of inebriate randiness which made him feel it would be better for him to go to bed with me than with no-one at all. It did not take us long to discover that the move had been a disastrous one. A certain coolness prevailed between us for the next day or two, but no grudges were borne and the incident seemed promptly forgotten.

8. Afterword to *Collected Journals*, 347–8.

Initially, the rent proved less of a problem, since in January Orage had been sufficiently impressed by David's contributions to his paper to appoint him as its art critic. This was no mere gesture. According to Eliot, Orage had 'the finest critical intelligence of our days',[9] and he had earlier employed the innovative novelist Storm Jameson to cover fiction. Gascoyne's brief was to cover London exhibitions plus significant art criticism, which in practice meant the 'Criterion Miscellanies' Faber was currently issuing each month. He adopted an assertive attitude and tone, laced with a little of Grigson's mustard. As his subjects soon discovered, he was prepared to sting several well-known artists, including his friends, Grigson himself, and even Orage. Rather than display an all-round susceptibility to everything modern, he made a great show of not being taken in, even by Herbert Read, whose enthusiasms he now pronounced promiscuous. Gascoyne announced his overall theme in his very first piece as 'The Significance of English Art': the Pre-Raphaelites, he opined, were 'abominable' and Turner was 'a man of colossal bad taste, who sometimes painted great pictures as if by accident'. The national genius, he then contentiously announced, was for caricature, which meant that Hogarth scored highly, and Blake also ranked high.[10] The trouble with English artists was that they were forever aping the Continentals several decades after the event. And they did not do abstraction well: ' "Look!" says Mr Ben Nicholson, proudly, I have painted two circles, just two plain little circles all by themselves! And we are supposed to say "How quaint!" I suppose.'[11] Some artists escaped this severity: Hayter with some of his pupils exhibited at the Leicester Gallery in March, and he earned his protégé's approval, both for his eclecticism and for his teaching of artists like Ernst and Trevelyan, who however engraved better than he worked in cork.[12] When Trevelyan held a one-man show at the Bloomsbury Gallery in July, Gascoyne dwelt on this inconsistency in him: his Jekylls, but also his Hydes. The only contemporary artist to win this 17-year-old critic's unqualified praise was Picasso, a giant among pigmies. The bête noire was imitation: the Cubists should not have attempted to learn geometry from Cézanne. If there was hope, it lay in the transformation of the real through inner concentration, the process that had once enabled Van Gogh to see his boots as 'strange, terrifying, monstrous creatures'. The same process had

9. Quoted in P. A. Mairet, *A. R. Orage: A Memoir* (New York: University Books, 1966), 121.
10. 'The Significance of English Art', *New English Weekly*, 11 Jan. 1934, pp. 306–7.
11. 'New English Art', *New English Weekly*, 29 Mar. 1934, p. 563.
12. 'Some Recent Exhibitions', *New English Weekly*, 1 Mar. 1934, pp. 473–4.

enabled Isidore Lucien Ducasse (1846–70), known to literature as le Comte de Lautréamont, when locked in his Parisian garret, to observe 'delirious crises in his subconscious; and he recorded them in strict mathematical language as a scientifically-minded observer might record the customs of some tribe in a newly-discovered land. The process by which the marvellous becomes real and the real marvellous are closely related; there are certain moments of hyper-aesthesia in which such processes take place in nearly all works of great art.'[13] Gascoyne called this transformative act 'Transcendental Realism', a synonym for Surrealism and the only method for this reviewer so universal and yet so original that imitation for once seemed no threat. There was only one proviso: however wild the transformations of reality were, they had to be rendered with the precision of a Vermeer.

At the same period David was reviewing fiction for Grigson on the *Morning Post*. For Eliot's *The Criterion* he assessed *Rimbaud Vivant* by Robert Goffin; and there were pieces in *The Everyman* and *John o' London's Weekly*. When not busy with such work, the two friends explored the city, sampling 'sometimes separately, sometimes together, the labyrinth of ill-lit and mysteriously pungent lanes between the warehouses then situated between the fire monument and the Prospect of Whitby, or the even less familiar south-bank docklands east of Southwark—nocturnal prowlings in a dark, Eliotic mood.

One person they had not been able to invite to their warming party was Kay Hime who had only recently returned from Paris, and was hanging out at her parents' house near Farnham. One evening while Roger was out, David asked her over to inspect the apartment. It was March, and they were in a room alone together for the first time since the debacle in the Dôme the previous October. Her memory of that episode inevitably coloured what happened next. While practising dance steps to the gramophone, David guided her towards the sofa and 'for a moment succeeded in persuading her to lie down by my side'. The encounter was no more satisfactory than the recent misunderstanding with Roughton. At the safe distance of fifty-five years, Gascoyne was later free to speculate: 'Had she been a few years older, more experienced, more attracted by my elongated, rather skinny physique than by that of one of Augustus John's sons whom she had just started going out with (a handsome, muscular and laconic type whose ambition was to become a professional boxer), who knows how the rest of

---

13. 'Pierre Roy and Transcendental Realism', *New English Weekly*, 5 July 1934, p. 281.

my life might have turned out?'[14] The possibility that Kay, whose fashionable good looks attracted several rich men, might also have been put off by
his relative poverty, seems not to have occurred to him.

Never again did they repeat this experiment, but they continued to see
one another as members of a loosely knit, sociable but safe since uncommit-
ted, circle of friends. In August Cyril and Jean Connolly planned a day out
in the car, and invited David and Kay along with Dylan Thomas. The mood
was boisterous and quite tense. They drove from south London through
Hindhead, Liphock, Midhurst, and Chichester. David, Kay, and Dylan, all a
decade or more younger than their hosts, sat together in the back of the car.
An account of the expedition by Gascoyne in later life captures the dynamic
of the occasion, its mixture of nerves and heedlessness. Kay started spinning
Irish yarns, slipping as she did so from her Surrey drawl into 'what seemed
to me a pretty good imitation of a broad Colleen accent'. The laughter died
when Cyril, who was at the wheel, turned round and rebuked her. Connolly
was half-Irish, and the hush that followed seems to have been prompted by
a suspicion that they had inadvertently offended his patriotism. Nothing
could have been further from the truth. A descendant of the Anglo-Irish
Ascendancy, Cyril had spent his childhood holidays at Clondaff Castle, a
property belonging to his mother's family the Vernons, who were descended
from Cromwell's quartermaster. A jotting from Cyril's childhood diary captures his attitude: 'Ireland = Aunt Mab, Castles, Holidays, Riches, Upper
Class',[15] It had been Ireland that had turned Connolly into a snob: the
group had just felt the brunt of his disdain. When they arrived at Selsey, they
picnicked on the beach, setting empty bottles up afterwards as effigies to be
aimed at. They threw shoes at them: at Edith Sitwell, Virginia Woolf, John
Lehmann, Michael Roberts, and Engels. It was a holiday from gratitude, as
well as from subservience. They journeyed back through Arundel, Amberley,
Pulborough, and Leith. After dropping off Gascoyne near London Bridge,
they returned to north London. Dylan stayed the night at Connolly's flat.[16]

Technically Thomas was arguably the most consistently Surrealist poet in
Britain, though he had complete disdain for the Surrealists themselves, as for
all artistic movements. That year Archer added to what would eventually

14. *Collected Journals*, 349.
15. Cyril Connolly, *Enemies of Promise: A Criticism of Modern Literary Tendencies* (London: Routledge,
    1938), 198.
16. Cyril Connolly, *Journal and Memoir*, ed. David Pryce-Jones (London: Collins, 1983), 268.

become a triumvirate of volumes by new poets by bringing out Dylan's *Eighteen Poems*, many of which displayed an inspired, associative, and slightly tipsy logic associated on the European mainland with Tristan Tzara or Benjamin Péret, though cast in well-organized stanzas and infused with that form of verbal gusto known to the Welsh as *hywl*. Gascoyne, in stark contrast, still required principles to underpin his practice. If the movement were ever to take off in an organized form in England intervention, he felt, was required. The preconditions for such a development were already present. There were critics and commentators—Grigson, but more emphatically Read—who were acutely aware that remarkable things had long been afoot across the Channel. There were writers—poets such as Thomas and, more self-consciously, Gascoyne himself, novelists such as Elizabeth Bowen— writing in a recognizably Surrealist vein. There were also a few British artists—Trevelyan, for example, and Roland Penrose, both of whom lived in Paris—who breathed the living atmosphere of the European movement which, however, they by and large regarded as local and probably untransportable.

These were settled attitudes that needed a fit of enthusiasm to shake. In this respect Roughton would prove vital. Though lack of funds caused him and Gascoyne to give up their lease in Pond Street after a few months, they remained in close touch. Like Gascoyne Roughton was a manic-depressive by temperament, but the psychological phases of the two friends did not usually coincide. When Gascoyne was down, Roughton was sometimes up, and vice versa. As a consequence Roughton occasionally tended to chivvy Gascoyne into courses of action he might not otherwise have taken (it is noticeable that, with Roughton's death in 1942, Gascoyne's role as catalyst and practical activist more or less came to an end).

There was one more liberating element. Before Gascoyne had left Paris, Ernst had given him the address of Paul Eluard, and in the early months of 1935, the two poets began to correspond. Gascoyne was always to acknowledge Eluard as the single most important influence in his pre-war literary development.[17] He was also a generous, at times a self-denying, man, artistically versatile though ideologically constant. Until his early death in 1952 he was to remain faithful to Surrealism, long after many of his colleagues had absconded in sympathy or in person. Throughout he would manage to reconcile this alliance with a commitment to Communism of an orthodox

17. BL Sound Archive, Robert Fraser Collection, C1081/08/0103/D1.

Russian brand, in the teeth of Soviet distrust and an eventual embargo of Communism by the high priest of the French Surrealist group, Breton. Eluard seems to have managed this balancing act precisely because in essence his lyrical poetry remained untouched by dogmas of any sort. As Gascoyne himself remarked when reviewing Eluard's latest collection *La Rose publique* in *New Verse* that very year, 'Eluard's poetry...is so pure and concentrated that it requires no ideological framework, no explanation. Every line means exactly what it says: the imagery becomes completely free of symbolism and refers to nothing but itself.'[18]

If anybody could convince Gascoyne that his poetic instincts were compatible with a cause then, it was Eluard. A double approach was needed. First, the English had to be introduced to the achievements of, and the sometimes fractious thought behind, Surrealism. With this end in view, and benefiting from the reputation of his published art criticism, early in 1935 Gascoyne persuaded Cobden-Sanderson to provide him with a contract to write a short book surveying the movement, and funds covering a second trip to Paris to research it. Secondly, there would need to be some kind of announcement that British Surrealism was under way. There was no point in signalling this fact in an insular arena. At Eluard's suggestion, Gascoyne chose *Les Cahiers d'Art*, a well-respected and high-profile periodical run in Paris by the Greek-born impresario of modern art criticism, Christian Zervos, which had recently issued a lavishly illustrated double-issue covering the work of Picasso. There was an element in this choice of showcase of reaction against British parochialism. In May 1935 Gascoyne seemed hemmed in on every side by rising hysteria connected with the approaching Silver Jubilee of George V. Against this jingoistic backdrop, he sat down in Leslie and Win's tiny flat in Twickenham, and wrote in French:

A FIRST ENGLISH SURREALIST MANIFESTO

Surrealist groups exist today throughout Europe, in America, in the Canary Islands and in Japan. Only England—one of the last remaining nonfascist countries—is without one. It seems to us that the moment has come to plug this gap.

Let us at the outset declare our resolve never to yield blindly to what is commonly known as 'the Great English tradition'. Surrealism is no exotic import that this tradition is free to accept or to reject. Neither is it a literary

18. *New Verse*, 18 (Feb. 1935), 18–19.

school. *It is an international system of ideas determined by conditions peculiar to our age.* And, so far as the tradition is concerned, it is there in Swift; Edward Young; Monk Lewis; William Blake; Lewis Carroll, whom we acknowledge as precursors, apart from whom we salute all of those living writers who have given proof of their devotion to the revolutionary cause. We affirm nonetheless our autonomy from all foreign critical 'standards'; our intention is resolutely to pursue our road undaunted by onslaughts we may attract either from individual writers or from members of the international society of authors.

At the very moment at which we are composing these lines in London (May 1935), the whole of England—orchestrated by the capitalist press—is preparing for an hysterical frenzy of the most futile and dispiriting kind: the Silver Jubilee. May one not discern in this fact a manifestation of historic justice? Just when the country is enjoined by its government to a travesty of rejoicing in the names of patriotism and imperialism, despair is the principal reaction of the poets.

Surrealism is the Dialectical Solution to the Problems of the Poet

While allocating a pre-eminent place to class struggle, Surrealism is by its very nature antithetical to the Leftish attitude according to which proletarian literature and propagandist art are the sole permissible revolutionary means of expression. Qualified poets are not confronted with a stark choice between two directions: on the one hand the pursuit of a simplified art, populist and proletarian and possessing no purpose beyond the efficacy of its propaganda or, on the other hand, depoliticised art, subjective in the extreme, aspiring to nothing save the personal self-expression of the writer. *Surrealism indicates a third way, the only authentic one, leading victoriously out of the twin traps on which the first two approaches are impaled.* We, the Surrealists, believe in a future in which the Revolution will reveal to mankind the real, the *surreal*, extent of his faculties for life, love and thought, where the chains that shackle us are broken forever.

Poetry must not be confused with propaganda. It is the act by means of which mankind comes to the fullest awareness of itself.

The Aims and Methods of Surrealism

The fundamental ambition of Surrealism is to dismantle all formal distinctions between dream and reality, and subjectivity and objectivity, so that, out of the detritus of these worn-out antimonies, the future conditions for which all revolutionaries strive may emerge into daylight.

The means employed by Surrealism to reach this goal are, above all, automatic writing and experiences characteristic of automatic creation. Surrealism is an instrument through which a voice both universal and pure speaks. Surrealist texts concern themselves only with thoughts in their nascent state, not intercepted by reason or logic. Important theories on Surrealist techniques have been developed over the last decade.

'To compare two objects as unlike one another as possible or, by another technique, to bring both within the range of a sharp and striking effect, remains the highest task towards which poetry can aspire. To this its unrivalled and unique power increasingly tends: to reveal the concrete unity of two terms placed in contact and communication with one another, so as to lend them a power which each lacks when viewed in isolation. What must be severed above all is any formal opposition between these two terms; what is clear is that their seeming incompatibility stems from an imperfect or immature sense of their nature derived from the externals of time and space. The more blatant their apparent incompatibility appears, the greater the need to suppress and annihilate it. Everything conspires to dignify the thing that is in play. Thus two objects, when rubbed together, achieve in the flash of a spark the supreme unity of fire; iron and water reach a complete and estimable resolution in blood, etc. Excessive particularity should constitute no stumbling block to this way of seeing and feeling: hence architectural ornament and butter marry sublimely in the Tibetan *torma*' [André Breton].

The Pronouncements of Surrealism

1. We declare ourselves to be in perfect agreement with the principles of Surrealism as initially set out by André Breton.
2. Relying absolutely on the proletarian revolution for the liberation of man, we proclaim our unswerving adherence to the historic materialism of Marx, Engels, and Lenin.
3. We calculate that an extensive field of action—poetic, plastic, philosophical, etc.—will open up to Surrealism in England.
4. We dedicate ourselves to a relentless fight against Fascism and War, Imperialism, nationalism, humanism, liberalism, idealism, anarchist individualism, the doctrine of art for art's sake, religious fideism, and dogmas emanating in general from any party or person capable of exploitation by capitalism to justify its perpetuation.

DAVID GASCOYNE.[19]

It was only a fragment of what he intended, but it would do. He packed the typescript in his suitcase, and set out once more for Paris.

---

19. 'Premier Manifeste anglais du surréalisme (fragment)', *Cahiers d'Art*, 10 (June 1935), 106.

7

'The Tears of Heraclitus'

Since losing his wife Gala to Salvador Dalí, Eluard had been living in an austere flat in the Rue de Legendre behind the Gare Saint-Lazare. His companion there was Maria Benz, a street performer, model, and sometime collagist from Alsace known to the world as 'Nusch', whom he had married the previous year. She was petite with wavy hair and wiry puppet-like limbs; when she leant back in his embrace, it seemed as if she would break. Nusch was out when Gascoyne called, but there were plenty of sketches and photographs of her about the apartment, mostly by Man Ray who was fond of portraying her in bizarre positions: as a giant nude reclining along le Pont d'Avignon, or in the quasi-lesbian embrace of his own, Guadaloupienne, mistress, Adrienne Fidelin. The pictures were much needed since the walls were bare of the works by Ernst and others Eluard had owned in more affluent days: he had put them in store, and many would later be purchased by a well-to-do British resident in Paris whom Gascoyne had yet to meet: the artist Roland Penrose. It was morning, and after coffee Eluard read aloud to him from several living poets he admired: Loys Masson, Raymond Queneau, Edmond Jabès, André Frénaud.[1] These were comparatively minor figures compared to Eluard himself, but they included several writers Gascoyne would later translate, and the reading broadened his sense of contemporary French poetry: as diverse as anything in England, and far less class-bound, less obviously stacked in generations or penned into cliques or schools. He spent the next couple of months amplifying his appreciation of French artistic life in all its aspects: poetic, graphic, sculptural, and polemic, collecting as he did so tracts, manifestos, programmes, and other ephemera.[2] By the end of July he knew as much about evolving artistic culture in France as anybody in England.

---

1. BL Lives, F1381, Side B.
2. David Gascoyne, *Scrapbook*, National Galleries of Scotland GMA A42/1/GKA005.

As he soon discovered, he had returned to Paris at a critical moment. To be sure, the Surrealist movement had always been in crisis; the extracts from the Second Manifesto that had appeared in Titus's English translation in the September 1932 issue of *This Quarter*, with a volley of attacks by Breton on all manner of opponents or backsliders, would have informed David adequately of that. Since this memorable fusillade, there had been further defections and purges. In 1931 the poet Louis Aragon had caused a minor furore by bringing out in a French edition of the Soviet periodical *Literature and the World Revolution* a prose poem called 'Front rouge' that even his keenest admirers recognized as the most artless form of tub-thumping Marxist propaganda. When this publication was seized by the police, Breton had written in its defence in his pamphlet *La Misère de la poésie*, but he had done so in such guarded terms—claiming so many special privileges for art as distinct from politics—that Aragon had felt obliged to disassociate himself from the apologia. The result had been Aragon's summary dismissal from the group.[3] By 1935 the memory of this inglorious episode was fading slightly. However, the question of the political responsibilities of Surrealism had since been brought into sharper focus by the inexorable rise of Hitler and the growing fracas in Spain between the elected Socialist government and its right-wing opponents. Never very keen on the wilder antics of this unruly bunch of painters and poets, the authorities in Moscow were insistently demanding where Breton and his associates would stand in the event of an out-and-out fight between right and left. Breton's successive replies, with their proviso that political contingencies should always be subordinated to the wholesale liberation of the human personality and mind, had done little to reassure party officials. More than ever, Surrealism was on the rack.

In this connection one person to whom Gascoyne was keen to be introduced was René Crevel, a controversial figure who had participated in several of the earliest experiments in automatic writing, and had since produced poems that reminded Gascoyne of snowflakes suspended in glass, some autobiographical fiction,[4] and a study of Paul Klee. The fiction was troubled, unsurprisingly since Crevel's father had hanged himself when the boy was 14, and his mother had forced him to look at the body dangling from a beam. Crevel was narcissistically handsome with intense grey eyes, a broad

---

3. *Short Survey*, 82–8.
4. René Crevel, *La Mort difficile* (Paris: Simon Kra, 1926) See also René Crevel, *Difficult Death*, trans. and introd. David Rattray with a foreword by Salvador Dalí (San Francisco: North Point Press, 1986).

jaw-line, and neatly coiffed russet locks. His looks were one with his moodiness: suicide, his friend Dalí later wrote, ran in the Crevel family like red hair. He was also determined in his attitudes, and was with some diffi-culty attempting to keep the lines of communication open between the Surrealists and the Soviets. As subsequent events were to prove, Moscow was in no mind for compromise. Nonetheless, Crevel was one of the few in the movement who believed there was a chance the apparatchiks might be per-suaded to view social and political issues from a Surrealist angle. The feelers he was putting out were, however, flailing around fairly ineffectively, and the effort had already turned him into an embattled figure. Sick with creeping tuberculosis and tormented by doubt, Crevel was also alone among the Surrealists in his declared bisexuality. For all his problems and perplexities, he was a force to be reckoned with, as his fellow Surrealists conceded, even those—like Breton by and large—who considered him misguided.

An incident in late May was etched onto Gascoyne's memory for ever. One rainy evening he was sitting with Reavey over drinks in the Café Flore opposite the church of Saint-Germain-des-Prés, when the swing doors opened and a small but dramatically beautiful figure entered the *salle* and sat alone for a few minutes. Almost anorexic in her slimness, she had the arms and legs of a doll or finely wrought marionette, and her clothes were of the most expensive cut, a fashionable hat topping her lustrous and abundant, swept-back dark hair. Her face in repose was almost hard, but it brightened to delight when the doors opened again to admit a quick and urgent figure wearing a cyclist's raincoat and no hat, and bearing in his hands a bunch of anemones, which he presented to her with a short word, then abruptly left. A little while later Man Ray, whom Gascoyne already knew from Atelier 17, entered the café with a crowd of friends and informed Gascoyne 'that the woman I had been watching was Nusch Eluard, and the young man who had spoken to her, Crevel'.[5] It was the only time Gascoyne ever saw him, yet this divided figure was to preoccupy him much in the ensuing years. Nusch he saw once more, on a return visit to Paris in 1937, but again he dared not approach her. Perhaps he was too shy, perhaps the sexual chemis-try was all wrong, but the whole brief cameo somehow encapsulates his position in those midsummer weeks in 1935 as an enraptured onlooker, appreciative of what these people had to tell him about literature and allied

---

5. *Journal 1936–1937*, 55–6. Compare BL Lives, F1381, Side B, where the flowers are violets.

arts, excluded all the same from the socio-sexual force field that bound many of the more gregarious Surrealists into a homogenous, mutually self-regarding, group. Crevel too was thus excluded. Perhaps that was the point.

Gascoyne's status as outsider did not last. After a few days he visited Christian Zervos, the Greek-born editor of *Cahiers d'Art*, and handed him the text of his 'Premier Manifeste'. Zervos was an energetic, if not exactly a glamorous, figure. 'Short, tough, *costaud*', as Gascoyne described him, 'with strong, thick, white hair', he resembled a well-dressed docker or perhaps nightclub owner. Zervos let nothing stand in the way of the artists he believed in, and he was largely responsible for Picasso's growing reputation in France. When the following month he published the Manifesto in his magazine, it was accompanied by a double expression of cross-linguistic homage: a poetic tribute by Eluard to his old friend Ernst, accompanied by another tribute by Gascoyne printed in Eluard's French translation.[6] 'Charity Week: To Max Ernst' took its title from Ernst's pictorial novel of the previous year, *Une semaine de bonté ou les sept éléments capitaux*[7] with its seven episodes compared by Gascoyne to 'medals of mud | One for each day of the week | One for each beast in this sombre menagerie'. The fact that, sometime before its British appearance, Gascoyne's accolade appeared in a French version by international Surrealism's most accomplished poet was testament to the fact that, in Paris at least, this 18-year-old enthusiast was starting to be taken seriously.

Slowly he resumed the strands of his former visit. Paris society, he soon found, had moved on slightly in the interval. Trevelyan had moved back to England in the aftermath of a failed affair, though Reavey was still running an international literary agency in the Rue Bonaparte. After a few days, Gascoyne made a return call to Atelier 17 where Hayter slightly took his breath away by suggesting they visit André Breton forthwith. He accompanied David to the Rue Blanche in Pigalle and up the street to where Breton lived with his wife Simone in a fourth floor apartment at 42 Rue de la Fontaine. It was a gaunt building overlooking a courtyard tucked behind a one-storey cinema. 'As we came into the courtyard, because it's some way off the street, a dog started to bark and I looked up, and there was Breton on this little balcony at the top floor looking down on us.'[8]

6. *Cahiers d'Art*, 10 (June 1935). The original English version of 'Charity Week: To Max Ernst' first appeared in *Man's Life Is This Meat,* and was later included in *Collected Poems* (1965), 9–10.
7. (Paris: Editions Jeanne Bucher, 1934).
8. BL Lives, F1381, Side B.

It was an impressive moment, since Breton was the undisputed leader of the movement in France, and by extension throughout Western Europe. 'Looking down' is an expression Gascoyne repeatedly used to describe the posture on his first appearance that day of a man sometimes facetiously described as Surrealism's Pope, and indeed there was something quasi-papal about the square, the veranda, and the attitude *urbi et orbi*. Breton inspired loyalty, fear, and resentment among his associates in almost equal measure. Eluard for one was no longer talking to him (an inconvenient fact both had managed to hide so far from their enthusiastic young guest), and neither was the Romanian veteran of Dadaism Tristan Tzara. For the previous four years Breton had also expelled the avowedly Stalinist Louis Aragon from his inner circle. He had little time for dissenters, and Gascoyne was predictably on his guard against a man with such an exaggerated proprietorial instinct, combined with such a capacity for taking offence. Breton led them inside the flat, its walls, shelves, and desktops 'covered by a prodigious number of paintings, drawings, carvings, objects, cases of butterflies and of fishing hooks…arranged in such a way as to make their complementarity apparent'.[9] The focal point of this *cabinet de merveilles* was Breton's oldest, most cherished possession: de Chirico's painting of 1914, *The Child's Brain*, in which a moustachioed, middle-aged man with a bare torso also looks down, at an unopened book that appears to represent the unexplored future he envisaged when a boy. This was the canvas that in 1922 had famously converted Yves Tanguy to painting when, travelling down the Rue de la Boitié in a bus, he had glimpsed it in the window of the gallery to which Breton had graciously lent it. Graciousness remained a prominent aspect of Breton's manner. As Gascoyne carefully noted that evening, 'He bowed a great deal'.

The influence and the splintering, the inclusiveness and the exclusiveness, of French Surrealism were twin expressions of its relative longevity. It was sixteen years since the founders of Dada had decamped from Switzerland to form the nucleus of the movement. Since then it had opened out all over Europe: in Germany, Belgium, in Romania, in Italy, and most spectacularly in Spain. England was one of the few countries to have so far substantially resisted it. France, though, regarded itself as the nerve centre, and would do so right up to the Second World War. Both Dalí and Picasso were in Paris in May 1935, though for understandable reasons they mostly kept out of Breton's way. Breton's immediate group of affiliates was in fact quite

9. 'André Breton', in *Selected Prose*, 450.

small, a microcosm of the larger network. They met at six o'clock every evening round the corner from his flat at the Café Cyrano, which faced the Moulin Rouge across the Place Blanche. Within a few days Gascoyne was invited to join them. The café management had an arrangement for placing tables together for up to twenty people. Breton sat at the top end and to his side usually Jean Bernier—a former editor of the journal *Clarté* and ally of Aragon who, despite this, had retained Breton's support. The left-wing cartoonist Maurice Henry attended frequently, as did the satirical poet Benjamin Péret, and the essayist Georges Hugnet, a poet and historian of Dadaism who was collaborating on a set of photomontages with another of the group's habitués: the designer Oscar Dominguez, soon to attract attention with *Brouette*, a silk-padded wheelbarrow. Man Ray came less often and Eluard never, his tiff with Breton tactfully unmentioned. People talked and had drinks until it was time for dinner, then Breton went home to his wife, while Gascoyne and the rest would go on to a local bistro: 'generally Georges Hugnet and his wife Germaine and Henry with his young and charming wife. And Péret would often come with us.'[10]

Gascoyne attended these sessions almost daily. It was the ideal listening post for the gossip, the toings and froings, the fallings-in and fallings-out. By the time he left Paris he had acquired something he would subsequently and spectacularly forfeit: Breton's respect, a commodity fastidiously granted and easily lost. The secret, he soon realized, was that there were in effect two Bretons: a private individual of much warmth and charm—of sharp scientific as well as artistic intelligence—and the public defender of a movement embattled on several fronts, trapped between cultural reactionaries on one side and intolerant left-wing ideologues on the other. The need to maintain the integrity of this chosen middle ground explained his fractiousness, and most of his quarrels. 'He forced himself to be authoritarian because he felt, I suppose rather like Freud, that in order to lead and pioneer this psychoanalytical movement you had to be authoritarian to keep the whole show going.'[11]

David received some insight into the private individual several afternoons later when it was Breton's turn to act as unpaid assistant at a *librairie* around the corner. The shop was called *Gradiva*, after a dream-filled novel by the German writer Wilhelm Jensen analysed by Freud in 1907. Gascoyne called

---

10. BL Lives, F1381, Side B.
11. Ibid.

in and found himself, for the first and only time, alone with the great man. The public bearing, the grandeur, the pose, had dissolved to be replaced by a presence still dignified and distant, but 'cordial, agreeable and helpful'. Within days, what is more, Breton had earmarked David as a translator of his lectures and addresses into English.

A more immediately useful commission came through the offices of Eluard, who recommended Gascoyne as a translator to his friend Dalí. At this period Dalí and Gala, his 'midwife, monitress and muse', lived apart from the main hub of the movement in a studio flat at 7 Rue Gauguet, a cul-de-sac in the fourteenth arrondissement just north of the Parc Montsouris. It was a modern whitewashed building designed by Zielinski in 1930 with high windows looking southwards across roofs to the suburb of Mont Rouge beyond. Dalí was more than usually busy. After two successful exhibitions in New York, he was planning a third later that same year at a Manhattan gallery run by the dealer Julien Levy. The catalogue, which was to be printed in both French and English, was to carry thirty-five black-and-white illustrations of his recent work, together with the text of Dalí's essay with poems 'La Conquête de l'irrationnel'. Gascoyne agreed to spend every morning for a week in the apartment turning Dalí's inventive but somewhat scientistic French into English, taking advice on difficult words as he did so either from Dalí himself, whose thick Catalan accent however made this awkward, or from Gala as she drifted solicitously in the background.

He sat at a desk facing the window and the southerly summer light. Behind him was the studio space in which Dalí worked, and beyond that a hallway dominated by *The Great Masturbator*, Dalí's canvas of 1929—the year of his meeting with Gala—in which a female wraith with her auburn hair and pallid features emerges from the severed neck of a stone profile resembling Eluard's. The profile's nose is buried in the ground, whilst hers sniffs at the crotch of an unidentified male to her right. Gascoyne could observe both painting and painter, since a sliver of glass next to his desk afforded a reflection of the artist at his easel wielding a magnifying glass and an extremely fine brush of three camel's hairs. Dalí appeared in an 'outwardly calm frenzy' or trance, 'completely absorbed in what he was doing and totally unconscious of me or anybody else. Maniacal almost'. The concentration of the man was as absorbed as the prose and poetry that Gascoyne was labouring to render as faithfully as he could: difficult and sometimes clotted sentences evoking, for instance, the melting transience, the ripe 'Camembert' of all natural and artistic forms. The essay was all the odder since throughout Dalí had referred to himself in the third person. The last section was called 'The Tears of Heraclitus'. Gascoyne translated: 'THERE exists a perpetual and synchronic physical materialisation of the great simulacrums of thought, in the sense in which Heraclitus already understood it when he wept intelligently and with warm tears for the auto-pudency of nature.'[12]

One day Eluard came to lunch with his and Gala's 18-year-old daughter Cécile, very shy, very devoted to both of her separated parents. Dalí sat moodily at the head of the table crumbling his baguette, an obsessive ritual of his. (The maid could never seem to purchase loaves long enough.) As he did so, Cécile endeavoured to attract the attention of her mother: a hopeless task since, almost devoid of maternal instincts, Gala only had eyes for her past and present husbands. Halfway through the meal Gala demanded, 'And which are the most wonderful love poems that I have ever heard?' Then Eluard rose from his chair, took down from the bookcase his 1932 volume *La Vie immédiate*, and read aloud the prose poem 'Nuits partagées' (Shared Nights), a sequence about an idealized woman whom Nusch probably imagined was Nusch, but which Gala was quite sure was Gala:

Au terme d'un long voyage, je revois toujours ce corridor, cette taupe, cette ombre chaude à qui l'écume de mer prescrit des courants d'air purs comme de tout petits enfants, je revois toujours la chambre où je venais rompre avec toi le pain de nos désirs, je revois toujours ta pâleur dévêtue qui, le matin, fait corps avec les étoiles qui disparaissent.[13]

Dalí carried on, silently crumbling bread.

That month the Surrealist group was planning a sequence of public lectures and shows to coincide with an 'International Congress of Writers for the Defence of Culture' that was taking place at the Place Maubert, a brisk walk along the Boulevard Saint-Germain from Gascoyne's hotel. An ornate invitation card had been drawn up in Breton's meticulous handwriting, framed

---

12. Salvador Dalí, *Conquest of the Irrational*, 35 photographic reproductions and an *hors-texte* in colours, text trans. David Gascoyne (New York: Julien Levy, 1935), 24.

13. Paul Eluard, *La Vie immédiate* (Paris: Editions des cahiers libres, 1932), 34. 'At the end of a long voyage I always see again this passage, this moleskin rug, this warm shade for which the sea spray prescribes breezes pure as small children, I see again this bedroom in which I came to break with you the bread of our desires, I see again your unclothed pallor which each morning blends with the fading stars.' The incident is recalled at BL Lives, F1381, Side B, and in Gascoyne's obituary for Dalí, *The Independent*, 24 Jan. 1989; *Selected Prose*, 254–8.

with miniatures by various contributing artists. Dalí's contribution was to be a lecture with dramatic interludes, the scenario for which he imparted to Gascoyne: 'On the platform with him he was to have an old woman, and he explained to me that he was going to have pink tape on her arms from her fingers, and at one point he was going to have a spirit lamp on stage, and he was going to make an omelette and put it on her head, and that he was going to tear off her fingernails by pulling off the pink tape.'[14]

To this end Dalí had contacted a theatrical agency to supply him with an actress to enact the elderly lady. One morning when his host was out, Gascoyne heard from his desk the ring of the doorbell and the maid—a tremulous employee much in awe of Gala—appeared to announce that somebody had arrived to audition for the part. So Gascoyne walked to the door and attempted to explain to the frail and diminutive person standing out on the landing what was required of her, as she peered timidly past his legs at the flagrant presence of *The Great Masturbator* beyond. As he reached the climactic moment of the superimposition of the omelette, the actress let out a strident Ave Maria, crossed herself, and fled.

Placing fried omelettes on the heads of old ladies was doubtless fun and liberating for the unconscious mind. It was, however, unlikely to attract the respect of the Communist Party with its relentless drive towards justice and realism. The discrepancy of attitude was becoming more and more obvious with each successive session of a conference. The Congress has gone down in history as a left-wing free-for-all and rehearsal for the ideological clashes of the later 1930s. In conception it was broader than that, an organized expression of protest at recent events in Germany attracting people of such different political persuasions as H. G. Wells and Thomas Mann. At the centre of it, however, a storm was brewing. Though the Soviets had not—contrary to widespread impression—been instrumental in planning the meeting, they were beginning to dominate its proceedings through the presence of their forceful delegate: the prolific Russian novelist Ilya Ehrenburg. Ehrenburg possessed strong views on the connections between literature, art, and politics, and he did not take kindly to being contradicted. Above all, he had very little time for the attempts being made by the Surrealist delegation, which included Breton, Crevel, and Eluard, to swing discussion towards their own brand of general mental emancipation.

14. BL Lives, F1381, Side B.

When he had finished each morning's translating stint, Gascoyne took the metro back to the Latin Quarter and walked across to the conference hall, where he was able to attend the afternoon sessions, and to follow the progress of a spectacular row. A few days into the event, riled by their defiance and apparent hedonism, Ehrenburg issued a pamphlet in which he denounced the Surrealists, in a deliberately wounding phrase, as 'pederasts'. Polymorphous perversity is what he seems to have meant, but the phrase sent a bolt through the Surrealist group who were especially outraged because these were the very terms in which their movement had been attacked in the recent past by outright enemies such as the *droitiste* Catholic poet Paul Claudel. Breton possessed a fastidious dislike of homosexuality in all its forms, and Crevel was almost bound to regard the insult as a thinly veiled attack on himself. A couple of days later, Breton and the others were making their way to the Congress on foot when they passed the doors of Les Deux Magots just as Ehrenburg was emerging dressed in his fur-collared jacket. 'Voilà Ehrenburg!' Breton exclaimed. Walking across the street to the astounded Soviet delegate, he slapped him four times across the face announcing as he did so 'Mon honneur est en danger!'

Unsurprisingly, this occurrence soon reached the ears of the conference organizers, who banned Breton personally from attending all future sessions. The declaration he had prepared to deliver a few days afterwards was read out by Eluard instead: bitter consolation for either man, since on Communist–Surrealist diplomatic relations they agreed not at all. Besides which, by this stage Breton was almost as suspicious of Eluard as of Ehrenburg. The speech was boycotted. 'They arranged for it to be the last in the evening, and it was interrupted at midnight when everything closed down. It was only half way through, and he had to finish reading it for Breton the next morning, before anyone turned up.'

Something much darker was to follow. Nobody had felt Ehrenburg's attack more bitterly than Crevel. Increasingly ill, disturbed by his worsening medical condition, at odds with the Surrealist group and the Communists to both of whom he was nominally affiliated, he spent the whole of the plenary session of 17 June pleading with Soviet officials to readmit his friends, to the congress if not to the party. He failed utterly, and at eleven that night he returned home in a mood of deep dejection. The following day he went to the doctor about his worsening symptoms, and was informed that the TB had reached his kidneys. The prognosis was one of wretched, painful, and humiliating physical decline.

The following morning at ten, Gascoyne went out to the Rue Gauguet to continue work on his translation. In the hallway he was met by an unusual and touching sight. Dalí had his overcoat on, and Gala was beseeching to him over and over again 'Embrasse pas!': 'Do not kiss him.' After Dalí left, Gala explained that her husband needed to visit a friend of theirs lying dangerously ill in hospital. It was not until Dalí returned at lunchtime that the circumstances became clear. The previous night Crevel had stuffed newspapers under the door of his flat, and turned the gas full on. When he was found early in morning there was a note on the table containing a single repeated word: 'Dégoûté, dégoûté'. Disgusted, disgusted. Whether with the attitude of his fellow Communists or with his own slow physical decline, nobody could tell.[15]

That night the Surrealist faithful met as usual in the café on the Place Blanche. For the first time Gascoyne or anybody else could remember, Eluard was there, in a condition of excited indignation over the funeral arrangements. Crevel had died in a hospital run by Catholic sisters who, he thought, would naturally wish him to receive a requiem mass. 'Eluard was very shocked and scandalised,' Gascoyne recalled, 'They were all scandalised. They immediately decided that he was going to make a tremendous "bagarre", a row, and smash up the chapel. And I said, oh, well, I'd like, you know, I thought it would be exciting to come.' It says something about the distance Gascoyne had by now travelled from his devout Anglican background that he felt able to endorse this stunt, even to derive pleasure from the prospect of taking part. In the end Breton dissuaded him from attending by telling him that, if the police were called and he was discovered to be there, he would be deported as an undesirable alien. The following morning, the 'bagarre' went ahead without him. But when the Surrealists turned up at the mortuary chapel, full of Buñuel- or Péret-like contempt for the ceremonial they were about to disrupt, they discovered that as a suicide Crevel had been denied Catholic rites. The brief committal was a secular one. There was nothing to break up.

Of course, Breton had been right in one respect. Gascoyne did not belong among these indigenous breakers of chapels. He had come back to France with the specific brief of finding more about a very particular movement and with the object of introducing it to, and interpreting it for, his native

---

15. BL Lives, F1381, Side B.

land. In his own eyes he was an explorer. Several Britons like Herbert Read had been following Surrealism from afar, and others like Trevelyan had made the Channel crossing to collaborate at close quarters. Despite this, the idea of a transfusion of cultural blood does not seem yet to have occurred to several individuals placed to effect it. One exception among the resident English community in Paris was the 35-year-old artist Roland Penrose. The product on his mother's side of a family of wealthy Quaker industrialists, Penrose had studied architecture at Queens' College Cambridge while designing resourceful sets for university productions. He had come to Paris in 1922 to study and paint, meeting there the slender and serious poet Valentine Boué, whom he had married in 1926. The marriage was in diffi-culties, and he was contemplating the—to him—dread prospect of return-ing home. Penrose knew several of the Surrealists personally: the promotion of Ernst's *Une semaine de bonté* the previous year had, for example, been largely his doing. Yet even Penrose, who had been living at the movement's heart for thirteen years, had so far done nothing to introduce its thought or practice to his family and friends back in England, with whom he had largely lost touch, and whose 'belief in a gentle liberal reform contrasted inevitably with the Surrealist revolution which was becoming the impetus behind all my thoughts and actions'.

The catalytic moment of change can be pinpointed with some accuracy from Penrose's memoir *Scrapbook*. In July 1935, deep in conversation with Eluard, he was turning the corner into the Rue de Tournon leading from the Senate on the north side of the Jardin Luxembourg towards the Rue Saint-Sulpice. In the opposite direction came Gascoyne, to whom Eluard introduced him. They instantly recognized one another as seekers on the same quest:

> By chance my reluctant return to my native fog coincided in a meeting with the young English poet, David Gascoyne. It was an encounter of two explorers who had discovered independently the same glittering treasure. David's explo-sion 'Why do we know nothing of this in England?' was echoed immediately by me, who rejoiced in the prospect of turning what had seemed like a gloomy retreat into an attack on indifference and ignorance at home, an affirmation of that which had made life in France so enjoyable and full of purpose.[16]

Later that year Penrose returned to London, where he and Valentine took a house off Haverstock Hill. The plan of an English Surrealist group along the

16. Roland Penrose, *Scrap Book 1900–1981* (London: Thames and Hudson, 1981), 56.

lines of, but with an emphasis slightly different from, the cells recently formed in Brussels and Tenerife began slowly to form.

Dalí and Gala were now making arrangements to move from their apartment in the Rue Gauguet to a larger and more expensive studio in the Rue de l'Université, at the heart of Saint-Germain. Before they moved, Gascoyne walked with Gala up the Rue de Maine and delivered to the printers at La Maison Ramlot the text and illustrations of *Conquest of the Irrational*. The front cover would bear a photo of Dalí himself, his moustache trim, his black hair artificially lengthened by shadow. The frontispiece was his painting of Gala, wearing an embroidered, quilted jacket and viewed from the back as she contemplates another, face-on image of herself seated on a wheelbarrow; behind them hangs one of Dalí's favourite pictures: Millet's *Angelus*.[17] In August Gascoyne took the boat train back to England, unpacked his souvenirs, and began with speed and clarity to write the book he had promised to Cobden-Sanderson before the year's end.

17. *Gala and the Angelus of Millet*. For Gascoyne's discussion of this painting, see *Selected Prose*, 255.

8

'This Meat'

A *Short Survey of Surrealism*, which appeared in November of 1935, occupies
a unique position in the history of the English movement: as a bird's-eye
view of one of the most energetic cultural stirrings of the twentieth century, and
as a snapshot of a particular moment in time. Julian Trevelyan, who was around
at its inception, was to judge it 'the best book on Surrealism that I know',[1] and
the Dalí scholar Dawn Ades would later remark of its style: 'The order, structure
and language are so beautifully judged that one is barely aware of their role in
carrying the reader to the heart of the movement.'[2] At the moment of his maximum exposure as an advocate of the most adventurous trends in contemporary
art, Gascoyne had achieved a feat of stylistic near-invisibility.

Gascoyne had been as much struck by the lucidity of Eluard's expository
prose—a trimmer critical idiom than Breton's opaque, associative flow—as
by the lucidity of his poems. The result was a concise book, 168 pages long
in its first edition and as clear as the Avon running over chalk. There was
little verbal excess anywhere, and little attempt at high-flown writing. In
other words, though its subject was Surrealism, its mode of address and the
organization of its material were not in the least surreal. The one exception
was the long opening sentence of the Introduction, almost a prose poem in
itself, which dips the reader briefly into the disorientating pool of dream
before whipping him out again onto the dry land of common sense:

> Confined from early childhood in a world that almost everything he ever
> hears or reads will tell him is the one and only *real* world and that, as almost
> no one, on the contrary, will point to him, is a prison, man—*l'homme moyen
> sensual*—bound hand and foot not only by those economic chains of whose

---

1. Julian Trevelyan, *Indigo Days: The Art and the Memoirs of Julian Trevelyan* (London: Scolar Press,
   1957/1996), 71–2.
2. *Short Survey*, 10.

existence he is becoming ever more and more aware, but also by chains of second-hand and second-rate *ideas*, the preconceptions and prejudices that help to bind together the system known (ironically, as some think) by the name of 'civilisation', is for ever barred except in sleep from that other plane of existence where stones fall upwards and the sun shines by night, if it chooses, and where even trees talk freely with the statues that have come down forever from their pedestals—a world to which the entrance has generally been supposed, up till now, to be the sole privilege of poets and other madmen.[3]

Thereafter the structure is straightforward, and the advocacy works by stealth. Gascoyne briefly describes the literary and artistic antecedents of international Surrealism, its roots in Dada, the early experiments in automatic writing by Breton and his circle, and the First Manifesto of 1924 with its defence of 'the advantages of madness, a form of freedom that is also, unfortunately, a tyranny, because one cannot control it at will'. Until then, Breton had argued, this avenue of awareness had largely been disregarded by all but poets and scientists (Gascoyne, it has to be said, in 1935 and later, would place far less emphasis on the science). Now this double-edged sword was available to everyone. Gascoyne proceeds to quote at length from the cantankerous Second Manifesto of 1929, in which Breton had attacked several defectors, before examining the implications of the Aragon affair. He alludes specifically to the suicide of Crevel, still vivid in his memory, without going into its causes, at the time still unclear. He closes his account by hinting at the prospect of a future Surrealist group in London, and a forthcoming visit by Breton and Eluard (whom he still assumed to be mutual friends). An appendix adds samples from the work of Breton, René Char, Salvador Dalí, Paul Eluard, Georges Hugnet, and Benjamin Péret, translated either by Gascoyne himself or by the Scottish poet and scholar Ruthven Todd. The last item in this mini-anthology is an extract from *The Immaculate Conception*, the rhapsodic prose work jointly written by Breton and Eluard in 1930—several years before their present tiff—in which they had expounded the artistic possibilities, and the potential dangers, inherent in harnessing the resources of the psychotic mind. There were nineteen black-and-white illustrations, including Man Ray's photographic close-up of dust gathering on the surface of Marcel Duchamp's large glass construction of 1920 *The Bride Stripped Bare by Her Bachelors, Even*. All this was presented with a cover design by Ernst suggestive of cross-national fraternity, in which

---

3. *Short Survey*, 23.

pairs of pigeons rub breasts, and human hands join in greeting, across a set of radiating geometric lines.

At one strategic point Gascoyne draws what with hindsight is a revealing distinction between two varieties of Surrealism. First, there is Surrealism in the broadest meaning of the term. In this sense, he observes, 'All drawing, painting of sculpture that is not primarily or exclusively pre-occupied with aesthetic form ("pure form" in the Roger Fry sense) or with the mere reproduction of the bald external appearance of objective reality, may legitimately be termed surrealist.' In the narrow sense of the word, however, 'Surrealist art with a capital S should refer to the work of those that belong, or have belonged, to the specific Surrealist group.'[4] Though consistent with Breton's own statements about the matter in the First Manifesto, the broader definition was far more in line with what Herbert Read, for example, had said about Surrealism in *Art Now*. It represented a way of regarding the whole subject that would become natural to, and quite characteristic of, the British arm of the movement. While Continental apologists continued to stress the potential of the artistic vanguard to overturn just about everything in the existing social and cultural order, English proponents would always be keener to emphasize Surrealism as a permanent substratum of the human mind, one potentially expressed in all true art, though frequently suppressed, and newly set free.

Mutatis mutandis, much the same was true of Surrealist poetry. In tracing the literary antecedents of the movement, Gascoyne trawls with a broad net. His inventory of French writers who had demonstrated a surrealistic tendency in the past includes de Sade, Louis Bertrand, Charles Baudelaire, Arthur Rimbaud, Lautréamont, Stéphane Mallarmé, J. K. Huysmans, Alfred Jarry, Raymond Roussel, and Guillaume Appollinaire. Several of these had featured forty years before in Arthur Symons's book on Symbolism, where Gascoyne had first encountered them. Others, specifically Lautréamont and Rimbaud, had already been claimed as Surrealist forerunners by Breton. Gascoyne's choices are so inclusive, however, that he almost seems to be concerned to trace some kind of retrospective canon. Of the presence of surreal tendencies in classic English literature he remarks, 'One need quote only Shakespeare, Marlowe, Swift, Young, Coleridge, Blake, Beddoes, Lear, and Carroll.'[5] Surrealism, then, entailed both tradition and rebellion, both a

4. Ibid. 79.
5. Ibid. 94.

permanent state of the mind and a revolt. It was potentially as active in Edward Young's eighteenth-century meditation on death, *Night Thoughts* (which, somewhat to Gascoyne's surprise, had earned the Surrealists' respect) as it was explicit in the work of René Char or Dalí.

This view of Surrealism as less a school than an ubiquitous tendency is apposite to the poetry Gascoyne was himself writing at the time. After delivering the typescript of *The Survey* to the publishers, he had resumed his attendances at the Parton Street bookshop, where he now had acquired a reputation as an egregiously accomplished Francophone and Francophile. His fluency much impressed his monoglot friend Barker who fifteen years later, with characteristically generous hyperbole and whimsy, would recall 'I really can never remember whether David Gascoyne really spoke only in French at this time, or whether he merely happened to give his impression'.[6] At the Parton Press Archer had already issued Barker's *Thirty Preliminary Poems*, then *Eighteen Poems*, the first book by the even younger Dylan Thomas. He now followed these initiatives with a proposal for a book by Gascoyne. Stuck for a title, David took the Northern Line up to see Grigson in his house in Keats's Grove, Hampstead. As in old age he recalled for Mel Gooding, 'Grigson at that time had a book of printer's types. And we opened it at random and in one set of letters there was this quotation, a line from a book that ended with the words "Man's Life Is" and then at the top of the next page the words "This Meat".'[7] The conjunction supplied the desired title, with just the right mixture of arbitrariness and fortuitous meaning. Here was an example of a verbal 'found object' in the spirit of Duchamp. Its title fitted the serendipitous aspect of the exercise neatly: *Man's Life Is This Meat*.

The last poem in the book was the first to have been written, dating from a few months before Gascoyne's first visit to France, and initially published in his absence there.[8] 'And the Seventh Dream is the Dream of Isis' is rife with beautiful and sinister disquiet, and it ripples with images that remind one of a classic Surrealist film scenario. With its piquing of sanctimonious priests, its slitting of eyes and general iconoclasm, it recalls especially Buñuel's *Un chien andalou*, the scenario for which David had found in the fourth number of *Surréalisme au service de la révolution* picked up in Zwemmer's, and

6. George Barker in *Coming to London* (London: Phoenix Press, 1950), 54.
7. BL Lives, F1382, Side A.
8. 'And the Seventh Dream is the Dream of Isis', *New Verse*, 5 (Oct. 1933), 157–8.

to which he alludes in the *Short Survey,* as well as its sequel *L'Age d'or.* The same magazine had provided him with the epigraph for the whole book, a quotation from Eluard at his most aggressively political: 'Of course I hate the reign of the bourgeois | The reign of cops and priests | But I hate still more the man who does not hate it | As I do | With all his might | I spit in the face of that despicable man | Who does not of all my poems prefer this *Critique of Poetry.*' All but six of the poems in *Man's Life Is This Meat* were designated Surrealist exercises, but it was 'And the Seventh Dream' that carried the unmistakably Buñuelesque and Dalí-esque bearing of anarchic jubilation and destructiveness.

Of what does the Egyptian goddess Isis dream? In *Isis and Osiris* Plutarch tells of her devotion to her brother and husband Osiris, trapped in a coffin and set afloat by his jealous brother Typhon, and subsequently dismembered into fourteen separate pieces by his ever-vengeful sibling when Isis recovered his corpse in Byblos in the Lebanon.[9] Isis then went in search of the body parts throughout the land of Egypt, and buried each where she found it. 'However, the genital member of Osiris had been eaten by the fishes, so Isis made an image of it instead.'[10] Gascoyne's poem is a collage of such dismembered limbs:

> white curtains of infinite fatigue
> dominating the starborn heritage of the colonies of St Francis
> white curtains of tortured destinies
> inheriting the calamities of the plagues of the desert
> encourage the waistlines of women to expand
> and the eyes of men to enlarge like pocket-cameras
> teach children to sin at the age of five
> to cut out the eyes of their sisters with nail-scissors
> to run into the streets and offer themselves to unfrocked priests
> teach insects to invade the deathbeds of rich spinsters
> and to engrave the foreheads of their footmen with purple signs
> for the year is open the year is complete
> the year is full of unforseen happenings
> and the time of earthquakes is at hand[11]

---

9. *Plutarch über Isis und Osiris,* ed. G. Parthey (Berlin: Nicolai, 1850), 12–20.

10. J. G. Frazer, *The Golden Bough: A Study in Magic and Religion,* pt. IV. *Adonis, Attis, Osiris,* vol. ii (London: Macmillan, 1913), 10.

11. David Gascoyne, *Man's Life Is This Meat* (London: Parton Press, 1936), 41; omitted from *Collected Poems* (1965); *Collected Poems* (1988), 25.

Because of its position right at the end of the book, this torrential tour de force was clearly designed to take the breath away—there was, after all, in 1935 nothing quite like it in British poetry. In retrospect it is partly remarkable because written by a verbal artist whose eyes were as wide open as his ears. In it, the poet and the art critic join hands. Elsewhere in the book there are *hommages* to particular painters: to Ernst, to Yves Tangy, and most famously to Dalí. In each case the tribute is couched in terms designed to evoke the painter's own style. Dalí, of course, also wrote verse: in French and, less often, in Spanish or Catalan. In the anthology at the back of the *Survey* Gascoyne had translated a fragment from his 'Amour et mémoire'.[12] The poem to Dalí draws on ideas from *Conquest of the Irrational* that Gascoyne had translated the previous year. Images melt into one another suggesting pictorial compositions, as in the first stanza where children who are chasing butterflies turn round to see Goliath advancing towards them with the poet's own body growing out of its head, like the graceful neck of Gala emerging from the husk of the decapitated Eluard in *The Great Masturbator* that had so discombobulated the elderly actress outside the painter's Rue Gauguet studio the previous June. Then the children disappear into a set of catacombs where they cry for help to mirrors suspended from the rocky walls: scenario melting into scenario: kinetic Dalí reminiscent of effects by Buñuel.[13] Other poems such as 'The Rites of Hysteria' are in a recognizably Dalí-esque mode, full of lines you feel he might well have painted: 'An arrow with lips of cheese' that is 'caught by a floating hair'; an 'ashtray' that 'balanced a ribbon upon a syringe'.[14] But the origins of this particular poem were literary as well: the most famous use of the term hysteria in French literature had occurred, as Gascoyne well knew, in Baudelaire's *Journaux intimes*: 'J'ai cultivé mon hystérie avec jouissance et terreur.'[15] Both Breton and Dalí had flirted with hysteria as a productive condition, though Breton for one insisted that artistically creative hysteria needed to be channelled and controlled. In Gascoyne's case, its cultivation would later have destabilizing effects.

These were poems very much of their time. In later years, when Gascoyne prided himself on having moved on, he would evince some reluctance to have them collected, embarrassed to have his name so automatically associated

12. *Short Survey*, 104–5.
13. *Man's Life*, 36; omitted from *Collected Poems* (1965); *Collected Poems* (1988), 46.
14. *Man's Life*, 39–40; omitted from *Collected Poems* (1965); *Collected Poems* (1988), 56.
15. Baudelaire, *Journaux intimes*, 23 Jan. 1862.

with a fad of his early youth. In reality his tastes were already broader, and less modish, than such occasionally derivative torrents of disparate images would suggest. Throughout both the poems and the criticism of this year you can already sense an admiration for two rather different styles: on the one hand the cascade of horrors characteristic of early experiments in automatic writing like Breton and Philippe Soupault's *Champs magnetiques* of 1919 or Tristan Tzara's poem *L'Homme approximatif* (a long fragment from which he had translated at the back of *The Short Survey* without Tzara's permission[16]); on the other, the limpid lines of Eluard. Clearly Gascoyne was torn temperamentally between a publicist in him determined to blazon the achievements of what was still, in the eyes of many insular English people, an unacceptably foreign and deliberately scandalous movement, and a quieter self, anxious to express all that its growing awareness meant to him individually. *The Survey* dwells approvingly on Surrealistic violation, yet the most approving word in its vocabulary is 'pure'. Accordingly, the contents of *Man's Life* alternate between the disorientation and radical *jouissance* of the *quais* and a persistently introspective, and far more English-feeling, mood of solipsistic stillness. Gascoyne had journeyed on from the imagistic delicacy and grace of the 'Five Netsukés of Hottara Sonja' three years before, yet he was still the same mystically inclined, deeply impressionable person.

Thus, while the identifiably Surrealist pieces in this book are impressive for their versatility of surface, there are other poems that aspire to a Dalíesque delirium while making coherent emotional sense at a level not far beneath their disjointed outer parade. If these poems tell us quite a bit about the period, they are far more revealing of the 19-year-old, slightly insecure, Gascoyne. 'Antennae', for example, is a description of lovemaking between partners of uncertain gender who remain remote and psychologically estranged from one another. It is not without relevance to Gascoyne's own unsatisfactory experience of sex at the time: urgently desired in theory, in practice leaving him stranded on the 'sonorous island' of self-conscious solitude. This is a poem about the near-impossibility of people blending:

> The timeless sleepers tangled in the bed
> In the midst of the sonorous island, alone
>
> The tongue between the teeth
> The river between the sands

16. At Tzara's insistence, a second impression was hastily issued minus the poem.

> Love in my hand like lace
> Your hand enlaced with mine.[17]

The mood is post-coital, with a forlorn feeling reminiscent of the meaningless love scene between the young man carbuncular and the bored typist in Eliot's 'The Burial of the Dead', though without its implied moral judgement:

> So evanescent that which binds us
> That more is meant, regret is absent…
> Our burning possession of each other
> Held in both hands because it is all we have.

The confession is personal though universal. It is also elusively phrased (though not so elusively as to yield to fairly ready interpretation), enigmatic in the style that is closer to a de Chirico than to a Dalí.

The most successful poems in the book, as well as the most characteristic, are those in which these two veins come together in an allegory about a self who is isolated in a landscape seething with change. There are several like this ('The Unattained' is a good example) but best is 'Unspoken', a poem recognizably about the slippage of language from meaning to meaning. Dating from November of the previous year when Gascoyne was wrestling with the translations for *A Short Survey*, it is a poem about the challenge of translation, of negotiating a no-man's-land between linguistic systems. Words refuse to attach themselves reliably to subjects, there are no limits to count on, definitions forever swarm and dissolve. This is a condition well known to all who have ever attempted to turn a phrase from one language into an equivalent phrase in another, too often having to make do with an approximation that may not mean the same to the reader as to the translator, and may further convey different connotations to different communities of readers or hearers:

> Travelling though man's enormous continent
> No two roads the same
> Nor ever the same names to places
> Migrating towns and fluid boundaries
> There are no settlers here there are
> No solid stones.[18]

17. *Man's Life*, 33; *Collected Poems* (1965) 18–20; *Collected Poems* (1988), 53. For a French trans. by Yves de Bayser, see *Nouvelle Revue Française*, 357 (Oct. 1982).
18. *Man's Life*, 22–3; *Collected Poems* (1965) 10–12; *Collected Poems* (1988), 42. Originally published in Dec. 1935 in *The Year's Poetry 1935: A Representative Collection*, Denys Kilham Roberts, Gerald Gould, and John Lehmann (London: John Lane, The Bodley Head), 147.

Gascoyne must often have experienced this sort of verbal vertigo. Unsurprisingly the semantic and linguistic theories underlying it were to make a frequent appearance in his notebooks in the years to come, years in which he was to make a name for himself as a translator. They were to resurface again in his work when post-structuralist linguistics became the rage in the 1980s.

Gascoyne was learning the hard but useful fact that the strongest poems often arose from his very difficulties, the resistant facts that troubled him. Historically speaking the most interesting item in the book derives from a celebrated Surrealist fracas, but his use of it illustrates the limits of his sympathy when it came to the more callous aspects of collectively organized anarchism. To appreciate what is happening in 'Lozanne' you have to go back two years. Violette Nozières was an 18-year-old from Neuvy-sur-Loire who had taken revenge on her much-resented parents by living as a prostitute in their home, maintaining her lover Jean Dobin from her earnings. When she had contracted syphilis, she had convinced her mother and railway engineer father the disease was inherited from them. On 21 August 1933, she persuaded them to cure themselves by imbibing a medicinal concoction. In fact it was the poison Somenal. She had then blocked the door and the windows, and turned on the gas to disguise the double murder as suicide. Her father had died, though the mother was revived and pleaded for her daughter's life at the trial. As a result, Violette's death penalty was commuted to a prison sentence, but the case had attracted the attention of the newly formed Surrealist group in Brussels under the direction of E. L. T. Mesens. The subsequent collation of poems, prose and artwork with its contributions from Breton, Char, Eluard, Maurice Henry, Péret, Dalí, Tanguy, Ernst, Magritte, and Giacometti had been seized by police at the French border.[19] It contained a mixture of responses and styles, but running through all of them had been the suggestion that Violette was not simply a victim of—but a warrior in the movement's ongoing struggle against—the 'bourgeois family'.

Gascoyne was naturally interested in such anti-family sentiments, but his reaction to them owed much to his own. Though Leslie and Win had left Bournemouth fifteen years before, they continued to keep up with events in this respectable seaside resort, including its occasional scandals. Bournemouth had been much in the news during 1935. In Madeira Villa in Manor Road had

19. *Violette Nozières* (Brussels: Editions Nicolas Flamel, 1933).

lived Alma Rattenbury—a fashionable beauty and amateur composer who
wrote light songs under the pseudonym 'Lozanne'—and her distinguished
architect husband Francis, thirty years older than herself. Early that year they
had hired as chauffeur and odd-job man a 17-year-old named George Stoner,
with whom the wife had become sexually involved. In March, unable to bear
the thought that he might be sharing her favours with her husband, Stoner had
attacked Mr Rattenbury with a mallet, shattering his skull. Anxious to share in
his fate, Mrs Rattenbury had initially claimed to be a willing accomplice to the
crime, a confession she had withdrawn at a late stage in the ensuing Old Bailey
trail. When Stoner was sentenced to be hanged, Lozanne had taken herself out
onto the banks of the River Avon, where she stabbed herself repeatedly through
the chest before drowning herself in its brackish waters.[20]

Naturally Win had followed the trial in the newspapers, and she and Leslie
had absorbed the local shock from their Bournemouth friends. David's prose
poem 'Lozanne' is an attempt to rework the Bournemouth tragedy—which
forty years later was to provide Terence Rattigan with the plot for his last
stage play, *Cause Célèbre*—in terms that align Alma's crime with Violette
Nozières's infamous parricide. It draws on the mood of 'Seaside Tragedy'
from *Roman Balcony* three years before, while endowing a provincial English
scandal with a sort of Surrealist frisson. Accepting Mrs Rattenbury's initial
confession as authentic, it portrays her too as a victim of oppressive family
circumstances (though all the signs are that Francis Rattenbury had truly
loved his wife). It ends with a description of her drowning:

> The dusty and ashen residue of a passion that now raged
> elsewhere, but still raged, rose slowly upwards to the surface
> of the lake as your blood sank slowly through it. And the
> other returned to ice. Oh, I can see through your eyes now
> and I can see what flame it was that melted everything before
> it! (Though the obstinate sod refused to become softened by
> the rain of thaw.) But you were spared passing through the
> black box where a masked man kisses his victim before her
> death. I ask the glass again: Who gave the victims right to
> refuse life to those who refuse to be victimised?
>
> Those who damned shall be damned.[21]

20. *The Times*, 30 Mar.; 3, 12, 17, 25 Apr.; 2, 24, 28, 30, 31 May; 1, 7, 25 June 1935. For Mrs Rattenbury's
    death while 'of unsound mind', see *The Times*, 10 June 1935. Stoner's sentence, like Nozières
    was subsequently committed to imprisonment.
21. *Man's Life*, 35; *Collected Poems* (1965) 20–1; *Collected Poems* (1988), 39.

There is a moral unease that complicates and embarrasses the revolutionary indignation of these closing lines. Gascoyne has phrased his expostulation so that the status of victim can ambiguously be claimed for all concerned: by Alma Rattenbury herself, for the young lover who wielded the weapon, the murdered husband, for the poet viewing himself in a looking glass (as Alma had viewed herself in the surface of the lake), even for society itself, and the legal authorities who have just passed judgement on its behalf. The poet's vocal protest arguably applies to the latter group most of all. His double use of 'damned' deploys a religiously loaded word that potentially gathers in most of the above. This theological epithet, however, is quite antithetical to Breton's sort of language. It is quite close to Cardinal Newman's.

9

'The Queen of Unrest'

In January 1936 Leslie and Win were able to escape from their cramped quarters in East Twickenham. Upriver at Teddington they found a two-storey terraced house in 'The Grove', an estate built in 1928 to accommodate employees of the petrol firm Shellmex. A few streets from the Thames, Teddington Film Studios, and the lock, 21 Grove Terrace was a sub-Lutyens, Hampstead Garden Suburb-style corner dwelling with a brick front, shutters, a false Georgian portico, and a garden with a mature yew tree. In this environment David seemed exotic. The painter Bettina Shaw-Lawrence, then a kittenish convent-educated 14-year-old living with her family round the corner in Grove Gardens, was told of his arrival by the admiring twins. She called round and found a cosmopolitan sophisticate who 'stood at the top of the stairs against the light as tall as a church steeple' and discoursed of Ernst, Eluard, and Henry Miller.[1] She invited him back to her own house where he noticed the piano and outraged her stolid engineer-manager father by launching into a mini-recital of Bartók.

It was in Teddington, in the early months of that year, that David received a letter bearing the unfamiliar postmark of the *département* Puy-de-Dôme. The sender was Roland Cailleux, a doctor with a summer practice in enteric medicine in the spa town of Châtel-Guyon, from which he annually travelled to London for a winter break. He had, he claimed, known René Crevel well, and now wanted to talk about him. Though David had never actually spoken to Crevel, his association with whom was confined to having once observed him present violets to Nusch Eluard, the message was intriguing enough for him to agree to meet this stranger a few evenings later at the Café Royale.

---

1. Letter from Bettina Shaw-Lawrence to Robert Fraser, 22 Jan. 2009.

Cailleux turned out to be in his late twenties, charming though elusive, suave, and 'good-looking in a very French and an entirely masculine way'.[2] The close connection with Crevel was probably a pretext or a sexual signal, though Cailleux had indeed known him slightly while training in Paris during the late 1920s when he had hung around the nascent Surrealist movement and met Breton. He also possessed credible aspirations as a writer. They chatted in French, though Cailleux's English was more than competent, since after qualifying he had worked for several months as a houseman at the French hospital in Hackney. After dinner he took Gascoyne to 'Park Royal', a large block of service flats near Marble Arch that was his regular base when in London, and there they spent the night together.

In the morning Cailleux read him some passages from his novel in progress, *Saint-Genès ou la vie brève*, that followed in thirteen chapters the literary evolution of a young man of about Gascoyne's age finding his way to liberation via Stendhal, Gide, Dostoevsky, and Rimbaud. Then he showed him a set of transparencies of his home town of Châtel-Guyon. An image of a row of trees at the edge of a wood reminded Gascoyne of the pine coppice unforgettably described in Alain-Fournier's novel *Le Grand Meaulnes* shortly before the narrator's first meeting with the beautiful Yvonne de Galais, a being almost as slippery as Cailleux. The novel was already favourite reading matter for Gascoyne, who took to handing out copies to friends as pledges of intimacy.[3] The association with Cailleux's slides, depicting a quite different part of France from Fournier's Normandy, implied a similar understanding. Gascoyne was to frequent the Frenchman's pied-à-terre on several occasions in 1936 when not busy with furthering the cause of Surrealism and with his major project in progress, a life of Rimbaud.

There cannot have been much spare time. Towards the end of the *Short Survey* Gascoyne had announced 'It is within the bounds of possibility that a Surrealist group may be founded shortly in London. André Breton and Paul Eluard have declared their intention of visiting England in the spring of 1936, and there is talk of a large Surrealist exhibition being held at the same time.'[4] By the New Year, informal meetings were under way in Hampstead, where Penrose now occupied a large double-fronted Georgian house on Downshire Hill, the top floor of which Constable had once used

2. Afterword to *Collected Journals*, 365.
3. For example, a few months later to Bettina Shaw-Lawrence. Letter of 22 Jan. 2009.
4. *Short Survey*, 92.

as a studio.[5] The first full meeting was held there on 6 April, and soon Gascoyne was attending quite regularly, along with Penrose, Read, Ben Nicholson, and Trevelyan, and the Cambridge don Hugh Sykes Davies. Rupert Lee, who headed the London group, was in the chair.[6] Aware that Surrealism was about to mount an opening assault on the English, Gascoyne now began expanding the slender body of translations published at the back of the *Short Survey*. Herbert Read, who knew Eliot well, had also persuaded Fabers to commission from him a translation of *Qu'est-ce que le Surréalisme?*, a lecture that Breton had delivered in Brussels in 1934 at the time of the formation of the Belgian group. Eliot was fond of pinpointing his authors with a telling phrase. His secretary-assistant at the time was Anne Bradby (the poet Anne Ridler), in talking with whom he invariably referred to David as 'that gloomy boy' (Barker was 'a most peculiar fellow'). When the said gloom called to deliver his typescript at Russell Square, Bradby went down to collect it in the small lobby next to the rudimentary telephone switchboard, staffed by a Miss Swann. She dared question Gascoyne's understanding of the technical terms Breton used in his talks: 'I remember querying what he meant by "white as alburnum"—a word which signifies "the sap-wood in exogenous trees". I supposed he meant "laburnum", but then that was not white but yellow. Could he have been thinking of the white acacia? My query, as we stood in the waiting room next to Miss Swann's box seemed to puzzle him, and I think we left the word as it stood.'[7]

Another platform for his translations and poems was a new London-based journal specifically devoted to Surrealist writing, foreign or home-grown. David's one-time flatmate Roger Roughton was its editor, *Contemporary Poetry and Prose* its name. Its makeshift offices were two doors down from Archer's shop at Meg's café, otherwise known as the Arts Café, in the basement of 1 Parton Street ('Home-made cakes; Morning Coffee'), where Roughton could now be found daily, editing among the cups.[8] Roughton is the mystery man of British Surrealism, though he was one of the movement's most accomplished poets, and to his contemporaries a vivid presence. He shared with David a capacity for the rapid absorption of tendencies he would then work through quickly, as if through some promising

5. Antony Penrose, *Roland Penrose: The Friendly Surrealist* (Munich: Prestel-Verlag, 2001), 70.
6. Michel Remy, *Surrealism in England* (London: Ashgate, 1999), 73–4.
7. Ann Ridler, *Memoirs* (Oxford: Perpetua Press, 2004), 107.
8. A. T. Tolley, *The Poetry of the Thirties* (London: Victor Gollanz, 1975), 199, 121, 224, 227, 228, 230.

geological seam. During Gascoyne's absence in France he had visited the United States with Dylan Thomas's friend (and later collaborator) John Davenport. There he had got to know e.e. cummings, and had worked as an extra in Hollywood. Joining the Communist Party, he had then journeyed to the Soviet Union and, his commitment still intact, had returned to London in January 1936 to review books for the *Daily Worker* while publishing prose and poetry in *The Criterion*. A little short of his twenty-first birthday he had gained access to a trust fund established for him by the Lancastrian father whom he had scarcely known before his death on the Western Front. It was enough to bankroll a lively magazine of which translations from a variety of European languages soon proved to be lifeblood.

An extra impetus to internationalism came from a third Parton Street habitué, the slightly older Albert Lancaster Lloyd, whom Barker was to describe as 'a rubicund sheep farmer from the hinterland of Australia who really did know the words and the tune that the fishy girls sang and how Achilles hid himself among the women...singer, scholar, whaler'.[9] In fact Bert Lloyd was English, the son of an invalided ex-serviceman. Born in Wandsworth in 1908, at 16 he had sailed for Australia under a scheme run by the British Legion, and there had picked up a love of folk singing on remote sheep stations. Acknowledged now as the man who rescued English folk music from the gentility of Cecil Sharp's generation, Lloyd was a lot more besides. His singing was earthed in his demotic politics, which in turn influenced his openness to other languages and cultures. He was to prove the most versatile of all Roughton's translators, rendering Dalí from Catalan, Kafka and Max Ernst from German, Saint-John Perse from French, as well as presenting 'Traditional Country Ballads' from America and Australia.

Reavey, who was back and forth from Paris to London at this time, supplied translations from Picasso's Spanish and Ernst's German. Of all the translations that appeared in the ten issues of this handsomely produced magazine (eight monthly numbers, and two quarterly) between May 1936 and September 1937, the largest number, however, were Gascoyne's: over twenty, in addition to his own poems. All were from French, and they included Benjamin Péret, Breton, Georges Hugnet, Alfred Jarry, and the teenage Greek-born Gisèle Prassinos, a writer of prose poems whom the Surrealists had recently discovered, showering her with much the same enthusiasm for youth as they had recently shown Gascoyne himself.

9. George Barker in *Coming to London* (London: Phoenix House, 1950), 55.

The originals were exceptionally various. Diversity of style, after all, had been one way—licensed even by the normally dictatorial Breton—for the worldwide community of Surrealists to resist the standardization and drabness fostered by the Communist Party. Péret's, for instance, was the funny face of French Surrealism. Traumatized by serving in the Great War, he was anti-authoritarian in every fibre of his being, and profoundly hostile to Church and State. A pet hate was Raymond Poincaré, President of France during the First World War, whom he blamed for most of France's ills, including the collapse of the franc in 1924. In an early issue of *La Surréalisme au service de la révolution* he had been photographed haranguing a priest in the open street. Admittedly in the picture he had not looked especially defiant, or the priest especially put out, but the cheekiness pervaded much that Péret did, and everything he wrote. Eluard, alive to both his strengths and his limitations, once said of him, 'One of the chief properties of poetry is to inspire in humbugs a grimace which unmasks them and allows them to be judged. The poetry of Benjamin Péret is particularly liable to cause this reaction, which is as fatal as it is useful.'[10]

For Gascoyne, the serviceman's son, the one-time cathedral chorister, such insolence was liberating. He had grown up among part-time humbugs, and here was a chance to be rude. But the abuse could itself cause problems, as Roughton found out that June when under the alias of the Europa Press he brought out a collection of Péret translations by Gascoyne and Humphrey Jennings under the title *A Bunch of Carrots*. Whimsically satirical poems pilloried Christianity, ex-soldiers, and several politicians. When the book appeared it was disfigured by horizontal black lines across several pages, since Roughton had been obliged to submit it to the censors. A sacrilegious piece about the Eucharist was defaced by several such scars, as was a squib about a war veteran. A similar smudge had removed a fraternal reference to a small lion that in the original had been depicted 'pissing on the head of the same Poincaré'. Several months later Roughton rushed out a second 'uncensored' edition under the revised, mock-reverential, title of *Remove Your Hat*. There had been compromises on both sides. The leonine gush had been unstopped, but for the most part the de-expurgation took the form of withdrawing whole poems and replacing them by less offensive ones. It was the first of several such brushes between the magazine and the law.

10. 'A Note by Paul Eluard', in Benjamin Péret, *A Bunch of Carrots*, trans Humphey Jennings and David Gascoyne (London: CPP Editions, 1936), 6.

At the same time Roughton assembled a group of writers including notably Gascoyne and Samuel Beckett, to translate a medley of Eluard's poems
taken from four different volumes. The title, *Thorns of Thunder*, was derived
from a tribute by Eluard to Ernst as translated by Reavey, the volume's editor.[11] Eluard was technically from the same national stable as Péret, but he
was about as different in character as it was possible to be. If Péret had one
tone of voice, mocking and unrepentant, Eluard's was as various as his politics were constant. 'Poetry', he had written, 'is perpetual struggle, life's very
principle, the queen of unrest.'[12] Endlessly versatile, he evoked art and artists,
was philosophically sophisticated and knowledgeable about many fields, and
he remains one of the most delicate voices of heterosexual eroticism in
twentieth-century French poetry. How could any one person translate all of
this? Beckett had set a high standard in 1932 when he had published some
Eluard versions in *This Quarter*. Reavey now took on most of the erotic
poems. A poem about Man Ray was translated by—well—Man Ray.
Gascoyne himself concentrated on poems about painters: Arp, Braque, de
Chirico, Masson. The one love poem on which he worked was called
'Necessity' and, tellingly perhaps, it is the most abstracted one, a study of
sensual aloneness:

> Between the carotid and the ghost of salt
> Between the auracaria and the head of a dwarf
> Between the branching rails and the speckled dove
> Between man and woman
> Between my solitude and you.[13]

Roughton issued all of these books of translation quickly so as to meet the
deadline for the forthcoming exhibition, now scheduled for early June. The
committee had worked fast, and it had quite a lot of experience behind it.
Lee, for example, had already organized several large shows, including an
open air exhibition of British art on the roof gardens of Selfridges in 1930.

11. Paul Eluard, *Thorns of Thunder: Selected Poems*, with a drawing by Picasso, ed. George Reavey,
    trans. Samuel Beckett, Denis Devlin, David Gascoyne, Eugene Jolas, Man Ray, George Reavey,
    and Ruthven Todd (London: Europa Press and Stanley Nott, 1936). Devlin's translation of
    'Nakedness of Truth' on p. 6 features the line 'DESPAIR has no wings', which Gascoyne
    would later answer in a line from one of his most quoted translations from Pierre Jean Jouve:
    'Despair has wings.'
12. The English words are actually Beckett's in his translation of Eluard's essay 'Poetry's Evidence',
    This Quarter, Surrealist Number (Sept. 1932).
13. *Thorns of Thunder*, 46.

They now drew up plans for a show along the lines of the Brussels exhibition that had coincided with Breton's trip there in 1934, and the Prague and Tenerife exhibitions of the following year. With Penrose providing £200 of working capital,[14] they booked the New Burlington Galleries (a now demolished building immediately behind the present Royal Academy of Arts) for five weeks in June and early July. Works were to be imported from all major Surrealist painters and sculptors; members of the committee and friends like Roughton were invited to submit collages and miniatures, and there was to be an associated programme of readings and lectures illustrating the aesthetic range of the movement, its ideology, and its connections with psychology and science. There were to be special sections devoted to the insane, and to children.

It says something for the atmosphere of British Surrealism at the time—tolerant or lukewarm, depending on your point of view—that these energetic organizers so seldom fell out. The natural leader was Read, a sure-footed Yorkshireman with a wide knowledge of modern art, a taste for administration, a secure reputation as a critic, contempt for established privilege, and a faculty for what his friend T. S. Eliot liked to call 'wisdom'. From the outset Read and Penrose got on famously, establishing a professional understanding that would later inspire the founding of the Institute for Contemporary Arts in 1947, thus perpetuating this earlier impulse.

Perhaps the most quixotic member of the committee was Sykes Davies. A versatile mind with a Cambridge double first in classics and English, by his mid-twenties he already held a tutorial fellowship at St John's where he would remain for the rest of his academic career. Podgy, pipe-smoking, softly spoken though unstoppable, he had published a quasi-Surrealist *conte* the previous year called *Petron*, blending echoes of Bunyan, Ovid, and Lewis Carroll with a mock belletristic style ('Dear Reader'; 'Our Hero').[15] Gascoyne had reviewed it in *New Verse*, opining, 'One cannot help wondering whether Peron genuinely is an "interior hero", a projection of genuine obsessions and conflicts, or whether he is merely an ingeniously manipulated puppet, made to dance to a tune Mr Davies once overheard in the

---

14. *Roland Penrose: The Friendly Surrealist*, 72.
15. Hugh Sykes Davies, *Petron* (London: J. M. Dent, 1935). It was addressed to 'those who used to enjoy Milton and Thomson's *Seasons* at school: for those upon whom Shakespeare was not wasted: for those who once liked the early poems of Shelley: for those who find little time for reading nowadays ...For those who have once read Poe'.

library.'[16] After a few more years he would lose interest in the movement, from which he would abscond almost as rapidly as he had latched onto it. A colleague later remarked of him that he 'was most fascinated by things he could not quite do: like writing fiction or playing the accordion'. He seemed to others to resemble Groken, the morose Clown. He had once been married to Kathleen Raine, and after four more marriages—two to the same woman—would ultimately comment, 'I am pleased to report that I parted on terms of perfect bitterness from all of my wives.' He would spend much of his retirement in solitude, fishing.[17]

Read and Penrose constituted the hanging committee, with freedom to select as broad and representative a display of international Surrealism's varied strengths in painting and sculpture. Davies and Gascoyne assumed responsibility for the programme of peripheral events and lectures, readings, and talks, to which they would both contribute personally. The initial plan was to invite the whole European elite corps of Surrealist practitioners in various genres to attend the event at the same time, but it soon fell foul of the recognition that, for example, six years after co-writing their masterpiece *The Immaculate Conception*, Breton and Eluard were still not on speaking terms. If Breton was to open the proceedings on 6 June, Eluard would therefore have to lecture on 'Poetic Evidence' on the 22nd, allowing a decent interval for the departure of one, and arrival of the other. Dalí fortunately was still cordially disposed towards both of them, but he too would appear towards the end, staying with Gala at the home of the American millionaire art-lover Edward James before lecturing on the unconscious, a climax to the entire event.

In the first week of June E. L. T. Mesens, head of the Brussels group, showed up. A one-time composer and follower of Erik Satie, a close associate of Magritte, he seemed to Gascoyne as controlling as Breton, but without the manners. He had firm ideas on how exhibitions should be run, since he had directed his own gallery for several years, and had masterminded the Brussels exhibition in 1934. He was not universally welcome in London where he would however make his home for the rest of his life, assuming the leadership of the English group.[18] Mesens carried around with him an

---

16. *New Verse*, 18 (Dec. 1935), 19.
17. George Watson, 'Remembering Prufrock: Hugh Sykes-Davies, 1909–1984', *Sewanee Review*, 109/4 (Fall 2001) 573–80.
18. For whom see George Melly, *Don't Tell Sybil: An Intimate Memoir of E. L. T. Mesens* (London: Heinemann, 1997).

air of well-fed, dapper, slightly whimsical self-satisfaction; he wanted, and demanded, efficiency and dispatch. Mostly he got what he wanted, usually by exhausting everybody else's patience so they gave in. He was, in Gascoyne's privately held view, smugly condescending and grubbily lecherous. Once on the committee, however, he had his way over many things, including the disposition of the pictures, which at the last moment he insisted were rehung to alternate between small and large items so the public would be obliged constantly to adjust their focus for viewing, even if they constantly bumped into one another in the process.

A few days short of the opening on 11 June, Gascoyne recalled a fan letter he had received the previous winter from a young woman living in a bedsit in Earl's Court. He paid her a visit and discovered Sheila Legge to be a robustly beautiful girl of 22 with fashionably long blonde hair and an attractive self-containment. He decided the best way of employing her was to convert her into a living exhibit, a walking 'surrealist phantom'. Adopting an idea from one of Dalí's canvases, he contacted the theatrical designer Motley with whom his family had had dealings in the past and who supplied costumes for the Old Vic, instructing them to run off a white wedding dress. 'And then I got a Mayfair florist to make a mask of roses, and we took her out to Trafalgar Square and had a photograph.' The picture appeared on the cover of the next issue of the *International Surrealist Bulletin*, and shows the phantom among fountains and pigeons and against the blackened backdrop of the National Gallery, her face covered by flowers.[19]

Afterwards Gascoyne led her up the Haymarket and Piccadilly to the gallery where the opening was in full spate. The right- and the left-wing press, unsympathetic almost without exception, claimed few people had turned up. In fact there were 2,000. Dressed in green, Breton made a speech, for which a translation by Gascoyne was supplied in the catalogue. Sheila circulated among the crush, carrying a prosthetic leg in her right hand and a pork chop in her left. But the afternoon was sultry. When the chop started to stink, it was abandoned. Dylan Thomas circumperambulated carrying a teapot full of boiled string and asking anyone he met 'Weak or strong?' A protuberance on a Miró sculpture was too tempting to be ignored by the composer William Walton, who suspended a kipper meticulously from it.

Visitors averaged a thousand a day at 1*s*. 3*d*. a head to see a mixture of work by Continental masters alongside English artists prepared to appear

19. *International Surrealist Bulletin*, 4 (London, Sept. 1936). BL P.423/60.

under the Surrealist umbrella. Breton had lent de Chirico's *Child's Brain*, a Head by Picasso, and *After Rain* by Picabia; Paul Nash had lent five paintings by Burra; Gascoyne himself had provided Dalí's *The Horseman of Death*; and Eluard had sent across Ernst's *The Elephant Celebes* and Picasso's *Le Rayon qui parle*. There were seven etchings by Hayter (who behind everybody's back was berating the whole exercise in contemptuously worded letters to Trevelyan). From Paris too came several canvases by Magritte loaned by the Galerie Simon; André Masson's *Man Eating Fishes* was lent by the poet Georges Hugnet, and nineteen Mirós came from from the Galerie Pierre. Penrose had provided four oils and two objects of his own, and Man Ray six of his rayograms. There were twelve Tanguys, and the Museum of Archaeology and Ethnology in Cambridge had supplied fifteen objects from New Guinea. Rupert Lee's wife Diana curated a sideshow of paintings by children.[20]

Four of the items were by Gascoyne, the most striking at object 113 being a collage based on a classical theme, *Perseus and Andromeda* (see Plate 11). Following Ernst he had collated it from newspaper cuttings, but the myth of the Greek hero releasing a captive girl from the clutches of a sea serpent had been treated in the past by Rubens, Tiepolo, and Veronese. Gascoyne almost certainly knew the Titian version in the Wallace Collection in London, though his realization of the legend was closer to Tiepolo's, while drawing on Surrealist bathos and free association. There were bizarre differences from the myth: the sea serpent was represented by a school of basking seals beneath a canopy of coral; Perseus was dressed in a Pierrot's uniform and held in a contraption resembling a body brace or iron lung, and Andromeda had diminished to the minuscule head of a girl with an Eton crop suspended on a badminton racket. She looked very much like Win's friend Tiny, with whom Gascoyne was staying at the time. The effect was one of tentativeness and lethargy, seabirds gathering and dispersing in the bleak headland beyond.[21]

Gascoyne attended the exhibition for the whole run, coming in by bus over Lambeth Bridge from Tiny's new flat in Kennington. The catalogue advertised all of his recent translations, including his rendition of *Qu'est-ce que le surréalisme?* which Fabers had now issued to coincide with the show

20. *The International Surrealist Exhibition*, Thursday 11 June to Saturday 5 July 1936 (New Burlington Gallery, Burlington Gardens, W1), Catalogue Price Sixpence, pp. 14–30: 392 numbered objects in all.
21. Now in Tate Modern, T05025.

in a volume with five more of his translated Breton essays. They were force-ful and quite faithful, though Breton was as sceptical as Anne Bradby about Gascoyne's grasp of technical French. At one point the original had com-pared the delicacy of the Surrealist imagination to the slow drip of water on an oval stone Breton had seen in a grotto at Fontaine-de-Vaucluse. 'The apotheosis of "Prince Rupert's drops" [*larmes Bataviques*]', he had written, 'seemed to me to dwell in this glimmering light.' Gascoyne had not heard of these crystal distillations, impermeable to pressure but exploding when struck, invented in the seventeenth century by Prince Rupert of the Rhine. He had construed the phrase as 'Dutch tears', and compounded the slip by referring in a footnote to chandeliers.[22]

Breton pointed out the blunder with exemplary tact, but there were other oversights he found harder to forgive. On the way to and from the Gallery, Gascoyne had been continuing his preparations for his biography of Rimbaud by reading a recent study of the poet lent to him by Reavey. It was a rejoinder to an earlier study of 1929, *Rimbaud le voyant* [*Rimbaud the Visionary*] by Rolland de Renéville, that had taken the French poet much at his own early exalted estimate in *Illuminations*. The new study, *Rimbaud le voyou* [*Rimbaud the Hooligan*], was by the Paris-based Romanian poet and philosopher Benjamin Fondane. In stark contrast, it took its cue from *Une saison en enfer*, the self-debunking sequence in which Rimbaud washes his hands of his early pretensions to exceptional inspiration. Fondane had por-trayed Rimbaud as a rebel against all systems, including by extension certain modern schools of thought. These included—most damningly—the Surrealism of Breton's Second Manifesto, which it accused of intellectual pretension and woolliness. This therefore is the diatribe Gascoyne found himself reading on the bus:

> I do not wish to discourage those who, following in the footsteps of Rimbaud, and believing their grasp over the Unknown secure, imagine themselves to have found a magic road to it, one of so-called 'mental dictation' (or was it perhaps of dictatorship?): even though it leads nowhere and even though, once their progress has ground to a halt, they of necessity have recourse to a modi-cum of reality. Reality, that is, of the most banal and inimical kind: factories rather than the multifarious mosques of the mind.

22. André Breton, *What Is Surrealism?*, trans. David Gascoyne (Criterion Miscellany, no. 43; London: Faber, 1936), 40. According to p. 9 of the exhibition catalogue it was 'prepared espe-cially for this exhibition'.

If such followers of Rimbaud wish to make their point candidly, if they wish to avoid intellectual confusion, they would do better to recognize that nowadays the theory of the Seer is to be classed among artistic regressions like Surrealism. They should address the resulting ethical contradictions directly, a challenge from which at the moment they appear to flinch. Otherwise what is the meaning of these lines from Breton's *Vases Communicants*: 'Just so that nobody can accuse me of having given way to stupefying despair…was I not the very first to acknowledge that at the instant I felt seized by an overwhelming bolt of sensation, the critical faculty was virtually destroyed in me.' Read these words again, I beseech you: do they not constitute one of those very ethical contradictions that nowadays people suppose to have shrivelled before our more advanced appreciation of Beauty? Are we not therefore justified in reproaching Breton for encouraging us to take wing once more, at the very moment at which he himself is returning to the prison house? To excuse himself, so as to exculpate the past, through an absence of the critical faculty—the only sort of vacuity that could possible endorse the value of visions or automatic writing—was this not, Monsieur Breton, an unpardonable lapse?

The real inconsistency between Rimbaud and his disciples, however, lies elsewhere. Rimbaud owned up to his mistakes, while Breton attempts to disguise his. What is more, Rimbaud travelled to the very end of his journey; he did not give it up at the very moment when he became wise to his own lunacy. Lunacy! This is the condition in which his followers have placed Rimbaud, once they have pursued him up to that point. Who then has transformed himself into the most debased sort of servant? Besides, there was really only one way in which such a person could protect his visions without entering the prison cell once more. That was to recapture the experience of sinking below the horizon of thought by going mad himself.[23]

One morning in the first week Gascoyne was strolling up Piccadilly on his way to the show, with Fondane's book under his arm. Coming along the pavement towards him he spotted Breton. Breton took a deep bow. 'Ce livre-ça', he remarked, indicating the volume beneath David's arm, 'est dirigé tout à fait contre *moi*!' ['That book is aimed entirely against *me*!']['24'] It was a turning point of sorts.

---

23. Benjamin Fondane, *Rimbaud le voyou* (Paris: Editions Denöel et Steele, 1933), 53–5. Fondane is playing with the French near-pun between *dictature* [dictation] and *dictateur* [dictatorship].
24. BL Lives F1382, Side B.

10

Engagé

By the end of June Gala and Dalí had come across from Paris, and were spending the weekends in East Sussex at Monkton House, the orange-and-mauve-painted country home of the American art patron Edward James, and their weekdays in James's curtain-draped flat in Wimpole Street. Breton now having tactfully departed, Eluard also put in an appearance, and gave a dignified and rhetorically phrased lecture on the subject of Surrealist poetry on 24 June. The arrival of these friends brought Gascoyne further into the limelight. He was in any case scheduled to run a poetry reading at the gallery on the evening of 26 June following Hugh Sykes Davies's academically incisive talk on 'Biology and Surrealism' (execrated in print by Jennings, who considered Sykes Davies's whole approach over-intellectual and mild). Eluard read extracts in French from Lautréamont, Baudelaire, Rimbaud, Jarry, Breton, Mesens, Péret, Picasso, and himself. Translations, mostly from a Surrealist double number of *Contemporary Poetry and Prose* timed to coincide with the exhibition, were then delivered by Gascoyne, Jennings, and Reavey, who followed them with poems of their own.[1]

Dalí was scheduled to give the culminating talk on Wednesday 1 July on 'Authentic Paranoid Phantoms', about a philosophy student who subsists for a month by eating his way through a mirror-fronted wardrobe. At James's suggestion, he chose to deliver this in Catalan from inside a diving suit purchased from the marine outfitters Siebe and Gorman, after entering the gallery grasping a billiard cue in one hand, with two of his patron's Afghan wolfhounds on a leash held by the other. James hovered close to the speaker, endeavouring to translate a text soon punctuated by Dalí's cries for help, while Penrose and Sykes Davies in the front row noticed the speaker's face was turning puce. To release him from imminent asphyxiation, Gascoyne

---

1. Michel Remy, *Surrealism in Britain* (London: Ashgate, 1999), 78.

was dispatched to fetch a spanner, and returned to wrestle with the screws at the base of the helmet, while James prised open the window at the front with the billiard cue. Dalí then continued, illustrating his fable with slides assembled in an arbitrary order, with several upside down. At the end a group photograph was taken, but Gascoyne had already disappeared to return the spanner, and his place was taken by Reavey.[2]

That Saturday the exhibition closed, but for Gascoyne the stand-off between Breton and Eluard had left its mark, all the more so because it reinforced the tension between the alternative routes of high art and political commitment he had charted in his 'First English Manifesto' of the previous year. The issue had not entirely been clarified by Eluard, who in his recent speech at the Exhibition had dexterously evaded the problem of what exactly the Surrealist poetry was supposed to do, and what exactly it was supposed to deal with, by playing verbally on the notion of the 'purity' of art:

> Pure poetry? The absolute force of poetry will purify men, all men. Listen to Lautréamont: 'Poetry must be made by all. Not by one.' All ivory towers will be abolished, all words will be sacred and man, brought into accord with reality at last, which is his own, will no longer need to do anything but close his eyes for them to open up the doors of the marvellous.[3]

Despite such sanguine finesses, the middle way of scrupulous but sensitized engagement was clearly going to be difficult to hold. If he had to turn in one direction or the other, David was temperamentally more inclined to side with the still resolutely Communist Eluard. Appropriately, overcoming his distaste at the execution on 25 August of Gregory Zinoviev—a former member of the Society *troika* and an early victim of Stalin's show trials—he joined the Twickenham Branch of the British Communist Party (CP) on 29 September.[4] His initial contribution involved standing outside Hounslow Station for a few afternoons selling the *Daily Worker*.[5] Once back in the Surrealist bubble, however, the upshot was a dressing-down from Mesens, who harangued him for several hours on 21 October 'about my having joined the CP, the Moscow Trial, the 4th International etc.'. Gascoyne had

2. Ibid. 77–8. Compare Antony Penrose, *Roland Penrose: The Friendly Surrealist* (Munich: Prestel-Verlag, 2001), 73.
3. Paul Eluard, '"L'Evidence poétique": Conference prononcée a Londres, le 24 juin 1936, a l'occasion de l'Exposition surréaliste, organisée par Roland Penrose', *Œuvres complètes* (Paris: Gallimard, 1968), i. 513–21.
4. David Gascoyne, *Journal 1936–1937* (London: Enitharmon, 1980), 23–4.
5. BL Sound Archive, Robert Fraser Collection, C1081/08/0103/D1.

just started to keep a journal, in which one of the early entries is a snarling reaction to this humiliation: 'Infuriating little man!'[6]

It was, however, not only politically that he was split. Roland Cailleux was back in town, picking David's brains for his novel and entertaining him at night in his Park Royal apartment. Then in late September the new journal records an unprecedented turn of events: 'A woman of 37—a woman who has had three husbands and two children, has been in an asylum, is being psycho-analysed and, having been living alone for about a year, is starved not so much of sex as of simple affection—has fallen in love with me.'[7] This lady was the novelist Antonia White, to whom Gascoyne had been introduced by a mutual friend and neighbour of hers in Chelsea: the torridly loquacious American writer Emily Holmes Coleman. On 18 September, all three had sat up until four-thirty in the morning in Coleman's flat in Oakley Street with Jennings and Emily's on-and-off lover, the senior civil servant Samuel Hoare. Jenning's conversation had been full of scintillating and disconnected images; Gascoyne and Hoare were both writing about Rimbaud, and Antonia, freshly infused with the Surrealist habit of bizarre association, was writing her own Surrealist poems. Luckily for this exercise, she had an exotic subjective world to draw on, having endured an early marriage to an impotent friend, a period in St Bethlehem's Hospital during which she had been straitjacketed, and the birth of two daughters, one to a mining engineer whom she had failed to marry, the second probably (though not certainly) to her second husband, the journalist Tom Hopkinson, from whom she was now estranged. Her literary reputation owed most to her early semi-autobiographical novel about education in a convent, *Frost in May*, but she was currently blocked and attempting to dig herself out of this hole of non-productivity through successive—or even synchronous—love affairs, and a course of Freudian analysis with the psychiatrist Dr Dennis Carroll.[8]

The late night discussions continued but now took the form of intimate têtes-à-têtes in front of the gas fire in Antonia's flat, where she and David sat *à deux* in a frenzy of soul-baring for many nocturnal hours, she impelled by her misery, he one suspects partly by the practical fact that, once he had missed the last train out to Teddington, he might as well stay the whole night. After one such session on 25 September lasting until six in the

6. *Journal 1936–1937*, 38.
7. Ibid. 26.
8. For all of which, see Jane Dunn, *Antonia White: A Life* (London: Virago, 2000).

morning, he let out a groan: 'She wants to explore, not so much my body as
my soul! (And she had only met me once before). My reactions to all this
were chaotic and I am hardly proud of them. Terror, pity, self-mistrust, mis-
trust of her, etc. I simply did not know how to adapt myself to the situation.
There is not the least possibility of my ever loving her, I am far too conscious of her age and she has no physical attraction for me. All she asks for
though, as far as I understand her, is a close spiritual intimacy—or, at least,
that first—and I do not know whether I can really give her even that,
although there is no reason why I should not, even if I do not "love" her.
But why, O why, has all this come upon me, the egoist asks.'[9]

Yet was he *quite* an egoist? Certainly he was obliging and courteous, and
there was something yielding in him that encouraged confidences from
women. Thus out of simple politeness he found himself involved in further
marathons of all-night disclosure: 'Entrails, entrails...'. After one such in
early October, Hopkinson, who had called round to collect the little girls to
take them to school, put his head round the door to see his wife and David
curled up in an affectionate platonic embrace on the divan 'like babes in the
wood'. He reddened slightly, then nodded and withdrew 'in slight surprise',
moved it would seem not so much by the intensity of the sight as by its
innocence, a fact more or less clear to both the main participants. Interestingly
Gascoyne was soon comparing their 'gentle and wistful' liaison with one in
a novel Antonia was then reading with some appreciation: Breton's *Nadja*,
in which a middle-aged man of letters befriends a 24-year-old mental
patient of wavering artistic potential. There was much to make such a com-
parison apposite, 'though Antonia', as David remarked in his journal, 'is
hardly a Nadja'. Such a qualification missed the point: given their mutual
ages, but reversing the genders, it was surely he who was the thoughtfully
lost Nadja, and Antonia the tender but concerned Breton. Besides, Antonia
too was drawing on archetypes, imagining herself as Yvonne de Galais in *Le
Grand Meaulnes*—another shared literary passion—though apparently she
could not decide whether he resembled the perplexed adolescent hero of
Alain-Fournier's title, with whom Yvonne is sexually involved, or the book's
besotted narrator—with whom she is not.

The ambiguity could not last. One morning, encouraged by a satisfactory
session with Cailleux in the Park Royal flat, David soldiered forth to Oakley
Street, determined to prove his manliness by satisfying White. By his own

9. *Journal 1936–1937*, 26.

later account the attempt was a disaster; he even told Bettina Shaw-Lawrence that White had laughed in his face, a reaction scarcely likely to fortify his performance.[10] In any case he had been motivated partially by misplaced chivalry while, as her biographer admits, Antonia was frigid at the best of times, having a squeamish horror of sex, an experience she seems princi-pally have used to assert her power over men, or to reassure herself that they valued her. Neither the frolics with Cailleux nor the physical fiasco with White feature at the time in David's journals. In any case the latter seems to have been felt, at least by her, as something of an irrelevance: they had, after all, been making love energetically with their minds, with their respective capacities for intelligent intuition and observation. The rewarding fruit of their involvement hence consists in their written comments on one another.

Hers permit us to observe Gascoyne at this transitional point in his exist-ence as viewed by a verbally gifted older woman. After several weeks of their inconclusive affair, White summed him up in her dairy. She noted his 'warm impulsive quickening towards someone combined with a cold, rather cruel drawing back'. Then there was his 'tendency to let other people do everything for him—guilt about it, but no strong effort to change the situ-ation'. She found off-putting his 'peculiar physical slovenliness, though he is vain', and his 'tendency to hero-worship'. His reputation amongst their cir-cle was not, it seems, as unanimous as one might have thought. 'He is', she sharply observed, 'accused of being a "climber". He may be. It is not very important. Provided he does nothing ugly or dishonest in order to meet people he wants to know.'

Last for her came his appearance as inspected by gaslight: his mouth with its atrocious teeth, 'very bad, obstinate, sulky, peevish and despondent. His forehead very broad and low: slopes back suddenly and disconcertingly. The chin too small…it can look very weak from some angles.' He was himself consumed by thoughts of his body, and talked of it much: 'Imagines his nose is too big (it is not). Dislikes allusions to his eyes which are singu-larly beautiful; is very self-conscious about his hair which is also very beau-tiful, though he does not seem to know it. Quite rightly he admires his hands (nails always dirty)…' There he is: a narcissistic—if occasionally conscience-stricken—malcontent, shrewdly portrayed as by a kindly nurse.

10. Interview with Bettina Shaw-Lawrence, 24 May 2009.

And there is a flash of foresight in her last remark: 'In spite of his youth and freshness, often something dusty and wilted about him ...'[11]

There was enough to encourage sobriety. He went round one night to Roland Pensrose's flat in Hampstead, where he dropped off some copies of the September issue of the *Surrealist Bulletin* covering the exhibition. On the way back, ruminating on the Heath, he had a vision of north London strafed by enemy planes. He had just turned 20, and tensions were rising all round him. In his new capacity as CP member he attended two anti-Mosley demonstrations in Cable Street in the East End; experiences that confirmed an impression, common in England at the time, that Europe had simply split into two camps: the workers, the party, and Jews on the one hand and, on the other, Hitler, Mussolini, and Franco. When on the 13th Roland and Valentine Penrose announced that they would be visiting Barcelona soon on behalf of Fenner Brockway and the Independent Labour Party (ILP), Gascoyne hatched a plan to go with them, oblivious as yet that the ILP, who had aligned themselves in Spain with the Partido Obrero de Unificación Marxista (POUM), a Trotskyite group of anarchist persuasion, were at loggerheads with the official CP, which he himself had just joined. These were arcane distinctions, incomprehensible then to most in Britain, where only two scenarios seemed to be accessible: on the one hand the so-called United Front against Fascism, to which both the CP and the ILP nominally still clung, and whose version of events was peddled weekly by the *Daily Worker*; on the other hand, the lurid propaganda against 'The Reds' regularly churned out by the *Daily Mail*. Meanwhile highbrow weeklies such as the *New Statesman* favoured by liberal intelligentsia were scrupulously maintaining the fiction that the revolutionary cause and the defence of the legitimate socialist government of Spain were in effect the same. There was no doubt, if the conflict was this straightforward, which of these pressure groups Gascoyne should support. So, visiting the offices of Cobden-Sanderson, he negotiated a £20 advance. 'I am going to Spain!' he ecstatically announced in his journal.

The practical arrangements were not so easy. The government in Catalunya (the Generalitat de Catalunya) was still in October 1936 in the hands of the United Front, which had set up an overseas office in Paris where those wishing to lend their active support needed to obtain visas. Appropriately, after a gushing farewell from Antonia at Waterloo, he took the night train via

---

11. Antonia White, *Diaries, 1926–1957*, ed. Susan Chitty (London: Virago, 1992), 82–3. See also Lindall P. Hopkinson, *Nothing to Forgive* (London: Chatto and Windus, 1988), 146–56.

Dieppe on 23 October, and joined Roland and Valentine in their hotel in Montparnasse. Together they went to see Zervos at the offices of the *Cahiers d'Art* to discuss plans. Zervos's wife was also there; they fell into discussion about party alignments in Spain. 'I did not follow the conversation', noted David in his dairy, an early confession that realities on the ground in continental Europe were a little more complicated and fraught than readers of the *New Statesman* realized. That evening he took a taxi to see the Eluards in the Rue Legendre. Paul had just finished a rapturous poem about a naked Nusch emerging from the sea during their summer holiday that June, which they had shared with Picasso. Picasso had etched an illustration to be printed alongside it, in which Nusch's pubic hair is plainly visible, as are a pair of horns on her head.[12] But now she lay moaning on a couch in the living room with her jaw swathed in bandages as she recovered from an operation for an abscess in her mouth, occasionally raising her eyes to cast baleful glances at her mother-in-law. After obtaining their visas from the Catalonian People's Bureau—an improvised emporium in a single room hastily coordinated by Zervos—Gascoyne and the Penroses alighted the following morning at the Gare d'Orsay on a train to Toulouse, where they boarded a plane bound for Barcelona. It was Gascoyne's first flight, and next day they were met at Barcelona airfield by officials of the government, and soon installed in a small hotel off the Ramblas, not knowing quite what to expect.[13]

The Catalans had assigned to Gascoyne a job as a translator attached to the Ministry of Propaganda. Each and every morning, news bulletins and upbeat impressions from the Front were compiled in Spanish and Catalan. These were then rapidly put into as many European languages as possible to be broadcast that evening on a local radio station for the growing international brigade in the city, and on the overseas service for the wider world. After breakfast Gascoyne took a tram from his hotel to the Ministry and spent his day translating these screeds into English from a French version earlier compiled by a young Englishwoman, also a CP volunteer, working alongside him. At six in the afternoon he went to a studio located in the Ministry of Marine down by the Port, and broadcast the result. The potential audience was considerable. That month Stephen Spender was passing through Barcelona on a journalistic assignment with the *Daily Worker* to

---

12. 'Grand Air' in *Les Yeux fertiles* (Paris: Gallimard, 1936), 71; also in Eluard, *Œuvres complètes*, i. 509.
13. Gascoyne's account of the Barcelona episode, written in retrospect in 1979, and interpolated in 1980 into his published *Journal 1936–1937*, 43–50.

investigate the torpedoing of a Russian vessel in the Mediterranean by the Italians. He was relaxing over a drink one evening in the Plaça surrounded by tall buildings festooned with banners and tannoys:

> I heard a rather languid English voice broadcasting from loudspeakers attached to the eighth-story windows of a building above me and, listening hard, I suddenly recognised it as that of the poet David Gascoyne.[14]

He was far from being the only British listener: in distant Teddington, Leslie and Win were surprised to hear their son's voice emerging from their bakelite wireless set as the autumn shades closed in around them.

The message conveyed was the official line of the government, that all factions and persuasions had put their shoulders behind the common cause and were supporting the elected representatives of the people against the Fascists. Yet, even as he advertised these claims, the realities of the situation on the ground were rapidly becoming as obvious to Gascoyne as they would to George Orwell when he joined the POUM militias a couple of months later.[15] After a few hours working alongside his British female CP colleague at the Ministry, it became apparent to David that she—longer established in the Party than himself and already several weeks into her own stint in Spain— regarded him as something of a political *naïf*, if not an outright renegade. Like Orwell, Gascoyne was instinctively drawn towards the Trotskyites (who, after all, had so far shown far more sympathy for Surrealist art than other leftish groups) and, beyond them, to the anarcho-syndicalists who for the time being held the balance of power in the administration. Yet these very groups were increasingly regarded as traitors by hardliners of Gascoyne's own party, who liked to portray them as fifth columnists at very best. After a few days toiling over his communiqués, two facts became obvious to Gascoyne: the first was that his CP girl comrade at the office despised him. The second was that, rather than aiding the anarchists, the trade unions, and the people to welcome in the Promised Land, the apparatchiks of Moscow and their local supporters were now actively committed to forestalling the Revolution, the time for which they did not consider to be yet ripe. In brutal fact, as Gascoyne later wrote, 'I came to find out that the Communists hated the Anarchists and the POUM much more than they

---

14. Stephen Spender, *World Within World* (London: Hamish Hamilton, 1964), 218.
15. See George Orwell, *Homage to Catalonia* (London: Penguin, 1962), 46–70.

hated the Fascists; and I think this was the beginning of my disillusionment with Communism as a means of creating a better world.'[16]

By the time he left Barcelona the United Front had in any case catastrophically come apart at the local level. In the meantime, the city itself was a source of some fascination to him. Though the churches were all closed, Gaudí's innovative architecture, as yet little known in the rest of Europe, surrounded him. In lively sherry bars off the Ramblas, refinements of local politics and culture were loudly discussed. From the perspective of mainland Europe, activists at home soon came to seem to him to have been both parochial and mistaken; in any case, the cosmopolitan community in Barcelona seemed to know far more about developments in Britain than the British people themselves. It was for example from the young Yugoslavian journalist Vladimir Dedijer, later a biographer of Tito, that Gascoyne first gleaned the surprising information that King Edward VIII was presently enjoying a cruise around the Adriatic in the company of the twice-divorced Wallis Simpson. Dedijer was covering this scandal for a Bucharest daily, but a news blackout at home had so far prevented Gascoyne from learning of it. In the Plaça Sarrià he sat discussing the international situation with Josep Vincenç Foix i Mas, pastry cook of renown and perhaps the most acclaimed poet in Catalan of his generation. Foix maintained a careful ideological neutrality, though he lived in an affluent suburb rife with supporters of Franco. As they talked, bullets ricocheted in the gardens to every side.

Foix was at least consistent in his neutrality. A rather different sort of encounter was with the incorrigibly chameleon Tristan Tzara. Tzara had been the *chef d'orchestre* of Dada in Zurich during the Great War. After a certain amount of tergiversation he had subsequently aligned himself with Breton's Paris-based Surrealist group. Through it all he had retained his membership of the more orthodox and severe wing of the Communist Party, stubbornly adhering to the PCF even after the suicide of his friend Crevel. Fairly soon, like so many others, he had fallen out with Breton, some insulting remarks of whom at his expense he had insisted on having removed from the first edition of the *Short Survey* in addition, somewhat illogically, to Gascoyne's translation from one of his own poems. Gascoyne had so far managed to avoid him, yet he now appeared, genial and beaming, at the head of an ambulance unit funded and supported by the official CP. Somehow Tzara managed to reconcile within himself classic Leninism with

16. *Journal 1936–1937*, 45.

imaginative free play even, as Gascoyne would soon discover, with a grudging respect for Christianity (or rather for his take on Christianity). Unlike Breton, Crevel, or even Roughton, he seemed to be serenely capable of living through these contradictions and to inhabit them all quite comfortably, despite his occasional outbursts against those who tried to caricature him, or to tie him down to one consistent logic. In Barcelona he oozed affability: even in the thick of the storm he contrived to rise above it. Gascoyne found these paradoxes a little bewildering. He was charmed nonetheless.

It was Zervos who arranged many of these meetings, and Zervos too who was responsible for Gascoyne's most memorable visit in Barcelona—to the apartment of Picasso's sister, where he and the Penroses were introduced to the painter's mother and namesake: the redoubtable octogenarian Maria Picasso y López. The old lady chattered on in Spanish that Gascoyne could only just about follow, illustrating each anecdote with vivid hand gestures. From these he gathered that her son had originally started painting after passing a test set him by his art teacher father José Carlos to depict a dead pigeon lying on its back: 'and you should see the fragile little claws sticking up in the air: so wonderfully expressive and pathetic'. They could indeed observe this touching effect, because she then showed them the picture, though David for one had not quite followed the story. In fact it had been Ruiz who had commenced the still life, and Pablo who had completed it unprompted when his father's back was turned, duly impressing his progenitor in the process. The eventual consequences for European art, however, had been much the same.

But the family ambience in this home—its closeness, loyalty, and pride—affected David deeply. Mother and daughter were out of touch with Pablo who was in Paris: they were concerned about him and, more painfully, were concerned he might be worried about their welfare in this war-torn city. It is characteristic of Gascoyne's obliging nature—though no doubt he also felt flattered by the request—that he now undertook to drop in on the painter to reassure him on his way back home through Paris. He had, in any case, volunteered to ferry some posters to Brockway for a benefit show in London, so in the second week of November he and Dedijer took the train back to the French capital together. The following morning he set out alone to the Rue de la Boétie, where Picasso was renting a flat above the Rosenberg Gallery. A clanking lift carried him up from the ground floor and, as the metal trellis doors slid apart, the painter was waiting on the landing. The flat was large, dusty, and stacked with paintings by Picasso himself or by others: a Cézanne, a Renoir, and Douanier Rousseau's *The Wedding Party*. Picasso seemed subdued: he had not been painting since the spring of that year when he had executed instead a sequence of largely unpunctuated prose poems 'full of colour adjectives', five were to be translated by Gascoyne the following month in a Picasso double number of Roughton's journal.[17] Picasso was further distracted by the behaviour of his dissolute 15-year-old son Paulo, an enthusiast for motorcycles rather than art or dead pigeons, later his father's chauffeur, drawn disconcertingly to raffish elements on the Right. The confession of these troubles, and David's attentiveness to them, created a bond.

Gascoyne returned to London by boat train on 16 November[18] to discover an England plunged in the midst of the Abdication Crisis, since the news embargo on the king's continuing romance had now dramatically lifted. At first he had no time to concentrate on this fracas, since he had a long-standing engagement to lecture on Surrealism on the evening of 17 November to the English Club at Oxford.[19] A room had been hired in the Taylor Institution, where he was met by a committee consisting of Esmond Romilly's brother Giles and the impetuously wordy, incorrigibly anarchic, and reputedly lesbian, Audrey Beecham, niece of the celebrated conductor, presently engaged to tubby Maurice Bowra, homosexual fellow in classics at Wadham College, later its flamboyant warden. Beecham was as embarrassed by this emotional experiment as was Bowra himself, who is reported to have offered the explanation 'Buggers can't be choosers'.[20] The relationship would come asunder a few months later to their mutual satisfaction, but for the next months she would tag along intermittently with David, attracted by his reassuring capacity to lend a sympathetic ear to the sentimental quandaries of others even if—perhaps because—he could never seem to resolve his own.

For his theme he had chosen the uncontroversial title 'The Future of the Lyric Imagination', but he now felt duty-bound to drag in the tenuous but topical connection between Surrealism and the crisis in Spain.[21] It was a rhetorical sort of an exercise and, bearing in mind the expectations of a student audience no younger than himself, it is instructive just how quickly he managed to slip back into the benevolent simplifications of the British

17. *Contemporary Poetry and Prose*, 8 (Dec. 1936), 163–4. See *Journal 1936–1937*, 49.
18. Gascoyne's movements were duly tracked by MI5. See list of participants in the Spanish war, National Archives KV/5/112, identifying Gascoyne's as case 162 (96) 48a.
19. *Oxford Magazine*, 2 Nov. 1936, p. 141.
20. See Leslie Mitchell, *Maurice Bowra: A Life* (Oxford: Oxford University Press, 2009), 144–6.
21. *Selected Prose*, 25–34.

left-leaning bourgeoisie. 'In a word', he announced at the outset, 'we are wit-
nessing, and to a great or lesser extent taking part in, the conflict between on
the one hand, exploitative capitalism fast becoming Fascism and on the other,
Communism.' This sentiment was greeted with mild applause and approving
smiles, but it was not what he had observed in Spain. Keeping to a careful
middle path, he continued by quoting Eluard, whom he could still just about
endorse without tripping over Breton. Poetry was still 'a perpetual struggle,
life's very principle, the queen of unrest'. As such it came into conflict with
conventional education (at least as practised in Regent Street) and with the
spiritual apathy of the bourgeoisie. Come the revolution, he implied, we shall
all be poets. But, returning to Breton's golden mean, he went on to argue that
poetry should never reduce itself to mere propaganda: 'It still remains for
someone to write a revolutionary poem in which the word "comrade" does
not appear in every verse.' To clarify this point he contrasted two snippets,
one by Dylan Thomas, the other by Clive and Vanessa Bell's son Julian, his
elder by eight years. Bell would die the following year as an ambulance driver
at the battle of Brunete but had already, in his recent volume of poetry *Work
for Winter*, produced one or two commendably polemical but verbally cack-
handed verses. Bell would, of course, never be described as a Surrealist by
anybody, then or now. What was interesting here was Gascoyne's implicitly
claiming Thomas for the Surrealist camp—an act of shrewd appropriation
since, though arguably a more consistent Surrealist in approach and method
than even Gascoyne himself, Dylan would have been extremely loath to
acknowledge a label he seems in retrospect most richly to have deserved.

Back in London, the hives of the media were abuzz with the dynastic
crisis. Anthropologically viewed, here was a clash between two taboos: the
sanctity of kingship and the holiness of marriage. The dilemma of loyalty
thus stirred among the king's subjects was proving of absorbing interest to
a mutual friend of Gascoyne and Jennings. Charles Madge, a minor Surrealist
poet and journalist on the *Daily Mirror*, was currently the second husband
of the poet Kathleen Raine, with whom he had fled Cambridge and she the
arms of her first spouse, Hugh Sykes Davies. On Monday, 30 November he
invited Gascoyne and Jennings over to their house at 6 Grote's Building's,
Blackheath for the first planning meeting for a new project already called
'Mass Observation'. The immediate purpose was to observe systematically
the reactions of the British population to the constitutional debacle as it
unfurled. It was as yet unclear whether Edward would step down from the
throne; he would sign the deeds of abdication on 10 December. In the

meantime the nascent Mass Observation (or M-O) Group busied itself over method and procedure. Madge's plan was to use unpaid researchers all over the country to send in reports on the unfolding drama. A letter inviting the participation of these volunteers was to appear in the *New Statesman and Nation* on 2 January. Among the respondents was Tom Harrisson, another Cambridge dropout, an ornithologist with experience of the Far East, now doing social work near Bolton.

In the short term, Harrisson agreed to take soundings among the Bolton community, while Madge set about recruiting a team of national volunteers. The 12th of February was selected for the first sampling of the public mood, followed by 12 May, the date fixed for the coronation, now to be of George VI. There was a collective feeling that a document enunciating a set of principles was necessary. Madge and Harrisson agreed to draft one, and to read their drafts for discussion at meetings between January and April. Their declaration—a manifesto in all but name—was published the following May in the first of Mass Observation's shilling bulletins, and it clearly bears the marks of the disagreements within the organizing committee between Madge and Harrisson on the one hand, and Gascoyne and Raine on the other. It is even more or less clear what each side had said, and just why Gascoyne and Raine's misgivings had been modified or overruled.

After stressing the need for the modern researcher to observe the survival of superstitions such as respect for the king, Madge and Harisson go on to debate the respective diagnostic claims of art and social science. At this point Arthur Rimbaud puts in an unexpected appearance with his celebrated boast from *Illuminations*: 'J'ai seul la clef de cette parade sauvage' ['I alone hold the key to this barbarous parade']. That ambition, the authors concede, had been valid for its time as a 'pre-scientific parallel' to Freud, but in a post-Freudian age, the relevant issues were a lot clearer. Indeed, 'many modern poets and painters have turned instinctively to anthropology and psychoanalysis as sources. The result has not been altogether happy ... All that such art can hope to effect is to make clear to other artists the immense importance of science. Because Rimbaud precedes Freud, his works have a historical significance far beyond those of the post-Freudian Surrealist writers and painters.'[22]

22. Charles Madge and Tom Harrisson, *Mass-Observation*, with a foreword by Professor Julian Huxley (London: Frederic Muller, 1937), 26.

It is easy to overhear in such passages the confident voices of the Wykehamist Madge and the irascible Harrisson as they slapped down the diffident interventions of a 20-year-old secondary school-educated poet, and Madge's increasingly disillusioned wife. Madge for one would later desert poetry and end his career as the first professor of sociology in Birmingham University, and Harrisson would gain distinction and notoriety as a museum director in Sarawak. Between them, these two convinced empiricists had taken J. G. Frazer's well-known schema of human intellectual development from *The Golden Bough*—Magic through Religion to Science—and replaced Art, poetry included, as the middle term. Neither Gascoyne nor Raine was likely to accept the proposition that poetry was a transitional stage on the way through to some positivist panacea. The results of this disagreement were to be, first, the eventual unravelling of Raine's marriage to Madge and, second, the lifelong mental affinity she would establish with David, whose vulnerable sensitivity compared to her assertively patrician husband is evident from her account, given several decades later, of those early Mass Observation meetings: 'I remember how beautiful he was,' she recalled in 1975, 'how gentle and defenceless, but, like a wild animal who has never had cause to fear man, open and expectant only of receiving the same goodness and out-flowing love that was in him.'[23]

On one impression, however, all were agreed. The royal crisis, the war in Spain, the threat of Hitler, all boded ill. As Gascoyne took the train from Blackheath back towards Waterloo after that inaugural meeting at the end of November, he had looked to his left and noticed a bright glow on the horizon. On the very crest of the North Downs, the Crystal Palace was burning in Sydenham.[24] 'For most of us', he wrote later in life, '—the Mass Observationists that is to say—it represented in some symbolic way an image of world conflagration which we were already beginning to think of as about to break out, and we felt that it meant this unconsciously to the general public, hence the unusual fascination it seemed to have for everyone at the time.' It was not the first foreboding of an approaching worldwide conflict he had experienced in the auspicious and eventful year of 1936. From a popular point of view, however, it fixed itself in his memory as among the most powerful.

23. Kathleen Raine, *Autobiographies* (London: Skoob, 1991), 226.
24. Introductory Notes to *Journal 1936–1937*, 9. For the fire itself, see Alan R. Warwick, *The Phoenix Suburb: A South London Social History* (London: Blueboar Press, 1982), 241. On the other side of London, Winston Churchill observed it as he returned from a long weekend in Chartwell.

11

Journal of a Disappointed Man

After the social whirl of 1936, the New Year found Gascoyne increasingly turning towards his own thoughts. If 1936 had been full of dramatic social activity, 1937 seemed set to resemble a tormented soliloquy. He was leaving an increasingly impressive paper trail, if not an entirely consistent one. Into his piled-up notebooks went poems, drafts, stories, book lists, and plans for projects. Into his journal meanwhile he poured his self-dissatisfaction, his frustration with his work, his circumstances and general progress, interspersed with an account of his days at home or in town, and observations on his friends. On a visit to Antonia White's flat he had borrowed her copy of *The Journal of a Disappointed Man* by the Devonian author Bruce Frederick Cummings (1889–1919), written under the double shadow of the First World War and advancing multiple sclerosis. Cummings had adopted a nom de plume bristling with baneful forenames—Wilhelm Nero Pilate Barbellion—and his journal was itself modelled on *I Am the Most Interesting Book of All* by the Ukrainian diarist Marie Bashkirtseff, who before dying in 1884 from TB at the age of 25, had been consumed by 'the fear that all her living and feeling might be wasted, that all her passionate days might pass and never leave a trace behind them'.[1] Reading her in his turn, Gascoyne saw that he too had plenty to probe.

He was perplexed on at least two counts. Fondane's caricature of the Surrealists—and Breton in particular—as a pack of self-deluded megalomaniacs had hit him hard, since it drove a wedge between them and his admired Rimbaud, and in any case it penetrated areas of vulnerability in the movement he had already observed at first hand. There was also the nagging problem of sexual drives which, if weak in intensity, seemed to be propelling him in contrary directions. In a journal he wrote, 'Falling in love with or

1. *Journal 1936–1937*, 53.

mentally forming a mental (Platonic) attachment for a woman is almost always followed by an almost entirely physical relationship with, or at least attraction towards, a man.'[2] Sex with Cailleux had apparently proved quite satisfying, but his recollection was of dirty sheets: Roland, he soon wrote, 'has despair in him; he prefers to evade it'.[3] Antonia on the other hand possessed an 'extraordinarily lively intelligence',[4] but their experiments in bed had been a literal flop.

His social life seemed to be drifting. Down in Middlesex he had made the acquaintance of Philip Marsh, an almost exact contemporary. Marsh worked in Fleet Street for the publishers Benn Brothers, whose sixpenny paperbacks were forerunners of Allen Lane's Penguins.[5] In his turn Marsh had introduced him to a pretty but conventionally minded 20-year-old, Joan Scully. By May, as an italicized entry in the journal announces, he had *fallen in love*. Joan and he had spent much of the previous five days together, culminating in a session of several hours on the embankment in Chelsea, where they had held hands and watched the river course past them. Back in Teddington he recorded it all: 'The grand old impatience once again upon its rocking horse; the not-so-grand difficulties that seem to have got us ... on skewers.'[6] Then, reaching for another notebook, he drafted a 'Proem: For J.S.':

> In all this peace (a man walks his dog down the road,
>   The wireless softly sings,
>   Night concentrates its blue),
> I think of you, and long with fascinated dread
> For all the noise and punishment of Facts:
>   And all that we could or could not know.[7]

Among the difficulties with Joan was his politics, since she found Communism unsympathetic, and he had just implicated himself further by joining Eileen Agar, Meryl Evans, Paul Nash, Penrose, Read, Trevelyan, and Sykes Davies in signing a two-sided manifesto from the Artists' International Association headed 'We Ask Your Intention' and calling on His Majesty's Government to intervene in Spain. He was drafting a letter to Joan enclosing this screed and justifying his own involvement when through the letterbox dropped

2. David Gascoyne, *April: A Novella*, ed. Roger Scott (London: Enitharmon, 2000), 111.
3. Ibid. 122.
4. *Journal 1936–1937*, 25.
5. Philip Marsh to Jackie Sims, 26 Oct. 1993, OUP PB/ED/013460, Box 1788.
6. *Journal 1936–1937*, 96.
7. *April*, 125.

her mild and very British rebuke. 'Why', she had written, 'can't people let one another alone? Why can't they resign themselves to the intactness of their mental cubicles and leave one another in peace?' It was the end of their temporary understanding though, again in his journal, he hints at other impediments: 'On a bench on the Chelsea embankment, in the nocturnal rain, she dazed or half-asleep in my arms, I kissed her; and how well she must have known at that moment—from the reluctant pressure of the lips and teeth, the hand's detached caress, the gaze wondering over the shoulder—the chilly truth!' 'And yet', he continues, migrating to the candour of French, 'I still protested. To remember in future: "Ne fais de bêtises que celles qui te font réellement plaisir".'[8]

All this while his creative energies were going into a project that reflected the dilemmas of his private life. Provisionally entitled 'A Quiet Mind', its purpose was to portray the reticence he sensed all around him in England: with his family, amongst his friends, everywhere in fact beyond that coterie of artistically and politically committed individuals associated with the Surrealist group or the Communist Party. Accordingly he had been working on a novella, the theme of which was not so much the feeling of politics, as the politics of feeling. Judith Irwin, an English girl in her twenties, lives with her mother in an apartment in the Faubourg Saint-Jacques. She has been in France since she was 5, when her recently deceased father was appointed to the British Embassy. Judith has the haziest notion of her native land, and what little she knows from visits to her well-bred country cousins does not inspire her. Unsurprisingly she feels adrift: 'She thought in French, which she had spoken with perfect fluency, and perhaps more often than her own language... The French seemed to think that she was English, and the English that she was French.'[9] And yet her temperament as presented by the book's narrator is utterly English. She has Joan's personality and political detachment, but her situation resembles a more acute, less intensely felt, version of Gascoyne's own identity crisis.

The keynote of Judith's critically examined national temperament is reticence, an emotional fastidiousness wary of any kind of involvement, emotional or political, that might compromise her condition of carefully maintained calm. In the evenings she teaches English at the Institut Britannique, where among her pupils is Frédéric Delaunay, a law student from a

8. *Journal 1936–1937*, 101.
9. *April*, 36.

middle-class family in Lyons and a covert rebel, attracted by her youth and her laconic, English rose, good looks. She offers Frédéric friendship but little more; she will not spend the night with him. When he introduces her to Max Vanderveld, a German Communist, her reaction is one of fascination and modified support; the ardour of his cause, however, is beyond her. Hence England and its children represent 'the dead land' of Eliot's 'cruel month' in *Burnt Norton*: accordingly the story was soon retitled *April*, the month in which David finished it. Judith is the perfect, securely wrapped, exemplar of such deadness. Her refusal to reciprocate Frédéric's feelings has tragic consequences: a diabetic, he ceases taking his medication, and dies in a coma in hospital. Chastened by his death, and convinced by now that 'acts have consequences', Judith decides to make a willing sacrifice of her jealously preserved virginity. She attends a political rally in the working-class Bastille *quartier* where she gives herself casually to a stranger in a side street.

The theme of cultural transplantation and Judith's inhibitions owe something to Henry James's *In A Cage*, which Gascoyne was reading at the time. Frédéric's fate also arguably owes a little to the suicide of Crevel, the rationale behind which Gascoyne must have discussed with Cailleux the previous year, and whose novel of bourgeois entrapment and suicide, *La Mort difficile*, Gascoyne had recently read. Crevel's death had, we now know, partly been a reaction to the inexorable progress of a tubercular condition. Symbolically at least, however, it had also represented an escape from deep-seated political contradictions. When in 1925 Breton had proposed the question 'Is suicide a solution?', the 25-year-old Crevel had been one of the few to answer yes. Like Frédéric, like Julien Sorel in Stendhal's *Le Rouge et le Noir* whose rise and fall Gascoyne analyses in a memorable passage in the journals, Crevel had been ill at ease with his own family background, a conflict exacerbated by the homosexuality that had him at loggerheads with his fellow Surrealists. The implicit theme of *April* is the capacity of human beings for passive self-destruction. Frederic's diabetes is an equivalent of Crevel's TB; Judith's self-prostitution too is a carefully judged act of self-mortification. These are private states or acts, yet as Gascoyne chooses to portray them, they are also political responses or statements. In the words of Gascoyne's journal, which traces connections with Crevel and with Stendhal, 'Frédéric's ideal of passion is the same as Sorel's, with an added surrealist feverishness. No doubt it is not so splendid to die of diabetes as to kill oneself and the woman one loves in a church. That is all the difference between the beginning of capitalist industrialism and the end of it. The modern romantic is far more likely to come to his end in a diabetic coma of excess of sugar.'[10]

David's own distress is increasingly obvious from a second volume of his journal, which he started in July. On 1 August—the tail end of summer and never his favourite month—he is agonizing over his state of mind, and toying with Crevel's way out: 'Even those nearest me, my family with whom I so unwillingly live, have not the faintest idea of my despair...If this gets any worse, if I do not manage to get away, do something, explode, during the next few days, only the most contemptible cowardice and weak-will can prevent me from suicide.'[11]

Instead he wrote a letter in French to Benjamin Fondane via the Paris publishers Denoël and Steele describing his career, his reading, his progress through Rimbaud, Pascal, Dostoevsky, Papini and Baudelaire, Kierkegaard, Unamuno, and the Russian philosopher Léon Chestov, and dropping hints as to his growing disenchantment with the Surrealists. A few days later, he was packing his bags for France when he received a signed copy of Fondane's recent collection of essays *La Conscience malheureuse* with a covering letter he would carry around in his wallet for years. 'God knows', Fondane had written, 'if in following the path of surrealism you were far off the mark.'[12] By the 6th he was in Paris with Joan and Marsh, whose presence smoothed over the embarrassment caused by the end of the affair. The overt purpose was to view the great European cultural event of the year, L'Exposition Internationale des Arts et Techniques dans la Vie Moderne. National pavilions had been erected all along the Seine from Notre-Dame to the Trocadero. On top of the Soviet building reared statues of factory workers wielding hammers and sickles in defiance of the German tent opposite, which bore an enormous Nazi eagle. Neither exhibit impressed him as much as the much-frequented Pavillon de Paix with its murals in honour of international workers' cooperation.[13]

When his friends returned to London, Gascoyne stayed on. Through e.e. cummings, to whom Roughton had given him an introduction, he had found an attic room at 11 Rue de la Bûcherie (now part of the Hôtel Colbert), out of whose single frosted window could be glimpsed 'one fragmentary cornice

10. *Journal 1936–1937*, 68–9.
11. *Journal 1937–1939*, 13.
12. 'Rencontres avec Benjamin Fondane', *Arcane*, 17 (Oct. 1984); 'Meetings with Benjamin Fondane', trans. Robin Waterfield, *Aquarius*, 17/18 (1986–7), 23–6. *Selected Prose*, 133–6.
13. BL Add. 56044, fo. 7^v.

of a corner of Notre Dame', across the roofs of Le Quai de Montebello. The novelist Rétif de la Bretonne had lived in the building in the eighteenth century, Simone de Beauvoir was to be a later resident; cummings and his wife now lived downstairs. The rent was 50 francs a week payable in advance to the landlady Mademoiselle David, and by late August she was pushing letters under his door demanding it. The reason for his non-payment is skated over in his journals. In a letter to Henry Miller written a few years later, but maybe not posted, he is far less coy:

> On the very first night after finding myself completely alone in Paris with hardly any cash and no plans for the future except a grim determination to go on being there even at the cost of starvation, I got myself picked up as I was going back to my attic by a couple of whores, who seemed to think I was a wealthy, soft-hearted, innocent English schoolboy tourist (I may even have looked like one). I went off with them to a little hotel, not because I wanted to fuck them—as you can well imagine from what you already know of me: I have not got a furious appetite for fucking, certainly not with two whores at once, and I'm not really interested in quite that way in the female sex, anyway—but because I had some crazy, pseudo-Dostoyevksian idea that the occasion might afford me with an opportunity to explore certain 'lower depths'. I suppose it was, in fact, quite an interesting occasion, really: I told the whores I simply wanted a friendly chat, and they thereupon behaved in a typically curious way, pulled my hair, had mild hysterics, squatted on the bidet, wept on my shoulder, told me sentimentally decorated and therefore doubly horrible life-stories, and so on. We all drank a lot of bad wine, and finally we parted on quite friendly terms and went our ways, I with a lucky charm in my pocket made out of a lock of the girls' hair tied through a *sou,* and the whores with all my money except the fifty francs with which I was supposed to pay the first week's rent on my attic.[14]

With its bathetic close the incident had savoured more of George Gissing or Patrick Hamilton than a Gorky. It had also left him with a hole in his income and continuing misgivings about his sexuality, exacerbated when a few days later he received a wistful letter from Kay announcing her imminent marriage in Brighton to Walter Gilbey, heir to a gin empire, a fanatical sportsman, but in all other respects, so she claimed, a man who physically resembled him.[15] The news was preceded by a dream in which he attended a ballet and performed a *pas de trois* with the leading couple. It had finished

14. 'To H.M.', Beinecke, Box 5, Folder 63, fo. 5.
15. Charles Devenish to Robert Fraser, 14 June 2009.

with the ballerina on his knee discussing their respective designs on her departed partner.

On the 11th he wrote a second letter to Fondane, quoting Conrad's 'In the destructive element immerse'. A few days later he received an invitation to Fondane's holiday home at La Varenne Saint-Hilaire on the river Marne. Within the week he had boarded a train at the Gare de Lyon. On his arrival, the poet-philosopher made him tea and rowed him around the lake discoursing on the meaning of life, and the limitations of our descriptions of it. For decades after his untimely death, Fondane was to become an almost forgotten figure in France, but he had much to give Gascoyne in the August of 1937. Son of an intellectually distinguished Jewish family from Moldavia, he had achieved repute in pre-war Bucharest, as poet, collector of Moldavian folklore, critic, and theatrical manager. In 1923, at the age of 25, he had moved to Paris and embraced Dada and Surrealism in passionate succession, in Gascoyne's words,

> becoming a friend of Brancusi, his fellow Romanian, and following the Surrealist movement from its earliest days with great interest, and feeling great sympathy with it. But then, after his encounter with the great Russian philosopher Léon Chestov, he began to think seriously along the lines of the revolt against reason, which seems to be parallel with that of the Surrealists. It's not just...seen to be irrational for the sake of irrationality, not at all; it was a realisation that we are tyrannised by reason to the extent of sheer scientific materialism dominating the whole of the world outlook that is accepted by everyone everywhere now. And he felt that the Surrealists' revolt against reason was too reasonable![16]

Currently Fondane was earning his living writing film scripts whilst immersing himself in mystical Catholic theology, and meeting with Chestov, who lived to the south of Paris, on a regular basis and writing a series of densely argued philosophical works, including a pioneering study of Heidegger. The rumpus and hypocrisy of the Aragon affair had exacerbated his disillusionment with the Surrealists, whose politics now struck him as posturing and ineffective in their opposition to Nazism, the dominance of which in Germany deeply offended Fondane's inquisitive Jewish soul.

Fondane's talk and example were to take Gascoyne further and further away from his previous Surrealist involvements. In any case, as the absence of expected names in the journal makes clear, Gascoyne had since his arrival

16. BL Lives, F1382, Side B.

been avoiding former Surrealist contacts. In September he notes 'Ambiva-
lence of my attitude towards Breton (as towards everything important to
me)'. He had, he declares, 'become keenly critical of [Breton's] pretensions,
sceptical of his undertaking (Fondane)'.[17] Instead, the notebooks are full of
new projects. Poor as he was, his determination was mounting. 'Il s'agit
d'agir,' he wrote, 'Write masses of rough notes on anything, everything of
interest. Write masses of letters. Pile up material. Release the vital sensitivity,
feed it, be attentive all the time. Eat and sleep as much as possible. Get drunk
more often. The fire is there: give it a chance to blaze.' As the metro and
buses were eating into his slender budget, he took to walking everywhere,
becoming a *flâneur* round the *quartiers* of the Rive Gauche. One evening he
stalked down the Rue Saint-Jacques to pay his respects to Miller with an
impromptu visit to the Villa Seurat, which lay to the north of the Parc
Montsouris in a cul-de-sac back to back with Dalí's former street, the Rue
Gauguet. Finding Miller out, he loped back via Montparnasse.

Daily along the quais he now roamed in search of bargains at the bookstalls of the *bouquinistes.* On one such expedition in early September, he
picked up an item that would revolutionize both his art and thought. It was
a 1930 paperback of poems by the late eighteenth-century German poet
Friedrich Hölderlin (1770–1843) in a French translation made by Balthus's
brother Pierre Klossowski and the French novelist and poet Pierre Jean
Jouve. Within a few days Gascoyne was translating the French into English,
interspersing the texts with five original poems of his own. What emerged
was a sequence called *Hölderlin's Madness*, in which twenty lyrics at two
removes from Hölderlin's German are juxtaposed with pieces by Gascoyne
in a complementary style. The Hölderlin poems had passed across languages, Klossowski acting as Jouve's linguistic consultant. Jouve had
Gallicized the result; now Gascoyne, consulting when he needed to with a
couple of German acquaintances in Paris, brought an English sensibility to
bear on the mix.

Hölderlin's poetry belongs to the first flush of German pre-Romanticism,
but it also coincides with an almost contemporaneous development: the
Enlightenment's discovery of ancient Greece as a, partly researched and
partly imagined, landscape. In the work of scholars like Johann Winckelmann
(1716–68), this had led to an idealization of the Aegean as a sublime absolute,
the 'sweetness and light' of the Hellenism praised in the intervening century

17. *Journal 1937–1939*, 20.

by Matthew Arnold. Alongside Blake, Hölderlin had been one of the great pre-Romantic mental travellers. It was not, however, quite the serenity of Winckelmann's Greece these poems had captured, but something more inclusive and disquieting. From the Gospel of St John and Epistles of St Paul, Hölderlin had absorbed a vision of Christianity transfused with a revitalized, half-pagan, Hellenism. Christ and the heathen Gods had become coexistent and co-eternal. Their dwelling was the 'Patmos' of Hölderlin's poem of that title, as Gascoyne now rendered it:

> Asia, before my eyes. I blindly sought
> For some familiar image,
> A stranger to those wide streets where there descends
> From Tmolus to the sea the Pactolus adorned with gold,
> And the Taurus rises with the Messogis,
> And the flowering garden like a peaceful fire,
> But in the light on high, the silver snow
> And sign of immortal life, on the unscaled wall
> The age-old ivy grows, and on living pillars
> Of cedar and of laurel
> Stand the solemn places the Gods have built.[18]

These are poems that appeal as much to the inner ear as to the inner eye. He had manifestly responded to the aural quality of Jouve's translations. As he was soon to find out, Jouve had a very acute musical ear, and his lyrics, in the words of a later Jouve protégé, the Lebanese poet Salah Stétié, were steeped in music of a 'radiant and grave profundity, like that of the playing of an organ, music in which there mingle rural reaches, tall mountains and lakes, immense trees in a rain-soaked summer, whose country of origin remains obscure, such is the intensity of its burning and crystal to both eye and ear'.[19] In the lyrics Gascoyne himself supplied to accompany Hölderlin's, he evoked a music of his own, music in a minor key, solemn and apocalyptic. In the liturgically entitled 'Tenebrae':

> The granite organ in the crypt
> Resounds with rising thunder through the blood
> With daylight song, unearthly song that floods

18. David Gascoyne, *Hölderlin's Madness* (London: Dent, 1938), 25, translating 'Patmos', *Poèmes de la Folie de Hölderlin*, trans. Pierre Jean Jouve, with the collaboration of Pierre Klossowski, *avant-propos* by B. Groethuysen (Paris: J. O. Fourcade, 1930), 32. *Collected Verse Translations*, 97.
19. Salah Stétié, 'La Lettre P: Pierre Jean Jouve', *En un lieu de brûlure* (Paris: Robert Laffont, 2009), 920.

> The brain with bursting suns:
> Yet it is night.[20]

These were poems both of empathy and detachment in which a stricken singer laments over monumental presences sometimes indistinguishable from himself. 'Figure in a Landscape', for example, had been entitled in draft 'Poet in a Landscape';[21] in it a figure—half-monolith, half-man—lies recumbent in an ageless, mythologized setting:

> The valley rivers irrigate the land, the mills
> Revolve, the hills are fecund with the cypress and the vine,
> And the great eagles guard the mountain heights.
> Above the peaks in mystery there sit
> The Presences, the Unseen in the sky,
> Inscrutable, whose influences like rays
> Descend upon him, pass through and again
> Like golden bees the hive of his lost head.[22]

The resulting sequence possessed the air of a song cycle. Hölderlin's poetry had already been set by Brahms, Richard Strauss, Stefan Wolpe, and Paul Hindemith. It has since attracted the attention of Britten, Henze, and Luigi Nono. Gascoyne treated the German originals like lieder, interpolating lyrics in a comparable blended idiom.

The majority of the poems selected by Klossowski and Jouve had been written after the onset of Hölderlin's madness in 1801. A preface to the French book had thus been commissioned from the Paris-based German philosopher Bernard Groethuysen, pointing out the connections between the poet's creativity and his insanity, interpreted as a form of radical existential instability. To it Gascoyne now added a biographical introduction placing the German poet in historical context. With hindsight, it seems strongly prescient of Gascoyne's own life. 'During his childhood,' we read, Hölderlin 'was brought up exclusively by women.' He wandered far afield but 'was forced . . . to return once more to his family. He had lost much strength, both physical and intellectual, and his temperament had become dangerously unsteady . . . His style changed, his speech and manner became strangely inconsequent and abrupt. A chasm was beginning to open between him and

---

20. *Hölderlin's Madness*, 41. *Collected Poems* (1965), 38. Tenebrae is a liturgical office for Maundy Thursday.
21. BL Add. 56044, fo. 24.
22. *Hölderlin's Madness*, 19–10. *Collected Poems* (1965), 37.

the outer world…A period of hallucinations and of furious agitation ensued. After a time, Hölderlin recovered slightly, and was able to do a certain amount of work on poems and translations. But finally…Hölderlin had to be sent into an asylum…For some time he was capable of writing only fragments, obscure and lacerated.' 'He still loves music', wrote a contemporary called Waiblinger. 'He has retained the technique of playing the piano, but this manner of playing is extremely strange.'[23]

Gascoyne was soon acquiring everything by Jouve he could lay his hands on. As he rapidly discovered, nobody was remotely writing like him in English, combining as he did Catholicism, sex, and Freudian psychiatry in equal measure. The psychiatry derived from his second wife Blanche Reverchon, a former student of Freud's and one of the most advanced psychoanalysts in Paris, who had systematically investigated the links between the unconscious mind and the creative process. Jouve was also the music critic of *La Nouvelle Revue Française* and an opera-lover whose enthusiasms ranged from Mozart to Alban Berg.

After reading his way through Jouve's poetry, Gascoyne went in search of his novels, which he found in a bookshop near the Luxembourg Gardens with a well-stocked lending library. Jouve himself, who lived just round the corner at 8 Rue de Tournon, was a frequent customer there. In quick succession David borrowed *Hécate* (1928) and *Histoires sanglantes* (1932), novels portraying the effects of psychoanalysis on the growing mind. Recognizing this pattern of interest, the female proprietor soon introduced them. It cannot have been a comfortable first meeting. Jouve was 50 and had a sort of gentle solemnity, invariably dressed in grey with an unobtrusive purple tie, his unsmiling countenance permanently drawn in seriousness, his penetrating eyes melancholy behind the thick lenses of his spectacles. He had little small talk (but then Gascoyne had none), and almost never laughed, except with asperity. A creature of habit, he always took one expedition a day at exactly the same hour, normally to the Bois de Boulogne, to which he was driven by his Chinese manservant. He seldom wasted words on anything but the most demanding subjects which, fortunately for David, included music—Mozart and the Second Viennese school especially—modern art, theology, and European literature, leaving aside English literature outside of Shakespeare, about which in any case Gascoyne was less inclined to talk.

---

23. *Hölderlin's Madness*, 1–14. *Selected Prose*, 155–62.

It soon became clear that he and Gascoyne shared a kinship of outlook. Jouve, for example, was currently writing written an elegy for Berg, who had died in December 1935. Gascoyne meanwhile had been wrestling with one of his own, and in his notebook he had recently inserted remarks on Erik Satie and Les Six, and observations on the structure of the Berg Violin Concerto, its first movement building on the bare fifths of the solo's strings in its opening bars. These elementary intervals, Jouve had independently observed, were in subsequent movements 're-engendered in multiple fashion in every register of the orchestra'. Gascoyne was attempting to construct his poetry like this, along lines that were second nature to the Frenchman. Within a few days he had been invited to attend the weekly salons Jouve and his wife held in their well-appointed flat.

The Rue de Tournon is a broad street leading south towards the back of the Senate on the northern edge of Le Jardin de Luxembourg. There in their spacious second floor apartment, every Thursday from nine until midnight, the Jouves were at home to painters and architects like Balthus, writers and philosophers like Jean Wahl—a leading proponent in France of Kierkegaard—designers like Elsa Schiaparelli and musicians. Several were Blanche's patients. The ambiance impressed Gascoyne as a mixture of luxury and austerity, reminding him of the atmosphere of the house described by Henry James in *The Ambassadors*.[24] On the thickly papered walls were hangings with paintings by Balthus and Josef Šíma, and in the living room that overlooked the street stood a baby grand on which guests were invited to play. Gascoyne took the opportunity to execute simple pieces by Schoenberg, and others from Bartók's *Mikrokosmos*, the early volumes of which he had taught himself back in Surrey. One evening, after a concert, an earnest and reserved-looking guest walked over to the instrument and executed some trickier pieces from the Bartók *œuvre*. It was Bartók himself, invited back with his pianist wife Ditta after the French première of his *Sonata for Two Pianos and Percussion*, which Jouve and Gascoyne had just attended. 'He seemed at home', Gascoyne later told a correspondent, 'realizing that Jouve really appreciated his music, then reputed to be impossible dissonant and rebarbative. Rare and unforgettable occasion!'

Thus, even as he mantained his curious stand-off from the Surrealist high command, Gascoyne's social life diversified between French writers and

24. David Gascoyne, 'A Paris, en 1937', *Revue l'autre*, Jouve special issue (Paris: Editions Arfuyen, June 1992), 11.

intellectuals on the one hand, and the lively expatriate, English-speaking community on the other. He had finally made contact with Miller. The American writer Anaïs Nin was living in a candlelit and scented barge moored on the Seine 'in the Moorish décor with which she surrounds herself, the "barbaric" jewellery, the incense-burning, the glass tree, the other exotic stage properties that she requires in order to convince herself that she is leading an intensely interesting "inner life" '.[25] They read one another's journals in manuscript and, when she had finished with his, he sent it to Lawrence Durrell, whose novel *The Black Book* he had also recently read. 'You are an expert on the English death,' he told Durrell, 'and what I have written here seems to deal almost entirely in one way of another...with precisely that.'[26] Recognizing an affinity, Durrell published an extract in his magazine *The Booster*. He and his wife Nancy were now at home to him in their flat close to Miller's, where most days the perennially hard-up Gascoyne went for his meals.

His growing familiarity with French-speaking intellectuals, a formalized milieu with its soirées and salons, furnished his mind and soul, yet it hardly provided the sort of easy social network he needed day by day to alleviate his moods. With the Jouves, appointments had to be made by phone the day before, but he could simply 'drop in' on the block at 44 Rue du Bac rented by the wealthy Etonian Victor William Watson, known to all as 'Peter'. Watson was the most elegantly attired Englishman in Paris, but he owed his considerable wealth to the commercial savvy of a father whose Maypole Dairy Company had cashed in on the need for margarine during the Great War. Peter by contrast was pure, refined butter. At 23 he had inherited £2 million, sported a black-and-orange Rolls Royce with a chauffeur formerly employed by the Prince of Wales, and was adored by Cecil Beaton. His clothes were famous, and he resembled a fastidious fawn. His posture relaxed, hair oiled and slicked back, silk tie neatly knotted, pocket handkerchief impeccably in place, Savile Row tailored suit fitting perfectly around slender shoulders, eyes serious and often lowered, mouth pursed in appreciation and discriminate choice, he reminded Stephen Spender, a frequent guest, of a 'handsome young Bostonian'.[27] He filled his Rue du Bac apartment with

25. David Gascoyne, quoted in Noel Riley Fitch, *Anaïs: The Erotic Life of Anaïs Nin* (Boston: Little, Brown), 203.
26. *Journal 1937–1939*, 30.
27. Quoted in Clive Fisher, *Cyril Connolly: A Nostalgic Life* (London: Macmillan, 1995), 186.

paintings by de Chirico, Gris, Klee, Miró, and Picasso, and with a louche American bum boy called Denham Fouts, a drug addict and former lover of the King of Greece. A lower floor was sublet to the American abstract expressionist painter Buffie Johnson, and English-speaking visitors were constantly in and out of the building, notably Peter's fellow old Etonian, Brian Howard.

David had also met Anne, 16-year-old daughter of the British conductor Eugene Goossens, who following her parents' divorce was living with her mother, two sisters, and stepfather—a commercial attaché at the American consulate—at 36 Rue Fleurus. Anne had formed a friendship with Bettina Shaw-Lawrence, no longer an awkward adolescent but studying painting in Paris with Fernand Léger, and currently dating the American sculptor Robert Burns Motherwell III. Gascoyne would bump into these young folk at the American Artists' and Students' Centre, at Café Flore or the Select, or would drink with them until the small hours at nightclubs like Le Bœuf sur le Toit. Anne and Bettina amused and titillated him. To them his poverty was alarming, his sex life a mystery. Despite his seeming lack of funds he always turned up immaculately dressed, wearing a dapper bow tie. Anne for one found him dashing but disembodied, as sexless as an archangel.[28] To Bettina he handed a visiting card in which his name was reversed as 'G. David'. Sensing in her a worldliness in advance of Anne's, he played games with her, fantasizing alternative identities, aspiring incongruously to the gallant. As she remembered in her eighties:

> David used to take me to Montparnasse parties, but when I came across men kissing on the floor he'd hurriedly take me home and go back for the 'fun'! We'd meet next day at the 'Select' and he said 'I'm going to change my type for you, get a Burberry mac, smoke a pipe and have a spaniel.'[29]

These *jeunes filles en fleurs* encouraged a jokiness, a sly and self-depreciating humour in him, stirring beneath his intent demeanour a compensatory gregariousness and self-satire. Mercifully, they cheered him up.

28. Interview with Anne Goossens, 3 June 2008.
29. Bettina Shaw-Lawrence to Robert Fraser, 10 Dec. 2008.

12

The Leap of Faith

Confessional in intent they may have been, but Gascoyne's journals often worked as strategies of disguise, or perhaps of displacement. The truly nourishing streams sometimes went underground, not to emerge until much later in his life. Apart from that fleeting mention back in September, for example, there is no reference anywhere to Benjamin Fondane. Yet, all that autumn and the following winter, Gascoyne had been visiting the Romanian on a regular basis. Forty-two years later he would dilate on these almost weekly meetings, which took place in Fondane's apartment at 6 Rue Rollin, over and after supper, from ten until well after midnight. After a brisk stroll from his attic room, up the darkened Rue Monge and past the Gallo-Roman amphitheatre known as Les Arènes de Lutèce, Gascoyne would mount steep, balustraded steps to the cobbled, lamplit impasse above:

> In an old building, next door to the one in which Pascal died, one reached his little flat at the top of some stone stairs. To be greeted at the door by the philosopher poet, smiling as usual, but at the same time obviously serious and to my eyes somewhat mysterious. He led me in semi-darkness to his own sitting room, which was also his workroom whose décor was remarkable for the magnificent illuminated aquarium let into one of the walls. He then began the little ceremony of making Turkish coffee. After that we settled down to talk until midnight, sometimes much later. As a matter of fact most of the time I listened to him talking about all sorts of things, a bit of politics, the latest news which became more and more sinister, and finally always on philosophy.[1]

Gascoyne later talked of his host's manner of 'sang-froid'. Fondane unbent slowly, but once released his conversation ranged widely, spiced with dark

---

1. David Gascoyne, 'Rencontres avec Benjamin Fondane', Arcane, 17 (1984). The translation given is by Robin Waterfield in 'Meetings with Benjamin Fondane', Aquarius, 17/18 (1986–7), ed. A. T. Tolley, 23–9. Also in Selected Prose, 133–9.

humour that appeared to his guest 'so distinctive it...could perhaps be described as Romanian-Jewish, but for the fact that it was, more than anything, sardonic'. Such sober wit served as a savoury accompaniment to Fondane's 'poetry of cries, of suffering and often despairing or ironically bitter songs, full of obsessions and fears...The landscape that it evokes is for the most part grey and misty, sordid and alienated, and one of the commonest images from the vegetable world is that of the stinging nettle.'[2]

Despite, or perhaps because of, his proud isolation, Fondane himself possessed a marked capacity for hero worship. His early admiration for Brancusi and Breton had since been replaced by emulation for a fellow exile with whom for several years he had been conducting an intense conversation, partly in person and partly by letter: the Paris-based Russian Jewish philosopher Léon Chestov.[3] Chestov's work was not entirely unknown to David, who had already read his book *All Things Are Possible,* published in English translation in 1920 with a Foreword by D. H. Lawrence. As a result of these visits, he was soon to learn a lot more about the Russian thinker, with long-lasting effects. 'I have had', the elderly Gascoyne confided to his old friend Robin Waterfield in August 1987, 'various "passions" in my life, some of them permanent...especially Chestov and his follower Fondane.' It was an auspicious trick of fate that brought him in the autumn of 1937 to Pascal's former street to hear at one remove, night after night, the thoughts of one he came to consider the great twentieth-century witness to Pascal's vision of occlusion and hope. Who was this Chestov, philosopher as Gascoyne later called him 'of Tragedy and of Paradox'?[4]

Lev Isaakovitz Shestov was born in Kiev in 1866, the son of affluent secularized Jewish parents. After studying at a military academy, where he had mixed in anarchist underground circles, he entered the Law Faculty at Moscow University where in 1900 his doctoral dissertation had been refused on the grounds of its opposition to the czarist labour regulations. There had been several moments of keen intellectual awakening in his life. The first had occurred when, reading a book on Shakespeare, he had realized that Hamlet's line 'The time is out of joint' could be applied to contemporary

---

2. Preface to Benjamin Fondane, *Le Mal des fantômes* (Paris: Editions Plasma, 1980). English trans. by Roger Scott and Catherine McFarlane, *Selected Prose*, 174–85.

3. A résumé of which, entrusted to Fondane's Argentine friend Victoria Ocampo, was published as *Entretiens avec Léon Chestov*, ed. Nathalie Baranoff and Michel Carassou (Paris: Plasma, 1982).

4. 'Léon Chestov: After Ten Years' Silence', *Horizon*, 118 (Oct. 1949), 213–29. *Selected Prose*, 79–93.

pre-Revolutionary Russia. In 1900 he had read Nietzsche, adopting that philosopher's open-ended aphoristic style as his own. From Nietzsche too he had borrowed the idea that God in the traditional sense of the term is dead. Thenceforth Shestov had transferred his earlier anarchist ideals onto this absconded deity. In much of his subsequent writing, God features as a subjectively apprehended condition of absolute mental freedom.[5]

In 1920, in reaction against the growing repression of the Bolsheviks, Shestov had moved to France where he became known as Léon Chestov. Four years later he met Fondane, newly arrived from Romania and working as a film director. Chestov had been 58, Fondane 26. The result had been a multi-layered friendship, a fifteen-year-long conversation, to which Fondane had clung though successive phases as Dadaist, Surrealist, and post-Surrealist mystic. In the 1930s Chestov had encountered the work of the Danish philosopher Søren Kierkegaard, in the light of whom he now reinterpreted the thought of Pascal. Kierkegaard's 'leap of faith' had become for him a modernized form of the wager, or act of free will, by means of which Pascal had rediscovered God as a chosen presence. Not for nothing in *The Myth of Sisyphus* does Albert Camus recognize Kierkegaard and Chestov as progenitors of Existentialism (a term which, however, Chestov himself seldom used). By 1937 Fondane was in the midst of a renewed debate with his master, principally about Kierkegaard and religion, the contents of which he now conveyed to his young English friend. In effect, as Gascoyne came to realize, there were two Existentialisms, the divide between which could be traced back as far as Pascal and Descartes. It was as Pascalian or religious, and Cartesian or secular, Existentialism that he came to think of these two tendencies. His sympathies were entirely with the first.

Gascoyne's conversations with Fondane seem to have been a cross between a tutorial and a confession. The effect was a course of induction into the philosophy of Chestov, whom in an essay in 1949 Gascoyne depicts as an 'arch-anti-idealist', by which he means an enemy of systematizing thought. This estimate was based partly on Fondane's account of Chestov's conversations. *All Things Are Possible* is a series of aphorisms, each of which meticulously turns through about 170 degrees, and ends up almost contradicting itself. Chestov had derived this paradoxical method of reasoning partly from Kierkegaard, with whom he had come to share contempt for all

---

5. Benjamin Fondane, 'Léon Chestov et la lutte contre les evidences', *Revue philosophique*, 126 (1938), 13–50.

peremptory judgements, and for the authority of both the academy and the
Church. The iconoclastic nimbleness of his approach entranced Fondane,
who now conveyed its attractions to his young British visitor. David thus
encountered a mystical version of Continental Existentialism well in advance
of his countrymen's limited awareness of it. One result of this was that he
was soon to be at loggerheads with the very different, secular, version of
Existentialism articulated in France by Jean-Paul Sartre, whose first novel
La Nausée he would encounter the following summer.

Such intellectual excitements buoyed him up over the early months of 1938,
in which the public and private spheres both darkened. As ever, his personal life
was in turmoil. Antonia White wrote to say that she had finally renounced love,
and 'What a huge relief it is'. Cailleux threatened to appear from Châtel-
Guyon, 'but Roland in Paris will not be the person he is in London'. In October
Kay turned up, having deserted her gin manufacturer fiancé on the eve of their
wedding and eloped with an affluent, yacht-owning type called Freddie
Devenish. In the light of all these developments, Gascoyne felt more than ever
excluded and alone. When he eventually got round to visiting Kay in her flat
on the Right Bank, the sound of her and Devenish billing and cooing over the
phone in her room made him feel ever more isolated. As he was leaving she
remarked, 'Now don't go and do anything *queer*.' As he walked back to his bleak
attic through the chilly streets, he overheard a passer-by in the Champs-Elysées
comment 'Le pauvre jeune homme!'

Perhaps in need of reassurance, in March he cut and ran for home for a
few weeks, but in Teddington, he reported, 'I don't belong . . . any more. I am
a stranger. I am absent.'[6] In Grove Terrace he occupied his hours making a
translation for Penguin of *Foules d'Asie* by the eugenicist Etienne Dennery,
a scaremongering work about the Yellow Peril. The sombre hackwork cannot have been congenial; indeed it must have been more than a little repulsive to him. But then spring broke, he was back in Paris again and,
unexpectedly but this time emphatically, enamoured.

In the journal he confides this intimate information in French. Bent von
Müllen was a 20-year-old art student from the well-to-do seaside suburb of
Skodsborg, twenty miles north-east of Copenhagen:

> a young Dane with large and dreamy eyes, tall, and with an upright and noble
> bearing, much like his character. He has a clear complexion, full-fleshed lips,

6. *Journal 1937–1939*, 39.

and sturdy hands like those of a worker. His voice is soft and gentle. From the outside he can seem a little withdrawn, shrouded in silence. But he has a generous nature and spontaneously refined manners. In all that he does he manifests exquisite taste, possessed as he is of a fine sensibility, an uncorrupted intelligence, and a spirit undaunted by its own depths. He is never vain, though with a proper self-regard. His turn of mind is imaginative, lively though mingled with an estimable Nordic austerity. He is an artist.[7]

One evening in May they sat together under the blossoming chestnut trees of the Place Dauphine, where 'even the *pissoir* near-by sounded like a fountain playing in an Italian piazza!' By early June he had done nothing for a whole month 'except be in love'. Perhaps his condition was an expression of the season; certainly there was something hectic and fragile about it, conscious as both parties were of Hitler's threat to Czechoslovakia and European peace stirring in the background. 'If Bent were to be killed today', he wrote with his usual singular prescience, 'or were to send a note and disappear, I should still have had an experience of inestimable value: the materialisation of my most secret dream.' Then on 9 June they went together to the Salle Gaveau to hear the European première of Stravinsky's neoclassical chamber concerto *Dumbarton Oaks* performed in the same programme as his *L'Histoire du soldat,* with the composer himself on the rostrum. There was an atmosphere around Stravinsky's music and physical appearance about the diminutive, jowly man himself, that unnerved David. His journal entry for the evening contains an unforgettable mini-caricature of both:

> there is something diabolic in him,—a streak of real evil in the R.C. sense,—cold, heartless, intellectual. In his appearance there is a mixture of mediocre respectability, of a Victorian melodrama-villain (or the 'sinister master in Jean Vigo's *Zéro de Conduite*), and of a rat. Expressionless face, pokily precise movements of the wrist, a crouching backward slink followed by the calculated pounce of a little fencing-master spy. I am sure, too, that there is something 'bad' about the music of the *Soldat*, with its acid waltzes and raucous ragtime ('*C'est abominable*', hissed a lady in the loge behind us) and its wicked parody of a Bach chorale.[8]

The following night they went back to hear Hermann Scherchen conduct Bach's *Musical Offering* and Eric Satie's symphonic drama *Socrate*, which proved more to his taste. By Tuesday, 5 July, the love of his life had departed for Denmark. 'Ever since, it has been raining.'

7. Ibid. 42.
8. Ibid. 46.

Hemmed in by desolation and disappointment, a regular end-of-summer feel, he escaped once again, to the village of Grez-sur-Loing on a tributary of the Seine close to Fontainebleau. It was a pretty village which in the 1880s had been discovered by painters who delighted in the neighbouring fields, and in the subtle light as it glistened on the shallow river flowing sluggishly beneath the ancient bridge. The composer Delius had later made his home there. Perhaps because of these associations, which continued to attract a small colony of artists, Gascoyne decided the town was sufficiently to his taste for him to install himself in the Hôtel du Vieux Pont for a couple of months. It was here he read for the first time one of the literary successes of the year: that masterpiece of provincial boredom, Sartre's bilious, properly speaking pre-Existentialist, La Nausée. Its protagonist's disgust with life was close enough to his own forlorn mood for him to feel a need to translate it. (Indeed, he was later to obtain Sartre's permission to do so, only to find that at that stage no British publisher was keen.)

He was not quite alone, followed as he was from Paris by a young Irish associate of Pierre Jean Jouve's (and patient of his wife's), the 26-year-old Irish painter Charles Ryan, who with his sister Leona took a studio room in the garden of the hotel, and by a clutch of other friends. One day young Anne Goossens turned up, and to her astonishment discovered them all huddled in the dark around what she took to be an Oujja board, but was far more likely to have been a revived experiment in Surrealist automatic writing.[9] It was at Grez too that Gascoyne first had recourse to narcotics: three cachets of opium supplied by his friend Rollo Hayes and taken over one night, partly out of curiosity, and partly to alleviate his *cafard*, his dull mood.[10] The result was not propitious: fitful sleep with some slight heightening of his sensations (the tap dripping in his room appeared louder), followed when the maid Roberte arrived with his *café au lait* in the morning by a violent fit of vomiting, then a whole day of nausea. His prostration seemed to mirror the mood of Europe in those days following Munich. Disconsolately in his lonely room he followed it all, with Chamberlain politely explaining the sell-out of Czechoslovakia on one station, and Hitler loudly boasting on another.

But at least the summer and its solitary reading had confirmed him in a sense of artistic direction. After receiving through the post from Faber the

9. Interview with Anne Goossens, 3 June 2008.
10. *Journal 1937–1939*, 58.

latest volumes of verse by Auden, Spender, and MacNeice, he grew ever more convinced that his own path of development lay via the European school. MacNeice's work with its verbal tricks, its university-bred cleverness, he seems to have found particularly annoying. More generally, he could not help suspecting that the 'New Country poets'—even at their most accomplished— were producing something closer to social analysis, or polemic, or ever a higher sort of light verse, than poetry as he and the European writers he admired understood it: 'The tradition of modern English poetry', he insisted, 'is really something quite different from the tradition of Hölderlin, Rimbaud, Rilke, Lorca, Jouve—I belong to Europe before I belong to England. The values I believe in are European values and not English ones.'[11]

As the summer visitors drifted away from the hotel, and the international situation worsened, he was left with only Ryan for company, and the imminent problem of how to settle his accumulating bill. He took long ruminative walks along the Loing, and occasionally bestirred himself to row solo on the river. Eventually, at the beginning of October, rescue arrived in the shape of his mother and Tiny, who were on a short visit to France. In another journal entry he resolves to try a social experiment, to confront Win in an attempt to break down her English passivity: 'break down her reserve...get her to talk about her life, to find out how far she realises Father's terrible weakness, the living sacrifice he has made of her life'.[12] He decided it was 'too cruel' a ploy; in any case, in his present condition of economic dependence, he was in no position to dictate terms. Once Tiny had settled the hotel bill he and Ryan could to return to Paris. His studio room in the Rue de la Bûcherie was still free, but the atmosphere of the French capital had definitely changed for the worse. He found himself in a city subdued by the aftermath of Munich, and occasionally breaking into fits of hysterical compensatory exhilaration. One afternoon on the Champs-Elysées he dropped into a news theatre, staying for the newsreels and half of the main feature. 'The audience', he observed with some disquiet, 'applauded everything...about the crisis, even Hitler and Mussolini, and the film which followed, all about White Russians, was so disgusting I went out in the middle in a chilly rage. A stupid, ugly, smug Saturday afternoon crowd was surging slowly up and down the boulevard under the dreary sky.'[13] The result of all

11. *Journal 1937–39*, 55.
12. *April*, ed. Roger Scott (London: Enitharmon, 2000), 123.
13. *Journal 1937–1939*, 73.

this vacuity was to precipitate him into a decision he had been postponing for some time. If he could not cure the malaise of Europe, at least he could have a go at curing his own. He decided to undertake analysis with Jouve's wife Blanche Reverchon, at their apartment in the Rue de Tournon.

Blanche later destroyed her notes, and David's own description of these sessions in his journals is fairly intermittent, but from a range of evidence it is fairly easy to reconstruct what transpired. They met every two days for an hour, usually at eleven o'clock in the morning, unless Blanche had another appointment. Almost certainly David, penniless as usual, did not pay, her fee being met by her more affluent patients, of whom there was no lack. Occasionally the proceedings were interrupted by a rising whine from a nearby street, since the authorities had recently instituted mock air raid warnings in expectation of hostilities. Blanche's consulting room lay at the end of a darkened corridor into which was let a shallow alcove containing a miniature statue of the Virgin, an effigy at once Christian (since Jouve and his wife were both at least nominally Catholics), pagan (since both were also well read in myth), and archetypal (since Jouve's vision of spirituality was Freudianized and sexual, and Blanche's understanding of the structure of the mind had much in common with that of Jung, whom however she insisted she had not read). Free association was the common opening gambit among therapists at the time; instead Blanche seems to have asked Gascoyne to state directly what he thought his problems were. We can glean some sense of his reply from a set of notes he made for himself the previous January in London. Headed simply 'sex', they enumerate a number of personal difficulties, including an incapacity to produce as much creative work as he would have liked—at 22, with five well-reviewed books to his credit, he was already convinced he was under-performing—some confusion as to his sexual identity; listlessness; and an impotence, creative as well as sexual.[14]

To understand Blanche's approach to these problems it is helpful to bear in mind her background, broader in many respects than that of many therapists, her orientation being in almost equal measure literary and medical. Well before her marriage to Jouve in 1925 Blanche had worked on the boundaries of science and poetry. The scientific bent came through from her father, who in the 1880s had studied neurology with Charcot at the legendary Hôpital de la Salpêtrière, where the young Freud had been one of his classmates. After undergraduate studies in philosophy, Blanche had

14. *April*, III.

been drawn to medicine and, once qualified, practised neurology in Geneva while writing a descriptive thesis on Parkinson's disease. In her thirties, she seems to have experienced some sort of epiphany, or at least a dramatic opening up of possibilities. In 1921, whilst staying in Florence, she met Jouve, five years younger than herself but already an established novelist and poet, married with a daughter. They had surreptitiously lived together while collaborating on a series of projects that would dynamically change the nature of both their work. In 1923 with the help of their mutual friend the German-born philosopher Bernard Groethuysen (later the author of the *avant-propos* to poèmes de la *Folie de Hölderlin*) she produced a translation of Freud's *Drei Abhandlungen zur Sexualtheorie* (1905), the work which had laid the foundation for an understanding of sexual sublimation in art and culture. When it appeared in print, *Trois Essais sur la théorie de la sexualité* bore her name and Groethuysen's, yet there is little doubt that, from the beginning, almost as much of Jouve went into Blanche's work, as hers fed into his.

The year 1925 had been a watershed in both of their lives. In that year Jouve obtained a divorce from his first wife, and he and Blanche married. Jouve renounced all his writing to date, dedicating himself to fresh perspectives that owed much to Blanche's influence. Thenceforth this devoted couple set their seal on a creative union of minds that would remain constant until her death in January 1974. In 1927, in Vienna, Blanche had at last met Freud in person: he had encouraged her to undergo analysis and devote herself to psychotherapy. She had chosen to undergo a course of analysis with the Polish practitioner Eugene Sokolnicka, another doctor of a literary bent who had given instruction in the elements of analysis to the group of intellectuals and writers (the so-called Club des Refoulés, or Society of the Repressed) clustered around Jacques Rivière and André Gide at *La Nouvelle Revue Française*. Along with Sokolnicka she was a founder member of the Société psychanalytique de Paris in 1932, though—partly one suspects as a result of her own humanistic leanings, and partly under the influence of Jouve's preoccupation with the transforming potential of the imagination— she was increasingly developing theories that diverged from the Freudian mainstream. A renewed emphasis on the 'mirror stage' of infantile development is usually attributed to Jacques Lacan. At first however, it seems to have owed more to the innovative, but publicity-shy Blanche.[15]

---

15. For Reverchon's background, see Elizabeth Roudinesco, *Lacan & Co: A History of Psychoanalysis in France, 1925–1990* (Chicago: University of Chicago Press, 1995), 94–100.

Other facets of her personality and professional conduct set her apart from the better-known Lacan. Blanche's routine was exacting; she always gave her patients a full hour and charged what they could afford for her undivided attention, sometimes not charging at all, in contrast with Lacan who according to his detractors was wont to bring his appointments to an abrupt end when he felt like it, and had been known to have his hair cut during consultations. Blanche also routinely broke with one of the most sanctified of Freudian taboos by befriending her patients. Many of them attended the Thursday salons, where they mixed freely with the assortment of artists gathered there— that is when they were not themselves artists, which was often the case. Throughout the thirty years of their relationship, it is unclear whether Gascoyne was principally Blanche's friend, her patient, or both. He certainly began as the first, graduated to being the second, and, by the end of the war when they met again in Paris, had certainly become the third. They became in their mutual, and rather formal, way quite devoted to one another, though associates of each were not always convinced that this policy was wise.

Her method of treatment varied from patient to patient. With Gascoyne it rapidly turned into a mixture of classical Freudian technique with personal hunches and insights, often rounded off with a salutary dose of common sense. She asked him to recount his childhood memories and dreams and he duly provided her with a stream of Freudian specimens, beginning with a recollection of sharing a double bed with Win in Bournemouth one summer night during one of Leslie's absences. A cow from a neighbouring field had stuck its horns through the open French windows and frightened him. Blanche provided a conventional Oedipal reading of this event, still unfamiliar enough in 1938 to appear surprising. Gascoyne took the interpretation seriously, understood the connection between Leslie and horns, but seems to have resisted the notion that he had ever desired his mother. Instead he talked about Florence Mole, of whose grave in north London he constantly dreamed, and of Tiny, always in his thoughts even when she was not, as so often nowadays, defraying his expenses. A classic Freudian interpretation of his sexual inhibitions with women acquaintances was then forthcoming. There is little evidence that it cured him, although the attribution to him of a form of impotence was not as insulting as it would have been for many patients: Chestov and Fondane had both attributed this condition to Kierkegaard, whose genius they thought was integrally connected with it.

Blanche then addressed herself to Gascoyne's purported artistic sterility. Applying the thesis of sublimation that had loomed large in the *Trois Essais,* she convinced him such a capacity was unusually developed in him. The suggestion, with its implications of appreciation for his versatility, impressed him. It also placed him on an even keel with Jouve, whose understanding of art was almost entirely based on this hypothesis. For Jouve, art and religion were both refinements of baser urges: 'celestial matter'. As he had remarked in a well-known Preface to his volume *Sueur de Sang* (1933), which condensed much of Blanche's thinking on the Freudian polarity of sex and death: 'Capable of vast transformations in quantity, and in kind, capable also of inventing its quality, and finally of transcending itself, such is the Libido... The poets who since Rimbaud have striven to emancipate poetry from the rational know very well (even if they don't fully believe in the explanation) that they have rediscovered themselves through the unconscious, or at least through thoughts influenced as far as is possible by the unconscious, that ancient and revitalizing source, and that they have thereby approach the world from quite a fresh angle.'[16]

Accordingly on 31 October, while recovering over a solitary drink at La Source after a particularly revealing evening session, Gascoyne noted down in his journal, 'Mme. Jouve says I have an exceptional faculty of transformation. I suppose this includes a particular aptitude for sublimating sex urges; because when I read novels about adolescence, confessions of sex experiences etc., it seems to me that I must be undersexed, if anything, so little have I suffered from the usual assault of tormenting carnal desires that most young men appear to have to cope with.'[17] This insight appears to have helped him understand why, for example, he had thought so seldom about sex since Bent's departure in late July. It did not, however, quite account for his poetic dearth over the same period, since according to this theory his art should have benefited accordingly. To clinch the diagnosis therefore, Blanche hit on a traditional proverb that epitomized the resulting problem. Since all of David's energies were now concentrated on the practice of writing, this offered outlet had become excessively attractive and important to him, and he was suffering from the writerly equivalent of priapic collapse after an inconvenient onset of honeymoon nerves. Disrobed, his art had disarmed him. As an old French saying has it, 'La marieé est trop belle': 'the bride is just too lovely'.

Whether in obedience to these directives or not, Gascoyne's social life now seems to have picked up for a few weeks. The anglophone crowd at the Rue du Bac were yielding an ever-widening range of contacts. Buffie

16. Pierre Jean Jouve, *Sueur de Sang* (Paris: Gallimard, 1933), 13–15.
17. *Journal 1937–1939*, 82.

Johnson had spent the summer months in Dalmatia where she had met Ingrid, a beautiful German girl anxious to escape Hitler's regime with the help of a British passport; marriage to an Englishman would supply her with one. Conscious by now of Gascoyne's sexual leanings—and thus the probably technical nature of any arrangement between the two of them— she suggested a union of convenience, such as Auden had contracted three years previously with Thomas Mann's daughter, Erika. When he acceded to the idea, Ingrid wrote enthusiastically, and even David himself seems to have been briefly entranced. In early December Auden himself turned up and pontificated impressively for some hours at Watson's apartment. Later in a café opposite the Opéra, Gascoyne absorbed a vivid impression of him, soon to become one of the most sharply drawn portraits in the journals:

> *Auden:* Even at the age of 40, he will carry the head of an undergraduate on his shoulders. At 31, he still has an air of disguising only with a difficulty acquired social manner the petulance and embarrassment of an adolescent.
>
> When delivering an opinion, he throws back his head, contracts the brows above his sloping, close-set eyes, and looks at you down his nose, holding a smile in reserve at the corners of his mouth.[18]

The Watson ménage was at sixes and sevens, as more and more hangers-on arrived to benefit from Peter's hospitality, including Cyril and Jean Connolly, who were on the verge of splitting up, but seemed unable to make the final break. As a result the Rue du Bac 'had the air of a stage set, an extraordinary collection of people wandering in and out all day long, dubious friends of Denham, English pansy or café society friends of the Connollys', the actor Jean Marais, servants, detectives and police inspectors on account of a theft there at a party on Christmas Eve'.[19] Spender called round with his wife Inez and stayed long enough to inform Gascoyne grandly that he had been obliged to give a 'rather severe' review to *Hölderlin's Madness*, which had recently been published by Dent. Antonia was still writing letters, and at Christmas appeared one of her cast-off lovers: Nigel Henderson, younger of the two sons of the Fitzrovia hostess Wyn Henderson, with both of whom in 1936 Antonia had been conducting concurrent affairs in London. Consoling himself for the absent von Müllen, who had not replied to his letters, David had a morose fling with this comparative stranger, recounted

18. Ibid. 104.
19. David Gascoyne quoted in Clive Fisher, *Cyril Connolly: A Nostalgic Life* (London: Macmillan, 1995).

in the journals where Henderson features as an intense, confused young man. (After the war he would achieve some small success as an artist, and commit suicide after an unsatisfactory marriage.) Roland Cailleux also showed up, but Gascoyne was getting wary of his Don Juan-like deviousness, and kept him at a distance.

Paris, in any case, was growing claustrophobic; Anne Goossens can remember perambulating up and down the Boulevard Saint-Michel with an agitated Gascoyne as one of Hitler's increasingly threatening speeches boomed out from a public address system overhead.[20] Those who could escaped: David accompanied some friends for a few days' respite in neutral Switzerland, but after that it was back to the snow-filled streets of the Left Bank, where a mood of suspense and catatonic unreality had gripped the French. It is beautifully caught in the poem 'Snow in Europe' which, alongside Jules Supervielle's 'Rain and the Tyrants', later translated by Gascoyne, deserves recognition for its movingly straightforward evocation of a nation caught midway between Munich and the abyss:

> Out of their slumber Europeans spun
> Dense dreams: appeasement, miracle, glimpsed flash
> Of a new golden era; but could not restrain
> The vertical white weight that fell last night
> And made their continent a blank.
>
> Hush, says the sameness of the snow
> The Ural and the Jura now rejoin
> The furthest Arctic's desolation. All is one;
> Sheer monotone: plain, mountain; country, town:
> Contours and boundaries no longer show.
>
> The warring flags hang colourless a while;
> Now midnights's icy zero feigns a truce
> Between the signs and seasons, and fades out
> All shots and cries. But when the great thaw comes,
> How red shall be the melting snow, how loud the drums![21]

Something was dramatically changing in him. The coming war, of whose inevitability all around him were convinced, would he sensed prove an equivalent for him of the 'great earthquake' of which Kierkegaard had

20. Interview with Anne Goossens, 3 June 2008.
21. *Collected Poems* (1965), 80.

written in his journals. The threat would soon send him back to England, but in the meantime, two experiences in the closing months of 1938, point to a new direction in his life and work. In late November, probably on the 22nd, he had met Fondane mooning down the snowy Rue Saint-Jacques. 'Chestov est mort' Fondane had intoned, and then passed grimly on. Like so much that affected David at a deep level, the event goes unrecorded in his journals; it had sunk in nonetheless.

But there had been deeper signs still. At the end of October he had attended a performance of the *St Matthew Passion* given by the choir of Bach's former church of St Thomas's, Leipzig. The singing had taken him back to his days at Salisbury when those heart-rending chorales had been so well known to him. He had spent the following day looking at pietàs in the Louvre, and then fortuitously bumped into Tristan Tzara, who had also attended the Bach concert. The founder of Dadaism astonished him by confessing how moved he had been by the music, adding 'They crucified Christ who was fundamentally a worthy man, did they not? It is the protest of the unconscious against the injustice of that which has created religion.'[22] If Tzara, the godfather of Dada, could be moved by the plight of the crucified Christ, then surely now could Gascoyne.

The plan to marry Ingrid came to nothing, but at the end of January at last there was a letter in French from Bent:

> No, I have not forgotten your existence. But I have been so disgusted with myself for months that I have little that is positive to give you in a letter. In general, I confess, those months in Paris seem to me like a dream—quite a beautiful dream, but above all a full and lively dream. Often I see your beautiful eyes, also your decent and sensible hands on my body. And I think as well of the nights of our amorous friendship that I too thought had been impossible—also I am very weak, since a life of that sort would require of me all of my strength. So you see that for me it is almost impossible to survive in such a furioso atmosphere. Nonetheless I have great desire to return to Paris, but perhaps not before the Autumn, September–October, unless a war makes such an expedition impossible—Write to me and tell me if everything is working out with Madame Jouve. Following your example, I am going to commence analysis in two days' time, it is my main hope now. I have felt so out of joint for so long...[23]

Depth spoke unto depth.

22. *Journal 1937–1939*, 81.
23. Ibid. 118–19.

NIGHT
TWO

1939–1964

13

Clamavi

Poverty and the threat of war seemed likely to drive Gascoyne back to England shortly after the New Year. The first of these problems was alleviated by the intervention of a benefactor. For the better part of two months he was sustained through an unexpected injection of funds from a Madame Edwards, South American wife of the director of Les Magasins du Louvre.[1] This, however, was not the only reason he lingered. On the evening of Epiphany he dropped into le Bal de la Montagne, a raucous nightspot near his lodgings, where he was followed out into the street by an importunate young German.[2] Wolf Berthold was a minor writer and outer acolyte of the George-Kreis, the circle surrounding Stefan George, the aristocratic poet whose reluctance to let his work be claimed by the Nazis had led to his death in exile in Switzerland six years previously. Apart from his other qualities, George had been much admired by German Francophiles as a one-time translator of Baudelaire. More relevantly in this connection, his memory was revered by patrician opponents of Hitler, including the von Stauffenberg brothers who were later to make an attempt on the Führer's life. Resistance to the demands of the new state apparatus in Berlin was routine among aficionados of the George-Kreis; accordingly in 1935, when military conscription was reintroduced into Germany, Gascoyne's new acquaintance—a source of mystery to him on several counts—had defied it and, like Stefan George before him, fled into exile. His plan, should France fall, was to move to England. He now persuaded Gascoyne to follow him

1. Interview with Michel Remy, 25 Apr. 2008.
2. The incident is traced in the manuscript item 'Wolf Berthold: A True Story', Enitharmon Papers, Brown Stationery Notebook dated 26 Nov. 1995. See also Michel Remy, *David Gascoyne ou l'urgence de l'inexprimé* (Nancy: Presses universitaires de Nancy, 1984), 125. See also Gascoyne's article 'Le Surréalisme et la jeune poésie anglaise', in *Encrages*, 6 (Summer 1981), Université de Paris VIII, Vincennes à Saint-Denis, 22.

back to his room in the Hôtel Roger Collard, an establishment between the western gate to the Luxembourg and the Colline Sainte-Geneviève favoured by wealthy Germans, where he was living with a friend called Jo, a medical doctor and, like him, a right-wing refugee from the regime in Berlin.

The night stretched into several weeks during which Gascoyne gave up his tenancy in the Rue de la Bûcherie, not without some misgiving. 'I've suddenly become involved in a rather strange and quite unexpected love-affair', he wrote in his journal on Wednesday 25th, with a mixture of surprise and misgiving.[3] The involvement, in which Berthold took the initiative at all times, caused him little happiness, though it went on for some six weeks. Spring that year was late in coming, with storms and sub-zero temperatures into early March. Shortly after the thaw he was making his way back to the hotel from a Montmartre nightclub in the early hours of a morning, and skirted the Luxembourg. Its trees were still quite bare, and gardeners had strewn ash over the footpaths to prevent walkers from slipping in the slush. In 'Winter Garden' Gascoyne depicts himself as a lone and listless figure excluded from the mild upturn, one whom 'no-one sees' as he passes across the frost-drenched grass.[4]

In any case, Berthold and his friend disconcerted him. With one part of his mind he suspected them of being Nazi agents, an impression intensified as pressure was brought to bear on him to secure their passage to England. By the time his money at last ran out at the end of the month and he took the boat train to Dover, he had given them some kind of assurance that he would contact officials in London who might arrange for immigration visas. In the event he did very little about it, disconcerted by the thought of their arrival, and in particular by Wolf's continual attempts to boss him around like a governess. (He had, he thought, had enough of such treatment from Florence Mole.[5]) Half-hearted attempts to reach the Foreign Office through Antonia White came to nothing, somewhat to his relief. When the following August the German armies marched across the frontier, Wolf and Jo fled to neutral Portugal, where they were not given permission to settle. They travelled onwards to Yugoslavia where, on the Nazi invasion in April 1941, they both took their own lives.

Characteristically, when the import of these facts sunk in (they featured minimally in some British newspapers) Gascoyne blamed himself for the

---

3. *Journal 1937–1939*, 119.
4. *Poems 1937–1942*, 11; *Collected Poems* (1965), 50.
5. BL Add. 56056, entry dated 5 Aug. 1947, Paris.

outcome. After the war he would constantly dream about Wolf, whom by then he was convinced he had ditched for his own convenience, just as he had symbolically (at least in his guilt-drenched subconscious) done away with Florence in 1930 for her £100 legacy. In 'Dichters Leben', a lied-like poem 'In Memoriam Wolf Berthold' published halfway through the war, he portrays his friend as a person burdened by contradictory feelings that only death could release: 'a grief which nothing could explain, but which some nights | Would make him cry that he could fight no more.' For all that, the ambiguities of his own feelings remained, and after two printed impressions of the book he removed the dedicatory line from the poem.[6]

This is a story that has had to be reconstructed from hints: jottings in later notebooks, fleeting references in superannuated editions. The name 'Wolf Berthold' is absent from the journal; it is expunged from the work. David's habits of involvement and contrition operated oddly, sometimes with a time lag, and often to his lasting disquiet. The same is true of an episode that occurred shortly after his return to England that came to mean as much—perhaps more—to the elderly man, or perhaps the recon- stituted and grieving boy within him. In late March he settled back into life in Teddington, and took stock of the world around him. For months during his absence Tiny had been supporting him with small amounts to defray his expenses in France. Faced with her physical presence, he now realized just how little she had been able to afford even these pittances. In the interval she had aged visibly, 'her smooth face...lined and wrinkled' with the unmistakable air of a 'sour old maid'. 'She had for some time been feeling increasingly tired and unwell; now the doctor diagnosed cancer.' Her illness and poverty placed Win and Leslie in a considerable moral dilemma. Leslie was still commuting to Pall Mall every day and the twins— 17 and about to leave their grammar school in Kingston—were weighing up possible careers. Though Tiny begged the Gascoynes for a room in the house where she might die in peace, there was little space for them to spare, and both Leslie and Win found her demands inconvenient and nerve- racking. In the short term they found her a cheap nursing home nearby, and then had her moved to the Middlesex hospital in Mortlake, where Win

6. *Poems 1937–1942*, 12. By the third impression of 1948 the dedication has gone, just as it has in *Collected Poems* (1965), 51–2. The title of the poem obliquely recalls Schumann's song cycle *Dichterliebe*.

visited her every day until she died the following year. They were all consumed with a deep, lasting, though for the most part unexpressed, regret.[7]

Not a word of this appears in the journal David was keeping at the time,
which as usual is far more concerned with his inner mental state. He was
reading more voraciously than ever, copying quotations into notebooks in
his neat and rounded hand: Kierkegaard, Miguel de Unamuno, and the little
of Heidegger that had so far been translated into French by the philosopher
and Islamic scholar Henry Corbin. For a while the entries sound almost
contented. 'Period of interior relaxation and repose,' he writes with momen-
tary optimism, 'Peaceful inactivity. The results of analysis taking effect.'

The plateau of relative calm lasted a few weeks, assisted by meetings with
various friends. One Saturday in May Roger Roughton put in an appearance at Teddington. At his side was Sheila Legge, the one-time phantom
from the Surrealist exhibition three years previously, whom he had just
accompanied to Kempton Park races. It was the last time David was to see
either of them.[8] In June he turned to the person among his English acquaintance most guaranteed to cheer him up: he went down by train to stay with
George Barker and his wife Jessica in their cottage in the village of Ball's
Cross in Sussex. Barker was Gascoyne's temperamental opposite in many—
though not in all—respects: witty, extrovert, confidently sexual, popular
with women. He was also a maverick who would not settle down finally—
to the extent that he ever settled—until much later in life. His apparent
happiness with Jessica masked considerable unease; they had recently had
their first child adopted through a Catholic agency, and in a little more than
a year their marriage would be on the rocks as a result of Barker's affair in
America with the Canadian writer Elizabeth Smart.[9] Gascoyne followed
the tergiversations of his friend's heterosexual existence with some fascination, and a certain humorous appreciation for its ups and downs.[10] But he
also, at least at this early period, had a tendency to project his frustrated
ideals onto his mercurial friend, including—however improbably in the light
of subsequent events—that of the sanctity of marriage. In the poem 'The
Sacred Heart', written either during this visit or an earlier sojourn with the
Bakers in Dorset, he views his friends as guardians of a domestic tranquillity

---

7. Afterword to *Collected Journals*, 379.
8. Ibid. 396.
9. Robert Fraser, *The Chameleon Poet: A Life of George Barker* (London: Jonathan Cape, 2001).
10. Interview with David Gascoyne, BL Sound Archive, Robert Fraser Collection C1081/08/0103/D1.

and erotic equilibrium that always seemed to elude him.[11] The impression was an illusion, an expression of his thwarted need for emotional completion, the more beguiling for all that.

On his return from this refreshing respite, he was once more sucked down by worry, fear, dread. The journal sounds an ominous note of complaint: 'The symptoms: nerves, moods, nostalgia, restlessness, periodic exaltation and depression. Its idiosyncracies: "insatiability", quasi-schizophrenic duality, an acute instinct for self-dramatization and self-analysis.'[12] These remarks are pitilessly honest, though there is some wishful thinking in that 'quasi'. This was his emotional situation for ill or for good and, for better or for worse, he knew that he must not only live with it but to some extent make art out of it. It was, after all, the best material that he had. 'Earlier this year', he observed, 'I came to see that my only way of dealing with "depressions", "inadaptability", etc. was to *accept* them, as being to some degree necessary... Possibly the *only* solution left to me, now, to the problem of living, is to *write*; and the only way I can write is, to let writing become neurotic symptom.'[13] Barker, with one of his habitually self-debunking, self-deflating, and always comical stylistic grimaces, had been writing to him about the responsibilities of the '*powet*'. For richer or for poor, this was the kind of '*powet*' David now knew himself to be.

Despite or perhaps because of these disturbing psychological symptoms, it was turning out to be a bumper year. His mood, for one thing, chimed resoundingly with the zeitgeist. As the prospect of war neared, the predicament of central Europe was weighing ever more on his soul as—largely thanks to Berthold's residual influence—was Stefan George. For four years he had been struggling with an elegy for the composer Alban Berg who even more than Schoenberg epitomized for him the achievements of the Second Viennese School. He had begun it in 1935 in the immediate aftermath of the composer's death and a rush of enthusiasm for the leftward-leaning opera *Wozzeck,* which he had heard several times. Two drafts in English had so far come to nothing, but back in Teddington he found he could rework the exercise in French, basing its structure on that of Berg's *Lyric Suite* for string

---

11. David Gascoyne, *A Vagrant and Other Poems* (London: John Lehmann, 1950), 10–11, where its positioning immediately after the title poem implicitly contrasts the author's recurrent rootlessness with his friend's domestic fulfilment. *Collected Poems* (1965), 101–2.
12. *Journal 1937–1939*, 120.
13. *Journal 1936–1937*, 121–2.

quartet, which had a 'secret text' by George.[14] The choice of language medium was arresting and appropriate to the theme: for the first time in his poems as distinct from his journal, where passages in French had been occurring for months at moments of solemn or embarrassed disclosure, the use of French released him. Two months before his death he explained to his editor Roger Scott that 'there were things that I wanted to say in French at the time'; the distinguished British poet and translator from German Michael Hamburger later explained further that 'French is a more abstract language than English, and therefore more congenial to David in his search for transcendental spirituality'.[15] In any case the medium, and the comparative ease with which he carried out this exercise, were further vindication of his self-image as a European poet, as was its publication in January of the following year in the Marseilles-based magazine *Cahiers du Sud*. He resisted attempts to let the sequence appear in English, explaining that the lines 'Les sons d'une musique énervante et câline, | Semblable au cri lointain de l'humaine douleur' (in the section 'Intermezzo') were a direct quotation from 'Le Vin' in Baudelaire's *Les Fleurs du mal*, parts of George's translation of which, *Der Wein*, had been set by Berg in a concert aria for soprano and orchestra in 1929. The quotation afforded a clue to his own approach, since he had verbally evoked three movements from Berg's suite, just as Berg had set three portions from *Der Wein*. The sense of these almost untranslatable lines, descriptive of 'The sounds of a music chafed and snug, like a distant cry of human distress', was moreover a wonderful summation both of Berg's style, at once soulful and austere—as if late Romanticism had passed through some sort of a strainer—and of the sincere yet distanced effect Gascoyne was reaching for in his own text.

The success of this long-deferred project did little to calm his nerves. By July he was beginning to ask himself, initially with a guarded curiosity, whether his quasi-schizophrenic symptoms were quite so quasi after all. On Monday, 3 July he sounds the disarming and prophetic note: 'I begin to wonder, with a half-fascinated, vague anxiety, whether it is possible that a schizophrenic *split* is going to carry me further and further way from the

---

14. 'Strophes élégiaques à la mémoire d'Alban Berg', *Cahiers du Sud* (Marseilles), 220 (Jan. 1940), 49–52. *Poems 1937–1942*, 25–9. The first abandoned English version may be found in BL Add. MSS 56041 and 56043, the second in Berg. They were published for the first time in Pierre Jean Jouve, *Despair Has Wings: Selected Poems*, trans. David Gascoyne, ed. Roger Scott (London: Enitharmon, 2007), 168–74.

15. *Despair Has Wings*, 17, quoting Michael Hamburger to Roger Scott, 22 Feb. 2002.

outer world,—whether being able to write as I want to, entails a further-outlook of ever-increasing ups and down, fugues, swinging from extreme to extreme—an intensity of solitude immuring one beyond all human contact?—Painful lucidity.'[16] The lucidity was half chastened, half brash. After all, had not Breton and Dalí talked of the uses of paranoia, of the potential for psychopathology to seed the creative mind? At least in Breton's case, this recognition had not entailed the corollary that one should actually go mad. But if one did?

Bit by bit, though with worrying speed, the symptoms worsened and diversified, unrelieved by love or society. A little over a month later, his path crossed again with a passing fancy from the Paris years. On Friday 11 August he met up with Nigel Henderson, once more in London and, as ever, in a state of professional and sexual flux. After they spent the night together in Charlotte Street, Gascoyne wandered footloose through the West End:

> As I walked through the streets, the brilliant unfamiliar sunshine falling on the faces of the crowd, became the hallucinating light of a despair so extreme as to appear *gay* in its nihilism. Sat on a bench in Leicester Square gardens, realizing that I have definitely 'been called' to be one of those who are to announce the true underlying event taking place during this century; aware of being perhaps the only human being there, in the middle of London, with any idea of what is really happening at this time upon this planet...[17]

For once this entry makes London seem like Paris. The experience of exceptional prerogative and unique vision was artistically orientating per-haps, but there is little doubt of its connection with other, less exalted, facets of his life that summer. Toothache had for long been plaguing him, because he had not visited a dentist since leaving school. He was also dogged by intermittent catarrh, which worsened as autumn approached. A new rem-edy for such ailments had recently come on to the market in the form of the amphetamine Benzedrine Sulfate, launched by the Philadelphia firm Smith Kline and French Laboratories in 1933 and now available in handy inhalers—gold-coloured cylinders with a silver cap at each end—that could be purchased over the counter of any corner chemist. In Britain, the prod-uct had recently been the subject of an extensive advertising campaign on public hoardings and in the newspapers, stressing its decongestant and

16. *Journal 1937–1939*, 122.
17. Ibid. 124.

sedative properties.[18] The euphoric side effects of this readily available form of self-medication were obvious to those who had recourse to it, though medical science would take some years to consider the potential of the drug as a recreational stimulant, or to recognize its varied side effects, of which euphoria was among the least serious. Barker took it on occasions, though he seems to have avoided the more drastic of its consequences. With a slightly more addictive personality, and subject to various inner strains, Gascoyne proved more vulnerable. For several weeks he had been benefiting from its salutary soothing of his blocked nostrils and bronchial tubes, and its ability to take his mind off his aching teeth. His use of it had not stopped there. Before long he was sniffing Benzedrine to alleviate his recurrent depressions, or to keep himself awake and alert during the lengthening nocturnal hours when so much of his intensive reading, and his best creative work, was done. In such circumstances he would stay awake all night, buoyed up on a chemical tide, then sleep for much of the day. Sometimes he hardly slept at all. On the morning of Wednesday, 16 August two otherwise inexplicable entries appear one after the other in the journal: '*spiritual crisis*' and '*White Nights*'. The double entry occurs on the very day in which he records his experience of personal vocation and elated singularity in Leicester Square.

He was fast projecting his mental condition on to the world, not that the world needed it. In the last week of August, just a few days before the declaration of war, he writes this related entry, involving Europe in his predicament, and his predicament in Europe: 'The only thing that reassures me, is my completely detached and objective conviction to the effect that '*schizophenic*' is one of the fundamental hallmarks of everything important that is happening in the modern exterior world, so that one ought surely not to avoid *insisting* on it. (Being a schizo type, though, perhaps I am more inclined than I realized to exaggerate this?)'[19] Six days later, the world seemed to have reached nadir, the 'zero hour'. On Saturday, 2 September, Barker came up from Ball's Cross for a brief visit. They took the bus to Hampton Court, and sat in the gardens overlooking the river discussing the course of political events, hurtling now towards a confrontation the inevitability of which had been obvious to both of them for months, and to David in particular since his last

18. Nicolas Rasmussen, *On Speed: The Many Lives of Amphetamine* (New York: New York University Press, 2008), 22, 37–8, 40–4.

19. *Journal 1937–1939*, 126–7.

weeks in Paris.[20] When the declaration arrived the following day, it was almost a relief.

In the event the phoney war—as the early, largely eventless, months of the conflict in Britain soon came to be called—turned out to be a mixture of apprehension and fun. Every evening at a quarter to seven he helped Win to pin brown paper across the windows in accordance with the new blackout regulations; eventually she sewed thick woollen curtains for all of the windows. David helped Leslie and the twins to dig an air-raid shelter in the garden; hoping to grow vegetables for themselves, they also put up a small greenhouse. By October the nights were well and truly drawing in, and in order to visit his friends the Shaw-Lawrences round the corner he had to fumble his way through almost impenetrable darkness. On his arrival he was met by a torrent of patriotic sentiment from the Shaw-Lawrence parents that disheartened him slightly. He escaped by taking Bettina and her brother Peter down to the Angler's Arms overlooking Teddington Lock. When they drove across to Richmond they were greeted by a violent electric storm that seemed to express much of the pent-up fury that was lacking elsewhere.

The daytime hours, though, were mellow, sunny, and uncannily calm. One day David slung his smelly gas mask around his shoulders, took the footbridge across the Thames, and walked north along the Surrey bank, past the disused gravel pits running like a gully towards the east, and onwards to the outer fringes of Richmond Park. He lay under the tree contemplating all of this incongruous and Keatsian ripeness. As he clomped back down towards the river, he met an old man sitting on a bench who pointed with premonitory finger towards the Star and Garter veterans home up on the ridge. 'You don't belong in there, do you?' he enquired. 'You haven't let them put you in there?' Gascoyne blurted out, 'Not yet.'[21]

His poetic response to the emergency was prompt and distinctive. He had been reading about the Great Pyramid at Giza in Egypt where, according to some interpretations, postulates were obliged to descend into the inner obscurity, dwell there for three days, and then ascend into daylight through a tunnel on the other side. The parallels with Christ's three-day entombment fascinated him, as did the promise of some eventual resurrection. In

---

20. BL Sound Archive, Robert Fraser Collection C1081/08/0103/D1.
21. *Journals 1937–1939*, 138.

the magazine *Nineteenth Century and After*, he issued two short poems, 'The Descent' and 'The Open Tomb' recounting this ritual, letting the hoped-for parallel with Europe's emergence from present darkness suggest itself uninsistently.[22] As the New Year of 1940 dawned, he hymned the departure of the thirties in 'Farewell Chorus', in which the ending of an excitable decade is memorably portrayed as a troop train pulling slowly out of a terminus:

> And so! the long black Pullman is at last departing, now,
> After those undermining years of angry waiting and cold tea;
> And all your small grey faces and wet hankies slide away
> Backwards into the station's cave of cloud. And so Good-bye
> To our home-town, so foreign now its lights no longer show;
> And to old lives already indistinct as a dull play
> We saw while staying somewhere in the Midlands long ago.

It remains one of the most effective accounts of that moment in time, more effective arguably than Auden's more famous valediction 'September 1st, 1939' with its picture of a lonely poet slumped in a 'low dive on forty-second street' and its questionable, and later rescinded, characterization of the period since 1930 as 'a low dishonest decade', leaving Gascoyne less to regret, nothing to alter.[23]

Unlike some, he would not slink away. He was well aware that, unlike Leslie, he was smack in the middle of the target age group if, as expected, conscription was to be introduced. He took to considering the possibility that he might soon be placed in uniform as perhaps the least likely recruit in the British army. He did not baulk at this. Barker had soon taken an academic post in Japan (not, as it transpired, the wisest choice of direction at the time), and Auden and Britten would take the boat to America. Gascoyne was resolved to stay put. He rejected in advance any notion that he might appeal from exemption as a conscientious objector, uncertain that he could construct a coherent defence of this position. In any case, as he confesses disarmingly in his journals, with his temperamental tendency to claustrophobia he dreaded a prison cell more than even the most gruelling of barracks.

22. *Poems 1937–42*, 18–19; *Collected Poems* (1965), 58–9.
23. *Poems 1937–1942*, 51–4; *Collected Poems* (1965), 82–5.

14

Paul Gravey

A s invasion threatened, Paris was a city of high apprehension. Pierre and Blanche Jouve listened to the radio bulletins daily, determining to flee should the Germans arrive and, as expected, target the intelligentsia. Eluard hung grimly put, resolved on poetic and active resistance. Breton was temporally conscripted into the army medical corps. Despite Jewish blood and Romanian nationality, at 42 Fondane was drafted into the French army. He had finished transcribing his conversations with Chestov and, before leaving the Rue Rollin, entrusted the typescript to his Argentinian friend Victoria Ocampo, who took it for safe keeping to Buenos Aires. David's expatriate friends too were dispersing. The Durrells were already in Corfu; Miller and Nin had gone back to the States. Gascoyne's co-analysand Desmond Ryan had quit his sessions with Blanche Jouve, and come home to take a job on the Isle of Wight as ship's cook on the yacht *Llantony*, requisitioned by the Merchant Navy to inspect shipping entering the Solent and Southampton Water.

Les jeunes filles had made their own arrangements. Anne Goossens, whose diplomat stepfather would soon be posted to the Pétain, government out at Vichy, also opted for England. She registered for an acting course at RADA where, habituated to diplomatic life in the States and France, she at first felt something of an outsider, until the college worked to purge her of her American accent.[1] Bettina Shaw-Lawrence joined with two Bedales-educated friends: David Kentish, painter and dramaturge, and Lucian Freud, painter grandson of Sigmund. Together they migrated to Benton End in Suffolk where Cedric Morris, Welshman, one-time singing student, now botanist, landscapist, and portrait artist, was running his grandly named East Anglian School of Painting and Drawing with his partner Arthur Lett-Haines.

1. Interview with Anne Goossens, 3 June 2009.

'There was no real curriculum,' she told me. 'Every morning Cedric just told us to go out into the fields and paint.'[2]

Slowly 44 Rue du Bac, hub for many months of David's set, emptied. Buffie Johnson followed her compatriots back to America. Sending the increasingly opium-addicted Denham Fouts to New York for his own good, and leaving much of his precious art collection with a Romanian friend for safe keeping, Peter Watson reluctantly made for London, where he rented a spacious flat in Berkeley Square, the walls of which he hung with his remaining Mirós, Klees, and Picassos. Watson had recently branched out into the acquisition of British art with the purchase of Graham Sutherland's canvas *Entrance to a Lane*, a quasi-abstract, Samuel Palmer-influenced landscape of paraphrased yellow and black shapes painted by Sutherland in Sandy Cove, Pembrokeshire, and the subject of one of Gascoyne's later poems.[3] He was also deep in discussion with Cyril Connolly about the foundation of a new magazine to replace those including Eliot's *Criterion* that had foundered since the declaration of war. Watson would clearly have to bankroll the enterprise: he was loath at first, especially when Connolly proposed the ideologically excitable Stephen Spender as a co-editor. He was won over by Connolly's persistence, his charm, and an eclecticism in the proposed editorial policy that some were to find flabby, but which at least had the merit of finding acceptance by contributors and authors across a broad political front. Connolly and Spender had two meetings about the project in late September, and on 10 October Watson had lunch with David, telling him of the plans. The magazine's title *Horizon* certainly suggested openness: towards Europe as well as authors of a variety of persuasions. It would carry a cover design by John Piper, Connolly and Spender would co-edit, and the offices would be situated in Spender's flat in Lansdowne Terrrace, Bloomsbury, empty now of Inez, with whom his marriage had just broken up.

David had left his journal in abeyance since the confused weeks of late October, since he had been concentrating on a prose work called *Blind Man's Buff*, with the Existentialist theme of a blindfolded tightrope artist crossing a chasm, and trying to decide which foot to put down next. But on New Year's Eve he opened a new volume of the journal with a resolve to base its entries on a different plan, with different ends in view. No time now for the self-infatuated Barbellion. What was needed was 'A journal more of

2. Interview with Bettina Shaw-Lawrence, 9 June 2010.
3. *Collected Poems* (1988), 227.

the Kierkegaard type (Appalling ridiculous presumption!) than the one I kept before. Corresponding to a new and radically different phase of my life, with new and peculiar problems of its own.'[4] That evening he went up to town for the first time in weeks to attend a party with Watson, Spender, and Tony Hyndman, and stayed on at Watson's spacious apartment for the rest of the month. Connolly was another intermittent guest, and upset Gascoyne by telling him that he could only ever be a 'literary writer'. 'In fact', he tactlessly added, 'you are much *worse* than *literary* really', sending his interlocutor into a spin of self-doubt unmitigated by Connolly's insistence that he had not intended the term in a pejorative sense. 'What exactly did he mean?' Gascoyne worried to himself. Could he have been referring to the 'long-winded, complicated style altogether unlike that of spontaneous speech' in which his philosophical speculations were increasingly involving him?[5] His stay was rendered uncomfortable for another reason. At that New Year's party he had clapped eyes for the first time on the 31-year-old married heart-throb Michael Redgrave. Redgrave had been an occasional habitué at Parton Street where somehow Gascoyne had missed him, but he now became hopelessly enthralled. The debonair actor had just finished touring as the errant spouse in Benn W. Levy's romantic comedy *Springtime for Henry*, and was involved in Liverpool with someone called Tommy. He paid no attention to Gascoyne's cow eyes, and was probably unaware of his plight. By mid-January he had left London for five weeks. 'I must admit', David mooned in his journal, 'that it still seems, to the detached part of myself, indescribably silly and unmentionable to be "in love" with M at all,—to be unable to expect him to respond in any way except with embarrassment if ever he were to become aware of my state—to be solemnly sitting here writing entries in a secret journal about it, like an infatuated schoolgirl.'[6]

At Lansdowne Terrace, they were now preparing the second issue of *Horizon*, buoyed up by sales of 7,000 for the first. Gascoyne was to appear alongside Barker and Kathleen Raine, C. Day Lewis, MacNeice, and Spender with a translation of Jouve's essay of 1937, 'Grandeur actuelle de Mozart'.[7] Its theme was that appreciation of even the greatest art changes with time. Three years previously Jouve's ears had been newly opened to the tragic

---

4. *Collected Journals*, 276.
5. Ibid. 280–1.
6. Ibid. 278–9.
7. *Nouvelle Revue Française*, 290 (1 Nov. 1937). Gascoyne's translation, *Horizon*, 1/2 (Feb. 1940) 84–94.

strain in Mozart through performances by the Vienna Phil under Bruno Walter: a Requiem at the Théâtre Champs-Elysées in June, followed by a *Don Giovanni* during the Salzburg Festival in August. His essay had set aside the dainty Rococo Mozart in favour of a religious artist 'under the sign of death'. 'Rupture', he had declared 'is the law of his supreme harmonic art...His work is baroque and also Greek, classical but also modern.' *Don Giovanni*, an opera that Jouve would soon link to Berg's *Lulu* as a dramatization of the tormented bourgeois sexual ideal, was its supreme expression. 'Thus Don Juan, at the end of the first act, bends his sword against his breast, while singing against the chorus of lamentation, fury and remorse.' The appearance of Gascoyne's translation implicitly extended this argument: Mozart was a composer for wartime.

Kierkegaard had also written memorably about *Don Giovanni*, which in his books *Either/Or* and *Stages On Life's Way* he sees as the summation, and the terrible denouement, of the aesthetic as distinct from the ethical and the religious life. Watson, who was in constant touch with David over this busy period, was aware that he had been involved with the work of Kierkegaard for some months. On 1 March Watson presented him with the *Journals* in a newly published English translation. As soon as Gascoyne opened them, there is in his own journal an immediate surge of renewed identification. 'What a figure!' he exults. 'Tremendous, even terrifying in complexity: a sombre palace full of mirrors, traps and winding corridors—I can see hardly any other figure so outstandingly remarkable in the whole of the 19th century.' Kierkegaard was helping Gascoyne find his way towards an authentic autonomous spirituality, beholden to neither Church nor State. The identification was almost uncanny. 'About K. I now feel as though an integral part of myself had always been waiting to understand him perfectly; as though that part of me were somehow inseparably bound up with his character.—*I understand him through myself. I understand myself through him.*'

Dangers lurked in this enthusiasm. Kierkegaard was an author of many aliases, each of which represented a facet of himself. Gascoyne felt himself pulled in too many directions at once. Acutely, even morbidly, sensitive to the versatility, the Protean variety of a writer that certain European intellectuals were slowly coming to terms with after more than a century of neglect, he blanched at the prospect of his own personality coming apart:

> As an influence upon a certain type of mind, the danger of K's thought is this: that in certain ways it may tend to encourage and thus aggravate the auto-destructive, ie. *demoniac* element that forms one of the principal distinguishing

features of this type; may encourage and aggravate its innate psychic complexity, inter-division, indefinitely repeatable 'sub-detachment', etc.[8]

Schooled by Kierkegaard's writings aided and abetted by Fondane and Jouve, Gascoyne was discerning bit by bit the possibility of introducing religious Existentialism of this kind to his native land just as, a very few years before, he had introduced Surrealism. In *Blind Man's Buff*, he had compared himself to Charles Blondin, the French tightrope walker who in 1859 crossed the Niagara Falls blindfolded. An Existentialist philosopher—perhaps more especially an English Existentialist philosopher—he seemed to be arguing, would be undertaking an equivalent feat, suspended above the empty spaces of public ignorance, the roaring rapids of war. He was resolved to be that intrepid 'subjective' risk-taker, to follow this philosophical balancing act through to the end.

Mundane risks, however, could not be postponed. On Monday, 6 March he presented himself at a tribunal in Kingston-upon-Thames for his army medical:

> After having been kept waiting all the morning, I was told to come back two days later, as I had not got my glasses with me (the oculist had been unable to finish my new pair in time). I went back on the 8th, with my glasses, and to my great surprise, found the doctors quite kindly and sympathetic. They ended by classing me in Grade III. The chairman of the board told me 'If you're in a job, don't leave it. Grade III are not being called up. If they are ever called, it won't be for a long time yet; most probably *never*. In any case you are only fit for work of a sedentary nature.'[9]

The advice made all the more necessary the acquisition of a paid position connected with the war effort. Gascoyne was helped in this by developments across the channel. Desmond Ryan had grown increasingly concerned over the predicament of the Jouves. At the end of March he decided to quit his chef's job on the *Llantony*, volunteering to meet them in Paris, and to drive them to safety in the South, from where they would eventually escape to Switzerland. In his absence he offered his post aboard the yacht to Gascoyne. For the whole of April he was based in Yarmouth on the north-west tip of the Isle of Wight, a tiny grid of streets behind a historic harbour within sight of Hurst Castle. The yacht was berthed alongside Yarmouth

---

8. *Collected Journals*, 288.
9. Ibid. 295.

Pier, from where David was sent every morning to fetch provisions in the town's few shops. He had twenty-four hours on, and twenty-four off. On working days he would toil in the restricted galley below decks, attempting to conjure haute cuisine out of wartime rations. Every few hours an unidentified vessel appeared, and the skipper would hail it through a loud-speaker, then they would pull alongside and inspect its papers. In between lay stretches of boredom during which the crew did petit point and the cockney engineer complained about David's complicated meals, which he compared to 'Chinese messes'. Culinary triumphs, it is true, were few and far between, 'though,' as Gascoyne later boasted, 'I did manage a fair steak-and-kidney pie on one occasion'.[10] In the evening the crew retired to Yarmouth to drink in the small town's many pubs: the George, the Bugle Inn, or the Wheatsheaf. Afterwards Gascoyne dreamed of wombs and entombment: 'Unconscious (a ship, the sea,—mental attention entirely devoted to, diverted by, exterior and practical affairs,—each night, a flood of extraordinary vivid and cogent dreams)'.[11]

Above deck, however, a fine spring was breaking, all the more welcome, and all the more unaccountably, since the skies over southern England were louring with German war planes. In the poem 'Spring Mcmxl' Gascoyne portrays the season as Persephone, a 'punctual goddess', regarded with amazement by those who scarcely recognize, and certainly do not compre-hend, her gift of perpetual hope. But in May ownership of the *Llantony* was transferred to the Royal Navy, making it impossible for a classified civilian to remain a crew member.[12] He left the island, not to return for a further twenty-four years, and in very different circumstances. He was officially free once more, though he was careful not to hang around London. Watson, in any case, had just evacuated *Horizon* lock, stock, and barrel to near Salcombe in south Devon, where its editorial offices occupied Thatched Cottage at Thurlestone Sands, with a cook hired for the summer. Connolly brooded on the bed and complained about the food, then went back and forth to London, as Watson groused about the lack of privacy and Spender kept the office running. Gascoyne joined them as soon as he could.[13] 'From the cliffs at night', Spender wrote later, 'we could see air raids on Plymouth, the black

10. BL Lives, F1383, Side A.
11. *Collected Journals*, 305.
12. As HMS *Llantony* the vessel would soon play a valuable role in the evacuation of Dunkirk.
13. Clive Fisher, *Cyril Connolly: A Nostalgic Life* (London: Macmillan, 1985).

sky seemed a background to the fires and bombs and shells, shaken like spangles out of it, and criss-crossed by the straight lines of searchlights.'[14] Gascoyne's great-uncle Cyril Maude was now widowed and living in retirement in nearby Dartmouth, the trials and excitements of his career long past. It was close enough for Gascoyne to be able to walk east across the headland to visit him one afternoon. The occasion, and the inevitable talk of the Emery clan, rekindled his interest in the theatre.

The general evacuation from London had given rise to some unpredictable but rewarding cohabitations. Roger Roughton, for example, had moved to Ireland, but he had left behind the travelling companion of his Hollywood months, John Davenport, to whom he had already introduced David. Davenport was a burly, irascible, and clever man who for much of his life would earn his living as a schoolteacher. He was also however, a practised critic and journalist with interests that ranged right across the arts. As versed in contemporary music as in literature, during his American months he had met Stravinsky, Schoenberg, and Aldous Huxley. He had recently invested his Hollywood fees in purchasing the Malting House in the Cotswold village of Marshfield twelve miles from Bristol, moving there in the late spring of 1940 with his striking American wife Clement, a set designer and portraitist, and their baby daughter Natalie. They filled the other rooms with a sometimes riotous assembly of artists in almost every medium. He invited Gascoyne down there over that Whitsun weekend to talk about music, to hike around the hills, and to lend a hand in the kitchen. David came and went throughout the latter part of the year and the early months of 1941, and when in residence, drawing on his recent experience of catering for a small community, he became the household's unofficial cook.

The house was hugger-mugger with talent. A desperate, comradely spirit of *carpe diem* prevailed. Lennox Berkeley, soon to join the RAF, was engaged on his coolly contrapuntal second string quartet. Humphrey Searle, a onetime pupil of Anton Webern, was writing a symphony in the weeks before joining Bomber Command. The Yorkshire-born composer Arnold Cooke was composing a piano concerto while waiting to be called up by the navy. Antonia White arrived with her two daughters and stayed for several weeks before moving out to a nearby farm. Like Gascoyne, Dylan Thomas had

14. Stephen Spender, *Journals 1939–1983* (London: Faber, 1985), 57.

been classified Grade III on account of a weak chest: in July Davenport
lured him across to escape his debts at Laugharne with his Irish wife Caitlin
and their young son Llewellyn. They stayed three months. There were jokes,
there were japes, and there were inevitable tensions. A 32-year-old musical
all-rounder called William Glock, who had studied piano with Artur
Schnabel and was later to come to national prominence as the organizer of
the Henry Wood Promenade Concerts, set several female hearts aflame: at
different times he was involved with Caitlin and Clement Davenport, with
whom he later absconded. All four musicians shared Gascoyne's enthusiasm
for Bartók, the full edition of whose *Mikrokosmos* pieces had newly appeared
in America. Two grand pianos, and the double beds upstairs, were in pretty
well constant use.

In the pub over the road in the evenings Searle played his admired Liszt,
while Caitlin pirouetted to the music. In the afternoons she danced to
gramophone records in an outhouse whilst her husband and Davenport
exuded mirth over a literary project they had in hand. *The Death of the
King's Canary* was a *roman-à-clef* and spoof detective novel. It was also a spirited hatchet job on the contemporary artistic world and its fads, including
the Surrealism that Dylan deprecated in theory whilst honouring it in practice. The socialite poet Hilary Byrd is elected Laureate; he invites his disappointed rivals down to his rural seat to celebrate. Byrd is murdered overnight,
but who has done him in? Poets are parodied and artists and composers
lampooned, each in a negative snapshot recognizable across seventy years.
Albert Ponting is Barker; Wyndham Snowden is Auden; Christopher Gorvin
is Spender; John Lowel Atkins is Eliot (his celebrated celibacy and symbolic
self-castration castigated in the mock Quartet 'East Abelard'); Limpit is
Michael Tippett; Lady Lucretia is Edith Sitwell; Hercules Jones is Augustus
John; Bernard Berkely is Lennox Berkeley; Tom Agard is Tom Harrisson.
Gascoyne, of course, is lurking in the shadows, though he is not easy at first
to spot.

At one point in this recreational romp a circumspect English artist called
Oliver Fry—cynosure perhaps for the recently dead Roger Fry—is attempting to force his native talent into a fashionable mould of Surrealist extravagance by composing a collage on his worktop table. To induce the required
state of oneiric instability, he brings to mind the unsparing strictures of
Breton. Paul Gravey is the name of their English translator, with a nod
towards the anthologist of the *Golden Treasury of English Verse*, and a brisk
sniff at Gascoyne's questionable abilities as a chef:

Oliver Fry was making a surrealist object in his neat, clinical studio. On the polished work table lay a Victorian corset, a moose's head imported, at considerable cost from North America, several abominations, a pair of spiked steel garters, dog's teeth plaited on a string and a woollen banjo. They were to be elements in Oliver's new creation: 'Imprisonment of a Nail'.

It was past midnight. 'When evil and disorder are not abroad, no artist should lift the somnambulist mountain of his brush', Breton had said, translated by Paul Gravey. Oliver, who always felt dull and sleepy by half past eleven, could not forget these apocalyptic words. Well fed, unemotional, wanting to go straight to bed where he knew he would dream about dividends and decent young women well brought up, who kissed him on the forehead and told him not to bother any more, he sighed, compressed his lips, and began again the bewildering task of erecting an obscene monument to disorder out of his clean, unhappy mind.[15]

The murder at the book's heart possesses a distinct air of Surrealist anarchy, as does much of the behaviour on display in the house. Arguably *The Death of the King's Canary* is the highest comic achievement of British Surrealism, though few have acknowledged it as such. It was not published until 1976, when most of those caricatured were past caring.

Caricature the reference to Gascoyne surely was. By 1940 he had long since ceased calling himself a Surrealist, determined as others were that the label should stick. To a certain extent this was the penalty of his own early success; it was also a sign of intellectual laziness on the part of readers and opportunism by his contemporaries: a stereotype limits a poet, prevents him developing in directions that others neither welcome nor predict. The imaginative daring of Surrealism, its ways of seeing the extraordinary in the ordinary, however, were strengths he would never renounce or let go. One early evening in March 1941, while staying back in Teddington with Leslie and Win, he strolled downriver to the gravel pits that yawned grimly on the Surrey bank of the Thames, a quarter of a mile or so to the north of Teddington Lock. It had recently rained, a stiff breeze was blowing overhead, and the visibility was unusually sharp, as it often is under low-lying cloud. Gascoyne was in a mood of heightened visual alertness, almost certainly assisted by the Benzedrine he was now sniffing daily. The scene that met him was mundane in the extreme: bare twigs, assorted rubble, and shards of bone sticking out in a higgledy-piggledy jumble from the base and

15. Dylan Thomas and John Davenport, *The Death of the King's Canary* (Harmondsworth: Penguin, 1976), 53.

rim of a crater patchily covered in grass, in this unpretentious and unpromising suburban setting. He carefully noted the prosaic details of the scene, but in the poem that resulted, 'The Gravel-Pit Field', the very dourness is transformed by an arresting clarity of vision. However one chooses to interpret that process—as mystical, psychedelic, or even psychosomatic—the detritus had been transformed into a precisely evoked, almost supernal beauty:

> So these least stones, in the extreme
> Of their abasement might appear
>
> Like rare stones such as could have formed
> A necklet worn by the dead queen
> Of a great Pharaoh, in her tomb...
> So each abandoned snail-shell strewn
> Among these blotched dock-leaves might seem
> In the pure ray shed by the loss
> Of all man-measured value, like
> Some priceless pearl-enamelled toy
> Cushioned on green silk under glass.[16]

For many of Gascoyne's readers (such as the novelist Olivia Manning, who chose to have it read at her funeral), this was to be Gascoyne's most satisfying poem, perhaps because it opens itself up to such a range of interpretations, and reconciles so many of the poet's contrary impulses and styles. It is both a poem about the surrealism of the object, and an exercise in mystical second sight (Gascoyne had recently discovered Traherne). Even the most hardened materialist, after all, occasionally experiences what religious people call transcendence. Gascoyne was still seeing with Dalí-esque eyes, as when rain water trapped in some stagnant puddles is compared to 'scraps of sky decaying in | The sockets of a dead man's stare.' Nascent somewhere, however, there is a suggestion of another scale of value entirely.

16. *Poems 1937–1942*, 59–61; *Collected Poems* (1965), 90–3.

15

'Multiplicity is My Daemonia'

S hortly before the outbreak of war Gascoyne had got to know Enid
Starkie, the colourful, Irish-born, reefer-jacketed, sailor-capped Fellow
in French at Somerville College, Oxford. She impressed him as 'a mercuri-
ally mischievous woman with an unmistakably Irish gift of the gab, formidably scathing when roused, and given to a flamboyance of attire not limited
to her well-known matelot get-up'. Starkie had persuaded Gascoyne to lay
aside his long-mooted and part-drafted study of Rimbaud so as to make way
for her own biography of the poet, published in 1938.[1] He had perhaps
given way too easily: there was room for more than one book on Rimbaud
in English, just as there had been in French, and his own would have been
bracingly different from hers. But Gascoyne was in touch with the Parisian
nineteenth century through other means. In Teddington his circle of
acquaintance had widened to include a septuagenarian Frenchman who
had known Marcel Proust in his childhood in the late 1870s, when the two
of them had played together in the Champs-Elysées. Alphonse Kahn proved
a source of fascinating anecdote, and a link with a Parisian life with which
David seemed temporarily to have lost contact. They dined together with a
group of friends in the Mitre Pub opposite the main gates of Hampton
Court palace, where the flow of reminiscences made up for the restricted
menu. Also present was a young man called David Carr, whose parents lived
in an elegant house in the village of Petersham a short walk across the fields
from Richmond. Soon he and David had achieved a friendship *à deux* with
'Sunday afternoon walks, visits to Hampton Court and Kew...evenings
together in town, etc.'. Somehow these sessions seemed awkward since he

---

1. Afterword to *Collected Journals*, 341–2, citing Enid Starkie, *Arthur Rimbaud* (London: Faber,
   1938). For a less magnanimous impression of Starkie, see Julian Barnes, *Flaubert's Parrot* (London:
   Picador, 1984), 74–6.

could not read Carr's intentions: an embarrassed and cumbersome sentence in the journals hints at 'a relationship, *enfin,* not altogether devoid, perhaps, of latent possibilities'.[2]

Such new friendships could not quite compensate for the loss of old ones. Nothing was to bring home so sharply to Gascoyne the extinguishing of the intellectual atmosphere of the thirties than the news, at the end of April 1941, that Roger Roughton had gassed himself in a boarding house in Dublin, leaving behind a passionate essay in which he pleaded with his friends to recover the innocent vision of a child.[3] Roughton had in many ways epitomized the febrile certainties of the decade just passed: 'The Communist Party, with its policy of instant recall and maximum discussion of all issues before decisions are taken', he had confidently declared in December 1936, 'is the most democratic organisation today, and those who, claiming to be communists, remain outside the party and criticise it, show not their independence but their irresponsibility.'[4] Nine months later, already a little discouraged, he had called a halt to his lively magazine *Contemporary Poetry and Prose*, announcing that 'the editor is going abroad for some time'.[5] Roughton had then wondered aimlessly through France, America, and Ireland; at his last meeting with Gascoyne shortly before the war the two already seemed strangers to one another. The Nazi-Soviet Pact of August 1939 seemed the living refutation of everything in which he had plighted his troth; he was not to live to witness its abrogation that July. Gascoyne's elegy for him was as much a threnody for an epoch as for a cherished friend:

> I'll say not any word in praise or blame
> Of what you ended with the mere turn of a tap;
> Nor to explain, deplore not yet exploit
> The latent pathos of your living years—
> Hurried, confused and unfulfilled—
> That were the shiftless years of both our youths
> Spent in the monstrous mountain-shadow of
> *Catastrophe* that chilled you to the bone:

2. *Collected Journals*, 306–7.
3. Published as Roger Roughton, 'The Human House', *Horizon*, 4/19 (1941), 50–7. Roughton's death is announced on p. 8 of the same issue.
4. Roger Roughton, 'Surrealism and Communism', *Contemporary Poetry and Prose*, 8 (Picasso Poems Number) (Aug. Sept. 1936), 74–5.
5. Roger Roughton, Editorial to *Contemporary Poetry and Prose*, 10 (Autumn 1937).

> The certain imminence of which always pursued
> You from your heritage of fields and sun...[6]

Old hopes laid waste, he was drawn into fresh spheres of activity. War was having a mixed impact on the professional stage in Britain. During the blackouts of late 1939, the theatres had temporarily closed. When they opened again the following spring, the plays on offer had adjusted to the public mood. New scripts were scarce, nor was there that appetite for troubling drama from the European continent that had existed during the last few crisis-ridden years of peace: for Chekhov, for example, who had experienced a revival during 1937. Now the English classics came into their own; Shakespeare enjoyed a field day, with the emphasis placed on his Englishness. Otherwise, audiences wanted light relief, distraction, tipsy hilarity. Vaudeville and farce both thrived.[7] Anne Goossens had now spent eighteen months as a listless student at RADA. On leaving, after working briefly in rep for a few months, she was faced with a decision. Many unmarried women were working as signalmen on the railway, driving trucks, or toiling in the munitions factories. 'I could either work as a bus conductor, or else get a job with ENSA. Personally I was tempted to work on the buses.' Priaulx Rainier, the South African composer whom both she and David had known in Paris in 1938, and who was now living in London, persuaded Goossens the buses were unworthy of her. She took a job with ENSA (the Entertainments National Service Association), and found herself unexpectedly in the same company as David.[8]

ENSA had been founded in 1939 by Basil Dean, who was to oversee the operation for the duration of the war from its headquarters at the Theatre Royal, Drury Lane.[9] Its scope was as broad as the theatres of military engagement, its purpose to distract bored servicemen at home and abroad. Dean himself had a background in light theatre, having worked with Gracie Fields and George Formby. His ambitions in this new enterprise were purely recreational. With government funding he provided solace and raucous fun, on a very large scale. War, which was to transform so much in society, had this further effect: it was to witness the first—not universally welcome—move

6. 'An Elegy (R.R. 1916–41)', Poems 1937–1942, 37; Collected Poems (1965), 69.
7. John Graven Hughes, The Greasepaint War: Show Business 1939–1945 (London: New English Library, 1976), passim.
8. Interview with Anne Goossens, 3 June 2008.
9. Basil Dean, Theatre at War (London: Harrap, 1956), 1–15.

towards the subsidy of the arts. As professional actors were conscripted into the forces, opportunities were created: for those younger than themselves— several careers got off to a precociously early start—for the professionally unqualified, and for others unavailable for military service who would under other circumstances not have considered the theatre as a way of life. The scale of the operation was vast, the standards were variable. It has been calculated that by the end of hostilities 300 million people had seen an ENSA produc- tion of some sort, and performances exceeded 2 million in six years.

Gascoyne had been biding his time for much of 1940, writing the occa- sional poem, turning out articles and reviews for the increasingly indispen- sable *Horizon*, and reading, reading. Since 1939, however, he had expressed a growing interest in his great aunt's profession. His opportunity occurred in the summer of 1941 when John Davenport, well connected with the arts in the West Country, introduced him to a German producer living and work- ing in exile. Dorothea Alexander's father had been one of the most com- mercially successful producers during the Weimar Republic in Berlin. She had fled to England at the start of the war and started her own company touring in the provinces, specializing in classic British plays or adaptations of novels, often performed *in situ*: Jane Austen in Bath, Shakespeare in towns associated with his plots. For some years there had been the beginnings of an arts festival in Bath, twenty miles from Davenport's home in Marshfield. The Bath Festival proper would not get off the ground until after the war, but in June 1941 a proto-festival was already in the offing. Benefiting from the general nostalgia for the classics, Alexander planned an adaptation of Jane Austen's *Persuasion* there, performed in the Pump Room and drawing its cast from a mixture of recent graduates from the London drama schools, of amateurs, and—for mature parts—men and women beyond military age. Gascoyne, who was alerted to the production by Davenport, went down from Marshfield to audition, and was given a couple of walk–on parts. He had not acted for ten years, had gangling limbs, noticeably rotten teeth, and no formal training. Alexander put him through his paces and, responding as he often did to the authority of a strong and assertive woman, he learned to respect, even to revere her. Her power over him was palpable. 'He always', Goossens recalls, 'spoke of her with the greatest fondness and admiration.'

Alexander presided, he soon found, over a company of slightly more than repertory standard. Not all of them were raw recruits, by any manner of means. Among the female leads was Joan Greenwood, then a 20-year-old graduate of RADA. Joan was petite (at five feet nothing), with a face that could switch in an instant from mock seriousness to flirtatious mischief. Her principal asset, as throughout her career, was her voice: deep, throaty, and employed to seductive effect. Later in life Greenwood would be described as 'gargling with champagne', but in 1941 she was perfect casting for the landowner Charles Musgrove's teenage daughter Louisa, who distracts the course of Austen's narrative when, on being jumped down from the cobb in Lyme Regis by Wentworth, she leaps too soon, and is stunned on the flag-stones below.

Gascoyne too seemed stunned. Despite the fifteen-inch difference in their height, they took to one another, and David was soon writing in his diary of an 'intimation of something special' with Greenwood he could not quite spell out. The feeling, sentimental on his side, protective on hers, per-sisted when, after a period of rehearsal in London in July, the company moved on to Welwyn Garden City to perform three plays in repertory. They were joined there by Goossens, herself just out of RADA, and not at this point certain whether she wanted to be an actress or a painter. In the rudimentary green room the three of them got into a huddle and discussed the uncertainty of the future, and the importance of keeping one's options open while maintaining 'continuity' through all these changes and chances. Alexander was modestly encouraging, advising him that, 'having made an apparently promising start at *anything*, it's a pity not to go on with it, some-how until one feels proficient at it. But of course', Gascoyne added in his journal, 'I don't at present think of myself as being an *actor* in the same way as I've always thought of myself as a *writer*... Have laid the foundations of a clear theoretical and practical approach to the problems of dramatic tech-nique and of acting psychology (introspective habit and training useful while actually on stage performing, in this respect).'[10]

It was a poet's attitude to the stage. Already he had dropped his surname and elevated his middle name of 'Emery' to an official stage alias, appearing on programmes as 'David Emery' as if a linear heir to great-aunt Winifred. And characteristically he was reading up on the subject too, immersing himself in Stanislavsky, with the result that he was developing a technique quite distinct from his great-uncle's who had always constructed his crowd-pulling caricatures from the outside in, from gestures, costumes, and props. Gascoyne wanted to work outwards from a process of introspection, as if writing in the first person. From a reading of Jung he had absorbed a view

10. *Collected Journals*, 311.

of the personality, including his own, as almost endlessly protean. He was also attending to Kierkegaard again, quoting with approval an observation from the journals 'One ought to be able to write a whole novel in which the present conjunctive was the invisible soul, the light and shade in painting.' All this time, too, he was working on a third novel, *Benighted in Babylon*, in which a character called Simon visits an infernal city in search of his lost twin brother, uncovering in the process myriads of alternative selves, selves as various as Jung's multifaceted understanding of the mind, or Kierkegaard's spouting aliases: 'a poor student, a libertine (Aragon), a homosexual, a *noctambule,* a wealthy man of fashion and dilettante, a member of a fascist type of secret society (Cagoulards), an unsuccessful poet and literary failure, an anarchist conspirator, a drug-addict, a "hermit" or mystical fanatic, etc.'.[11] Doubtless he had observed his own twin brothers, very different in their temperaments; yet all these diverse personae could be found in himself.

For her next venture Alexander staged *The Merry Wives of Windsor* in the Theatre Royal in that royal town. She cast 'David Emery' as the irascibly jealous husband, Master Ford. There were a lot more words to learn than before, including two obsessive soliloquies, the gloomy mood of which she may have thought suited him. By early September he was swotting his lines and orientating himself into the period by poring over Eliot's *Elizabethan Essays*. At the dress rehearsal on the 13th he disgusted himself as 'shaky, uncertain of my way about the stage, of acoustics, etc.'. He recovered his composure in time for the opening on the 16th. All this exposure to practical stagecraft was getting him used to the theatre as a multidimensional space. He decided that, if he were ever to assume the mantle of a director, he would like to put on the death-infatuated Thomas Love Beddoes's last and uncompleted play *Death's Jest Book*—on which the author had been working in 1846 at the time of his suicide—with stylized movement and diction in the manner of Antoine Artaud, a commissioned score from Constance Lambert—to whom Lennox Berkeley had introduced him— and a set and costumes by the camp British artist Edward Burra, who had exhibited with the Surrealists in 1936. Perhaps in reaction against the austerity around him, he was consumed with a craving for outré ideas, for high and feminized style, for the *entre-deux-guerres* sophistication of Ronald Firbank, for the sorts of 'costumes, decors, mannerisms, glamour-ideas, etc.' found in successive albums by Cecil Beaton, epitomized for him by a

11. *Collected Journals*, 307–8.

portrait of the cosmetics tycoon Helena Rubinstein, 'the face-pack queen, *chez elle*', in the pages of *Life* Magazine. For all that, his poetry was moving in a contrary direction: towards 'bareness, sobriety, simplicity, formal discipline, clarity of pattern...a certain blunt, chill, "pensive" interior music'.[12]

The Merry Wives went off sufficiently well for him to consider acting in the longer term. Bettina Shaw-Lawrence had just put him in contact with her current fiancé David Standish, a talented painter-turned-actor currently touring the North with his sister Elizabeth in a production of Larry E. Johnson's pre-war three-act hit, *It's a Wise Child*. The Coventry Theatre Company show had the advantage of funding from ENSA, giving company members a weekly wage of £6. On 28 October, after a fleeting visit to David Archer who had moved his bookshop and arts centre to Sandyford Place in Glasgow, Gascoyne went along for an audition at the ENSA headquarters in Drury Lane. The theatre had received a direct hit from an enemy bomb in 1940 which had wrecked the circle and part of the stalls. The proscenium arch stage was roughly partitioned into cubicles to provide makeshift offices, in one of which the impresario Henry Oscar gave him a brief audition and offered him a part. Within a few days he had joined the rest of the company in Darlington, where he was put through his paces in a series of impromptu rehearsals. He was understandably jittery, confiding to Leslie and Win in a letter back home:

> My first week of actual acting was really rather agonising and I was very glad when it was over. I don't think I've ever had such bad stage-nerves in my life as I had on the first night, and what made it worse, I didn't fully realise this until I actually got onto the stage. I gave a frightful performance. Somehow it was so much more intimidating than any ordinary first night,—everyone else in the company being highly experienced and efficient and, of course, all knowing their lines backwards, many of them having been acting in this same play for a whole year now. It wasn't until the end of the week that I began to be able to do my part at all competently; the first two or three nights I was so bad that I really was quite afraid of getting sacked!—though I must say, everyone in the company was as nice about it as they could be.[13]

He soon recovered confidence, though Stanislavsky proved of little help. *It's A Wise Child* had been a Broadway success of the late 1920s when at the Belasco Theatre on West 44th street it had secured a 376th successive

---

12. Ibid. 313–14.
13. Ibid. 317.

triumph for its profit-minded producer David Belasco. Humphrey Bogart had taken one of the romantic leads. The *New York Telegram* had called it 'the heartiest laugh in town' and the *New York Daily News* had remarked that it was 'funnier than it is naughty—much funnier'. In 1931 a Hollywood movie had brought it to the attention of British audiences; great literature, however, it was not. The plot centred around Joyce Stanton, a giddy girl from a middle-class household, who attempts to extricate herself from engagement to a 55-year-old banker by claiming to be pregnant by an unidentified lover. She succeeds, but in process brings down a cloud of suspicion on her current heart-throb, on her respectably married cousin, even on the cantankerous and self-righteous banker himself. All of them disown her in turn; only the dependable but slightly boring family lawyer stands by her.

It was the sort of vertiginous farce homesick troops adored: mildly risqué but fundamentally decent, disturbing the social and moral just long enough to deliver a belly-full of mirth before confirming the status quo. The family's maid Alice, for example, is throughout genuinely pregnant. Her lapse gives rise to less concern: illegitimacy is more tolerable among the lower orders. Henry Oscar had matched the man to the part. He cast Gascoyne as Joyce's dissatisfied younger brother Bill, a junior employee in the bank, keen to achieve promotion, 'spoiled' and with a 'sulky temperament'. The sulks went on for much of the play:

ROGER: How are you feeling this bright and glorious day?
BILL (still with enthusiasm): Rotten.
ROGER: That's the cigarettes; they sap your vitality. You take my word for it—I've had a lot of experience. You cut out the cigarettes and inside a week, you'll feel another man.
BILL (Gloomily): What other man?[14]

Gascoyne needed do little more than impersonate a younger version of Leslie. He cannot have been stimulated by this mild fare, yet he threw himself into it with seriousness, if not exactly abandon. After Darlington came Bridlingon in Yorkshire and Northampton then, after a short pre-Christmas break, Aylesbury and Colchester. At each stop he was given digs, at which he ate his daily supper before taking the coach with his fellow actors to some encampment on the edge of town, where they would perform on

---

14. Larry E. Johnson, *It's a Wise Child: A Comedy in Three Acts* (London and New York: Samuel French, 1937), 16–17.

an improvised stage in the communal hall. On the way to and from the performances the cast sang songs to keep their spirits up: Bettina Shaw-Lawrence who joined them to be with David Kentish, recalls the forced merriment as the bus rattled along the darkened roads.[15] If basic living conditions proved oppressive, they could dip into their wages and sign in at a hotel. David took this option with increasing frequency.

His voracious reading was influencing his acting, and both were changing the ways in which he looked, heard, and felt. Just before Christmas, when the company was performing in Northampton, he went to the cinema to see one of the successes of that year, the early film noir *High Sierra*, an apotheosis he thought of the gangster movie. He was struck by its inexorability, its tension, and an artistry 'which suggested both Aeschylus and Webster to me'. He was attracted by the trip wires of its plot, and by the atmosphere of the culminating scene in which Roy Earle, the 'mad dog' criminal played by Humphrey Bogart, is holed up in the mountains after a botched raid on a Californian casino. As a ring of police closes in, taking pot shots at him through the encroaching darkness, one hears 'the voice of the radio commentator, pouring an ecstatic eyewitness account of the situation into his microphone, keeping the nation's eager, vengeful masses informed as to the approach of the sacrificial victim's certain death'. As he watched spellbound, some lines from Rimbaud's *Une saison en enfer* drifted into his mind: 'When still a child, I admired the hardened criminal on whom the prison door is forever closing. I saw the universe through his eyes.' The *poésie du mal* connected the scene with other recent artistic manifestations of such dark power: with Theodore Dreiser's novel *An American Tragedy*, with James Cain's hard-boiled *The Postman Always Rings Twice*, and with cabaret songs by Brecht and Jacques Prévert.[16] Part of him was ineluctably drawn towards these shadows.

During the long, vacant provincial afternoons he rummaged in local bookshops, rejoicing in out-of-the-way finds. In Ipswich he discovered the whole of Henry James's correspondence for 8s. 6d., especially lucky since— with dubious effects on his prose style—James was a current infatuation, along with the writings and paintings of Blake's friend Samuel Palmer. A book on Palmer by Grigson had just appeared. By the time he got round to mentioning this fact to Grigson himself, his one-time mentor had

---

15. Interview with Bettina Shaw-Lawrence, 24 May 2009.
16. *Collected Journals*, 319–22, quoting Rimbaud 'Mauvais Sang', vi.

typically lost faith in the subject, returning an acidulous reply leading to a rift that took months to heal.[17] The collecting advanced a step when in March the company reached Tunbridge Wells with its welter of second-hand bookshops. Gascoyne was in a highly excitable state. One day he discovered on a fishmonger's slab 'a rare and delicious fish, probably a rainbow trout',[18] at a bargain price. Spending a sizeable proportion of his weekly wage, he bought it on an impulse. Realizing the artist Graham Sutherland, whom he had known since the 1936 Exhibition, lived nearby with his wife Kathy at the White House in Trottiscliffe, he rang them up, invited himself along, and on his arrival presented Kathy with the fish, which he insisted she cook for supper. They were alarmed, though probably more at Gascoyne's manner than by his gift.

By the first week of May when, six months after his joining the company, the tour came to an end, the book collecting had assumed manic proportions. Of all the Romantic poets he was, with his addictive habits, his erudition, his moods, and his drugs, coming to resemble Coleridge more than any other. As with Coleridge, his reading fed into a marked mystical tendency. Like Coleridge he was drawn towards the arcane: towards the classical Christian mystics, but also towards figures like Jakob Boehme, the seventeenth-century German who had discovered God in a ray of light in a pewter dish. This in turn led him to reconsider English verse in the light of such influences, uncovering in the process a disregarded underbelly of indigenous cultic thought and expression running beneath the main body of English tradition. As his fragmentary war diaries draw to a premature close, he sets out a procession of names that amount to an alternative literary legacy. There are canonic names amongst them, but the combination suggests a new insight and a new pattern of literary descent. He had been collecting books by all of them over the previous six months: Langland, Surrey, Wyatt, Drayton, Campion, Waller, Marvell, Crashaw, Vaughan, Traherne, Smart, Blair, Chatterton, Emily Brontë, Poe, Emily Dickinson, Beddoes, Landor, Arnold, Clough, Patmore, Christina Rossetti, Meredith, James Thomson, Edward Dowden, Ernest Dowson. Each Friday he dispatched the week's acquisitions in an immense parcel addressed to Teddington, where Leslie and Win piled them up in forlorn heaps across the carpet of his bedroom.

17. BL Lives, F1382, Side A.
18. *Selected Prose*, 266.

An especially exciting discovery had been the seventeeth-century poet Francis Quarles, whose *Emblems, Divine and Moral, together with Hieroglyphics of the Life of Man* he stumbled on in Cecil Court that summer. Orthodox scholarship by and large held that Quarles's grand compilation of scripture and invention was saved in the eyes of posterity, if at all, only by virtue of its illustrations, which are by quite another hand. To Gascoyne, however, it came to seem that Quarles was a representative of that very otherness within tradition that he was always seeking to find, all the more attractive to him since his own access to this source of inspiration had been the product, not of tradition, but of his own restless auto didacticism.

A note in his journal the previous July gives some indication of a perspective that these preoccupations increasingly confirmed. 'As I see it now,' it observes, gravitating into the past tense, 'the Surrealist Movement represented nothing less than an instinctive Twentieth-century attempt to fulfil an equivalent social and historical function to that fulfilled by the Alchemists during the Middle Ages and early Renaissance.'[19] For the time being, he could leave such influences aside, their place filled with modern tendencies which in time would blend with them to yield a twentieth-century variety of mysticism. Presently, he was absorbed in Jung and Heidegger and, as volume after volume was translated from the original Danish, with the growing revival of interest in Kiekegaard. In the dying days of 1941, in his bedsit in Colchester, he was immured with Walter Lowrie's recent English translation of Kierkegaard's *Stages on Life's Way*, with its adumbration of three realms through which the developing mind must pass: the aesthetic stage (the stage of *Don Giovanni*), the moral stage, and lastly the stage of the spiritual man. All of these tempted him. With their competing allure, augmented with an actor's necessity to play different roles, they threatened to pull him apart. 'Multiplicity', he observed in the last journal entry of this eventful year, 'is my daemonia.'

19. *Collected Journals*, 302.

16

Portrait of the Artist
as a Young Sneeze

The tension and constant shifts of place, the minimal living conditions and imperfect security of theatrical touring, were doing little to assist Gascoyne's mental or physical well-being, which by the early months of 1942 was precarious. He wasn't eating sensibly for one thing. Life on the road did nothing to encourage regular meals. Goossens, who was also travelling at the time with a different show, recalls some of the deleterious effects: 'Food was expensive, and people didn't have time to sit in restaurants.'[1] Drugs were cheaper than snacks, and they could be taken on the move. If David's suitcases had contained nothing but books, the results would have been mostly beneficial, but they often contained more worrying loads. By the early spring his amphetamine addiction had reached such proportions that he needed to conceal it. Along with several of his contemporaries, he had worked out that the stimulant properties of Benzedrine could be intensified if, hacking off the metal cladding of the inhaler with a knife, he released the drug-saturated wadding inside and, steeping the contents in warm water, took the infusion as a drink. He was then faced with the problem of what to do with the resulting piles of accumulating metal husks, too many to be disposed of incrementally at each stage of the journey. The dilemma, and the forms of subterfuge to which it led, go unmentioned in his journal. Forty years later, he was more forthright about this particular nightmare: 'I still', he then confided, 'have a distinct recollection…(and it is of the kind that it is natural in such cases to repress) of finding myself confronted, in one of the theatrical lodging bedrooms allotted *weekly* to members of the company I toured with for ENSA, with the problem of how to dispose inconspicuously of half the contents of a small suitcase: an accumulation of dozens of ripped open Benzedrine inhaler cases.'[2]

1. Interview with Anne Goossens, 3 June 2008.
2. Afterword to *Collected Journals*, 386.

He was no longer undertaking analysis; instead he had been referred by a number of friends to a mysterious character practising medicine from a Notting Hill address called Dr Karl Theodor Bluth. Sixty years of age, Prussian Protestant by birth, bald and stooping in appearance, Bluth was a Svengali of the period, a contributor to *Horizon*, an expert on the works of Novalis, and an acquaintance of both Heidegger and Brecht. Unlike Heidegger, he disapproved of Hitler, and had moved to London in 1934, one year after the burning of the Reichstag. Among his patients were Peter Watson, whom he treated for drug addiction, Julian Trevelyan, who had suffered a breakdown after the abrupt end of his first marriage, and George Barker, who had just returned from America in a nervous state to join the Canadian writer Elizabeth Smart. Highly sympathetic to the plight of artists, he was also treating the novelist Anna Kavan, whose testimony gives some indication of the trust his manner could inspire: she called Bluth 'the only one who has ever made me feel as though I really mattered as an individual or as a person'.[3] Several of his clients were addicts of one substance or another, and his usual course of treatment consisted in prescribing, and sometimes administering, more of the same. He was fond of giving injections: he injected Barker with a cocktail of drugs in a base of ox blood, and he regularly shot crude heroine into Kavan's arm, an act her biographer compares to 'sex of a highly sublimated Freudian' sort. For Gascoyne Bluth prescribed a brand of the amphetamine-derivative methamphetamine that was now being marketed by the British firm Burroughs-Wellcome under the brand name 'Methedrine'. Methamphetamines possessed a slightly dodgy reputation: during the Blitz they had been widely taken by Luftwaffe bomber pilots, who had swallowed 35 million tablets of the stuff in a form manufactured by the drug firm Temmler under the brand name Pevetin. It was Pevetin-puffed pilots who had laid waste the streets around St Paul's. The RAF had admired the associated pluck, and by late 1941, when the Germans were already worried by the addictive properties of this particular narcotic, Methedrine was being handed out to boost the morale and high-altitude flying skills of British aircrews on long-range night missions. Both Churchill and General Montgomery were enthusiasts: the victorious army at El Alamein may have been inspired by patriotic zeal, but they were also high on speed.[4] The drug's adaption for civilian use was equally swift. It had

---

3. Quoted in David Callard, *The Case of Anna Kavan: A Biography* (London: Peter Owen, 1992), 78.
4. Nicolas Ramussen, *On Speed: The Many Lives of Amphetamine* (New York: New York University Press, 2008), 54–5, 59, 61, 64, 66, 68, 72–3, 76–8, 82.

a practical advantage over Benzedrine: the top of each inhaler could be unscrewed, and the contents replaced by refills obtainable at local pharmacies. 'The problem', as Gascoyne later explained, 'now became one of having to avoid purchasing refills too often from the same chemist so as not to arouse suspicion.' He had a further dilemma: how to hide his growing addiction from Win and Leslie, with whom he was again lodging when his ENSA tour finally drew to a close in June 1942.

His reading was growing increasingly weird and mystical, and this, possibly in combination with the drugs he was taking, was giving rise to moments of epiphany he was inclined to view in a religious light. In May, for example, he records a sense of 'Serenity, confidence, richness, resilience, control! (Control, i.e. over the daimoniae of disintegrating multiplicity, of melancholia, of weary and sick-hearted lubricity, of suicidally precipitous febrility, etc. etc.)— A sense of reawakened strength, uprising, like a dear strangely, touchingly familiar Angel, from the seldom-stirring, ageless obscure depths of latency within me. Oh! like a wonderfully fresh, invigorating upland wind!'[5] Drug-induced such moods may have been, but they were also in tune with an aspect of the times. Mysticism was in the air in the early 1940s, as warfare nurtured in many thoughts of compensating sublimity, an eternity to set alongside loss. It was to be found increasingly, for example, in the art of Gascoyne's friend Graham Sutherland, a Catholic convert now working as a war artist. It could also be detected in the poetry of the period, and in its drama. Mysticism of a quasi-religious sort had in fact been around since the early thirties, when it had taken the form of a protest against the pervasive Marxist materialism of the left. 'Time present and time past | Are both perhaps present in time future | And time future contained in time past': So ran the opening of 'Burnt Norton', the first of T. S. Eliot's *Four Quartets*, published in 1936. The lines are frequently quoted as expressing Eliot's personal preoccupations in the late 1930s to early 1940s, but they also draw on philosophical concepts current in the period. The illusory nature of time's passage had been a key concept of the Cambridge philosopher J. M. McTaggart; in 1927 it had secured popular awareness in J. W. Dunne's best-selling *An Experiment With Time*, which had argued that our dreams possess in equal measure experiences of present, past, and future. The implications of this potentially mystical theory quickly influenced drama, including Eliot's own *Family Reunion* of 1939 and the middlebrow plays of McTaggart's one-time student J. B. Priestley,

5. *Collected Journals*, 334.

notably *Time and the Conways* of 1937 and *An Inspector Calls* (1945).[6] They even infiltrated commercial theatre of the period, and were parroted in some West End plays, endowing them with an appearance of profundity sometimes deserved, frequently not.

In the spring of 1939 Eliot's *Family Reunion* had been staged to great effect at the Westminster Theatre, where Michael Redgrave, soon to be David's heart-throb, had played the role of Harry, Lord Monchensey. Possibly in the light of its success, the Ambassadors Theatre decided in October 1942 to stage another, far less worthy, dramatization of the paradoxical effects of time, Ronald Millar's comic thriller *Murder from Memory*, hoping that it would see them through the Christmas season. Gascoyne went along for an audition.

Millar's potboiler opens on Christmas Eve in a train stuck in deep snow. Six passengers decide to hoof it to the nearest town and, after they have set out, a corpse is discovered by the guard in the adjacent compartment. The passengers shelter in a deserted country house where they are encouraged by the sleuth among them—Kyanston Carver of the Royal Psychical Society—to take part in a paranormal experiment. Painstakingly they reconstruct a crime that occurred in this place twenty years previously when the elder son and heir, with the assistance of the family butler, poisoned his father, whom he believed to be about to alter the will on behalf of his younger brother. Carver establishes that the elder son has since been done away with by the butler, who promptly appears to be confronted with crimes that Carver carefully re-enacts. The younger brother Frank Maitland then appears with his daughter, just before Carver—like a student of McTaggart or Priestley—articulates his salient and fashionable idea. 'Time is measureless,' he declares. 'The past, the present, and the future are all one. One has but to lift the curtain and the past is rediscovered.'[7]

One of the travellers is a 'tall pale youth' by the name of Fothergil. Fothergil opens the action with a resounding sneeze. He is required to sneeze a further twenty-nine times during the first act. When the travellers reach the deserted dwelling, he makes them tea and then retires upstairs with a temperature of 103. His role for the rest of the play consists of telling everybody he meets that his surname is spelt with one 'l', and twice sleepwalking draped in a

6. For a summary of this strand of popular thought, see J. B. Priestley, *Man and Time* (London: Aldus, 1964).
7. Ronald Millar, *Murder from Memory*, BL Lord Chamberlain's Collection LCP 1942/20, p. 16.

sheet, once in Act Two when he is mistaken for a ghost, and once in Act Three, when he inadvertently captures one of the fleeing accomplices, who gets entangled in his bedclothes.

Gascoyne was tall and pale, and as usual that winter he was suffering from catarrh. On the strength of his sneezing ability he got the part, and for the first time found himself in a fully professional company. The American movie actor Ernest Milton, once a blood-curdling Robespierre in *The Scarlet Pimpernel*, was the devious Carver. Roy Emerton, whose wife Catherine Lacey had enjoyed triumph as Agatha in *The Family Reunion*, played Brown, a proletarian stranger who is later discovered to have murdered the victim on the train. Peter Ustinov's wife Isolde Denham was Frank Maitland's daughter. The play received mixed reviews, and was not helped by the heavy smog that descended in early November. Intended to fill the Christmas slot, it soon, despite its heavy-handed notions about time, exhausted its appeal. After twenty performances it was taken off on 14 November.[8]

Gascoyne had spent enjoyable hours after each evening performance drinking and dining in the West End with Ustinov and Denham, but his affability hid deep-seated medical problems. Stress and irregular eating combined with a regular intake of amphetamine infusions had given him stomach ulcers, one of which burst in early December to agonizing effect. One morning three weeks after *Murder from Memory* closed, Win came upstairs to find him lying face down on the landing. She called the family doctor who diagnosed a ruptured stomach ulcer with uninterrupted loss of blood. Rushed to Mortlake Hospital, Gascoyne was given an immediate blood transfusion. Word of his condition spread via a sort of bush telegraph through the London acting fraternity. Redgrave soon learned of his illness. So did Roy Emerton, who informed Catherine Lacey. She came round to the hospital and pleaded with him for several hours to give up his debilitating and now evidently dangerous dependence on drugs. Her homily did little good. After six weeks Gascoyne discharged himself on an impulse, quitting the hospital in his dressing gown and slippers and travelling back to Teddington by bus. Win went back to collect his clothes. She was brusquely informed by the duty nurse that the hospital was glad to be rid of him.[9]

8. J. P. Wearing, *The London Stage: A Calendar of Plays and Players*, 4 vols. (London and Metuchen, NJ: Scarecrow, 1991), iv. 152.
9. Afterword to *Collected Journals*, 387–8. Also BL Lives, F1386, Side B. According to this later account, the matron on his ward told Win, 'We will never have him back again, even if he is dying'.

He was increasingly mercurial, and the chameleon qualities of his personality were now often evident to others. In the spring of 1943 he spent two weeks in Lewes in a house rented from Peter Watson by the artists Lucian Freud and John Craxton, to whom Watson had introduced him. Freud sketched three head portraits of him in charcoal and chalk, vivid in their contrast. In the first, Gascoyne is bespectacled and earnest, an open book at his side. In the second (see Plate 15), his eyes are closed and inward-looking, his hair neatly combed, his nose pointed and elongated, ears fastidious and small, mouth sensitively pursed, the hint of a scarf wrapped around his neck and Adam's apple. He could be praying or meditating. In the third (see Plate 16), his eyes are open and averted furtively to the left, his hair tight and African, his left ear swollen like a cauliflower ear, his right ear minuscule, almost stunted. The lips are full and sated, the neck straight and strong, the collar of the coat louche and loose. He seems like a trapped animal, or perhaps a con man on the run. That one of the most perceptive portraitists of the twentieth century could represent the same subject as scholar, mystic, and ruffian says as much about the temperamental changeability of the sitter as the versatility of the artist.

On Elizabeth Smart, to whom Barker introduced him that summer, he also made a multiple impression, by turns withdrawn into 'educative silences (Like brackets enclosing | Enormous sympathy | Too huge to speak)', irresponsible and tenderly kind. In July he came to stay with the two of them in the Cotswolds, where he broke a pane of glass in the basement and earned a polite but stern reprimand from a fellow tenant. By October they had moved with two young children to Hammersmith, where they occupied a house near the Thames loaned from A. P. Herbert, close to Trevelyan's home on Durham Wharf. Gascoyne came to stay on a night interrupted by V2 rockets. Sensitive to the apprehension around him, he calmed Smart and her babes by reading Baudelaire aloud to them, then as their fear grew more intense, graduated to the solemn hopefulness of Jouve, as forty years later Smart recalled:

> As the flames leapt
> And people ran with water
> I clutched my daughter
> And son, and wept.
> You said: 'Le désespoir a des ailes
> L'amour a pour aile nacrée
> Le désespoir

Les sociétés peuvent changer.'
You quoted Jouve.[10]

After the raid was over, Smart put the children to bed. She returned to the sitting room to find Gascoyne staring intently at a little dead mouse.[11]

The lull did not last long. Benefiting from his spell in the West End, Gascoyne now signed for a further tour of duty as an actor. His employers this time were not ENSA with their amateurish jinks before bored servicemen, but CEMA (the Committee for the Encouragement of Music and the Arts), a government-assisted organization aiming to bring work of high cultural value to the masses. CEMA had been formed in the early years of the war with the assistance of a grant from the Pilgrim Trust. It had a more elevated conception of its role than ENSA, concentrated on classical drama, and performed for the most part for workers in munition factories rather than troops. Its activities attracted jealous asides from commercial theatre managers in London and the provinces who pointed out that, while competing with the mainstream theatre in the material it offered, CEMA did so unfairly by citing its educational brief to avoid Entertainment Tax. The organization's cultural remit was broad, supporting musicians such as Imogen Holst on tour as well as assisting theatre companies: in 1946, under the direction of John Maynard Keynes, it would morph fairly naturally into the Arts Council of Great Britain. In early 1943, however, its aims were more modest and its arrangements sometimes makeshift.

Walter Hudd was a 47-year-old actor with a wide experience of rep, and a lively career taking supporting roles in films. He had first come to notice as Guildenstern in a modern-dress West End production of *Hamlet* in 1925, and had consolidated his reputation in 1931 by taking the role of Private Napoleon Meek, 'a Shavian notion of genius' based on T. E. Lawrence, in Bernard Shaw's *Too Good To Be True*.[12] In the summer of 1943, with CEMA backing, Hudd formed a company to take Shakespeare round the factories. His first production was *Hamlet*, in which he cast Gascoyne in the role of the Grave Digger. 'It was rather apt actually,' recalls Goossens. In the interval between painting sets in the Old Vic, she had joined Hudd's troupe as assistant stage manager, and remembered Gascoyne's lugubrious singing of the Grave

10. Elizabeth Smart, 'To David Gascoyne on his 65th birthday, some blue Himalayan poppies, first found on the roof of the world by an intrepid plant-hunter, and these inadequate verses by his friend Elizabeth', *Collected Poems*, introd. David Gascoyne (London: Paladin, 1992), 136–8.

11. Robert Fraser, *The Chameleon Poet: A Life of George Barker* (London: Jonathan Cape, 2001), 221.

12. See Michael Holroyd, *Bernard Shaw* (London: Chatto and Windus, 1997), 636.

Digger's song 'In youth when I did love, did love'. For *Twelfth Night*, his next production, Hudd gathered together quite a distinguished company. Thirty-year-old Wendy Hiller, an actress with classically severe features who had risen to prominence with her performance as Sally Hardcastle in the drama-tization of Walter Greenwood's *Love on the Dole* and Eliza Doolittle in *Pygmalion*, and had been directed by Shaw himself in *Major Barbara* and *Saint Joan*, was cast as the spirited Viola. Gascoyne had the sober role of the Priest. One evening the editor of Penguin New Writing, John Lehmann, found himself in the 'buried concert hall' of a munitions factory in the midlands watching this particular production. In Act V he was surprised to 'see the tall, bowed figure of a well-known poet cross the stage with painful nervousness, clad in the priest's robes, and a few minutes later, with even greater nervous-ness, stumble through his half-dozen lines: David Gascoyne'.[13]

Anne Goossens's principal memory at this period is of a harassed young man in a mackintosh dashing to meet a train, encumbered by large bags full of assorted volumes, with which he had to be helped in and out of the doors of carriages. 'I used to run after him. He always had ten, twelve or twenty books and as I was the ASM I had to get him on and off trains all of time, with all these books.'[14] In this manner he ferried his growing library from various far-flung cities to London, arriving unpredictably at any hour of the day or night to spread out his trophies on the limited floor space in Teddington. At equally unsociable hours he would turn up in Richmond where Bettina Shaw-Lawrence had now moved with her parents, occupy-ing an impressively fronted Queen Anne residence at 30 The Green. The family got used to David appearing out of the blue in a grubby mackintosh, clutching bulging bibliophiliac acquisitions that he then spread on the car-pet before talking excitedly for hours, or else sinking into an imponderable brown study.

His amphetamine dependency had not abated. To Goossens he seemed a 'lost soul. War was wearing him out. And he didn't do himself any favours by these drugs. What was he doing?' she asked me rhetorically, 'destroying himself because the world was being destroyed? He had started to halluci-nate too.' The answer is that, along with several writers of his own genera-tion and the generation above it—Muriel Spark and Evelyn Waugh among them—Gascoyne was now paying the price of his self-medication with

13. John Lehmann, *I and My Brother* (London: Longman 1960), 251.
14. Interview with Anne Goossens, 3 June 2008.

morbid drug poisoning.[15] It was to be another twelve years before amphetamine psychosis was fully recognized as a medical condition—though warning sounds had already been made, especially in America—but the symptoms are already detectable in several accounts of David's behaviour at this time. On one occasion when staying at 30 The Green he insisted on addressing his remarks to an invisible Irishman. On another even more distressing afternoon, Bettina was upstairs in the studio that occupied most of the second floor of the house when her mother entered hurriedly, locked the door behind her, and announced that David had just attempted to strangle her.[16]

It is a moot point how much the intensity of his poetry at this time owes to such seizures, and how much to the influence of Jouve, so central to his thinking that year. His poems were becoming more mystical, close in mood to Jouve's redemptive Catholicism with its images of hope swelling out of darkness, despair sprouting wings. Perhaps his best known poem of the period adapts some lines of Jouve's about the compassionate power of Christ, directing them at the hanging figure of the Saviour on the Cross recalled from the Isenheim altarpiece by Grünewald, to a reproduction of which Christian Zervos had drawn to his attention before the war, the central panel of its triptych showing a pockmarked, skinny, victimized Jesus, shocking in His total vulnerability. 'Ecce homo', however, was far from being a Christian poem in any doctrinaire or sectarian sense. Its Jesus, 'Christ of Revolution and of Poetry', is a figure of universal sympathy, compassion, and understanding, closer to the radical humanitarian Tristan Tzara had commended to Gascoyne in Paris six years previously than to the numinous person of the Trinity alluded to in the creeds. Like Michael Tippett in *A Child of Our Time*, the topical and ecumenical oratorio of 1941, Gascoyne was seeking salves for a moment of crisis, a gospel for outcasts, a reproof for unthinking conformity:

> Involved in their own sophistry
> The black priest and the upright man
> Faced by subversive truth shall he struck dumb,
> Christ of Revolution and of Poetry,
> While the rejected and condemned become
> Agents of the divine.[17]

15. See Evelyn Waugh, *The Ordeal of Gilbert Pinfold: A Conversation Piece* (London: Chapman and Hall, 1957); Martin Stannard, *Muriel Spark: The Biography* (London: Weidenfeld and Nicolson, 2009), 151–7.

16. Interview with Bettina Shaw-Lawrence, 24 May 2009.

17. *Poems 1937–1942*, 5–7; *Collected Poems* (1965), 44–6.

Other poems hark back more explicitly to the celebrations of the Eucharist at Salisbury. One of the most puzzling is 'Mozart: Sursum Corda', written for the South African composer Priaulx Rainier, whom Gascoyne had met when she was studying with Nadia Boulanger in Paris before the war. It derives from Jouve's appreciation of the darker shades in Mozart, which David shared. The oddity unnoticed by some readers is that the 'Sursum Corda' is one section of the ordinary of the Mass which Mozart himself never set. Few composers have done so, for the reason that its invocation 'Lift up your hearts' is addressed—or more usually intoned—by the celebrant priest to the people at the moment of the elevation of the host. The 'Sursum Corda' as such requires no choral embellishment. Gascoyne's poem is an evocation of some awful silence, imagining music Mozart—or, strictly speaking Jouve's Mozart—might have supplied to clothe meanings 'beyond our speech':

> Filters the sunlight from the knife-bright wind
> And rarifies the rumour-burdened air
> The heart's receptive chalice in pure hands upheld
> Towards the sostenuto of the sky
>
> Supernal voices flood the ear of clay
> And transpierce the dense skull: Reveal
> The immaterial world concealed
> By mortal deafness and the screen of sense
>
> World of transparency and last release
> And world within the world. Beyond our speech
> To tell what equinoxes of the infinite
> The spirit ranges in its rare utmost flight.[18]

Happily he had just discovered an editor of fitful brilliance. Meary James Thurairajah Tambimuttu was a fair-to-middling poet with an astute eye for merit in others, and an uncanny instinct for bringing it to light. In too many memoirs of the period the editor of *Poetry London* features as a sort of obliging oriental marionette, or else a sociable bar fly with a tendency to lose manuscripts in taxis. But Tambi was from one of the most intellectually distinguished families in Ceylon; his uncle was the eminent art critic and philosopher Ananda Coomaraswamy, and since arriving in London in 1938 he had built a reputation, a magazine, and a publishing house. The headquarters

18. *Poems 1937–1942*, 14; *Collected Poems* (1965), 53.

for all three were in one of the most elegant districts in London, at 27 Manchester Square to the north of Wigmore Street. The building was later to be destroyed by bombs, and in 1943 the brilliance of its surroundings was dimmed: the Wallace Collection opposite had moved into storage, and many of the offices around were temporarily unoccupied. But Tambimuttu had flair as well as flamboyance, sureness of ear along with civility, generosity as well as charm. He also possessed an understanding financial backer in Peter Watson, who bankrolled both the magazine and the associated book imprint Editions Poetry London while allowing Tambi unfettered artistic control. The only palpable influence Watson brought to bear was an enthusiasm for the graphic arts and vocal and financial support for the house's on-going programme of marrying poetry with visual art. It was Tambi's idea that a painter should be brought in to design and illustrate each of his books. Thus Barbara Hepworth illustrated Kathleen Raine, and Henry Moore a book by John Maynard Keynes's poet son, Nicholas.

When Tambi accepted Gascoyne's *Poems 1937–1942* that summer, he asked him which artist he would like to illustrate it. Watson had moved his collection of modern art from Berkeley Square to a house in Queen's Gate, where among the exhibits was *Entrance to a Lane*. Gascoyne already felt an affinity with Sutherland's work: he asked Watson to approach him, and the typescript was sent to the White House in Trottiscliffe.

The poetry invited illustration. Gascoyne had brought together his most intense poems of the previous five years, positioning them as a series of five themed sequences. 'Ecce Homo', for example, now stood as the culmination of the seven-movement sequence 'Miserere', in which phases from Christian liturgy and art—the Tenebrae of Passion week, the Pietà of Michelangelo, the De Profundis of Psalm 130, the Kyrie of the Latin mass, Lachrymae or 'Tears'— led up to this moment of sacrificial and inclusive expiation. 'Miserere' was followed by a series of 'Metaphysical' pieces mostly written in Paris between 1937 and 1938, including poems for Wolf Berthold, Fondane, and Rainier, and translations from Jouve's volume of 1937, *Matière celeste*. There ensued the elegiac stanzas for Alban Berg in their French realization of 1939, then a further set of 'Personal' poems and elegies, including the elegy for Roughton. The book closed with a set of meditations on 'Time and Place' following the progress of the war beginning with 'Snow in Europe' and ending with 'The Gravel-Pit Field' and a translation of Supervielle's 'Rain and the Tyrants'.

The disposition of these pieces was highly musical, radiating outwards from the stanzas to Berg, themselves scored as a set of contrasted movements along the lines of the composer's own *Lyric Suite*, to encompass a larger, equally varied form akin to an extended work of chamber music. Sutherland perceived the form, but he also delved into its sad heart. For each movement he provided a titled graphic frontispiece employing a mixture of gouache, inks, and coloured chalk (see Plate 18). The frontispiece to 'Miserere' showed a comet in mid-air, its tail behind it like the shaggy locks of a decapitated head, suspended over a wintry, mountainous landscape soaked in blood: the comet reminded Gascoyne himself of the Bayeux Tapestry, and the atmosphere of the rending of the veil of the temple following the death of Christ. The introductory page to the 'Metaphysical Poems' was more elusive, displaying a shrouded form whose blank face resembles the Sacred Heart of Catholic iconography, above which rise three plumes which Gascoyne thought 'could well be transmuted flames, appearing against a pink-tinged sky'.[19] The plate supplied for the Berg elegy was the most figurative and Blake-like. A prostrate, skeletal figure like those to be seen on medieval sepulchres, but disconcertingly alive and alert, lies beneath an upper panel displaying a riot of clashing shapes suggestive of an iceberg about to strike an ocean liner by night. In the frontispiece to the 'Personal Poems' a horseshoe-shaped ivory claw extends from the right. Along its upper side clambers a waif-like figure reduced in scale so that the claw seems like a vast coil or circular ridge he must surmount or, as the poet himself put it, 'the labyrinthine path of one both on the horns of a dilemma and preoccupied with the thorn in the flesh'. In the subtitle page to the poems of 'Time and Place' two stone monoliths rose like giant incisors above a sea creature with writhing arms forming a rough-and-ready swastika. They are joined at the top by a bracket fastened to each by an eye-shaped bolt, the one on the left resembling a crescent moon and that on the left a stricken sun.

The dust jacket was equally striking. The front cover displayed a range of four volcanic peaks skewered by a horizontal spear or, as Gascoyne thought, a pen. The back cover derived directly from Gascoyne's version of Jouve's poem 'Les Papillons' from *Matière céleste*. In French the title means butterflies but, perhaps thinking of the frolicsome piano accompaniment to Debussy's song of the same name, Gascoyne had rendered it as 'Moths', mindful of Freudian echoes and Jouve's implied evocation of rising sexual sensations,

---

19. For Gascoyne's account, see David Gascoyne, 'PL Editions and Graham Sutherland', *Tambimutu, Bridge Between Two Worlds*, ed. Jane Williams, introd. Robin Waterfield (London: Peter Owen, 1989), 112–18.

'celestial matter'. Sutherland had transmuted the moths into a cluster of insect forms silhouetted against the sea and an enormous, liquidly descending sun. Winged and vengeful, they resemble a flight of armed hornets, or possibly bombers departing on a night raid.

This after all was war poetry in a special, though admittedly a civilian, sense. To accompany it Sutherland has supplied a post-Surrealist vision of wartime. Undeniably their collaboration was enhanced by a common religious response to the unfolding tragedy. The combination hints at a theological interpretation of suffering akin to the prison writing of Dietrich Bonhoeffer, an ethical rejoinder to a variety of evil very much of its time. The influence between poet and painter was mutual, and Sutherland gained as much as he gave. Interestingly, the one poem of Gascoyne's he did not illustrate directly was 'Ecce Homo', with its echoes of Grünewald's altarpiece. Yet a little more than a year after the book's publication Sutherland produced a painting called simply *Crucifixion* in which the posture of the body and the upturned hands irresistibly recall Grünewald, just as they recall Gascoyne's poem. In the same year, Sutherland's friend Francis Bacon produced *Studies for Four Figures at the Base of the Cross*, the contorted lines of which resemble the limbs of the Christ figure in Sutherland's painting, and the twisted girders of his warscapes. Isolated Gascoyne may have been. He was far from being alone.

17

Exit Pursued by Poles

Gascoyne's latest volume was received more warmly than anything he had so far written, though naturally he had to share the plaudits with Sutherland. The *New Statesman* praised him for 'an astonishing purity of diction and command of the long swift line', and enthused: 'Style! Its appearance today rouses an incredulous pleasure.' In *Time and Tide* C. Day Lewis observed that 'his verse rings true and speaks unequivocally from the heart of his personal conflict'. 'The drawings', he added 'are symbolic, sombre, finely illustrative of the poems' moods.' Even Spender, inclined to be sniffy in the past, pulled out a few organ stops of appreciation. 'David Gascoyne', he announced in *The Tribune*, 'is perhaps the one outstanding pure poet among the young English writers living today . . . The great virtue of Gascoyne's poetry is that it makes one feel that what is said could not have been said in any other way. It is eloquent, without being facile, sensuous, moving and perfectly sincere.' In a late night radio broadcast on the BBC Home Service, Cyril Connolly introduced a personal selection from the poems by calling attention to their astringent music, their uncompromising artistic courage. 'They take us', he observed, 'in their chill, calm, sensitive language as near the edge of the precipice as a human being is able to go and still turn back.' As one of Watson's familiars, Connolly had been privy to the book's mode of production, so he went on to deliver an implied compliment to Sutherland and Tambi for the visual values of a publication 'illustrated in a way which makes the book a delight to possess, and which holds out a wonderful prospect of future collaboration between publishers, poets, and artists'.[1]

---

1. Quoted on the dust jacket of the third impression of *Poems 1937–1942* (London: PL Editions, 1948), transcribed from Robin Waterfield's personal copy, marked 'Isfahan, 1962'.

Such comments might well have cheered Gascoyne up. Instead he was consumed with shame, and a feeling of having realized neither his early promise nor his own high standards. So certain was he that he had disgraced himself that when Connolly's radio programme was broadcast in the first week of January 1944, he could not bring himself to tune in. Afterwards he wrote to Cyril:

> This is just a brief line of thanks—for all the agreeable things I'm told you said about my book of verse over the air the other night. I do wish I'd been listening. I should have been had I realized you would be giving a talk at that time.
>
> For quite a time now I'd been feeling a little regretfully that you were, if anything, disappointed in my work, and considered I had failed to live up to whatever small precocious promise I may have shown at the time you first knew me (just over ten years ago, I realise to my astonishment!). So it gives me a very real pleasure that you should have spoken about me so kindly and encouragingly.[2]

In attributing his own perceptions of blighted promise to Connolly, Gascoyne was responding partly to ongoing private despondency, and partly to a genuine hiatus in his public image. Certainly, he could now appear very differently to different people. In a set of publicity shots with Tambi taken that month in Hyde Park, he looks masterful beside the shorter editor: legs astride like flying buttresses, hands clasped smartly behind his back, woollen tie flying stylishly in the breeze, he resembles a confident squadron leader in mufti. Off camera, however, and especially with strangers, he could seem far less self-assured, the grandeur touchy and jumpy, the apparent gloominess a pose. For some time he had been in correspondence with the poet Derek Stanford, who was working for the Non-Combatant Corps and co-editing the short-lived magazine *X6*. Early in 1944, with Charles Wrey Gardiner, editor of the *Poetry Review* in tow, Stanford arranged to meet him in a milk bar situated off Leicester Square. It was during the nightly blackout, and central London was 'taxi haunted':

> There, in an illuminated cavern, sat Gascoyne looking rather like a moth dazzled with excess of light. My friend, who knew him, introduced us, the poet seeming nervous and tense. He had the kind of unhappy good looks attributed to heroes of the Romantic Movement. His hands were 'pale-aesthetic looking'

2. Gascoyne to Cyril Connolly, 5 Jan. 1944, Berg, Box 44.

and the line of his nose proclaimed a certain hauteur...Gascoyne indeed is a curious mixture of the aristocrat and the republican. Plagued by tiresome women, he once resorted to the royal plural and ended the palaver with the statement 'We have spoken'...I was told how, once, he had been seen at a fancy dress party, standing in the corner with a rope around his throat. As he was wearing an ordinary lounge-suit, a friend asked him whom he was representing. 'Don't you see the rope?' Gascoyne replied. 'I'm Gérard de Nerval', naming a nineteenth-century French poet who had hung himself one night from the window of his lodgings. The *humeur noire* is typical of him.[3]

The humour could also be frivolous, closer to irrepressible private fun. Priaulx Rainier accompanied him to the Wigmore Hall in October 1944 to hear a performance of Benjamin Britten's recent cantata *Rejoice in the Lamb*, a setting of an ecstatically devotional poem by the eighteenth-century scholar, poet, and asylum inmate Christopher Smart. The text with its multiple eccentric aphorisms provoked in this habitually melancholy poet, as she reported to her sister afterwards, a 'wonderful mood of witticisms, making nonsense rhymes and inverting the proverbs'.[4]

With those who knew him intimately, these varied masks could slip completely, revealing a profoundly destabilized state of mind lurking beneath. Kathleen Raine had known him in his decorous incarnation during the late 1930s as Boy Wonder of the Surrealist Movement and Mass Observation. She encountered him again at the time of the publication of *Poems 1937–1942* and, unaware as yet of his drug habit, was astonished and shocked at the change, 'for now he looked racked, tormented, his large hands forever moving nervously, twisting a handkerchief, his deer-like eyes haunted; his teeth were decayed, his skin grey. He still had no mask or defensive barricade, and he still had the same sweetness; and where he sensed sympathy he assumed in others a truth of feeling equal to his own.' It seemed to her little short of miraculous that someone so overwhelmed by life could have produced those recent poems. How had a 'sensitivity so vulnerable as his survived and found eloquence in a world so ruinous'?[5] Yet he had, 'the greatness...apparent to all who care for poetry'.

3. Derek Stanford, 'David Gascoyne: A Portrait', MS and TS, Berg, Box 44; published in *The Scotsman*, 3–4 Aug. 1965; reprinted in revised form in Derek Stanford, *Inside the Forties* (London: Sigwick Jackson, 1977), 109.
4. Priaulx Rainier to Nella Rainier, 7 Oct. 1944, quoted in June Opie, *'Come and Listen to the Stars Singing': A Pictorial Biography* (Penzance: Alan Hodge, 1988), 31–4.
5. Kathleen Raine, *Autobiographies* (London: Skoob Books, 1991), 226–7.

If Gascoyne was sending out mixed messages, the reactions to—and expectations of—him flooding in from the wider world were similarly contradictory. Those trickling through with difficulty from mainland Europe were especially so. From Châtel-Guyon a fitful message arrived, a blast from the past: Roland Cailleux sent him a prospectus for his recently published first novel with the cryptic appeal 'Dear David, write to me. Here is my first book. I have found you again by sheer luck.'[6] Wary of Cailleux's foxiness and his intentions, he did not reply. Then from Switzerland in August he heard from Blanche Reverchon, spurred into communicability by the Liberation of Paris that month. She and Jouve were now planning on returning to Paris in September. Meanwhile she sent him a plight of her faith: 'Someone', she wrote 'has written that these recent times should have been dedicated to poets—I believe above all that they have been times in which "poetic souls" (God alone knows who these are) have been most cruelly bombarded.' When David responded, she eagerly wrote back, 'My friend, your letter arrived here miraculously and has given me the strongest desire to see you…But where, and how?'[7]

It was not going to be easy to repair these human bridges with Europe. The Continent was still in turmoil, and recreational travel was out of the question for all except the very rich. Voices flickered out of the general darkness like probing searchlights and then, as like as not, they faded. The following year with the liberation of the Eastern Front, Gascoyne and Herbert Read each received a heartfelt typed appeal from the Czech Devětsil Movement. Founded in Prague in November 1920 under the leadership of Karel Teige, Devětsil had hosted one of the earliest Dada events. It had since diversified to embrace Futurism and Constructivism, and had always prided itself on its spreading network of international connections. In 1935, Gascoyne had talked with Teige and several of his colleagues during the Conference for Cultural Freedom at L'Odéon. Since the invasion of 1940, however, its leaders had spent the duration under official embargo, cut off from what had remained of the artistic vanguard in Western Europe. Many outsiders had simply assumed that the movement had petered out. Unleashed from official restraint, the leading lights of the movement were now desperate to get in touch, and Teige and two colleagues wrote to David: 'Locked up deeply in the grey centre of German Europe and cut off for six years

6. Roland Cailleux to Gascoyne, Beinecke, Box 1, Folder 2.
7. Blanche Reverchon to David Gascoyne, 7 Aug. 1944, Beinecke, Box 1, Folder 11.

from the whole world, we are not at all informed about the present state of the group of surrealists in England and because it was impossible for us until now to get in touch with André Breton, we don't know anything at all about the situation of this movement in the world in general. To our friends who remained in France and whose addresses we did not know we could write only this month. We would be very happy if you would be so very kind as to inform us as precisely as far as possible about the present situation in England as well as about the situation of Breton and about his relation to those who remained in France. We are sure that we will be able to establish permanently collaboration with you and expect impatiently news from you.'[8]

Breton had in fact moved to the United States in 1941, boarding the same crowded steamer in Marseilles as Claude Lévi-Strauss, who had found him 'very much out of place *dans cette galère*...wrapped in his thick nap overcoat, he looked like a blue bear'.[9] Passing through Martinique, he had discovered yet another Surrealist *ingénu* in the poet Aimé Césaire, whose *Cahier d'un retour au pays natal* he had soon seen into print. By the close of hostilities he was back in France, but Gascoyne had long since lost touch with him. Nor was David himself swimming any longer in the Surrealist mainstream, or interested in so doing. He had lost whatever faith he once tentatively held in the integrity of the movement, and his preoccupations in any case had turned elsewhere: towards Existentialism and new ways of expressing religious faith. This fundamental reorientation of direction was as yet known to and appreciated by only a limited number of individuals, almost exclusively in England. He was thus faced with an acute and growing inconsistency between the way that he saw himself and the ways in which he was regarded by many others, especially abroad. Connolly for one knew this better than most, and had been at pains to follow his spiritual progress. To the wider international circle, though, conscious of his pre-war reputation but ignorant of the inner movements of his mind, he was still— and perhaps always would be—the wunderkind of Surrealism.

There were other, more personal reasons, why he was coming to feel more and more disorientated. Up until the summer of 1944, whatever the

8. Karel Teige, Toyen, Ludvik Toman, and Jindřich Heisler to David Gascoyne, 24 Sept. 1945, Beinecke, Box 1, Folder 14.
9. Claude Lévi-Strauss, *Tristes Tropiques*, trans. John and Doreen Weightman (London; Penguin, 1973), 26.

ups and downs of his condition, Gascoyne had one constant recourse and resting place: he could always spend weeks at a time quietly if uneventfully at home with his parents in Middlesex. But in 1944 Leslie Gascoyne retired from the bank. On their modest savings, and relying on their residual vigour and health, he and Win decided to emigrate to British Vancouver where they could be close to her only sister, who had spent much of her life in Canada after a childhood being cared for by their mother's relatives in Yorkshire. Tony—the younger of the twins, still serving with the armed forces—promised to join them there after his demobilization. The move left David with no permanent address in London, and more exposed than ever to the vicissitudes of his own moods, circumstances, and income. He also became distressed on learning that, whilst sorting through their effects in Grove Terrace, his parents had found it necessary to dispose of the contents of a large tallboy in his bedroom containing precious ephemera brought back from Paris in 1935. The small loss exacerbated the greater. By Christmas, his friends were slowly becoming aware that something was more than usually amiss with David. It had long been his habit, for example, to visit the Shaw-Lawrence family in Richmond every few weeks. He had not been there for months, so in December Bettina sent him a card of Carlo Crivelli's *Annunciation* with the concerned message 'Everyone is very sorry to hear you're ill david dear. Do get well quickly.'[10] In Canada too, Leslie and Win, though now scarcely able to help, became aware, mostly from his silences, that David's habitual depression was fast turning into something approaching a breakdown.

It was in these circumstances, and in this state of mind, that he was standing one morning in the outer office of Poetry London in Manchester Square when someone handed him an envelope postmarked 'Skodsborg, Denmark'. He knew the place name since several months earlier, in an attempt to ease his loneliness and to piece together the disjoined segments of his pre-war existence, he had sent an enquiry to this affluent coastal suburb of Copenhagen addressed to the one individual with whom he was convinced he had once established a near-perfect mental and physical accord: Bent von Müllen, from whom he had not heard for five and a half years. The message inside the envelope was from Bent's mother. As he later recalled the contents, they starkly informed him that, in the closing months

---

10. Bettina Shaw-Lawrence to David Gascoyne, Dec. 1944, Beinecke, Box 1, Folder 13.

of the Nazi Occupation, Bent, his father, and four of their neighbours had been rounded up by the authorities in reprisal for the assassination of a Gestapo officer by a group of the Danish Resistance. They were summarily hanged. This is not the version of Bent's death preserved in the archives of the Danish Resistance Movement in Copenhagen, which have an even more gruelling tale to tell. Gascoyne was never to learn the full horror of the truth. Yet even the milder version that he absorbed was fast plunging him into night; it was deepened by the revelations now emerging about the fate of internees in the German death camps, including Benjamin Fondane, gassed at Birkenau on 3 October 1944.[11]

His emotional decline steepened. By the summer of 1945 Tambi, who had been in touch over the second impression of *Poems 1937–1942*, had become sufficiently concerned to intervene. He wrote to David on 8 June, remarking 'I understand how you must be feeling after this period of nerve strain and I do see that we must arrange for you to have a rest.' He offered to contact 'a friend, Dr Wells, who is a painter and writer as well as a good surgeon, of the Scilly Isles' to see if he could arrange for a period of recuperation for Gascoyne in a cottage in the Scillies.[12]

Tambi had posted his letter to Teddington, but to his surprise the reply came from Downside Crescent Gardens in Hampstead. Rescue, it appeared, had arrived in the shape of the latest of David's devoted and strong women. Gascoyne owed this particular introduction to a strong-minded editor, Gwendoline Murphy, who in April had written to him from Cornwall requesting permission to include three of his poems in an anthology. She had added a postscript: 'My friend Mrs Eric Crozier is also extremely fond of your poetry. I can't find the letter at the moment where she writes at length upon it, but I have a later one where she is speaking about a bad anthology: "It seems guarded, half-hearted, almost mean verse. No magic. No goodness. No Poetry. So shut it and open the Gascoyne."'[13]

Biddy Crozier, born Ada Margaret Johns and, a year older than David, had trained as a stage designer, and had also been an actress. In 1936 she had married the producer and dramaturge Eric Crozier, who had returned from studying drama in Paris. From 1939 they had worked together at the Old Vic, he as assistant to Tyrone Guthrie, she as a teacher at the London Drama Studio

---

11. Afterword to *Collected Journals*, 397–8.
12. Tambimuttu to Gascoyne, 8 and 11 June 1945, Beinecke, Box 1, Folder 10.
13. Gwendoline Murphy to Gascoyne, 13 Apr. 1945, Beinecke, Box 1, Folder 9.

run by the French acting theorist Michel Saint-Denis with George Devine and Marius Goring. Since 1942 she had been working as a staff director at the Sadler's Wells, where her husband had produced Smetana's *Bartered Bride* with Peter Pears in the tenor lead. Pears had introduced him to his friend Benjamin Britten, who had recently asked him if he would direct at the Wells his new opera *Peter Grimes*, with a libretto by Montagu Slater from a poem by George Crabbe, with Pears in the title role. In June 1945 the three men were deeply involved in rehearsals for this, the theatre's latest, risky production. Britten and Pears had formed a vibrant working bond with Crozier, who like them had been a conscientious objector, a fact which rendered them all unpopular with demobbed members of the cast, management, and stage crew.

Peter Grimes is a work about social ostracism, mirroring as it happened the sexual isolation of composer and lead singer and, as it now transpired, the political isolation of both, as well as of their increasingly overworked director. The friction had taken a toll on Crozier's marriage, which was fast falling apart. Early in June Mrs Murphy put David in contact with Biddy, who offered him a room in her home with her preoccupied and alienated husband, and their two daughters. On 7 June, the day before the first of Tambi's two sympathetic letters, she and David attended the première of Britten's opera together. He continued staying on and off at her Downside Crescent Gardens flat for much of the next nine years, using it as a London base even when, from 1947, his visits to France resumed.

The address was highly convenient for maintaining cultural contacts. William Glock, now married to John Davenport's estranged wife Clement, with whom he had eloped in the early years of the war, was living just up the hill. There were concert parties and soirées. David slept for much of the day, and read for much of the night. Abstruse volumes crowded the table-tops, and his notebooks abounded with references to an impressive and proliferating body of reading: to Kierkegaard, to Heidegger and Heidegger's French disciples, to Chestov and his fellow Russian exile and sage Berdayev, to the theologians Martin Buber and Karl Barth; to the mystics Paracelsus and Swedenborg and Boehme and Thomas Traherne. Biddy herself brooded over these philosophical problems, strong but herself quite moody, as a friend remembered her, with an 'air of great distinction and fastidiousness: tall and thin, with large burning eyes, she had a look of being expensively dressed, even in time of penury'.[14]

---

14. Paddy Fraser, 'G. S. Fraser: A Memoir', *Jacket*, 20 (Dec. 2002), http://jacketmagazine.com/20/fraser.html/

She was also, and usefully, quite habituated to the vagaries of poets, having at various times given house room to W. S. Graham and even Tambi, whose attentions she had sometimes needed to fend off. She had little need to fend off David's. Some indication of his self-image at this time emerges from a reply to a letter received from Sheila Legge, one-time Surrealist Phantom of the Burlington Gallery, now a married book collector living with her two children in St Mawes, Cornwall. In November 1945 she wrote requesting his assistance in procuring a signed first edition of Sartre's *La Nausée*. Gascoyne replied that he had lost contact with Sartre, who had once been quite happy for him to translate the book provided a publisher could be found for the result, which at the time had not been possible. But Sheila's personal circumstances stirred in him mixed feelings of envy, wistfulness, and emotional reluctance:

> I am awfully glad you're—I nearly said settled down, which is an odious phrase and not what I mean, which I'm sure you know (what I mean)—to a husband and children. I envy you very much; still, I suppose there's still time for me to emulate—I don't know about children, though I think that the older I get the more sentimental about them I become—I certainly don't want to remain single all of my life. I'm dreadfully backward, though, in some ways.[15]

If this was intended as a confession, it was an oblique and guarded one, and even avoided the main point. Biddy and David were growing increasingly, if not quite contentedly, close. By mid-1946 Crozier, who was much involved with Britten projects, including the opera *The Rape of Lucretia* and the film *A Young Person's Guide to the Orchestra* (for which he had written the script), had withdrawn from the family home in high dudgeon, convinced Gascoyne and his wife were lovers. This was almost certainly not the case in any technical sense. The fact remained that from that moment on David was, as far as many observers were concerned, living with another man's wife. Two years later Crozier, now Britten's regular librettist, was to find a second spouse in the mezzo-soprano Nancy Evans, for whom he and Britten were to write the opera *Albert Herring*. The two children by his marriage to Biddy, however, remained with her, and however improbably, with Gascoyne.

Further light on their relationship is shed by a vivid recollection of the Welsh-born poet and physician Dannie Abse who, towards the end of this

15. Gascoyne to Sheila Legge, 1 Dec. 1945, Beinecke, Box 1, Folder 8.

period, was living in a flat in nearby Belsize Park with his wife and young daughter. One afternoon, the bell started insistently ringing downstairs. Abse went down and opened the door to reveal Gascoyne, whom he vaguely recalled from a reading at the Crown and Greyhound pub in Dulwich, standing out in the road:

> Before I could say a word he, 'wild of eye', agitated, began to babble, 'I'm being pursued by a Pole. Ever since I left the midwifery hospital, he's been following me.'
> 'Midwifery hospital?'
> I searched his haunted, rather handsome face.
> 'They locked me up there in a padded cell. I escaped. Please let me in. Please, please, please. . . .'
> 'He chased me all the way,' David Gascoyne continued desperately. 'That Pole can't be far. He can't be far.'

Upstairs, Abse introduced Gascoyne to his family. He ignored them, pleading, 'Ring Biddy Crozier, ring Biddy. Tell her I'm besieged.' Abse, who had heard the name somewhere, looked her up in the directory and phoned. 'When I did speak to her,' he later recalled, 'Biddy Crozier asked for my address. 'You're not too far away,' she said. 'I won't be long. Tell David I'm coming. I'll come at once.'[16]

Biddy was, albeit exasperatedly, fond of this intermittently demented man. In these circumstances his attitude of semi-involvement—somehow there, yet not there—sometimes infuriated her. As for the children he told Sheila that he was growing sentimental towards, he was having to cope with hers while remaining in an essential inner part of his mind detached from this whole makeshift setting. The arrangement had seen him through a breakdown, and it had put a roof over his head. Biddy was almost certainly more committed to the relationship than he could ever be. As her demands on him grew, so did David's resentment of her.

The rows were intensified by Biddy's uncertainty as to her position: was she platonic spouse, secretary, or nurse? He could pick a quarrel when he needed to, and so could she: as one friend remembered, 'her voice was soft and deep with an occasional high, cracked note at moments of crisis'. One day she borrowed one of David's crammed commonplace books, and scrawled across the page an accusatory message: 'Ages ago you asked to stay here . . . the sort of ménage where there are children and not "unwanted"

---

16. Dannie Abse, *The Presence* (London: Hutchinson, 2007), 220–1.

ones is rather an eccentric taste and not everyone's cup of tea. We are both too conjugally nervous to live well in an atmosphere charged with emotion and are both most ourselves when the general atmosphere is quiet and friendly and thus quiet friendliness exists only when there is real confidence and a single openness between persons. It is not lack of probity but the capacity for probity that makes between person and person the continually recreated relationship we call friendship.'[17]

Yet Biddy too was interested in philosophy, now his abiding concern. His mysticism, however, flummoxed her. His interests, to those unaware of their intellectual roots, were increasingly strange. Charing Cross Road and Cecil Court lay a convenient tube ride away down the Northern Line. He haunted basements of books, rummaging for oddities and arcana. One morning, delving into the lower shelves at Watkins' Bookshop, he came across a heavy tome entitled *OAHSPE: A New Bible*, written in 1891 by the cranky Ohio-born dentist and mystic John Ballou Newbrough, reputedly via automatic writing assisted, as Gascoyne came to surmise, by an intake of anaesthetic ether. He found the passage:

> The end of the dawn is near at hand: I will give a feast, a very great feast. Go ye and survey the ground from Croashivi to the Lakes of Oochi-loo, in ethereal and for the length thereof make ye a width in the form of Fete; and the road of the Fete shall be sufficient for the passage of twelve avalanzas abreast; and the depth of Fete shall be as from the surface of the earth unto Chinvat.[18]

He acquired the book, but took it back after a few days as unsuitable reading matter for someone in his state of mind. He was, he was quite aware, growing more and more suggestible, and the atmosphere of post-war tension did not help. In January 1946, he applied for a reissue of his reader's ticket at the British Museum Library. The application form has survived, countersigned by Connolly.[19] Next to the question 'Profession of Occupation', Gascoyne has entered 'Poet-Seer'. Against the query 'Purpose or kind of books for which the library is chiefly required' he has written, in a neat hand, 'Preparation of case for Prosecution of the Last Judgement'. It is a wonder they let him in.

17. Biddy Crozier, comment inserted in Gascoyne's *A Little Book of Odds and Ends*, BL Add. 56047, fo. 52.
18. *Selected Prose*, 141.
19. Application for British Museum Library Pass, Beinecke, Box 7, Folder 79.

18

Ayer Absconditus

The Last Judgement had certainly become for him a matter of overriding concern. Six years previously, under the threat of impending war, Gascoyne had begun drafting a prose work with that exact and apocalyptic title. Now there loomed a fresh set of dangers in the shape of the mushroom clouds pluming over American atom bomb test sites in the South Pacific. In the autumn of 1945 Gascoyne, who seemed to be 'in an extremely nervous condition', buttonholed Stephen Spender. The nuclear explosion at Hiroshima, he explained, had been no isolated event. It had set off 'an explosion inside people's heads'. There was as a result 'a new unity of human consciousness' unknown to any previous period of human history.[1] As, early in 1946, preparations got under way in the Marshall Islands for the series of tests known as 'Operation Crossroads', he revived the typescript of *The Last Judgement* and noted down on its title page each test date as it was announced. As each one came and went without world-shattering incident, he disconsolately crossed the date out.

A few weeks later he was sitting in the front room of Downshire Crescent Gardens clasping a fountain pen in his right hand and the seat of his chair with his left, and thinking about Blaise Pascal. The passage he had in mind was Proposition 205 of the *Pensées* in which the French philosopher shudders at the thought of the immense, dark interstellar void. But there was also a void within:

Pascal towards the end of his life appears to have become obsessed by the consciousness of his own inner existence; he is said to have referred continually to what he described as an 'abyss' on his left side and to have had always to protect himself from giddiness by holding onto a chair placed on that side

---

1. Stephen Spender, *Journals 1939–1983* (London: Faber, 1985), 292.

of his body. The chair which *we* hold onto, to save ourselves from an under-lying sense of the 'bottomlessness' of our existence, is the intellectual, rational commonsense side of our mind. I have myself, for instance, a secure hold of my chair while writing this page; for not even an existential philosopher can write reasonably and communicably about 'the existential moment' and allow himself to re-experience it (except dimly, in imagination and memory) at the same time.[2]

Another way of describing this sensation of emptiness was of a sort of cos-mic blank or 'nothingness'. During one of the early nocturnal blackouts in March 1940 he had wandered outside his parents' home in Teddington and stared up at the night sky, its stars for once sharply visible. The experience, he had then noted, was 'like entering an exteriorization of that unwalled intimate dark space with which I am so familiar *within* myself'.[3] Such quasi-Pascalian moments of dread and aloneness revived a recollection of those evenings in the Rue Rollin in which he had discussed Existential philoso-phy with Fondane in the house next door to Pascal's. He was also reading Heidegger's essay 'What Is Metaphyics?' in French, and worrying about 'Negation. *The Void, das Nichts, Nada, le Néant.* Practically the only image that presents itself at all strongly to me', he had remarked on that occasion, 'is *a black vacuum in (or through) which two eyes are fixedly staring.*'[4]

Common sense provided an antidote to this destabilizing sensation; the problem was that common sense also seemed to dispel poetry. Gascoyne was perfectly well aware that his mystical and disturbing sensations of emptiness emanated from much the same source as his best work. The challenge seems to have been to fend off the void without arresting the poems. There was at least one school of contemporary philosophy that might have offered a grammatical way out of this impasse. The proponents of the Logical Positivist school stressed clarity of language, and they were certain that abstractions such as 'Nothing' were linguistic fictions, belonging to the category of asser-tions they liked to call 'pseudo-statements'. Among Gascoyne's notebooks is an emerging essay entitled 'Logical Positivism and the Void' in which he considers this clash of ideas. At one point he begins a paragraph on 'The Provincialism of English Philosophy' by copying out an abrupt dismissal of that Heidegger essay on metaphysics by A. J. Ayer, the Oxford philosopher

---

2. *The Last Judgement*, Beinecke, Box 20, Folder 398, fo. 18.
3. *Collected Journals*, 292.
4. Ibid. 256.

who to his mind epitomized the unimaginativeness of the Positivist approach. 'In general', Ayer had insisted in his *Language, Truth and Logic*, 'the postulate of non-existence results from the superstition that for every word and phrase that can be the grammatical subject of a sentence, there must somewhere be a real entity . . . To this error must be attributed the utterances of Heidegger who bases his metaphysic on the assumption that "Nothing" is a name which is used to denote something ultimately mysterious.'[5] By 1946 Gascoyne had formulated his own rejoinder to this position of intellectual self-limitation. 'It is to be suspected', he now wrote, 'that the Logical Positivist state of mind—for it is a state of mind that produced it, far more than an act of thought—is in reality the involuntary expression of a *silent despair*. The Logical Positivist is inhibited in his thinking because of an abnormally sensitive and typically English *pudeur* which shrinks from examining anything so *asocial* and melodramatic as a state of despair.'[6] In a slightly later notebook he goes as far as to castigate the whole Logical Positivist stance as 'the rational systematisation of a neurotic defence-mechanism'.[7] Proponents of this school of thought, it seemed to him, had too firm a grasp on the chair.

Ayer's attitude appeared to epitomize what elsewhere Gascoyne had called 'the rational common sense side of our mind', and there was something insular and British about it. Gascoyne was both wrong and right in this. He seems to have been unaware of Ayer's roots in the Vienna School, and his verdict completely bypassed Wittgenstein. But he was certainly correct in suspecting that the leading lights of contemporary British analytical philosophy were blind to every variety of Existentialism. In the whole of Bertrand Russell's *A History of Western Philosophy*, published the previous year, there is no reference to Kierkegaard, whom Russell probably did not consider a philosopher at all. Thus between Kierkegaard and Heidegger to the south, and Russell and Ayer to the north, an Iron Curtain seemed to have descended over the continent of Philosophy. Acutely conscious of this condition of intellectual Cold War, Gascoyne was minded to appoint himself an intermediary between the parties. Ten years before, he had made a highly effective Surrealist ambassador in London. Might he not, in the face of this new embargo, make an equally efficacious Existential emissary to England?

5. A. J. Ayer, *Language, Truth and Logic* (London: Gollancz, 1936), 35–6, quoted in BL Add. 56045.
6. BL Add. 56053, fo. 44.
7. BL Add. 56052, fo. 5.

In any case there was for him no way back to Surrealism, since he had now lost social contact with both the British and French wings of the movement. The fast dwindling English group had barely survived the throes of a bitter wartime feud between its nominal leader E. L. T. Mesens and an acrimonious Russian-born young pretender with the grandiose moniker of Toni Romanov del Renzio dei Rossi di Castellone e Venosa.[8] Mesens, 'that horrible little man' as Gascoyne had once called him, was now more of less back in control, but his position had been weakened, and there is even some sign that he was slowly losing faith in the cause himself: his previously impressive network of contacts had been replaced by the likes of George Melly, a former naval rating and would-be jazz artiste who was currently rogering both Mesens and his wife Sybil.[9] Mesens had, nonetheless, regained contact with Breton who following his return to Paris had thrown himself into organizing an International Surrealist Exhibition there to coincide with the tenth anniversary of the London show. It opened in the Galerie Maeght on 20 June 1946, and for it Breton commissioned a manifesto from the English group. Mesens and the film director Jacques Brunius came up with a form of words in which they loudly dissociated themselves from several of those whose organizational efforts Mesens had usurped ten years previously. With savage glee they rounded on Gascoyne, Henry Moore, and Humphrey Jennings for retrograde tendencies: Gascoyne for the sacred imagery of *Poems 1937–1942* with their 'very peculiar kind of Christian moral oppression', Moore because his reclining female figures reminded Mesens of Madonnas, and Jennings for accepting an OBE for services rendered by his documentary films to British wartime morale.[10] As a result, as far as the Surrealist movement was concerned, Gascoyne was now *persona non grata* in both cities.

Since his former paths of communication were now closed, he pursued new ones. His first communiqué as an Existentialist advocate was entitled 'A Little Anthology of Existential Thought' and it appeared that year in the journal *New Road* published by the Grey Walls Press from Crown Passage off Pall Mall.[11] The general editor of *New Road* was a solemn and lecherous

8. For which, see Silvano Levy, 'The Del Renzio Affair: A Leadership Struggle in Wartime Surrealism', *Papers of Surrealism*, 3 (Spring 2005), 1–34.
9. Or at least according to Melly. See George Melly, *Don't Tell Sybil: An Intimate Memoir of E. L. T. Mesens* (London: Heinemann, 1997).
10. Michel Remy, *Surrealism in Britain* (London: Ashgate, 1999), 281–2.
11. *New Road*, no. 4 (London: Grey Walls Press, 1946), 176–206.

weasel of a man called Charles Wrey Gardiner, former editor of the *Poetry Quarterly*, who had started his publishing and bookselling business in 1939 from the front room of his seventeenth-century cottage in Billericay in Essex, and since moving to London prided himself on running a concern staffed exclusively by poets. Nicholas Moore typed out copy, and office errands were run by 26-year-old medical student and amateur poet, later to win notoriety as a prophet of sexual liberation, Dr Alex Comfort. Also on the staff was Fred Marnau, an Austro-Hungarian who wrote poems in German, which were then translated for inclusion. Derek Stanford later recalled Gascoyne wafting to and fro from the office looking impressively grim, 'like the Prince of Aquitaine from Gérard de Nerval'. He was in any case in step with the editorial policy of the press, which had just published *Outlaw of the Lowest Planet*, his own selection from and admiring introduction to the work of the American poet Kenneth Patchen, with a Preface by Comfort and an Introduction by himself in which he characterized Patchen as a kind of latter-day American Dadaist. The link with Gardiner's magazine was maintained for some time, and would produce in the autumn of 1947 a special number devoted to Stanford's appreciative essay *David Gascoyne: Poet of Crisis*.

It was no. 4, edited by Marnau, that carried the 'Little Anthology'. Strictly speaking, it was less an anthology than a collage of passages, and its Existentialism was closer to 'Existential thought' (a term he sometimes used to distinguish the mystical intimations of Chestov and Fondane from Sartre's trendier secular variety). At the very end, for example, he had juxtaposed a passage from the Gospel According to St John—Christ's interview with Nicodemus—with Roger Roughton's message from the grave in *Horizon*. Thus Christ's enjoinder 'Without a new birth no man is able to see the Kingdom of God' was brought into harmony with Roughton's arresting observation 'It is no coincidence that the most perfect love produces the most astonishing creature, the human child... An articulate babe could topple empires'. Alongside passages from Kierkegaard, Chestov, Fondane, and Buber, he had placed others from the notebooks of the eighteenth-century physicist and mathematician George Christopher Lichtenberg, jottings by the nineteenth-century moralist and essayist Joseph Joubert—the organization of both which somewhat resembled his own—and extracts from the work of the British autodidact and pioneer of linguistics Lady Victoria Welby. The context for this eclecticism is obvious from one of the quotations from Joubert: '*I, whence, whither, why, how?* These questions cover all philosophy—existence, origin, place, end, and means.' These, furthermore, were questions that Kierkegaard would have considered as pressing, and Ayer as meaningless. There was little doubt whose side Gascoyne was on, or on whose definition of philosophy he had chosen to rely.

At much the same time he was also conducting a complementary exercise in which he tried to trace the origins of modern mysticism through the native English tradition. Strongly indebted to Francis Quarles (1592–1644) in its title and orientation, *Emblems and Allegories* was a thematically organized anthology of indigenous devotional poetry and prose, following what Quarles would have called 'the Hieroglyphics of the life of man' through extracts from Herbert, Traherne, John Skelton, Vaughan, Hopkins, Blake, Shelley, Tennyson, Henry Wotton, Chaucer, Tennyson, Yeats, and many another author. Again the complete typescript was sent to Graham Sutherland who, pronouncing himself delighted, produced an accompanying sequence of original lithographs, some of which were to appear separately in *Poetry London*. Gascoyne, however, had got himself into a not untypical contractual muddle over the publication. He had committed himself both to Tambimuttu and to the firm of Frederick Muller, who expected to publish this highly attractive illustrated tome in their series 'New Excursions into English Poetry'. The book fell between stools, and is even now a highly inviting typescript held at Yale.[12]

Gascoyne was distracted from these negotiations by an opportunity once more to visit France. Shortly before the war in Paris, he had occasionally spoken to a 'slightly enigmatic' young married couple whom he saw drinking every evening on the terrace of the Café Flore. They were American by nationality, and the husband was William Le Page Finley, a playboy in his late twenties who laid claim to an exotic, mixed-race background that included pre-Columbian Indian blood. Gascoyne had since lost sight of them, though in 1940 Finley had written, inviting David to join them in the States. In the summer of 1947 Finley, who had by now split up with his spouse, arrived at Downshire Crescent Gardens and asked Gascoyne to accompany him to Paris. He accepted, unaware of the fact that the bisexual Finley was in the throes of a whirlwind affair with the tempestuous 51-year-old shipping heiress and poetaster Nancy Cunard. In an unguarded moment Finley communicated the substance of his invitation to his possessive and

12. Beinecke, Box 5, Folders 54–60.

bangle-braceleted mistress. As Gascoyne later recalled, the upshot came close to farce. The bracelets rattled: 'When she heard that there was a possibility of my going to Paris with him...Nancy became absolutely furious and rang up and said "I'm coming round to fight you!" And I said "Well come round then!"' [13] No Nancy appeared. Despite these vocal threats, Gascoyne and Finley left for France by boat train. When they reached Paris, Gascoyne—who would always insist that his relationship with the charming but feckless Finley was altogether platonic—was installed in a house his companion had rented for the summer season near the Champ de Mars. Finley then promptly disappeared, as Cunard had been hot in pursuit. She had a taken a double room for herself and her lover at Hôtel Montana in the Rue Saint-Benoît, where Finley took to spending his nights. Every few days he would drop round for a chat with Gascoyne, who in the meantime was left contemplating the watery sun as it hovered over the Seine northwards towards the Trocadero:

> Magnificent strong sun! in these last days
> So prodigally generous of pristine light
> That's wasted only by men's sight who will not see
> And by self-darkened spirits from whose night
> Can rise no longer orison or praise... [14]

Eventually Finley's visits ceased. He had driven south with Nancy and, careless of Gascoyne's predicament, was now accompanying her through Perpignan and Toulouse towards Andorra, where they were to spend their time consorting with some Spanish Republican refugees whose cause Lady Cunard's munificent daughter had thoughtfully adopted. [15] Back in Paris, he had neglected to pay the rent.

Without money, and ejected from their house, Gascoyne took to the streets. 'I wandered about,' he later told Mel Gooding, 'and in fact for a couple of nights I even slept under the Pont Royal...at the end of the Rue du Bac.' He had been penniless, and footloose too, in Paris before, but never before had he been without a roof over his head. He spent his thirty-first birthday amid the dust, spit, and piss of the *quais*. There he improvised a dramatic monologue in the voice of an itinerant, as if one of Browning's

13. BL Lives, F1384, Side A.
14. 'September Sun: 1947', David Gascoyne, *A Vagrant and Other Poems* (London: John Lehmann, 1950), 22; *Collected Poems* (1965), 109.
15. Anne Chisholm, *Nancy Cunard* (London: Sidgwick and Jackson, 1979), 280–1.

soliloqists was down on his luck. First published in *Horizon* the following year, 'A Vagrant' would make an aptly named title piece for his next collection:

> 'They're much the same in most ways, these great cities. Of them all,
> Speaking of those I've seen, this one's still far the best
> Big densely built-up area for a man to wander in
> Should be have ceased to find shelter, relief,
> Or dream in sanatorium bed; should nothing as yet call
> Decisively to him to put an end to brain's
> Proliferations round the possibilities that eat
> Up adolescence, even years up to the late
> Thirtieth birthday...'[16]

His situation was dire. Enter, therefore, the seventh of Gascoyne's strong-minded, middle-aged benefactresses. Jenny de Margerie was the wife of the senior diplomat Roland Jacquin de Margerie, who following several years in China had returned to play a key role in the formation in June 1940 of the Anglo-French Supreme War Council, and the negotiations between de Gaulle and Churchill at Briare and Tours; he had since served as his country's representative in Thailand, earning some obloquy for apparent collaboration in so doing.[17] High-minded Catholics, they lived with their daughter Diane and son Bertrand in the Rue Saint-Guillaume, off the Boulevard Saint-Germain. A casual meeting apprised them of David's predicament. They hired a room for him in the Hôtel Pas de Calais in the Rue des Saints-Pères that ran parallel with their own street, from where he could walk round to lunch two or three days a week. By November, helped by food parcels from the Rue Saint-Guillaume, he was working on a typewriter borrowed from Diane at further Jouve translations. His letters breathe gratitude: 'How', he wrote to Madame de Margerie, 'can I ever thank you enough for your kindness—Your wonderful parcel on Saturday evening was such a lovely surprise. I hope that I do not seem ungrateful in not having written more promptly to express my thanks. As I shall not be seeing you till tomorrow, I am sending this inadequate note.'[18] Perhaps affected by Jenny's devout Catholicism, he was rereading Herbert, whose tone of intimacy with the

---

16. *Horizon*, 18/104 (Aug. 1948), 75–6; *A Vagrant and Other Poems*, 7–9; *Collected Poems*, 99–100.
17. Roland de Margerie, *Journal 1939–1940*, ed. Diane de Margerie (Paris: Editions Grasset et Fasquale, 2010).
18. David Gascoyne to Jenny de Margerie, 12 Nov. 1947, courtesy of Diane de Margerie.

Divine came together with Jouve's highly charged mysticism, and some-thing of his own personal wretchedness. He typed out a prayer:

> O Thou to all eternity God of my love,
> My prayer beholds Thee in this silence dense and dark
> Whereunto I after yet one more day am come:
> Sacred the dark, wretched the ragged wound,
> Wound wedded to the darkness and with peace welded as one.[19]

He was stung to the quick by the plain manifestation of concern by his new Catholic friends and the contrast it emphasized with the anonymity and exclusiveness he seemed so often to have encountered back in England. Cunard's recent behaviour may have had something to do with it but, be that as it may, he was now drafting a play with a contemporary setting called *The Quick and the Dead* about what Durrell had once called 'The English Death' and about the iniquities of the British class system. At the centre of the plot was Beatrice Carving, the widow of a military man living in reduced circumstances with her scholarly elder brother and supressing her rather mixed feelings after the reported wartime death of her son Donald. Donald sounds as if he is partly based on Giles Romilly: a public school renegade, he is a Communist, and has fought in Spain whence he returned to marry the wife of a former comrade. The wife now turns up to announce Donald still lives and is hard at work on an apologia for his life containing a strongly worded attack on 'the snobbery and distorted values of his background' and, by implication, on his mother's way of life.[20] Beatrice's brother reads some of it out loud, scarcely able to disguise his glee at this assault on the smug-ness of his younger sister, who refuses to be reconciled either to the pres-ence of her radicalized daughter-in-law, or the continuing social aberration of her son. At his point, like so many of Gascoyne's projects at the time, the play peters out. He had dedicated it to a differently disposed member of the European bourgeoisie, 'to Jenny de Margerie in gratitude and more, and much, much more'.[21]

Gradually he was reconstituting his Parisian social life. In 1944 he had received two letters from the Jouves, and in February of the same year he had sent them a copy of his *Poems 1937–1942* signed to 'Pierre Jean Jouve—to

19. 'Evening Prayer: After the French of Pierre Jean Jouve', Beinecke, Box 13, Folder 292. *Selected Poems*, 238.
20. Synopsis in BL Add. 56060, fos. 6–10.
21. Partial draft in BL Add. 56056, fo. 2.

whom I owe infinitely more than I could express—with all my gratitude, admiration and affection'. Since 1939 he had had very little contact with them. Late in 1947 this was put to rights when Pierre and Blanche, who had been unable to resume the lease on their Rue de Tournon flat, settled into a large apartment in the Rue Antoine-Chartin in the fourteenth arrondissement, near Alésia, from where Pierre resumed his daily drives in the Bois de Boulogne. In June 1948 Gascoyne recommenced his now daily therapeutic sessions there with Blanche, and his literary dialogue with her husband. The spate of Jouve translations during 1948 are testament to the continuing efficacy of that spell.

Not all his reunions were so blessed. From the Rue des Saints-Pères it was a simple metro ride out to Pigalle where, after returning from the USA, Breton had settled back into his flat in the Rue de la Fontaine and relaunched his daily soirées on the terrace of his neighbourhood café. Breton was now 51 and, as Gascoyne had recently noted, while in America had been considered 'sufficiently respectable to deliver an official address to the Year's Leaving Class at Yale'.[22] In New York he had consorted anew with the much-feted Dalí, whom he had taken to referring to cynically as 'Avida Dollars', but he had also made new friends, among them Lévi-Strauss whom he had continued to see, and a Polish semiotician called Roman Jakobson. He had inspired in both men an interest in the deep underlay to the human psyche, 'la pensée sauvage'—the wild pansy or savage mind—thus sewing the seedbed for one of the still unacknowledged intellectual affinities of the mid-twentieth century: between Surrealism and Structuralism.

In the meantime, however, Breton had read the maliciously worded Manifesto by Mesens commissioned for the brochure of the 1947 exhibition, with its lofty dismissal of Gascoyne's new interests and beliefs. Breton had not sought to look behind the malice, nor were either he or Mesens well equipped to distinguish between the radical religious humanism of 'Ecce Homo', with its Grünewald-derived sacrificial imagery, and the authoritarian Roman Catholicism they both despised. When Gascoyne next attended a drinks session at the Café de la Place Blanche, the rebuttal was instantaneous: 'I am given to understand', remarked Breton grandly, 'that you have recently become a Roman Catholic.' Nothing more needed to be said.

---

22. David Gascoyne, 'Introducing Kenneth Patchen', in Kenneth Patchen, *Outlaw of the Lowest Planet*, selected and introd. David Gascoyne with a pref. by Alex Comfort (London: The Grey Walls Press, 1946), xiv.

After this abrupt anathema, Gascoyne was no longer officially a Surrealist of any water, having been excommunicated from both the English and the International groups in quick succession. The experience does not seem to have upset him unduly. He had long ceased being Surrealist in his ideological sympathies and, besides, Breton was forever ejecting people from the movement. In the eyes if his more disillusioned former acolytes, he had even by now succeeded in expelling himself.

There were, however, new gurus. One afternoon an ascetic-looking priest joined them for lunch at Jenny de Margerie's flat. The de Margerie family had got to know the Jesuit scientist and writer Pierre Teilhard de Chardin in the thirties during Roland's prolonged diplomatic attachment in Peking. During those years Chardin had been involved in a series of geological expeditions, and he was already developing his highly personal, heterodox theology.[23] By the late forties, they were all back in France, and the Jesuit was still energetic, if a trifle elderly: still not respectable, still mistrusted by the Holy See. He had long ago written his masterpiece, *The Phenomenon of Man*, and, though the Vatican would ban its publication until after his death, its theories permeated his conversation. A leading palaeontologist, he believed in the God-directed processes of human evolution towards a future 'Omega Point' of reconciliation with the Divine. There was much in his thinking that chimed with Gascoyne's own, in particular the idea of an incremental moral consciousness operating through the transcendent zone that Chardin termed the 'noosphere'. They talked across a social and religious divide, but the effect on the development of Gascoyne's subsequent thought is easy to trace.[24]

And then there was the Russian Orthodox émigré and mystic Nikolai Berdyaev. An almost exact contemporary of Chestov, with whom he had been an ally in the forward march of theistic Existentialism in France, Berdyaev was a widower in his eighties and was being looked after by his daughter in a flat to the south of the Porte d'Orléans. Chestov had been dead for nine years and, despite the affinity of their thought, the two men— as Fondane had carefully recorded—had argued interminably. It had been a dipute between spiritual brothers. Berdyaev was still at the epicentre of the small circle of expatriate Russian intellectuals in France. One day, Jenny

23. Conversation with Diane de Margerie, 7 June 2010.
24. BL Lives, F1384, Side A.

drove Gascoyne out to meet him. 'It was a Sunday afternoon, and he had a lot of Russian people there. We had tea with him and afterwards he took us into his study. And I was immediately struck by the fact that all around the room there were portraits of Tolstoy, Chekhov and other Russian writers. And the largest picture of all, over his desk, was of Chestov.'[25]

25. Ibid.

19

A Bridge Too Soon

Gascoyne's exposure to the commercial theatre during the war years had left him with a distaste for the West End and the repertory circuit, the dramatic and social illusions fed by drawing room comedies and the like, in which seated members of the audience gawped at the antics of the privileged through the empty 'fourth wall' of a Proscenium Arch. In 1949 he decided to do something about it. On his return to England at the turn of that year, he started work on a play entitled 'Talk, Talk, Talk', or 'The Hole in the Fourth Wall' intended to satirize the mainstream British theatre of the period and to explore alternative modes of dramatic writing, production, and stagecraft. As usual he was far ahead—perhaps too far ahead—of the pack. This was a full six years in advance of the establishment of the English Stage Company at the Royal Court Theatre under George Devine, and seven years before the success of *Look Back in Anger* by another former repertory actor, John Osborne. Though the script was characteristically British in its dismemberment of the class system, its methods of theatrical experimentation were French, closer to Sartre or Ionesco than to anything to be seen in London. He was feeling in the dark, and he knew it.

His notebooks again became crowded, more so than in any previous year except 1938. Their recurrent themes were sex, marriage, Shakespeare, and humour, and sometimes the relationship between these four. He had enjoyed a front stalls seat from which to observe the interaction of the first two topics whilst watching the acrimonious decline of the Croziers' marriage. The marriage was now emphatically over, but its demise had left Biddy feeling vulnerable and apt to take her frustrations out on David, who did not know how to respond. Soon he and Biddy were 'throwing things at one another'. More and more it came to seem that *chez Crozier* consisted of a prolonged scene from a play by Ibsen, with Biddy a Hedda Gabler figure, manipulative and destructive of everything she touched. 'And', David gasped in a notebook, 'I used to think of her as Candida!'[1] He had no intention of play-ing the role of Hedda's protégé Eilert Lovborg, uncertain of his moods, his precious manuscripts in danger never of seeing the light of day. He was, in any case, no more able to assist Biddy in her distress than he had been to prevent the collapse of her family. Marriage, he now thought, could only be a vocation, and not everybody had it. 'Only the gentle should marry,' he noted in a journal, 'Only those who love children should wed.' Besides, sexual desire as a foundation for social relationships was coming to seem to him flawed. This was the year in which proposals were first seriously mooted to introduce sex education into the British school curriculum. Unless it was placed in the context of the morality of human relationships in the broadest sense, such instruction was, he felt, bound to fail:

> Until it is generally recognised and accepted that all marriages based merely on sexual attraction are bound to be based, before they are a year old, on deep disguised or even overt sexual antagonism. This antagonism, everyday conflict between man and woman that goes on as a rule below the immediate surface level of consummation, is very often the sole cause of marital infidelity. One partner commits adultery as a rule, not because of someone else providing an overwhelmingly irresistible temptation but in order to score a point against the other partner, or because the other partner wishes it, and has done every-thing possible without actually making it explicit to suggest it, in order to score a counterpoint by reproaching the other partner with infidelity. Nothing can be done to mitigate this perfectly natural state of affairs until both man and woman are above all anxious to be perfectly truthful to one another, and are sufficiently aware of themselves and the elementary facts of human psy-chology to know that every fully developed human being is psychically bi-sexual.[2]

There was one other marriage in which David had potentially constituted a third party, though less centrally. William Empson was then lecturing in Peking where he and his stately South African wife Hetta were observing the invasion of the Communists—whom Hetta at least openly supported—and the establishment of the new China that year. Empson was subtle, pro-fessorial, and egregiously clever; he was also bisexual in an oblique way not everybody could follow. The 'everybody' included Gascoyne, who respected his intelligence while finding his academic airs tiresome and excluding, suspecting Empson of regarding him as 'a semi—or half-educated duffer'.

1. BL Add. 71704E, fo. 59.
2. BL Add. 71704A, fo. 49.

Despite these barriers, there had been an attraction, at least in David's mind. It also seemed to him that the majestical Hetta—whose name lay uncomfortable close to 'Hedda'—had kept the two of them apart. In his notebook he asked himself ruefully: 'Does she know that for her presumed sake I regretfully resigned hope of a loving friendship with someone who might perhaps have not been altogether ruined if he had allowed his extremely nice kind of homosexuality to have more open and fearless expression in his life?'[3]

By December 1949 the friction with Biddy was intense, cursed with patches of mutual temper, even of violence. Without warning either her or any of his other friends, he took off to Paris alone over Christmas, re-establishing contact with the de Margeries. His arrival in a highly fraught state found Jenny at a loss, so she entrusted him to her 22-year-old daughter Diane, who took him out for a few days to the relative tranquillity of l'Abbaye de Royaumont, a former thirteenth-century Cistercian foundation set amid forest and wetlands. Back in Paris, he clapped eyes on a young American called Dan. He saw him again on the ferry back to Dover, and then in the restaurant car of the train up to London, but still had not the courage to introduce himself. Enraptured he mooned, 'I know I am myself a sick and worthless creature, but I want to be a human being strong and loyal and affectionately unselfishly loving enough to be worthy of Dan's love.'[4] Though they eventually got to know one another in London, Gascoyne had to rest content with advising Dan on the poems this literary hopeful was attempting to write. His advice was encouraging; 'Dan' was not.

Restlessness consumed him. In January he went round to see John Lehmann who, following his successful wartime career as the editor of *Penguin New Writing*, was thinking of setting up a publishing firm with his sister Rosamond:

> He suddenly rang the doorbell of my house. All the worst forebodings of the sick age in which we live seemed to writhe like snakes in his ever-changing expression. He came in, and poured out a fevered story of his recent life, a Cassandra-like cry into the void. I calmed him down as best I could, and suggested he should collect together the poems he had written since his wartime, Sutherland-illustrated volume, and let me publish them. *A Vagrant* was published at the end of that year.[5]

---

3. BL Add. 71704I, fo. 49.
4. BL Add. 71704E, fo. 59.
5. John Lehmann, *The Ample Proposition* (London: Eyre and Spottiswoode, 1966), 107–9.

Unable to face Biddy, David now contacted Kathleen Raine, who had taken a large Georgian house at 9 Paultons Square, just off the King's Road in Chelsea. For several weeks, as he prepared the poems of *A Vagrant* for publication, Gascoyne was her non-paying lodger. Raine was struck by his protean nature filled with light and dark, humour and despair:

> He was, at that time, even more ill than he had been at the time of *Poetry London*. He used to say that it was as if his brain 'leaked'; (he later described it as 'like a transistor set inside his head,' on which all kinds of voices not his own spoke, wept, declaimed, argued, chanted; while others would say, 'we are the gods, the gods'). But he read continuously, widely and deeply in works of mystical philosophy, and existentialism, and talked, rapidly, and eloquently, of the divine vision which haunted his darkness, like the sun at midnight—an image he himself used.[6]

Gascoyne had known Raine since the Mass Observation days in the late thirties. She had since left her husband Charles Madge and set up house with her two children by him, Anna and James. She had endured an unreciprocated infatuation with a man called Alastair, who had left her feeling high, dry, and unwanted. A bird of spiritual passage, she had since flitted in and out of the candlelit certainties of the Roman Catholic Church then, like the sparrow in Bede's *History*, flitted straight out again into the spiritual dark. She too was sick of the sex war which Gascoyne had been eviscerating in his diaries, and craving peace of mind and body. In this they seemed at one: outcasts in a world of conflicting passions that would not admit them. They also had definite interests in common: Gascoyne's preoccupation with the emblematic movement was leading him towards alchemy, while Kathleen was spending her days in the British Museum Reading Room absorbing the intellectual antecedents of Blake. She was much taken with the work of the eighteenth-century translator and Neoplatonist Thomas Taylor, in whose English versions Blake had encountered the philosophy of Plato. Now 40, Kathleen's dove-grey eyes seemed constantly to peer beyond the shapes of the tawdry actual towards some mystical reality beyond. Gascoyne had swapped Hedda Gabler for somebody more closely resembling a latter-day Hildegard of Bingen.

Shelf loads of books passed between Watkins' occult bookshop in Cecil Court and Chelsea to service their respective obsessions. But the two of

6. Kathleen Raine, *Autobiographies* (London: Skoob, 1991), 227.

them, in lighter moments, also shared a kind of multi-layered levity. One day David rushed to the Tavistock Clinic to pour out his problems to a staff psychiatrist who, after listening to him patiently for close on an hour, remarked 'I am afraid I can do nothing for you'. In a characteristic mood of sombre irony, Gascoyne replied 'Then perhaps you will pray for me'. Gravely and somewhat pompously the doctor replied 'I am afraid I do not believe in prayer'. Afterwards, when Gascoyne described the episode to Raine, they were convulsed in mirth for several minutes, as much one suspects at the absurdity of Gacoyne's conduct as by the priggishness of certain expressions of non-belief.[7] The levity, and his gratitude to Raine for their growing friendship, emerged in a gift to her, a posy of poems entitled 'A Little Zodiac for K.J.R.', covering the astrological signs from hers, Gemini, to his, Libra. He was in a relaxed mood, and the exercise found him at his most playful. These were Gemini:

> Each looks towards his brother and sees yet one more than him;
> In friendship with each other sealed, they both remain unmet.
> Their eyes still gaze towards the misty heights that precede Time;
> Whatever one of them looks on, the other will forget.

And this was Libra:

> O unjust man behold
> How she must stand blindfold
> Who personates the word
> *Justice*, and in one hand
> Wield naked sword as wand
> Who with the other lets
> Two equidistant plates
> Dangle, while she forgets
> Which yours is, which your fate's.[8]

For Kathleen such neat verses, with their attention to assonance, metre, and rhyme, appeared to be a form of liberation. Following the near-hegemony of High Modernism, it was feasible to write structured poetry like this after all. In the margin of his notebook, next to this sequence, she wrote 'Strong, clear vowel music. And it hasn't turned you into a Fascist.' Some years later

---

7. Raine, *Autobiographies*, 227–8.
8. David Gascoyne, *A Vagrant and Other Poems* (London: John Lehmann, 1950), 38, 40; *Collected Poems* (1965), 121, 122–3.

they were set to music by David's former schoolmate from Salisbury, Geoffrey Bush.[9]

But Raine's was perhaps too powerful a personality for her to live contentedly at close quarters with another adult for very long. She eventually put Gascoyne in contact with two neighbours of hers, the brothers John and George Russell, who offered him a room in their house a few doors away. Living thus in semi-cohabitation, their relationship proved a source of solace. David even established an avuncular attitude towards her children. Fourteen-year-old Anna found him a gentle, reassuring presence: she recalls him calling round unannounced on one overcast, squally August afternoon. He put onto the gramophone a 78 of Brahms' Clarinet Quintet in B Minor (Opus 115), and they sat silently, absorbed in the music.[10] For Raine, too, in his calmer moments he seemed an occasional oasis in a city of strife. After more than a decade of spoiled marriages and physical malentendus, she had come to value the company of homosexual men as soulmates, provided she was not in love with them. Having observed David's more moody and self-destructive side at close quarters, there was little possibility she would fall for him in such a way. 'I had been wounded in the sexual hunt when I was young', she observed in 1977, 'and had by now become wary at evading any sexual approach. If a homosexual man likes the company of a women it is for other (and better?) reasons.'

Chelsea brought out the dandy in Gascoyne. He took to attending Edith Sitwell's regular lunches at the Sesame and Pioneer Club at 31 Grosvenor Street, where his eccentricities did not go unnoticed. Another frequent guest was Stephen Spender's second wife Natasha, a former concert pianist with an eye for the bizarre. One afternoon she sat opposite Gascoyne who 'every minute would swivel violently from the table to repudiate some imaginary persecutors in the empty space behind his chair'. Edith's kind enquiry elicited from Gascoyne the explanation that 'these dreadful people won't ever leave me alone'. With benign authority she declared, 'My dear, take absolutely no notice of them. They only do it to annoy and will go away if you ignore them.' Thus he did and thus, to all appearances, did they.[11]

---

9. Geoffrey Bush, *Signs of the Zodiac for Voice and Piano* (London: Novello, 1956).
10. Conversation with Anna Hopewell, 12 July 2010.
11. Natasha Spender, 'Lady Natasha Spender remembers Edith Sitwell', *Daily Telegraph*, 8 June 2008.

After his recent spells in Paris, his head was full of cabaret songs. In Chelsea he tried his hand at the genre. One result concerned a 'Bland Maid of Kensington' of uncertain gender, who cohabited with a 'Bluff Ex-Young Ladies Man' and who 'Continued in Kensington | To Adorn every Day | The Saloons of Three Locals | Well-known to be Gay.' 'What A Way to Walk into My Parlour, Little Man' was along the lines of 'The Minute You Walked Into The Joint'. 'Au Café Cosmopolite' was full of cross-linguistic puns:

> J'aime bien la chanson réaliste;
>   But life's so life-like too;
> So I sing this irreal song
>   Just to the unreal you.[12]

Then, anticipating Yale's bestowal that year of the Bollingen Prize for Poetry on Wallace Stevens, he composed a tribute to the Connecticut poet in the form of a parodic pastiche. 'Un Vers de Circonstance' he called it, or 'This perfectly awful attempt at a parody', but it was full of the sort of spirited verbal play Stevens had called his 'jocundissima'. Lastly, relying 'more on Mischief than on Manet', he polished off a 'Déjeuner Sur L'Herbe' in verse, seating a naked 'belle-dame sans mercerie' (a young lady without haberdashery) next to a gallant and clothed 'Comte d'à côté' and an equally gallant, and sideways-looking, 'Le Duc de Profil'.

By March *The Hole in the Fourth Wall* was ready for production. Since it lampooned all conventions of the mainstream theatre, including the institution of the Lord Chamberlain's Office, it was thought unwise to approach his Lordship for a seal of approval: a commercial performance in the West End or even in rep was out of the question. Instead, on the first of the month the play opened at the Waterfield Theatre Club beneath the arches of Charing Cross station, in Villiers Street off the Strand. In 1950 there were over thirty such private theatre clubs in London, affording the only feasible way of evading the jurisdiction of official stage censorship. For 5s. members of the public were granted annual membership and admission to what was in theory a private performance, staged under studio conditions. (The strip clubs of the period often operated under an analogous system.) In these circumstances Gascoyne's satirical squib was performed by a cast of drama students and young professionals. Surviving drafts suggest a formal experiment at least half a decade ahead of its time: a blend of Ionesco, Pinero,

---

12. *A Vagrant and Other Poems*, 60; not in *Collected Poems*.

Beckett, and the yet-to-emerge Harold Pinter.[13] The set is a tennis court, with a net across. Around stand a cast representing the stock characters of West End comedies of the day: 'A Woman Of A Certain Age' (called in Gascoyne's early drafts a 'Grand Dame', and probably based on Beatrice Carver in *The Quick and the Dead*); 'The Unavoidable Female Interest' (earlier called 'A Moll', and perhaps a recollection of Marie in *High Sierra*); and 'A Young Man With A Note of Urgency In His Voice' (earlier styled 'A Sneaking Intellectual'). At the end of the first act the action shifts back in time to a wartime bomb shelter, where these personalities, divided by class, are forced to confront one another. The well-born 'Woman Of A Certain Age' is mocked by both the Female Interest and the intellectual young man, who brusquely inform her that for women of her ilk, 'there will not be another tomorrow'. Over this comedy of death-in-life, of bad and good faith, presides a masked figure ultimately revealed as the Lord Chamberlain, still empowered in 1950 to scrutinize, comment upon, and considered necessary, to excise all proposed scripts. His intervention is symbolized by a blackout, during which a disembodied voice comments on the end of these social and moral arrangements. In the Waterfield production the voice was Michael Redgrave's; the part of the Lord Chamberlain was given to Buck Hurst; Joy Adamson was the 'Unavoidable Feminine Interest'; Geoffrey Best played 'A Young Man With A Note of Urgency In His Voice', and Janet Joye the 'Woman Of A Certain Age'. Production was by Elizabeth Sprigge, translator of Ibsen and Strindberg, later biographer of Gertrude Stein and Cocteau. The run lasted a week, and on its slender proceeds Gascoyne ordered himself a bespoke black corduroy suit.

The England he so vividly satirized was hemming in once more. That month he applied for a travel bursary of £200 being offered by the shipping heiress, lesbian writer—and long-time partner of Hilda Dolittle—'Bryher' (Annie Winifred Ellerman), another of Sitwell's circle at the Sesame. On April Fool's Day Sitwell discussed the list of applicants with John Lehmann, resolving Gascoyne should have it.[14] He decided to tour Provence, still unvisited, by way of Paris. There was, however, no relief from his tormentors. In the bar of the train ferry at Dover on 6 June they hounded him: 'It is very peculiar,' he wrote in the notebook perched on his knee, 'though

13. BL Add. 71704B, *passim*. Also BL Lives, F1385, Side A.
14. John Lehmann, Diary B2, entry for 1 Apr. 1950, John Lehmann family papers, 1649-1990, Princeton University Library, Manuscripts Division, CO746, series 4, box 74.

familiar enough to me, but my "delusions" by which I have been haunted
continually during the last few days are doing their best to persuade me that
I am surrounded by louche and sinister figures who know all about me, are
hostile to me, and seem to be trying all the time to scare me, or intimidate
me, and seem to be trying all the time to intimidate me with meaningful
phrases or warnings... The strange fiction-like atmosphere, complete with
characters out of one of the Greens [Graham or Henry], persists; and I do
not care for it at all. Ridiculous! Persecution-Mania! How idiotic.'[15]

In Paris he settled into the Hôtel Jacob, place of sojourn on his first
arrival in this city seventeen years before, hoping the familiar surroundings
might soothe his nerves. The following evening he was sitting in the lobby
overlooking the street. 'It goes on', he wrote in the notebook 'and is now
much worse than before. The whole of the Rue Jacob is... full of agitated
young men and women with American voices who for the last hour or
more have been walking up and down and continually calling out in a fearful state of urgent excitement all kinds of things, all completely unintelligi-
ble, hysterical and certainly pifflingly stupid, which they seem determined
that I should hear. How much longer they can keep it up I don't know. I do
know, really, that they are no more than daemonic fragmentary pseudo-
beings created by my nerves and disintegrating brain for the sole purpose of
driving me into a state of intolerable exasperation, which I shall presently
bring to an end in some violent way if I can find one.'

While in Paris he met up with Humphrey Jennings, who confided in
him his decision to become a painter. (A year later, Jennings was dead.)
Then he set off for Avignon on the overnight train from the Gare Saint
Lazare. He overslept and found himself in Aix-en-Provence, from where he
struck out for Marseilles. At the end of his first week he was in Cassis, feeling a little more rational. Phantasmagoria had been replaced by a sense of
emptiness and desolation so complete it sealed him off from the beauty
around him. He made for Nice and then Vence, where he left a pot of cycla-
mens in memory of D. H. Lawrence, who in 1930 had died in nearby Villa
Robermont. In Villefranche on the 23rd he wailed 'I have more than once
this week, surrounded by the most magnificent landscape of the Azure
Coast and in glorious sunlight, felt the most profound desire not to go on
living.' Gascoyne was in the condition evoked by Coleridge in 'Dejection:
Ode': 'I see, not feel, how beautiful they are.'

15. BL Add. 71704F.

Plate 1. Florence Mole in middle age.

Plate 2. Rebbie Freuer ('Tiny') Wright in the year of Gascoyne's birth.

Plate 3. The Harrow school for young ladies, 1910. Middle Row: 'Tiny' Wright sits fifth from left, and Win Gascoyne fourth from right.

Plate 4. Win and David Gascoyne, Bournemouth, *c.*1919.

Phoebe Lollipop.
David Gascoyne

Plate 6. David Gascoyne as Phoebe Lollipop in *At Ye Sign of Ye Sugar Heart*, Salisbury Cathedral School, January 1926.

Plate 5. Win Gascoyne in costume as Winifred Emery's Lady Teazle, *The School for Scandal,* Salisbury 1920.

ford. Earl. Rose. Gascoyne. Jeeves. A. Fermor. Raven. T. Packer. K. Packer. Swinstead. Wells. Sutton. Moss.

Plate 7. Salisbury cathedral choir on the wall outside Canon Robertson's house, Salisbury, 1928. David Gascoyne fourth from left, Bernard Rose third from left.

Plate 8. David Gascoyne at 15.

DAVID GASCOYNE
From a Drawing by STUART A. RAY

Plate 9. The Author of *Roman Balcony*, 1932. From a Drawing by Stuart A. Ray.

Plate 10. 'Four Surrealists', Paris, 1930. Photo by Stefano Bianchetti. From left to right: André Breton, Salvador Dalí, René Crevel, Paul Eluard.

Plate 11. David Gascoyne, *Perseus and Andromeda*, collage (1936).

Title: Group of friends with Zervos and David Gascoyne - (Valentine Penrose sitting second from the left)
Location: Pedralbes, Barcelona, Spain
Date: 1936
Artist: Roland Penrose
Negative Number:
Notes: VN CR
Credit Line: © Roland Penrose Estate, England. All rights reserved.

Roland Penrose

The Roland Penrose Collection
Photographs and Works by Roland Penrose 1900-1984

This photograph/document/art work is the copyright of
the Roland Penrose Estate.
© The Roland Penrose Estate, The Roland Penrose Collection,
Farley Farm House, Muddles Green, Chiddingly, East Sussex,
BN8 6HW, England.
Tel: ++44 (0) 1825 - 872 691 Fax: ++44 (0) 1825 - 872 733
E-mail: archives@leemiller.co.uk

Plate 12. Group of friends with Gascoyne (standing at the back), Valentine Penrose (sitting second from left), and Christian Zervos (standing second from right), Monestir de Pedralbes, Barcelona, Spain, November 1936. Photo by Roland Penrose.

Plate 14. Benjamin Fondane.

Plate 13. Léon Chestov in Paris, 1927.

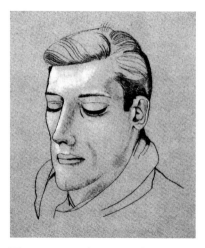

Plate 15. *David Gascoyne* by Lucian Freud, 1943.

Plate 17. David Gascoyne and Tambimuttu, Hyde Park, London, 1943.

Plate 16. *Head of a Man (David Gascoyne)* by Lucian Freud, 1943.

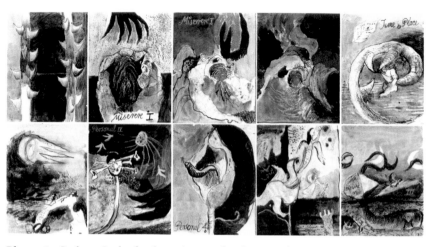

Plate 18. Graham Sutherland, ten images for Gascoyne's *Poems 1937–1942*, 1943.

Plate 19. David Gascoyne at la Tour de César, outside Aix-en-Provence, 1956.

Plate 20. David Gascoyne, *Woodcut*, gouache and ink, 1961.

Plate 21. David Gascoyne, *Blatant Invention*, gouache, *c*.1961.

Soleil de paon ovale

David Gascoyne

Plate 22. David Gascoyne, *Soleil de paon ovale*, gouache, *c.*1961.

Plate 23. David Gascoyne, *Impacts*, gouache, *c.* 1963.

Plate 24. L'Asile de Vaucluse, Epinay-sur-Orge in the nineteenth century, showing the line of *pavillons* on the crest of the hill.

Plate 25. John Martin, *The Destruction of Sodom and Gomorrah* (1853).

Plate 26. David Gascoyne alone in the sitting room at 48 Oxford Street, Northwood, 1965.

Plate 27. David and Judy Gascoyne conducting a joint reading, Durham, 1979.

Plate 28. David Gascoyne with Christine Jordis, Paris, November, 1979.

Plate 29. François-Xavier Jaujard (far left) David Gascoyne (centre), Jean-Claude Masson (right), and John Edwards (far right) at the launch of *Miserere,* the Village Voice bookstore, Saint-Germain, October 1989.

Plate 30. *David Gascoyne* by David Stoker, Leamington, 1989.

His plan was make for Genoa, but he overslept again and missed the bus. Instead he took the train straight to Milan, and thence to Venice. In the dining car he found himself sitting opposite a 25-year-old Californian from Pasadena with the sort of mild, sensitive manners that often attracted him. Richard P. Beedle was an aspiring actor overshadowed by the career of his elder brother William who, three years later, under the screen name 'William Holden' was to find fame as the star of *Sunset Boulevard*. In that very same year Richard would reach the summit of his own career in a cameo role as an unnamed Prisoner of War in the film *Stalag 17* where the heroic lead would once again to be taken by his brother, to whom he almost certainly owed the part. In July 1950 these disappointments were a few years ahead of him: he was 'doing Europe' and, once they reached Venice, Gascoyne, captivated yet again, pleaded with this fetching wannaby to stay. For several nights they shared a bed in the Hôtel Valise. But Beedle planned on his way east to take in Oberammergau, where the Passion Play was being presented in one of its decennial seasons, and would be detained no longer. Gascoyne found himself alone once more, in Venice at the height of the tourist season. And he had miscalculated his finances. To his alarm, he realized he could not settle his half of the bill.

His bounty from one millionairess exhausted, he had recourse to two others. The first, 70-year-old Princess Marguerite Caetani, was an Italian aristocrat by marriage, though she had been born in Waterford, Connecticut in 1880 and was a distant cousin of Eliot's. For two years she had edited her multilingual review *Botteghe Oscure* from Rome. Gascoyne sent her three atmospheric Nocturnes set along the canals, full of mystery, flickering lights, and fugitive glimpses of girls, like one who floats

> Reclining in a gondola alone and with the tide
> Being borne across the Bacino towards where all the stars
> In heaven like spilt pearls blur on the black robe Venice wears
> Slackly undulating round her when as a nocturnal bride
> She mourns her morning glory long drowned in the sea of years.[16]

A rapidly dispatched cheque from the princess helped fix the hotel bill. For a second source of sustenance he perhaps remembered how, fifteen years before, his friend George Barker had been sustained for several months by the New York metallurgy millionairess and benefactress of modern art,

16. *A Vagrant and Other Poems*, 27; *Collected Poems* (1965), 112.

Peggy Guggenheim. Peggy had spent the war years in Manhattan and had briefly been married to Max Ernst in 1941. In 1948 she had exhibited her priceless collection of Surrealist, Dadaist, and Futurist paintings at the Venice Biennale, and in the same year had acquired the Palazzo Venier dei Leoni on the Grand Canal, which she was planning to convert into the significant gallery space it remains. Hers was a natural port of call for Gascoyne, who had to tread carefully however since, despite several contacts they had in common—Antonia White and Djuna Barnes amongst them—he had not as yet met this 52-year-old bejewelled bohemian, then busy hosting a private exhibition of the work of Jackson Pollock. 'So I kept on putting off going to see her, I don't know why, and finally I did. I went to lunch there and she said "Well do come back for dinner." And I went back to my hotel for a siesta, and lay down on my bed, and suddenly one of the bed posts broke, and I was precipitated onto the marble floor of this room. So I went to dinner with Peggy, and during dinner I began to feel very uncomfortable, and explained to her what had happened to my back. And she said "Oh you must stay the night and have my masseur to see you tomorrow." And in the end it became a week staying at the Palazzo Venier dei Leoni, the truncated palace towards the Salute.'[17]

Together they visited the Biennale where there was an exhibition of Cubism. The Belgian tent was devoted to the work of James Ensor. At La Fenice an English company were performing *Twelfth Night*. Celia Johnson was Olivia, Ernest Milton Orsino. Gascoyne and Milton went out drinking together. David last remembered him in *Murder from Memory*, muffled in snow. Now Milton was an amorous duke, feeding on lutes and on love.

17. BL Lives, F1385, Side A.

20

Humpty Dumpty and
the Cuckoo

A *Vagrant and Other Poems* took some readers and reviewers by surprise. Few
Surrealist poems were to be seen in any sense of that elastic term, and the
avowedly Christian—and when not Christian, more broadly spiritual—
meditations seemed to have gone temporarily underground. Many of the
items were poems of place—London, Paris, Venice—and several, in the fullest
sense of a commonly abused expression, were poems of occasion. Poems of
place were balanced by those of displacement, and the interplay between these
two forces of attraction—the centripetal and the centrifugal—defined the
book's theme. For once, especially in the 'Make-Weight Verse' towards the end
of the volume—the parodies and nightclub songs—Gascoyne had given his
latent humour free reign. The reception raised his cachet more than his confidence. After the book had been lauded by Edwin Muir in the *Sunday Times*,
Lehmann arranged for a reading at Rhodes House in Oxford, attended by
Oxford students and outsiders to the university such as Dylan Thomas and
George Barker. To this very mixed audience Gascoyne delivered, not a selection from the book, but a lecture on Christian Existentialism, as he stood
beneath a portrait of Rhodes, mumbling and staring at his shoes. At first only
two or three rows seated towards the front could make out a word. By the end
everybody behind them had shuffled forwards, cocking their ears in the hope
of catching a few sentences. They included several of the next generation of
young British poets, like Alan Brownjohn, then a student of English at Merton.[1]

New poems were coming slowly against a background hum of psychic inter-
ruption. In the midst of one of his amphetamine-induced possessions on
27 April he scrawled: 'This poem will never be completed since whenever

---

1. Conversation with Alan Brownjohn, 28 Mar. 2008.

I attempt to write some further lines, I hear an incessant clamour and laughter and snarling and urgent cries of advice and abuse... *Je m'en fous d'ailleurs.*' When verse writing proved difficult, he turned to prose. On his walks along the river his eye had been caught by the 1882 statue of Thomas Carlyle by Joseph Edgar Boehm in Cheyne Walk Gardens, and soon he was at work on a book-length essay on Carlyle. Kathleen Raine was writing on Coleridge, their essays ultimately appearing as supplements to *British Book News* and in the British Council's series *Writers and Their Work* (his as no. 23, hers as no. 43). Gascoyne's set Carlyle is a wider context than Scotland or even Britain, aiming at nothing less than 'a re-interpretation, relating him to the great nineteenth-century thinkers who represented the living spiritual consciousness in exile in the Egypt of bourgeois capitalist society—"a castle-builder's world"—to Kierkegaard above all; to Joseph le Maistre and Baudelaire, to Tennyson, Browning and Arnold, to Nietzsche, Whitman and Ibsen. To Ruskin and perhaps to Kingsley.'[2] Here was Carlyle, to adapt one of his own phrases, as Existentialist precursor and hero. As ever, Gascoyne could not keep personal anxieties out of the exercise. The more he thought about Jane Carlyle—with whom Thomas had lived on terms of chaste mutual recrimination for thirty years—the more she came to resemble Hedda Gabler, and by extension Biddy Crozier, against whom he was still ineptly chafing. Applying the plot of Ibsen's play to this insight, he was soon writing one of his own entitled *The Holly* [Jane] *and the Ivy* [Thomas]. Jane stung; Thomas clung. In this revision of history it is not John Stuart Mill's unfortunate housemaid who has flung the priceless manuscript of volume i of *The French Revolution* onto the parlour fire, but Jane. Following this Ibsen-like act of gender liberation, she persuades the maid to own up.[3]

David was now reading much contemporary and traditional literature through equivalently dark lenses. After Sitwell lent him a copy of her recently published *Notebook on William Shakespeare*,[4] he went along so see Peter Brooke's production of *The Winter's Tale* at the Phoenix Theatre, with John Gielgud in the role of Leontes, Flora Robson as Paulina, and Diana Wynyard as Hermione. In his notebook he interprets the play in the light of Sitwell's reading of *Othello*. Projecting as ever his own angst, he detects a 'demoniacal mystery in Shakespeare'.[5] 'The theme of treachery,

2. BL Add. 71704 G, fo. 41, discussing David Gascoyne, *Thomas Carlyle* (British Council Writers and Their Work, 23; London: Longman, 1952).
3. BL Add. 71704 H, fo. 21.
4. Edith Sitwell, *A Notebook on William Shakespeare* (London: Macmillan, 1948).
5. BL Add. 71704 J, fo. 13.

duplicity and gratuitous impulsion to ruin', he observes, 'must now be sought for in other plays and one might at last arrive at a sensational new interpretation of Shakespeare's work which would at the same time shed new light on the hidden mystery of Shakespeare's mid-life and duality', including his sexuality. This was scarcely an original line: its unusual ingredient was that he went on to attribute this destructive tendency in *The Winter's Tale* not to the overheated imaginings of Leontes, but to Hermione herself, complicit all along in the suspicions levelled against her. And when Chatto and Windus issued Empson's *The Structure of Complex Words* that year, he examined chapter 11 on 'Honest *Othello*', only to upbraid his friend for failing to acknowledge the repressed homosexuality in Iago's— and by implication in his own—temperament.

For years now he had also been wrestling with an ambitious theological work called *The Sun at Midnight* in which he announced the dispelling of the darkness of modern man by the glowing star of a forthcoming Theocratic Revolution.[6] The project was grandly conceived, frequently announced and discussed. He had already poured its intimations of futurity into Lehmann's uncomprehending ears.[7] He now buttonholed Julian Huxley to expound his cosmic theory of Dialectical Super-Materialism (the conception of which sounds a little like Teilhard de Chardin's noosphere), and one Boxing Day he prevailed on his long-suffering brother John to drive him to Oxford, where he trespassed on the festive celebrations of a member of the university's Physics Department in order to expatiate on much the same theme. The physicist sat stony-faced, then showed them politely to the door.

He was still typing out revised drafts of this magnum opus when in July 1951 Sitwell announced at one of her lunches the imminent arrival of two interesting guests from America. Tennessee Williams had settled in at the Cavendish, and the novelist Carson McCullers had taken a room at the Dorchester which, Gascoyne soon noted, 'she did not like'.[8] Instead he found a room for her with the Russell brothers in Paultons Square where he himself was staying, and escorted her around a London where the Festival of Britain was in full flood, misfits together. McCullers had a number of medical complaints including the aftermath of a series of strokes which had left her hyper-nervous

6. Extensive typescripts and drafts are to be found at Beinecke, Box 6, Folders 69–73. Other sheets at Box 2, Folder 24.
7. John Lehmann, *I and My Brother* (London: Longman, 1960), 33.
8. BL Lives, F1538, Side A.

and with a marked tremble; like David she was subject to fits of convulsive and confessional speech during which others found it difficult to interrupt her, or even to connect. On 20 August Lehmann gave a dinner party for them both, with Henry Yorke, Bill Samson, and Moura Budberg, 'a strange party that never coalesced as one, everyone having their own lunch party, Carson looking sometimes with astonished misery at Bill and Henry cracking jokes together, David suddenly making some mysterious rapid low-toned conversation that nobody could understand, and Carson suddenly announcing that her husband was an epileptoid alcoholic—nobody quite knowing how to take it.' Between them their candour could be alarming, but it was often at cross-purposes. Five days later they came to dinner with Lehmann again, and this time they brought along Tennessee who was, Lehmann noticed, 'in great form . . . As usual Carson and David talked across one another, David muttering madly on until I rudely asked him to shut up because I wanted to hear Carson—and he went off, and I had to wheedle him back and ask forgiveness . . . In the end . . . we jumped into a car and toured round and round and over the bridges to see the lights of the Festival and Funfair . . . Carson surprised me by talking quite openly of Tennessee's habits and compulsions.'[9]

As his edition of Patchen and the recent Stevens pastiche had suggested, Gascoyne's interest in American writers went back decades. American verse had been a feature of the public readings at Harold Monro's bookshop. As a teenager he had read 'Calamus' from Walt Whitman's *Leaves of Grass*, a satisfying contrast to the copy of *Les Fleurs du mal* he had scoured in Kew Gardens: a 'Jamesean juxtaposition', he had considered it to be: 'innocent Whitman, corrupt Baudelaire'. He had first acquired a volume by Stevens from Sylvia Beach's shop in Paris in 1933: it was the 'chic Knopf first edition of *Harmonium*' in its white dust jacket, an act both of faith and of discernment: this would have been one of the remaindered copies at 11 cents apiece the publisher had disposed of twelve years before after the first hundred had been sold, thus placing it within the means of a 17-year-old bibliophile of limited funds.

During the war the American bug had almost bankrupted him, since he took to dispatching copious lists of book requests to Gotham Book Mart at 51 West 47th Street, ordered on credit. He had run up a bill of 200 dollars,

9. John Lehmann, Diary B4, pp. 52 and 55, John Lehmann family papers, 1649-1990, Princeton University Library, Manuscripts Division, CO746, series 4, box 74.

and in 1945 ordered for them fifty complimentary copies of *Poems 1937–1942* in a vain attempt to settle the debt.[10] His credit had promptly been wiped out by another huge order: Marianne Moore, Lowell, Emily Dickinson, Frost, Crowe Ransom, Richard Eberhart, cummings, Gertrude Stein, more Stevens. All ticked off, all dispatched. Frances Steloff, the shop's poetry-loving proprietor, later told Raine that she had countenanced the debt 'just because he showed such good taste—all the best poetry as it appeared—She said that when he won his recognition, the Gotham would be proud that he should owe something of it to them.'[11] For months he had been preparing an annotated anthology of American verse ranging from Archibald MacLeish though Richard Eberhart to Pound, Lowell, Frost, and Conrad Aiken,[12] 'my mind's eye', as he later told Allen Ginsberg, 'familiar with a vision of a continent teeming with cement canyons, back lots, prairies, swamps, small towns, city slums, drugstores and deserts'.

It was thus in a receptive state of mind that summer that he received an invitation from John Malcolm Brinnin, who had already organized several reading tours of the United States for Dylan Thomas, to tour with Raine, suggesting they join up with 33-year-old Glaswegian poet W. S. (Sydney) Graham. Raine was less enthusiastic, involved as she was in a complicated passionate if platonic relationship with the homosexual naturalist and author Gavin Maxwell, to whose home off the coast of Scotland she was constantly commuting. She elaborated on her reluctance in a letter to her friend the Romanian Sephardic Jewish writer Elias Canetti, with which she opened a fresh journal that month, addressed throughout to Canetti as soulmate and confessor. (Canetti was fulfilling this role for several friends at the time, including Irish Murdoch.) Though she respected David's work, the prospect of being cast in his and Graham's company for weeks on end frankly appalled her. 'I will not', she asserted to Canetti, 'go with David and Graham . . . they are both Bohemians and accept a scale of human conduct that I cannot accept—not at least humanly . . . for the poetry I can accept, but how I despise them otherwise! My peers were Charles [Madge], Humphrey [Jennings] and William [Empson], and I can't when it comes to the point go off with men so much *their* inferiors.'

10. David Gascoyne to Gotham Book Mart, 18 Aug. 1945, Berg, Box 44.
11. Kathleen Raine, Journal for 1951, BL Add. 80783B, from which all subsequent quotations from Raine in this chapter are taken.
12. BL Add. 71704K, fos. 20 ff.

Overcoming her misgivings, however Raine flew out with her fellow poets in November,[13] with David taking the typescript of *The Sun at Midnight* in his luggage. She insisted they stay at different addresses in New York. David found a room with Stella Erskine, a British-born poetry lover at whose house in Brooklyn Heights, he was glad to learn, Hart Crane had earlier stayed. On the first foggy morning he woke up to the strain of sirens from the nearby Navy Yard that reminded him of the fragmentary, acerbic music of Edgar Varèse. Raine lodged with Ruthven Todd, now running the Weekend Press in New York and preparing a scholarly edition of Blake. The flat was cramped: Ruthven shared the one bedroom with his partner, the sculptress Joellen Rapee or 'Jody'. Raine slept on the sofa.

Their first engagement was a reading and symposium at the Poetry Center at the Young Men's and Young Women's Hebrew Association on 92nd Street, of which Brinnin was director. It was a near fiasco for David since, as he later told the speed-addicted Ginsberg, 'I had been rushing about that day trying to get a fix to boost me for the evening, and arrived strung-up and late.'[14] But the appreciative audience included Marianne Moore, the Grand Old Lady of American poetry, who invited them to pay a call on her at her tiny Brooklyn flat. Raine and David went by taxi with Ruthven and Jody, who to Raine's annoyance chain-smoked throughout. But Moore inspired her with envy: a sort of female T. S. Eliot, she received them politely 'in her little old maid's apartment, full of old furniture and a stable past, old photographs, little antique elephants, quantities of little tables and old mahogany chairs... David talked freely as he always does on literary occasions, and I looked with modified admiration at this very perfected character who had never made errors of taste or judgement as I have, in her life or in her poetry, who has expressed passion by reserve (if at all), never by violation (as I have), who is a lady and now sits enthroned on the bric-a-brac of a virtuous and honoured literary career.'[15]

On 8 December there was a two-day colloquium at Bard College up the Hudson, where they conferred with senior American poets. When each was asked to explain their approach to writing, a difference of philosophy

13. Philippa Bernard, *No End to Snowdrops: A Biography of Kathleen Raine* (London: Shepheard-Walwyn, 2009), 85.

14. 'Anniversary Epistle to Allen', in *Kanrecki: A Tribute to Allen Ginsberg*, pt. 2, ed. Bill Morgan (New York: Lospecchio Press, 1986), 48–52, at 48.

15. BL Add. 80783 B.

became apparent. Graham had been increasingly preoccupied with technique and verbal texture since the magazine publication the previous year of his poem 'The Nightfishing'.[16] The overt mysticism of Gascoyne and Raine he found puzzling and irrelevant. 'David and I', Raine summarized afterwards, 'believe in an objective reality, the revealing of which is the task of poetry and the arts; Sydney takes the Humpty Dumpty view of words—that the poet is the master, and can make with words what he likes. A domineering attitude, yet in a way a workmanlike approach, if he were not so insensitive towards the whole central purpose of poetry, the uncovering of the face of a Platonic universe of eternal essences. He blusters about the technique of writing, and I must grant that he is more skilled and conscientious than I am about learnable rhetoric, but he has no conception of Metaphysics.'

The following morning John Berryman gave a talk on the relationship between poetry and prose. As Raine recorded, 'David then said, in his Sybiline way, that poetry has to do with the Redemption, prose with the Fall of man. I said prose communicates to the Ego, poetry to the whole personality of man, at deeper, almost unconscious levels. Graham did not know what we were talking about.' On such subjects she sided with David, with whom she also agreed 'that the language of human wholeness is poetry'. She was, she now acknowledged, 'less of an artist by instinct than David; W. S. Graham obviously thinks that I have no rhetoric, and William [Empson] obviously thinks the same'. That night she had a dream 'in which I tried to kill a woman who mocked at me and told me how David was the only true poet here, and that my appearance with him was a laughable insult to him and myself'.

They had hooked up with the 55-year-old American poet Louise Bogan and with Lys Connolly, Cyril's New York residing sister, who on the 12th threw a dinner party for them all, together with Auden and a former boyfriend of Peter Watson with his current male lover. 'David', Raine observed, 'is going from strength to strength, and Auden, like Pound, is a big figure in these days. One can hear his voice on the telephone three rooms away; and his face is deeply scored with lines that passion and experience and an active consciousness have written there.' 'David in New York', she extolled a couple of days later, 'becomes more and more extraverted. Everybody loves him, and his poetry.' Ruthven planned to honour the memory of their com-

---

16. Eventually published as the title poem of *The Nightfishing* (London: Faber, 1955).

mon friend Humphrey Jennings, who had died that summer while filming in the Aegean: seeking a wider angle for a shot, he had moved backwards across a mountain ledge and disappeared over the edge. As well as documentary films, he had left a clutch of unpublished poems, of which Todd was running off a selection at his Weekend Press. One midnight he turned up clutching the first two copies, one for Raine and the other for Frances Steloff. 'David and I', recorded Raine, 'went off to the Gotham Book Mart with them, and Frances was delighted and proposed a party after Christmas to launch the book, at which we will give a reading of Humphrey's poetry. Wonderful!' That night Raine dreamed Charles Madge and then David attempted to rape her. The second apparition especially appalled her. 'Instead of Charles being the incubus alone whom I fought off, it was David—I fought him off with all my strength for what seemed an age, succeeding at last in keeping him away sexually . . . I have to fight them off because in my dreams (as in reality) I have a physical horror of them—no, not of Charles, only an indifference (physical), but of David a stronger distaste if only because proposals of marriage from David are still recurrent possibilities and I have a certain sense that he would like to take possession of me and suck me dry (he is—all unconsciously—a spiritual vampire and utterly exhausting to be with for long) and allow me to look after him in my way—for he has the instinctual egotism of an animal—a cuckoo I meant to write. Sexual demands are the only ones he would not make.'

Seeking images for her resistance to Gascoyne, she drew on her knowledge as a naturalist (twenty years before, Raine had sat part 1 of the Cambridge tripos in botany). David, she now decided, was a sort of parasite that 'like a tropical pitcher plant or mistletoe must find a tree on which to root himself. That is, in no way blameworthy, on the contrary I wish he could find one always, because the flower produced by David's epiphytic existence is one of rare beauty. And apart from that aspect of David, there is another, that of friendship, pure and simple, which I value indeed at its true worth, for his unfailing generosity, gentleness, humour even, imagination, everything one could desire at the higher level. He ought however to be epiphytic not on another poet but on some good motherly soul like Mrs Erskine whose existence is justified, in her own eyes even (principally) by being able to contribute to the creation of works of genius that she admires.' These were prophetic words.

Two months later she would wonder whether dreams such as hers originated in the mind of those dreamed about. If David stalked her dreams, did she herself stalk Gavin's? Her apprehension of male poets soon received ratification. The following week she went to dinner with George Reavey, who had also moved to America. Afterwards there was a gathering at which an increasingly sozzled Graham made half-serious advances to every woman in the room. When he reached Raine, he lurched across and breathed, 'Why should you and I not get married?' Raine laughed him off. Later that week Djuna Barnes invited them to join her in a café on West 8th Street. David breezed in, manically expansive. He was bearing 'an orchid tied up with mauve ribbon—David has no taste in flowers, but I will say he brings them—and to David this was a full-blown literary occasion—as all David's meetings are. I had been talking to Djuna about common friends...but David was in a very confident mood and kept on interposing literary references: "I used to live on the same staircase as e.e.cummings in Paris, etc." Then some reference to marriage arose—I said that I would never marry again, and David, just to show off in front of Djuna that he has the right to propose to me, made a tentative "Are you sure you would never change your mind?" approach, not realising that I only tolerate him from a sense of responsibility that I have assumed towards him, and I would never marry him if he was the last man alive—hateful thought. If I hold David's hand and give him a friendly kiss, it is only to comfort him and show him that he is not really repulsive.'

In certain respects Raine found Gascoyne absurd. His politics, for example, appeared to her a sham. She had been invited to Washington for Christmas, and whilst there proposed to visit Ezra Pound, incarcerated in St Elizabeth's hospital after pleading insanity after his wartime radio broadcasts on behalf of Mussolini. David now protested he would never visit someone of Pound's ideological complexion. 'He hates Confucius and Socrates as well as Pound,' Raine noted, 'and authoritarian theories of any kind. Perhaps he's right about Fascism, but I feel that David's Leftism is so very largely a personal insubordination, mixed up with his homosexuality and his shame because he has lived for years by taking money from people who could afford to give it, and many who could not, that his political affiliations have no objective significance.' 'Really,' she went on, 'David's political talk is neurotic drivel, but lots of people will take it seriously because it has all the earnest high mindedness of neurotic thought.' His disapproval of her for planning to visit the author of *The Cantos* provoked a sharp response: 'Why does David think I have taken so much trouble with him?' she fumed to Canetti. 'Is he not also a criminal lunatic?'

At a quarter past ten on the night before she set out, Gascoyne loped up the stairs to Ruthven's flat. Raine was in no welcoming mood. 'I merely said "I am just going to bed, David" and shut the door...I hope David stays in America, my patience with him is at breaking point.' In Washington she lodged with Charles Empson, brother of William and currently British minister at the Embassy, and his wife Monica.[17] When she got back to the Big Apple in early January, she learned that David had been haunting the Todds' flat over the holiday, complaining about having no money, and looking for her. He had already quarrelled with his hostess Mrs Erskine, 'and his life is again in decline'. She was still furious with him over his public proposal of marriage, however light-heartedly meant. When they met, she told him that she had bought her passage by sea back to Southampton, and he replied he did not see how he could afford it. Then he asked her 'dramatically' for some paper on which to write to Florida about a forthcoming engagement, only to be told to wait until the New School of Social Science paid him for a recent event. Over Christmas Gascoyne had been to visit Auden at his apartment on the corner of Seventh Avenue and 23rd Street, where he had lent him the typescript of *The Sun at Midnight*, and stayed overnight. Kathleen herself now went along to lunch. For twelve years Auden had been a communicant Episcopalian and lived, she appreciatively discovered, 'largely on Italian music and his Anglicanism'. He 'obviously respects people who can behave well, but also spoke very kindly about David...He likes his poetry and says what an innocent he is (and what a naïve book *The Sun At Midnight*, because David has no idea what has been thought and said before) and asked me if David is capable of doing even the simplest job, like working in a bookshop. I said no, someone will always have to look after him. Auden said he was not good enough to find (as Joyce did) a disinterested patron, and that there is always a price to pay for patronage if one is less than great, personal conditions attached, pity or sex, or some such thing.'

Then she was off by train to Harvard to lecture, staying with Empson's old Cambridge supervisor I. A. Richards, with whom she bewailed the absence of any responsible generation between Eliot and 'the guttersnipe poets (Barker, Graham + Dylan Thomas + poor David): none of these have a responsible attitude towards society'. As if to prove the point, David came round as soon as she got back 'very depressed because he has not got his fare to Philadelphia

---

17. Bernard, *No End to Snowdrops*, 86.

next day to read his poems there. He moped and I was schoolmistressly and unresponsive, but finally asked Jody to lend me five dollars.' She asked him why he had made no effort to sell his latest poems to the *New Yorker*, and he replied that he had no copy to send, 'so I suggested he sat down and typed them out, which he did. When I gave him the 5 dollars he cheered up and went off to get his ticket.'

On his return from Florida there was the launch of Jenning's poems at the Gotham, where David read some of his friend's work aloud in a 'good clear voice'. 'Beautiful' Frances Steloff presided; as a parting gift she gave Raine a volume of essays by the Japanese scholar Daisetsu Teitaro Suzuki on Zen Buddhism, in which she and David had both expressed an interest. On her last day David called round at the flat to say farewell. Aboard the *Queen Mary* she paid £20 she could ill afford to upgrade from steerage to cabin class. The move, she informed Canetti in a candid aside, permitted her the privacy she sorely needed, away from the sort of people she had been obliged to consort with in the States, including 'Sidney Graham, who made his circles with people he could drink or sleep with; and David who is, although a fine poet, what he himself calls—a vagrant'. In the luxury of her private cabin she concluded 'I have done all I can in America. Unless you say I have neglected David. Well, if I have, I have. It can't be helped, and I can do no more.'

The Suzuki essays proved a topic of conversation when David called round the following month to the see the 'quiet, kind and cagey' composer John Cage in his East Side apartment, furnished in 'typically austere minimal Japanese style'. That year Cage was embarking on his first experiments with prepared tape and, as David later recalled to Ginsberg, it must also 'have been at the time when his "interest in" (J.C. seems to me to be too cool to have admitted to a "passion for") Zen Buddhism was probably at its height'.[18] When Gascoyne mentioned his own amateur interest in Zen, Cage told him that Suzuki was visiting professor at Columbia for the semester just commencing, and offered to take him along to hear him lecture. They found two seats near the podium. 'Suzuki', Gascoyne would later recount to Ginsberg, 'began his discourse by telling us just how many sermons the Buddha delivered, and at which places; we were then told just how many people had been privileged to be present at each sermon (little or nothing regarding the teaching).

---

18. 'Anniversary Epistle to Allen', fo. 50.

Then came an enumeration of those followers from whose heads lotus plants had emerged during the course of the sermons, how many lotus-leaves had emerged from each plant (my chin was already beginning to droop intermittently), and how many celestial beings were seated on each lotus-leaf; then how many lotuses emerged from the head of each celestial being (bodhissatva?), how many minor celestial beings were seated on the leaves of... but by this time I was sound asleep, not to awaken until Cage gave me a dig with his elbow and the lecture was over.' The purpose of this teaching method, he decided, was to dissuade trendy dilettantes from attending the rest of the course. 'On the whole,' he confessed to Ginsberg, 'I guess I'm allergic to gurus.'

One day the painter Nico Calas drove him out to Rutherford, New Jersey to visit William Carlos Williams, who had only just retired as one of the town's doctors. They found plenty in common: both distrusted Pound (Williams for his eclectic allusions, Gascoyne for his politics) and both had mingled with the Surrealists, several of whom Williams had encountered in New York during the war. His conversation was 'mild, wise and sometimes tetchy'. There was something genuinely and authentically American about him, a contrast in style to e.e.cummings, whom Gascoyne called on at Patchin Place in the early summer. Cummings seemed still to be mentally half in Paris: he asked about their landlady at the Rue de la Bûcherie, fallen on sad times since the Occupation. She had, he told a touched Gascoyne, latterly displayed a copy of his Hölderlin translations on her dining room table next to some of cummings's own work.

It was cummings who brought to Gascoyne's attention the availability of artistic residences at Yaddo in Saratoga Springs in upstate New York, where he spent two months in the late summer.[19] The Korean War was at its height, the McCarthy persecution just ending, and General Eisenhower canvassing for the Republican nomination with the slogan 'I like Ike' and an implied promise to bring an end to the war and prosecution of leftish leaning intellectuals. At Yaddo feelings ran high. Among the writers was the inappropriately named Kenneth Fearing, co-founder of the *Partisan Review*, later an early influence on Ginsberg. Fearing was Illinois-born, and represented a different aspect American authenticity to Doc Williams. His Chicago accent was so thick Gascoyne almost could not make out his words, and he carried

---

19. Berg, Yaddo Collection, Guest Files A, Box 247, Folder 21.

with him an aura that was urban, bitter, and forlorn. He was a pessimist at heart, with a dark Swiftean wit and a deep distrust of the structures of capitalism. In *Fearing* two meanings of depression seem to have enjoined; he epitomized a period and a mood. During the McCarthy period he had survived through guile; interviewed by the FBI in 1950 and asked whether he was a Communist, he replied 'Not yet'. Gascoyne and he struck up a deep, dour, and slow-moving accord. He was, remembered Gascoyne, 'of a mellow disposition, though inclined to be taciturn'. When he did talk, Gascoyne listened enthralled, in touch with a peculiarly American sort of bleakness, an atmosphere conveyed by a sound Gascoyne heard for the first time at Saratoga: 'the occasional approaching then diminishing of 9 late night goods train bound for far places'.

On the day Eisenhower won the nomination, Gascoyne boarded a greyhound bus to Chicago on the first leg of a journey northwards to join Leslie and Win on Vancouver Island. On the hottest day of the year he presented himself at the offices of *Poetry* (Chicago) where, after taking him to lunch, Isabella Gardner, the editor's secretary, introduced him to a wealthy patroness of the magazine. She drove him round the windy city in her chauffeured limousine and asked which cultural sites he would like to see. Gascoyne was in no mood to be patronized, and keen to shock. He asked to be shown the homes of Richard Loeb and Nathan Leopold, the homosexual couple who in May 1924 had murdered Bobbie Franks, the 14-year-old schoolboy son of a local millionaire. Afterwards he said that he would like to see 2122 North Clark Street where at the garage of the SCM Cartage Company members of Al Capone's North Side Gang had systematically mown down seven aficionados of Bugs Moran's South Side gang during the St Valentine's Day Massacre of 14 February 1929. His hostess expressed 'real disappointment' that a visiting English poet should regard her city in that way. Instead he was taken to the university, where Loeb and Leopold had once studied, then to the Art Institute where 'I sat a long time in air-conditioned contemplation of Seurat's *La Grande Jatte*'.[20]

The greyhound took him onwards via Minneapolis Saint Paul, and thence to Seattle 'that civilised city with its beautiful Sound', where he was due to catch a boat to Canada. In New York Louise Bogan had encouraged him to pay his respects to Theodore Roethke, a former lover of hers, now poet-in-

20. 'Anniversary Epistle to Allen', fo. 51.

residence at the University of Washington. Roethke's reputation was a little
unsteady: he had progressed from the brief, compact, flower-studded lyrics
of *Open House* Bogan had admired so much in the forties towards the looser,
more elliptical structures of *The Waking*. After a day at Mount Rainier
National Park, a woman colleague drove Gascoyne up to Roethke's 'cabin
on a green cliff top overlooking the amethyst sound. That this poet should
have been known as Teddy is a funny coincidence: he was indeed very bear-
like, though not like the old grizzly I had just seen shambling up the lower
slopes of Mount Rainier, but a burly bear whose honey was alcohol.'[21]
Roethke had hosted Dylan Thomas the year before, so had a healthy respect
for the constitutions of British poets. As the sun slowly sank over the Pacific,
they sat downing glass after glass of increasingly strong cocktails of martini
and bourbon. After a wine-fuelled dinner, Gascoyne was taken down to the
Faculty Club where the English Department were holding an end-of-year
party and where again 'booze was as abundant as the brouhaha'. In the midst
of the shindig he suddenly recalled that his boat to Victoria left at midnight.
Roethke drove him down to the docks and settled him into his cabin, where
he rolled into a bunk and awoke the next morning in Canada. It was, he
later enthused to Ginsberg, 'a glorious way of ending my first stay in the
States'.

21. 'Anniversary Epistle to Allen', fo. 52.

21

Megalometropolitan

In the autumn of 1952 Gascoyne flew back to Britain from his parents' home in Canada. He re-entered an ambience whose poetic and intellectual tone seemed to him subtly to be changing. It was to be a further two years before, in an anonymous article in *The Spectator*, the magazine's literary editor, J. D. Scott, would identify a shift in national literary life towards what came to be known as 'the Movement',[1] a mood that would be characterized later in the decade by Charles Tomlinson as that of a 'Middlebrow Muse' compounded of parochialism, irony, and a distrust of rhetorical thought and expression.[2] 'A new type of poet', Tomlinson then sagely opined, 'has impinged on the literary scene.' With his hypersensitive cultural antennae Gascoyne had already picked up this change before others had sensed—still less labelled—it. In the New Year of 1953 he wrote a letter to Raine bewailing the narrowing of literary horizons, and reaffirming a commitment to broader vistas. His exemplar of what could be achieved with more mental ambition was the philosopher Simone Weil, Jewish-born, mystically inclined, politically active, ecumenical in persuasion. Since her death at the age of 34 in 1943, Weil's notebooks had been published in French and then English translation: *Waiting on God* in 1951, then in 1952 her *The Need for Roots: Prelude To A Declaration of Duties Towards Mankind*, with a Preface by Eliot. These edited, exploratory texts had been sympathetically reviewed by Raine; they were a lodestar to Gascoyne.

On Sunday afternoons, which they were regularly spending together, one or the other of them would walk round the corner to Carlyle Mansions off the Chelsea Embankment, where Eliot shared a large flat with John Hayward, omnivorous literary scholar and acerbic wit, who was confined to a wheelchair. They would then push Hayward round to Paultons Square

1. 'In The Movement', *The Spectator*, 1 Oct. 1954.
2. Charles Tomlinson, 'The Middlebrow Muse, *Essays in Criticism*, 7/2 (1957), 208–17.

and devote the afternoon to conversation. After one such session discussing Weil, Gascoyne wrote to Raine that the talk had impressed on his mind the importance of maintaining a 'religious position', and suggesting an exchange of letters that might help them to clarify their ideas. He went on to express his personal frustration at the lack of a contemporary public platform open to these ambitious perspectives: 'I am at the present considerably perplexed and dissatisfied with myself because of a feeling of having no specific audience to address. One has no pulpit. It is not that I have an urge to preach, but that I have a sense of the need—I suppose I really mean *duty*—to testify.'[3]

Of late, frictions in America having cleared the air, Kathleen and he were certainly growing more open with one another. One of the matters they argued out, sometimes with heat, was David's sexuality. Raine's platonic love affair with the homosexual Maxwell was growing more fraught by the month: when in London she was inclined to take her frustrations out on David as the nearest homosexual male. Early in 1953 this tendency led to a row during which she inveighed at length on the unnaturalness of same-sex love. Realizing she had gone too far and attacked the wrong person, she promptly wrote a tender letter of apology: 'I hate to think how fierce and horrible I was to you the other evening. You know I respect your embracing of the cause of *all* the outcast and oppressed more than anything else you hold by, and I know how true and sincere and full of love your motives are. Christ descended into Hell, and I often think of you as sharing that descent, and carrying through the darkness your affirmation of love. I know you are right—who can doubt it?'[4]

By 1953 Raine had reached the conclusion that, whatever Gascoyne's shortcomings and perplexities, one needed to accept him on his own uncomfortable terms. When that July she was awarded the annual Arts Council Prize for Poetry, she promptly passed on to him as much of the money she could afford. She had duties towards her children, she explained in her covering letter, and a necessity to keep a home going. Yet, 'little as it is, this is the only cheque I have written this morning that has given me real pleasure. The rest has already disappeared.'[5]

As soon as he could, Gascoyne headed once more for Paris, where for the next few months he moved from address to address, footloose, lonely, but always resourceful. One evening he shared a bed in a small hotel in the Rue

3. David Gascoyne to Kathleen Raine, probably early 1953, Beinecke, Box 11, Folder 253.
4. Kathleen Raine to David Gascoyne, n.d., probably early 1953, Beinecke, Box 10, Folder 208.
5. Kathleen Raine to David Gascoyne, n.d., probably July 1953, Beinecke, Box 10, Folder 208.

Molière with a 25-year-old actor from the Comédie-Française called Claude. He slept and, when he awoke, found his lover had fled. The letter he wrote in French later that morning plays compulsively with various meanings of the words 'honesty' and 'acting'. It also tells us a lot about the difficulties Gascoyne experienced in speaking truthfully about private matters, hamstrung by scruples of various kinds. Before sending it, he had wrestled with this heart-searching draft:

> Dear Claude,
>
> I woke us this morning in a pensive, if quite exalted, state of mind.
>
> True honesty is seldom coarsely stupid, and entertains no conception—or strives to entertain no conception—of what is means to take advantage of another.
>
> I'm sure you yourself are not dishonest, but I sense you have taken insufficient account of just how hard it is to be truly honest with someone else. And I also suspect that you must have found me lacking in sense, for all my 'artistic intelligence' and so on.
>
> To be honest means to be sincere; which in turn means looking life straight between the eyes without flinching, discomfort or evasion. Responding to life without hesitation or defensiveness. When it comes down to it, I am sure you recognize this just as well as I do. But it involves scrupulous alertness every hour of the day.
>
> Such vigilance and care are not products of pain. Pain only comes from carelessness. The skill of the greatest acting lies in the balance between honesty and contrivance. A great actor is never deliberately dishonest, especially when not on stage.
>
> To be dishonest without realizing it, intending it, or seeking to confront it—nothing could be more disastrous, more completely ruinous or conducive to unhappiness. It is the most absolute form of moral misery known to the human condition. Probably this is simple enough to say (Which is as much as to say: that truth is reluctant to recognize itself, with ultimate candour anyway, without seeking to dress itself up just a little...)
>
> On what subject are the worst actors (who are not always the least adept ones) able to dilate most freely, spontaneously and to most effect? You must know the answer, dear and lovely boy (though your naked and beautiful body knows nothing of all this, naturally). Are you any sadder today: are you any wiser, for instance? To enact a charade without a conscious decision to do so, through mere abandon—that is the quickest way to turn oneself into an indifferent young actor. Don't say I never told you so. I wish you well. I hope that one day you will learn just what real 'love' involves![6]

6. David Gascoyne to 'Claude', probably late 1953, French MS in Beinecke, Box 11, Folder 258.

He had never ceased thinking about the theatre or the potential of performances of various kinds. By February he had decamped to the Hôtel de Louisiane in the Rue de Seine, and was considering the possibilities of radio. The occasion was another loss: Paul Eluard, unrepentantly Marxist to the end, had died on 18 November at the age of 57. For Gascoyne the event signalled the disappearance not merely of an important mentor but of a particular presence and integrity, the withdrawal of a distinctive, deep-throated sonority. He was now working on an 'Elegiac Improvisation on the Death of Paul Eluard', the text of which was to appear in Princess Caetani's *Botteghe Oscure* the following April. He was also contemplating its radio transmission, appropriately enough since the poem concentrates on Eluard as an almost disembodied voice. In a passage playing with the manifold expressive possibilities of the adverb, he evokes Eluard's mouth declaiming

> Warmly and urgently
> Simply, convincingly
> Gently and movingly
> Softy, sincerely
> Clearly, caressingly
> Bitterly, painfully
> Pensively, stumblingly
> Brokenly, heartbreakingly...[7]

On 16 February 1954 he wrote to John Davenport investigating the possibility of having the elegy broadcast on the BBC Third Programme, to which Davenport was now attached as producer. He added that there were more recent French voices of a different sort deserving a hearing: 'There are a number of singers to be heard in Paris now who are highly intelligent artists specialising in a type of poetry which has virtually no equivalent in England.'[8] These were the new breed of nightclub performers, entertainers but also poets and consummate word-setters. Among them, and to be heard nightly at Les Trois Baudets or at the Harlequin Club beneath the all-night Pergola Café in Saint-Germain, was the velvet-voiced Catherine Sauvage, who sang settings of Aragon, Baudelaire, Brecht, Colette, Desnos, Eluard, Jarry, Lorca, Hugo, Prévert, and Soupault. On the right bank, in the club Milord l'Arsouille, named after an eccentric nineteenth-century English resident of Paris who had impersonated the King of the Carnival in around 1838,

7. *Collected Poems* (1965), 129.
8. David Gascoyne to John Davenport, 16 Feb. 1954, Beinecke, Box 11, Folder 236.

Michèle Arnaud sang settings of Apollinaire. On Davenport's commission, Gascoyne spent the early months of 1954 recording and interviewing several of these artists for a programme broadcast at the end of May.[9]

Contemporary French theatre too seemed to possess a vitality and originality still lacking in Britain two years short of the Royal Court revolution of 1956. Gascoyne reported back to Davenport on these further developments. Contemplating his own waning precocity he was, for instance, much taken by a powerful allegory of ageing in the form of a play by the 49-year-old Alexandria-born Lebanese dramatist Georges Schehadé, an admirer of Rimbaud, Lautréamont, Eluard, and Perse. Schehadé's 'superbly acted and produced period play *Soirée des Proverbes*' had just opened at Jean-Louis Barrault's recently established Marigny Little Theatre.[10] It concerned the boyish hunter Alexis, who, hearing of an entertainment being mounted in a glade in the Forêt des Quatre Diamants, attends it enthusiastically, only to find that the performers are all old. One of them is his elderly self, who raises a gun and shoots him so he may always remain young.

Schehadé was one of the small and active group of francophone Lebanese artists and poets educated in Beirut during the short-living French mandate from the League of Nations, now living and writing in Paris. He lodged at 40 Rue des Saints-Pères to the immediate north of the Boulevard Saint-Germain, eating his lunch every day without fail at Le Rouquet on the corner of the boulevard. Jouve considered Schehadé a 'butterfly', but then Jouve was growing increasingly inward-looking, self-absorbed, and prone to peremptory opinions: the eccentric and world-roving Belgian author Henri Michaux was a mere 'cosmopolite', the idealistic and now dead Jean Giraudoux had been a 'walking crown of thorns'. Jouve had also grown puritanical. One day he expressed disgust at a lurid passage in a magazine article devoted to him, until Blanche pointed out that it was a quotation from one of his own essays.[11] He had a tendency to adopt waifs and strays who reminded him of the self he might have become had Blanche not rescued him in early middle age. Blanche's own clientèle continued for the

9. 'Parisian Cabaret', dialogue composed and read by David Gascoyne, produced by Anna Kellin, BBC Third Programme, Monday 30 May 1955, 9.45–10.25 p.m., BBC archives, Caversham Tape CTFR 18426.

10. David Gascoyne to John Davenport, 16 Feb. 1954, Beinecke, Box 11, Folder 236. See Georges Schehadé, *La Soireé des proverbes* (Paris: Gallimard, 1954).

11. Conversation with Salah Stétié, 8 June 2010.

most part English-speaking and homosexual, many convinced against all the evidence that she could 'cure' them. Gascoyne was still consulting her daily.

The social life of Paris was just as clique-ridden as previously, just as much under the thumb of its 'grandes dames'. Schehadé and his younger compatriot Salah Stétié, who was studying in Paris prior to a double career as diplomat and poet, were both drawn into the circle around the wealthy Suzanne Tézenas. Her 'salon fermé' on the Rue Octave Feuillet in the sixteenth arrondissement included poets such as Jules Supervielle, Octavio Paz, Henri Michaux, Yves Bonnefoy, Gascoyne, and Stétié; as co-founder of 'le domain musical', the society for the private performance of avant-garde music, she was also home to composers such as Francis Poulenc and Pierre Boulez; along with theatrical types such as Barrault and Ionesco. The 28-year-old Boulez, who was experimenting with *musique concrète* and working on his song cycle *Le Marteau sans maître* to texts by René Char, directed the music at Barrault's theatre: he was one of the few people around with whom David could discuss John Cage. The others called him 'boubou'. At weekends all were invited down to a substantial property Tézenas owned on Lake Annecy, at Veyrier-du-Lac in the Haute-Savoie. The whole gabbling crew would resort there, the poet Yves de Bayser, a discovery of Char's who published in *Botteghe Oscure*, turning up in a battered *deux chevaux* with Gascoyne as his sole passenger.

To the younger members of this set, Gascoyne appeared impressive if enigmatic. In the eyes of Stétié, there seemed something thwarted about him, something ultimately self-involved, unable to escape a mystery he craved but also feared, unable maybe to confront his own God. 'David was', Stétié told me in 2010, sitting on the terrace of the café he and Schehadé had frequented the fifties, 'like a caterpillar that wished to become a moth without the bother of sleeping, and all the time dreamed of becoming a butterfly. Always he was trying to mix sand and water, but the water obstinately remained water, and the sand, sand. He needed yet lacked the female element in his life: all his women friends were substitute mothers, or perhaps nurses. He lacked the courage to be an outright homosexual, yet would not risk a fully-fledged relationship with a woman. Like his poetry with its slightly démodé vocabulary, his life lacked tenderness, the common touch, even slang.'[12]

Gascoyne's diffidence could affect the ways in which he committed himself to practical applications of his craft. Jouve, he well knew, was using radio

---

12. Conversation with Salah Stétié, 8 June 2010.

with increasing effectiveness and by June 1954 had completed a series of ten interviews for Radio France.[13] David proudly informed his father that he was himself being touted for a production job on French radio which might have suited him (only a financial crisis at Radio France prevented it.) In London too, Douglas Cleverdon, who had recently joined the Third Programme as an arts and drama producer, was urging him to work with the composer Humphrey Searle, innovative modernist, former student of Webern, whom David had met a few years previously at one of Sitwell's lunches. The collaborative scheme was very much of its time. One of the insufficiently recorded cultural aspects of the late 1940s and early 1950s remains the pervasive influence of the radio over two generations of intellectually adventurous Britons, instigated by the creation of the Third Programme in 1946 as a vehicle for serious thought, debate, and music. A generation of producers was pushing back the frontiers of the medium, among them the poet Louis MacNeice and the music producer Hans Keller, appointed by Gascoyne's friend William Glock and a champion of several twentieth-century composers, including David's beloved Bartók. Searle himself had a versatile background, and much in common with Gascoyne. Both were austere experimentalists in their respective spheres, eclectic in taste, unbound by convention. Raised in the Far East, with an Oxford degree in classics, Searle had devoted a two-year spell at the BBC between 1946 and 1948 to promoting works that employed the serial method. He continued to sit on the BBC's music reading panel and advise on the choice of modern works; he was used to thinking in medium-specific, as well as synaesthetic, terms. More perhaps than any other living British composer, Searle thought radiophonically.

Their first tentative act of collaboration brought together Gascoyne's love of American poetry with Searle's musical daring and a shared appreciation of modern art. *The Old Guitarist* had been painted by Picasso during his so-called Blue Period in 1903, and in 1937 had inspired Wallace Stevens's poem 'The Man with the Blue Guitar'. On 24 May, while back in London, Gascoyne recorded the poem for the Third, his voice accompanied by a solo guitar part composed by Searle and played by Freddie Phillips.[14] The script bears musical directions in Gascoyne's own hand so Phillips and he could

13. David Gascoyne to Leslie and Win Gascoyne, 28 June 1954, Beinecke, Box 11, Folder 239.
14. BBC Archives, Caversham, Tape TLO 79754.

keep time: 'accel' at one point.[15] Fortuitously the transmission served as a valedictory tribute to Stevens, who died on 2 August.

The grander ongoing scheme was a 'radiophonic poem' in three movements which Searle and Gascoyne discussed in Paris that June. With an eye to literary precedent Gascoyne had named it 'Night Thoughts', since it was under this title that Edward Young's poem *The Complaint* of 1742–3 was best known in England. Rendered into French as 'Les Nuits de Young', this devotional work had been an iconic text for the Surrealists. Gascoyne was aware that its Continental vogue was founded on a misunderstanding. Basing his impression on an inaccurate French prose translation, accompanied by woodcuts depicting ladies in graveyards fainting at the sight of reinvigorated skeletons, Breton had interpreted the work as Gothic fantasy; the original had been a pious piece of advocacy of the compensations of Heaven for the disappointments of earthly existence. With a further twist of metaphorical fancy, the title 'Nuits de Young' had since been appropriated as the name for a purple rose, probably under the misapprehension that the phrase referred to what the young do at night. But the nocturnal theme attracted Searle: his Op. 2 in 1943 had been *Night Music*, written for the sixtieth birthday of his old teacher Webern. The theme of dementia also appealed; his Op. 1 had been a setting of Gogol's *Diary of a Madman*. This was to be a work not so much written as jointly composed: less a radio play with incidental music—or even a set of words intended for musical setting— than a seamless event in which spoken, sung, and played sounds combined. Through it Britain's leading (if lapsed) exponent of Surrealism joined hands with Britain's principal proponent of Serialism.

It was a work that explored the conditions of its own reception. 'Night Thoughts' had been planned with Cleverdon as a solstitial transmission, to be relayed during the darkest weeks of 1955, towards the end of the broadcasting evening (the nightly 'closedown' with the national anthem then being at eleven). After several delays caused by Gascoyne's dilatory progress (a state of affairs brought to end by the encouraging payment of a BBC advance), the work was recorded at the Maida Vale Studios on 6 December, and broadcast the following night between 9.40 and 10.30, with a cast of eleven speaking voices, and Searle himself conducting the Symfonia of London, with James Blades on percussion.[16] It remains a highly effective

15. Beinecke, Box 5, Folder 65.
16. Ibid., and Box 14, Folder 302.

piece: in itself, and in its use of the medium. Fully to register this fact nowadays you need to transport yourself to a room late in the evening and in the
dead of winter. You need to close the curtains, turn out the lights and pref-
erably the central heating, and listen to a recording, seated in imagination in
the quasi-candlelight provided by the illuminated panel at the front of a
radio or crystal set of the mid-fifties. You are in a sort of modernist cell:

> Let those who hear my voice become aware
> That Night has fallen. We are in the dark.
> I do not see you, but in my mind's eye
> You sit in lighted rooms marooned by darkness.
> My message is sent out upon the waves
> Of a black boundless sea to where you drift,
> Each in a separate lit room, as though on rafts,
> Survivors of the great lost ship, *The Day*.[17]

There are no characters in this scenario, no actors as such, no narrator.
Instead there are voices that weave in and out, prompt or interrupt one
another, creating an all-embracing atmosphere of shared solitude. Some of
the voices (A, B, and C) are lyrical in tone, others (D, E, and F) colloquial
representatives of a community seized by loneliness and fear. They are ava-
tars of an all-embracing paranoia in the sense in which Dalí had used the
term in his pre-war essays: a paranoia with philosophical depth. In the first
movement, 'The Nightwatchers', these contrapuntal voices reveal themselves as citizens—this is a poem both of cosmic dread and of the city:
London and everywhere. Several of its interjections are drawn from
Gascoyne's notebooks: the neurotic interjections of Voice E, for example
(*The war? What war? We've had too many wars! The last war's over*) had originated in early sketches for 'The Hole in the Fourth Wall'. Some sound
rather like the broken, febrile voices that featured in Eliot's *The Waste Land*
(once entitled *He Do the Police in Different Voices,* and itself a proleptic radio
play). The second movement, 'Megalometropolitan', is full of cues for the
composer. It is a sort of *Walpurgisnacht* or urban Witches Sabbath set—like
the fifth movement from Berlioz's *Symphonie fantastique*, 'Songe d'une nuit
de Sabbat'—to the Gregorian chant *Dies Irae*. Searle combined these sombre strains with the children's jingle 'Girls and Boys Come Out to Play' in a

---

17. *Collected Poems* (1965), 134.

piece of bitonal counterpoint that built in intensity until abruptly brought to an end. Against such effects Gascoyne deployed his speaking voices as if instruments in a vocal ensemble, as in the Train-Wheels Chorus ('*Hurry Up and Get On Hurry Up And Get On*') which, even as it recalls Eliot's 'Hurry Up Please, It's Time', achieves quite a different pace and effect.[18]

With Movement Three ('Encounter with Silence'), we are out in the countryside. Quietness prevails. In a garden a solitary walker (reminiscent of the night visitant in Gascoyne's 'The Sacred Heart', and played in the broadcast by Norman Shelley) stares up at the night sky, clear for once of the luminary fuzz of the city. We have been here before in Gascoyne's work, in the terror of nothingness evoked in some of the earlier notebooks. But, instead of pervasive dread, we are met with a moment of mystical Pascalian-cum-Existentialist healing. The philosophical underpinning is implicitly that of Heidegger, a Heidegger most improbably rendered into flowing English free verse. Against a backdrop of silence, the solitary evokes his encounter with that lingering entity Heidegger had termed *Dasein*, an intimation of a common ground of being that alone can save us from the threatening abyss of nothingness. The result is that difficult, embattled thing, modern prayer:

> O Being, be! O be what faces me, to whom my heart may speak.
> Almightness, O be the Face that bent over me, O be aware and hear.
> Acknowledge me, accept me, and may my response responded to help me
>   slowly to realize how we are thus akin.
> O be the One, that I may never be alone in knowing what I am.
> Let my lost loneliness be illusory. Allow to me a part in Being, that I may thus
>   be part of One and All.[19]

In *Night Thoughts* Gascoyne converted his individual isolation into a universal condition, sharing it with thousands of listeners, each of whom he imagined sitting alone in a dark night, maybe of the soul, but also of a bedsit or suburban drawing room. It was a work he was uniquely qualified to write: through his recurrent depressive condition, which became a creative opportunity; through his sexual loneliness (and thus his empathy with various kinds of loneliness in others); through his self-imposed course of reading in literatures and schools of thought, and his sensitivity to the alienated and

---

18. Taped broadcast at BL Sound Archive T138W and Beinecke, Box 19, Folder 304.
19. *Collected Poems* (1965), 161.

uncertain mood of the times. With hindsight it appears surreal in method and effect, though it was characteristic of the author that he had achieved this in a medium few paid-up Surrealists used, and sometime after he had lost faith in the Surrealist creed. It is a poem for all times and places, and yet one that could almost only have been written towards the beginning of the cold war; in Western Europe in its first pervasively secular phase; in singular financial insecurity, frustration, weariness, and countervailing hope. Within a very few months André Deutsch had published it. It would feature as the climax and culmination of Gascoyne's first *Collected Poems*.

He was working with other composers. In 1938 he had written for Priaulx Rainier, while both were in Paris, a prophetic poem of war, 'Requiem'. She had spent fifteen years mulling over the work and was now living in a studio in St Ives close to Barbara Hepworth, whom she was helping to create a sculptural garden adjoining her studio above the town. On 3 January 1956 she wrote to say she had finished a full draft. 'I find the Requiem a very great poem,' she told Gascoyne, 'living and working with it day and night for three months—its profundity is revealed and remains inspiring. I hope to present the meaning with the fullest intensity, for its statement is one which we all need at this time—at any time.'[20]

Rainier's setting for tenor solo and a cappella choir was performed during a series of Museum Gallery Concerts at the Victoria and Albert Museum on 15 April 1956 under the auspices of the Chamber Music Society. Imogen Holst conducted, Peter Pears—whom Gascoyne had known since his Crozier days—took the solo part, and the chorus were the Purcell Singers. In long, echoing, filigree lines suited to Peter Pears's light yet resonant voice, Rainier had captured much of the poem's anticipatory sense of menace and underlying compassion. The accompanying chorus part was for the most part in block chords, or else in unison.[21]

Most requiems are for the recently deceased, or perhaps for the survivors. Gascoyne's had been written in the immediate lead-up to the war, and was specifically intended for the prospective victims of a conflict then felt to be inevitable. The text was therefore of as much relevance to 1956 as to 1939. The work was reviewed favourably by *The Spectator* and the *Manchester Guardian*.[22] It was the *New Statesman*'s critic, however, who put his finger

---

20. Priaulx Rainier to David Gascoyne, 3 Jan. 1956, Beinecke, Box 10, Folder 209.
21. Taped broadcast at Beinecke, Box 19, Folder 395.
22. *The Spectator*, 20 Apr. 1956; *Manchester Guardian*, 17 Apr. 1956.

firmly on the particular strengths and weaknesses of this unaccompanied cantata. Quoting some of the text, he concluded that 'The musician has not yet been born who could find a natural musical equivalent, making sense on its own account, for a sentence so long and involved. In Miss Rainier's setting the tenor plays roughly the role of cantor, with the chorus sometimes "responding to him" and sometimes tagging along a few bars behind with the same words. This layout complicates the composer's already difficult task, and the music tends to lapse into an isolated mood or word-painting sometimes very striking in itself.'[23] Without the skill for framing or offsetting words possessed by Searle, whose model in this respect had been Schoenberg, Rainier had also been bold enough to do what he had avoided: she had set, word for freighted word, lines by Gascoyne that already possessed their own intrinsic, distended music:

> [Choir]
> Tenebral treasure and immortal flower
> And flower of immortal Death!
> O silent white extent
> Of skyless sky, the wingless flight
> And the long flawless cry
> Of aspiration endlessly!
> [Voice]
> The seed is buried in us like a memory; the seed
> Is hidden from us like the omnipresent Eye; it grows
> Within us through Time's flux, both night and day.[24]

The work was repeated at a recital at the Wigmore Hall later that summer and, with the same forces, performed again at the Maltings, Snape during that year's Aldeburgh Festival. It crowned Gascoyne's poetic and musical year. Such collaborations with composers drew on his inborn musical sense, and thirty years' experience of musical and theatrical expression. Searle for one was enthusiastic to continue their working relationship. For two years he had been corresponding with this peripatetic poet at a series of temporary addresses around the Faubourg Saint-Germain. By the early summer of 1956, however, shortly after Rainier's requiem received its first performance, he was surprised to find himself writing to Gascoyne at the poste restante of a café in deepest Provence.

23. *New Statesman and Nation*, 21 Apr. 1956.
24. *Collected Poems* (1965), 95.

22

A Surrealist Cookbook

Though Paris would remain his centre of activity throughout the 1950s, he was often tempted further afield. For all his preoccupation with the 'Christ of Revolution and of Poetry' in the poem 'Ecce Homo', Gascoyne had never for example set eyes on the Grünewald altarpiece on which its poignant vision of the crucified Christ is based, having to remain satisfied with black-and-white reproductions Christian Zervos had shown him before the war. But early in 1954 he was introduced to the art critic Brigitte Leclerc, later to become a Picasso expert, and her brother François. They volunteered to drive him to Colmar in West Germany in the Leclerc parental car to see Grünewald's triptych in the Unterlinden Museum in Isenheim.[1] They motored through northern France and Germany, arriving at Isenheim on Saturday 10th shortly before the museum closed. Gascoyne stood quietly before the famous—and famously imagined—retable, its Christ figure thin and pallid, skin disfigured by the ergotism rife among those once served by the monks at the monastery of St Anthony who had commissioned the sixteenth-century masterpiece. In the evening they went to the Municipal Theatre to hear the Vienna Octet play Beethoven and Schubert. They returned via Strasbourg, whose cathedral seemed to him made out of terracotta, then through Nancy and back to Paris.[2]

Early that summer Gascoyne also met two lively Paris-based Americans who were to change the course of his troubled life. The painter Sam Francis had mounted his first two solo exhibitions at the Galerie Nina Dausset and the Galerie du Dragon that year. An abstract Expressionist, he was at 31 progressing towards the technique known as *tachisme* in which blobs of brightly coloured pigment are allowed to set once they have dripped down

---

1. BL Lives, Tape 1384, Side A.
2. David to Leslie and Win Gascoyne, 12 Apr. 1954, Beinecke, Box 11, Folder 239.

a canvas. In July he rented a stone farmhouse, le Mas des Roches, in the hamlet of Les Granettes to the west of Aix-en-Provence with the Jewish American art critic and philosopher Rachel Jacobs, and they invited Gascoyne to join them. His recordings of cabaret songs for the BBC done and dusted, David hitched a ride south with two lorry drivers on their way down to Marseilles. On 14 July, after a spectacular overnight drive along the banks of the Loire and then the Rhône, he was for the second time in his life breathing the air of Provence.

Four years earlier, in the depths of drug-induced paranoia, the South had seemed a disappointment, its midsummer tints almost drab. Now, flushed with his broadcasting successes, Gascoyne was far more receptive. Aix, he enthused to Leslie and Win, was a revelation: 'full of fountains, old court-yards, seventeenth century mansions and magnificent plane trees'. The annual music festival was in full flow and in the first week he attended *Don Giovanni*—a speciality of the Festival—in the open courtyard of the arch-bishop's palace: 'first rate singing, and beautiful décors in perfect taste'.[3] Around the farmhouse 'chestnuts, cypress, fig trees, olives and willows' grew to profusion, while the surrounding fields were rife with 'vines, garlic, arti-chokes, tomatoes and corn'. 'All day long a chorus of cicadas', he exclaimed, 'and at night the frogs!'[4]

Almost as vocal as the cicadas and frogs was Rachel Jacobs, with whom he soon discovered points of precarious affinity. A specialist in the theoreti-cal implications of contemporary painting, she was already a recognized interpreter of stylistic practice among American artists resident in France. Jacobs was a protégée of the Byzantinist and art critic Georges Duthuit, son-in-law of and expert on Matisse, and *copin* of Samuel Beckett to whom, somewhat belatedly, he had introduced Gascoyne.[5] She was preparing a thesis at the Sorbonne on the aesthetics of modern American painting. In her short life Jacobs was to complete several essays that remain important sources for the American art of the period.[6] She was articulate, politically well to the Left, an admirer of the poetry of Jouve, and, intellectually and personally, fairly volatile. By mid-August it is clear that she and David were

3. David Gascoyne to Leslie and Win Gascoyne, 4 Aug. 1954, Beinecke, Box 11, Folder 239.
4. David Gascoyne to Leslie and Win Gascoyne, 14 July 1954, Beinecke, Box 11, Folder 239.
5. For Duthuit, see Hilary Spurling, *Matisse the Master* (London: Hamish Hamilton, 2005), 257–65.
6. See esp. Rachel Jacobs, 'L'Idéologie de la peinture américaine', *Aujourd'hui: Art et Architecture*, 6/37 (June 1962), 6–19.

involved in an uneasy, verbally boisterous, and not entirely platonic love affair. Almost certainly she was more caught up in the relationship than was he: in her eyes, after all, he was a published poet with a radical reputation in at least two countries who could command a swathe of philosophical and critical reading, and that summer he was keen to communicate all of this to anyone who would listen. David's postcards back home at this time appear buoyant with geographical adventure: Ramatuelle beside its very blue sea is sprouting with 'palms and pines, cypress and olive, cork-trees and cacti, pink and ochre villas, pink and white laurier roses, azaleas and geranium'; even under a scything mistral, Arles is 'a very fascinating old town, rather gloom-ier than Van Gogh's paintings might suggest, because it is so ancient and full of Roman remains'.[7] Almost certainly this confident mood was boosted by the flattering, unfamiliar sense of having attracted the devotion of a fetch-ing, highly intelligent if unstable woman in her twenties, even if he did not know at first quite what to do with it or, indeed, to her.

Since the others were paying the rent, he cooked. One evening in late August they entertained two affluent bohemian women friends from the vicin-ity, and Gascoyne conjured from crushed garlic, egg yolks, and glistening virgin olive oil a large bowl of bright aioli sauce. The guests, both ex-wives of celebrated painters, were warmly appreciative. By far the elder of the two in her late seventies was Gabby Picabia, the pensioned-off spouse of poly-philoprogenitive, racing-car-driving Francis Picabia (who now had a new wife as well as a new car). As over most summers, she was staying outside Aix with her friend Meraud Guevara, widow of the Chilean artist Alvaro Guevara. Meraud had briefly been introduced to Gascoyne two years previ-ously by Mary Hutchinson, an art-loving barrister's wife, one-time mistress of Clive Bell and now of Sam Beckett. Like Hutchinson she was in her early fifties, and decidedly unflagging. Irish by birth and nationality, she was the elder of two daughters of the drinks magnate Benjamin Guinness, from whom she had inherited the small fortune she was fast diminishing through artistic benefaction. Meraud had grown up in stilted high society, against which she was still in partial reaction, having been partly raised when a girl by Mr and Mrs Anthony Eden. She had long since gravitated from being the flapper waspishly portrayed in 1930 by Evelyn Waugh in *Vile Bodies* as one of the 'Bright Young Things', a period when she reprimanded the supercilious Marquess of Donegall for asking her why she carried a suitcase

7. David to Leslie and Win Gascoyne, 4 Aug. 1954.

round with her rather than a conventional handbag with the snub 'because the damn thing holds more, you fool!'[8] After studies at the Slade, and participating in the exhibition of 'Thirty One Women Painters' at Peggy Guggenheim's Art of This Century gallery in New York in 1943, Meraud was now a modestly successful painter in a post-Impressionist representational style, as well as a generous supporter of younger artists from whose styles of experimentation she was keen to learn. A rare combination of practitioner and patron, bilingual and protected by her Irish passport, she had remained in France throughout the war. Following Alvaro's death in 1951, she now lived during the summer months on her rambling estate in hilly pinewoods to the north-east of Aix. In the winter Meraud stayed in her garishly decorated top-floor Paris flat just behind the Gare d'Orsay.

Late that September David wrote home to say that he had been invited to stay with Meraud Guevara at her summer home for a few weeks after the lease at Les Granettes had expired. He soon became an annual fixture, invited back over the next ten seasons, arriving just as spring enlivened the pine woods and departing with the autumn mists. Meraud's property covered two acres of sloping ground on the southern escarpment of a low crest crowned by the stark Gallo-Roman relic known as La Tour de César, from which it took its name. Aside from the main house, the terrain was scattered with cabins that accommodated a gaggle of artists in various mediums: painters, writers, restorers of harpsichords. Meraud was its pauper-dressed princess: 'she covered the walls with frescoes,' remembered a contemporary, 'painted all the furniture, and surrounded herself with forty cats'.[9] Her flat in Paris was decorated with similar, bright-coloured, élan in flagrant violation of the good taste she despised. As well as the pets at Aix there were the guests, resident or transient, several distinguished in their respective spheres. They included Lady Churchill when she accompanied Sir Winston on his occasional painting expeditions to Aix, the portraitist and sculptor Jean Dubuffet, a keen admirer of Meraud's work; the lawyer and painter Jean Follain; the Swiss writer and musician Charles-Albert Cingria; and the English painter Matthew Smith, who rented a studio in the town. There was even talk of an 'Aix School of Painting', centred around the local celebrity 'Tal Coat', combining bold, broad shapes with bright colours in a variant of what Dubuffet liked to call 'l'art brut'. From the nearby woods you had a

8. 'Art Anarchist', *Time*, 4 Apr. 1939.
9. Monica Ceño Elie-Joseph, *Woman's Art Journal*, 21/1 (Spring–Summer 2000), 20.

clear view of the western face of Mont Saint-Victoire, and the spirit and example of Cézanne—who had painted the mountain over and over—were everywhere.

Throughout much of October David was still enmeshed in his nervous on-and-off relationship with Jacobs. Mary Hutchinson saw them together in Paris that month, and argued with them about the merits of Jouve, about whom she was sceptical. On 14 November she wrote from London to say that they had converted her. 'His poems', she enthused, 'have an intoxicating power. Please tell Rachel that I feel this.'[10] A week later Gascoyne was back in London, already hinting at impediments. 'Last week', recorded Lehmann in his diary on the 22nd, 'David Gascoyne came to see me suddenly, after a long absence in France...He had a good colour, looked even leaner in the face nevertheless, more anguished, but not so mad...averting his eyes one moment, then facing one with his light blue eyes, flinging them up then flinging them down again to the ground. He said he had seen no one but me. He had written no poetry, was waiting for someone to give him a crystallization point. We talked and then I said "write about the destruction of love"— and he said the *ob*struction of love—yes, I could write about that.'[11]

Gascoyne spent the winter in England, on the understanding that he would join Jacobs in France again in the spring. But when he arrived back in Paris at the end of May 1955, Rachel had disappeared on a tour of Italian galleries. From the flat of her friend Georges Duthuit he moaned to Meraud, who had already left for Aix: 'After waiting frantically week after week all this spring to get back to France and rejoin Rachel, at last I have returned to Paris. But there is no Rachel here: she has gone off to explore Italy they tell me and she does not seem to have received my messages.'[12] By the second week of June he was back at the Tour de César and, as he prosaically informed his parents, 'My friend Rachel has arrived from Italy to stay for a little while'.[13] Jacobs had in fact rented a house for them in the centre of Aix, into which she expected him to move. Gascoyne, however, preferred the hospitality—and safety—at the Tour. In Meraud he had met someone who would never attempt to mould, control, or seduce him, only require he

10. Mary Hutchinson to David Gascoyne, 14 Nov. 1954, Enitharmon Papers.
11. John Lehmann, Diary B9, p. 46, John Lehmann family papers, 1649–1990, Princeton University Library, Manuscripts Division, CO746, series 4, box 74.
12. David Gascoyne to Meraud Guevara, TGA 9326/1/39.
13. David Gascoyne to Lesleie and Win Gascoyne, 18 June 1955, Beinecke, Box 11, Folder 239.

be his complicated, solitary, unpredictable self. Meraud expected artists to behave oddly: she had grown up among the *haute bourgeoisie*, and was heartily sick of good manners. At the Tour they were soon joined by her 24-year-old daughter Alladine or 'Nini', who thus enjoyed a ringside seat for the sequel in the saga of David and Rachel. In her memoir Nini narrates the relevant episodes as slapstick farce, but through her comic hyberbole one can sense an ill-at-ease Gascoyne vainly attempting to deal with his emotional embarrassments with what, in that letter to a recent male lover, he had called 'honnêteté':

> Rachel was madly in love with him and reproached him for refusing to go and live with her … One day when she was feeling especially piqued, she asked a sturdy acquaintance of hers to accompany her to the Tower to 'beat David up'. Since she had forewarned Meraud of her intentions, my mother advised David to keep a low profile. Rather than follow her hint, David went out as soon as he heard the sound of the car. He asked the driver 'Are you by any chance the individual who wishes to beat me up?' When this young chap saw how delicate David was, he refused point blank to carry out his mission. Filled with indignation, Rachel followed them into the house calling them every name she could think of. Seeing that neither was paying the least attention, and that my mother was standing there calmly offering her a drink, Rachel grabbed everything within reach of the doorway and started to hurl it at David and her friend, while Meraud bustled the two men into a side room. When she had run out of things to break, Rachel simmered down and left.[14]

Violence did not come naturally to David, except at the manic peak of his bipolar cycle. On the next occasion when Rachel turned up to protest at his neglect of her, he was in just this excitable condition, and for once he slapped her. This Rachel would not forgive.

But the Tour de César proved an excellent base from which to explore the surrounding country with its complex of artistic culture and ancient woodland. Gabby Picabia had by now joined the small community at the house. On Midsummer's Eve she turned 80 and she and David clambered to the very top of the Mont Saint-Victoire to observe the St John's Day fires. There were continual expeditions to the opera: Gluck's *Orphée* and Mozart's *Figaro* and *Così fan tutte* in July alone. Nini observed Gascoyne's bursts of energy and enthusiasm for these various excursions with a quizzical eye. She further perceived his countervailing bouts of melancholy, and

---

14. Alladine Guevara, *Meraud Guinness Guevara, ma mère* (Paris: Editions du Rocher, 2007), 173–4.

the mixed results of his labours in the kitchen. All winter he had been obliged to put up with tasteless fodder served in skinflint London. But in 1950 Elizabeth David had begun to open British eyes to Continental cooking with her *Book of Mediterranean Food*, published by Lehmann in London. Gascoyne approved of her recipes, occasionally cutting them out of the English newspapers. But he preferred his own, which he now needed to serve in considerable quantities, since in the evenings the whole boisterous community at the Tour ate al fresco on the terrace on tables lit, as a tardy dusk fell, by candles set in wine bottles. With rabbit, for example, Elizabeth David had recommended a purée of brown lentils, or else a mallow soup. Gascoyne proved as inventive:

> LAPIN AUX PRUNES
> One jointed rabbit
> Prunes, soaked overnight and stoned
> Butter
> Chopped rashers of bacon
> Flour
> Red wine (and water or stock)
> Seasoning, thyme, bayleaves.

He let these ingredients slowly simmer in a casserole for two and a quarter hours, adding potatoes after the first hour. He then served the meal and awaited comments from the assembled guests. These were original recipes seldom served a second time round. Each dinnertime thus became the culinary equivalent of a painter's *vernissage*. As Nini grimly noted, the participants were expected to be critical but appreciative:

> When he concocted a dish that satisfied everyone, he categorically refused to make it again. To him this was a matter of principle. Keen to try out new combinations, he never made the same dish twice. He was furious when nobody praised him. If the members of the household chatted away without paying any attention to their food, he mumbled over and over again: 'Talk, talk, talk!' until someone remembered that no one had complimented him on the dish they had been eating. On one occasion he angrily picked up his plate still full of food and set it down for the dogs.[15]

Nor would many present would have recognized 'Talk, talk, talk' as the title of one of his plays. Each recipe went into his private cookery manual, 'Food Notes', between drafts of literary work, projects for books, sketches, and

15. Ibid. 173.

observations on the still approaching millennium.[16] As Suzanne the maid vociferously complained, it often took her longer to clean up after him than to have prepared the meal herself.

Gascoyne passed the autumn house-sitting for Meraud on the top floor of 69 Rue de Lille, where the decor was as vibrant as in Aix, with patchwork curtains she had sewn together from brightly coloured fabrics from Le Bon Marché. He returned to spend Christmas with his parents, now back in England, at their house near Godalming, with intervals in a London that seemed, he told Meraud, like 'a damp grey mass full of flickering souls'.[17] On 18 February 1956 he turned up at Lehmann's house with Laurie Lee, and they all discussed the election for the Oxford Chair of Poetry, which Auden had just won, and the oppressive hegemony of the Movement. 'David', Lehmann observed, 'looked less racked with terrors than I have seen him for a long time; still, in a neurotic tick, twisting his head over his shoulders to look for shadowy assailants, but brightening up, laughing and making shrewd comments as the conversation developed...Both of them spoke very bitterly and contemptuously of the so-called "new movement"...in poetry. But why aren't their voices heard? It's our fatal silence that allows these toadstools to grow so rapidly.'[18] Following the success of *Night Thoughts*, which André Deutsch were now keen to publish, Cleverdon had commissioned from him and Searle a second radiophonic poem to mark the tenth anniversary of the Third that September.[19] The advance supplemented Gascoyne's cheque for *Night Thoughts* repeats. After the performance of Rainier's *Requiem* in April, he was free once more to go south. Rachel, he now learned, had been staying at the Rue de Lille in his absence: 'I often ruminate about her,' he wrote to Meraud in March, 'hoping that she may have recovered a serener equilibrium, and that she won't think of me with loathing ever after.' Meraud reported back that Jacobs was still seething. 'I am so sorry', he wrote in return, 'to hear that Rachel wants to go on being elephantine. I must try to find some really winning way of erasing from her mind the resentful recollection of that most unfortunate but not, surely major, incident...My great mistake, of course was not to have gone and

16. 'Food Notes etc', Beinecke, Box 12, Folder 263, from which all of the recipes in this chapter are drawn.
17. David Gascoyne to Meraud Guevara, 25 Jan. 1956, TGA 9326/1/39.
18. John Lehmann, Diary B11, pp. 17–18.
19. Humphrey Carpenter, *The Envy of the World: Fifty Years of The BBC Third Programme and Radio 3* (London: Weidenfeld and Nicolson, 1996), 195.

grovelled on her doorstep the next morning. Do help me if you can by suggesting to her that I am still heartbroken about her attitude, and presently I shall make some very touching gesture and I am sure that her natural good sense and fundamental tender-heartedness will do the rest! Or is this only sentimental dream?'[20]

In late April Meraud exhibited her recent paintings at the Galerie Guénégaud in Paris: moonlit glades as Gabby Picabia described them, and pallid jungles. Afterwards she left for Aix and, braving Rachel's disapproval, Gascoyne caught a plane to Paris at the end of May, venturing down to Provence a few days later. By the 14th he was fully installed once more, and could report triumphantly that 'Yesterday I gave a most magnificent dinner party, cooked entirely by myself'. Some feat for Paul Gravey:

CASSEROLE PRINTANIÈRE:
Veal
Ham
Spring Onions
Butter
Stock
Herbs
Seasoning

Cook for An Hour
Add: small new potatoes
Peas
Beans
Carrots
Asparagus

Cook for Another Hour

He was not always the cook. His local fame as a poet had spread, and on 27 June the editorial board of *Les Cahiers du Sud*, the Midi-based magazine devoted to Surrealist and post-Surrealist verse, threw a dinner in his honour in Marseilles at which he delivered a speech in French, fortified by *un picher de rouge*. André Masson, erstwhile Surrealist and one-time confidant of Breton who was designing sets for the festival, had taken a house with his wife in the village of Le Tholonet about ten kilometres to the south-west of Aix. Meraud and Gascoyne drove over to see them in her jeep, and all the

20. David Gascoyne to Meraud Guevara, 22 Mar. 1956, TGA 9326/1/39.

talk was of literature and philosophy. Masson liked his art red and raw: musically he was an admirer of the wilder shores of Stravinsky, and he had no time for the stylistic and political temporization of Shostakovich, whose work was featuring at the festival that year.

On other mornings before the heat of day struck, or in the cool of the early evening, Gascoyne the urban *flâneur* turned hiker, following a variety of routes into the centre of Aix, either by way of suburban by-roads or by a longer and undulating route past Bibemus and Le Barage Zola, the water reservoir built by the novelist's engineer father. He collected his mail at the Café Leydet at the corner of the Cours Mirabeau and the Rue Leydet, bought in provisions for his great feasts, or secured a drug supply at one of the local pharmacies. He would then dawdle at the café hoping that one of the other residents would give him a lift back to the house.

Though the Tour was peaceful, it was hardly cut off, and communications with the greater world, and the coming and going of guests, were constant. On 12 July the BBC committed a temporal solecism by repeating the wintertime *Night Thoughts* at two-thirty on a summer's afternoon. A week later George Barker turned up with his current live-in lover Betty Cass, fancifully renamed 'Cashenden' or 'Casseopia'. David escorted this modern-day Don Juan and his Donna Elvira to see *Don Giovanni* at the Théâtre de l'Archêveché in the courtyard of the Archbishop's Palace, with tall, lean, droll Antonio Campo as the Don and Marcello Cortis as Leporello. Afterwards, they drank in one of the teeming *terrasses* along the Cours Mirabeau, staring up at the stars. The 'Barkers', as he restyled them for his parents' benefit, were en route for Bormes near Toulon, where he joined them for several days. In August Peggy Ashcroft came to stay, and Nini and Gabby Picabia each rolled up for their annual *vacances*. David and Meraud went to pick up Gabby in Avignon; on the way back they enjoyed a *casse-croûte* in a little abandoned hut by the side of the road near Paradou.

And in early September Searle flew in with his wife Leslie to discuss the new programme for the BBC. Provisionally entitled 'Celebration for a Festival', it took its cue from the Aix event, now in its eighth season. Gascoyne presented Searle with his script, culled from his commonplace book and consisting of linked quotations around the theme of celebration. Unused to this collage technique, and expecting all the words to be Gascoyne's own, Searle expressed his disappointment and dropped out of the project.[21]

21. Humphrey Searle, 'Quadrille with a Raven', ch. 12 'Breakthrough?', http://www.musicweb-international.com/searle/break.htm/.

Perhaps, after all, jollification was simply not Gascoyne's forte. Instead, Searle spent two weeks hammering out his Second Symphony on an ancient piano upstairs in a café on the Cours Mirabeau, socializing with Matthew Smith and picnicking with David and Meraud in 'extraordinary old Les Baux. Unfortunately everywhere we go there seem to be clouds of mosquitoes!'

David celebrated his fortieth birthday by taking an early morning bus with Meraud to Sisteron in Haute-Provence, and lunching on shrimp tarts and white wine. Later that week, they made a late seasonal visit *au Tholonet*, where they discussed Heidegger and Jouve with Masson. Heidegger, he told them, had once visited him and talked of the humility necessary in the face of death, not an attitude of which Masson seemed to approve. Gascoyne asked him what he thought of Jouve; he replied that Jouve strove for perfection rather than progress, tradition rather than innovation. Figuratively Jouve was a *cuisinier* too, but his work was invariably 'a reheated if immaculately served dish'.[22] As ever, it was fierceness in art and thought that Masson valued.

On 29 October Meraud drove David back to Paris via Vienne, and that night, hit by an unseasonal snowstorm, they were holed up in Sanlieu. They had grown closer: so much so that many now mistook them for a couple. David stayed on at the Rue de Lille for much of the winter. When Meraud was away, he looked after her dog Tarzan, and cooked for Nini and her guests:

FISH A LA ASTURIA
One lb of fish
A half a glass of white wine
Two onions
One teaspoon of grated chocolate
Four ounces of butter
One glass of water
Twelve small mushrooms
One tablespoon of flour
Salt and pepper
Put the butter in a casserole and when hot add the fish, the finely shredded onions (previously cooked) and the flour. Then add hot water, wine, chocolate, salt and pepper, and simmer till the fish is tender. Add the cooked mushrooms 10 mins before serving.

Thus he continued as a kind of resident cook-cum-caretaker in the flat all winter, attending the Peking circus, visiting Nini in her new home near

22. *Meraud Guinness Guevara, ma mère*, 214.

Dreux in the Beauce, and enthusing over Vincent Minelli's *Lust for Life*, his film of the life of Vincent Van Gogh based on Irving Stone's book of that title, with Kirk Douglas as the tormented painter. The changing palette of the film brightened up the grey of the wintry city, relieved otherwise by the crowds in the Tuileries gardens over on the Right Bank: 'people with dogs, people with children, children with boats, balloons and balls and aeroplanes!' As in the thirties Gascoyne described the metropolitan merry-go-round with fascination, but now it was as if it was all taking place on the other side of a screen that cut him off from the living, pulsating world. He was growing steadily more remote and strange.

He constantly promised to return to Surrey, when Leslie had now contracted the diabetes that would eventually kill him, and which David himself would one day inherit. However in February 1957 he was still ensconced in the Rue de Lille gazing out of the window as migrating storks started on their yearly procession back to Alsace. He did not seem to be part of any of it. In March he went to a fancy dress ball in the country, dressed as a Chinese mandarin. Why not? The same month he saw *Capriccio*, Richard Strauss's final opera, at the Opéra-Comique. A 'conversation piece', its theme was the relative strength of words and music. It was a theme that impinged on his late collaborations with Searle, but by the late 1950s Gascoyne felt himself to be contributing to neither, except in the most passive of senses, an observer for the time being. In the mornings he discovered himself 'sitting outside without a coat and it was almost comfortable in the sun. The willows by the Seine are bright green already and the chestnuts are in full bud.' His frustrated creativity was going into a series of meticulous and bright hued gouaches at which he worked in odd hours, and, of course, into his culinary experiments. 'I have', he told Leslie and Win with feeble pride, 'been doing the cooking for quite a lot of smart dinner parties.'[23] His recipes were spreading outwards from the cookbook to other notebooks, even to the backs of letters:

BAKED CORN (for 4):
1 tin of sweet corn (or six cobs—boil for 7 mins)
1 cup of milk
2 eggs
1 sweet pepper
1 onion

23. David to Leslie and Win Gascoyne, 22 Mar. 1957, Beinecke, Box 11, Folder 243.

2 tomatoes
Half a pound of pork, diced or minced.
Seasoning.
Fry pork till slightly brown, add onion, pepper, tomatoes chopped. Cook till tender.
Add beaten eggs and milk to strained corn, all this to vegetables in pan and stir till
thickens. Pour into buttered dish, put in oven until slightly browned.

He was growing steadily less rebellious, less engagé, less inclined to kick against the pricks of tradition, or indeed of anything. When in April 1957 the young English queen and her naval officer husband arrived on a state visit to the French capital, the spectacle evoked in this one-time member of the Communist Party of Great Britain a surge of suspiciously patriotic loyalty. To his surprise and excitement, he was unaccountably moved. 'Had two glimpses of the Queen—leaving the Opera she was quite radiant,' he rhapsodized to his mother, 'something magical one really can't explain.' The mental scene was being set for mystical veneration that would later bear strange fruit.

He spent all summer with Meraud in Aix, accompanying her and Tarzan in the car that September to visit her sister Tanis in Biarritz. When they got back to Paris in October, it was to the news that he had been awarded the Guinness Prize for Poetry for the year. Despite Meraud's maiden name, there had been no complicity over the result, as David stressed.

23

Animal, Vegetable, Mineral

Though his relationship with Rachel Jacobs had long since foundered, Gascoyne was mixing with art critics such as Georges Duthuit during the winters in Paris; during the long summers in Aix he was cast amid painters. A revival of interest in making art of his own was the unsurprising result. Already by the mid-1950s he had learned from Matisse, who in 1952 had developed the technique known as découpage, essentially a trick of cutting out shapes from a sheet in one colour, then gumming them onto a background sheet in a contrasted shade. Three years later Gascoyne's *Anarchist Arabesque* shows an organic-looking, almost amoeboid, cut-out in red against a black ground.[1] There is a kinship between such works and the collage technique he had been using intermittently since 1936. Gascoyne had never lost faith in such *bricolage*. He had, for instance, been collecting pictorial bric-a-brac for a projected edition of the complete works of Baron Friedrich Leopold Von Hardenberg (1772–1801), known to history as Novalis: geologist, mystic, and poet and a specialism of the drug-dispensing Doctor Blüth. The restless, eclectic intelligence of this contemporary and acquaintance of Hölderlin's—together with the intermittent death wish expressed in works such as 'Hymns to the Night'—appealed to something deep in him, representing as it did the omnivorous activity of the sharpest kind of post-Enlightenment mind, including a putative synthesis of art and science. To illustrate it he brought together woodcuts by Albrecht Dürer, and reproductions from artists as various as Lucas van Leyden, Henri Rousseau, Samuel Palmer, and Picasso.[2] The atmosphere of the Dürer prints in particular echoed configurations within Novalis's and Gascoyne's own poetry. From the *Engraved Passion* he had taken images depicting 'The Entombment', 'Christ

1. Beinecke, Box 17, Folder 358. Compare Henri Matisse, *Black Leaf on a Green Background*, 1952.
2. Beinecke, Box 20, Folders 400–2.

Descending Into Hell', 'The Resurrection', and 'St Peter and St John Healing
A Cripple,' a procession intended to illustrate the fifth of Novalis's six
'Hymns of the Night', where the death and re-emergence of an unnamed
Christ-like figure are evoked. Such images recalled the Bruegel visions he
had admired as a young man, and could well have served as accompani-
ments to Gascoyne's own poems from the 'Miserere' section of his wartime
volume, and to Sutherland's illustrations to them. There was thus an implicit
line connecting this early sixteenth-century north German painter, print-
maker, and depicter of—possibly sufferer from—Gascoyne's own complaint
of *Melancholia Imaginativa*, to Novalis the nineteenth-century visionary and
to himself, a broadly Continental or perhaps more locally German axis
equivalent to the English artistic-cum-religious descent he had traced in his
projected anthology *Emblems and Allegories*. The conjunction was to remain
a fascinating possibility until, in active collaboration with the poet Jeremy
Reed, Gascoyne returned to the work of Novalis in his seventies.[3]

Collage was currently experiencing a revival. Having largely abandoned
painting, Roland Penrose, now settled in a large country house near Muddles
Green in East Sussex, had decided to concentrate on collages when not
running the ICA. Meanwhile in Aix, every Saturday morning in summertime, Meraud would go down to the weekly flea market on the Cours
Mirabeau to purchase old postcards. She used them to gather ideas about
the costumes and headdresses of the peasant women she was fond of depicting, but she also employed them, along with marbled paper she manufactured herself, for collage borders with which she framed her paintings. It
was just one of several respects in which she and David were learning from
one another. Meraud was no intellectual; her reading was for the most part
confined to detective stories, *romans policiers*. In other respects she was eager
for instruction and Gascoyne was an assiduous teacher, guiding her taste in
music especially, buying her 78s of works by Bartók and Berg which she
learned to enjoy while trying out new painterly methods in her studio in
the Tour. Nini's memoir recalls that in 1954, the year of David's first stay
there, 'my mother began to experiment with new techniques such as collage, mixtures of ink, gouache and acrylic, sometimes on a base of coarse
uneven plaster, as in the technique of Dubuffet'.[4] Gouache, more workable
than oil yet with something of its surface finish, was a technique she in her

3. See also Beinecke, Box 20, Folders 400 and 401.
4. Alladine Guevara, *Meraud Guinness Guevara, ma mère* (Paris: Editions du Rocher, 2007), 269.

turn introduced to Gascoyne, who was using it fairly regularly from the late 1950s. Over the next few years he was to produce a number of works in this medium, and in an abstract Expressionist style. *Couches persanes*, for example, features strips of black, grey, aquamarine, jade, and pink against a background of pink blotches that recalls Meraud's distressed plaster grounds.[5] Another gouache from the same period is set against a vivid light orange above which swirl a medley of ellipses, medallions, and streaks in a variety of shades.[6]

Their shared understanding of art was thus of the essence of their relationship; its emotional timbre is less easy to locate. Meraud and David had never been lovers in any technical sense, but she respected, protected, and to some extent too she clearly needed him: 'I miss you' runs the constant refrain of her news-packed letters and postcards to him, though like phrases occur less frequently in his to her. To her he is 'Dearest' or 'Darling' David; to him she is simply 'Dear Meraud'. For all that, there was in her eyes, something mysterious and unrepeatable about him. In her journal she wrote, 'I am almost not a "human being" at all. I am half angel and half animal. David is no longer quite human either, but he has a smaller dose of the animal in him than me. Something of the angel, yes, of the vegetable and the astral maybe, with possibly a touch of something chemical or pharmaceutical—a sort of un-oxidizable acid . . . David is a brain, like a flower at the end of a long stem.'[7]

Yet he was her most assiduous and perceptive critic, whose educated eye detected developments in her painting, schooled, encouraged, and promoted it. Meraud's early portraits, often of women in domestic settings, had inclined towards pastel colours and prettiness. Frequently, though, she had caught a hint of exoticism in her subjects' very ordinariness. From the beginning she had sought an effect of calm, whether in her portraits of domesticated women with their pets or in still lives such as *Intérieure* of 1952 or *La Chaise dorée* of the same year, compared by her biographer Ceño Elie-Joseph to the *natures mortes* of Zurbarán. Her women sit or kneel in repose; their faces, however, are frequently haunted, as if their thoughts are elsewhere. The subject of *Femme assise avec un chien*, now in Tate Britain, has a far-away expression as if her mind is dwelling on some undeclared sorrow, a quality

5. Beinecke, Box 17, Folder 360.
6. One of six gouaches in Beinecke, Box 17, Folder 362.
7. Quoted in *Meraud Guinness Guevara, ma mère*, 202–3.

interestingly Meraud's former husband Alvaro seems to have noticed in her too, reproducing a similar effect in a portrait he painted of her soon after they met in 1929. In Alvaro's painting there is a melancholy in the eyes of the one-time 'Bright Young Thing' as she squats against cushions in her fashionable clothes. She has shed her shoes, and her large, vulnerable feet are curled up on a chair. By the time Gascoyne got to know her, Meraud had learned to impose the surface serenity of her pictures onto her own social life, where she had become an uninsistently effective manager of others. She was, however, no stranger to distress, succumbing towards the end of her life to a calamitous nervous breakdown during which she sold off La Tour de César. When that occurred, Gascoyne was vocally taken aback. He had always needed her to be calm.

Her landscapes, painted during her early years in Aix, possess a more flamboyant feel, exploring a Provençal ambience to which Gascoyne too was growing increasingly attracted: in them, as he pointed out, she 'created a world both distinctively specifically her own, and that of le Midi'. Meraud was now exhibiting almost annually, her productivity a reproach to him, whose poetry seemed temporarily to have stalled. In March 1956 she had a show at the Galerie Guénégaud in Paris. Her art was in a quietly representational phase, though the polyglot Polish-born critic Waldemar George, editor of the journal *Prisme des Arts* and an enthusiastic supporter of several women artists, praised her for distilling a formal serenity from the jostling panorama of Provençal life. In his review George quoted some lines from the sonnet 'La Beauté' in *Les Fleurs du mal* in which Baudelaire—himself no mean art critic—had praised a particular kind of remote, almost ideal, formalism: 'Je hais le mouvement qui déplacent les lignes, | Et jamais je ne pleure et jamais je ne ris.'[8] In Meraud's recent pictures, he went on to remark, were 'peasant women of Provence meditating in their homesteads with their limewash-whitened walls, Arlesienne dancers, bird women, or bird-crested women, domestic goddesses over whom messenger pigeons might hold watch'.[9]

Gascoyne followed her progress keenly, but he was now splitting his years three ways, between London, Paris, and Aix. In England he stayed either with his parents near Godalming or with Elizabeth Smart, who had a large

---

8. It is Beauty herself who speaks: 'Disdaining motion that ruffles lines | I'm one that never laughs and never weeps'.
9. Quoted in *Meraud Guinness Guevara, ma mère*, 193–4.

flat in Westbourne Terrace near Paddington. Separated from Barker whose four children by him she was struggling to bring up, Smart was working as desk editor for both *Queen* and *House and Garden*. Strapped for time and cash, she nonetheless gave him a room next to that shared during the boarding school holidays by her sons Christopher and Sebastian—known to the family as 'Bashie'—who recalls the oddness of the arrangement, and of Gascoyne himself: 'He was like a fellow in the same dormitory, except that there was this wall between us...It was all very interesting: he was a man, what was he doing there? But he was very much like that: he was a sort of hermit.'[10] Gascoyne's existence was not, however, quite as hermetically sealed as it seemed to some. He and Smart had a common friend in Mary Hutchinson who that spring held a dinner party in her flat at 21 Hyde Park Square, and invited along both of them to meet T. S. Eliot and his young second wife Valerie, whom he had married on 7 January. Gascoyne's dealings with Eliot had been fragmentary and unsatisfactory. Eliot had employed him as a reviewer for *The Criterion* in the mid-thirties, but had later rejected his poems on the grounds that they lacked 'negative capability'. Gascoyne had not seen him since those tea sessions with John Hayward during the period when Eliot and he had shared a Chelsea abode. Though they shared views of the relationship between religion and poetry that were in certain respects akin, their dealings had always been nervous and inhibited, Gascoyne daunted by the senior poet's reputation, Eliot uncertain of the younger poet's worth. On this occasion all such constraints were swept away by the tide of Eliot's late-found and very evident personal happiness. 'Eliot', Gascoyne later recalled, 'was mellow and more benign than I had known him during our previous brief encounters: in a word, he was typically, uncondescendingly generous.'[11]

In March and early April 1957 Meraud was one of eight artists showcased at the Galerie R. Creuze in the Rue Beaujon. After spending the summer with her in Aix, Gascoyne was back in London again for much of the winter, spending weeks at a time in Smart's flat, talking with her through the night and accompanying her each weekday morning to Muriel Belcher's Colony Club in Old Compton Street, where she parked him in a corner and collected him again when her day's work was done. She had already caught from him something of his cooking bug, and had published with

10. Conversation with Sebastian Barker, 24 June 2010.
11. 'Elizabeth Smart', in *Selected Prose*, 211.

Paul Hamlyn a wittily worded and practically resourceful manual called *Cooking the French Way*. In the meanwhile David did what he could to promote Meraud's painting, discussing it with the ever-helpful Mary Hutchinson and with Freddy Mayor at his gallery in Cork Street. In early September they accompanied the poet Stevie Smith to spend the day with the poet Patrick Swift and his wife Oonagh in north London. They picked mushrooms: 'a fairy ring, boleti, button mushrooms, and even the rare and startling *Phallus impudicus* hiding under a bush'. They ate the mushrooms for dinner, exchanging culinary tips. Later that evening they walked Stevie back to her Palmer's Green house from the tube station, marvelling at her independence and seemingly unaffected originality of mind.[12]

With Hutchinson's eagerly offered help, other plans were now afoot. Gascoyne had long talked of launching a counter-offensive against the Movement, which seemed to him to be taking the Continental lifeblood out of English poetry. Early in 1959 this at last became possible. Patrick and Oonagh Swift were now heavily involved with the South African poet David Wright in launching a literary magazine called *X*, named after the unknown quality or ingredient the Movement and its supporters seemed to them to be leaving out of account. Hutchinson was the financial backer, and an *ex officio* member of the editorial board. She resolved that Gascoyne should be involved in the capacity of translator and reviewer of foreign books. Matters looked brighter for several other reasons: he was, for example, involved with negotiations with Longman to bring out his *Collected Poems*. But on a visit to Leslie and Win in Surrey he attended an optician's appointment and was diagnosed with a slipped retina in his right eye. Taken into the Royal Surrey County Hospital in Godalming that evening, he had an operation on the 30th. He stayed there for a further five weeks, recuperating whilst listening to Berg on the radio and sketching through his good left eye. 'Apparently,' he informed Meraud, 'I had been going around going blind without knowing it.'[13] 'Poor dear David', she consoled him from a distance, 'I'm terribly sorry about your eye. I do hope it is quite cured and alright now and as beautiful as ever, and that you did not suffer too much.'[14] On 7 September, Hutchinson wrote: 'Poor dearest David! So distressed I feel about you! But your mother tells me that the doctors are pleased with the

12. Ibid. 210.
13. David Gascoyne to Meraud Guinness, 15 Nov. 1959, TGA 9326/1/39.
14. Meraud Guinness to David Gascoyne, Oct. 1959, Enitharmon Papers.

result after the operation and this is good news. I know how patient you must be and how trying it is to lie still and not to be able to read.... I hope you have some more ideas about X, which we will discuss when we meet.'[15]

That December Meraud was to have had a solo exhibition in Biarritz; at the last moment, however, with Hutchinson's help she secured instead a space for forty-five of her pictures at the Jacques O'Hana Gallery in Carlos Place in London. No sooner was David out of his bandages than she was fondly badgering him for a catalogue entry for the show. To rest his eyes, she enclosed with her letter a multiple answer form compiled by herself—and, she said, by Tarzan—on which he could either accept this commission or reject it by crossing out A or B:

A

I would be delighted to write your preface and feel flattered to be asked. I don't know how it will turn out but will do my best. As you know I am quite capable of turning out a few beautiful sentences.

B

I can't possibly write your preface and you know why I can't write it; but I am grateful that you understand and say you won't mind.

The trick worked and, after a little more gentle persuasion, Gascoyne sent the required Preface directly to the gallery. It concluded with the remark: 'A period of experiment and research, during which she has incidentally made some remarkable discoveries of a technical order, has led her, through to a phase of austere abstraction, to a finely redistributed equilibrium of the objective and the subjective.' Pattern, coloration, and atmosphere: all had now adhered.

Gascoyne might just as well have been writing of himself, since the sketching in hospital had produced unexpected results. He had begun to realize that gouache could be used to produce a particular kind of austere miniature. To begin with he produced a panel two inches by four on which bloom-like patches of pink, black, cobalt blue, and grey blossomed on the paper: the effect was modest, almost self-effacing, but satisfying when viewed up close. In another such miniature, a striking mixture of hieroglyphs and kinetic lines were traced in black and red against a plain, cream ground.

---

15. Mary Hutchinson to David Gascoyne, 7 Sept. 1959, Enitharmon Papers.

Once he had perfected such effects, Gascoyne began to combine gouache brushwork with woodcuts. First he carved a maze-like interconnected pattern on a block which, inked and stamped on a piece of absorbent paper, gave the effect of dark tracery, as if representing a maze of stark winter trees. When he filled in the vacant spaces with abstract patches of contrasted colour in gouache, the darker outline resembled leading, and the whole composition bore a resemblance to a sombre, yet vividly stained, window. It was a style he now made his own, turning out a number of such miniatures in quite rapid succession (see Plate 20). In the best of them the slightly ecclesiastical atmosphere is offset by vivid contrasts of coloration and an often bewildering variety of the forms. With their sombre palette, their implicit spirituality, and their overall constraint, these small and concentrated works represented a sort of updated Abstract Impressionist Dürer. They were poems in paint: in their tidy form and encapsulated, almost allegorical meaning. Therapeutic in intent and in effect, they were, like his best verse, sober, intense but calming. In this respect at least, though very different in their idiom, the balance they achieved between serenity and suppressed inner turmoil was not that dissimilar to effects achieved by Meraud, in whose work her daughter detected 'la tranquillité des tourments sublimés', the tranquillity of sublimated torments. Though the view of the artistic function was quite consistent with that of Blanche Jouve, whom Gascoyne was also seeing at this period whilst in Paris, Meraud knew exactly what she was doing in encouraging such work.

As Gascoyne's confidence in this medium grew, the works increased in scale and in boldness, while the meanings that could be extruded from them sometimes grew more explicit. Perhaps the densest was an allegory on a Jungian theme that represented nothing less than a map of the striving mind, probably his own. To it he gave the self-mocking title *Blatant Invention*, and he prepared himself by drawing a pen sketch of its schema, to which he attached the subordinate title 'Doodle of things to come'. Segments to the left and right of an amoeboid form were labelled 'Animus' and 'Anima'. From the top of the main body extended a folded protuberance labelled 'egg' while, banished to the far left, above a limb-like feeler, he placed the phrase 'Reflector of Rubbish'. The preliminary sketch illustrated the balance in the human personality that Gascoyne in his more visionary or heightened moments projected onto a future age: a bisexual personality enfolded within a living form. In the completed painting (see Plate 21) the labels have disappeared, the allegory subsumed within a riot of beige, crimson, pink, jade, and purple strips, all which are outlined within his ubiquitous sable tracery. Thus bedecked, it is a lot more than an illustration to Jung.

Of all the paintings Gascoyne turned out at this period the most striking is a large composition entitled *Soleil de paon ovale* (see Plate 22). Quite unlike anything he had done before, it is a vision of the sun at its zenith, but it is also a visualization of a peacock's crest, with beams of gold, purple, aquamarine, jade, and blue streaming out from a solar oval of dark pink towards the top left-hand corner. The central orb is dancing with grey sunspots such as he may have experienced during his recent spell of eye disease. The colour of each beam is distinct, but all shimmer and ripple with a visual, visceral heat haze. Round the sphere of sun itself is painted a penumbral black circle, itself a clue to the meaning of the work. Here is the 'sun at midnight', the moment of solar illumination in the dark night of personal and social eclipse of which Gascoyne had often dreamed, and about which he was still writing.

By the end of 1960 Gascoyne had enough of these artworks to think of mounting an exhibition. The contacts he made while helping to promote Meraud's work now assisted with the promotion his own painting. During his periods in London he had kept in fairly constant touch with the well-connected Mary Hutchinson, who had visited him several times in Paris where she was close to Beckett and Georges Duthuit (who at long last introduced David to Beckett[16]). Now 51, Hutchinson was tirelessly active on behalf of artistic good causes, including at this time a fund to support the ailing David Archer. She was also active in advocacy of several lesser-known and individualistic painters, including Meraud. In the spring of 1961 she persuaded one of her aristocratic friends, Barbara Countess Moray, to host a show of thirty-four of David's recent artworks at her Chelsea home at 174 Ebury Street. On 23 April Hutchinson wrote to him in Paris enclosing a letter from Lady Moray and adding 'My dear David. I have been trying to arrange an exhibition of your "miniatures" ever since I saw you in Paris and brought some of them over. Everyone I have shown them to who is sensitively visual has admired them with real enthusiasm. Now I am glad to send you this letter and I feel sure that the little exhibition will bring many more admirers. Barbara . . . is a collector of works of art and she has a most charming house . . . where the pictures will glow in all their beauty.'[17]

16. Roger Scott to Robert Fraser, 2 June 2008.
17. Mary Hutchinson to David Gascoyne, 23 Apr. 1961, Enitharmon.Papers.

Lady Moray herself collected the works from the Rue de Lille and transported them back to London where they were framed by Tooth's at £1. 5d. each. To Hutchinson the Countess had written, 'I find this work beautiful and poetic and strong and unlike anything that I have ever seen before.'[18] The private view was scheduled for May, but a disagreement with her landlords about using the Countess's residence as a 'place of business' delayed the opening until December. But by reclassifying what was in essence a commercial show as a private exhibition, the prohibiting clause in the lease was at length satisfied, and the exhibition of Gascoyne's woodcuts and gouaches opened at Ebury Street on 5 December. Hutchinson wrote the catalogue.

During the two-week display, and following a good notice in the *Art Review*, much of literary artistic London attended, and many brought pictures at £10 each.

Cyril Connolly and Douglas Cleverdon came and bought items, as did Julian Trevelyan and Priaulx Rainier. David Jones, the mystically inclined Welsh poet and painter, was especially drawn to what he evidently felt was a religious undertow beneath some of this work. Elizabeth Smart acquired a small oblong entitled *Carpentry*, the linear configurations in which resembled joinery. Kathleen Raine was about to depart for America to deliver the tenth annual series of A. W. Mellon lectures in the Fine Arts at the National Gallery of Art in Washington. Her subject was to be Blake; David's pictures with their clean shapes and ambient mysticism put her, she told him, in an appropriate frame of mind. Shortly after the show closed on the 19th she wrote:

> Your spirit was clearly there in your work, which has the same sombre visionary radiance as your poems, and spoke from the spirit *de profundis*. The paintings seemed to be in some way like the Book of Kells and the other great gospels, those pages of elaborate intricacy that took years to complete. Do you think you were ever a monk-artist in Ireland or elsewhere?[19]

Kathleen had recently been up to Scotland to see Edwin Muir's widow Willa, 'and to live in her ambiance and among Edwin's books, was a great joy. I gave her *Night Thoughts* to read, and she agreed with me that it is poetry in the sense in which Edwin and I understand it; what the "new"

18. Barbara Moray to Mary Hutchinson, 20 Apr. 1961, Beinecke, Box 10, Folder 199.
19. Kathleen Raine to David Gascoyne, 30 Dec. 1961, Beinecke, Box 10, Folder 208.

poets seem to be writing is to Willa (and to me) incomprehensible, through, beyond any doubt, its absence of intelligible content, vision or soul.'

After the exhibition closed on 19 December, Barbara Moray wrote to him, enclosing a welcome cheque for £300. Thirty of the paintings had been sold, she told him, and only four remained. In London art circles Gascoyne had created a mild stir. The only interested party who had never once put in an appearance at Ebury Street, however, had been David Gascoyne himself. The clue to his absence lay deep in the paintings sold and unsold, for at this time Gascoyne reached perhaps the greatest crisis of his long life. In the early 1960s he had glimpsed the luminous darkness of Novalis. Beyond it, he had glimpsed the peacock sun.

24

An Incident at the Elysée

By 1961 Benzedrine and other associated amphetamine products had been on the European market for twenty-two years, but the long-term effects of reliance on these drugs was only just beginning to be fully appreciated. Rumours had been rife since the late 1930s, especially in the United States, about hallucinations and persecution mania among habitual users. A Kansas patient complained of his thoughts being telepathically controlled by his enemies; a man from Massachusetts insisted that six police vehicles were following him round Boston; a woman from New York was convinced that radioactivity had invaded her skin.[1] None of these victims was schizophrenic, any more than was David; all had been taking recourse to Benzedrine inhalers for several years past, and in all them the symptoms ceased once the amphetamines were withdrawn. In 1958 the British clinical psychologist Philip Connell placed these observations on a scientific, empirical footing in a celebrated Maudsley monograph entitled, after the condition itself, *Amphetamine Psychosis*.[2] Had Gascoyne consulted a doctor at this period, the chances are that the source of the recurrent delusions recorded in his many notebooks might have been diagnosed. However, with the one exception of Karl Bluth, who had treated his addiction by indulging it, Gascoyne had never sought appropriate medical advice, even at the time of his near nervous breakdown in 1949. As a result, his condition had gone undetected, whilst he himself preferred to rely on the classical Freudian psychotherapy offered by Blanche Jouve, whom he was still seeing fairly regularly during

1. Nicolas Rasmussen, *On Speed: The Many Lives of Amphetamine* (New York: New York University Press, 2008), 138–40.
2. P. H. Connell, *Amphetamine Psychosis* (London: Oxford University Press, 1958); an earlier, more tentative, hypothesis had been made in A. H. Chapman, 'Paranoid Psychosis Associated with Amphetamine Usage', *American Journal of Psychiatry*, 111 (1954), 43–5.

his months in Paris. Meraud, Hutchinson, and Raine all harboured doubts about the wisdom of this policy; each had privately expressed her suspicion that over the last couple of decades Blanche had been doing David active harm, turning a temperamental introvert further in on himself. None of them had felt able to intervene.

Since 1939, moreover, Smith Kline and French Laboratories had been experimenting with a modification of their best-selling narcotic, employing an isolated right-handed 'isomer' or variant of the amphetamine molecule.[3] Known generically as dextro-amphetamine, it had been launched commercially in 1943 as 'Dexedrine', and by the mid-1950s it was available under a range of brand names including 'Adderall', and in France 'Maxitone'. Maxitone had fast become the narcotic of preference for young Frenchmen and women; in April 1956, *Time* magazine published a feature pointing out that during the annual examination season in Paris demand for it doubled from 10,000 to 20,000 boxes per month, converting headstrong and highly strung students, *petits mentaux*, into temporary mental cases or *grands mentaux*.[4] Maxitone delivered twice the mood uplift per gram as classic racemic amphetamine, and it was reported to produce fewer 'jitters'. Gascoyne could easily lay hold of it while staying in Paris, and in Aix it was obtainable from several pharmacies in the city centre. His habit perpetuated itself, and so did its sometimes dramatic consequences.[5]

The swings in his temperamental pattern were thus intensified, and over the months Paris reflected his moods. Meraud's spacious apartment at 69 Rue de Lille, where he was always welcome, served as his base and sanctuary there, its shutters giving onto the broad street and the eastern approach to the back of the busy Gare d'Orsay, beyond which coursed the Seine. Meraud's sister Tanis rented a flat on the floor below and, between them all, they had a constant flow of visitors. Hutchinson came two or three times a year on her clandestine trysts with Beckett, with whom she discussed books Gascoyne might translate. She possessed an almost limitless faith in Gascoyne's powers, if her letters are anything to go by. 'There is', she enthused at one point, 'no one who has such a true, original and bountiful poetic gift as David Gascoyne who is also a seer . . . I think of the mysterious content and

3. Rasmussen, *On Speed*, 51–2.
4. 'Medicine: La Maladie de Boheme', *Time*, 9 July 1956.
5. BL Lives, F1383, Side B.

form of your work—of its inspiration that will touch others and myself.'[6] One evening in 1961 Allen Ginsberg came to dinner on one of his trips to Europe. Aware that Ginsberg delighted to 'épater les bourgeois', Gascoyne warned Meraud in advance that their visitor was likely to deface—or at least climb up onto—the walls. Bucking his reputation, Ginsberg proved a model of restrained conduct, much to Meraud's disgust. 'She loved artists and their fits of madness,' explains Nini of her mother, 'probably because as one herself, she consorted more comfortably with them than with the aristocrats and high bourgeois from whom she stemmed, but with whom she had little sympathy.'[7]

Now 31, and divorced with a small daughter, Nini had recently married Martin Lacroix, son of Alvaro and Meraud's painter friend, Pierre Lacroix. Most years, when Meraud left Paris in mid-March for her emporium in Aix, the couple house-sat for her, sharing the flat with an increasingly restless and moody Gascoyne, who concocted elaborate meals for them, but otherwise worked quietly in his small room. Each year therefore, between Meraud's departure for the South and his own, there was this awkward period of cohabitation with a young couple who were, to Gascoyne, little more than friendly strangers. His behaviour at such times could be a source of puzzled amusement to them, of irritation to the maid Josette, of resentment to the hired cook who had to clean up after his culinary experiments, and of complete exasperation to the concierge downstairs, who was supposed to deal with his visitors. It could even be alarming to those who knew him quite well, and to the young, including his friend's children. There was, for example, the small matter of his moral obligations to Elizabeth Smart, with whom he had now lodged free of charge for several successive winters in London. In April 1961 her younger son Sebastian turned 16 and, selling off all of the toys of his childhood, chose to spend the proceeds hitchhiking to Paris over the Easter holiday. Smart have given him David's address at the Rue de Lille, where on an impulse Sebastian decided to visit him. At the entrance he described himself as 'Mr Barker'. The concierge came upstairs to where the poet was tinkering with a poem: was this, he was wondering, the long-delayed moment of creative release? When the concierge announced the stranger's presence in the lobby, he assumed him to be Sebastian's father—his old friend and contemporary George—and told her

6. Mary Hutchinson to David Gascoyne, 26 Mar. 1964, Enitharmon Papers.
7. Alladine Guevara, *Meraud Guinness Guevara, ma mère* (Paris: Editions du Rocher, 2007), 237.

to direct him to take the lift up to the second floor, where he would greet him out on the landing.

When the lift doors opened, Sebastian found himself confronted by a tousled and abstracted Gascoyne, evidently in a 'petulant and spitty' frame of mind. Nor did the poet recognize the casually dressed young man advancing towards him. Assuming this youth to be some obscure relative of the Barker clan or, worse, a parasitical hanger-on, he asked him a few brusque questions, complained that he had interrupted his work, then asked him to leave. 'He looked', recalls Sebastian, 'somewhat angry to be interfered with. It was as if he was saying "Why don't you piss off? Why don't you get out of here? What do you want with me?" Well, I didn't stay long, as you can imagine.' Seeing he was unwelcome, and a little put out by the unaccountably 'spikey and self-congratulatory' behaviour of this close friend of his family's, Sebastian fled down the stairwell, and out into the open street.[8]

A few moments later Gascoyne came to, realizing whom he had just rudely ejected, and what a repudiation of cherished obligations this rash act had entailed. It was too late for him to follow his fleeing guest into the busy Rue de Lille. Mortified by the emotional and moral implications of this comedy of errors, he sat down and composed the following contrite 'Document Memento Mori' to Smart:

> This is a difficult letter to write—it is a delicate thing to say and I only hope I may be imagining that I have done real harm to Sebastian, but this afternoon when the concierge came up and told me that there was a Mr Barker downstairs and he sent him up, I immediately supposed it must be George passing through Paris on his way somewhere. Also, just at this time I had been living under considerable strain, being able at last to write for the first time, and was at that moment completely preoccupied in attending to something in my mind, and when that angelic child appeared out of the lift, shy and trembling, I simply failed to recognize the Bashy I used to know. What I thought was my sensitive love of human beings was obviously a partial delusion, because instead of immediately loving him unhesitatingly and taking him into my heart and asking him in at once, I stood there half thinking of something pseudo-scientific and, what is worse, asked him, are you one of George's nephews, and then, and I am so ashamed of this because it should have been impossible, I said 'Who is your mother?' still half thinking of something else. I am in a really horrible state of anguish about it now. What can I do? If only I knew his address, I should have rushed after him after a minute or two, but God gave me

---

8. Conversation with Sebastian Barker, 24 June 2010.

the chance and I lost it, and now I find that I am not the person I thought I was, and it is a terrible punishment, because I am sensitive, but obviously not *that* sensitive. I have judged myself and there is no way to make reparation.[9]

By now the long-suffering concierge was quite used to these visitations and their unpredictable results. She had long since developed a line of preliminary defence designed to dissuade all but the most intrepid visitors. On another occasion when David was sharing the flat with Nini and her husband in Meraud's absence, an unnamed British acquaintance turned up unexpectedly, and asked if the poet was in. Afterwards, the concierge reported their conversation to Nini:

'Mr Gascoyne. How should I know? He is in Loony Land [*dans la lune*]!' retorted the concierge.
'Ah, and when does he get back?' asked the visitor, unperturbed.[10]

As his moods soared and dipped, his physical surroundings appeared to reflect his state of mind. In May 1962 as the blossoms emerged from the trees along the Seine, he wrote to Meraud who had just left for Aix: 'Paris is really beautiful just now, when the sky is blue, which it has been quite recently—new leaves out, lilac and chestnut blossom. Only I do wish you were here still. I don't really like living alone.'[11] He was working at his paintings, and Barbara Moray had written to say that she had sold the last four pictures from the exhibition the previous December, yielding a valuable £40, which she enclosed. He had also made a graphic design for Nini and Martin: it was for a large *tapisserie* destined to cover the top of a footstool: Nini would do the needlework, and the result would be installed in a country house they had recently taken in La Beauce. He was, he told Meraud, exhibiting again at a small neighbourhood gallery, Chez Papille. Hutchinson, always active on his behalf, had come over from London and accompanied him to the *vernissage*: he was sharing the show with a number of other artists who were displaying work inspired by the poetry of Paul Valéry, of whose worth both Mary and he were both uncertain: 'a kind of French Bernard Shaw, Mary thought', Gascoyne told Meraud, then added 'but a lot more subtle'.

Once more this year, there a trickle of visitors. The Filipino poet Jose Garcia Villa, a friend of Barker's whom David had met a decade previously

9. David Gascoyne to Elizabeth Barker, Apr. 1961, Beinecke, Box 11, Folder 255.
10. *Meraud Guinness Guevara ma mère*, 195.
11. David Gascoyne to Meraud Guevara, 10 May 1962, TGA 9326/1/39.

during his tour of the States, turned up unexpectedly at Easter time. He resembled, David told the absent Meraud, a Chinese sage 'and has been keeping me up quite a lot, as he likes conversation and beatnik cafes'. Predictably, however, the letter describing this visit turned into a begging one: he was longing for Aix again, but had she house room? She had, and David went back down there to stay on 17 May. He was keeping in touch with developments in England, where once more the tide of poetic taste seemed to have turned against him as the Movement and its advocates seemed to dominate the media-driven debate as to poetry and its purposes. For four years X had seemed to keep alight the candle of an alternative sort of poetry. X had created mild ripples, and its editorial board had discovered fresh talent: the Yorkshire poet Brian Higgins who a few years later would die of a heart condition and, more lastingly, the one-time civil servant and versatile translator Charles Sissons. X however had bitten the dust, and there seemed little likelihood of a successor. Gascoyne mourned its going, though with a sinking sense of the inevitable. British poetry, it seemed to him, was in the doldrums. To make matters worse, after a long period of prevarication and indecision, Longmans had turned down the option on publishing his *Collected Poems.*

At the very moment when all seemed plunged into gloom, however, there was a twinkling in the darkness. The Yorkshire-born poet Robin Skelton had recently quitted the University of Manchester, where he had been lecturing in English literature, and taken up an appointment at the University of Victoria in Canada, where, as editor of the *Malahat Review* he would henceforth publish and promote an alternative version of British poetry to that currently prevailing in England. Skelton was widely read, artistically resourceful, and sympathetic towards the occult, but he was also a man of great energy, persistence, and organizational skill. Even more usefully, he was a persuasive lobbyist. Strongly drawn to Surrealism, inclined to regard his own practice as Surrealist in kind, he was by 1963 editing for Penguin books a refreshingly challenging anthology entitled *Poetry of the Thirties* offering a far more rounded account of the poetry of that decade than the widely shared view that Auden and his circle were all that were worth preserving from that time. In his Introduction Skelton called attention to the influence of Freud, recalled the Great Exhibition of 1936, and discussed the contributions made by Gascoyne, Reavey, and Jennings to translation. Privately he had also noted that Gascoyne's reputation seemed to be in decline. Via the Oxford University Press, over whom he had some influence, he was determined to do something about it.

In the 1960s Oxford University Press, unique in this respect among uni-versity presses in Britain, were stewards of a poetry list commanding the respect both of academics and of living poets. By 1961 it included James Baxter, Austin Clarke, Padraic Colum, Tony Connor, Allen Curnow, Christopher Hassall, John Heath-Stubbs, Thomas Kinsella, James Kirkup, Douglas Livingstone, Edward Lucie-Smith, John Press, Tom Scott, Anne Sexton, Anthony Thwaite, Charles Tomlinson, Keith Wright, as well as Skelton and the New Zealand-born poet Jon Stallworthy, who together with John Bell of OUP's London office oversaw the operation. Bell was paying Skelton a small annual retainer to act as a talent scout for the series, and it was in this capacity that in 1961 Skelton approached the Press to enquire if it might be interested in taking up the baton of Gascoyne's *Collected Poems* which Longmans seemed unaccountably to have dropped.

That very year another anthology had appeared that had made quite a difference to Gascoyne's general cachet. Elizabeth Jennings was a quietly articulate poet associated in many critics' eyes with the Movement; she was furthermore a devout Roman Catholic, and had herself suffered from peri-ods of mental illness. In 1961 she published *An Anthology of Modern Verse, 1940–1960* which made room for a different kind of Gascoyne poem: the meditative and undogmatically religious pieces he had been writing since his Surrealist phase abated.[12] When he received Skelton's proposal, Bell had just been reading this well-constructed anthology.[13] He was much impressed by what he had seen of Gascoyne's verse, and by Jenning's defence of it in her introduction. There were several problems. For a start, Gascoyne had covered his tracks so well that nobody—including David Higham, nomi-nally his agent—knew where he was. Bell sent a letter to the only person he thought might know. Anne Bradby had been T. S. Eliot's secretary in the mid-1930s, at the time when Faber had published Gascoyne's translations of Breton. She was a niece of Sir Humphrey Milford, Publisher to the University of Oxford between 1913 and 1945, and in 1938 she had married Vivian Ridler who shortly after the war had become head of the Press's printing department. It was to the poet 'Anne Ridler' that in October 1961 Bell's first enquiry went. Ridler delayed for a while, then furnished the address of the only person who she suspected might be of any help in this

12. *An Anthology of Modern Verse 1940–1960*, chosen, with introd., by Elizabeth Jennings (London: Methuen, 1961).
13. John Bell to Robin Skelton, 9 Oct. 1961, OUP PB/ED/017417.

search: Kathleen Raine. Once Raine had given the Press Meraud's address in Paris, they contacted Higham, and in principle negotiated terms. The Delegates of the Press agreed to the proposal in Oxford. A contract was drawn up, subject to Gascoyne's signature.

To accept the book and to find Gascoyne were two comparatively straightforward matters; to make contact with him a much more difficult third. In April 1962 Bell wrote to him care of the Rue de Lille: 'I wonder if you would consider allowing the Oxford University Press to publish a volume of your collected poems and translations? Several of us feel that it is time that your work was brought together and made more easily available than it is now and that you may be in agreement.'[14] In May Gascoyne boasted about this letter to Meraud; he then joined her in Aix and forgot all about it. Nine months passed, and Bell wrote again. Once more, there was no reply. In despair he turned to the one person in the office who might possess the presence of mind to sort Gascoyne out. She was the foreign rights manager, she possessed the promising-sounding name of Ilissa Bossy, and she agreed to visit Gascoyne in an attempt to persuade him on one of her overseas trips in January 1963.

The year 1963 did not bode well for Gascoyne. His state of mind at the time can be inferred from a vivid gouache he had recently completed (see Plate 23). Called *Impacts*, it displays a striking forest of black, yellow, and orange shapes. *Impacts* is markedly more aggressive and wildly threatening than any of his other pictures. Gone is the restrained grid work of symmetrical lines. The dark uprights and horizontal lines are thicker than before; they twist, distort, and writhe; in places they even seem to attack one another. They have also expanded outwards so as to cover much of the surface with a pall of cloud, as if a storm is just about to break out. If his earlier miniatures had reminded Raine of an updated Book of Kells, this was closer to a sort of Abstract Expressionist Francis Bacon. The dominant shades are burned sienna and carmine red, and there is precious little light anywhere.[15]

When Bossy paid a call to the Rue de Lille in January to speak to Gascoyne, she did not find him in an accommodating frame of mind. Braving the unsympathetic and hatchet-faced concierge, she ascended to the second floor where she discovered the poet sitting in his room in a state

---

14. John Bell to David Gascoyne, 18 Apr. 1962, OUP PB/ED/017417.
15. Beinecke, Box 17, Folder 361.

of absolute mental prostration.[16] He was almost completely silent. She urged the great advantages of being published by Oxford, and set out the financial terms of the contract she bore in her handbag. Gascoyne was not to be bossed.

A further communication from Bell on 18 February elicited no response. He eventually concluded that the only feasible way to clinch a deal was to send Skelton, who had already undertaken to edit the proposed *Collected Poems*, to France with the paperwork. £30 plus expenses was agreed to cover the trip. Coming after a severe Canadian winter, an offer to spend several days with his young wife Sylvia in Paris in April at OUP's expense met with little resistance from Skelton. He went, and on 9 April jubilantly cabled back to Bell: 'Mission Accomplished.' The surviving contract is signed in Gascoyne's wavering hand; the witness is Sylvia Skelton.

Social withdrawal was one extreme end of Gascoyne's mental pendulum. His mind driven by inner and outer pressures, at some of which that baneful recent gouache had hinted. The causes had much to do with a sense of imaginative constraint, a writer's block or *crampe* for which he illogically blamed Meraud. One day early in March 1964, driven to an excessive of frustration by his continuing inability to write, he attempted to strangle his benefactress and hostess.[17] The climate of public affairs in France was another contributing factor to his dismay. Politics, it seemed to Gascoyne, were approaching a climax in France. President de Gaulle was beset by opponents to right and to left. To the left were the Algerians, who were demanding independence at the end of a long drawn-out war. Well to the right was L'Organisation de l'Armée Secrète or the 'OAS', an extremist white settler group who were setting off bombs in France in an effort to keep Algeria French. Somewhere in the middle were the British, still ineptly suing to join the European Common Market in the teeth of continuing resistance by de Gaulle. Motions of censure on the French government for the severity of their policies in Algeria had been proposed at the United Nations, supported among other nations by the British.

The left-wing press in Paris were continually on de Gaulle's capacious back. Prominent in its opposition was the satirical and anticlerical weekly *Le Canard enchaîné*. *The Manacled Duck* (or the *Stifled Rag*, as its punning banner could variously be translated) had for months had been running a series

16. Conversation with Jon Stallworthy, 15 Feb. 2010.
17. *Meraud Guinness Guevara, ma mère*, 233.

of articles lampooning the President's regal style, which they unflatteringly compared to that of the Sun King—Louis ('L'Etat, c'est moi') Quatorze—and comparing the Elysée Palace to the pre-Revolutionary court at Versailles. In a long-running cartoon series 'La Cour'—a spoof on the *annales* of Saint-Simon devised by André Ribaud and the artist Moisan—de Gaulle was sarcastically referred to as 'His Eminence', and the pretentious ceremonial of his regime as 'Illuminations'.

In March 1964 Gascoyne was yet to leave the Rue de Lille apartment for his annual sojourn in Aix. In the immediate aftermath of the throttling incident, Meraud had already left to make the Tour de César ready for her summer guests. This time she had taken Nini with her, leaving Gascoyne alone in the flat with Martin, whom he hardly knew. Martin was slightly at a loss. One evening, as he later recounted in a horrified tone of voice to his wife, he invited this distracted poet to dine with his friends the Bassouls. When they arrived, 'the poet stopped in front of the door announcing that something terrible had just occurred inside, and that in any case he would not be taken into their apartment'.[18] Martin took him back to the Rue de Lille instead.

Gascoyne spent the next few days listening to ever-more alarming news bulletins on Radio France. As March advanced, he grew ever more convinced that the OAS were agents of Satan, and that their violent activities signalled the approach of the Last Days. On the 18th he wrote to his old friend and former BBC producer Douglas Cleverdon in London with a very particular request. Could Cleverdon possibly ferret out a copy of the 'old medieval mystery play called "The Harrowing of Hell". I am almost certain it is contained in a collection of mysteries in the "Everyman Series".' By way of explanation he added a rider, stating that 'I write to you at present because *at last* recently I have been able to see again, and consequently to believe myself capable of something worthwhile.'[19]

Then his mood turned, calamitously, towards mania. Stirred by amphetamine-fuelled psychosis, voices in his head proclaimed the end of all things and his mission to inform the powers-that-be of the imminent end of history. By the morning of 8 April, the whispered confidences proved impossible to resist. Armed with his message from on high, Gascoyne set off for the Elysée Palace with the intention of conveying it to the Head of

---

18. *Meraud Guinness Guevara, ma mère*, 233.
19. David Gascoyne to Douglas Cleverdon, 18 Mar. 1964, TGA 9326/1/39.

State. Skirting the grounds, he arrived at the lofty wall along the Rue d'Elysée to the left of the main gate. With some difficulty he scaled it. He was making his way across the cobbled courtyard towards the palace buildings when his presence was noted by some plainclothes policemen patrolling the grounds. They asked him what he was doing there. He replied that he was a messenger from the Messiah and wished to speak with the French President concerning the imminent Apocalypse, of which he alone was apprised. The guards asked him to accompany them to the guardhouse to clarify the nature of his mission. He refused and, when they laid hands on him, struggled to break free and once more reach the palace.

Reinforcements were called up, and Gascoyne started to fend them off with legs and fists. He was eventually overcome by force of numbers and escorted to the medical post attached to the local police depot, where he was held overnight. The following morning he was transferred to the Centre Hospitalier Sainte-Anne in Rue Alésia, Paris's largest psychiatric facility where, pending an interview with a consultant, he was restrained in a straitjacket and kept in a padded cell for a day. After a further interview with a specialist, he was diagnosed as suffering from mania, sedated, and dispatched by ambulance to L'Asile de Vaucluse, a large nineteenth-century asylum to the south of Paris in the suburban riverside town of Epinay-sur-Orge.

The incident did not go unnoticed in the wider world. Staying round the corner from the presidential palace at the Hôtel Continental along the Rue de Castiglione had been the freelance journalist Janet Flanner, who on 15 April submitted her report to the *Manacled Duck*:

HE TAKES HIMSELF FOR THE MESSIAH

The police at the Elysée have been accosted by a messenger from God—who wanted to force an entrance into the presidential palace—and have taken him to the infirmary attached to the guardhouse.

Take comfort, this was no action by You-Know-Who, but a British citizen's who, purporting to be an envoy from His Eminence Yet More High, desired to assist His Majesty You-Know-Who with his Illuminations.

An Englishman who takes himself for Joan of Arc—and in Joan of Arc's own country! These British folks certainly have some cheek. Rest assured: Mon Général was quite right to vote against them at the UN.[20]

---

20. *Le Canard enchaîné*, 15 Apr. 1964.

NIGHT
THREE

1964–2001

25
Post-Apocalyptic

L'Asile de Vaucluse, the largest and most impressively situated of Paris's suburban psychiatric hospitals, stands along a low ridge overlooking the left bank of the River Orge to the south of Paris, just a few miles from Orly. Though much expanded since its foundation in 1869 as a safe haven for the mentally disturbed of the capital, the main lines of its deceptively serene architecture were still visible when Gascoyne entered it a century later. From the eighteenth-century villa at its centre, a line of *pavillons* or circular-shaped wards stretched eastwards and westwards, joined by corridors. Each pavilion was divided into several cell-like rooms that accommodated three to four patients, and was arranged around a courtyard. To the north of the complex a broad driveway flanked by gardens swept down towards the river, with a working farm beyond that. Apart from the occasional growl of jets taking off from the airport, it was a peaceful place, and in April lushly beautiful. During his years as a medical intern, André Breton had worked there, and it was here he had placed the treatment—or as he preferred to view it the incarceration—of the troubled waif Nadja in his classic Surrealist tale of that title in 1928. Gascoyne might have derived comfort from this coincidence. Under dramatic, and what increasingly came to appear to him ludicrous, circumstances he had now reached a crisis that been in the offing for years, and his immediate reaction was one of relief. Six days later, in precocious spring weather, he was sitting up in bed writing:

April 16, 12.55 p.m.
Just received crucial visit of verification and recognition from Meraud and Giselle. Extraordinary increase of feeling of normality and fulfilment. Impossible to write more at this moment. Superabundance should (and does) equal silence equals contained tranquillity.

★

(Later)
Now I want my glasses back. Both pairs.

★

I can still make lists of projects.

April 16 on p. 303
Yesterday I saw the first bee here, *inside* the window-pane, and redirected it on
its way out and back to its swarm, with a message about globular hives suspended from hoops and combs with hexagonal cells.[1]

The 'projects' were characteristically ambitious. They included a plan 'to be
allowed to direct and produce in collaboration with the conductor and
composer Pierre Boulez, *Turandot*, at the Milan Scala, with Callas in the title
rôle, and with décor and costumes by the (quasi-unknown) Swiss, Meret
Oppenheim'.[2] In consoling fact, as he concluded, 'all this experience since
my release from the *Dépôt*, has simply represented a psychological and physical "check-up", before I can properly assume my personal vocation. That is
quite clear to me today.'

He was certainly receiving a gratifying amount of attention. Word soon
reached Blanche Reverchon, still semi-officially as his analyst and, it now
seemed to him, 'one of the true 20th century Scientific (Freudian) Sybils.
And a Sybil is an incarnation of the Divine Total(ly) Human (or Collective)
Unconscious.' Her reaction was one of brisk common sense: the hospital
should contact the British Consulate immediately with a view to his repa-
triation. 'It is very important', she told the authorities, 'that upon his release
he is put in charge of someone answerable to his mother.'[3] Meraud had
rushed back up from the South: she brought him his much-needed spectacles, and a little blue notebook in which he was soon jotting down ideas for
poems. He requested his paperback editions of Rimbaud, Lautréamont, and
Eluard, his New Testament, and a copy of *The Tempest*. Desmond Ryan, his
old friend now settled back in Paris, came to see him on the 23rd as did, he
told Meraud, 'a nice lady I had never seen in my life before, from the British
Consulate'.

1. David Gascoyne, 'My First Post-Apocalyptic Notebook', Tulsa, Box 2, File 3, from which all
   subsequent quotations in this chapter are taken.
2. (1913–85). Painter and sculptor, associated particularly with the creation of Surrealist objects,
   such as her *Fur Cup and Saucer* (1936). Subject of a number of photographs by Man Ray in the
   thirties.
3. Blanche Reverchon-Jouve to Meraud Guevara, 17 Apr. 1964, TGA 9326/1/39.

He had been placed under the care of a Dr Carrère, who diagnosed mania, and prescribed a regime of 'injections, transfusions, pills, potions and sleeping pills'. It included a regular intake of the tranquillizer Equanil, and of Largactil, a drug pioneered at the Hôpital Sainte-Anne ten years previously. The latter was intended to flatten out his moods of elation, but it soon produced unfortunate side-effects including, he complained to Meraud, 'an acute hypersensibilité', especially in his thighs 'so that I couldn't sit still for more than five minutes at a time and had to keep on walking, walking, walking'.[4]

For all these medicaments, delusions and paranoid obsessions still hung about. He christened a fellow patient 'Judas' for his habit of spying, and perhaps reporting, on fellow inmates. By contrast, his next door neighbour appeared to him endowed with remarkable, if *naïf*, artistic gifts; 'I am going to write to Jean Dubuffet about the man in the bed to the right of mine', he observed carefully in his journal, 'I mean Jacques Derune who is discovering in himself today a primitive graphic artist of a certain natural talent.' On inspecting the results a little later he added a corrective observation to the effect that 'This was perhaps? a piece of generous self-deception'. Others meanwhile were paying attention to *him:*

There is someone watching me write whom I am still not at all sure I altogether understand...He *can't be* Judas.

★

Nocturnal Obsession (night of 16th/17th): The Dream Story and Meaning of Charles the Incest Prodigy and his Bucking Broncho [*sic*].

★

(yesterday) April 17th/18th.

★

Marvellous thought for the French about the Common Market and All That (borrowed from Paul Jennings' *The Penguin Jennings*, that I am reading in bed— Desmond R. brought it for me yesterday): 'Les amis des Fritz sont des Amis à Nous!'

★

A Third Banal Observation to complete my notes for this completely banal (medicarefully) day: the poor (in France) undoubtedly eat far better, in the

---

4. David Gascoyne to Meraud Guevara, 13 May 1964, TGA 9326/1/39.

poor districts, than the rich who live in the rich districts; and for less than half the price.

★

Dream Complications of Oriental Miracles.

★

Saturday morning. April 18th/19th.
I feel today will somehow be a better day than yesterday. I started shaving again this morning! There seems to be a lot of shifting about going on in the dormitory.

★

Monday. April 20th.
After siesta.
A fine day, a rich morning. Talked satisfactorily to 2 doctors. Sent letter to Mother. Shaved completely. Sat in the courtyard. Feel very fit.

★

Now I can see at last what use my lit. agent, David Higham Associates, may be going to have for me!

With returning calm, he slowly grew habituated to the place. The food, he remarked with some satisfaction, 'is extremely good here. And the chap I thought was "Judas" knows far more about French History than I do.' His nights were in effect more eventful than his days, filled as they were with such apparitions as, on the night of 24–5 April, a 'Dream about Divine justice literally interrupted by infernal roaring of night flight jet planes'. On waking, however, he found little to do but read between six when he got up until lights out at ten. A temporary distraction was a welcome visit by Mrs Barney 'from the British Consulate...It seems I am quite a notability, of a kind, after all!' Otherwise he endured more or less gracefully a procession of empty hours. '*Evénement*,' he exclaimed on the 25th, 'The *petit déjeuner* was 25 mins. late this morning.'

On the 28th he was moved to another and larger pavilion ward. It was better equipped with 'two shops and a cafeteria; and television'. On the other hand he had to put up with his bed being parked in the corridor. Besides, his loquacious neighbour Jacques Derune, in whose *faux-naïf* talent he now totally lost faith, had been moved across as well, and kept on spouting dire uneducated wisdom. Gascoyne was edgy, restless, and he had difficulty in concentrating or sitting still for more than a few minutes at a time. The doctors had been told that he might be out in a week, but there was little sign of a reprieve. Moreover, he had no money with which to purchase even the modest merchandise at the hospital shops, and was obliged to beg Meraud for a cheque to relieve his difficulty.

As April turned into May, Martin Lacroix and their friend Georgette Camille came bearing a traditional Mayday nosegay of *muguet*, lilies of the valley, 'especially white and perfumed this year' according to the French newspapers. Lacroix bore away a new poem, promising to type it and, what seemed just as useful, cashed Meraud's cheque. She meanwhile had retreated to Aix, whither David wrote soliciting yet more funds, by *mandat* or postal order this time, and evoking for her the deleterious side-effects of Largactyl. At one especially low point, on Monday, 11 May it had, he told her, caused him 'most miserable and frightening day of my life':

> It suddenly occurred to me that I was going to be more or less permanently a *malade mental,* that I should never be able to use my talent, and should have to spend a large part of my life in institutions (and consequently hardly be able to see *you* again.) I realize perfectly now that all this was a delusion, an artificially stimulated one, actually enhanced by actual financial insecurity. And it was actually *necessary* for me to pass through that ghastly day...in order for me really to understand what was happening to me and to become objective about it.[5]

By way of compensation he was writing once more; his latest poem, he now claimed, being 'something quite new for me, very *gnomie* [*sic*]...but almost as simple as nursery rhymes (which are not always so simple as they seem, except in form)'.[6] The result, when Lacroix delivered the typescript, was a kind of blend of Jung and early Blake, its theme the passionate intercourse of two impulses that were eating him up: Memory and Desire:

> Our gentle sister Memory,
> Our brother Brother Brute desire,
> Conspire from time to time in Time
> To set the World afire.
>
> They never can destroy this World,
> The strange incestuous Pair:
> Their loving intercourse takes place
> Within their Father's care.
>
> Their Father is a whoring man,
> Although his hair is grey.
> He will not set his scythe aside
> Till he has had his play.

5. David Gascoyne to Meraud Guevara, 13 May 1964, TGA 9326/1/39.
6. Ibid. He means *gnomique*, as in 'Poésie gnomique', defined by *Le Petit Robert* (1990 edn.), 872 as an 'ensemble de maxims, de précepts, de conseils pratiques versifiés'.

He loves his fornicating Twins,
He loves to watch them sin;
But hammers at the window-pane
And breaks out once he's in:

'How dare you break my sacred laws!
How many times a day
Have I had to repeat to you
What all the Great Books say:

'There is a limit to all things,
Thou can'st not but comply.
What I have told you once for all
Thou shalt believe or die.'

'You shall not suffer in your bed,
But only in the Bath
Which I am going to prepare
As for an aftermath.

'This afternoon, before the Sun
Has trod his wearying way
Towards his final resting-place,
You shall resume your play.

'But first I'll strip you to the bone
To see in what clean dew
You have been washing in like snow
No spring rains can renew.

'There *is* a mighty mystery,
In spite of your belief
That Time and old Eternity
Were nothing but a grief.

'The griefs that come, the joys that go,
The vague material things,
Are nothing to the forms of me
Our greater Future brings.

'So get ready for your Bath
Of Blood you're going to take,
Since as I happened to pass by
I saw your Great Mistake.'[7]

---

7. David Gascoyne, 'Part of a Poem in Progress', Beinecke, Box 15, Folder 344. Published in the *Malahat Review* (Vancouver) 7 (1968) and in *The Sun at Midnight* (London: Enitharmon, 1970), 53–5.

If this lyrical performance were indeed *gnomique*, it was also driven by compulsions and certainties: the necessity for—nay the relish of—sex and of strife, and a strong, Neoplatonic sense that beyond 'these vague material things' lay some grand sacrificial design. At this crisis of his mortal life he was suddenly been gripped by a conviction, Equanil-induced perhaps but still profound, of the operations of Providence. It was the material processes that now seemed vague: destiny on the other hand appeared as certain and as definite as a pinprick. Kathleen Raine would have appreciated all of this, and even more so certain other directions his mind was now taking, spurred on by memories of reading Martin Buber on the sanctity of the human relation between *ich und du*. Thus:

> I have been thinking about God and the gods; Prayer and Inspiration; I, Thee and the 'Thou', and dialogue; the mind, the heart, the soul.
>
> I have my own five special secular saints, five special pagan gods. Paracelsus, Luther, Shakespeare, Rimbaud and the author of the Greenberg mss.—Minerva, Ceres, Mercury, Pan and Athena.
>
> The rainbow: Tranquillity, my soul.

But there were reductive thoughts as well, by means of which he could perceive himself satirically from the outside as a middle-aged man simply enduring a rough passage. Some of his symptoms he found reflected in *Le Fanal bleu*, the sickness-haunted final volume of Colette's autobiographical sequence of novels, which he was now reading. At other moments, what he was experiencing resembled more prosaically a variety of male menopause, a description of which he had found in Simenon's *Le Grand Bob*, which Meraud had lent him:

> **May 8th. Friday.**
> '*Il attaignait l'âge où on commence à avoir des ennuis. Je prétends que les hommes passent par les mêmes périodes difficiles que les femmes, vers quarante-cinq ou cinquante ans, et, si j'en juge par ce que j'ai en à souffrir avec la patronne . . .*'—*dixit* a Simenon character, *patron* of a Montmartre café-bar, in *Le Grand Bob*.—I shall be forty-eight this year.
> **9 a.m.**: Have become unusually talkative today. *Bon signe, sûrement.*
>
> ★
>
> One of my fellow-inmates, in *Pavillon VI*, is the nephew of Georges Sorel (war experience; consequent drunkenness).

At other times his moods seesawed wildly, to almost comic effect. At least Meraud's postal order had arrived, though it proved more complicated to cash than he had hoped. But he was also compelled to look into causes: his unrelieved isolation, a crushing sense of sexual failure, and a conviction that that the only fulfilled love that he had ever known—his affair with Bent von Müllen, the memory of whom continued to haunt him—had been violently snuffed out almost before it had begun. He was, then, a sort of widower:

> At no time have I really suffered from 'delusions of grandeur'. I now know and understand what it means to say that Christ is resurrected in me.
>
> ★
>
> *May 13th. Wednesday.*
> *8 a.m.*
> Today again I have woken up to find myself unusually loquacious.
> I now at last am really more fully able to understand what is meant by the animus-anima relationship in the individual spiritually conscious man. I owe a lot of this understanding to having read Jung.
>
> ★
>
> *May 14th. Friday.*
> I now really am beginning to feel better in every way, every day.
>
> ★
>
> The fears which so much conditioned the subconscious of my youth, had a perfectly real origin. After all, the most beloved friend of my life was hanged by the Nazis as a hostage (so was his father).
>
> ★
>
> A slightly difficult day, owing to *mandat* trouble. At any rate the money is *here*. Am bearing-up fairly well.
>
> ★
>
> *May 16th. Whit Sunday.*
> This morning I woke early again, and had an unmistakably clear realisation about the nature of my true vocation.
> Attended Mass in the little hospital chapel, and afterwards met an extremely sympathetic Dominican with whom I am going to have a little talk about ecumenism later in the week.

Moreover, in Cyrano de Bergerac mode, he was making himself useful:

> This afternoon, one of my fellow patients asked my help in writing a love letter, which gave me extraordinary pleasure. Together we were able to compose *un billet vraiment doux et tendre*.
>
> ★
>
> *May 18th Whit Monday*
> *6 a.m.*
> Today I have awakened to the realisation that I am now my true self. I now know who I am and what I am meant to do with my life. All through my

present strange and wonderful experience, one of the several words most fre-quently recurring to my consciousness has been Preparation.

★

I am gradually destroying my fear of the word 'destruction'. Destruction, as a necessary phase of true Creation, can never be destroyed, any more than the sun can suddenly go out. (Death of Eros).

★

Destruction does not mean annihilation (It means transformation, even in atomic physics.)

★

May 19th. Tuesday.
Day of gradual improvement. Coping.

★

May 20th. Weds.
It is easy now to see the simple problem of my life: how to achieve true self-*consistency*. (What is the etymology of this word?)

★

This is certainly a sort of Red Letter Day for me. The *interne* I met by chance while strolling this morning informed me that I shall be leaving before the end of the month, that my passport is already here, and that I can make a trip to Paris to collect my books and things.

And I've written another love-letter for *l'affreux Jojo* to send to his nurse-friend.

★

May 21st. Thurs.
'Vieilles évocations de firmament, mirages de mers, ce que nous tenons pour éternel est volontiers bleu...' Colette. (*F.B.* p.35).

★

What is the real meaning, the correct spelling and etymology of the word feasible/able? Future reference *Ox. Dict.*

★

It's just as well for me to remember for the time being that I am still a convalescent.

★

I'm afraid that Jojo's nurse-friend was only in his imagination. Mysterious business, of a kind probably well-known here. I wish I could help...

★

After lunch:
Now I know that I am definitely embarking for Dover on the 26th. I hope I can visit Paris first.

Reality gripped him by the throat. For two decades now he had been on a search for grand metaphysical insights. Perhaps through his conversations with doctors, the recognition was growing him that his eventual salvation might actually lie via an embrace of the very ordinariness his *enfant terrible*, Surrealist self had once spurned. The enigma of his sexuality remained. Physically uncertain with women, he knew he still needed them desperately: perhaps the solution for his difficulties lay after all through the domestic calm he had once found so dull:

> *May 22nd. Friday.*
> I love my father deeply and tenderly. I genuinely, spontaneously realised it this morning. I need no longer feel any shyness about it…
>
> ★
>
> The truth about my sex-life: I cannot stand up for ladies, and I have an innate sense of chivalry.
>   I rather wish I could one day marry an understanding, wealthy widow.

Arrangements were being made for his departure. Win had already contacted the hospital authorities about arrangements for bringing him back to England. She was also in touch both with the British embassy in Paris and with Meraud, who was keeping a tactful and concerned eye on developments from what David refers to in the journals as the 'imperial Ivory Tower' of Aix. From the practical point of view matters could not have been more difficult. The doctors wanted Gascoyne to be taken straight from the hospital to England under medical supervision. But most of his personal effects were still in the Rue de Lille. And Leslie and Win had recently moved to the Isle of Wight, where with their slender savings they had purchased a modest semi in the village of Northwood, just a few miles inland south of Cowes. Leslie was still suffering from recurrent eye trouble as a result of his diabetes, and was at the time of his eldest son's breakdown in Moorfield's eye hospital in London. For all the practical challenges, Win pluckily informed Meraud:

> We all think that it is better for him to come here, and my nephew who is a doctor says that the National Health Service will look after him 'til he has recovered… You know of course that he had a breakdown after the war, but he did get over it though he had no proper treatment then—because he just would not co-operate.[8]

Perhaps because there was so little that he could actually do, and certainly because those he trusted were taking events into their resourceful hands, Gascoyne felt more at peace than ever:

---

8. Win Gascoyne to Meraud Guevara, 16 Apr. 1964, TGA 9326/1/39.

May 24th. Trinity Sunday.

Yesterday, spoke with the Dominican briefly. Today, he is going to say at Mass a prayer for my intention; and for me this represents a reconciliation with the country where once my ancestors were persecutors.

★

May 25th. Monday.

This is my last day at Vaucluse.—It has been an enforced stay here, and I have been under a complicated involuntary treatment, which has had various not all at all [*sic*] pleasant side-effects. It is a dull rainy morning here today (6 a.m.). But I lift up my heart to the Creator. I have learnt much that is of deep value during my stay. Most of the *sociothérapie*, although I have not officially been put to work in that department, has taught me better to love and understand my relations, friends and brothers—I should simply say my fellow-men. So much is lasting and positive. What the effects on my nervous system of the Largactyl [*sic*] treatment will have been remains to be seen. They can only have been curative, that is obvious, whether I have liked it or not at the time.

★

I hope to visit the Isle of Wight *bénédictins* sometimes. If I have to see a psychiatrist, I shall insist on a Jungian. It seems to me this ought to be my constitutional right.

★

May 26th. Tuesday.

My intelligence and my sense of humour have been somewhat in abeyance during my illness. Argactyl [*sic*] and previous insidious intoxication have curious side-effects—among them a deformation of creative impulse and a diversion (inverted sublimation?) into negative channels of normally coherent elements of the balancing power of personality. I suppose the cure is meant to make one find one's own feet by one's (true) self.

The authorities embargoed any suggestion that he might call in at the Rue de Lille to collect his typewriter, his papers, and his books. Instead he was taken straight to the ferry that morning in the company of an orderly, Win making the complicated journey by public transported transport from the Isle of Wight to meet them. As she later told Meraud: 'I met him at Dover on May 26th. He was escorted by a male nurse. It was a long journey from here and an ordeal—but everything went off well thanks to my kind friend Mr Kennedy who phoned the Emigration Officer beforehand, and he was so kind and helpful and rushed us through customs etc. We arrived home about 11.45 p.m. after an exhausting journey.'[9] As Gascoyne related in his journal the following day: 'My

---

9. Win Gascoyne to Meraud Guevara, 26 May 1964, TGA 9326/1/39.

journey was long and a bit complicated and of course I was tired and so was Mother, but we both got home with providential ease, in reality.' At least a belief in Providence remained.

He persisted in thinking all was for the best. But, briefed by Blanche Reverchon, who had watched his ups and downs across several decades, the French doctors had made one fact abundantly plain before he left. As with unfeigned candour Gascoyne later informed an interviewer, they instructed him that 'You must go back to England, and no account must you live alone'.[10]

---

10. BL Lives, F1383, Side B.

26

Enter Zuk

The village of Northwood straddles the undulating main road between Newport, capital of the Isle of Wight, and the quaint, busy, yacht-haunted harbour town of Cowes facing the Solent and Southhampton on the island's hilly north coast. It is a modest and reasonable place and even now, away from the steady hum of traffic along the main road, it is hard to make out much sound beyond the voices of children in the primary school, and the occasional subdued chatter from nearby gardens in summertime. Indeed, as Gascoyne himself was soon to find out, to call it a 'village' as such was something of a misnomer, for it had little centre apart from a huddle of shops with a pub near the bus stop. On the southern fringe of the settlement a rural track called 'Chawton Lane' led to the pretty, much modified twelfth-century parish church of St John the Baptist, beyond which lay the open fields of Chawton Farm. To the north of that was a string of fairly recent houses spread out along the place's few, well-spaced streets. 'Oxford Street' was the inappropriately metropolitan and commercial-sounding name of the double line of well-kept bungalows and semis running west-wards into countryside where Leslie and Win had chosen to spend their last years in a brick two-storey turn-of-the-century dwelling known, suitably enough, as 'The Haven'. The house had a pleasant bay-windowed sitting room at the front, while to the rear lay a surprisingly rambling quarter-acre garden, somewhat neglected of late but which Win with characteristic tenacity was working to bring back to life with beds of lemon blossom, fuchsia, wild geraniums, rhododendrons, and purple azaleas around a frog pond shaped like the island. If Gascoyne craved peace of mind, he had come to the right spot: spiritually, mentally, and socially it was about as far away fom the loquacious experimentation and social daring of Paris's Faubourg Saint-Germain as it was possible to reach.

To begin with, he relished the sheer tranquillity, the domestic ordinari-ness. He had not seen either Leslie or Win for some five years, and all of his recent correspondence with them had been addressed to his mother alone, since Leslie's eyesight was now too weak for him to read, and his mind wandered at times. Win, though, was as brisk and supportive as ever, exuding the no-nonsense confidence and affection she had acquired from Florence Mole. His post-apocalyptic notebook soldiers on for a few more entries, all of which breathed uncomplicated gratitude. On Wednesday, 27 May he records a 'wonderfully rich, calm and happy day'. Friends had soon caught up with him, and there were a couple of solicitous and helpful postcards from Mary Hutchinson. She spoke encouragingly of his 'new voice' which, he consolingly told himself, was unexpectedly that of 'an experienced married man, for I am spiritually now a widower, or rather a man with a good many ex-mistresses once more looking for a mate'.[1] She also told him that 'Rosamond Lehmann ("now there's a really beautiful person," I've always said, tho' I've never had the chance to know her at all well) is coming to the Island early next month, and may be wanting to see me. I have heard or read somewhere that she is at present engaged in finishing a long new novel about modern man and his difficult search for God.'

He was still fascinated by his inner processes, but more inclined than before to acknowledge that help was more likely to arrive from professional medicine than from the artistic process itself. He diagnosed himself with 'curative/creative paranoia (ex-homosexual variety)' but, for all that, he went to see the local GP in Cowes. While waiting his turn in the consulting room, he browsed through the book that he had with him: it was an Everyman edition of Shelley's translation from Plato's *Ion*.

> When I opened it at random, almost the first words to meet my eye were these:
> SOCRATES: Has the rhapsodist or the physician the clearest knowledge of what ought to be said to a sick man?
> ION: In that case the physician.

What the doctor could not supply, religion possibly could. On Wednesday, 3 June he visited the Benedictine abbey on the north coast of the island and was interviewed by Father Ziegler, 'a German convert who reminded me somehow of Francis the Pole and to whom I read some extracts from this journal. His spiritual presence seems to have helped restore me a little further to my true native reality, insofar as I have been alienated from it

---

1. David Gascoyne, 'My First Post-Apocalyptic Notebook', Tulsa, Box 2, File 3, from which subsequent quotations in this chapter are taken.

during the past until fairly recently—who can say until when?—by various suppressed poisons and delusions in my own unconscious.' Slowly he was establishing some sort of routine and sense of detachment. His composure, however, was not assisted by a letter he received from Meraud. It may well have been the product of conversations with Blanche, and it was certainly meant to temper kindness with realism. Its well-meant advice, very different in its sense of his future from Mary Hutchinson's, was devastating nonetheless:

> To me 'David the Poet' is a real person who exists apart from my friend David Gascoyne—I think I should describe him as 'un état, d'esprit' or a sort of state of great excitement and enthusiasm which you can probably provoke artificially through drink or drugs, and that you can only write creatively when you are in this state—That is why I say that David the poet has to be *really* and properly buried by you, with a stake through his heart—I imagine that the voices have something to do with David-the-poet who was trying to come back and inhabit your body and mind—He did come back but he drove you mad—I feel sure that if he comes back again he will kill you and that is why I want to believe that he is properly buried—I didn't like him but I am quite prepared to shed a few tears on his grave because he was a genius.
>
> My friend David Gascoyne is young and handsome and very intelligent, sensitive and delicate. I hope that he will find a way to go on living and to recapture the joie de vivre which he has lost—He is capable of many things such as painting, being a wonderful art critic or a professor of literature if he had the tiny bit of energy necessary and the 'will to live!' The fame and genius of David-the-Poet will help him to get a job anywhere.[2]

If some friends in their misplaced concern were anxious to see David's gift well and truly interred for his own good, there were others equally determined to revive it. The most palpable sign of this was the promised appearance of the *Collected Poems* which the Delegates of the Oxford University Press had accepted the previous May. On 9 June, Bell wrote officially from the Press welcoming Gascoyne back to England. At the end of the month he communicated with Meraud to report proudly that 'When I go to London, I shall be going to lunch with the Oxford University Press. They say that they are treating my *Collected Poems* as "an important book", and so for some reason it cannot come out until early next Spring. Better late than, etc.'[3] Progress on the book was undeniably slow; it was also exceptionally

---

2. Meraud Guevara to David Gascoyne, Tuesday, 2 June 1964, Enitharmon Papers.
3. David Gascoyne to Meraud Guevara, 27 June 1964, TGA 9326/1/39.

thorough. One problem was that his poems were scattered all over the place: in separate, and sometimes almost unobtainable, volumes, journals, and small magazines. Another was that earlier publishers held rights in some of them; André Deutsch, for example, still had *Night Thoughts* in print, and was reluctant to relinquish it until an agreement was reached that the *Collected Poems* should be brought out jointly. In some instances Gascoyne could not even remember who had issued his earlier work. An enquiry from Stallworthy as to who had published *Roman Balcony* provoked the blank response 'I can't remember'.[4] 'Requiem' existed only in typescript, and Priaulx Rainier had to make a photocopy so it could be included.

In effect the book turned into a labour of love shared by two fellow poets who, temperamentally and in appearance, could scarcely have been more different, even if each of them represented an aspect of Gascoyne's enduring appeal. Jon Stallworthy was a 29-year-old desk editor working in the General Books Department of the London offices of OUP in Amen House, close to St Paul's Cathedral. A New Zealander by birth, a published poet, an Oxford English graduate and former winner of the Newdigate Prize, he combined efficiency and courtesy in the office with a scholarly interest in twentieth-century verse, and an individual poetic voice of charm and dexterity. For several months, ever since Gascoyne had been prevailed upon to sign the contract, he had been corresponding over the forthcoming book with Robin Skelton in Canada and England. Skelton was 39, softly spoken, incipiently bearded, fussy, gently humorous, and exceptionally hard-working. At Victoria University, British Columbia he had converted himself into a one-man literary industry. Volumes of verse and criticism and anthologies streamed from his unresting typewriter, and it was in Canada that he would establish an influential magazine of new verse, the *Malahat Review*, that was soon including Gascoyne's work. For some time he had busied himself academically with English poetry of the immediate pre-war period, and in 1964 he had just published his well-publicized compendium *The Poetry of the Thirties*.

Skelton believed strongly that the responsible, sensitive handling of poetry by others amounted in itself to a form of art. He applied to such tasks the collage technique that Gascoyne had practised as a younger man both in his miniature pictures and in his poems. 'The art of selection and arrangement', Skelton declared in his introduction to his recent anthology 'is also an act of judgement.' Manifestly absorbed by the larger-than-life personalities that

---

4. David Gascoyne to Jon Stallworthy, 19 June 1964, OUP PB/ED/017417, Box 2353.

had dominated the 1930s, Skelton was also acutely aware that the most interesting talents are frequently those who transcend period, and that as a consequence all decades constitute melanges. Of no slice of time was this truer than a decade seemingly dominated by W. H. Auden and writers of his clique. Even Auden had been a bundle of contradictions, and the nimbus surrounding his name was more spectrum than shade. In his Introduction Skelton took apart the journalistic myth of thirties poetry as a platform for fashionable political sentiment to reveal something more complicated and interesting underneath:

> The question of the poet's image was very important to the men of the thirties. It almost seems as if the main task of many poets was to make an assertion about the poet's function, rather than to perform that function. Some of the propagandist poems convince us more of the writer's belief in the importance of writing propaganda than of his emotional commitment to his statements. Frequently the image of the poet gets in the way of the poetry. The new-style laurel wreath is worn self-conciously, and with the fashionable tilt to the left. It is, however, difficult to keep on when you are not used to it, so the conversation often becomes stilted. While the thirties men had all of the advantages of sharing (generally speaking) a social credo they had also to suffer the disadvantages of being members of a group that demanded they play a particular role. This role, however, could be interpreted in several ways, and as the thirties progressed some poets took the general belief in the importance of individual fulfilment to its logical extreme, and became involved in the use of dream-language, automatic writing, and all of the paraphenalia of Surrealism. Nothing could be more opposed, one would imagine, to the tenets of the left-wing poets who made up the *avant-garde* of the first years of the decade, and yet it seems that when in 1935, the younger poets began to produce this irrational, nightmarish, outrageously introverted poetry, the Old Guard were far from dismayed.[5]

The thirties had therefore manifested no simple turning of the tide: from the subjective to the objective and then back again, or from the stridently committed to the oblivious and wilfully detached. There had always been a blend. In his choice of contents Skelton had reserved for Gascoyne a special and privileged place as 'the youngest poet of any weight to publish a volume before 1940'. He concluded the anthology with the grand lowering of the curtain in 'Farewell Chorus', placing it after Auden's better-known viaticum 'September 1939', conveying an impression that David's poem represented the more satisfactorily inclusive statement of closure. In the

---

5. *The Poetry of the Thirties*, ed. Robin Skelton (Harmondsworth: Penguin, 1964), 30.

body of his anthology he showed a partiality for a particular kind of Gascoyne poem in which the personal note strove to be representative, the visceral to be universally true. And he found room too for the scattered poems—far stronger than most people remembered—of David's long-dead contemporary and collaborator, Roger Roughton.

Skelton's was a versatile literary personality, among whose many projects featured a sustained self-disguise as the fictitious 'Georges Zuk', middle-aged French Surrealist poet and survivor of the 1930s Left Bank. Zuk was Skelton's surrealist alter persona. He was everything Skelton in life was not, and quite a lot besides. He was indolent where Skelton was industrious, sad where Skelton was merry: he was also lecherous with a lechery that bordered on legend. In successive volumes published under this nom de plume, Skelton posed as translator and editor.[6] He had, he told Zuk's readers, been seriously interested in the work of this benign dinosaur since 1963: the year in which he had first interested himself in the neglected importance of Gascoyne. Born in Algeria in 1918 (and thus two years Gascoyne's junior), Zuk had, so Skelton claimed, moved to Marseilles with his parents in the early 1930s. Urban life had drawn him out, but in 1934 the young man began to suffer severely from attacks of asthma, and he had been obliged to spend the following four years with relatives in the country. During this period he had learned English and then read *Sartor Resartus* by Gascoyne's admired Carlyle, a work that had influenced him deeply. At 17, like Gascoyne, he had experienced his first serious love affair, after which—in a reversal of Gascoyne's history—he had spent the war years in Paris, having been rejected for military service on account of his asthma: years in which, like Paul Eluard, he had worked conscientiously for the Resistance, though in a different capacity: as a forger of passports for the activists of Le Marais. Zuk had spent the rest of his life in Left Bank cafés writing witty libidinous verses, and picking up girls.

They had first met, claimed Skelton, in the Café Baie in the Place Denfert-Rochereau near the entrance to the catacombs. Like Gascoyne, Zuk had been perplexed by the apparent interest taken in him. 'When I suggested that I might translate some of his poems, he seemed more amused than anything else.' Yet it had decidedly been Zuk—or rather the Zuk side

6. See esp. Georges Zuk, *Selected Poems*, trans. Robert Skelton (San Francisco: Kayak Books, 1969) and *Zuk* translated from the French of Georges Zuk, introd. Robin Skelton (Erin, Ontario: Porcupine's Quill, 1982). Apparently taken in by the hoax, the British Library catalogued both under 'Poetry in French: Algerian Writers 1960– .'

of Skelton's protean personality—that had first awoken to Gascoyne's appeal, and it was with an ear and an eye thus schooled that Skelton now set about editing the *Collected Poems*. The book appeared under the double imprint of Oxford and André Deutsch and within an austerely sable jacket on 29 July 1965, in an edition of 1,000 copies priced at 30s., half of which were taken by OUP's New York branch. Feeling too low to oversee the proofs, Gascoyne had trusted Skelton to get on with much of the selection and arrangement. Skelton had responded with his own Zuk-like being and compounded a sequence that perfectly expressed what he took to be the essence of Gascoyne's evolving personality. He had trawled periodicals for vintage early pieces, some of which had never been collected before, and passed on to the best of *Man's Life Is This Meat*, then the original poems from *Hölderlin's Madness*, *Poems 1937–1942*, and *The Vagrant and Other Poems*. He had ended with the whole of *Night Thoughts*, presented as the logical, spiritual, and emotional climax to the whole.

The book created slow but deep ripples in the poetic world. By 28 September the edition was sold out, and a reprint was ordered. It was while negotiating corrections for this reprint that in December 1965 Stallworthy at last met his monastically shy author. They had lunch together in London, with Kathleen Raine in attendance to break the ice. 'I was', Stallworthy wrote appreciatively to Skelton afterwards, 'of course greatly taken with his remarkable presence and gentleness.'[7]

The year 1965 had proved to be something of a turning point in British verse. It was, for example, the year of T. S. Eliot's death. The Movement was still in evidence, though voices were already to be heard challenging its hegemony. One way of assessing the way Gascoyne's new book fitted into its temporal context is to look at the reactions to the year's offerings from one of Eliot's tender nurselings.[8] The Poetry Book Society had been running since 1954, and had since been awarding plaudits in two categories: as either 'choices' or 'recommendations'. In 1965 the choices could scarcely have been more different: they included Kathleen Raine's *The Hollow Hill* as well as Sylvia Plath's *Ariel*, posthumously introduced in the society's *Bulletin* by her husband Ted Hughes. Before publication, Stallworthy had been careful to submit the proofs of Gascoyne's *Collected Poems* to the society: on 15

---

7. Jon Stallworthy to Robin Skelton, 1 Dec. 1965, OUP PB/ED/017417, Box 2353.
8. The idea for the society was Stephen Spender's; Eliot, however, had been a founder member and its director in two successive years: 1954 and 1955. White was its first secretary and later first literature director of the Arts Council.

December 1964 its secretary Eric Walter White had written to say that the book was to be one of their recommendations in the following spring's quarter. Stallworthy wrote to Gascoyne jubilantly: 'as I expect you know, this is the highest honour they can pay to a *Collected Poems*; only new volumes are eligible as choices'.[9] The following autumn, Raine wrote a notice in the society's *Bulletin* introducing her own *The Hollow Hill*, and devoted much of her allotted space to declaring herself Gascoyne's ally in the battle of the poetry books. 'I am in fact', she asserted, 'in the tradition of Spenser, Vaughan and Traherne, Coleridge, Shelley, a Platonist; and (in consequence, since that philosophy implies the concordance of the visible with invisible forms) a symbolist. Among the modern poets I admire chiefly Yeats, Edwin Muir, Vernon Watkins and David Gascoyne.'[10]

Raine was in an advantageous position: she had observed Gascoyne grow as a poet, had been privy to his swaying moods, and had an acute sense of the influences his magnetic being had picked up over the years. The anonymous review the *Collected Poems* received in the *Times Literary Supplement* that August was also hers. It described cross-currents within the culture of the thirties and the forties that few before her, and not many since, have been able to discern.[11] Raine's verdict was all the more welcome since she herself, despite—or perhaps because of—her exposure to the work of her former husband Charles Madge—was deeply unsympathetic to Surrealism. She might therefore have been expected to overlook the merits of Gascoyne's early work. Instead, she interpreted the whole of his writing as one integrated development in which she isolated an unsuspected quality: provocatively, she talked of its 'objectivity'. This particular strength, she argued, had been there from the very beginning, but it had been accentuated by perturbations in Gascoyne's temperament and in British culture: 'If from the Surrealistes Mr Gascoyne learned to find everywhere the reflection, in objective reality, of subjective intuitions, it was not only or principally his own subjectivity that he there discovered. From the first…we find a remarkable imaginative objectivity. Whatever that "other mind" may be that speaks in such poetry, it is not the personal subjectivity of the poet: the extroverted

---

9. Jon Stallworthy to David Gascoyne, 21 Dec. 1964, OUP PB/ED/017417, Box 2353.

10. *Poetry Book Society: The First 25 Years 1954–1978*, ed. Eric W. White (London; Poetry Book Society, 1979), 37.

11. An exception—setting out the connections between Surrealism, Mass Observation, and the documentary movement in the thirties more generally—is Rod Mengham, 'Bourgeois News: Humphrey Jennings and Charles Madge', *New Formations*, 44 (Autumn 2001), 26–33.

social realist is neither more or less subjective than the "intensely personal" poet of introverted imagination…One of the most consistently imaginative of modern poets, he writes with equal objectivity of the world's visible and interior aspects.'

Hence if Skelton had perceived in the imagination of the thirties a constant forwards-and-backwards movement between object and subject, to Raine these were very much sides of the same cultural coin. Her argument depended on a redeployment of critical terms of much potency in the years immediately before and following the war, in the discussion of both literature and painting. Several observers of the artistic scene from Herbert Read onwards had then spoken of the 'image' and of the 'object'. The use of these terms had, moreover, depended to an unusual extent on viewing the object as a sort of image, and the image as a sort of object. As far as Gascoyne and Raine were concerned, this equation had depended less on Breton or Eluard than on Humphrey Jennings, as both writer and film-maker. The crucible for this experiment in poetic and social perception had been the Blackheath drawing room in which the defining lines of Mass Observation had once been forged. In this development Jennings had been far more instrumental than either Madge or Tom Harrisson. Raine wrote:

> Above all Jennings talked of 'the image', not in Freudian terms as personal and objective, but as the language of the collective subliminal consciousness of a nation. Both Mr Gascoyne and Jennings were friends and associates of Charles Madge at the time he conceived Mass-Observation, which was (especially for Jennings, Mr Gascoyne and Mr Madge himself) much more a kind of poetry than (as for Tom Harrisson) a kind of sociology: a way of reading the signs, the oracles. The images thrown up by the unconscious mind of the nation were those the poets must recognize and use. Such images Jennings held to be valid insofar as they were not 'invented' but discovered. Never must a poet 'invent' an image, because the kind of truth poetry exists in order to communicate was, for him, prophetic and public. Thus in Jennings the *surréaliste* search for 'unconscious' images met the Prophetic vision of William Blake's 'I see London, a Human Awful Wonder of God', the minute particularisation of Stubbs and Gainsborough, the imaginative patriotism of Purcell and Dryden.[12]

Raine went on to place a passage from one of Jennings's documentary-inspired, Mass-Observation-orientated *Reports, I See London* side by side with a speech from the first movement of *Night Thoughts*, both being

---

12. 'The Orphic Voice', *Times Literary Supplement*, 12 Aug. 1965, p. 656.

descriptive of the Embankment by night. In both, she concluded, there had been a marriage between inner and outer worlds, 'interpreting the scene of the outer in terms of the inner meaning'. The sociological and the personal, the documentary and the visceral experience, were not antithetical to one another, but seamless aspects of one and the same enterprise.

It was a way of claiming Gascoyne for sanity, and for England. Raine was not alone in this. Someone else who had been privy to Gascoyne's recent breakdown had been the profoundly deaf South African-born poet David Wright, who had been in Paris at the time but unable to contact him. In 1965, just a few months after the appearance of the *Collected Poems*, he brought out a different but equally well-distributed Penguin anthology that once again shifted Gascoyne's work in relation to its period and surroundings. *The Mid Century: English Poetry 1940–60* was dedicated to David Archer, and it was admirably non-partisan. It printed five of Gascoyne's post-Surrealist poems alongside others by Auden, Graves, Empson, Dylan Thomas, Thom Gunn, Larkin, and emergent figures such as Anthony Thwaite.[13] Wright had no axe to grind, and he was careful to avoid poetic politics, or the animosity of opposing 'schools'. The resulting approach had the effect of nesting Gascoyne in a securely inclusive English scene. There was, then, a limit to seeing David as an 'exotic'. By the mid-sixties, troubled as he was in mind, he had come home in a double sense. There were even paradoxical, though welcome, senses in which Gascoyne could now belatedly be regarded as that surprising creature: a patriot.

13. *The Mid Century: English Poetry 1940–60*, introduced and edited by David Wright (Harmondsworth: Penguin, 1965) 138–47.

27

An Incident at Buckingham Palace

Shortly before arriving to live on the Isle of Wight, Gascoyne had experienced a dream about the island 'in which drab suburban villas appeared to be filled with sleepy inertia and boredom as though with poisonous gas'.[1] The image spoke loudly of the way in which he had anticipated residence in the place. At first it had proved both quiet and disconnected. His unease was somewhat relieved when a car drew up outside The Haven and disgorged the thin, earnest shape of Edward Upward, novelist and Marxist, with whom he had kept intermittently in touch since the 1930s. Upward lived with his formidable wife Hilda in the coastal village of Sandown on the island's south-east coast. It says much about their politics that they had both quitted the Communist Party of Great Britain in 1948, considering its policies not to be radical enough. These were not nowadays Gascoyne's sort of convictions but, as long as they kept off areas of contention, the two men found that they had sufficient in common to maintain a diverting and, to both of them, welcome friendship. Upward took Gascoyne on a series of expeditions in the car around the island and 'my eyes began to open to a scenic environment clearly related to the part of the mainland, Hampshire, Wiltshire and Dorset, that I had known so well and deeply loved when a child'.

Gascoyne, however, was not an entirely insular being, and London was always going to be necessary for him. Shortly after settling in Northwood he had journeyed up to the capital for a diagnostic appointment with a Dr Dewsbury at the Maudsley Hospital in Denmark Hill. Dewsbury advised him, for the sake of his mental health, to move to London.[2] The best

1. David Gascoyne, Introduction to *Facets of an Island: New Poetry from the Isle of Wight*, ed. Brian Hinton (Freshwater I-O-W: Isle of Wight Poetry Society, 1983), 4.
2. Mary Hutchinson to J. G. Broadbent, n.d., RLF, David Gascoyne file 3806.

he could manage in that direction was to spend short periods staying with Kathleen Raine or with the poet and translator from the German, Michael Hamburger. Reluctant to overstretch his welcome with such hosts, he later took to making occasional sorties up to the Chelsea Arts Club at 143 Old Church Street where he spend days at a time in a condition of studious meditation interspersed with the odd orgy of socializing. He was acquiring ever more—and ever more recondite—books: books on alchemy together with works by Jung, the late Jung from *Seven Sermons to the Dead* onwards. He absorbed especially the works written after the sage of Geneva had broken with Freud and metabolized forms of neo-Gnostic, mystical wisdom. What emerged from all this reading was an interpretation of alchemy interpreted in the light of Jungian lore. There were few friends with whom he could discuss these matters on the island, and not many apart from Raine with whom he could speak of them in London. As a result he became from the mid-sixties onwards ever more withdrawn, with an inwardness that occasionally broke surface in bouts of enthusiastic communicability that would sometimes prove alarming, and certainly seemed puzzling, to many of those close to him.

His movements were also limited by his relative impecuniousness. He was earning very little from his writings: 5 per cent royalty on the *Collected Poems*, even when sold out, only yielded £75. Back in October 1949, thanks to peristent lobbying by Biddy Crozier, John Lehmann, and G. S. Fraser, the Royal Literary Fund (RLF) had given him a small one-off grant of £200. As soon as he reached England again, the lobbying resumed. With support from Hutchinson and Raine, backed by a medical reference from Dr McNelly of Cowes, a further grant of £600 was made, £200 of which was paid immediately and a further £400 kept in reserve for later use. Since the RLF was responsible for recommendations to the Cabinet Office for Civil List pensions given annually to authors in need, his income was further augmented from 1966 by an annual income from the Crown, initially of £200.[3] Even with these disbursements, Gascoyne was less truly autonomous in his social life than he had been since the age of 16. Now in his early fifties, this erstwhile opponent of the 'bourgeois family' was in effect cohabiting with elderly parents to whom with some reluctance he now recognized himself as being deeply and inextricably attached. Escape to France—his constant recourse in years gone by—had for several reasons become problematic.

3. All details from RLF, Gascoyne file 3806.

When in late 1967 a young French scholar, Michel Remy—who was to emerge as a leading Continental student of English Surrealism and was currently writing his masters dissertation on Gascoyne—decided to visit the subject of his research, he was advised in the first instance to contact Raine, who warned him that he would find his subject clothed in an inpenetrable cloud of gloom. Remy arranged to call on David at the Chelsea Arts Club. When he was shown up to the poet's study bedroom, he discovered as predicted that Gascoyne was unwilling or unable to answer his keenly phrased questions. Happily, Remy did not lose heart and was soon pursuing enquiries elsewhere, seeking out manuscripts that enabled him to follow the course of what was to remain to him—despite his initial disappointment with the subject himself—this elusive poet's fascinating if undulating career.[4]

Such researches proved possible since an archive documenting the poet's past was beginning to form. Whilst in France Gascoyne had entrusted his papers to his friend Robin Waterfield, now an Anglican missionary in Persia, who had kept them ever since in a small apartment he maintained on the Edgware Road. In July 1966 Waterfield was on leave in England. With mediation from John Bell of the Oxford University Press, a meeting was arranged between him, Stallworthy, and Eric White in his capacity as literature director of the Arts Council. Once the value of the papers had been estimated at £1,000, White made a successful offer on behalf of the Council, under whose aegis the trove was subsequently sold to the British Museum Library.[5] Among those to consult it there was someone who was to have a decisively practical effect on Gascoyne's presence in the world of literature. Alan Clodd was a grandson of the eminent Edwardian banker (1840–1930), man of letters, folklorist. and freethinker Edward Clodd, associate of Thomas Hardy, Edward Fitzgerald, and Sir James Frazer of *The Golden Bough*.[6] As a boy he had been deeply impressed, during visits to his octogenarian grandfather's Suffolk retreat, Strafford House in Aldburgh, by the sight of shelves packed with signed books and manuscripts by eminent writers of the late Victorian age. A circuitous and in some ways unsatisfying early career had since led him back to this bibliophiliac inheritance. Born in 1918 in Dublin, where his mother's family the Alexanders were rooted, Clodd had missed out on a

4. Interview with Michel Remy, Nice, 2 May 2008.
5. Memo by John Bell, 18 July 1966, OUP file PB/ED/017417, Box OP 2353.
6. Robert Fraser (ed.), *Sir James Frazer and the Literary Imagination* (Basingstoke: Macmillan, 1990), v–vi.

university education owing to the precarious circumstances of his father, a businessman who prior to his marriage had spent several years as a rubber planter in the Malay archipelago. Instead, after a childhood spent partly in Ireland and partly in Welwyn Garden City where he had attended Bishop Stortford's College, he had embarked on a series of unsuitable clerical jobs interrupted by service with the Friends' Ambulance Unit in Egypt and the United Nations Relief and Rehabilitation Administration in Italy.[7] Afterwards he had spent five rewarding years on the front issue desk of the London Library, but by the mid-1960s he was working frustratedly for a luxury hire company in Piccadilly. Feeling more than ever out of the literary swim, he had in his late forties begun to issue under his own imprint pamphlets of the writings of Ronald Firbank, Kathleen Raine, and Christoper Logue. It was the second of these who encouraged him in 1967 to call his growing enterprise the Enitharmon Press. A Blake scholar, she had suggested he name it after the emanation of Los of the Prophetic Books, personification of space, the eternal female, wife, and muse. In that year Clodd set about seeking out Gascoyne's early editions and journals, beginning with a copy of the increasingly rare *Opening Day* and continuing with the notebooks recently deposited in the British Library. Like Gascoyne himself, Clodd had haunted the second-hand emporia of the Charing Cross Road since early youth. He read with the voracity of an autodidact, he hoarded, and the thought of throwing printed paper away inspired in him a condition of quasi-religious dread. Clodd possessed persistence, civility, and a voice that seemed to emerge from an earlier more bookish era, compared by some to aged parchment. An engaging obsessive with wide sympathies and the patience of six Griseldas, Clodd also at some significant and profound level simply appreciated what Gascoyne was *about*.

Developments in the poet's private life were, however, about to make his mission quite a lot harder. On 18 January 1969 Leslie Gascoyne died at home, with Win and David at his bedside. He had, David told Meraud, suffered from 'years of shingles, growing senility—and blindness, poor man. It had to come, but he was 83 and never had been strong'.[8] His going left Win feeling increasingly vulnerable, and dependent emotionally and to some extent financially on her eldest son, who henceforth made her a small weekly allowance from his already slender means. The short-term effect of

7. Stephen Stuart-Smith, obituary for Alan Clodd in *The Independent*, 26 Dec. 2002.
8. David Gascoyne to Meraud Guevara, 9 May 1969, TGA 9326/1/39.

this sequence of events was to plunge him into a bout of depression quickly followed by a condition of compensatory mania of the sort that he had experienced five years previously in Paris. Over the weekend of 2–5 May he took a a short recuperative break in Amsterdam, partly to cheer himself up with the sight of tulips in fresh bloom, partly in order to view pictures in the city's galleries. 'The gardens', he told Win in a postcard, 'were marvellous, the bulbs are just in full bloom. Amsterdam is fascinating'.[9] He spent much of Saturday 3rd in the print room of the Rijksmuseum sampling the land- and skyscapes of Hercules Seghers (1589–1638) with their dizzying atmospheric vistas, and on Sunday evening he flew back to London. As the plane lifted off from Schiphol Airport, he was granted a glimpse of one of Holland's overarching skies, with thunderous clouds of impending night crouching round the dying embers of the sun. His painterly eye picked up affinities with the Seghers prints he had just been viewing with their vaulted zeniths and endless horizons. The deep grey of the clouds also recalled the work of another Seghers: Bruegel's Flemish pupil Daniel Seghers (1590–1661), whose work features garlands of vased flowers, principally tulips, arranged around a central cameo featuring a devotional figure, often the Virgin, executed in monochrome grisaille (Daniel Seghers had been an ordained Jesuit). In his journal entry for this date, Gascoyne blends all of these visual sensations into one running commentary together with notes for future poems on 'The coastal map. The Channel. The cloudscape—grisaille de Seghers'.[10] Colour blended with the absence of colour, translucent monochrome.

As the aircraft approached Heathrow, darker panoramas succeeded, of 'ruins and desolation. The Sunset. The English coast. Vision of nocturnal London. Surpassing wonder. . . . London Pride [a beer of course, but also a mode of patriotism]. Evil and Civilization. . . . Pelican in the Wilderness. London birds at dusk. Their revelry among the cornices above the neon. Awaiting the dove's return.' His plane was the dove descending, and the aweful totality of these forlorn visual suggestions converged in his mind as an intensification of the apocalyptic premonitions seen in several of the canvases by John Martin (1789–1854), 'Mad Martin', the hypersentive Norfolk artist whose lurid visualizations of cosmic catastrophe in paintings like

---

9. David Gascoyne to Win Gascoyne, 5 May 1969, Beinecke, Box 11, Folder 245.
10. Beinecke, Box 12, File 263, from which subsequent journal entries in this chapter are all derived. Compare *The Sun at Midnight: Notes on the Story of Civilisation Seen as the History of the Great Experimental Work of the Supreme Scientist* (London: Enitharmon, 1970), 3.

The Great Day of His Wrath or *The Destruction of Sodom and Gomorrah* (see Plate 25) had once shocked and delighted a mid-Victorian England newly schooled on the terrors of late Turner.

Over the following week and a half, like images of fire and brimstone fused with Gascoyne's renewed reading in alchemy. He had been immersing himself in the arcane writings of this proto-science since the war years, when its inherent sense of history as a series of climaxes had seemed peculiarly appropriate. The outlines of this medieval craft had recently been reinterpreted by the German Swiss scholar Titus Burckhardt, great-nephew of the author of *The Civilization of the Renaissance in Italy*, and as 'Sidi Ibrahim', a convert to Sufism. Burckhardt's *Alchimie* had appeared in German in 1960 and been issued in English from Watkins' bookshop seven years later. Its exposition of an old and—to Gascoyne—familiar theme rekindled a lasting enthusiasm. That week, Gascoyne reopened a journal previously devoted to food recipes. At the back he wrote 'Alchemy is of such mysterious potency that no-one of any intelligence can come at all near to it or gain some familiarity with its symbolism without being affected by it, even without understanding it.' The purpose of it all, as he now realized and Burckhardt had explained, was a fiery union, a 'chymical marriage' between sexual opposites. Gascoyne saw in this fusion a symbol of the magical reconciliation of the male and female aspects of his own bisexual self, or in Jungian terms of his animus and his anima. This is how Burckhardt had put it:

> The marriage of Sulphur and Quicksilver, Sun and Moon, King and Queen, is the central symbol of alchemy. It is only on the basis of the interpretation of this symbol that a distinction can be made between, on the one hand, alchemy and mysticism and, on the other, between alchemy and psychology.
>
> Speaking in general terms, mysticism's point of departure is that the soul has become alienated from God, and turned towards the world. Consequently the soul must be reunited with God and this it does by discovering in himself His immediate and all-illuminating presence. Alchemy, on the other hand, is based on the view that man, as a result of the loss of his original 'Adamic' state, is divided within himself. He regains his integral nature only when the two powers, whose discord has rendered him impotent, are again reconciled with one another. This inward, and now 'congenital', duality in human nature is the result of its fall from God, just as Adam and Eve only became aware of their opposition after the Fall and were expelled into the current of genera-tion and death. Inversely, the regaining of the integral nature of man (which alchemy expresses by the symbol of the masculine-feminine androgyne) is

the prerequisite—or, from another point of view, the fruit—of union with God.[11]

The furnace in which this alchemic/mystical, psychic fusion traditionally took place was the alchemist's athanor or oven. As pressure and grief bore down on Gascoyne that late spring, however, this legendary receptacle seemed to occupy his own mind. The secret to the crisis of modern civilization, it now seemed to him, lay furthermore in the recent work of the Regius Professor of Modern History at Oxford, Hugh Trevor-Roper, whose *The European Witch-Craze of the Sixteenth and Seventeenth Centuries* had been published earlier that year. Witchcraft as presented by Trevor-Roper represented a dramatic rejoinder by the feminine principle to the brutal realities of male dominance. On Thursday, 15 May Gascoyne reported the emergence of a '*New Light on Western History*. Revelations of essential Evil. The witchcraft epoch (see Professor Trevor-Roper's recent work). When the feminine principle turns its back on the unjust male dominator and exploiter of Nature in just indignation, she becomes evil and revengeful. Satan comes, seduces her, betrays her and then exults in the bitter chain-reaction of poisonous cruelty that ensues. All this has happened throughout Europe [and] is now more clearly to be seen than ever. The "good" then also are infected and similary become monsters when this happens.' Here was a Gnostic interpretation of 'Genesis', a neo-Blakean scenario that seemed to be leading inexorably towards a Yeatsian, apocalyptic climax. The grand result, in tune with the mystical and sexual insights of alchemic science, would be a 'Golden Wedding' he was inclined to detect through an eccentric reading of Heidegger. The renewed marriage of the genders would, he thought, lead to a New Age when 'we know what being is, and who He is who gives it to us'.

There were stranger affinities than even these. On Friday 16th Gascoyne added 'A note on to Jehovah's witnesses. The Watch-tower. Christianity misundersood because of the prevalence of bad *preachers*. Otherwise, a great deal of what they are saying may be *true* in its own way (which is not exactly my own way). All I can say is "Good luck to them! I have perfect faith."' He thought quite otherwise of the Scientologists, whom he now grew convinced were partners in some cosmic cospiracy to rob the world of its ethnic integrity. Their gimcrack pseudo-sagacity reminded him in this respect of George Ivanovitch Gurdjieff, the sage of Fontainebleau whose

11. Titus Burckhardt, *Alchemy*, trans William Stoddart (London: Stuart and Watkins, 1967), 149.

pseudo-science, and worse pseudo-medicine, had deprived Katherine Mansfield of her life when in 1923 she had taken refuge in a clinic run by this charlatan in her last attempt to rid herself of tuberculosis. But 'I will say no more on this subject, as several friends and acquaintances happen to be involved (I do not suspect them, of any really evil intentions, however).'

He was consumed by visions of innocence and virtue perverted—sex especially. With his innate fastidiouness about personal relations, the permissiveness of the mid-sixties, confused and narcissistic, was plainly revolting him. The journal grew lurid as he railed against the exploitative and wasting nature of pornogaphy. It passed on to the inference that 'cosmic cruelty has caused the perversion of Nature and above all of human nature on our planet. Man is not the cause, but the vessel of Wrath, the diseased victim and the intended instrument of the temporarily disastrous working through. But the curse of man's great illness has been long revealed and known. Now is the time to *understand* how what we call Redemption really works.' Only by the reintegration of the sexes, he considered, could such blatant perversities be redeemed. In the original state of the world the genders had existed in a perfect harmony. The deity would, he devoutly hoped, presently step in to restore this harmonious state of affairs. 'God', he now declared, 'is the Greatest of Bi-Sexual Beings, who has two eyes in one, Left Right and Centre. All vision is an a priori preliminary to (the) synthetic judgement of God. God saw all things were good.'

All manner of things might be good again, with a little assistance from Gascoyne. He had been reading his recent reviews and taken them to heart. 'Today,' he declared, 'I shall begin by ceasing to use words like "great", "wonderful" and "extraordinary" for a little while, and simply state, quite soberly, that in me and myself, Subjectivity and Objectivity have been safely married. That is what I meant when I used the expression the "Golden Wedding".'

In the third week of May, Gascoyne determined to act on these intimations. Kathleen Raine, who might just have calmed him down, was away in Scotland, so he rounded up some other old friends. The translator and biographer Elizabeth Sprigge, who fifteen years previously had produced his play *The Hole in the Fourth Wall*, now lived in a large house at 45 Ladbroke Grove: on Sunday morning he paid a call to explain his evolving thoughts. On Saturday 17th he had lunch with Sprigge and Priaulx Rainier, both of whom he endeavoured to convince of the justice of his cause. Afterwards, he delivered an informal talk on Jakob Boehme and Pascal in the downstairs lounge at the Chelsea Arts Club. Preparing for the coming day of visitation, he then took delivery of a batch of calling cards on which he might post cryptic messages, prognostications, and warnings.

As the week advanced, matters became increasingly clear to him, or as we might think, increasingly muddled. He announced '*The Momentous Discovery. God has been dead in man. The Saviour has been dead in God after man's historical repetition of his betrayal, rejection and murder. The Lord of all Beings has come to the moment of His resurrection in all true human beings. He is what he was. He is the Saviour that he is. He shall be the Holy returned dove, the revenant Ghost of Himself. This is the ultimate spiritual meaning of the achieved Great Philosophical Work of Pre-Civilisation, the rehearsal of the World to Come.*' By Monday events were fast moving towards a climax. 'The day', he proclaimed, 'is today, 19th May 1969. We have been through the terrible crux of the crisis in the historic crucible, the dragon has been slain, the maiden rescued, the atom almost put together again though not yet understood—and we can now *relax.*' The following morning he imparted to an astonished Roland Penrose his apprehensions about an imminent confrontation of supernatural forces, concluding 'I have at last fulfilled the purpose of the Surrealist movement, and have achieved super-reality through understanding the full meaning of Blake's Vision of the Marriage of Heaven and Hell: the Upper Macrocosm and Lower Microcosm, which Hermes Trismegistus teaches is that which is above, for bringing to pass of the One Thing which is the Unity of God and Man, Word Re-integration and Re-birth.'

Accordingly Gascoyne now announced his 'Mission to London'. On Tuesday he met Penrose once more, this time in the company of his former radio producer, Douglas Cleverdon. He 'instructed' both of them in the incipient Mysteries. Early the following morning he rang Penrose, and agreed to meet for lunch. Then he phoned the *Sunday Times* to see if they might be interested in publishing his revelations. He spent the rest of the morning attempting to contact Sir Kenneth Clark, whose televisison series 'Civilization' he had been much admiring while watching it with Win back on the island. Clark he was sure would understand.

Another possible ally, he suspected, might be the popular philospher Colin Wilson, whose attention-grabbing bestseller *The Outsider* of 1956 had rehashed Continental Existentialism, of the Sartrean and secularist variety, for the paperback-reading British pseudo-intelligensia. Calling round at Watkins' bookshop to check up on relevant arcana, he buttonholed the hard-pressed proprietor (who was fortunately used to humouring excitable customers). He showed him his two hands, each of a different gender, and how their functions might be reversed. Later in the day he phoned 10 Downing Street. His purpose was to make contact with Mary, wife of the Prime Minister Harold Wilson, on the hunch that as a poet she might be sympathetic to his cause. Through her secretary, he endeavoured to make an appointment to see her just as soon as she was free. He hoped, he explained, to convince her that henceforth 'Theocracy is the only humanly possible form of democracy'. God, the Royal Family, and Harold Wilson might be trusted between them to administer the imminent Apocalyse, with a little assistance from himself. The forthcoming reign of God was, after all, likely to influence the material conditions under which the premier, among others, would in future be working. He was asked to phone again.

Gascoyne devoted the interval to making lists of potential allies in the great cause: Sonia Orwell, Keith Vaughan, and Graham Sutherland. The following day he called on Antonia White and her cats at 42D Courtfield Gardens in South Kensington, and afterwards recorded a 'Marvellous complete success!' He was shriving himself against the great day. At long last in the journal he came clean about his drug addiction, covering five closely written pages with a confession of his amphetamine habit, and regrets as to what this had cost him by way of a loss of poetic creavity. The confession clearly proved cathartic, but the ultimate confrontation was yet to come. 'When I see the poet Mary Wilson today,' he announced to himself, 'she will help me from now on to understand the practical difficulties and see them from a woman's point of view. Telephone for an afternoon interview at ten o'clock. Argue with secretary if necessary.'

He argued to little effect. After putting the phone down, Gascoyne was filled with charitable thoughts concerning this irresponsive official. He pondered ideas for a replacement. 'Personal secretaries', he wrote, 'may be devoted and competent (this is the optimistic view), or they may be very competent but not really devoted; or they may be absolutely devoted, yet strangely incompetent when it comes to things they think that people don't know about their employer. My own ideal private secretary would be someone like Christine Keeler, for instance, after her conversion. She'd know all the necessary things that are required.'

Gascoyne never did get to meet the premier's poet spouse. Instead, in the face of resistance from Downing Street, he had a change of plan. On Thursday, 29 May he made instead for Buckingham Palace to disclose his vision to the Queen, whom he now wished to convince of an imminent plot for world domination by the Scientologists. A quarter of a century earlier, on Christmas Eve 1944, Gascoyne had conducted a not dissimilar mission to confide in her father. In the present journal he records this earlier episode as a plain instance of lunacy. The sober recognition of its barminess does not appear to have inhibited him from a further attempt. On the earlier occasion a sentry posted at the gate had informed him that the royal family were at Sandringham for the Christmas season. This time the Sovereign was actually in residence, and Gascoyne was not so lucky. As he was later to inform Mel Gooding, 'after my father's death I was in London, and I tried to get into Buckingham Palace'.[12] In his later radio play *Self-Discharged*, based he told Gooding closely on the facts, he was to elaborate further: 'When I arrived early one morning at the gates of the Palace to communicate to the Monarch my inspired sense of the world's spiritual situation, I immediately found myself in conflict with the earthly powers in the person of a young guardsman.'[13] After a short struggle he was interviewed by a security officer, to whom he communicated the reason for his presence. Gascoyne was placed in a cell where he suffered several hours of claustrophobia, combined with hallucinations that appeared to emanate from the peep-hole in the steel door. The door opened to admit a plain-clothes officer accompanied by two medical orderlies. They informed him they were about to drive him 'to a place they were sure I would like to visit. Never doubting that this must be somehow connected with my supernatural assignment,' the playscript recalled, 'I went out with them into the yard: climbed into their van and was driven away.' Their destination, fifteen miles away, was Horton Psychiatric Hospital, Epsom, in the Surrey suburbs.[14]

12. BL Lives, F1383, Side B.
13. David Gascoyne, 'Self Discharged', *Resurgence*, 15 (Mar./Apr. 1986), 20; *Selected Prose*, 215.
14. Horton Hospital, General Register of Male Admissions 1969–1971, LMA H22/HT/B/02/008. and Admission register for male and female patients 1967–1970, H22/HT/B/10/006.

28

'Not Necessarily Silly'

When five years previously he had returned to England in mixed mood of elation and dismay, his consultant at the Maudsley Hospital had predicted, not unreasonably, that a proper reintegration into English life, diversified with wide-ranging literary contacts, would return Gascoyne to a full and productive existence. Following the tragicomical events of the summer of 1969, it was now no longer possible for him and his family to maintain this illusion. Alone in Northwood, Win grew, perhaps for the first time, truly frightened for him.

In the late 1960s London was ringed by psychiatric institutions placed at a safe distance from the centre in quiet locations like Banstead, Tooting, and Watford. Completed in 1902, Horton was just one of five such hospitals situated in the largest psychiatric complex within the conurbation, containing at its most flourishing as many inmates as there were 'normal' residents in this quiet, commuter town of Epsom. Like many built at the time, it had been designed according to a standard neo-Benthamite pattern by the architect George Thomas Hine.[1] An Italianate water and clock tower rose above a central block composed of alternating courses of yellow London 'stock' and red brick. Within sight of this ran an orbital corridor, open at the sides to form windbrakes and joining outbuildings within the spacious grounds. Thanks to the hospital's historian Ruth Valentine, we have figures for the year in question: in 1969, 26 per cent of admissions were first-timers, and 57.5 per cent were 'informal', that is voluntary patients. Both figures were well bellow the national average, suggesting that the hospital concentrated on the long-term ill.[2] Gascoyne had been escorted there under the

---

1. Iain Sinclair, *London Orbital* (Harmondsorth: Penguin, 2003), 345–6.
2. Ruth Valentine, *Asylum, Hospital, Haven: A History of Horton Hospital* (London: Riverside Mental Health Trust, 1996), 31.

1959 Mental Health Act, beneath the terms of which 'police officers could bring someone they saw behaving oddly to a mental hospital for assessment. Doctors had forty-eight hours to decide what to do'.[3] Accordingly on Thursday, 29 May he was voluntarily admitted, and placed in a reception ward where the consultant Dr Low Beer began the painstaking process of assessment, diagnosing what we would now call a bipolar condition with long periods of depression interdispersed with shorter surges of mania.

Win came in to visit him when she could, though she was harrassed and still grieving for Leslie. Weeks before, the twins had begged her to join them in America for the recuperative holiday she so sorely needed. On 19 June she applied for a passport to enable her to fly to San Francisco where John, the elder twin, was now living with his wife and two teenage children.[4] Anxious as to what would happen to David while she was away, four days later in her capacity as next of kin she arranged with the hospital to have him detained for his own safety under Section 26 of the Act. Accordingly he was regraded, and sectioned on 23 June.[5] Win was concerned, even so, that a further manic episode would lead him to squander money. Through her Cowes solicitors on 11 July she approached the Court of Protection and requested a certificate restraining him from ordering his own finances. On 15 July she left for California and 29 July the Official Solicitor was appointed as receiver, responsible for administering the modest income accruing to David from royalties, his Civil List pension, and the Royal Literary Fund's grant, £400 of which was still pending.[6]

The exact nature of the treatment remains confidential, but a year later Kathleen Raine, who was visiting him at the time, told the publisher Jamie Hamilton, a member of the RLF's supervisory committee, that Gascoyne had undergone several sessions of the 'shock'—that is electro-convulsive—therapy that Horton had been practising with some regularity since the 1930s.[7] After several weeks he was moved to an annex for rehabilitation where conditions were less draconian, and discipline more relaxed. Afternoons were spent in the adjoining Occupational Therapy Unit where patients could watch soap operas on a colour televison— still a relative novelty in 1969—were served with sweetened tea, and enjoyed the use of a piano and facilities for painting in Gascoyne's favourite medium of gouache, of all of which he availed himself. Though his treatment had left him

3. Ibid. 85.
4. Win Gascoyne, passport issued in London, July 1969, Enitharmon Papers.
5. LMA: H22/HT/B/02/008.
6. Court of Protection Order No. 1627 of 29 July 1969, RLF 3806, File 1.
7. Jamie Hamilton to Victor Bonham-Carter, 27 Nov. 1972, RLF 3806, File 1.

feeling low and confused, the anarchist streak of rebellion in him survived. How low he had sunk, and what form his remaining defiance took, can be gathered from the most touching document in the whole widespread Gascoyne archive. The main event of the afternoon was the dispensing of the tea under the watchful eye of a 'burly, good natured Central European' nurse on whom the inmates bestowed the half-affectionate, half-awestruck moniker of 'Budapest(h)'. It was to this lowly but in this context omnipotent functionary that in October Gascoyne addressed a patient's manifesto written in large and wavering characters across three folded A4 sheets. Thirty years after his First Manifesto of Surrealism, it was addressed to more immediate needs:

Freedom of Psychiatric Treatment in Our Hospitals

On some wards, they put the sugar in bowls. What we do, we put it in the tea. They should be separated. That's a very stupid system. We are not necessarily silly. The patients who are less ill can help the patients who are more ill. I've been educated in such a way. By the way, some people don't like sugar in their tea. In America, there are more per 100% patients. Please. Budapesth. Is it permissible to raise a personal question? Nothing ever happens. Sugar's not good for you. There is a solution. Not to go to the toilet for five days. Take cold water, anything [...] Of course some people have got the idea in Coronation Street.[8]

As in Epinay-sur-Orge, the ward became to him a world of its own, a civil society of sorts, with patients its citizens. Horton Hospital as evoked by Gascoyne reminds one of Florence Mole's school in Harrow, with its sudden infatuations and disagreements, its array of nicknames, its abrupt arrivals and equally sudden departures. Gascoyne was watching both patients and staff. Later these observations would cohere into an essay for radio entitled 'Self Discharged' that serves as a record of his six months inside Horton and a meditation on the one act he himself seems never to have been tempted to perform: that is, suicide. While in the reception ward he had noticed the presence of a young man who spent much of the day curled up in bed:

It did not take me long to discover that he was regarded as the most seriously disturbed of all my fellow detainees. Though from his appearance one might have thought him still in his teens, he was, in fact, about twenty-five. Most of the time he looked harmless, serene but not stupid. He paid scant attention to anyone, but occasionally we would exchange smiles. He was dressed by a nurse before breakfast, after which he would lie down and curl up in a corner. Two or three times a week he was visited by his parents, a quiet couple in whose

8. Manuscript in the collection of Marcus Williamson.

presence he became slightly more animated, though he would consume the biscuits and Mars bars they brought him only perfunctorily and scarcely responded to their efforts to engage him in conversation. Neverthless he seemed at least momentarily to regard his mother with something like normal affection. When the time came for the callers to leave, he would follow them to the door with his eyes, then relapse once more into listnessness.[9]

Because of his docility, his fellow inmates had christened this dispirited youth 'Larry the Lamb'. Yet Larry's apparent passivity hid violent depths. One afternoon in June, when the other occupants of the ward had been allowed out into the grounds for an hour or two for a communal stroll in the sun, he attacked the television set near his bed and reduced it to a mangled wreck. For the next few days, Larry was banished to a padded cell.

Once he reached the convalescence unit, Gascoyne found himself in the company of less withdrawn companions who, however, proved no less disturbed. In the early evenings the patients were allowed temporary exeats to visit the local pub, and it was during one of these excursions that he made the acquaintance of an affable and seemingly even-tempered woman in her early thirties, a Scottish reformed alcoholic of lesbian sexual orientation whom he calls 'Mac'. She was sociable, even slightly extrovert, and non-judgemental with, he says, 'a reassuring homeliness of manner,' all of which evidently drew him to her. It was quite otherwise with the unit's other homosexual occupant—a waspish and camp male known as 'The Rodent', financially maintained by an affluent Harley Street surgeon who sent across a chauffeur-driven Bentley to collect his lover each week.

In Valentine's history of Horton she reserves a paragraph or two for the circumstances under which patients left the hospital. In the 1960s, she observes, 295 were listed as 'undesirable discharges': men and women who 'absconded, or left without discussing their case, or against the doctor's advice ... The 29% also included suicides.'[10] The self-discharged of Gascoyne's semi-fictionalized account all belonged to this last category. The catatonic Larry survived in a state of near-vegetative calm for several outwardly peaceable months before breaking into the ward's cleaning cupboard, swallowing a bottle of concentrated disinfectant, and writhing in agony for some hours before choking his last. Mac was eventually allowed home to join her girl lover, who in the meantime had taken a boyfriend and moved in with him.

9. *Selected Prose*, 217.
10. Valentine, *Asylum, Hospital, Haven*, 31.

When she learned of this, Mac soberly took her own life. One day the Rodent set on Gascoyne as they were both waiting their turn to use the public phone, assaulted him, and brought him to the floor. Some days later he ended his own desperate, embittered life with a shotgun.

Each had found their own way out of the ward and out of life. Gascoyne's attitude to each is characterized by sharp, unsentimental compassion. There is no wringing of hands, and certainly no moralizing at their expense; in effect he deals with them as victims of what the philosopher Bernard Williams would later call 'moral luck'. The death of each is the arbitary result of a concatenation of circumstances not of their own making: no more of a judgement on them than death through cancer, or indeed the attack of pleurisy which, about halfway through Gascoyne's period in Horton, and somewhat to his relief, landed him in the relative seclusion of the hospital's infirmary for several welcome weeks. But the decision of each of these unfortunates to walk away from the unendurable—since that in each case is what their departure from life had amounted to—does shed some light on Gascoyne's own, less dramatic, gesture of rebellious defection.

Though some way towards a cure, he was still plagued by voices and paranoid delusions. While still in the reception ward he had grown convinced that his elderly neighbour was a clandestine adherent of the Essenes of Kosmon and kept a copy of OAHSPE, the 'new bible', sequestered beneath his bed. Gascoyne's spent one restless and with restrospect absurd night attempting to locate the suspect volume and confiscate it.[11] Some time afterwards an equivalent delusion lodged itself in his mind that the hospital staff were all secret devotees of the same scabrous sect, and that he owed it to himself and to a threatened society to make his escape. Dressing in his day clothes, evading the vigilant nursing staff, and pocketing his allowance for the pub, he slipped out of the hospital precincts and boarded a bus into central London. By midday he was in Chelsea where, entering the Markham Arms on the King's Road, he bought himself a barley wine and, engaging his fellow drinkers in intense conversation, endeavoured to convince them of the imminent social and spiritual danger that threatened to engulf them, and all England with them. Well before closing time he found himself confined once more, this time to Chelsea Police Station. He was returned to Horton, where he was immediately placed in what amounted to a punishment ward, from which his bout of pleurisy at length released him.

11. 'The Most Astonishing Book in the English Language', *Selected Prose*, 146–7.

And yet there was something within him that refused to be quelled. He might flee the ward: unlike Larry the Lamb, Mac, and the Rodent, he was nowhere near ready to quit life. There was even a kind of resistant logic forming in his mind. The experiences through which he was travelling may have been ghastly; yet he knew he was precisely the one who could and would write out, and pass beyond, this very ghastliness. *Self-Discharged* culminates with a couple of sentences from Sir Thomas Browne's *Urn-Buriall*, a work with which Gascoyne had been familiar since the months in 1946 when he had compiled his doomed anthology of metaphysical poetry and prose, *Emblems and Allegories*: 'Life is a pure flame, and we live by an invisible sun within us. A small fire sufficeth for life.' The quotation seems to have attracted him because of its kindling of Christian hope, but it could also bear an alchemic construction. Suffering, according to this reading, was the athanor or oven in which was smelted the precious metal of survival. The months in Horton were certainly Gascoyne's darkest hour, his midnight or winter equinox; yet in this dire season his sun was already imperceptibly turning. As always, he kept by him a small cache of favourite volumes and his ever-present notebooks. Among the books was Titus Burckhardt's work on alchemy, which had once deranged his thoughts, but which now helped him to organize them. Slowly he began to rearrange his impressions of his recent breakdown, numbering and dating them, converting them into an aphoristic sequence. On the last day of October Clodd, who had been visiting him throughout, was able to inform Jon Stallworthy that 'I saw David Gascoyne yesterday and am pleased to say that he seemed very much better: the hospital have high hopes that he may be discharged fairly soon. He seemed full of energy and was writing.'[12]

The result was a set of meditations that adopted the title *The Sun at Midnight* from Gascoyne's abortive manual of spiritual regeneration of the 1940s and added the amibitious subtitle 'Notes on the Story of Civilisation, Seen as the History of the Great Experimental Work of the Supreme Scientist'. It contained both an account of the chaotically euphoric weeks during May that had led to his incarceration, and related observations on the transformation of society. Part of it appeared in the winter number of the periodical *Two Rivers*; when Clodd asked if he could publish the whole text, the book that emerged, printed in a fine art edition with illustrations culled from Burckhardt by the Daedalus

---

12. Alan Clodd to Jon Stallworthy, Beinecke, Box 13, File 280.

Press the following November, was to be one of the key early publications of Enitharmon.

Since 1967 Clodd had been in constant communication, both with Skelton in Canada and with Stallworthy in OUP's London office, with a view to collecting together David's scattered verse translations. The initial spur to this initiative had been a programme on Gascoyne as translator that Skelton had compiled and introduced on the Third programme on 19 September 1967. Following its transmission, Stallworthy and Skelton wrote to Clodd, and by 25 October Clodd and Skelton had agreed to edit the book together. The following May, Skelton was back in England; he spent some of the time hobnobbing with John Betjeman and other poets with a view to his forthcoming sequel *Poetry of the Forties*; the rest he devoted to ferreting out Gascoyne translations in the library of the British Museum and elsewhere. When he and Clodd had conferred, it fell to Stallworthy to prepare a report for presentation to the Delegates of the Oxford University Press. Stallworthy was a poet of quiet technique and personal reminiscence who felt no immediate affinity with the French poets whom Gascoyne had rendered into English. His report was written with an eye both to his personal predilections and the desired catholicity of the growing Oxford poetry list, very much his baby. 'I must say at once', it began, 'that these translations are not my cup of absinthe (to Gascoyne a phrase), but then I have always been allergic to undiluted Surrealism. Gascoyne's poets—Unik, Giacometti, Emmanuel, Rosey, Breton, Char, Jouve, Reverdy—follow Eluard's prescription "Give influence free play, invent what has already been invented, what is beyond doubt, what is unbelievable, give spontaneity pure value".... This structured hysteria, however, is frequently shot through with beautiful, haunting, memorable images and statements, and there are a number of poems that even I can see are good.'[13] When C. H. Roberts, classicist, papyrologist, and secretary to the Delegates, presented the proposal to the board at the last meeting of the summer term on 3 July 1968, all of these reservations had been omitted in the service of a short and complimentary precis. Consequently Stallworthy was able to write to Clodd announcing the book's acceptance.

Neither Clodd nor Skelton had any idea just how much and how widely Gascoyne had translated. On 10 July 1969, following one of his visits to

13. Jon Stallworthy Report, 25 Sept. 1968, OUP ED/ED/BackA00595, Box BLA 132.

David in Horton, Clodd informed Skelton that he had stumbled across still more material in Wrey Gardiner's *New Road* and a week later Gascoyne himself was writing a letter in wavering handwriting giving Clodd access to furher notebooks in the British Library. By March 1970 it had been decided to present the translations straightforwardly with a minimum of editorial appararus, and no indication as to where the French originals had first appeared.

The book had a circulation and influence well beyond the small circle suggested by its modest print run. Above all, it set up Gascoyne as a historically prominent voice at the crossroads of languages and traditions. But it also highlighted problems of which Gascoyne himself had long been aware concerning the technical challenges involved in rendering into another language—especially a language as tactile and empirically based as English—certain kinds of subjectively experimental Continental poetry. A strong feeling of personal affinity between poet and translator was no guarantee of success, especially when it came to the modern classics of Surrealism. A Surrealist translation of a Surrealist original must of necessity prove an imperfect exercise. Effective Surrealist writing depends almost entirely on the magnetic precision of its very arbitrariness. Paradoxically, under these circumstances a translator arguably needed to restrain his own whimsy. The originals strove for luminesence; the translation must offer transparency.

From its roots in Dada, French Surrealistic poetry had moreover striven to be anti-literary and anti-poetic, not merely in its defiant eschewing of conventional lyricism and subject matter, but in its avoidance of the calculated effects of 'voice' and overtly symmetrical form. What was required of a translator was a style and approach that was true to the imagistic cruelty of the originals: as true as a de Chirico or Dalí painting was to the dreamlike texture of its subject matter.

The task was easiest when the original made clear its departure from lyric form by substituting the visual appeal of print layout. Giacometti, for example, was known first and foremost as a sculptor; his 'Poem in Seven Spaces', which Gascoyne had translated as long ago as December 1933 in the sixth issue of *New Verse*, consisted of seven clumps of text framed within a square, two of which adjoined smaller inner squares, so that Gascoyne needed do little more than recreate the graphic layout, and render the poet's phrases as literally as he could.

Relatively straightforward too were poems describing pictures, such as Eluard's tributes to Braque, Giorgio de Chirico, and André Masson—which in the *Collected Verse Translations* appear on facing pages. Here the oddness resides in the visual images evoked, and the artist-subject's trick of combining them: a translator had simply to be as true to both as feasible. In such cases, fidelity and accuracy were much the same thing. In other circumstances and with other poets, however, Gascoyne considered these to be very different desiderata: the maximum challenge arose when literal accuracy detracted from the spirit of the original. This was not usually true with Eluard; it was more often the case with Jouve, whose intense, abstract, and at the same time uncompromising sexualized spirituality needed careful handling. *Collected Verse Translations* includes two Jouve translations of 1946 which Clodd had recovered from an issue of *New Road* from that year; both are versions of items in Jouve's collection *Matière céleste* of 1937, the year which the two poets met. Both are poems of mingled desire and reverence for a woman who is fairly obviously Blanche, on whose Freud-derived ideas of the identity of the sex and death wishes they draw. By his own lights Gascoyne was well qualified to translate these pieces, being a close associate of Jouve's, and one of Blanche's long-term patients. Here is the opening of a lyric Jouve had simply entitled 'Poème':

> Le désir de la chair est désir de la mort
> Le désir de la fuite est celui de la terre
> L'excrément des villes c'est l'amour de l'or
> Le désir de la jeunesse est l'appétit du cimitière
>
> Les faims sont dures commes des femmes nues
> Sur le lit du jour j'aime épouse je souffre
> Les perles matinales dorment de lumière
> Le long du rivage ourlé vert de la mort.[14]

Here is Gascoyne:

> The desires of the flesh are a desire for death
> And the desire for flight is earthly, of the earth
> The love of gold is the great cities' excrement
> Desires of youth are all a greed for graves
>
> As hard some hungers are as a woman's nakedness
> I make love on the daily bed I lie in pain
> Drowsy with light the pearls of morn lie strewn
> Along death's green-marged shore[15]

14. Pierre Jean Jouve, *Matière céleste* (Paris: Gallimard, 1937), 53.
15. *Collected Verse Translations*, 41–2.

One fact is obvious: Jouve's stanzas have no commas, so his suggestions of lust and mortality flow into one another. Gascoyne recognizes that the phrase 'de la terre' can also be applied to the gold that is the city's excrement, so he has rendered it twice: as 'earthly' then, after an inserted comma, as 'of the earth'. The repetition does the same job as Jouve, but by different means. In Jouve the line 'le désir de la jeunesse est l'appétit du cimitière' is a terse paradox; Gascoyne's wording imports a colloquial note of camp and clevery mockery: 'Desires of youth are all a greed for graves'. The line 'Sur le lit du jour j'aime épouse je souffre' is almost untranslatable, since 'épouse' can be both a verb in the present tense—'marry'—and a vocative noun: '(oh my) spouse!' Gascoyne keeps the disquiet, but the marital gesture has disappeared, and so has the wife. 'Les perles matinales' are beads of semen, but 'The pearls of morn' are elegiac, as in A. E. Housman's phrase 'the tears of morning'.[16] Where his own subjectivity is engaged, as it always is with Jouve, Gascoyne is sometimes more ornate that his originals, and often more solipsistic.

Interestingly, among the most convincing moments in the *Collected Verse Translations* are the most grandiose. The translation of Pierre Emmanuel's 'Asie' had first appeared in the magazine *The Window* in February 1954, but its force derives from the fact that the Asia to which it bids farewell is not the geographical continent but the fabled, hallucinatory Orient imagined by Hölderlin. The most effective translation of all is 'Rain and the Tyrants: After the French of Jules Supervielle' that had appeared in *Poems 1937–1943* between the same covers as his own 'Snow In Europe', with which it shares a common reaction against Fascism, and faith in the earth's power to heal. Its composition, Gascoyne declared in 1980, had been one of the rare occasions when he had been able to convert a French original into a poem 'that might have been written in English':

> I stand and watch the rain
> Falling in pools which make
> Our grave old planet shine;
> The clear rain falling, just the same
> As that which fell in Homer's time
> And that which dropped in Villon's day
> Falling on mother and child

---

16. A. E. Housman, 'The sigh that heaves the grasses', in *Last Poems* (London: Grant Richards, 1922), 53.

As on the passive backs of sheep;
Rain saying all it has to say
Again and yet again, and yet
Without the power to make less hard
The wooden heads of tyrants or
To soften their stone hearts,
And powerless to make them feel
Amazement as they ought;
A drizzling rain which falls
Across all Europe's map,
Wrapping all men alive
In the same moist envelope;
Despite the soldiers loading arms,
Despite the newpapers' alarms,
Despite all this, all that,
A shower of drizzling rain
Making the flags hang wet.[17]

Clodd and Skelton had rounded off the book with the 'Strophes élégiaques: à la mémoire d'Alban Berg'—a poem that Gascoyne had first attempted to write in English and, having failed, been moved to recast in French. Before that, the editors had included the whole of *Hölderlin's Madness*, the work in which Gascoyne's character as poet and as translator had most perfectly been blended. It had also been the work in which he had come closest to the work of a fellow writer who had once crossed the brink into authentic madness. Now Gascoyne had himself gone off his head, at least for a while, and in his account of the episode he says that he feels glad of it. 'What I want to end by saying', he states in the penultimate paragraph to *Self-Discharged*, 'is that I do not regret for a moment having been out of my mind. It seems to me now that in fact that I went deeper *into* it than I'd ever been before; and that after having been able to return as sane as I am now, I can think of what happened to Larry, the Rodent and Mac in a way that helps me to understand the true cost of sanity better.' David stayed in Horton for a little under six months. All things considered, in later years he was almost grateful for 'La Folie de Gascoyne'.

17. *Poems 1937–1942*, 61–2; *Collected Verse Translations*, 77.

29

Under the Clock

Gascoyne was released from Horton into his mother's care on 18 November 1969, though by Christmas Kathleen Raine was still writing to him there, unaware of his return to the island. Nor did his move extricate him from the provisions of the court. As the Official Solicitor crisply informed the secretary to the Royal Literary Fund on 22 December, 'You will...appreciate that I still remain Receiver in this matter until such time as the Court makes an Order determining the proceedings and discharging me from my Receivership.'[1] Not that financially speaking there was much to administer, since David was still as poor as a church mouse, with little apart from his Civil List pension of £200, raised to £350 in 1974, and £60 annual interest on some Treasury Stock, to support him. Aware of his predicament, the RLF now paid over to the Solicitor as receiver the £400 balance of the grant awarded in 1964.[2] Even with this extra assistance, the RLF calculated his average annual income as £450, out of which the Court of Protection paid Gascoyne a personal allowance of £336, with a weekly allowance of £1 to Win 'for her maintenance'. (To place all of this in context, Gascoyne's income throughout the early 1970s was approximately one-tenth of what I was then paid as a very junior university lecturer.) His reputation was slowly growing in England, enhanced to some extent during 1970 by the *Collected Verse Translations*, though the tiny royalties from this publication had now to be paid over to the Court. In France, although his work remained a presence to those who knew it, his circumstances and whereabouts were matters of mystery. Many of those who continued to read him simply assumed that he had been permanently hospitalized, or else that he was dead.[3]

1. Official Solicitor to Victor Bonham-Carter, 22 Dec. 1969, RLF 3806, File One.
2. Official Solicitor to Victor Bonham-Carter, 9 Jan. 1970, RLF 3806, File One.
3. Conversation with Christine Jordis, 11 Aug. 2008.

Few people anywhere would have credited him at this period with any possibility of permanent recovery, and most who knew him tacitly took it for granted that he would get worse. His brothers, both living across the Atlantic, were vaguely aware of the situation as described in letters from Win who was, however, temperamentally disinclined to dwell on day-to-day problems. Distance, in any case, made concerted family intervention awkward. The general, not entirely inaccurate, impression was soberly summed up by John Brown, Publisher to the University of Oxford, the man ultimately responsible for Gascoyne's place on the Oxford list, when writing to the RLF: 'He is an invalid and is, I am afraid, likely to remain so. He doesn't answer letters. He lives with his parents on the isle of Wight and is more or less regularly in and out of hospital. The royalty cheque now due to him will amount to about £170, and his last account amounted to £18. His circumstances will not change, and he will continue to be a proper beneficiary of the RLF.'[4]

After a short period of illness, Win Gascoyne died in St Mary's Hospital, Newport on 29 May 1972 of a complicated mixture of colonic haemorrhage, diverticulitis, and diabetes mellitus.[5] Her going could only make a dismal scenario worse. As Gascoyne's friend Philip Sherrard wrote to him from Greece the following month, her departure 'must mean that you are more alone that ever'.[6] For the following six months David Gascoyne became as close to a hermit as his ambivalently sociable nature would permit. Once a day he would walk to the top of the street and spend a couple of hours drinking alone at the Horseshoe Inn on the main road, surrounded by nonplussed locals. Otherwise he spent his days reading and chain-smoking in the cramped house surrounded by his mother's belongings and by papers, notebooks, and volumes he had accumulated over the years. Even so, his library was depleted, since he had scattered ephemera all over England and France in the course of his travels, abandoning some of his library in Meraud's flat in Paris. His solitude was broken by very occasional visits from Clodd who was arranging to bring out the new *Sun at Midnight*. Having become one of Gascoyne's publishers, Clodd was now anxious to assume the additional role of agent. For the whole of this difficult period, however, he was working to establish his bookselling business in north London, and

4. John Brown to Victor Bonham-Carter, 21 Sept. 1972, RLF 3806, File One.
5. Death Certificate, 30 May 1972.
6. Phil Sherrard to David Gascoyne, 29 June 1972, Beinecke, Box 10, Folder 214.

could only make the journey across to Cowes by train and ferry for widely spaced weekends. During his long absences, one of the few human beings who had any contact with Gascoyne was Upward, with whom David resumed his welcome pattern of Sunday afternoon drives. The resulting expeditions became over this precarious few months a lifeline for a soul in torment.

Mercifully, strangers were looking out for him. Following Win's funeral at Northwood parish church in early June, David's neighbours at 50 Oxford Street, the Colvilles, had not set eyes on David for months. Milk bottles lay uncollected from the doorstep, empty cigarette packets accumulating in the bins outside. They informed the Cowes Social Services Department of this state of affairs, and it in turn reported it to the RLF. On 29 June Gascoyne was visited at home by Edith Gotch, an assistant from the RLF's offices in London, to assess his needs. But, as the secretary Victor Bonham-Carter then reported back to the committee, 'This was a most unprofitable inter-view, as Mr Gascoyne, whose mother died a few weeks ago has, at least at the moment, no idea of what is spent on anything.'[7] To the Official Solicitor Bonham-Carter wrote with more urgency, 'We have recently heard that Mr Gascoyne's mother died and as a result of a visit by my assistant we find that Mr Gascoyne is living alone at 48, Oxford Street and is not really capa-ble of looking after his own affairs. There is some plan afoot to sell his house and for him to go to America and live with his brother, but all of this is rather in the air and we are worried about what is to happen meanwhile.'

As a result of these communications, Gascoyne's financial affairs, which following his temporary recovery in November 1969 had been returned to his own control, were once again resumed by the Court of Protection, with the Official Solicitor again acting as receiver. On one question there could be little doubt. Win's death had placed the whole question of David's future in doubt. John in San Francisco and Tony in Canada had become vividly aware of this fact. Even so, it is doubtful if any course of action would have been taken, had it not been for the nagging question of Win's estate, which included her small legacy from Leslie, and the house. Win had died intestate, intending David, who was appreciably poorer than either of his brothers, should inherit 48 Oxford Street, but placing no words on paper to that effect. This was a state of affairs that was hard for other beneficaries to

---

7. Victor Bonham-Carter, Report of home visit to David Gascoyne, 29 June 1972, RLF 3806, File One.

ignore, even from America. As Bonham-Carter reported to John Brown on 27 September, 'we have more encouraging news from the Official Solicitor, to the effect that his brothers are now taking an interest in him'. That month John flew over from San Francisco, and found David, whom he had not seen for many years, in a state of complete physical and mental dereliction. He immediately proposed to take his brother back to America with him, provided the RLF, or some other charitable body, could find the fare. There were deep difficulties even with this compassionate plan, since the house, the market value of which had been calculated as £8,000, was the major item in the estate, which had yet to proceed to probate. Recognizing his eldest brother's greater need, John was now prepared to stand aside and wave his claim to the property, but his brother Tony was insistent that The Haven be placed on the market, and the sale price divided three ways.[8] Seeing no alternative, John had in the short term to agree to this plan, and the house was duly put up for sale, with Win's solicitors in Cowes, who were also in contact with the Court of Protection to defend David's interests, acting for the estate.

In October John was obliged to return to California with these problems as yet unresolved. The tacit understanding was that, once the financial tangle of the estate had sorted itself out, and provided the RLF and the Court of Protection both proved amenable, David would fly across and place himself under the wing of John and his wife Joan. There were, however, limits to John's practical, far-sighted concern. His 24-year-old son Edward was currently living in Hove while studying for an engineering degree, visiting his uncle as often as he could, and reporting back to San Francisco. The news was not encouraging, since Win's death had taken from David the only source of emotional stability that remained to him. In effect he was doing the one thing his doctors in France had warned him against: living alone. By the end of the year Edward, who was intending to move to a modest apartment in Guildford, became so worried about his uncle's health he suggested that, in the event of the sale of the house, and assuming the Calfornia plan was unlikely to materialize, David should move to an address close to him. He could then keep an eye on his uncle, a proposal he explicitly put before Raine as a family friend, to his father, and to the RLF, whom he approached with a view to their paying the rent. In San Francisco John Gascoyne remained deeply concerned about his brother's worsening condition, but he

8. Victor Bonham-Carter to the Society of Authors, 22 Sept. 1972, RLF 3806, File One.

was more exercised by the welfare of his son. On Boxing Day 1972, with understandable solicitude, he wrote to Edward in England:

> Your distressing report on David's condition prompts me to reply as quickly as I can, in order to prevent you (if I can) from taking some impetuous action that will not really solve any problems and may, in fact, only worsen them.
>
> You must know, of course, that I have been aware that David's health—both physical and mental—has been deteriorating rapidly since Grannie's death. You should know too, that David's condition is not the result of her death: rather, when she was alive she was able to give him the love and security which was needed to arrest for a while the deep melancholy from which he has been suffering for a great many years. His condition, then, is a natural consequence of the illness that has been with him for so long; its deterioration has merely accelerated in the last few months, as you may remember I predicted that it would. But you must also clearly understand that even the care he now needs would not cure his condition: it can only arrest it; and the time is bound to come, with or without that care, when he must deteriorate beyond the point of recall to normal rationality.
>
> I do not think you can have any clear comprehension of the difficulties which will accompany whoever has care of David. Resourceful as you are, you are simply not equipped with the knowledge to nurse him through what can only be a long but worsening mental illness. Your compassionate and emotional involvement cannot substitute for the expert understanding that is quite essential for the care of his condition. Think, too, of the possible effect it could have on your own life and that of others who are close to you.[9]

One way or another, the RLF was necessarily implicated. Its committee, however, was in several minds as to what was the best course to take, dependent as it was on conflicting representations from Raine, Clodd, and various members of the widely dispersed Gascoyne family. In January 2003 it was prompted into further action by Gascoyne himself who, with Clodd's help, completed an application form for further assistance. Seeking more information relevant to the application, and with the collaboration of Social Services, they approached Dr Thompson, senior consultant in psychiatry at Whitecroft, the island's psychiatric hospital situated to the south-west of the Newport, who visited Gascoyne and made a preliminary assessment. Through David's Cowes GP, he was furnished with the patient's medical history. Observing that Gascoyne's endemic depression seemed to be passing

---

9. John Gascoyne to Edward Gascoyne, 26 Dec. 1972, RLF 3806, File One.

through an acute phase, he advised a short period of hospitalization 'for a period of further evaluation and psychological rehabilitation'.[10]

Isolated in certain respects, the Isle of Wight is rich in the kinds of institution that traditionally benefit from physical seclusion: prisons, hospitals, and religious houses. Whitecroft Hospital—or to give it its full title the Isle of Wight County Lunatic Asylum—stood in spacious grounds about two miles to the south of Newport off a narrow road that ran between open fields, serving Carisbrooke Castle, Carisbrooke Priory, and the community of Verbum Dei. Closed as a medical facility in 1992, the complex lay abandoned for a decade and has recently been coverted into an upmarket housing estate, whose glossy introductory brochure makes no reference to its original function as a mental institution. Even so, the developers have not been able to disguise a basic physical layout that betrays its origins in 1896 as a facility inspired by post-Benthamite conceptions of social surveillance and benevolent social-cum-medical control. Though it was a lot smaller than Horton, its physical layout was much the same. A tall watchtower, with a clock once driven by a complex set of steel cogs, stood at the centre of a semicircle of lower outbuildings which in 1973 served as wards connected by an orbital corridor. The local expression for admission to this monument to Victorian philanthropy, or for simply losing one's mind, was to go 'under the clock'. The various wards were named after historic male worthies: seamen, colonizers, or poets, among whom numbered Shakespeare and Tennyson. In the 1940s, in an attempt to bring the place up to date, a ward had been christened 'T.S. Eliot'. Gascoyne was placed in 'Tennyson'.

Despite recent advances in medical science, it remained a depressing place, built for 650 patients, including those deemed by Victorian standards as guilty of 'moral turpitude', but now accommodating a couple of hundred men and women classified as mentally ill. It is recalled by Robin Ford, poet, teacher, one-time mayor of Medina, and a Whitecroft inmate several years after Gascoyne, as 'empty and echoing'.[11] During the long, purposeless afternoons men and women drifted around the cavernous rooms and the rambling grounds, wondering how to spend the hours before supper. The staff were well qualified and kindly, but even they could not relieve the near universal despotism of nothing to do. Though electro-convulsive therapy and surgical interventions of the cruder sort were already losing ground

10. Official Solicitor to Victor Bonham-Carter, 8 Jan. 1973, RLF 3806, File One.
11. Conversation with Robin Ford, 4 June 2009.

before the latest generation of pharmaceutical remedies, emergency treatment of the more draconian kind was sometimes performed in public. Occasionally there would be an emergency. A patient would arrive after a particularly grievous manic episode and be sedated in full sight of other patients on the ward though the administering of a 'liquid cosh', a concentrated cocktial of tranquillizers. Patients could work in the gardens, and hospital radio was provided via a link with nearby St Mary's, featuring record requests and chatty programmes with bracing titles such as 'Happy Talk'. Visitors were encouraged after lunch, and there was extensive provision for outpatients, who sometimes attended as often as five times a week. In these surroundings Gascoyne was kept under gentle observation and supervision, and given insulin for his diabetes, and valium for his depression. He received visits from the ever attentive Clodd on his rare visits to the island, and from Upward, who took him out for Sunday afternoon drives. Inevitably his mood varied. Some visitors, such as the local volunteer Caroline Buckland, found him so 'deep inside himself, as to be almost unreachable'.[12] On the other hand he responded favourably to younger visitors with whom he could establish some kind of cultural rapport. One afternoon a 26-year-old artist from Bonchurch called Roger Ackling, St Martin's graduate, sculptor, and later a professor at Chelsea College of Art, called round and was informed that there was a poet living on 'Tennyson'. He had not heard of Gascoyne, but was shown into an anteroom where an immaculately dressed gentleman treated him to a fluent lecture on Breton, de Chirico, and Dalí. Ackling left deeply impressed.[13]

Pyschiatric medicine in 1973 was slowly and surely being transformed. As Whitecroft was depleted towards eventual closure, the wards emptied, many of them already lying idle. Though the misnomer 'Care in the Community' was yet to be coined by a cost-cutting Thatcher government Gascoyne would come to despise, there was an active policy of interaction between the hospital and the wider society on the island. The charity National Association for Mental Illness had been founded as long ago as 1946. In 1973, having purged itself of an incursion of Scientologists whose presence would have gratified one of Gascoyne's recurrent phobias, it had just restyled itself as MIND. Dependent on contributions and bequests, with no support from national government, and maintaining a tactful distance from the

12. Conversation with Caroline Buckland, 3 June 2009.
13. Conversation with Professor Roger Ackling, 21 July 2009.

pharmaceutical industry, it operated through 200 local centres staffed by volunteers, organizers, and hospital visitors.

The island's own branch had been flourishing for several years. Among its most committed supporters, and its one-time chairperson, was a 51-year-old vet's wife from Yarmouth, that ancient, compact, and lovely harbour town at the island's north-west corner, overlooking Hurst Castle across the straits of the Solent. A broad-faced woman with a kindly, and deceptively brisk, cheerfulness of manner and a deeply affective love of English poetry, she had been visiting Whitecroft on a weekly basis for several years. Judy Lewis had her own reasons for showing practical concern for the mentally afflicted. She believed wholeheartedly in poetry as a form of therapy. After a gap of several months caused by family troubles of her own, she had recently resumed leading weekly 'classes' on Wednesday afternoons at Whitecroft, at which she read out poetry of her choice to groups of patients at various stages of treatment. Late in January 1973, her group was joined by a tall and disconsolate middle-aged man in a state of deep dejection, who said very little each week as he settled in a chair to her side. On the afternoon on 7 February, she opened her anthology of modern verse at a poem entitled 'September Sun: 1947'. Twenty-nine years later, in the year following his death, she recreated the moment when 'I told my class that it was a difficult poem by a poet called David Gascoyne', before reading it out to them in her subtly modulated voice, shaped and warmed by the enunciation of one who, like the recently dead Win, had spent several years working as a trained teacher of elocution:

> Magnificent strong sun! in these last days
> So prodigally generous of pristine light
> That's wasted only by men's sight who will not see
> And by self-darkened spirits from whose night
> Can rise no longer orison or praise:
>
> Let us consume in fire unfed like yours
> And may the quickened gold within me come
> To mintage in new season, and not be
> Transmuted to no better end than dumb
> And self-sufficient usury. These days and years
>
> May bring the sudden call to harvesting,
> When if the fields Man labours only yield
> Glitter and husks, then with an angrier sun may He
> Who first with His gold seed the sightless field
> Of Chaos planted, all our trash to cinders bring.

Characteristically, she had delivered the final angry line softly, as if it was a blessing rather than the modified curse implicitly intended. 'When I had finished reading', she later recalled, the 'tall sad-looking man' sitting to her left 'touched me on the arm and said quietly, "I wrote that poem. I am David Gascoyne." '[14]

'Yes, dear,' Judy Lewis replied softly. 'I'm sure you are', and turned the page.

14. Judy Gascoyne, *My Love Affair with Life: A Memoir* (Isle of Wight: Island Books, 2002), 24.

30

Dog Eats Sun

That Judy at first failed to make the connection between the patient and the poem is scarcely a matter for surprise. By 1973 the gulf between the individual David Gascoyne and the myth associated with his name had opened up so far that there were few—including himself—who seemed capable of bridging that divide. The myth had cohered around an internationally recognized writer and translator, prime instigator of English Surrrealism, magus, and latterly mystic. The man had to all appearances shrunk into a chronic mental case cooped up in a provincial hospital on an obscure island, and assumed by professional carers and family alike to be incurable.

But over tea after the class they talked, and Gascoyne said enough to convince her that she was indeed speaking to the author of the poem she had just sympathetically read. The succeeding events have won for themselves a small but memorable place in the history of modern twentieth-century poetry. Many of the existing accounts, however, slightly distort the context they describe. What is sometimes said to have occurred is a process of one-sided recognition in which a humdrum if vivacious vet's wife happened on a poet in a hospital and, through loving understanding and application, brought him gradually back to life. The suspect implication behind this chauvinistic legend is that there was nothing of any note that Gascoyne in the process recognized in her or, indeed, that she had no suppressed self which, in learning to love her, Gascoyne could bring to creative life.

The attitude of avid appreciation that she brought to the mix was in fact the product of a complicated and eminent background. Judy Tyler Lewis was born on 1 February 1922 at Mile End Farm on the high ground overlooking the town of Marlow in Buckinghamshire with its broad swathe of the Thames. Her mother Lorna had been one of eleven children of Frederick Slocock, vicar of Mottisfont in Hampshire, through whom she had imbibed an atmosphere devout, high-minded, politically progressive, but, for the women at least, not in the least literary. If Win's theatrical ambitions had been thwarted by her aunt when she was a girl, Judy's thirst for books had been staunched by an overbearing mother with a late Victorian understanding of the role and responsibilities of girls. In the early days of their relationship, Judy confided in Gascoyne that she had been discouraged from reading as a child. 'I think', she told him after sitting in the small hours over one of his early works, 'it's the first time in my life that I've been awake all night reading. My mother used to accuse us of wasting time if she ever caught us reading.'[1] Public responsibility and self-sacrifice, in stark contrast, flowed in the blood. Judy's maternal grandmother, after whom she was named, had been a sister of Charles Alfred Cripps, Lord Parmoor, who in 1923 had quitted the Conservative Party to join Labour: he was married to the sister of Beatrice Webb, both daughters of a radical MP. One of his sons, and thus Judy's distant cousin, was Stafford Cripps, Churchill's wartime envoy to Moscow, friend to Mahatma Gandhi and Chancellor of the Exchequer in the post-war Attlee administration. The families remained close, and in long summers of the mid-1930s, when Judy was in her impressionable teens, when cousin Cripps was endeavouring to hold together the Socialist League, the Independent Labour Party, and the United Front against Franco, and when the 21-year-old Gascoyne was working for the anarchists in Barcelona, Judy and her brothers had spent long weekend days at the Cripps country residence in Gloucestershire. In 1947, when Stafford Cripps was appointed Chancellor, there had been invitations to 11 Downing Street. Judy had been a Labour supporter for most of her adult life.[2]

Her paternal grandfather had been the society sculptor and Catholic convert William Tyler RA, among whose surviving works is a plaster bust of the poet Matthew Arnold that stands in the library of Balliol College, Oxford. Through her paternal grandmother, born Isabel Maria del Carmen Stubbs, she was descended from Peruvian supporters of Bolívar. The Catholicism had passed to Judy's father Guy, who after service under Baden-Powell in the Boer War had become a mounted policeman in Canada, then a rubber planter in Kuala Lumpur, then served in the Irish Guards during the Great War, winning the Military Cross. Wounded in the head, he had elected for a quiet life as a gentleman farmer on the outskirts of Marlow, buying the hundred-odd acres of Mile End Farm in 1919 so he could be

1. Judy Lewis to David Gascoyne, 8 Mar. 1974, Enitharmon Papers.
2. Conversation with Judy Gascoyne, 2 June 2008; Kate Griffin to Robert Fraser, 4 Dec. 2010.

close to his Slocock in-laws in Maidenhead, and diversifying into arable and dairy farming.

Though she clung to her mother's established religion, from her Catholic father Judy had inherited her tranquil and essentially sunny temperament, and a fruitily expressive speaking and reading voice. It was as a teacher of elocution that she was studying when in the closing years of the Second World War she was conscripted as a signalman and, after a week's training, found herself working the shuttle line between Marlow and Bourne End on a weekly wage of £5. 10d. Soon after the peace, a self-effacing agricultural student called Michael Lewis had come to the farm on an attachment prior to specializing in vetinerary medicine. Michael was the son of the eminent consultant psychiatrist Strafford Lewis ('Straff' to the family), whom Judy had found magisterial and daunting. The son by contrast seemed self-effacing and subtly amorous. He had wooed her with kisses and in 1950, after he had qualified, they had married and Michael had taken a partership in Stratford-upon-Avon, where they had started a family and Judy had gradually recognized in herself a love for the works of Shakespeare.

In the late fifties Michael had spent a few weeks as a locum in a practice in Ryde and, noticing the paucity of vetinerary provision in this overwhelmingly rural island, had decided to set up on his own in Yarmouth. In 1956 they had found a spacious and detached corner house along the coastal road to the west of the town and, with a loan of £3,000 from friends, they brought it. 'Westport' had a rambling garden and faced Yarmouth Common, with the ample views across harbour beyond, the regular toing and froing of the car ferry from Lymington on the mainland, and dramatic sunsets across the harbour with its castle and the adjoining George Hotel. They converted the ground floor into a surgery where, in between raising their four children and bouts of charitable work, Judy worked as a receptionist and general factotum, occasionally helping with the animals. Michael was a keen amateur painter who specialized in portaits; he was also generally popular in the island, especially with the farmer's wives into whose sedate lives he brought a quiet and ruminative charm. Life seemed set to continue like this: stable, efficient, affectionate, hard-working. In the early 1970s, though, discord had struck.

Even the relative somnolence of this unspectacular island community was no barrier against the stimulus and disruption of the sixties. In 1968, resolved to encourage further the steady but unspectacular flow of summer visitors, a group of enthusiasts had dreamed up a rock festival to be held in August. The first of these events had packed three fields and a hillside with cheese-

cloth-clad and hirsute youth. Judy was roped in to help with the organization and, following a shipboard accident in New York which had injured
one of Bob Dylan's children, found herself looking after Dylan, who had
arrived alone, his wife Sara when she followed on, and George and Pattie
Harrison, in a farmhouse in Totland. For a few weeks the island hummed
with unaccustomed and discreetly—and sometimes not so discreet—bohemian activity: parties at Westport, and a general relaxation of provincial
stuffiness that Judy and her childen welcomed. The hectic company had
been joined from Chester by a niece of Michael's, together with her French
boyfriend Michel Remy, a postgraduate who was writing his *maîtrise* dissertation on the English Surrealist movement in relation to the work of
Gascoyne, whom Judy had yet to meet.[3]

As one by one the elder chidren left home, the harmony in the Lewis
household remained to all appearances as peaceful as before. But Michael
too had found alternative outlets for his energies and by 1972, after several
transient affairs, was seriously involved with a woman in Newport. He was
genuinely torn. One day that summer he drove two large dogs to the car-
park on the sloping coastal ground at Compton, within sight of Freshwater
cliffs, and delivered injections to himself and the animals. The dogs both
died. He survived and was admitted to Whitecroft, spending some time on
Tennyson Ward, also occupied by Gascoyne. For a few weeks after their
first meeting, Judy Lewis thus had the embarrassed predicament of finding
her husband and her new and tantalizing friend as patients in the same
institution. At her lowest ebb she had even sought unofficial advice there
herself, only to be informed by the doctor that she was likely to weather
this and most future storms, engaged as she had always been in a 'love affair
with life'.[4]

At first, Gascoyne intrigued and moved her. Conscious he had nowhere
to go during the long weekends of his release from Whitecroft except the
barren and coldly empty rooms of his home in Northwood which in any
case he seemed likely soon to lose, she invited him to spend the period
between each Friday and Sunday evening with herself, her two younger
childen, and her husband, out at Westport. The arrangement soon turned for
both of them into a habit, then an oasis, and finally a source of emotional
nourishment and of joy. Her two daughters, one married and both living

3. Conversation with Michel Remy, 2 May 2008.
4. Judy Gascoyne, *My Love Affair with Life: A Memoir* (Isle of Wight: Island Books, 2002), 9.

away from home, found the new set-up puzzling, disconcerting, and even alarming: Sue taking the view that Judy needed looking after herself rather than spending her energies on others, and Jenny that she needed a 'different sort of a man' entirely.[5] Both were of the opinion that their mother had taken on more than she could comfortably manage: this lanky and for much of the time silent visitor seemed yet another of her lame dogs. That she was growing markedly more attached to him they could not deny, though unable to classify the relationship as it evolved. Milo, the Lewis's younger son, who was still at home, took to addressing the intense and gloomy stranger as 'uncle', unsure how to address this gaunt and elegant stranger.

Judy herself was unsure, though less of her growing feelings, than of their proper expression. At times, frustrated by his moments of solipsistic gloom, she would write letters to him when he was sitting silently a few feet away from her. At times she ventured into poetry of her own: what emerged was a sort of baffled, loving doggerel: 'How can I reach you | When you sit silent and constrained | With your thoughts all dried up | And your feelings all drained?'[6] As time went on she felt relieved by his intermittent presence, then exultant. As each and every Friday evening came round, as she wrote in her diaries, she realized that 'I was looking foward to the weekends when this sad looking giant would appear at the hospital gates, clutching a carrier bag containing all his possessions.'[7] She would sit reading his early work into the early hours of the morning. With a sort of guilty, furtive pleasure which she communicated to him in long, loop-handed letters, she absorbed his successive volumes of verse, then *Opening Day* which she got through while sitting out in the garage in her husband's car as Michael worked in his surgery with a female assistant, castrating calves. She felt 'embarrassed' by Gascoyne's literary skill, apologizing over and over again for her own butterfly mind. He was grateful for her attention and care, and responsive to her own response. A vicarious, mutually sustaining bond grew between writer and reader. One day he fished out of his bag one of the few remaining copies of *The Sun at Midnight*, and said that he would lend it to her if she would care to read that as well.

Her presence, and her persistence, slowly lightened his mood. In late March he ceased to be a full-time resident at Whitecroft, the doctors releasing him into the care of the medical social worker J. F. Cobb on condition

---

5. Conversations with Sue Oldershaw, 3 June 2009, and Jenny Lewis, 15 Feb. 2010.
6. Judy Lewis to David Gascoyne, 21 Mar. 1973, 3 a.m., Enitharmon Papers.
7. *My Love Affair with Life*, 24.

that he returned to the hospital as an outpatient for five, then for three, days a week. The pressures of his life had, however, far from abated. The clash of opinion between his twin brothers as to the dispensation of Win's estate had led to lingering stalemate, and for the time being The Haven was still officially on the market. Even now, it seemed likely that in the near future David would find himself without a roof over his head. Since nephew Edward's plan of removing him to Guildford seemed increasingly unlikely to succeed, Cobb was now corresponding with the RLF in an attempt to find Gascoyne shelter with a charity called GRACE, which provided modest, supervised accommodation for needy, deserving persons. When, one Saturday in April, one of Gascoyne's oldest friends, Eunice Black, turned up unexpectedly on the island, she found the curtains of The Haven drawn at midday. It looked, she reported to Edward Gascoyne, who in turn informed the RLF, as if nobody had been there for a long time—no answer to the doorbell—although the dustbin was filled with empty cigarette packets.[8] Gascoyne's absence from home at the weekends was a mystery, only explained when late the following month Alan Clodd received a request from a would-be customer in an unusual predicament:

> May 17, 1973
> I am a friend of David Gascoyne's and I have been helping him to recover from a severe attack of depression. He lent me his book *The Sun At Midnight* which was published by the Enitharmon Press in 1970. (I think that only a few copies were published.) Most unfortunately our puppy found the book and chewed up a few pages, and I am wanting to buy another book to replace it. Would you have any copies? Or would you know of anyone who might lend me his?
> I don't want to tell David Gascoyne about this because I feel that in his present state of depression he might get worse.
>
> Judy Lewis[9]

The dog-eaten copy was duly replaced. Later that month she persuaded David to read some of his work at the Southampton Literature Festival. By the year's end he was assisting her with her contributions at St Mary's hospital in Newport for the island's hospital radio. On 10 June 1974 she was able to report to Clodd that 'he is a bit lethargic, and easily dispirited, but I notice quite a change in him . . . Last night he read "The Lotos Eaters" on the hospital radio, and it really was excellent. Far better even than his Southampton

---

8. Eunice Gluckman [Black] to Edward Gascoyne, 3 May 1973, RLF 3806, File One.
9. Judy Gascoyne to Alan Clodd, 17 May 1973, Beinecke, Box 8, Folder 103.

performance. Of course, to my way of thinking it really is ridiculous that he should spend all day at that dreary mental hospital. Unfortunately I am going through a very tricky crisis myself, otherwise I would take him on. But it would cause great family friction if I did, although my husband seems to enjoy his company at weekends. I wish that he would have his house and garden "trimmed up" and a regular cleaner. He seems to hate his house, and he is not exactly hospitable!'[10]

The Sunday evening radio slot 'Poetry Time' became an improbable catalyst for a miracle of artistic reincarnation. Every week, disregarding patients' requests which he sometimes found irksome, and ignoring his own work, Gascoyne read aloud Keats, Herbert, and e.e.cummings. Recalling perhaps that long-ago recitation by Eliot in the room above Harold Monro's shop, he intoned Christina Rossetti. His manner of address was not unlike Eliot's: slow, drawn-out, seemingly diffident, attentive to detail and to nuance, as far from declamation as could be.

Recovery was not without its ructions: he could be touchy, and with strangers sometimes dismissive. One evening in July 1973, on his way back from visiting his nephew Edward, he stepped into a pub in Hove, ordered a beer, and fell into a conversation with two young men at the bar, one a British postgraduate in comparative literature at the newish University of Sussex, the other an Austrian philosophy student of Czeckoslovakian origin visiting from Vienna. Some years later, the Austrian had cause to remind him of what happened next:

> Soon a quarrel arose. The reason for this quarrel was the dissertation of the English student: you were not content with his describing his topic and what he intended to do. For me, the foreigner, it was quite unusual.
>
> I almost expected a fight between you two but finally both of you calmed down and you even bought us two pints of beer and then you started talking about your days in Vienna and about Wittgenstein's philosophy...and then you stood up, tapped my friend on the shoulder and wanted to go. My friend kindkly asked you for your name, you smiled and finally revealed your identity and then you walked out of the pub.[11]

Two years later the Englishman, Robert Lee, a poet and translator from German, died, his questionable thesis unfinished. His Austrian companion on that evening had been the poet Peter Bielesz, who then wrote to

10. Judy Gascoyne to Alan Clodd, 10 June 1974, Beinecke, Box 8, Folder 106.
11. Peter Bielesz to David Gascoyne, Beinecke, Box 10, Folder 164.

Gascoyne asking him to accompany him to the university's campus in Falmer and plant a sapling that he intended to bring from France next to a sycamore recently planted to Lee's memory outside the meeting house— the university's non-denominational answer to a traditional chapel. The sycamore and Bielesz's smaller tree, with an inscription to the memory of Lee, stand to the north of Falmer House.

Despite such downs and ups over the closing months of 1973 and the spring and early summer of the following year, Gascoyne mended: not dramatically but by degrees, patiently, and for the most part with a good grace, as Judy described each stage of his progress to the solicitous Clodd. In July an instalment of £100 from the RLF's grant arrived. Michael Lewis was still conducting his desultory affair with a woman in Newport. Between them, Judy and David hatched a plot. Clodd would arrange for them to spend a weekend together in London and, on their return, Judy would confront Michael for a firm decision on the future of their faltering marriage. 'David and I', she wrote to Clodd on 15 July [. . .], 'are planning a little holiday in London shortly and, while he is in the mood, I think that it would be wise to come. Have you any idea where we might stay?' Clodd booked separate rooms for them at the Basil Street Hotel in Knightsbridge, between the Brompton Road and Sloane Street. On the first morning Judy extracted from David Antonia White's telephone number, and phoned her to ask whether she would like to meet. White's reply—'I would go to the ends of the earth to meet David Gascoyne'—stayed with her for ever.

It was a well-chosen meeting. White and Gascoyne had known one another on and off for forty years. Besides, White was increasingly close at the time to Raine, about whom she had written the previous September 'I have become very, very fond of her; she is a rare, a unique person. I know no one else of that quality.'[12] Doubtless these two long-term friends had discussed David's predicament, and White, who had suffered periods of emotional instability herself, would have been strongly sympathetic to Judy's concern for David. When they all met at the hotel that evening, they were drawn to one another: two middle-aged souls so different in temperament and experience yet united by their shared and passionate Englishness, their capacity for doubt and for faith, a common sense of humour, an essential and frank outgoingness. David, Judy recorded in her diary, had difficulty inserting a word.[13]

---

12. Jane Dunne, *Antonia White: A Life* (London: Virago, 2000), 410.
13. *My Love Affair with Life*, 25.

The following day, Clodd called round and escorted them to an exhibition at the British Library in Great Russell Street on the theme of 'Poets of the Thirties'. Until that moment, Judy had possessed only a hazy conception of the extent of David's reputation: 'Much of David's work was on show,' she noted in quiet astonishment, 'with handsome photographs of him when young.' And more was in the offing. In the days before their arrival, Clodd had arranged with the committee of the Poetry Society, then housed in spacious quarters in Earl's Court Square, for David to give a reading there on their last night, 26 July. At three that morning, Judy lay awake in her room, writing to Gascoyne, who was slumbering next door:

> You said that I would find it frustrating to fall in love with you. And of course I do. I have waves of physical desire for you that make me feel so weak—but it really does only come in waves... I love you, David, and I want nothing in return but your friendship and your happiness. You are such a strangely Godlike creature, and you don't seem to mix with all the profanities of life. Perhaps I will sleep now.[14]

He had not been told that he would be reading that night, and was shepherded across to the Poetry Society under the impression he was to hear the work of others. On the way from Earl's Court tube station they fell in step with the poet John Heath-Stubbs who had been summoned to attend. As tall as David, Heath-Stubbs had very limited eyesight, and no notion of who Judy was. When she asked him if he too was a poet, he replied with his grandiose modesty, 'I leave that for others to decide.' David turned to her and added 'He has just been given the Queen's Medal for Poetry.'

Word of the event had spread rapidly. Neither Clodd nor Judy had expected much of an audience. When they arrived in the large room set aside for the event on the ground floor of the Society, every seat was taken. Clodd handed Gascoyne a copy of the *Collected Poems* he had brought with him, and told him it was he who was to read. It is surprising he could manage anything at all: in fact, as Judy duly noted, he performed in a strong and confident voice. Later that evening at the hotel, as they prepared for their return to the island the following morning, she wrote gratefully to Clodd:

> Dear Alan,
>   I feel very much in your debt. And I'm afraid that I didn't say goodbye and thank you properly tonight. Forgive me, it was because I was feeling so elated!

14. Judy Lewis to David Gascoyne, 26 July 1974, Enitharmon Papers.

It was wonderful that the little plot that I had hatched really did come off. And I was moved by the way people had seemed to come from high and low and wide to hear David. You see to me he is just a wonderful friend who has helped me through a crisis. I knew nothing of his genius or his poetry (which are both beyond me). And I think that we have helped in some tiny way to restore his self-respect is good. I think it was more exciting for me than anyone else because I know nothing whatsoever of the high regard these people have of his work. (He's just the guy I worship!). And really it's in such a holy way![15]

15. Judy Gascoyne to Alan Clodd, 26 July 1974, Beinecke, Box 8, Folder 106.

31

A la Terrasse

Two days later, back at Westport, Judy confronted her husband with an ultimatum as to the future of their marriage. When Michael replied that he was resolved to leave, she responded, 'That's fine, because I have fallen in love with David Gascoyne.' She 'waited until I took David his breakfast in bed at 8.30 am and told him everything. He listened and then said, "Well, I'll be a most frustrating husband, but if you are brave enough to risk it, so am I."'[1] One of the first people to be informed was Clodd, who wrote to congratulate them, despite some private misgivings. Judy replied, 'I am so glad that you are pleased with the news. We aren't really keeping it secret anymore, so you can tell anybody you like. (I feel like "shouting it from the rooftops"). My family are very good about it too, but I shall be thankful when I am able to be on my own with David in Oxford Street...'[2]

For most of his adult life Gascoyne had been seeking a companion: someone, he always seems to have assumed, who would serve as as soulmate, fellow sufferer, fellow doubter, fellow tragedian, fellow Christian Existentialist. Instead he had now met a resolutely cheeful, resourcefully practical, buoyant, ever-so-slightly bossy, down-to-earth friend who matched her capacity for devotion with the bracing attitudes of an insuperable, chivvying optimist. In the first months of their engagement, with divorce proceedings looming in the Lewis household, they were like adolescents in the first flush of excited love. 'Can we go out for lunch together?' she gushed. 'I'm having my hair done at 12, and I'll meet you at one in the Bugle.' He had released in her a complex, existentially reverberating, sense of identity she had not known she had. 'Whatever I do with you,' she solemnly declared, 'even if it's

1. Judy Gascoyne, *My Love Affair with Life* (Isle of Wight: Island Books, 2002), 25.
2. Judy Lewis to Alan Clodd, 19 Aug. 1974, Beinecke, Box 10, Folder 106.

pouring you a cup of tea, or standing by you in a crowded pub, I feel in a strange daze of happiness. I feel I can just "Be" without any pretensions. Please make me stay that way.'[3]

To those who had known him in and out of health and fame for decades, this development arrived as a profound, and not invariably welcome, surprise. A common reaction among his French associates when they came to hear of it, was 'David Gascoyne: *marié*?'[4] Among his English acquaintance too there was a general feeing that this solution, this entente, would fail in the long or even in the medium term, and not simply because of what was known of David's sexuality. The difference in height between the two of them, for a start, was almost as noticeable as it had between him and Joan Greenwood on stage in the early months of the war. The superficially ill-assorted nature of their backgrounds—vet's wife and poet—was assumed by many to entail an unbridgeable personal incompatability. Anne Goossens had known David in Paris and London before and during the war as one who aspired to the condition of being 'a lost melancholic poet of the night'. After marrying in Italy, she had followed her father, the conductor Eugene Goossens, to Australia, then back to London to support him in the final stages of his career. After his death in 1962, she had stayed on. One afternoon in the autumn of 1974, she was strolling down Cork Street after viewing some paintings in one of the many Mayfair galleries:

> Someone shouted out 'Anne!' and I looked across the street, and there was this very tall, very fat man standing there and I thought 'Oh God, who's that?' Anyway, the person came over and crossed the street, and of course it was David, and he had this extraordinary person next to him, and I couldn't work out...Well, we all went to a bar and had a drink together, and all the time I was talking to him, I found it difficult to recognize him because he had put on such a lot of weight, and that of course was the result of being in hospital where they feed people up...I just couldn't believe it. I couldn't believe that he could *be* with someone like Judy.[5]

On the island, reactions were mixed. In nearby Cowes, in a spacious house overlooking the quayside, lived the benign and kindly *littérateur* Neville Braybrooke, his novelist wife June Orr-Ewing, who published under the nom-de-plume Isobel English, and June's daughter Victoria. They were hospitable, piously Catholic, genteelly poor, perennially disorganized, and

3. Judy Lewis to David Gascoyne, 15 Aug. 1974, Enitharmon Papers.
4. Conversation with Christine Jordis, 11 Aug. 2008.
5. Interview with Anne Goossens, 3 June 2008.

recurrently superstitious. Neville especially was given to improbable flights of fancy. Their mutual friend Francis King later recalled that Neville had once claimed to have been visited, at a time of great despondency, by the ghost of E. M. Forster. 'Quite why', King puzzled, 'Forster should have chosen to visit a man and a house unknown to him instead of, say, his biographer and friend P. N. Furbank and King's College, Cambridge, was a question that I thought it kinder not to put.'[6] Despondency was something husband and wife both richly understood. June herself was regularly prostrated by periods of paralysing migraine during which Neville did almost all of the housework. They had been prominent amongst those who, in the tightly knit Roman Catholic community in London in the mid-1950s, had welcomed Muriel Spark during the difficult months following her conversion.[7] Later they were to collaborate on a biography of another prominent writer, occasional depressive, and fellow Gascoyne enthusiast, Olivia Manning. For these and many other reasons, they were well placed to understand and support Gascoyne during his own years of dejection, and the uplift that followed. Over this fresh alliance of his, however, the Braybrookes were very torn. Neville was glad David had discovered something like happiness; June was unconvinced that somebody of Judy's unintellectual turn of mind could ever truly satisfy him. There were other, more mundane, problems, once marriage seemed on cards. On one occasion, Victoria recalls Judy asking her mother, in confidence and over coffee, whether she considered it at all possible, given his intimate past, that David (sotto voce) 'might ever *change*?'[8]

Despite this mingled chorus of reception, the unlikely couple were by the early autumn of 1974 growing closer by the week. Tony Gascoyne had by now been persuaded to renounce his part-share in the house, leaving David in sole possession of the modest property. 'I must write to you to calm my nerves,' Judy scrawled to him as her family life collapsed around her. 'Selfishly I want to be alone with you now and forever. Away from Michael's endless restlessness and insecurity, and the demands of my family, and shut in your own dear little house in peace and quietness.' They settled in together on the chilly evening of 23 September, as the evenings closed in and Gascoyne's professional prospects unexpectedly opened out. Two years previously, when he had been in the Slough of Despond over Win's final

6. Francis King, Obituary for Neville Braybrooke (1923–2001), *The Independent*, 18 July 2001.
7. Martin Stannard, *Muriel Spark: The Biography* (London: Weidenfeld and Nicolson, 2009), 107–8, 156–7.
8. Conversation with Victoria Orr-Ewing, 5 June 2009.

illness, a letter had arrived from an old friend in Coventry about the precious manuscript of the Paris journal of the 1930s, on which Gascoyne had last set eyes during the war. While touring with CEMA, he had lent it to Monica Norres, an actress in Hudd's touring troupe. In the early fifties in Paris he had requested its return from Monica's husband Peter, who had thought it irretrievably lost. 'Two years ago,' Peter now wrote to say, 'it turned up on the front door-step as a brown paper parcel—Monica had lent it to a friend years before and had forgotten . . . I have now discovered your whereabouts, so at last the MS should be in your hands again soon.'[9] When the bulky package arrived, Gascoyne had morosely stuffed it in the attic. In August that year, Judy became its first ever reader. She wrote to him at once 'Your journal is *so* wonderful I read it over and over, and feel the same elation as I get when spiritually inspired. You *must* share it with the world.' She insisted it be sent to Clodd, who soon wrote to her 'The journal is being typed out, and is in very safe hands.' Two days later Gascoyne appointed Clodd his agent, in which capacity he was able to report on 18 October the sale of eight of David's drawings for a welcome £109, while also announcing that the freshly typed journal was on its way to Robert Lowell, who it was hoped would recommend it to publishers. In early December, Clodd arrived to discuss his new role. It proved an awkward occasion since David had recently tripped and broken the humerus in his right arm, and Clodd was uncertain as to how to react to Judy's friendly but ubiquitous supervision. On his return to East Finchley he wrote to Fred Marnau, a mutual friend of his and Gascoyne's who had once worked for Wrey Gardiner at the Grey Walls Press:

> As you know, he has broken his arm but he seems otherwise cheerful. It was difficult to get him on his own but I did manage to have a very short talk with him in which I expressed doubts as to the suitability of his marriage. He said that it would be a companionate marriage and he is quite determined to go ahead with it.[10]

Clodd was not alone in his misgivings. Once the journal was on its way to Lowell, Clodd sent a copy to Raine, who it was hoped would report favourably. She was not slow to react to its more revealing contents: the affairs with Müllen and Nigel Henderson, the abortive marriage plan with a German girl, the emotional impasse with Kaye Hime. Through Antonia White she

9. Peter Norres to David Gascoyne, 19 July 1972, Beinecke, Box 10, Folder 201.
10. Alan Clodd to Fred Marnau, 4 Dec. 1974, Beinecke, Box 10, Folder 123.

had been made aware of recent developments over in Northwood. She wrote in some concern:

> I did laugh at the saga of your crazy plan—Buffie's crazy plan—to make a husband of you! I very much hope that you are not going to venture yourself in that way again—it would be fatal, and ridiculous. No homosexual really takes the idea of marriage seriously, it seems so unreal to you. But don't underestimate 'the horror' (to borrow a cliché from Conrad). My dear, doomed, poet, how beautiful and dear you are to your friends; and yet there seems little we can do to help you.[11]

Once news of the engagement reached her, Raine wrote Judy a forthright letter in which she expressed her firm opinion that any marriage with David was bound to fail. As long and bitter experience had taught her, he required a nurse rather than a wife. She implored Judy to think again—to little avail.[12]

There were other impediments. Gascoyne's financial affairs were still in the hands of the Official Solicitor, who had therefore to approve any change in his personal circumstances. In March, an officer from the Court of Protection paid a visit to Northwood where, after requesting Judy to leave the living room, he interviewed David in private as to whether he was entering into this marriage of his own free will. He replied in the affirmative and, after a delay of a few weeks, the management of his bank accounts was returned into his own hands.

Professionally his life was taking a beneficial turn, since by 1975 the ambience of British poetry was, for the first time in decades, flowing in a direction favourable to him. For almost twenty years now, the mood had been one of retrenchment, national authenticy, and cautious craftmanship, epitomized by the poets—highly individual in their personal styles, if easy to caricature—of the Movement. By the 1970s the seeming hegemony of this group was gradually being challenged by voices of a more experimental, technically adventurous kind. An early symptom had been a 'Poetry International' event held at the Royal Festival Hall in the summer of 1965, succeeded by two well-attended events on the same scale in successive years. In 1968 a young Cambridge English graduate of German extraction, Richard Burns, had been living in Venice, where he had encountered the doyen of

---

11. Kathleen Raine to David Gascoyne, 23 Nov. 1974, Enitharmon Papers.
12. Conversation with Judy Gascoyne, 2 June 2008. This, it seems, was one of the very few letters that Judy Gascoyne tore up.

experimental and cosmopolitican verse, Ezra Pound, now released from St Elizabeth's. Further encounters with George Seferis in Greece and Octavio Paz back in Cambridge, where he had started lecturing at the polytechnic, had confirmed in Burns a conception of poetry as a vehicle of transnational accord. 'I was', he later recalled, 'reaching towards recreating a polyglot, multicultural energy, a cross-fire of "risk ideas" and "edge-talk" that to me was (and still is) the stuff of poetry. And I was drawn more southwards than westwards, and across and through language frontiers, rather than movements happening anywhere within the citadel of hegemonic English... I was a pluralist, and I had consistently opposed hierarchical and hegemonic models that interpret cultural transmission in terms of patterns emanating outward and as it were downward from an established "higher centre"... I was also especially suspicious of such notional centres when advocacy of them was couched in national or nationalistic terms, or tied to any kind of political or religious ideology. Another key idea was that "good" ("serious", "exciting", "vital", etc.) poetry is multiform, diverse, and sometimes necessarily reclusive and exilic...'[13]

On 24 March 1973 the poet and don J. H. Prynne—mentor to the British poetic avant-garde and a magnet for those distrustful of the power exercised by the poetry lists of metropolitan publishing houses—convened in his fellow's set at Gonville and Caius College a planning meeting attended by Burns, the assistant literary editor of the *New Statesman* Elizabeth Thomas, Anthony Rudolf of the Menard Press, and Martin Booth of the Sceptre Press. 'The idea', recalls Burns, 'was to focus energy and gather a working team.' With funding from the Eastern Arts Association, the first Cambridge International Poetry Festival was held over the last weekend of the Easter vacation of 1975, centred on the Cambridge Union building, with supplementary venues in Kettle's Yard, various consitutent colleges of the university, and some bookshops including Heffers, where Clodd had planned a display of Gascoyne's books. It became an important catalyst in the British Poetry Revival and, from the initial planning stage, the presence of Gascoyne was deemed essential to the exercise. The impact of his reading in Earl's Court the previous July had been noted. His re-emergence into the light and the resurrection of this new Blakean synergy in British poetry seemed beautifully

13. Richard Berengarten, 'The Cambridge Poetry Festival: 25 Years After', *Cambridge Literary Review*, I/I (Michaelmas 2009), 152–4. Conversations with Richard Berengarten, 12 May 2010.

to coincide, and now at last, his depressions and self-disparagements largely behind him, he was minded to respond. Burns, who was now coordinating the event, invited him to share the opening reading at the new festival from 7.30 to 10.15 on the evening of Friday, 18 April with Roy Fisher, Sorley MacLean, and Takis Sinopoulos. The previous day Judy drove him up to Cambridge in her trusty Skoda. On the morning of the reading, while crossing King's Parade, he was struck by a bicycle peddled by a heedless undergraduate and, falling to the ground, he broke his collar bone. He attended the reading with his arm in a sling.

David and Judy returned to prepare for their wedding on Saturday, 17 May. The skies above the island were overcast, and the rain persisted all day. After a civil cermony in Newport Town Hall in the morning, there was a reception back at the house. Neville Braybrooke made a speech. In the evening the couple dined at the Farringford Hotel, housed in Tennyson's grand former home near Freshwater. Back at the house, David retired to bed early. Later Judy joined him. 'I lay across him as he slumbered. We stayed like that,' she later told me, 'in a sweet embrace until morning.'[14]

Thus began a twenty-five-year marriage of rare complexity, full of subtleties, unconscious negotiations, and mutual replenishment. It was a marriage whose ultimate terms were perhaps unknown to all except husband and wife. As Gascoyne himself had written six years before, in admonitory anticipation: 'Everyone's marriage is a secret affair and their own affair and it is not to be interfered with, or spied on, or advised about.'[15] One who, in its later decades, was able to observe this rewarding though occasionally fragile relationship from the outside was Stephen Stuart-Smith, Clodd's eventual successor at Enitharmon. 'It is likely', he concedes, 'that she was expecting more from the relationship than she actually got from it. But she certainly did get very deep affection from David. It's also true that there were some periods of great strain in the marriage, not least quite late on. But basically it was a marriage of very very great affection, based on gratitude on his part part for what she did for him, and *vice versa*. She was suddenly swept from this very provincial society into . . . this exciting international poetry world. And he was very attached to his stepchildren too. He very much enjoyed being part of that family unit, accepted at first

14. Conversation with Judy Gascoyne, 2 June 2008.
15. David Gascoyne, *The Sun at Midnight* (London: Enitharmon, 1970), 30.

as this curiosity who had come into the family, but who went on to take a very great interest in them all.'[16]

It was also a marriage with social and cultural contexts of overlapping and mutliplying diversity. At the start, as letters backwards and forwards convey, the tactful, ever-attentive Clodd played an integral role as confidant, sustaining a trinity of mutually satisfying private and professional need. The mutual sustenance fulfilled all three of them: David in his newfound domestic security and emotional wellbeing; Judy to release her repressed love of literature and to heal emotional wounds received during the breakdown of her first marriage; Clodd to lend substance to his late achieved and quite precarious role as publisher and agent. In the ensuing months, all three of them threw themselves into the challenge of publishing the journals. In January 1975 David had received a communication from Lowell which, as Judy rapidly informed Clodd, 'cheered him up no end'. On the 13th Clodd spoke to Lowell who, he announced, 'has at last read your journals and told me he was impressed by them. He has promised to write to Charles Monteith at Fabers to recommend them.'

It is not hard to discern what Lowell appreciated in these forty-year-old diaries. A self-ackowledged manic-depressive since at least 1949—a decade after the older Gascoyne's first attack—he had been on lithium for the past four years, and was about to return from England to Boston, where an appointment at Harvard beckoned with its opportunities and anxieties. In all his moods and phases Lowell is a confessional poet, and Gascoyne's journals of the 1930s are highly intelligent and unflinchingly confessional documents, the self-evisceration of which lies somewhere between St Augustine, Rousseau, and Kierkegaard. Lowell had written:

> The journal rather bowled me over. It is the record of you changing under my eyes as I read—first, the long but clearheaded despair, no sign of [its] ending, then it does, then the almost merry times in Paris, the lover, the other writers etc., then the fevered prophetic thought as war begins—an amazing record, told without drama and flatly, with intelligent control. I find of course many parallels with my own experience. What struck me most was the strangeness of the light that morning in London and Leiceser Square.[17]

On 30 January Clodd wrote to Monteith at Fabers urging a response; on 2 February Monteith requested the typescript. He had, he added, no 'high

16. Interview with Stephen Stuart-Smith, 23 Jan. 2008.
17. Robert Lowell to David Gascoyne, 13 Jan. 1975, Beinecke, Box 9, Folder 121.

hopes'. The upshot was fairly predictable. An Oxford double first in English and Law, Monteith had been with the firm since 1954, the year in which he had fished William Golding's novel *Lord of the Flies* out of a slush pile and persuaded his fellow directors to publish it at the cost of toning down its Christian symbolism. He had a sharp eye for the market, and knew just how to cater for the requirements of intelligent middlebrow taste. He was, one obituary stated, 'prone to polishing his glasses when about to...sum up incisively the points for and against a borderline manuscript'. On 3 March he sent a rejection letter, explaining that 'though in some ways an interesting book, it seems to us much too highly introverted and, oddly enough, too monotonous in tone to stand much of a chance of reaching more than a very limited readership'.

By the end of the year, Clodd had come to the conclusion that he should publish the book under the Enitharmon imprint. Pasted into the front of the typescript was a poem by Lawrence Durrell from the *New English Weekly* of 7 September 1939, four days after the declaration of war between Britain and Germany. The poem was a technical tour de force which began by parodying Auden and ended by addressing the inconvenient opening question of Francis Bacon's essay 'Of Truth'. Dedicated to Gascoyne, its title was simply 'Journal':

> Monday escapes destruction.
> Record a vernal afternoon,
> Tea on the lawn with mother,
> A parochial interest in love etc.
> By the deviation of a hair
> Is death so far so far no further.
>
> Tuesday: visibility good: and Wednesday.
> A little thunder, some light showers.
> A library book about the universe.
> The absence of a definite self.
> O and already by Friday hazardous,
> To Saturday begins the slow reverse.
> A Saturday without form. By midnight
> The equinox seems forever gone;
> Yet the motionless voice repeating:
> 'Bless the hills in paradigms of smoke,
> Manhair, Maidenhair meeting.'
>
> And to-day Sunday. The pit.
> The axe and the knot. Cannot write.
> The monster in its booth.

At a quarter to one the mask repeating:
'Truth is what is.
Truth is what is Truth.'[18]

The closing question was Bacon quoting Pontius Pilate whilst interrogating Jesus at his trial, but it also pointed to a quality that Durrell had detected in these journals from the moment Gascoyne had first shewn them to Anaïs Nin in 1938: a determination to acknowledge one's demons, inner or outer, however threatening they might appear. On 27 January 1976, Clodd wrote to Durrell in Sommières requesting his permission to reproduce the poem as a frontispiece to the forthcoming edition, and asking him to write a short introduction. On 2 February, Durrell replied 'Yes, will gladly do a short introduction for David Gascoyne, whose work I have always admired: when do you want it by?' The Preface arrived a month later, and it contained an unforgettable portrait of the 23-year-old Gascoyne as he had appeared to his English expatriate friends on the brink of war, and an estimate of his place in poetic tradition:

> He himself describes his heritage in poetry as a European one, and this was a gift conferred on him by his mastery of French. He escaped the parochialism of so many English poets. It could not help but give him a larger vision and a glimpse of the more supple and subtle Latin sensibility. It was in Paris at this time that we became friends and Anaïs Nin persuaded David to give us a few extracts from his journal for THE BOOSTER, that irreverent little mag which we were editing from the Villa Seurat. It is impossible to describe the poet's good looks and charm which he disguized sometimes under an appearance of self-deprecating ineffectuality. But the tremendous sense of humour and the intelligence were always at hand to leaven his serious conversation. He managed in a strange sort of a way to be terribly preoccupied with himself without ever being self-centred in a tedious fashion.[19]

To enhance this sense of personality and period, Clodd then approached Julian Trevelyan, who had known Gascoyne during his first visit to Paris, for an image for the dust jacket. Trevelyan sent him a sketch of the 16-year-old writer as he had then seemed to him, seated alone on a Montparnassian terrasse: torso dapperly jacketed and seated bolt upright, bow tie spry beneath a tense chin, lips pursed in thought, brows furrowed, eyes trained pensively

---

18. Lawrence Durrell, 'Journal: to David Gascoyne', *New English Weekly*, 7 Sept. 1939; repr. in Gascoyne, *Journal 1937-1939*, 7.
19. Lawrence Durrell, Preface to Gascoyne, *Journal 1937–1939*, 6.

at mid-distance, hair slicked smoothly on either side of his parting, right hand grasping a pen a little too hard, left arm resting on a blank page whilst nursing a goblet of rouge. The portrait recalls the serious-minded, almost solipsistic young person captured in some of Lucian Freud's slightly later studies, tempering the intensity of attitude with a note of affectionate satire. The result was an almost cartoon set against a cold blue background: abstracted, austere, but at the same time humanly engaging.

32

'A Mouth Urgently Speaking'

Gascoyne's *Paris Journal 1937–1939* was published in August 1978. There was a clutch of reviews by friends or long-time associates—Neville Braybrooke in the *Daily Telegraph*, George Barker in *Aquarius*—which stressed the precocity of the author at the time of writing, and the near miracle of the manuscript's return. The most astute remarks, however, were Stephen Spender's.

There had always been a sense of unfinished business beween these two poets. A lot later, after reading a subsequent collected edition of the journals, Spender would privately admit to their author that, at the time covered, he had experienced towards Gascoyne a sense of unease, and even a tinge of envy. 'I was', he then confessed 'afraid of an attraction and an identity.' He had, he would go on to say, been 'totally blind to your situation of despair and poverty'.[1] The two writers also had a very different conception of the purpose behind a published journal. When in 1985, he came to edit his own journals for publication, Spender would deliberately, as he then informed Gascoyne, take all the *Innerlichkeit*, the internal landscape, out. In 1978, though, he reviewed the first volume of Gascoyne's journals with sympathetic interest. In places, he observed, the newly discovered journal recalled those of Durrell or Anaïs Nin, both of whom appeared in it:

> Yet despite its fitting so very agreeably into the conventions of the private confession which a public will be heir to, Gascoyne's journal seems different from the others. What makes it so is the quality of the writer's preoccupation with himself. The underlying theme of the book is the struggle going on in his mind between two kinds of self-involvement, the selfish and the heroic. The selfish, of which he himself is penetratingly critical, is pure self-absorption, what he calls 'being sunk in my own depths, inescapably locked up in my own

---

1. Stephen Spender to David Gascoyne, 2 Aug. 1992, Enitharmon Papers.

egotism', 'my miserable small misery'... The heroic aspect of his self-absorp-
tion arises from his deep conviction that he can only get away from selfish
self-regard by experiencing, and realising through language, the objective historical world as his own and most intense subjective experience. There is a
subjective self, and there is an objective non-self: but the not-self can only be
realised if it is to be experienced, not as something which is happening 'out
there', but within the articulate and eloquent poetic self.[2]

A different kind of impact was registered by notices from reviewers who
knew the author slightly if at all, but were struck by a subterranean stream
in twentieth-century British literature that seemed to have resurfaced in
this unknown work. In the *New Statesman* James Fenton, the weekly magazine's foreign correspondent and a poet with Continental affinities and
antecedents, welcomed the re-emergence of this, to him, unfamiliar and
cosmopolitan voice. In *The Observer* Philip Toynbee, who had known David
passingly during the heyday of Archer's Parton Street bookshop, set the
book in its historical context, but he also gave testimony to its honesty, its
individuality, its personal take on a—to Toynbee—familiar age.

The re-emergence gathered pace. Two months after the journal's appearance, Spender and Gascoyne read together at the Round House, the cavernous converted steam engine repair shed north of Camden Lock. The event
was preceded by an interview with Gascoyne in *The Guardian* in which he
recounted, for a generation unaware of them, the strange history of his early
life, his wartime adversities, his descent into madness, and his recent marriage and recovery. Among those to see it was a 29-year-old actor, Simon
Callow. Callow had first encountered Gascoyne's writings twelve years previously as a vulnerable and excitable pupil at the Oratory School in
Kensington. '*Ecce Homo*', he was later to write, 'had leapt out at the wavering
Catholic schoolboy that I then was' fulfilling his adolescent search for a version of his inherited faith in tune with the late 1960s realities of struggle,
engagement, and social justice: 'The Christ of Revolution and of Poetry
invoked... in the poem was... the only one we children of Vatican Two
were prepared to acknowedge.' His enthusiasm now rekindled, Callow
attended the reading:

> Moved on more levels than I could adequately express, I made my way to the
> Round House. It proved—how could it fail to? an extraordinary event. The
> two poets sat side by side at a table, carafes of water in front of them, looking

---

2. Stephen Spender, 'Out of the depths', *Times Literary Supplement*, 27 Oct. 1978, 1249.

somewhat stranded in that vast, scrubbed engine-hall of a building. Spender, with characteristic generosity, led the evening. Enormously tall, patriarchally handsome, himself a central figure of the literature and life of our times, he uttered his verse, some familiar, some new, but even the new somehow familiar, with professional skill and clear impersonal power. If Gascoyne was returning to public life, Spender *was* public life. Next to him his fellow poet, equally tall, perhaps even taller, insofar as one could judge from the slightly hunched seated position which he never abandoned, not even when reading, listened intently. His huge eyes framed and forward-staring, mouth sensually fastidious, formal suit offset by a bow-tie of floppy raffishness, only his fingers, restlessly wandering over and over his text as if it were Braille, betrayed any nervousness he might have felt. He had the air of a visitor from a distant age who had seen terrible things, and was about to give a report.

Here then, side by side, were the outer and inner faces of the thirties. The difference between the two poets, Callow found, was accentuated by Gascoyne's manner of reading:

> The voice that emerged from the hunched, haunted man was, by comparison with Spender's bold clarity, feeble, despite the microphone in front of him [...] The passion gripped him, a strange vatic figure, now become Beckett-like, nothing but burning eyes and a mouth urgently speaking of isolation endured and alienation transfigured, of pain universal and particular, of high noon and eclipse. He spoke of these things with a presentness and a personal truth which was more than moving: it was nearly unbearable. The man's life had been a sort of *via crucis*; he knew whereof he spoke... *Ecce Homo*. The memory of the generalised seventeen-year-old emotionalism I brought to the poem, seeing it as some sort of mirror of *my* supposed *via crucis*, made me blush in the face of this authenticity, these molten feelings poured into a cast of such precision. It was the stubborn pursuit of the precise word, the exact image as a conduit for the expression of experience that Gascoyne, in his reading, made so evident.[3]

One significant episode that evening occurred backstage. Another member of the audience was Sebastian Barker, now in his late twenties and resolved to follow his father and become a poet. Gascoyne noticed his presence and begged for a quiet word. When they were alone together, he recalled the ugly incident in 1963 when he had peremptorily thrown Sebastian out of the Rue de Lille, and went on to plead for forgiveness, 'You realise', he explained, 'my behaviour was controlled by amphetamines at the time.'[4]

---

3. Simon Callow, Introduction to David Gascoyne, *Night Thoughts* (Paris and London: Alyscamps Press, 1995), 11–12.
4. Conversation with Sebastian Barker, 24 June 2010.

Already, the notices for the journal appearing in newspapers had provoked an unforeseen consequence. Fenton's review was read by a boyhood
friend of Gascoyne's with whom he had long lost touch. James Rake had
been the son of the local doctor in Fordingbridge during the late 1920s
when Gascoyne had lived there as a boy with his parents. A keen amateur
painter, he had recently retired after a career as a GP. His French wife
Violette, who had died in the summer of 1978, had in the war years shared
a flat in Percy Street with Sonia Brownell, later to marry George Orwell but
working at the time as a secretary in the offices of *Horizon*. It was during
this confused period, when David's movements were exceptionally peripatetic, that he had lent Sonia the manuscript of an earlier journal covering
the years 1936–7. Unbeknown to him, Violette Rake had then borrowed it,
and held on to it for the next forty years. In the late summer of 1978 Rake
came across the battered notebook while sorting through his wife's effects.
One morning in September it appeared wrapped in brown paper on the
doorstep of David and Judy's house along with an explanatory letter.[5]
Gascoyne had long since reconciled himself to its loss.

The period covered by this, the earliest of David's journals, coincided
with the first of his serious depressions, but it also reflected some of the
most active months of his early life: the aftermath of the Surrealist Exhibition
of 1936 (immediately following which it opens), his brief involvement with
the Communist Party, his sojourn in Spain, planning meetings for Mass
Observation in Madge and Raine's flat in Blackheath, the writing of the
novella *April* (the manuscript of which had itself apparently since disappeared), a growing disillusionment with doctrinaire Surrealism, and the spell
of intense personal reflection between Christmas 1937 and his third departure for France. It bore testimony to an evolving temperament, a welter of
reading in English and French, and an individual perspective on the tensions
of that difficult, doomed time.

Clodd immediately decided to publish it, and asked Gascoyne to fill in
the occasional gaps: notably the crowded weeks in Barcelona in the autumn
of 1936 during which he had been too busy and precoccupied to keep a
daily diary. Gascoyne's memory proved uncannily clear: the internecine
bickering between rival factions in the Catalan capital, his first encounter
with Tzara, his visit to Picasso's mother, the nightclubs, the bars, the gun-
shots in the streets, then the slow return overland via Paris, where he had

5. David Gascoyne, 'Introductory Notes', to *Journal 1937–1939*, 7.

paid a call on Picasso in a tiny flat in the Rue de la Boétie. Passages of self-analysis and introversion jostled with a tableau of events and personalities. Auden, Isherwood, Antonia White, Jennings, Penrose, Zervos appeared in unfamiliar, and sometimes in intimate, guises. No less intriguing was the personality of the narrator, his persistent (and sometimes irritating) self-involvement counterpointed with observations of the social and political scene. Clodd published the journal together with two early pieces recovered from limbo. The first was a comic cameo of 1937 called 'Death of an Explorer' in which a clerk in a pharmaceutical company—an almost comically Wellsean figure—goes for a walk at twilight through the streets of a city and falls down a builder's shaft in a deserted house—an obvious cypher for the fatal attractions of the subconscious to which Gascoyne was prone at the time. There was also an essay on Chestov from a latish issue of *Horizon*. With a new cover illustration by Trevelyan showing a lanky and self-absorbed young Gascoyne standing with a book in his hands against a clutter of suburban houses, the book came out in October 1980 to respectful reviews.

In the meantime, Gascoyne's personal re-emergence from the shadows proceeded by a myriad of means. In the summer of 1977 George Barker had read to Cambridge Poetry Society and suggested Gascoyne, already familar to some in Cambridge from his appearance at the city's International Poetry Festival two years previously, as someone who might contribute to the society's programme for the following Michaelmas Term. The society's co-president was a third-year student of English at Trinity Hall: Stephen Romer, Hertfordshire-born, an aspirant poet. David 'a very frail, a tall angular figure' arrived escorted by Judy. After the reading he came to Romer's college rooms and invited Stephen and his girlfriend Bridget Strevens to visit them on the island over the following winter holiday. In the New Year of 1978 they turned up, having travelled down by motorbike. David was in a 'fairly compulsive state', alternating between 'extraordinary dialogues of rapid speech memory' during which the names of his extensive French connections came tumbling out—Tzara, Pierre Jean Jouve, Pierre Leyris, Jean Follain—and manic periods of compulsion or control when he would attend fixedly to his watch, or attempt to synchonize all of the clocks in the house. His easy command of cosmospolitan high culture, they soon found, coincided with some fairly demotic tastes. Every evening at six Gascoyne would insist that the television be turned on so that he could watch the latest episode of the soap opera *Coronation Street*. Though impressed by the elder man's talk, his guests eventually felt oppressed by all of this, and quitted the house after a few days for a whirlwind spin round the rest of the island.[6]

Gascoyne had not visited France since the crisis of 1964. In the interval, however, academic interest in the pre-war literary map had been growing in Paris, notably among a group of literary intellectuals within the ambit of the Beckett scholar and Sorbonne professor Jean-Jacques Mayoux. Among them was John Edwards, a Leeds modern languages graduate then lecturing in English at the Centre universitaire expérimental de Vincennes, later l'Université de Paris VIII, one of the institutions carved in the years following the student uprising of May 1968 out of the ancient Sorbonne. Edwards was preparing a *thèse* for his *doctorat d'état* on Isherwood and his circle, and in the summer of 1978 he travelled to Sandown to interview Upward. Their meeting was direct. 'I am Edward Upward,' announced the novelist, 'and I am heterosexual.' 'I am John Edwards,' retorted the scholar, 'and I am not.' He found Upward unrepentantly Communist, and his wife Hilda equally politically unbending. Yet it was Upward who alerted Edwards to the existence of Gascoyne in nearby Northwood, and invited the poet over for tea. The relationship between these two writers was a matter of some curiosity to the visitor, aware as he listened to their conversations that for Upward literature had always been a handmaid to politics, while for Gascoyne it seemed to have been very much the other way round. Edwards found David 'affable and utterly charming. Very dreamy and otherwordly; I failed to see what he could have in common with Edward and Hilda, apart from their being writers on a tiny island.'[7] Gascoyne intrigued him, and on his return to Paris he began to lay plans for a formal invitation for David to speak at a symposium on 'Littérature et Politique dans les Années 30', to be held at Vincennes in April 1979. David would talk about his 'Souvenirs de l'Avant-Guerre', and the event was to be coordinated by l'Institut Britannique in the Rue de Constantine, a body affiliated to the universities of Paris and of London and incorporating the Paris headquarters of the British Council.[8]

The person responsible for overseeing British invitees to the Council in the late 1970s was another student of Mayoux's, Christine Jordis. Jordis was an academic by training who, after writing a thesis on *humour noir* in British fiction at the University of La Sorbonne had spent several years in London

---

6. Interview with Stephen Romer, Amboise, 13 Aug. 2009.
7. Interview with John Edwards, Paris, 17 Aug. 2009.
8. Published in *Encrages*, 6 (Vincennes) (Summer 1981), 15–39.

lecturing at Queen Mary College. She had then returned to France, initially to a schoolteaching job, then to an editorial position with the *Nouvelle Revue Française*. Since January 1979 she had been in charge of English visitors hosted by the Institute, where her brief was 'to make British writers known to French intellectuals'. She possessed an avidity for experimental literature, an openness of attitude and educated, evolving artistic tastes. Jordis's involvement with Surrealism was partly nostalgic, and partly that of a writer determined to develop a style and vision of her own. The Council had previously hosted Raine, whose reputation in France was already well established, and she considered the prospect of arranging a visit by Gascoyne 'something very special'. Married to an Austrian banker with a daughter and a toddler son, Jordis lived in an elegant, warrenlike apartment high above the Boulevard Saint-Germain, next to the former Chambre des Propriétaires. She had personal warmth and intelligence combined with beauty, alertness, and efficiency. When they met in April, Gascoyne, always responsive to strength of personality in women, took to her at once.

For Jordis herself the encounter proved something something of a personal and artistic liberation. 'It was my first step in the literary world,' she recalls. 'I was very fresh and enthusiastic, ready to give a lot. David was very special in my life; I would never have done for anyone else what I did for him, to find outlets for his work, to have him published in France. Of course, I already knew the Surrealist movement fairly well, and was very much involved with it, regretting never to have been part of it. I found it an exhilarating adventure, really. And suddenly to have David coming in a way fresh out of it, because he had disappeared some twenty years previously and had been living in limbo ever since. And there he was in Paris again, and the link was made directly with the forties. When I was in the streets of Paris with David, and he was telling me "Just opposite here was Benjamin Péret telling me to cross", I was living the Surrealist movement as if there had been no gap. Because David had not lived in between. And I was directly in it too.'[9]

Once invited, the Gascoynes became regular visitors to Paris. They could, they soon found, make the trip with relative ease, either by car ferry from Portsmouth, or more usually by flying from Eastleigh Airport near Southampton, staying in modest hotels in the seventh or fifth arrondissements, eventually electing for periods of up to a week at the two-star Hôtel

9. Interview with Christine Jordis, 12 Aug. 2008.

Saint-Pierre on the Rue de l'Ecole-de-Médecine. There were two more visits in 1979 alone. In July the Gascoynes drove down to holiday with Meraud at la Tour de César, enjoying the dancing and drinking of the 14 July celebrations, then driving back through l'Isle-sur-la-Sorgue, Marseilles, Avignon, and the Luberon. In November, apprehensively braving the threat of terrorist attacks by the National Liberation Front of Corsica then convulsing Paris, they were back for a public reading and symposium on David's work at the Institute, attended by a posse of translators. Over lunch that day Jordis introduced Gascoyne to someone who would prove integral to his reception in France. François Xavier Jaujard was the son of the actress Jeanne Boitel of la Comédie-Française and of Jacques Jaujard, Directeur des Musées de France. An accomplished publisher, editor, and translator, he had for ten years been living in or near Chartres, with Diane de Margerie, writer daughter of Jenny de Margerie, David's saviour and benefactress from the late 1940s. He had a daytime job with the publisher Flammarion, and in his spare time he indulged his private literary loves by running his own, highly selective imprint, Granit. One of his keenest interests was in the work of Kathleen Raine, three of whose volumes he had already translated with supreme sensitivity, and whose reputation, largely due to his inspired if slightly haphazard advocacy, currently stood higher in France than in England. In 1978 with Diane he had translated Raine's first volume of memoirs *Farewell Happy Fields. Adieu prairies heureuses* had just won for her the Prix du meilleur livre étranger for 1979.[10] The irrepressible—though, as Gascoyne would discover by painful degrees, incorrigibly disorganized— Jaujard was soon enthusing about arranging for the entire Gascoyne *œuvre* to be translated into French. That evening Jordis and her Austrian husband Sasha threw a dinner party in their flat high above the boulevard. Afterwards David wrote to her from the Rue Racine acknowledging her 'letter of welcome, the crazy lunch with François Xavier Jaujard, the visit to the publishers, and then the grand dinner party at which I was able to meet Sasha (an unforgettable occasion!). We heard the bombs as we were leaving. It was good to remember that life cannot all be a constant round of champagne and poetry.'[11]

---

10. Published by Stock in Paris, The subsequent volumes were to be translated as *Le Royaume inconnu* [*The Land Unknown*], trans. Claire Malroux (Stock, 1980), and *La Gueule du lion* [*The Lion's Mouth*], trans. Pierre Leyris (Mercure de France, 1987).
11. David Gascoyne to Christine Jordis, 19 Nov. 1979, courtesy of Christine Jordis.

Word of this unlikely resurrection gradually spread in France. Gascoyne, Jordis discovered, retained many acquaintances in the country, but they were 'scattered all round the place. And really the thing to do was to find one or two of these people. It was like pulling a thread, you found a huge network again: Meraud Guevara, Madeleine Follain, the poet and translator Pierre Leyris, the poet Yves de Bayser, the influential critic and founder of *La Quinzaine Littéraire* Maurice Nadeau, Georgette Cannilly.' Among such friends his reappearance caused astonishment on several counts. For some it provided grounds for reconciliation after ructions caused, in Gascoyne's drug-fuelled middle age, by misunderstandings or various sorts of personal affront. Among them was Leyris, with whom David was now reconciled after a contretemps in the fifties over his treatment of Rachel Jacobs, who had since died of cancer.[12] Most were struck by his dignity and newly found calm. 'For them', John Edwards recalls, 'David was a ghost; many of them had not realised he was still of this world.' That he was present at all was a matter of some surprise, that he had a cheerful and assertive spouse on his arm provoked further astonishment. 'They had thought of him as not a sexual being or, if sexual, homosexual,' Jordis told me in her sitting room, from which an *œil-de-bœuf* afforded generous views across the roofs of the septième. 'It was very surprising to see David, whom everybody had thought of as an angel, with a wife. First he was not dead, and then with a wife!'

His air of heterosexual conformity, however, had its limits. As Edwards rapidly realized, in the emotional constitution of David Gascoyne there were few clear boundaries. Libidinously, 'L'un n'empêche pas l'autre.'[13] Sitting with us thirty years later, he recounted an episode of which even Jordis had not heard:

> I remember one night coming out of this house. We were sauntering down the Boulevard Saint Germain on the other side of the street, going back to David's hotel. And we were talking when all of a sudden he grabbed me by the arm. There were these young fellows on motorbikes. As they started to mount their machines, he gasped 'Oh John, I still *love* rough trade!'

In between these French forays Gascoyne reported to Jordis on the gradual restoration of his reputation in England. He had again been invited to the biennial Cambridge International Poetry Festival, which continued to introduce him anew to poets from all over Europe and beyond, and they to him.

---

12. David Gascoyne to Christine Jordis, 19 Nov. 1980, courtesy of Christine Jordis.
13. Conversation with John Edwards and Christine Jordis, 17 Aug. 2009.

The third such event in June 1979 was organized by Peter Robinson, and and was exceptionally inclusive in scope. Orchestrated by a large committee drawn from the University and the Cambridge poetry reading public, it featured poets from the USA, from France, Germany, and Greece. Edmond Jabès, Hans Eisenberger, Michael Schmidt, and C. H. Sisson—poets very different in style, origin, and temper—illustrated the range. Allen Ginsberg and his lover Peter Orlovsky flew in from New York. Knowing of Ginsberg's preoccupation with Blake, whom he claimed to have met in a vision, Richard Burns showed them the Blake engravings in the Fitzwilliam Museum. 'Jesus!' exclaimed Ginsberg to Orlovsky, 'these are Blake's illustrations to the *Book of Job!*' 'Wow!' responded Orlovsky, 'Who wrote *that*?' At a lunchtime event at Dillons Bookshop on Friday 8th, Gascoyne read and signed his work: in the front row sat the two Americans, looking up as if he were a deity. Sebastian Barker, sitting a few rows back from Ginsberg and his friend, remembered the performance as one of inspired chanting. The following evening in the Corn Exchange, the two Americans returned the compliment as Orlovsky read his 'clean arse' poems and Ginsberg performed on the bongo. 'Their performance', Gascoyne later reported, '(including shouting and singing and improvised dancing) upset a few possibly straight-laced people, no doubt intentionally, and was greeted with great enthusiasm by others.'[14] At the Hobson Gallery Michael Hamburger discussed the challenges of translating Paul Celan; earlier that Friday he had read his own work alongside the German graphic artist and winner of that year's Rilke Prize for Poetry, Christoph Meckel, and the Italian poet and Hölderlin and Baudelaire enthusiast Andrea Zanzatto. There were the stirrings of a feminist revolt, as on the second afternoon Hélène Cixous, soon to become the doyenne of Parisian literary feminism, discoursed on 'Women and Literature' with Wendy Milford, Anne Waldman, and the founder of the Virago Press, Carmen Callil. Bucking the general Larkin-wards trend towards English poetic insularity, the taste could not have been more eclectic.

Another younger poet who attended the festival was Stephen Romer who, following a year in Harvard studying prosody under the poet Robert Fitzgerald, had freshly embarked on a Cambridge doctoral thesis on the influence of French poetry on the early work of T. S. Eliot. Though still a long way from publishing his own first book of verse, Romer had already

---

14. 'An Attempt to Give a Report of the First International Poetry Festival in Rome', 28–30 June 1979, Beinecke, Box 3, Folder 36.

fairly firm ideas on the directions he wanted his life to take, plans that did not, at the time, include residence in England. 'I was', he recalled thirty years later, 'very slightly anglophobe at the time', and he was determined to move to France.[15] Gascoyne encouraged him, and furnished him before leaving with a list of recently restored contacts in Paris. Most were writers: among them Maurice Blanchot, Albert Birot, George Schehadé.

No sooner were David and Judy back from Cambridge than another invitation awaited. The Communist Commune of Rome had inaugurated an International Poetry Festival, free to all comers, and to it they had invited writers from far and wide whose transportation costs, and those where necessary of a minder, were met by the City Fathers. The first was held in the ancient port of Ostia, and Gascoyne, one of the only two British poets to accept, was booked to fly out on 27 June. 'During the night', reported David that morning, 'my wife dreamed that the Festival would take place somewhere at sea, with all the poets continually plunging into the waves in their spare moments.' He was careful to take with him a supply of valium 'which', he remarked gratefully, 'my broadminded doctor goes on prescribing for me since my psychiatric hospital days'. They were accommodated in a large, uncompleted hotel. 'There was no food', Judy recalled, 'so David had to go in search of breakfast on the beach.' The twenty-nine poets on the programme included the ubiquitous Ginsberg and Orlovsky, William Burroughs, and George Barker, who since they had last met had sprouted a moustache, and whose spoken Italian was more competent than he liked to pretend. Yevtushenko arrived from Moscow and was interviewed by Italian television; he was, Gascoyne found, 'a warm, multilingual, unassuming, courteous and charming human being, *à mon avis*'.[16] The poems were delivered on three successive evenings on a stage erected on the open beach and surrounded by food stalls. The audience consisted for the most part of locals with a limitless appetite for pasta, sea, and sand, but a limited patience with poetry: David and Judy christened them the 'Beach Boys'. All work by foreign writers was delivered in the original and then in Italian translation. Gascoyne was allocated a half-hour slot in which his Homage to Benjamin Fondane and 'Rex Mundi' were read in English by himself, and Italian by Delfina Vezzoli. When 'The Beach Boys' grew tired of the proceedings,

15. Conversation with Stephen Romer, 13 Aug. 2010.
16. David Gascoyne to Christine Jordis, 18 July 1979, courtesy of Christine Jordis.

they began to hurl rocks down onto the stage, shouting 'Basta! Basta!'
Ginsberg restored order by reciting and singing to them with his guitar.

On the last night, under the combined weight of poets and protesting
rocks, the stage collapsed, whereupon Ginsberg and Orlovsky helped
Gascoyne and Judy to safety down the steps. The Italian television crew
were delighted by this turn of events. They captured it all in a documentary
entitled 'Lunatics, Lovers and Poets'.

33

'Words, Words, Words'

Among the former friends Gascoyne had discovered lurking under various proverbial stones during his resumed trips to Paris was Yves de Bayser, whom he had last known as a passionately political poet in his early thirties, an experimentalist, a theoretician of language, an ally of Camus and protégé of René Char. Now 58 and in poor health, de Bayser lived with his devoted wife Clorette at 53 Rue des Petits Champs. He was mentally very close to Jordis, who recognized their kinship by calling Yves her 'cousin'. Deeply impressed by the strain of Neoplatonic mysticism in the work of Kathleen Raine, whom he had met during her recent excursion to Paris to collect her prize, he had just published a three-part mystical sequence of his own entitled *Inscrire*. In July 1979 Gascoyne wrote to Jordis from Aix saying that he was translating extracts, and a few days later de Bayser received a 'long and interesting' letter about the challenges involved in the act of translation, challenges with which the French poet was quite familiar: his French versions of some of Yeats's plays had appeared in 1974.[1] There ensued a dialogue by correspondence on the responsibilities of translators. De Bayser was attempting to render Gascoyne's poem 'Lozanne' from *Man's Life Is This Meat*, but could not find a French equivalent for the 'blemish' of which its suicidal subject complains. For his part, Gascoyne was intrigued by the tone, style, and vocabulary of *Inscrire*, and by its eccentrically religious point of view. De Bayser had developed a personal ontology quite as distinctive as anything in Yeats. Reality, he now believed, constituted a form of sleep from which we awoke into, not common-or-garden existence, nor into conventional religious experience (for de Bayser was no Catholic), but a revived and imaginative encounter with spirituality and the divine. The whole of his new sequence, he informed Gascoyne that September, was

1. W. B. Yeats, *Le Cycle de Cuchulain*, trans. Yves de Bayser (Paris: Obliques, 1974).

animated by 'a great and particular piety'. The purpose with which he had written was 'to wrong-foot our celestial and realist education, our ferocious historical instruction, since for my own part I consider that the basis of reality is sleep, that our cursed and ferocious reality is first and foremost a condition of sleep. As for poetry and its guardian angel music, I bow before them repeatedly, as if they had expressly arrived to assist me.' But what, Gascoyne then enquired, had de Bayser meant by a 'zénon', a noun not to be found in the dictionary? De Bayser informed him that it was a follower of the Presocratic philosopher Zeno of Elea. 'You must translate literally.'[2]

Inscrire went on to win the Prix de poésie de l'Academie Mallarmé in 1980. The honours were shared by de Bayser's publisher François Xavier Jaujard, 'our crazy publisher' as Gascoyne called him, who now had plans afoot for French translations of most of Gascoyne's texts. Nothing if not ambitious, Jaujard would, he proposed, mastermind a translation of all of the poetry. Jordis would take on the journals, beginning with an extract in the *Nouvelle Revue Française*[3] and proceeding to a complete translation to be issued by Flammarion. Thus there formed a kind of community of mutual interpretation, with Gascoyne rendering his favourite modern French poems into English, while like-minded French colleagues reintroduced—or in many instances introduced for the first time—his work to a French reading public. Wheels span within wheels.

After de Bayser, Gascoyne turned his attention to an old friend from his days in Aix: the lawyer and poet Jean Follain, scythed down by a speeding car in a Paris underpass eight years previously. Follain, who worked for much of his life in rural Normandy, is a poet of presentness, of the passing moment, of the changing seasons, of the fleeting perceptions of the bucolic scene. He was remote from Gascoyne in his subject matter, more turned outward to the transient world, but in his translations Gascoyne made him his own, as when he converts the title poem of the collection *Présent Jour* into an idiomatically English artefact:

> In the present day
> people flee
> biting right into bread
> the clouds change form

2. Yves de Bayser to David Gascoyne, 21 Sept. 1979, Enitharmon Papers. This did not prevent an over-zealous proof reader altering the word to the meaningless 'zero', *Selected Verse Translations*, 25.

3. David Gascoyne, 'La Mort anglaise', trans. Christine Jordis, *Nouvelle Revue Française*, 334 (Nov. 1980), 50–66.

in the low sky
a shivering of branches
gives rise to dreaming better or worse
a door opening onto the lane
shows a face
and two hands
one of them wearing a ring
the rest of the body is wrapped
in an unaged sheet.[4]

In all sorts of ways Gascoyne was newly alive to intellectual traditions in France, and keen to involve himself once more. In the interval since his last residence there in the mid-1960s, the French intellectual scene had developed in decisive and fascinating directions. The Surrealists and the post-Surrealists, the Marxists, even the Sartrian Existentialists, no longer occupied the centre of the cultural stage. Instead, the Structuralist insights of the comparative anthropologist Claude Lévi-Strauss permeated critical and literary discourse, drawing attention to the arbitrary constituents of all societies, languages, and texts. The rumblings of the post-Structuralists, with their deconstruction of thought and all language, were loudly to be heard. Gascoyne was fascinated by all this: as much by its implied anarchy as by its rigour. Over the next few months he put himself through a crash course in modern semantics, beginning with Ferdinand de Saussure's newly celebrated *Course in General Linguistics,* initially delivered at the University of Geneva between 1906 and 1911, then reconstituted from lecture notes by students after his death. He passed on to the modern classics of Structuralism and post-Structuralism. 'I now feel', he wrote to Jordis excitedly, 'that all poets should be aware of the "Language Revolution" that's been taking place since Saussure, and is now going on, largely under Chomsky, in the USA.'[5]

His reaction to all of this was a poet's one: such ideas possessed practical consequences for those who used language professionally, above all for translators. In 1975 George Steiner's seminal study *After Babel: Aspects of Language and Translation* had been issued by the Oxford University Press, Gascoyne's own publisher. Its contention that all human communication represented a form of translation—'To understand is to decipher. To hear significance is to translate'—proved strongly attractive to David, who

4. *Selected Verse Translations*, 52–3.
5. David Gascoyne to Christine Jordis, 17 Aug. 1979, courtesy of Christine Jordis.

likewise responded with empathy to Steiner's argument that complete and faithful rendition of meaning from one language to another—and certainly de Bayser's ideal of 'literal translation'—was little more than a pious hope. Authentic meaning was secret, and even the most sensitive and knowledgeable of translators invariably contaminated where he or she trod. Steiner's ideas, he told Jordis, were to him 'wonderfully well formed and exciting'.

Gascoyne was already responding to the world around him in the light of these insights. He spent the August Bank Holiday of 1979—a period he confessed to Jordis 'que je déteste d'habitude'—in Totleigh Barton in Devon, where Ted Hughes had established one of the three centres for the Arvon Foundation to provide master classes in writing for authors. Gascoyne had been apprehensive of the task of teaching, believing himself to be no more of a natural instuctor than he had been a natural student, but it seemed to go off well enough. On his return, he informed Jordis, he was prompted into composition by 'un assasinat insensé'. On 27 August, sailing with two of his grandsons on holiday in County Sligo, the Queen's cousin Lord Mountbatten of Burma had been killed when a bomb planted by the IRA exploded aboard his dinghy. On 5 September Mountbatten was buried with full military honours, the funeral procession wending to the droning of bells and the braying of naval brass bands from Wellington Barracks to a funeral in Westminster Abbey before interment near Romsey. David watched the proceedings on television with Judy. He was struck—as so many are on such occasions—by the inadequacy of words in the face of grief. His sense of generalized verbal impotence—as if the whole of British society was afflicted by some writing block—ritual and music standing office where speech failed—chimed with the reading he had been doing in structural linguistics and translation theory. What Saussure had stated about the essential arbitrariness of words, their tendency to slip and slide, was doubly true under such circumstances: the pitiful, resistant clamminess of human diction had, after all, been one of the principal themes of Eliot's 'Burnt Norton'. Gascoyne's response was to write an elegy, or perhaps an anti-elegy, that was in effect a poem about translation, not in this instance *between* different languages as between meaning—exceptionally solemn meaning—and verbal expression. Over and over again, during the broadcasting coverage of Mountbatten's obsequies, he had been struck by how far the dumb bereavement of the common man or woman—the foot soldier or naval rating in society's ranks—surpassed in its eloquence the posing of the poets. On 4 October *The Listener* printed 'Speechlessness':

A soldier at Mountbattens' funeral
To the interviewer from the BBC:
'I don't care what the poets will say,
Our fine old motto's good enough for me...'
I think he's right, of course he is.
'We love him,' said the Romsey paper's editor.
'But what does a word like love mean nowadays?'
'Words, words, words' Impatience or despair?
Mere worn-out husks, devalued, coinage, 'strain
Crack and sometimes break.'
Decay and imprecision.
'What can one say?' asks everyone.
Some withering wrecks. Inpenetrable memories?
Such is our every-increasing impotence.
Is this our more and more blood-reeking world.
Is silence therefore really best?
Even a poet can no longer *say.*

Translation was impossible but necessary, and Gascoyne was doing more and more of it. His notebooks from the early 1980s include transcribed quotations from Steiner, but they are also a mass of English versions of poets as diverse as the proto-modernist Swiss (the so-called 'left-handed poet') Blaise Cendrars, the rogue Surrealists Philippe Soupault and Georges Ribemont-Dessaignes, and the anti-Surrealist Roger Caillois. The best and most discriminating are of writers belonging to no discernible school, including René Guy Cadou (like Follain loosely attached to the so-called 'Ecole de Rochefort' with its cultivation of an intimate verse of friendship and oblique, bucolic grace), the deft craftsman of metaphysical verse André Frenaud, the dramaturge and musician Jean Tardieu. Together they consitute a virtual map of twentieth-century French poetry. Gascoyne had begun translating Ribemont-Dessaignes as long ago as 1933, though he would probably not have dreamed at that stage of tackling someone like Caillois.

Of the poets translated, de Bayser earned his respect as someone who worked between languages, and Tardieu as a writer who liked to think of himself as an artisan as much as a poet. By 1985, indeed, this is probably how Gascoyne chose to regard himself. He was, for example, more and more open to the idea of poems appearing simultaneously in several languages. When in 1981 he was coaxed into producing an anticipatory monologue entitled 'Prelude to a New Fin-de-Siècle' about the inadequacy of poetry in the face of modern reality, the poem appeared in English and Flemish, side by side.[6] Its theme was the linguistic debasement caused by casual hyperbole in the media and the overblown rhetoric of politicians, both of them constant refrains in the letters to and from de Bayser, who had been dilating on this particular theme since his book *Eglogues du tyran* of 1953. Power did not simply corrupt men of state, it corrupted words as well. In these circumstances, poetry had—as Eliot had previously stated—to strive for purity, to insist against the grain and the odds on integrity of meaning and intent: 'Mature awareness knows that poetry | Today demands the essence and the minimum; | That only Silence such as God's could say the Whole.'

In April 1980, ten years after publishing his own essay-memoir on the power of language, *Les Mots,* Jean-Paul Sartre died, and with his massively attended funeral in the Cimitière Montparnasse one phase of ideologically tinted post-war French literature seemed to be drawing towards a close. In all sorts of ways France already seemed to be re-evaluating its own recent past. One symptom was a facing up to the ambivalent legacy of the Second World War, a sometimes agonized revisiting of the myths and realities of collaboration and resistance. In the closing months of 1979 the Surrealist scholar Michel Carassou, friend of Michel Remy's and editor of the literary journal *Non-Lieu,* had sent Gascoyne a special issue of his magazine dedicated to Fondane's work and memory. A few months later the publishing house of Plasma, which Carassou also directed, brought out for the first time a transcription of Fondane's conversations with Chestov. The typescript had been entrusted by Fondane to his Argentinian friend Victoria Ocampo shortly before the war; it was now recovered from limbo after a forty year interval. At the same time Carassou reissued Fondane's 1944 sequence of poems *Le Mal des fantômes*, to which he invited Gascoyne to provide a preface in French. The timing, as far as Gascoyne was concerned, was near-perfect. 'Non-Lieu' is the title of one of Fondane's poems, implying in one multiple pun the no-man's-land or limbo exiles such as he inhabit, the vacant space lying between text and translation, and suspension of ethical or judicial indictment: (in French legal parlance *non-lieu* is the verdict invoked when a trial is abandoned for lack of evidence; 'case dismissed' would be an approximate English equivalent). 'Non-lieu' was a place or no-place where Gascoyne instinctually felt at home. He set about rereading Fondane's poetry and prose: the book-length essay *Rimbaud le voyou* which had drawn his

6. 'Prelude to a New Fin-de-Siècle', *Poetry in Town* (Kessello, Leuven: European Association for the Promotion of Poetry, Cahier No. 30, 1981), 34–6; *Collected Poems* (1988), 221–2.

younger self towards this Romanian artist, cinéaste, and thinker in the first place, the conversations with Chestov, the essays on Surrealism. The result was not simply the commissioned Preface but a series of translations, some since published, others still unpublished, through which Gascoyne came to terms with his memories, with what Fondane had once meant to him, with promptings and affinities long since repressed in a search for further self-definition. Among the memoirs printed in Carassou's magazine, for example, was a recollection by the Romanian philosopher and one-time Nazi sympathizer Emil Cioran who had visited 6 Rue de Rollin during the early days of the Occupation, in the months immediately after David had left France. Gascoyne set about rendering it into English, less apparently for publication than for himself. In translating this redolent piece, he was in a sense translating a slice of his own past:

> To *search* was for him more than an obsession, or something that he was haunted by; to search unremittingly, was a fatality, his fatality, perceptible even in his way of pronouncing things, especially when he got carried away or when he was oscillating without a let-up between irony and breathlessness. I shall always reproach myself with not having noted down his remarks his discoveries of idea or phrase, the leaps of a kind of thinking orientated in all directions, ceaselessly struggling against tyranny and the nullity of proofs, avid for its contradictions and seemingly terrified of *coming to a conclusion*.[7]

Cioran's evocations of Fondane's exploratory monologues, with their tergiversating tracts of sardonic irony, their quips and avoidance of anything as banal as a resolution, chimed precisely with what Gascoyne himself recalled. Another piece he translated for his own use at this time was a strongly worded rebuttal by Fondane of 'Légitime Défense', Breton's apologia of 1926 for the alliance of Surrealism and Communism. Gascoyne had long considered the marriage between anarchic Surrealism and disciplinary Marxism to be a historical absurdity; it helped (and also settled matters further in his own mind) that Fondane had reached this conclusion first. As far as Gascoyne was concerned, the position-taking, however, was secondary to Fondane's talk and to his poetry which, as he avowed in his Preface to *Le Mal des fantômes,* 'takes hold at the centre of our being, it sends a shiver down the spine, it makes the nerves quiver. At bottom, I believe that it is a question of voice: some voices possess a special, unique tone, which affects us in

---

7. David Gascoyne, MS translation of Emil Cioran, '6, Rue Rollin' from *Non-Lieu*, 2 (1978), 48–52, Beinecke, Box 4, Folder 38.

the manner of certain notes which have the power to make glasses shatter because of the remarkable vibration of their sound waves.'[8]

The question of voice straddled poetry and music. While thinking about Fondane's tone of address Gascoyne recalled the months in Paris in 1955 when he had recorded for the BBC a generation of nightclub singers—Piaf, Marianne Oswald, Brassens, Catherine Sauvage. The stoicism of Piaf had been apparent in her voice, and this is a quality that he now picked up from Fondane's *Ulysse*, a poem exploring the ambiguous legacy of exile for those with no abiding home. Fondane had revised it during the final few months of his life when languishing almost as a self-imposed prisoner in his Rue Rollin flat, immediately prior to his arrest and transportation to Drancy. It was full of a sense of foreboding, of what Gascoyne in his Preface calls the 'Eschatological Sense':

> The Earth was still there, she was firm
> Yet I heard these future cracks,
> — I don't have to linger,
> — I don't have to trust him,
> — something will happen. Something, but what?[9]

The tragic events leading up to Fondane's execution duly became the focus of a 'Louange à Benjamine Fondane' that Carassou convened at the Palais Pompidou on 28 February 1980, at which Gascoyne spoke of the long sessions with Fondane on those dark November evenings forty-two years before, and of the lasting effect of them on his thinking and work. He was, he now told Jordis, still consumed with 'gratitude I have always felt for the influence he exercised on me at a certain moment of my life—a spiritual turning-point honestly'.[10]

For all this hindsight and acquired wisdom, the elderly man could still be quaintly naive. In the late spring of 1980 he was invited by Sebastian Barker, now a poet in his own right, to read at Bracknell Arts Centre, where Sebastian was writer in residence. There were good reasons for accepting, since his appearance served as an apology for the faux pas of 1963, and the reading was scheduled for 17 May, the fifth anniversary of his marriage to Judy. Sebastian offered them hospitality in his flat along with one other guest, a

---

8. David Gascoyne, Preface to Benjamin Fondane, *Le Mal des fantômes* (Paris: Plasma, 1980), trans. Roger Scott and Catherine McFarlane; *Selected Prose*, 174.
9. Ibid. 177.
10. David Gascoyne to Christine Jordis, 17 Aug. 1979.

Pole named Edward Orlovsky, no relation to Ginsberg's partner in life. Sebastian was already aware that Orlovsky, a shady character but a personable one, was in the habit of 'stealing fur coats' from Oxford Street stores:[11]

> And we had a party in the evening which went on until the next morning and during the course of the evening I went into the kichen and found David in the arms of—and kissing—Edward Orlovsky... I found this extremely amusing. I thought 'What *is* going on here?' I wasn't shocked or surprised or anything like that. But I just thought, if they have come here to celebrate their wedding anniversary, it seems a little odd. It also seemed to be the most natural thing in the world. Later next morning I was talking to David... about Edward Orlovsky, who was a pathological liar. I said 'He is not what you think at all. He is not a photographer. He is not the author of various books and so on. He's a thief, and he steals fur coats'. David refused to believe me.

Gascoyne and Judy had agreed to return to Paris so that on 21 May Gascoyne the public man could deliver the second annual Claude Guillot Memorial lecture at the Université de Paris 3. He chose as his theme 'The Poet-Translator and His Problems', citing Steiner's work, but working in at the last moment a tribute to Sartre. There was, he declared, no obligation when translating poerty to reproduce the aural form—rhyme scheme, alliteration, and so on—of the original text (for this reason he approved of Jouve's translations of all of Shakespeare's Sonnets as a sequence of prose poems). Instead, what was required was an immersion in the depths of the original founded on an understanding of its author's subjectivity or, to use an image taken over from George Steiner—and with a nod in Gascoyne's case to Marcel Duchamp's painting *Nude Descending a Staircase*—a journey down a set of spiral steps into the psyche of a fellow poet. 'Translation as I see it', he declared, 'is a matter of atunement in view of a transaction. The more imaginatively delicate and close the atunement, the juster or more satisfactory the transaction.'[12] As Rimbaud had once said in a different connection, 'J'est un autre'. For this reason it was a decided advantage for a would-be translator to have known the author of the original personally: hence, he believed, his own relative success in rendering Eluard and Jouve. In any case, at the beginning of his translating career, 'I was always inclined to devote my attention to unrhymed verse, the form of which did not need to be strictly adhered to.'

11. Conversation with Sebastian Barker, 24 June 2010.
12. David Gascoyne, 'The Poet-Translator and His Problems', Second Claude Guillot Memorial Lecture, University of Paris 3, 21 May 1980, p. 22, Enitharmon Papers.

He finished by reading his recent translation of Sartre's nightclub song 'Dans la rue des Blancs Manteaux' describing the fate of hundreds of fine desmoiselles at the guillotine during the harshest weeks of the Revolutionary Terror. Sartre had given it as a 'petit cadeau' to Juliette Gréco: her interpretation of it, in a voice gravelly and light, had brought out its sinister humour. Gascoyne had wanted to convey that earthiness, that quality of 'satirical maudlin pathos' he had first recognized when, shortly before the war, he had heard the late and great Yvette Guilbert singing the part of Polly Peachum in Brecht and Weil's *L'Opéra de quat'sous*. There was something grimly Brechtian too about Gascoyne's version of Sartre:

> In the Rue des Blancs Manteaux
> There were trestles to behold
> And a pail well filled with bran
> And standing there was a scaffold
> In the Rue des Blancs Manteaux.
>
> In the Rue des Blancs Manteaux
> The executioner rose at dawn
> He'd a hard day's work ahead of him
> Generals', bishops' and sea-lords' heads
> To cut as one might mow a lawn
> In the Rue des Blancs Manteaux.
>
> In the Rue des Blancs Manteaux
> Many proper madams came
> With their best bits and pieces decked
> But without a head, once that had rolled
> Down from on high with hat still on,
> Not one of them looked quite the same
> In the gutter of the Blancs Manteaux.[13]

He had sacrificed the swaying rhythm of the original (like the swaying of the crowd, or the bodices as they fell), and he'd lost too the assonant play on 'bourreau' [executioner] and 'boulot' [job], but had sneaked in instead an echo from a well-known Beatles song to convey the carefree attitude of this Grim Reaper or mower of necks. The Beatles were favourites of Judy's; perhaps the *hommage* swung two ways, like the heads.

---

13. Sartre, trans. David Gascoyne, from 'The Poet-Translator and His Problems', TS, Enitharmon Papers.

34

'Diverlike Below'

Thanks to marriage and an appropriate round of medication, by the mid-1980s the intermittent dejection that had undermined Gascoyne's self-confidence for three decades was largely a thing of the past. In February 1981, with Judy at his side, he was back in the States. An invitation to perform at the City Lights Bookshop in San Francisco had been a boon of the latest of the Cambridge festivals, and David had not crossed the Atlantic for thirty years. He had been a nervous and fear-haunted young poet then; he was closer to a celebrity now. Their first ten days involved a stopover in New York where their hosts were the Beats, Ginsberg at their head. Judy was not sure what to make of them en masse, nor they of her. After some inititial misgiving—allayed by the fact that Ginsberg had saved them from a near riot in Ostia two years previously—she concluded that they were 'not very polite' and an unnamed Beat went so far as to address her as 'You stuck up prig'.[1] Gregory Corso offered David some hashish, but—according to Lawrence Ferlinghetti—'his old lady' firmly intervened. A truce was struck after the first few days, as the Gascoynes revelled in the luxury of a Fifth Avenue apartment before moving to the cultured scruffiness of the Chelsea Hotel on West 23rd Street. Gascoyne ribbed the Beats mercilessly at times, since they brought out both his fellow puckishness and his mock solemnity. He had himself photographed in a pork-pie hat, wrapped up against the winter cold; at his side slouched an almost self-effacing Ginsberg, clad in the deceptive respectability of a college scarf and tie. Before a talk at New York University on Surrealism and its influence, Ginsberg impressed Judy with his relative modesty by publicizing the event as 'The Surrealist and the Bumpkin', with himself cast in the bumpkin role.

---

1. Judy Gascoyne, *My Love Affair with Life: A Memoir* (Isle of Wight: Island Books, 2002), 30.

Once back in England, Gascoyne was at his desk daily: translating, reviewing, corresponding. The marriage established its own rituals: social, prandial,
and literary. A regime was established that visitors came to recognize and
respect: it allowed the poet privacy and time to study and write, while making him accessible to the increasing number of people who wished to interview him. As one visiting poet noted, Gascoyne was slow to appear in the
morning. 'He spent an age', remarked Alan Brownjohn after one visit to the
island to read, 'in fact he seemed not to descend the stairs from his bedroom
much before lunchtime.'[2] Gascoyne often retired upstairs again soon after
lunch, descending again for tea, some more talk, a ceremoniously proffered
drinks tray before supper, then an evening meal and a little television. Judy
and David often read to one another in the evenings, making their way by
this means in the first few months through the successive volumes of Proust.
Gascoyne was proud of his wife's ability as a reader, though he could be
waspishly sarcastic about it. Someone once remarked to him that she read
quite beautifully, whereupon he snapped back, 'Yes, and doesn't she know it.'
In several respects he was careful gradually to raise the cultural tone. Used
to catering for a large family, his wife kept him at first on a diet of fish fingers, which at least at weekends were soon replaced by *œufs florentines* or
asparagus and prawn *soufflé*, with plum and apple mouse with Calvados to
follow. At long last, Gascoyne had established a balance between society,
connubiality, and a jealously guarded solitude. As the torrent of typescripts,
letters, journals, and translations that emerged during these years attests, he
required space and time in which to think and to write. In Oxford Street,
downstairs was for talk, upstairs for work. His memories were fascinating to
others, but they relied upon a constant input of relevant reading and related
writing.

It had steadily become apparent that, whatever his personal reservations
about Surrealism as a school of thought, in the eyes of others—in Britain
and in France—he was both an authority on the subject and an indispensable link with a vivid past. Interest in the history of the movement was fast
growing across Europe amongst those too young to remember it, as evi-
denced by the publication in Paris in 1982 of the voluminous *Dictionnaire
général du surréalisme et de ses environs.*[3] On 29 July 1983 Gascoyne wrote to

2. Conversation with Alan Brownjohn, 16 Mar. 2008.
3. (Paris: Presses universitaires de France, 1982).

Alastair Brotchie, who had founded the Atlas Press in London that very year as a vehicle for Surrealist history, culture, and thought:

> I hope to be able during 1984 to complete the translation I have been working on intermittently and bringing out in instalments in various little magazines of Breton and Soupault's *Les Champs magnetiques* of 1919, part 6 of which has just come out in the last issue of *Ambit*. As soon as I have time to spare shall set about the last 30 pages—a short prose piece entitled *Gants Blancs*, then two sets of poems 'Le Pagure Dit', I and II (Le Pagure stumped me for a while: it turned out to mean 'hermit-crab').[4]

Les Champs magnetiques was the kind of text that suited Gascoyne. It was less Surrealist strictly speaking than proto-Surrealist, a product of what in chapter 3 of *A Short Survey* he had once called 'The Period of Sleeping-Fits' ('la période des sommeils'); that molten, excitable period when Dada was about to turn into something more systematic and perhaps straitjacketing: a harvesting of the freely associative processes of the subconscious mind unlimited by ideology or conscious commitment. It was a quirky text that abounded in unexpected turns of thought and phrase (like that zoologically exact 'Pagure': in modern colloquial French a hermit crab is 'bernard l'ermite'). Soupault and Breton had produced the ten-section text during several successive periods of 'automatic writing' some time before they quarrelled, and five years before the first of Breton's defiant manifestos. The work was thus evidence of the Surrealist process rather than the Surrealist cause (and Gascoyne, after all, had never quite abandoned the first even if he had jettisoned affiliation to the second). 'It is from here', Breton had written restrospectively in 1933, 'that Surrealism sets out.'

Breton had died in September 1966, though his widow Elisa continued to occupy their flat in the Rue de la Fontaine. Now 86 and still spry, Philippe Soupault was living out at Auteuil in the Paris suburbs. Gascoyne was one of a tiny band of survivors, and among the British contingent probably the most articulate. Soupault, with whom he remained in contact, had never accepted the political pretensions of Surrealism, though he continued to regard it as a force capable of liberating the human personality on every level. Latterly he had come to regard himself as a 'Surréaliste raté' (a misfiring or damp-squib Surrealist), much in fact as Gascoyne tended to regard himself. Gascoyne's translation became an act of reconciliation,

---

4. David Gascoyne to Alastair Brotchie, 29 July 1983, courtesy of Alastair Brotchie.

enabling him to think back beyond the authoritarian Breton who had expelled him publicly from the movement to the revolutionary leader and superlative writer of French prose who had always insisted, even at the period of his puppeteering pretensions, on absolute freedom of subjective expression as the indispensable source of all art. The *Magnetic Fields* was historically significant for several reasons. First, it represented a root from which both fully fledged Surrealism and a brand of psychoanalysis as practised in France since 1920 had drawn nourishment. 'The psychanalytical operation', wrote Gascoyne in the Introduction to his translation, 'is intended to bring mysteries to light in order to explain them. The purpose of automatic writing is to discover the marvellous, not to fabricate it deliberately.'[5] To that extent the continuing Surrealist tradition made common cause with the brand of highly influential psychoanalysis associated with the name of Jacques Lacan—a younger colleague of Blanche Reverchon some considered to have plagiarized her ideas. By the 1980s, what is more, Lacan's writings were already pervading several spheres of French culture and life, especially literary criticism. There were other aspects of the exercise of which Gascoyne personally might well have felt wary. The manifestations of an erupting subconscious mind included, after all, hallucinations visual and aural, paranoid obessions (which Dalí had made the foundation of his approach): the very phenomena in other words which, during much of the intervening period, had beset Gascoyne in his infirmity. To some extent Gascoyne was investigating through translation the common sources of his art and his one-time malaise.

With the help of a grant from the Elephant Trust, an organization dedicated to fostering Surrealist events and publications formed by Roland Penrose and Lee Miller in 1975 and funded through the sale of Ernst's painting *The Elephant Celebes* to the nation, Gascoyne's translation of *The Magnetic Fields* appeared in 1985, forty copies being signed by Soupault. Gascoyne had provided a sober and scholarly introduction. If Surrealism would remain for him a phase that he had long ago relinquished, the older man was able to recognize its general significance for the culture of the mid-twentieth century. There were other grounds of affinity, as exemplified by that troublesome hermit-crab as it crawled through the translated text: 'It gropes its way forward obtruding a fine pair of stalked eyes. The body in complet

---

5. André Breton and Philippe Soupault, *The Magnetic Fields*, 2nd edn. (London: Atlas Press, 1997), 47.

phosphorous formation remains half way between the day and the tailor's shop. It is connected by delicate telegraphic antennae to the sleep of children. The dummies down there are made of cork. Lifebelts. Those charming codes of polite behaviour are far away.'[6] Secretly subversive and yet alert, this all-seeing crustacean seems to have more than a little in common with the translator himself.

By the mid-1980s therefore, Gascoyne was among the leading world authorities on what had since become a global movement, as well as a living witness to its force. As he accommodated the curiosity of younger people, he relaxed with modest, self-directed humour, into the—for him always slightly suspect—role of survivor and sage. The many essays on Surrealism that Gascoyne published in his sixties and seventies entailed a searching re-estimate, both of the movement as a whole and of its practitioners. Gascoyne was singularly honest, sometimes forthright, about both, since he had ultimately come to regard Surrealism as both a creative force and an incidental blight. In reviewing a raft of Breton republications in 1991, he called attention to 'two emblematic images' epitomizing alternative facets of the personality of the magus of international Surrealism: the great anteater who features in the *ex libris* plate once designed for him by Dalí, and and knight errant as seen in a silhouette at the beginning of an essay on him by Julien Gracq.[7] The anteater noses out rare titbits from every corner: he is an eclectic. Meanwhile, the knight rides into battle.

For Gascoyne Surrealism had in its time been both method and a cause. In his critical writings of the 1980s and 1990s, it is the method—or rather methods—Gascoyne champions. He had been fascinated by the varieties of modern art since his precocious magazine articles of 1934. Now he revelled in this wealth: Ernst's bird paintings and his *frottages, grattages,* and decalcomania; Man Ray's rayogrammes, erotic female torsos, and fashion spreads; Apollinaire's *Calligrammes,* Duchamp's *objets trouvés,* his smashable glass exhibits; Picabia's early experiments with *tachisme,* his middle-period instantism, even his latter-day postcard kitsch. In the journalism Gascoyne poured out during this last and surprising period of hyperactivity, appreciation of this stylistic range is interspersed with recollection, gossip, and bons mots. The mystical sage is put on hold as he gives himself over to

6. Ibid. 117.
7. David Gascoyne, 'Alchemist of the Spirit: Breton's Esoteric Treasure Hunt', *Times Literary Supplement,* 23 Aug. 1991, pp. 14–15; *Selected Prose,* 446–54.

appreciation, his oldest and most reliable gift. There are moments in these articles, many written for the *Times Literary Supplement*, when he merits a plaudit paid in one of them to the elderly Gabrielle Buffet, as possessing 'a Voltairean spirit, sophisticated, tolerant and shrewd'. The tolerance and respect are especially notable in the case of Breton, whose philosophy of life he connects less with a desire to exercise control than with the omnivorous visual appetite apparent on the shelves of the Rue de la Fontaine apartment when he had first visited him there in 1933: its collection of 'paintings, drawings, carvings, objects, cases of butterflies . . . all arranged in such a way as to make their complementarity apparent'. Surrealism was abundance.

Gascoyne's mind had itself become equally miscellaneous and rich, its wealth sometimes hard to contain. Often, and to his own express annoyance, his mind spiralled off in a multiude of directions as it hunted after a menagerie of thought. Invited to speak at the Centre Pompidou on the work of Fondane, he feared—coining an adverb in a letter to Jordis—speaking 'trop vite et trop verbeusement', too quickly and verbosely.[8] As a result, he almost always scripted his talks. When speaking impromptu he would on occasions lunge in one direction after another, indulging each memory or insight as it occurred to him. Sometimes when writing he would allow every passing thought elbow room, giving rise to parentheses that threatened to capsize his sentences. In October 1983, I commissioned from him a brief seventieth birthday *hommage* to his old friend Barker; what arrived was a sprawling and magnificent essay that invited the pruning-hook (indeed, in his accompanying letter, he positively requested its use, confessing that the editorial faculty had long since deserted him).[9] At the *Times Literary Supplement* a succession of editors and subeditors found ample use for the blue pencil as they carved manageable essays from mounds of delectable prose, disentangling the main line of argument from a welter of subsidiary clauses. He was humbly aware of all of this, and the effort put in was invariably worthwhile.

In Paris Jordis was translating his journals, uncovering for French readers an intimate and personal perspective on a phase of their cultural history that, for most people living, had been consigned to the history books. She was helped by the fact that, shortly after the publication in England of the *Journal 1936–1937*, a third diary had come to light covering Gascoyne's early wartime experience, including his involvement with *Horizon* and his

---

8. David Gascoyne to Christine Jordis, 20 Dec. 1979, courtesy of Christine Jordis.
9. David Gascoyne, 'George Barker at Seventy', *PN Review 31*, 9/5 (1983), 59–60.

activities as a travelling actor. It was thus, and entirely in keeping with the tenor of his early life, that this phase of his self-analysis appeared in print for the first time in French as *Journal de Guerre 1940–1942,* the concluding part of *Journal de Paris et d'ailleurs.* To read these accounts in French was to be made aware of Gascoyne's close affinity with, for example, Baudelaire. To read them at one go was also to be made aware of continuities, not simply between the separate journals, but between the younger and the older man. Often his remarks about his own work seemed far more pertinent to French literature than to English. The only solution to being at the same time a neurotic and a writer, he had declared, was 'de laisser l'écriture devenir symptôme névrotique' ('to let the writing become neurotic symptom'), a remark much in the spirit of Baudelaire's 'j'ai cultivé mon hystérie avec jouissance et terreur'.[10] On other occasions he seemed to be anticipating his old age. In an entry for March 1937 he had recorded his need for solitude, repudiating the vivacious social persona of Antonia White with the words 'Rien à dire contre les Marie, mais, à la longue, je préfère les Marthe' ['The Marys are all very well, but give me the Marthas in the long run'].[11]

All this time, supported by Judy's Martha-like presence, Gascoyne was travelling ever more widely. Between 1981 and 1991 they took on a demanding schedule of tours, at home and abroad. Judy made the arrangements and did all of the driving, as she cajoled her dilatory and sometimes despondent husband into shape, much as his editors commanded his prose. For much of the time, especially in England, they read as a team, sometimes taking turns to perform his work. Their itineraries were extraordinarily ambitious for a man who ten years earlier had scarcely quitted the Slough of Despond, and a woman who previously had hardly left England. Following the renewal of his contact with Durrell, they were often in Sommières. In 1983 they were in Nantes, in 1984 in Bordeaux, then Nancy again, then Lyons, then The Hague where they stayed with David's old friend Salah Stétié, now Lebanese ambassador to the Netherlands. In 1985 they were in Cambridge again, then Milan for the Biello Prize, then on to Venice; in Sepember of that year to Glasgow followed by Iceland, where they read alongside Seamus Heaney; the following March to Corfu via Athens. Gazing back across to the mainland he descried:

10. David Gascoyne, *Journal de Paris et d'ailleurs 1936–1942,* trans. Christine Jordis (Paris: Flammarion, 1984), 324–5, translating *Journal 1937–1939,* 122. Compare Charles Baudelaire, *Journaux intimes,* entry for 23 Jan. 1862.
11. *Journal de Paris et d'ailleurs,* 73–4, trans. *Journal 1936–1937,* 55.

Two facing foreheads, one afforested,
The other sparsely greened as with Greek-hay,
An isthmus vista in between them hazed
By distant fluorescent shimmering
Of drowsy blended colours in which soot
Suffuses violet, peach and ivory.[12]

Then on to the Ninth World Congress of Poets in Florence; then Edinburgh, Belgrade, and Belgium for a colloquium on 'Le Gouffre' (The Void); in 1987 to Lugano for an international conference of PEN; in 1988 to Malmö in Sweden, then Paris again; then Edinburgh.

All of this time Gascoyne's literary reputation was expanding along two complementary fronts. In 1984 the Eliot scholar Bernard Brugière and a committee of French literary academics chose his *Collected Poems* of 1965 as a set text for that year's national *agrégation*, the competition sat by all students intending to teach professionally at universities, in colleges, or in the higher classes of *lycées*.[13] Those students specializing in English were obliged to answer written questions on the book and, in the final viva voce exam, to speak about it before the jury, should they happen to draw this particular title out of a hat. The selection was an honour and a sign of recognition in itself, and made Gascoyne's work familiar to a whole generation of French would-be teachers of English literature. It also involved the Gascoynes in an exhaustive and exhausting series of tours round institutions and departments entering students for the exam. As a result of this, Gascoyne became the subject of sudden and fairly intense academic interest in France. Michel Remy, now teaching at Nantes and an accredited Gascoyne expert, journeyed to Northwood to interview him to provide candidates with annotated answers to pertinent questions. They were published that year as an appendix to Remy's monograph *David Gascoyne, ou l'urgence de l'inexprimé*, the first full-length study of Gascoyne's work.[14] Three years later, curiosity as to his life and work having intensified in the interval, Michèle Duclos of the University of Bordeaux interviewed him for the journal *Cahiers sur la Poésie* in a slighly more personal style. In her opening description she gave an impression of just how his demeanour at the age of 70 came across to

12. 'A Further Frontier Viewed by Corfu, to Lawrence Durrell', *Selected Poems*, 248.
13. Conversation with Christine Jordis, 12 Aug. 2009.
14. Michel Remy, *David Gascoyne, ou l'urgence de l'inexprimé* (Nancy: Presses universitaires de Nancy, 1984).

someone newly alive to his life and work, a French intellectual attempting to view him against the backdrop of British literature and life:

> First impression: he is very tall. An expression of suffering in the fold of the mouth, but marked gentleness in his smile, the face framed by white hair. An 'Hebraic' temperament to use Matthew Arnold's terminology; an immense earnestness from which nothing either human or cosmic escapes in his constant endeavour to remain open, to be accessible to others; a tranquil, almost impersonal, detachment from superfluities; a lively sense of humour which however, when annoyed or aggrieved, gathering up the whole power of his existence, can sometimes grow uncontrollably violent.[15]

This academic attention was opportune in several ways. It arrived at a time when academic discourse in France was increasingly dominated by the language of deconstruction, and there was something about Gascoyne's carefully poised antimonies that lent itself peculiarly well to analysis via the style of discourse popularized by the writing of the philosopher Jacques Derrida, on which Remy's study, for instance, had implicity drawn throughout. But the interest in Gascoyne's work was a lot more than simply academic. Moves were afoot to translate the whole corpus of his poetry into French, the first stage of which was a project by François Xavier Jaujard for a team of translators to render the tormented and inward-looking *Poems 1937–1942*.[16] Jaujard was a meticulous if slow-working editor, and the preparation went on throughout the late eighties, with Gascoyne observing its halting progress with affectionate exasperation from the sidelines, and Yves de Bayser dropping sardonic asides on the slowness of the project in his regular missives to the Isle of Wight. In practice, Jaujard did much of the translating himself. Paul le Jaloux took on the opening sequence of religious poems, while Jaujard shared the metaphysical (or metapsychological) poems that followed with de Bayser; de Bayser translated 'Ecce Homo' with the Cambridge academic David Kelley (who in 1982, in his fellow's rooms—a sort of bohemian den across an archway to New Court at Trinity College—had introduced David to Derrida). The poems of a personal nature, as Gascoyne had called them, were rendered by Jaujard, with the exception of 'Apologia' ('only the poem that I can never write is true'),

---

15. Michèle Duclos, Interview with David Gascoyne, *Cahiers sur la Poésie*, 2 (Université de Bordeaux III, 1987), 10.
16. David Gascoyne, *Miserere: Poems 1937–1942 avec un portrait de Jankel Adler et un postface de Robin Skelton* (Paris: Granit Collection du Miroir, 1989).

which fell to Pierre Leyris. De Bayser did most of the 'Poems of Time and Place', and the stanzas to Alban Berg were left in the original. Promised year by year from 1984, *Miserere* was eventually launched at a reading at the Village Voice bookshop in Saint-Germain in 1989, without its dust jacket. Though the promised remainder of the French translation of Gascoyne's poetry was not to appear, the Existentialist meditations in *Miserere* represented, when all was said and done, the enduring kernel of his sensibility and his art.

At home too Gascoyne had become an object of curiosity ranging from the appreciative to the merely impertinent. By now he possessed the allure of the survivor, and nowhere was this truer than on the Isle of Wight, a location habituated to fossils. By the mid-1980s he was a local celebrity, and several poets, such as the Oxford graduate Brian Hinton—later an MBE and curator of the Dimbola Margaret Cameron museum—were drawn to live and work on the island by the aura of distinction his residence bestowed. The island had a flourishing poetry society, the presidency of which Gascoyne was persuaded to accept. The post involved him in an annual round of readings and meetings, but it also exposed him to the attentions of the importunate. Respect was welcome; adulation could be simply tiresome. In the late 1980s an enthusiastic local schoolteacher and poetry aficionado plied him with persistent enquiries about his personal relations with various Surrealists, a subject of which he was by then pretty tired. Short shrift was the only defence. When his tormentor put one further question about his association with Ernst, Gascoyne thundered back, 'Knew Max Ernst? *Knew* him? I had him over the back of a grand piano in 1926.'[17]

As the 1980s advanced, further evidence of Gascoyne's consolidated reputation in Britain was provided, first by Colin T. Benford's *Bibliography* of his work, then by a new *Collected Poems*. The *Bibliography*, issued from Benford's bookshop in Ryde, was intended as a gift on the poet's seventieth birthday.[18] It supplied for scholars and readers a detailed account of five-and-a-half decades of literary activity—books, pamphets, anthologies, anthology contributions, translations, and broadcasts—beginning with the choirboy's verses written in Salisbury in 1929, and ending with Gascoyne's recent poems, interviews, and reviews. It was published too

---

17. Conversation with Robin Ford, 4 June 2009.
18. *David Gascoyne: A Bibliography of His Works (1929–1985)*, compiled by Colin T. Benford (Ryde: Heritage Books, 1986).

early to cover the second *Collected Poems* which OUP had initially thought of as a fresh collection, but which burgeoned into a paperback of new and collected work, prepared by David in Northwood, and then knocked into shape by the New Zealand-born poet Fleur Adcock.[19] Each book gave the lie to the myth that Gascoyne's life had been overshadowed by silence.

Most productively of all, Gascoyne had swum into the ken of a diverse cohort of British writers, each of whom in their way seeking an alternative to the prevailing hegemony of the Movement and the Surrealist group. Stephen Romer, having graduated from Cambridge, had been on a fellowship at Harvard where he had studied prosody under Robert Fitzgerald. One September afternoon he had sat in his Harvard study imagining another poet in a winterbound room: a poet in turn imagining water lilies beyond his icebound windowpane. Both were cunning illusions:

> Except this heart's white face was seen
> Shy mouth pressed by the winter's cold,
> The question what could lilies mean
> That shades the glass with asking, might never be told.
> For he's at work, diverlike below
> The surface leaf, to sift and draw and turn to gold
>
> Between the time to strike a match and blow,
> Once, twice, you catch the spark and fix it,
> Burning beyond belief in a room returning to shadow.

Ten years later the revised poem would appear as 'Nénuphars, Nymphéas' in Romer's collection *Idols*.[20] Dedicated to Gascoyne, it is about craft, concentration, and the ability of art to dispel the tyrannies of place and time by working in the depths of a universal subjective stream.

At every turn Gascoyne seemed to offer an escape from the stultifying parochialism of certain aspects of British culture. The Jersey-born poet Jeremy Reed got to know him in the very late 1970s and immediately recognized a combination of personal affinity and indebtedness to a particular descent: 'his incandescent, powerful visionary poetry', wrote Reed, 'looks back to the tradition of Hölderlin, Baudelaire, Rimbaud, Lautréamont, and forward to the violently juxtaposed images of the French Surrealists.'

---

19. Fleur Adcock to Jacky Simms, 6 Aug. 1986, OUP PB/ED/013460, Box 1788.
20. Stephen Romer, 'Nénuphars, Nymphéas', *Idols* (Oxford University Press, 1986), 45, MS early draft in Beinecke, Box 16, Folder 353.

Gascoyne's work had been in its time 'tempered by his mystico-alchemical readings, and apocalyptically coloured by the 1939–1945 war'.[21] For his part, Gascoyne saw in the much younger poet an heir as much as a disciple, admiring from the outset his 'richness of imaginative range and...maturity of technical control'.[22] When in 1989 Reed brought out a sequence of translations from *Hymns to the Night* by Gascoyne's much-admired Novalis, Gascoyne supplied a biographical introduction very much along the lines of that which fifty years before he had added to his own versions of Hölderlin.[23] At about the same period as Reed, the Hackney-based writer Iain Sinclair, who had studied Gascoyne's writing whilst a student at Trinity College Dublin, met Gascoyne at a joint reading of their work and Reed's at the University of Essex in Colchester. Sinclair, then known as a poet rather than a writer of explorative prose, found in the radiophonic poetry of *Night Thoughts* and the evocative prose of *Opening Day* a topographical-cum-mythological evocation of the city of much relevance to his own work:

> *Opening Day* was full of the kind of tracking shots that you would not have found in the English writing of that time. It was a very French way of reading the city. It was cinematic, and I responded to that. He was also a dreamer and a mystic...I'd used bits and pieces of Rimbaud in the East End in my novel *Whitechapel*, which he responded to very much, as if they belonged to his own period. To him, it seemed like his own writing of the 'thirties. That was our point of contact, the sense of a wanderer, slightly on the edge of derangement, even over the edge. To both of us, the city was a mythical entity, a labyrinth.[24]

On Sunday evenings, when Judy was out at church, Gascoyne would ring Sinclair and discuss the early days of his wanderings around the metropolis. In these conversations two inveterate *flâneurs* were following directions that superficially owed something to what in the 1960s the French Situationists had dubbed 'psychogeography', though in both their cases their visions had just as much in common with those of that other great Londoner, William Blake. At much the same time, another London-obsessed poet, Aidan

21. Jeremy Reed, Introduction to Gascoyne's section of *Conductors of Chaos*, ed. Iain Sinclair (London: Picador, 1996).
22. 'Gascoyne's Choice', a review of Jeremy Reed, *Bleecker Street* (Manchester: Carananet, 1980), *Poetry London/Apple Magazine*, 2 (1982), 72–3.
23. Introduction to Novalis, *Hymns to the Night*, trans. Jeremy Reed (Petersfield: Enitharmon, 1989), 7–18.
24. Conversation with Iain Sinclair, 9 Dec. 2010.

Andrew Dun, drew inspiration from Gascoyne's offbeat view of the capital that would later emerge in his epic *Vale Royal* (1995), evoking the psycho-geography of King's Cross.[25] By the early 1990s it was the young who increasingly turned to Gascoyne as one who held a key opening the—to them—stifling cupboard of the familiar and the dull.

25. Aidan Andrew Dun, *Vale Royal* (London: Goldmark, 1995).

35

'Truth is What is'

New friends thus abounded, but Gascoyne was very grateful for old ones. In France Kathleen Raine's reputation had continued to grow alongside his own. Her opinion of his work remained high; at home, though, they were both aware that poetic fashion has passed them by. There was a need for a new focus, a new philosophy of art to sustain them. In 1979, on returning from the award ceremony for the Prix du Meilleur Livre Étranger, Kathleen Raine had contacted Philip Sherrard, classicist and poet, with whom she had discussed founding a journal in England as a platform for shared ideas and insights. It was Sherrard who had suggested the name *Temenos*, meaning the outer precincts of a Greek temple, to which all, not merely initiates, were allowed access.[1] They joined up with Brian Keeble who ran the Golgonooza Press in Ipswich, a concern like Enitharmon possessing Blakean priorities to go with its Blakean name and demanding graphic design. Keeble was a fine art printer with an understanding of literature and its place in culture in step with Raine's own. The magazine was housed in Raine's home, now at 49 Paultons Square, and Watkins in Cecil Court saw to its distribution. They brought out the first issue in 1981, resolving to publish once a year.

The driving force was Raine's Neoplatonic belief in art as the expression of transcendental ideals, a view she reinforced in an article on Blake in the very first number.[2] The group of artists and seekers surrounding her, contributors to successive issues of *Temenos*, were united in their respect for this guiding principle, but they were richly diverse in the ways in which they expressed it. In the fullness of time they included the composer and convert

1. Philippa Bernard, *No End to Snowdrops: A Biography of Kathleen Raine* (London: Shepheard-Walwyn, 2009), 146.
2. Kathleen Raine, 'Science and the Imagination in William Blake', *Temenos: A Review Dedicated to the Arts and the Imagination*, 1 (1981), 37–58.

to Eastern Orthodoxy John Tavener, the batik artist Thetis Blacker whose work adorned the naves of several English cathedrals, and the Orcadian Catholic poet George Mackay Brown, to whose island home Raine had been writing since the mid-sixties.[3] Alongside them appeared work by the Guyanese novelist Wilson Harris, the Jersey-bred poet, biographer, and performance artist Jeremy Reed, as well as the incumbent Dean of Winchester Michael Stancliffe, who contributed articles on David Jones, an interest he shared with Kathleen. Eventually they would be joined by Charles, Prince of Wales, who was introduced to Raine by another of his mentors, the South African explorer and mystic Laurens Van Der Post and was soon adopted by Kathleen as her very own 'sweet prince'.

Gascoyne had always been a reluctant joiner. He maintained an attitude of empathic distance from *Temenos*, making his commitment to their spiritual quest quite clear, while demurring from some of their declared beliefs. When Duclos asked him about Raine's Neoplatonism, he countered by saying that Raine had got Plato all wrong; the linear descendant of Platonic thought was not Neoplatonism as such: ultimately, it was Hegel.[4] Nonetheless, in July 1979 Gascoyne wrote to Jordis to say that he was translating Yves de Bayser's poetry for 'Kathleen Raine's new review'.[5] He soon became a mainstay of the journal, contributing his 'Prelude to a New Fin-de-Siècle', and several translations from the French of the Polish-Lithuanian poet Oscar Milosz (1877–1939), whose more famous living cousin Czeslaw Milosz, a recent Nobel laureate, both he and Kathleen had met in Paris.[6] He began, however, by setting out his own philosophical pitch in a transcript of an imaginary interview he had intended to give in Ostia two years previously. The non-existent interviewer, a putative and somewhat nosey Italian journalist, became in effect a mouthpiece for Gascoyne's own ideals and self-doubts. For this inquisitive and probing phantom he reiterated the Romantic view of the poet as one committed to Freedom, giving it an individual twist. The enemy of Freedom, he now declared, was fear, though it was important to distinguish between fears of particular eventualities and general anxiety or Dread. Dread was reaction to his old Heideggarian bogie: 'Le

---

3. Maggie Fergusson, *George Mackay Brown: A Life* (London: John Murray, 2006) 181, 206.
4. Michèle Duclos, Interview with David Gascoyne, *Cahiers sur la Poésie*, 2, Numéro Spéciale David Gascoyne (University of Bordeaux III, 1987), 43.
5. David Gascoyne to Christine Jordis, 18 July 1979, courtesy of Christine Jordis.
6. 'Prelude to the New Fin-de-Siècle', *Temenos*, 2 (1982), 65–7; *Collected Poems* (1988), 221–2. Oscar Milosz, trans. David Gascoyne, 'Unfinished Symphony', 'Canticle of Spring', and 'Psalm of the Morning Star', *Temenos*, 3 (1983), 81–5, 86–8, 88–90.

Gouffre', Nothingness or Emptiness. In essence it was an apprehension of Evil, a subject on which he felt unusually well informed:

> I think I can claim to know what evil is like, and if what we are at present menaced by can conceivably be described as an evil and destructive demiurge, then I dare say...that I have experienced evidence of the existence of some such force intimately and directly, this experience being a factual one, however 'merely subjective'. I do not understand this force. My own experience of it might seem to suggest that I am liable to be tempted into something like manichaeanism; yet I have always fought shy of heresies, at least in theory...What I can state positively is that I have been brought face to face with evil in *myself*; and while I know I cannot exactly be described as a common man, certainly not as a model of normality, I do not regard myself as being at all exceptional in this respect, though perhaps not everyone consciously realises to what extent they are capable of cruelty, violence and destructiveness.[7]

Gascoyne's religion was exceedingly personal—what else would it be?—but it also contained elements of canonical orthodoxy. As he informed his shadowy interviewer, 'I still believe, in fortunately still recurring moments of certain conviction, in the unprecedented occurrence of the Incarnation and in the meaningfulness of the term Resurrection. At the same time...Original Sin and the Fall of Man are undoubted facts to me. The question we seem to be facing, as we enter the "eighties", is whether or not we can collectively come once more to believe in the Redemption.'

Candour and confession had been attributes of Gascoyne since the early journals. The interval of time, the descent into madness and back to clarity, had done nothing to diminish their force. In the winter of 1980, a while after the debacle in his Bracknell kitchen, Sebastian Barker went down to Northwood to spend a few days with the Gascoynes. He was accommodated in the bedroom next to that in which David slept alone, divided from the guest room by a thin partition wall:

> Early in the morning, and late at night before I went to bed, I would hear him praying. And that I found deeply moving, because he was obviously sincere, and he was talking to God. It was quite clear to me that this dialogue would go on after he was dead. He wasn't fooling around. He wasn't doing it for effect. He was clearly on his own, and Judy was somewhere else. It was a kind of chanting that made your mind dilate. At that point my feelings for David Gascoyne deepened boundlessly because I realised that the person you encountered when you met him was not by any means all that there was. I also

---

7. David Gascoyne, 'A Kind of Declaration', *Temenos*, 1 (1981), 165–6. *Selected Prose*, 42.

came to understand why my mother loved him, and why she had such a deep regard for his mind, as had my father and many another.[8]

The solitariness of Gascoyne's devotion was a reflection of his temperament and his reading, but it was also a measure of his relative isolation from more conventional faith communities. Nominally he remained an Anglican, but he had read and suffered his own way to religious understanding through an encounter with Christian Existentialism in the persons of Fondane and Chestov, and the pervasive influences of Kierkegaard and Heidegger. Even by the mid-1980s, the Anglican hierarchy in general was loath to acknowledge such an approach. Only once had official Anglicanism taken cognizance of religious existentialism, when in the early 1960s the Cambridge New Testament scholar John Robinson had been appointed suffragan bishop of Woolwich, and shortly afterwards had published a short book discussing the significance to modern life of post-war central European theology. *Honest to God* had patiently explained to parochially minded Anglicans the import of Kierkegaard and Heidegger as it had impacted on the work of the Protestant theologians Paul Tillich and Rudolph Bultmann.[9] The book had, however, caused dismay among congregations brought up on a diet of muscular Christianity and parish breakfasts. Denied all further ecclesiastical preferment, Robinson had returned to lick his wounds in Cambridge, and Christian Existentialism had died a quiet death in England.

This had not prevented the Anglican establishment attempting to gather the mavericks into the fold. Back in the Isle of Wight, Judy was a robustly enthusiastic member of the congregation of St John's, the twelfth-century church down in the village. Gascoyne by and large kept back from full participation, his spirituality always having had as much in common with the Kabbalah as with the Prayer Book. 'As a goy,' he wrote in 1984 to the intellectual and journalist Clive Sinclair, 'I have long been convinced that Judaism contains an element absolutely essential to non-Jews' understanding of their own beliefs and present situation.' In the same year he prepared for the *Jewish Chronicle* an appreciation of the ecumenism in Martin Buber's writings, only to find the paper's general editor wary of so inclusive and high-flown a project.[10] Despite such reverses, Gascoyne persisted in presenting

8. Interview with Sebastian Barker, 24 June 2010.
9. John A. T. Robinson, *Honest to God* (London: SCM, 1963), 35, 47, 56, 59.
10. Clive Sinclair to Robert Fraser, 19 Feb. 2008; David Gascoyne to Clive Sinclair, 20 Feb. and 15 Mar. 1984. Courtesy of Clive Sinclair.

himself as a man of faith, though sometimes—as Judy herself occasionally conceded—it was a little difficult to tell exactly in *what*. His old friend Robin Waterfield was now back from Iran, where he had spent two decades building up a network of Christian bookshops, and had settled in Oxford, setting up an antiquarian bookselling business specializing in theology, at first near the city's railway station, then in the high street. Robin's erudite piety was far more conventional than Gascoyne's could ever be, but the two of them communicated across a common plateau of intelligent, well-read wonderment. Their letters to one another were full of affectionate rapport and mild reproof for positions with which both disagreed. 'Do you still see Dame Iris [Murdoch] from time to time?' Gascoyne enquired in a characteristic letter. 'I read the review in yesterday's *Independent on Sunday* of what sounds like an intimidating opus of hers disposing of God and Metaphysics very thoroughly, if not exclusively. I do not intend to read it, but wonder how she personally regards faith: as delusion, self-deception or exceptionally good fortune.'[11]

By the mid-1980s the Established Church, in the midst of Robert Runcie's liberal arch-episcopate, was lurching from mild crisis to crisis only slightly less mild.[12] Already in trouble with Margaret Thatcher for his failure to celebrate victory in the Falklands War in jingoistic style, Runcie had married Prince Charles to Lady Diana Spencer despite personal reservations about their suitability for one another, and the tendency of her eyes to glaze over in boredom when he explained to her the Christian teaching on matrimony. In an effort at outreach, he had appointed Terry Waite to liaise with the wider Anglican community, both at home and worldwide. In February 1984 he sought to involve the artistic fraternity in the Church's ongoing process of liturgical reform by convening a lunch at Lambeth Palace to which he invited six rare birds among the flock of contemporary British poets who could be described as in some sense 'religious'. These included Anne Ridler, Eliot's one-time secretary, now married to the Printer to the University of Oxford and a devotional poet in her own right, and Gascoyne himself.[13] Judy drove him along to the event, but was excluded from the guest list at lunch because she was not a poet. She ate downstairs in the kitchen with Waite, who seemed glad of the company. 'He made me cup-a-

---

11. David Gascoyne to Robin Waterfield, 12 Dec. 1992, Waterfield Papers, BL.
12. See Humphrey Carpenter, *Robert Runcie: The Reluctant Archbishop* (London: Hodder and Staughton, 1996).
13. Judy Gascoyne to Robin Waterfield, 7 Mar. 1984, misdated as '1983', Waterfield Papers, BL.

soup and we had bread and cheese,' she later recalled. 'One thing he said that amused me was "It's a question of Poets and peasants: Poets upstairs and peasants downstairs." '[14] At about four Terry sloped off 'to try and free some hostages in Beirut', so she boldly walked upstairs, knocked on the door of the dining room, and entered to discover an atmosphere of hushed and embarrassed constraint. 'I must say Runcie seemed relieved to see me. He sat me down with tea and cakes and asked "Why didn't you come in *before*? What do *you* think that poets could do for the liturgy?" So I said "Well, I don't really know. I leave that to the poets." '[15]

That night they were accommodated in the Palace guest house by its warden, Ross Hook, retired bishop of Bradford and, as Judy wrote gleefully to the Waterfields, 'his very charming and intelligent wife Ruth. David said she had a real grasp of what he wanted to say about Chestov. They got on splendidly!' They were joined for supper by Canon Anthony Harvey from Westminster Abbey and his wife Julian. The upshot was an agreement that, when they were next in town, they would stay with their new ecclesiastical friends at 3 Little Cloister, next door to the Abbey. Judy was delighted at this turn of events, enthusing in her diary 'one good thing always leads to another'. David, however, was well aware how such hobnobbing with the Establishment might seem in the eyes of his more radical young friends. The invitation was not taken up until 24 May, when David was due to read with Kathleen at the Poetry Society. On the 10th he wrote in some embarrassment to Alastair Brotchie, for whom he was preparing his translation of *Les Champs magnétiques*: 'It may seem rather odd, even scandalously unorthodox, for a one-time Surrealist, but my wife and I have been befriended by a Canon of Westminster Abbey, and we shall be staying with them this time.' But the poets and liturgy scheme proved a predictably Runcie-like damp squib. 'Nothing much came of it', as even the normally upbeat Judy confessed. In any case, Gascoyne's fundamental wariness of all kinds of alignment rendered his part in it unlikely. And though his poetry continued to be read in churches for seasonal or festal use—*Miserere*, for example, made a perfect Passiontide sequence—the very notion of his writing or even making recommendations for weekly worship had always been slightly preposterous.

14. Judy Gascoyne, *My Love Affair with Life* (Isle of Wight: Island Books, 2002), 42, where the visit is misdated as '1985'.
15. Interview with Judy Gascoyne, 2 June 2008.

Gascoyne had therefore not signed up to the Establishment, however liberal, nor had he made the fundamental mistake of so many Romantic or post-Romantic poets from Wordsworth to Auden of turning himself into one of literature's grand and grumbly old men. Very much to the contrary, the ideological drift of the time had confirmed him as 'a convinced and unrepentant socialist';[16] in so many ways the 1980s with their strikes, lock-outs, and continuing cold war seemed a rerun of the worst days of the 1930s. In this context, old work and deeply held attitudes possessed a new relevance. In this connection he was far more drawn to *Temenos* than to any conventional Church: ecumenical almost by definition, open—as Raine saw it—to all seekers after truth, whatever their creed or persuasion. Early in the new decade she had introduced Gascoyne to Satish Kumar, a former Jainist monk who had settled in north Devon, where since 1973 he had edited the journal *Resurgence* as a vehicle for ecology, alternative education, spirituality, and sustainable development. Kumar was a man after Gascoyne's own heart—a cheery warrior for purity and 'elegant simplicity' in an increasingly complex technological world. In early youth he had walked the roads of India clad in little more than Gandhian idealism and an unstitched white robe, dependent on the goodwill and charity of others. The beliefs supporting his multifarious activities were at one and the same time profoundly traditional and searchingly modern. His assumption of the editorship of *Resurgence* had occurred in the year of an influential collection of essays by the Galbraithian economist E. F. Schumacher entitled *Small is Beautiful*. Schumacher's reaction against capitalist excess or 'enoughness' had since been reinforced by alarm at the emerging monetarism and strident economies of scale of the new Tory government and its philosophical fathers Enoch Powell and Keith Joseph. In 1982 Kumar founded in the village of Hartland 'The Small School' for pupils between the ages of 11 and 16, whose parents wished their children to be educated locally rather than in a large urban comprehensive. In 1986, to help finance it, he commissioned seventeen poets associated with *Temenos* to contribute to an illustrated anthology, *Learning by Heart*. Since each one of them had been educated at a small, provincial school, they were asked to describe the experience. Raine evoked 'times tables in Northumberland', Reed his schooldays in Jersey, R. S. Thomas juvenile courting in Wales, George Mackay Brown recalled skirting the

---

16. *Temenos*, 1 (1981), 157.

harbour side in Stromness to enter a morning classroom 'amid twenty whispers'.

In February 1985 Gascoyne had taken Judy along to look at his choir school: 'David and I lunched at Salisbury yesterday,' she reported back to Robin Waterfield, 'and then had a good look around the Close and Cathedral, so beautiful in the early spring sunshine.'[17] For Kumar he now wrote about schooldays there beneath 'the tallest spire in England' and the watchful eye and ear of Walter Alcock. Since the poem was about discipline, he wrote it as a sestina, among the more demanding of forms because, though unrhymed, it offers the poet only six possible end words for each line, which occur in a different order in each six-lined stanza, with the optional extra of a three-line concluding envoi. The challenge was to maintain variety while ringing the changes on this limited menu of verbal choice, not unlike the variety attained by the skilful pointing of a psalm text as sung to Anglican chant. 'A Sarum Sestina' was a strict poem about rules:

> Grubby and trivial though our schoolboy lives
> Were as all are, we found in singing
> That liberation and delight result from lessons.
> Under the ageless aegis of the spire
> Seasonal feasts were ever-renewed games.
> Box-hedges, limes and lawns line Sarum Close.
>
> Choristers in that Close lead lucky lives.
> They are taught by a spire and learn through singing
> That hard lessons can be enjoyed like games.[18]

In November 1986, one month after Gascoyne's seventieth birthday, he and Judy decided to visit Kumar in Ford House, his cottage on a cliff top near Bideford, setting off early one morning in Judy's Skoda. It was Remembrance Sunday and, as they drove north from Plymouth, the car radio was on. David had last set eyes on Plymouth in April 1941 during the weeks in which *Horizon* was evacuated to South Devon shortly after the raids that had laid waste the docks and the church. The memory caused in him a spurt of residual anxiety about convoys or spies lurking among the dunes. Shortly before eleven o'clock they reached Launceston and the radio picked up the

17. Judy Gascoyne to Robin Waterfield, 2 Feb. 1985, Waterfield Papers, BL.
18. David Gascoyne, 'A Sarum Sestina', *Learning By Heart*, anthology ed. Satish Kumar with drawings by Truda Lane (Bideford, Devon: The Small School, 1986), unpaginated. *Collected Poems* (1988), 225–6.

strains of a military brass band in distant Whitehall as it broke into the sombre strains of Elgar's 'Nimrod'. It set off in Gascoyne a mental sepia snap of
himself aged 3 years and 1 month standing in the doorway of the house in
Bournemouth holding on to Win's hand as they listened to the very first
Remembrance Day service in November 1919. The recollection, the tune,
and the autumnal countryside around them then blended in his mind with
the words of the fourteenth-century North Yorkshire 'Lyke Wake Dirge',
included in his projected anthology *Emblems and Allegories* in the 1940s, and
revived in the popular mind by several folk groups in the 1960s: 'When thoo
frae hence away art passed | Ivvery neet an' all, | Ti Whinny Moor thoo comes
at last, | And Christ tak up thy saul.' As soon as they reached Kumar's house
near Hartland Point, Gascoyne got out of the car and asked his host to be
left alone for a while to pursue an idea surging through his mind. 'November
in Devon', a preparation for his own death, is the most accomplished of his
later poems:

> Now I know that to Whinny-moor
> Before long I shall come, as one more year
> Declines towards departure in deceptive calm.[19]

Soon Gascoyne was contributing essays on ecological themes to *Resurgence*,[20]
and extending his interests in animal preservation by penning a tribute to
the threatened world whale and dolphin population for the Greenpeace
Foundation. What stirred Gascoyne in the plight of dolphins in particular
was their possible kinship with the species bent on exterminating them:
from the late 1950s several attempts had been made in the United States to
construe the whistles and clicks articulated by this most enigmatic of marine
mammals as a linguistic system. If successful, these investigations would put
paid to the Chomskean notion of the human uniqueness of language. Such
a possibility reinforced the dolphin's mythic power as a symbol of playful
innocence, victim of the worst instincts of man. Here was yet more evidence of a decline from Grace:

> We've been turned out of Paradise; we've made the world
> into a shambles and a slaughter-house; we've lost
> the primal *Urspräch* which may once have been
> also an aid in our communion with the beasts
> we now exploit and prey upon. Polluted earth,

19. 'November in Devon', *Collected Poems* (1988), 229.
20. See esp. 'Long Live The Weeds', *Resurgence*, 124 (Sept./Oct. 1989), 6–8.

> polluted souls: Now finally, perhaps too late,
> we try to care, if not Pray, for some Salvation.[21]

Kumar's magazine had an ethical charge Gascoyne deeply respected, making it a natural setting for expressions of ruthless honesty or occasional confession. It was in *Resurgence*, for example, that he chose to publish the text of a radio play first broadcast on BBC Radio 3 in November 1985 depicting his harrowing but instructive incarceration in Horton. *Self-Discharged* was a first-person dramatization of those fraught months. Completely free of sentimentality, self-pity, or opportunistic indignation at his treatment, it was also a kind of declaration, and a meditation on madness as a useful coming to terms with personal demons.[22] If, as he had told the readers of *Temenos*, he had become acquainted with evil and chaos within himself, it was then that he had learned these sobering lessons. The play offered him the opportunity to air these thoughts: it also reflected the attitude of candid self-scrutiny that had come to dominate his view of the past, all the more possible because he was now able to contemplate these episodes from a position of comparative calm. Publication in *Resurgence* emphasized the frankness, all the more so since the text resisted the temptation to turn the exercise into a fashionable protest against psychiatric care of the sort epitomized two decades previously by Miloš Forman's 1975 film *One Flew Over The Cuckoo's Nest*, in which all of the doctors and nurses in an Oregon psychiatric institution had been portrayed as monsters, and all of the patients as victims. Nor had Gascoyne espoused the still widely credited doctrine of the Scottish psychiatrist and radical R. D. Laing that psychosis was a superior vein of sanity an uncomprehending society was determined to suppress. Instead, Gascoyne depicted his fellow patients with clarity and charity, the doctors with distant understanding, and his own predicament with wry humour. Madness was still madness, and a cure still a cure. Soon enough it was translated into French by Michèle Duclos as *Quitus*, a title with multifarious meanings and resounding with half echoes, since in medieval Latin a *quietus* is a discharge from debt (as in the phrase 'quietus est', he has paid), and the word furthermore obliquely suggested Hamlet's dilemma as to whether to 'his quietus make with a bare bodkin'.[23]

21. 'Whales and Dolphins: A Poem for the Greenpeace Foundation', *Collected Poems* (1988), 220.
22. 'Self-Discharged', broadcast on BBC Radio 3, 21 Nov. 1985 at 9.30 p.m.; *Resurgence*, 115 (Mar./ Apr. 1986), 20–5; *Selected Prose*, 215–27.
23. 'Quitus' in *Exploration*, trans. and pref. Michèle Duclos (Bordeaux: Dufourg-Tandrup, 1992), 43–68.

Gascoyne was equally forthright in his comments on the contemporary political scene. In 1982 Michel Remy had unearthed from one of his note-books a film script from 1936 entitled 'The Wrong Procession'. It was a classic Surrealist experiment, full of the sort of disjointed connections between images and scenes found in the work of Luis Buñuel, spiced with undeniable burlesque. Autobiographically, it drew on Gascoyne's experience of street violence such as the mob clashes he had observed at close quarters in Cable Street in the East End. The message had originally concerned the disruptive effects of Fascism on the fabric of social life, even in places remote from the conflict. However, as Duclos had recently noted, Gascoyne retained a capacity for timely anger. In 1984 he reworked the script to make the parallels with Margaret Thatcher's Britain quite clear.[24] Renamed 'Procession to the Private Sector', it was intended to feature 1930s footage and newsreel shots of scuffles as seen every evening during TV coverage of that year's miners' strike against the closure of pits in Nottinghamshire, Yorkshire, and South Wales. In 1998 Sean Street recognized its potential as a 'film for radio', and the BBC director Julian May cast Simon Callow as a camera aurally describing what it sees. The result was an acoustic representation of an essentially visual medium, the clinical detachment of the speaking lens as it cut between each disturbing manifestation and the next heightened by the grandiose tenderness with which Callow read its soliloquizing lines. Since two periods were brought together in the minds of listeners, the cumulative effect was of interpenetration, but oddly too of stillness. The broadcast fin-ished as it had begun with a high-pitched whistle reminiscent of a steam train passing through a station, against which Gascoyne had instructed an actor to read a quotation from Wittgenstein's *Philosophical Remarks* compar-ing ideas of temporal succession to a film rushing though the bracket of a projector. The quote questioned facile notions of the present as distinct from past and future. The present in that superficial and fleeting sense, implied the revised scenario, does not exist.

Then the voice recited the climactic moment of Nietzsche's essay 'How the "Real World" at Last Became a Myth' from *The Twilight of the Idols*, in which the abolition of reality is announced: 'the "real world"—an idea no longer of any use, not even a duty any longer—an idea grown useless,

---

24. 'Procession to the Private Sector', first published in Michel Remy, *David Gascoyne, ou l'urgence de l'inexprimé* (Nancy: Presses universitaires de Nancy, 1984), 157–74. Broadcast BBC Radio 3, 13 June 1998. *Selected Prose*, 357–72.

superfluous, consequently a refuted idea—let is abolish it'. With that the 'film for radio' faded out, as if itself a delusion.

Gascoyne could be equally pitiless with the past. It was now half a century, for example, since he had walked up the Rue du Maine with Gala Dalí and delivered the manuscript of his translation of her husband's *The Conquest of the Irrational* to the printers. Gala had died in 1982, long separated from Dalí, who then moved into the Catalan castle of Púbol to be close to her grave. When Dalí died in 1987, some months after a fire had ravaged the castle, Jamie Fergusson at *The Independent* asked Gascoyne for an obituary. In it, like Breton several decades previously, he accused Dalí of abandoning art for commerce: 'Dalí's *Conquest of the Irrational*', he wrote, 'was about to become synonymous with the conquest of the international art market and the media by the most assiduously exhibitionist showman of the century.'[25] That same year Tim McGirk published his iconoclastic life of Gala *Wicked Lady: Salvador Dalí's Muse*, and in reviewing it Gascoyne stressed Gala's deleterious influence, the 'ruination of whatever integrity Dalí had once possessed, and the rapid deterioration of his muse into a hardened mercenary virago'.[26] Gala, he ruefully disclosed, had been referred to behind her back by the younger Surrealists and by exploited art dealers, who nonetheless continued to play along with her game, as 'Gala la gale': 'Scabrous Gala' or 'Gala the itch'.

But in the same piece he evoked some pictures which in 1935 had sat alongside his translation in Levy's New York catalogue. One was the full colour frontispiece *Gala with the Angelus of Millet*, in which Gala the itch or witch sits on a wheelbarrow in front of Millet's painting of a potato-picking husband and wife hearing the angelus bell resounding across the fields, lowering their eyes in silent prayer. The man's hat covers his groin and, so Dalí had impertinently suggested, his sexual arousal.

Among the black-and-white reproductions in the same catalogue had been *Furniture Food* in which an old woman sits with her back to us on a beach, her hollowed-out torso supported by a cleft wooden prop, as fishing smacks loll along the bay. When in 1995 another lost film scenario of the same vintage as *The Wrong Procession* rose like a wraith from the archive, he immediately recognized it as an oneiric variation on this painting. In *History of the Womb or Nine Months' Horror*, based on that disturbing image, an old

25. *The Independent*, 24 Jan. 1989; *Selected Prose*, 255.
26. 'A Mercenary Madonna', *Times Literary Supplement*, 14–21 Apr. 1989, 393; *Selected Prose*, 429.

woman and a boy—probably her son or grandson—wrestle almost to the death, as her face is transformed into that of a snarling hyena. As they tussle, two fishermen in eighteenth-century dress approach in a boat. The boy releases the crone and walks towards them in indifference. The original conception had been full of unresolved anger or angst, possibly even at the cost of the much-loved, now long-departed, Win.

Gascoyne authorized its publication in 1998 with not a word altered.[27] Other twentieth-century poets such as Auden or Mackay Brown had tinkered with their early work in the light of more mellow attitudes. Gascoyne altered, or censored, nothing. He had been through much, he had endured much, but he was in no wise tempted to edit or meddle with the past. As Durrell had once written of his friend's journal on the cruel outbreak of war, 'Truth is what is'.

27. *Selected Prose*, 373–5.

36

The Dream of Gerontius

On a balmy late September evening in the 1990s Judy sat in the back garden at Northwood writing to Robin and Sophie Waterfield in Oxford:

> It is good to start preparing for the next life. But I am much enjoying this one. As I write I am in the garden with the birds singing their heads off, awaiting David's arrival for tea outside. We don't have many days quite alone, and I cherish them. But I am also thankfully aware that David has an enormous number of young admirers, and they often come to see us. How I would love to have a long talk with you about life.[1]

Reconciliation was in the air. When in 1992 all of the journals from the 1930s and 1940s were at last gathered together in one volume in English, Spender read them again and wrote Gascoyne a letter at last acknowledging that at the period in question he had not treated his fellow poet well:

> I won't ask you to forgive me because a) you have done so and b) my asking embarrasses you. Also the situation in relation to myself goes way beyond you and those particular circumstances. I must again and again have had an envious attitude towards people who were worse off than I was. It is the sin of the reviewer. Geoffrey Grigson certainly had plenty of this.[2]

The arrivals and departures continued, as more and more literary pilgrims found their way to Oxford Street. Every morning Judy propped to the right of the front door a large blackboard on which she wrote in chalk a message of personal and frequently rapturous welcome for the guests arriving that day. They came with cassette recorders, cameras, and notebooks, sometimes staying the night, more often than not putting up at local hotels under instruction not to tire an elderly poet who liked to stay upstairs for much of

1. Judy Gascoyne to Robin and Sophie Waterfield, 20 Sept. 1998, Waterfield Papers, BL.
2. Stephen Spender to David Gascoyne, 2 Aug. 1992, Enitharmon Papers.

the morning, came down for lunch, and often retired early. For all that, the reception was always courteous, and very few departed without receiving exactly what they were looking for, be it reminiscences, anecdotes, information, or critical insight.

Among the visitors whose name Judy inscribed on the blackboard in 1993 was a widely read and sympathetically courteous history graduate who was to do more for Gascoyne over the next few years than most. Stephen Stuart-Smith had headed history departments in a couple of Hampshire grammar schools before entering publishing in 1985, working alongside Clodd and developing his own lists and interests before taking over as director of Enitharmon two years later. He shared Clodd's enthusiasms for worthwhile but slightly out-of-the-way contemporary poetry and for fine-book production, and he was becoming ever busier as more and more mainstream London houses turned their back on poetry by living authors, leaving this precarious field to insecurely subsidized specialist presses such as his own. In 1993 Enitharmon launched a series of pamphlets artistically set 'in 10 point Garamond Light' and including in its first year C. H. Sisson, Martyn Crucefix, Norm Sibum, Marius Kociejowski, and Christopher Middleton. Stephen arrived at Northwood in June bearing champagne and copies of the latest publication: David's translations from Oscar Milosz, some of which had earlier appeared in *Temenos*. The translations were as lean and keen as Gascoyne himself:

> The garden descends towards the sea. Poor garden,
>   garden without flowers, blind
> Garden. On her bench, an old woman clad
> In glossy mourning, yellowed with the memento
>   and the portrait
> Watches the vessels of time departing.[3]

Stephen was repeatedly drawn back to the island on business, but also to converse with a dignified and much-valued author who retained an omnivorous mental alertness, for all his assorted ills. The old habit of gloom had not altogether departed, and silences would sometimes descend like a weeping cloud. They would invariably lift after a while to let the light through. 'David', Stuart-Smith was later to recall, 'had a formidably well-stocked mind and one of the keenest of intellects. Conversations with him were a

---

3. Originally from *Temenos*, 3. David Gascoyne, *Poems of Milosz* (London: Enitharmon, 1993), 5.

delight and a danger—a delight in that his conversation was spellbinding: a danger only in that few visitors could match the depth of his knowledge and the richness of his reminiscences. Certainly his publisher was hard-pressed to keep up. His memory was crystal clear, his observations brilliant, his stories sometimes implausible but always true. And of course it was part of his modesty and courtesy that he assumed you understood every reference, every aside. David was never boastful, never name-dropping to impress, and he was a rarity among great writers, in always being interested in the person he was talking to. A conversation with him was an interchange of views, not a monologue.'[4]

A second visitor of consequence in February 1994 was a tall, sharp-witted north-countryman, a Durham modern languages graduate who after three decades teaching Spanish and English in a Northumberland comprehensive school had decided in his late fifties to write a doctorate on Gascoyne's early work. Roger Scott was not alone in this ambition, but he was by far the most resourceful and determined among those who undertook it. He had first been drawn to Gascoyne's verse at school when he had encountered in an anthology the lines 'The granite organ in the crypt | Resounds with rising thunder through the blood' from *Hölderlin's Madness*. He had been 'hooked'. He now realized just how much of Gascoyne's work lay sequestered in libraries around the world, principally the British Library and the Beinecke manuscript collection in Yale, and how much of it was almost forgotten to its author. As he burrowed through chaotically organized notebooks, many of them written in green ink by Gascoyne's seldom resting fountain pen, plays, poems, essays, film scripts, and drafts of letters sent and unsent came to light, along with the entire text of the 1937 novella *April*. As Scott continued to scour the archive, the full extent of Gascoyne's early productivity emerged, fuelled as it had been by a bipolar temperament alternating between phases of manic activity and dolorous prostration. The mania had yielded the poetry, essays, and the plays: long and meditative journal entries stood witness to the depth and self-appraising intelligence of the dejection, and to its human cost.

Not everybody was consistently impressed. By the late 1980s Stephen Romer had finished writing his thesis on Eliot and the French and had found a permanent lecturing post at the University of Tours. He was married

---

4. 'Address for David Gascoyne's funeral by Stephen Stuart-Smith', Thursday, 6 Dec. 2001, reprod. in Judy Gascoyne, *My Love Affair with Life* (Isle of Wight: Island Books, 2002), 129–32.

with a son, and was busy building the foundations of an academic and writing career. By now he had spent almost a decade looking up to Gascoyne's example: the poems, the wide-ranging imagination, and, since 1978, the published diaries. In the mid-1980s he handed a copy of the much-admired, Kierkegaard-influenced, Paris journal to the poet and organist Keith Bosley, expecting him as a translator of Jouve and Mallarmé to be as affected as he had himself been when first encountering it. To his astonishment his friend burst into peals of derisive laughter after a few pages, gasping 'You can tell what's wrong with this fellow. Nobody ever blew his raspberry.' Romer had not thought Gascoyne could provoke such mirth, but on rereading this introspective document with something of the scepticism Charles Monteith had brought to it ten years earlier, he discovered an aspect of it that was newly disconcerting: the splendour and misery of a young man's 'almost willed descent into despair'. This was not a mood which Romer wished to indulge in himself at this stage in his life. He had experienced his own forlorn moments, and whilst pursuing graduate studies at Harvard had once suffered a mild nervous collapse. He had pulled himself out of this slough. For the next ten years he would learn to regard these once-admired diaries, productions as they were of a 'superb adolescent', as an 'almost forbidden book'.[5]

The impression of perpetual gloom was misplaced in several respects. Gascoyne's sense of humour may have been drowned out by his Existential despair during the late 1930s, but it had always been subtly present, as Priaulx Rainier had noted when after accompanying him to the Wigmore Hall in 1944 to hear a performance of Britten's cantata *Rejoice in the Lamb*, he 'launched into a volley of wordplay around Christopher Smart's text'.[6] Half a century later, he and Judy named their domestic cat after Kit Smart's Jeoffry, a rueful joke partly at asylum-dwelling Smart's, and partly at the asylum veteran Gascoyne's, expense. Stuart-Smith was to compare David's wit to 'a dry Sancerre', but it had come to be augmented by a developed sense of the absurd, not least in relation to himself and his own history. Someone who brought out this vein of drollery in him was the art historian Mel Gooding, one of the very few friends who could keep up with his scope of reference and cultural allusion. In March 1991 Gooding travelled down to Northwood to record a couple

---

5. Interview with Stephen Romer, Amboise, 13 Aug. 2009.
6. Priaulx Rainier to Nella Rainier, 7 Oct. 1944, quoted in June Opie, '*Come and Listen to the Stars Singing': A Pictorial Biography* (Penzance: Alan Hodge, 1988), 31–4.

of days of interviews for the British Library sound archive's series on Artists' Lives. Their talk ranged across David's childhood, his first few expeditions to Paris, the war years, and the trials and tribulations of the peace. Understandably, Gooding was curious about his subject's private life, and the direction of his sex drive, or perhaps the lack of it. He was, for example, rather taken with the theory that Florence Mole and Win's friend Tiny must both have been closet lesbians, and that this was the secret to his interviewee's emotional history. Their conversation revealed, not merely Gascoyne's freedom from false *pudeur,* but an absence in him of the faintest shred of vanity, or even of that thin layer of protectiveness most men and women interpose between themselves and the prying eyes of the world. Gascoyne was comically cour-teous, and comically candid as well, but the candour kept on getting in the way of the courtesy, and the courtesy of the candour:

GOODING: Well at that time in Paris you were, in any case... thinking of yourself as homosexual, weren't you?

GASCOYNE: Well, I've always thought of myself as essentially bisexual actually, though really the heterosexual part has not been very successful because... I mean the classic example of being born like that. I mean I've had relationships with women and not been able to go to bed with them successfully because of, you know... that's vice versa I mean. I don't want to go... it would take a complete session of recordings for me to discuss my sex life frankly.

GOODING: Certainly not, but it's something that occurs openly in the Journals; it's not as if we're broaching upon anything that hasn't...

GASCOYNE: No, of course not.

GOODING: ... been touched upon.

GASCOYNE: (*molto crescendo,* as both men endeavour to make themselves heard) I'm perfectly willing to discuss it as frankly as possible. (*Pause of mutual embarrassment*[7])

Judy found him amusing too, especially on occasions when he behaved like a camp parody of himself. She continued to drive him to engagements the length of Britain, not nowadays in the Skoda, which had given up the ghost, but in its replacement, a second-hand Nissan. In July 1992 they were invited to the annual summer garden party at Buckingham Palace. David bought a new suit from Simpsons in Piccadilly for the occasion, and afterwards they stayed in London overnight to watch Simon Callow's production of Sharman Macdonald's *Shades* at the Albery Theatre. On the way back south they called in for tea with Gooding in Barnes. Judy had neglected to fill the tank of the Nissan with water. Halfway down the

7. BL Lives, F1384, Side B.

recently constructed M3, she later recalled, 'we reached boiling point, and the whole car shuddered to a halt. No Automobile Association telephones had been installed on the new stretch of the motorway, so ...I climbed down a very steep slope across a field, and into a nearby house whose owner let me use a telephone...I hurried back to the car to find David had fallen asleep.' The dozing poet was woken by the arrival of a leather-clad AA mechanic on his motorbike, and emerged from the front seat like a wraith, gasping to the figure before him—an emanation of 'the rough trade'—, 'Take me...Take me to a *tea room!*'[8]

Small luxuries, in any case, were more affordable now. The RLF, which had recently received an influx of funds from the literary estates of Somerset Maugham and A. A. Milne, had renewed David's grant every five years, raising it annually from £350 in 1977 to £9,000 in 1999. They were rewarded by a letter of trumpeting gratitude each bountiful July. By the end of the century, helped by a Civil List pension of £2,750 and professional earnings of £1,000, the Gascoynes' yearly income had risen to an unprecedented £15,528. They were still far from affluent, but make-do penury was a thing of the past.[9]

The trips abroad were rarer now. An end-of-year visit to Paris in 1990 enabled them to view the eighteenth-century collections at the Musée Cognacq-Jay in the Marais, where Gascoyne identified the blood-soaked silk flag that had inspired Pierre Jean Jouve's poem 'A une soie'.[10] They managed one last international poetry festival in the Escorial palace near Madrid, before in December 1994 Judy returned late one night after reading on the island's hospital radio to discover David lying in the dark on the dining room floor: he had fallen while trying to put his supper tray on the table, and had fractured his pelvis. 'He was very cold, distressed and in pain.'[11] An ambulance was called and took him to St Mary's hospital outside Newport, where he was operated on the following day. His convalescence proved prolonged and uncomfortable, and he was placed on Luccombe, an orthopaedic ward, over Christmas, with one leg under constant traction. As Christmas turned into New Year with no sign of freedom, depression returned like persistent rain. His plight was intensified by the fact that the hospital's orthopaedic wing faced the gloomy precincts of Parkhurst Prison,

8. Judy Gascoyne, *My Love Affair with Life*, 85. Interview with Jenny Lewis, Oxford, 10 Feb. 2010.
9. RLF Archive, 3806, File 2.
10. David Gascoyne, diary entry for 30 Dec. 1990, Enitharmon Papers.
11. *My Love Affair with Life*, 96.

the searchlights of its perimeter fence clearly visible through the window at night.

Suddenly the world of his public successes seemed very far away. The *Independent on Sunday* devoted a column to his work, and BBC Radio 4 broadcast an hour-long feature, *A Burning Sound*, directed by Sean Street with contributions from Jordis, Judy, Reed, and David's childhood friend Philip Marsh. In February too, whilst he still languished in hospital, he received a letter from the French Embassy in London informing him he had been elected 'Chevalier' in the nation's Ordre des Arts et des Lettres. 'Chevalier' was the least elevated of the order's three ranks: Eliot had been decorated 'Commandeur' in 1960, as would Kathleen Raine in 2000; the actress Jeanne Moreau was 'Officier'. But the recognition did something to buoy him up during the early weeks of March, spent in the drab surround-ings of the Rockwood ward, which was reserved for elderly patients and the chronically disabled. Back in Oxford Street, Judy ordered a chair lift for the stairs and set about agitating 'for David's release'. He was eventually brought back by ambulance on 17 March, but the presentation ceremony for his French award had constantly to be postponed.

The investiture was eventually fixed for 27 June 1996. Before it, in short days at the beginning of that year, Jordis made the complicated journey from Saint-Germain to interview him for *Le Monde*.[12] Thirteen years had elapsed since, in the bistro 'Aux Fins Gourmands' on the boulevard, he had inscribed a book to her with the words 'with, and I really mean it, much love (agape et plus qu'un brin d'eros)'.[13] When she arrived in Northwood, it was cold and dark, and the house, which she had never visited before, seemed unwholesomely cramped and restricting. For the whole of the first day David mumbled in reply to her questions. The following morning he spoke with such grim irony of his recent incarceration in St Mary's that she imagined he must be speaking of his much earlier time in Whitecroft—thus inadvertently absorbing the growing myth that David had spent far more of his life in the island's mental institution than had been the case. A few miles from his home, he told her, stood the three baneful prisons of Parkhurst with their high security areas: 'At night they are ringed by floodlights. With the hospital where I was ill for so long, it is like a concentration camp. The house next door belongs to the prison governor. Hereabouts imprisonment

12. Interview with Christine Jordis, Paris, 12 Aug. 2008.
13. David Gascoyne to Christine Jordis, 13 Jan. 1983, courtesy of Christine Jordis: with 'agape and more than a sprig of eros'.

is a veritable local industry.'[14] For preference he would have chosen a house on the Île Saint-Louis, or a flat overlooking Le Jardin de Luxembourg.

Her article appeared a couple of weeks later in the same issue of *Le Monde des livres* as a feature on the cartoonist Hergé; on the front page Mark Gerson's profile of Gascoyne appeared looking superciliously down its nose at a disguised Tintin fleeing Shanghai from *Le Lotus bleu*. 'The Isle of Wight on the southern coast of England', Jordis observed in her profile, 'is not a place one would associate with someone who in his journal described himself as a blend of fire with ice, and whom his friend Lawrence Durrell called one of the finest and most authentic metaphysical poets of his epoch.' She went on to imply that the solstitial ambiance of 48 Oxford Street with its sickbed sadness and close domesticity had made of it a kind of annex to Parkhurst. It was a tribute to Gascoyne that he could sometimes rise above such circumstances, if only by squibs of irony. It was also to Judy's credit that, when Christine posted the published piece to them, she seemed to enjoy the joke. She was sure she was a liberator, no prison orderly.

For David to travel to Paris to collect his medal was an impossibility, so the ceremony was rescheduled at the Institut Français in South Kensington. They hired a wheelchair from the Red Cross, and David in a brand new blazer with Judy in a Pierre Cardin suit set out very early, arriving at 17 Queensberry Place three hours before the six o'clock start. Stuart-Smith turned up with a pile of Gascoyne's *Selected Verse Translations* that Enitharmon had with foresight brought out in time for the celebration. A hamper appeared from Fortnum and Mason: a characteristic present from Simon Callow. Against the grinding of gears outside and the clicking of cameras within, the Cultural Counsellor Olivier Poivre d'Arvor delivered the citation, expressing the hope that Gascoyne did not feel, as he had once dreaded in his journal, that he had arrived at some 'pantheon devoted to dead visionaries'. He had been a British Gérard de Nerval, a go-between across languages and cultures even—as Soupault had once remarked—'a French poet writing in English'.[15] Poivre d'Arvor then pinned the medal to the lapel of a seated Gascoyne. Polite banter ensued when it was David's turn to reply (Brisk Judy:'Would you care to stand up?'; Unsteady David:'Not really, no'). His throat, he explained, was too constricted by grateful emotion, and his mouth too dry, for him to address them all in French. He went on to prove

14. Christine Jordis,'David Gascoyne, de feu et de glace', *Le Monde des livres*, 8 Mar. 1996, p. v.
15. Taped proceedings of presentation ceremony, Beinecke, Box 19, Folder 393.

Soupault's point. Thirteen years previously, in December 1983, in the depths of the tragic Lebanese Civil War, he had penned a tribute in French to his friend Salah Stétié which had taken as its starting point a sentence from the *Sunday Times*: 'With all that is going on in the Lebanon right now, home might be just about everywhere.' He thereupon read his 'Arbres, Bêtes, Courants d'Eau: Improvisation', which began with his memories of several rivers—the Avon at Fordingbridge, the Thames, the Seine, the Medina on the Isle of Wight—then described the extra-territorial oasis that waters all poetry, 'reverdissante toujours peuplier, pin et cèdre, | oasis outre-lieu de tous nos terrestres'.[16] The 'outre-lieu', though he did not say so, was close to the 'Non-Lieu' of that other exile Fondane, a site of migration and of translation. He ended his address with a coded warning against violence: his translation of Jouve's meditation on that blood-soaked silk flag:

> That which first made my *heart stand still* was the crimson piece; not crimson though, no, rose-red, as of a rose with crushed and dried up petals; yet the rose-blossom red, did I say? not so; but in a sort of anguish verging on lilac, of a graver tone, that exquisite tone that the assassinated victim's blood has acquired at last, the blood of Marat.[17]

Then they gave him champagne for his dry mouth and someone proposed a toast, as Kathleen perched next to him on a couch. During the party Judy took the star-shaped medal with its ribbons off him, and stuffed it in her coat pocket to keep it safe. When they reached the hotel, they found it had tumbled out. They never saw it again.

Thanks largely to Scott's scholarly advocacy and Stuart-Smith's energy and dispatch, the publications kept on coming. Gascoyne's prose had always been pugnaciously lively and honest. The Oxford University Press, his principal publishers since 1965, might well have been approached to collect it, but their list of modern poets had been in jeopardy for some time. On Tuesday, 17 November 1998, Jacquie Simms, who had been David's editor at Oxford since taking over from Jon Stallworthy in 1976, was handed a letter that read 'Your worst fears all confirmed. We are selling off the poetry list by the end of March.' Three days later Gascoyne and the other writers on the list each received a letter headed by the university's coat of arms

---

16. *Cahiers du Désert* (Spa, Belgium: Editions de la Louvre), 'numéro spécial consacré a Salah Stétié' (Spring 1984): 'continually refreshing poplar, pine and cedar | oasis beyond nation or place'.
17. *Selected Verse Translations*, 98.

making it clear that the Press would be accepting none of their future work. Gascoyne had been touchingly proud of his connection with Oxford, dropping round to visit 'his publisher' whenever he and Judy stayed with her daughter Jenny in a converted pub in Jericho round the corner from the Press. He was disappointed, and Romer—another Oxford poet—furious. The public controversy that followed opened up some revealing fault lines in British cultural life. Peter Porter, whose *Collected Poems* OUP had scheduled for the following February, remarked drily that 'something in Britain is getting more and more frivolous'. Keith Thomas, eminent historian and a senior delegate of OUP, responded at length in the *Times Literary Supplement*, defending the decision on grounds of cost.[18] When a junior arts minister in the recently elected Labour government called the termination of the list 'barbaric' and 'an erosion of standards', OUP's public relations officer replied that for the Press to continue with something that always lost money was 'to invite it to subsidize creative writing, to behave as if it was an outlying department of the Arts Council...Writing poetry is a valuable activity, but it is not an academic one.'

The row laid bare differences in attitude between a subsidized publishing sector used to defending risky investments on grounds of their worth, and a historic institution pledged to defray the costs of an ancient university to which it was answerable, and of which it in effect constituted a department. But several poets were left in the lurch as a result. Some like Romer found shelter with the Manchester-based imprint Carcanet, whose director Michael Schmidt promptly inaugurated the pointedly named 'Carcanet Oxford Poets' to accommodate them. Smaller imprints such as Salt sprang up to serve others. Gascoyne himself was henceforth ever more reliant on Enitharmon, who had long anticipated this state of affairs. It was thus with Enitharmon that his *Selected Prose 1934–1996* appeared in the autumn of 1998. Edited by Scott, the book contained lectures, essays, radio plays, and interviews stretching back to 1934. It manifested the range of Gascoyne's mind, and it implicitly also engaged with the legacy of that troublous phenomenon Modernism, all the more so since Gascoyne, ever suspicious of academic labels, never once used the term. He emerged as learned, discriminating, wry, and far less reverential towards his fellow artists than in these later years his fans tended to be towards him. Typical of the restrained whimsy of several items was an unedited speech, 'Francis Picabia, funny-

18. Keith Thomas, 'The Purpose and the Cost', *Times Literary Supplement*, 5 Feb. 1999.

guy', delivered at the Royal Scottish Academy in Edinburgh in July 1986.[19] Picabia had been a chameleon, opportunist, and pleasure-seeker, as much at home behind the wheel of one of his sports cars or in bed with a succession of women whom he then dumped, as he was behind an easel. He had never properly belonged in the Surrealist camp, and his temporary alliance with the more consistently serious Marcel Duchamp had been a matter of expediency. The canvases of his last phase, featuring voluptuous pin-ups, had savoured in the eyes of many critics of the most vulgar kitsch. Gascoyne had never met Picabia himself, but he had climbed Mont Saint-Victoire with his octogenarian cast-off wife Gabby, in whose company he learned to regard the peccadillos of her runaway husband with affectionate indulgence. Gascoyne presented Picabia as a sort of running joke, alive to the fun of his life and its protean comedy of excess.

Gascoyne could be excessive too. As time went on, his study turned into a dishevelled mess, and Judy encouraged Brian Hinton to come over to help them sort through the books, to reshelve what needed keeping, and to dispose of the rest. During these sessions Gascoyne displayed the full gamut of his moods, sometimes expressing exaggerated grief at the loss of some quite minor item, frequently and self-mockingly sepulchral in tone, sometimes so dismissive towards his guest that the effect seemed to Hinton 'like being swatted, as if I was a fly'. Gascoyne was now amiably humble, now theatrically grand. He pointed to his modest working table and lamented 'Has any poet ever had to endure such a tiny desk?' One day Brian brought with him to help with the reshelving a South Asian undergraduate and poet of striking handsomeness:

> David looked like a worn-out crocodile, very old, very rigid. But when Judy left the room, he started flirting with this young man, started telling us these amazing anecdotes about his homosexual past, twinkling, flirting. As soon as Judy came back into the room, the lid came straight back down. Suddenly he was again the Solemn Old Man of English letters.[20]

The *Selected Prose* consolidated the official image of a Grand Old Man. When Enitharmon sent the 400-page volume to Tours so that Romer could cover it for the *Poetry Review*, Gascoyne's one-time protégé realized he had written off his former idol too lightly. The essays in this intelligently edited tome covered Chestov to Carlyle, Fondane to Van Gogh, Hayter to Ferlinghetti. As

19. *Selected Prose*, 404–26.
20. Interview with Dr Brian Hinton, 3 June 2008.

Romer rapidly inferred, 'there was a considerable body of work here', a strong recommendation for an academic in early middle age still nurturing his own poetic voice. If Gascoyne had sometimes been morose, he had been very far from idle. Romer had not contacted David now for the better part of a decade, but after posting his piece, he determined to make one more visit to the island. When he reached Oxford Street on 5 December 2000 the familiar blackboard was propped by the doorway, with Judy's unmistakable words of personalized welcome. 'I was glad I'd come', he admitted, 'pleased I'd made that last effort, before it was all too late.'

As the months passed and life grew more housebound, Gascoyne derived comfort from the ivy growing outside his bedroom window, ivy 'never sere' as Milton had put it, or as Gascoyne himself had described this particular clump in a new poem, with 'A patch of pale blue behind it suggestive of 'a persistent faint yearning | While the cloud crossing, grey as boredom | Is yet tinged with a flush of residual hope.'[21] He and Judy recalled these lines when in the summer of 1998 they received through the post from Sophie Waterfield a cheering gift in the shape of Herbert's poem 'The Flower':

> And now in age bud again.
> After so many deaths I live and write;
> I once more smell the dew and rain,
> And relish versing. O my only light
> It cannot be
> That I am he
> On whom thy tempests fell all night.[22]

In reply, Judy evoked their quiet life: 'I listen to the World Service during the night. Sometimes the sadness of the world is more than I can bear, so I will take your advice, switch off and think of my many dear friends that I know and love. Your broadminded view of Christianity cheers me! David wants to ring you this evening. In old age, he has become so easy to live with and his constant encouragement to me is a real joy.'[23]

Even now there were professional successes. In May 1998 Callow raced back from Los Angeles, where he had been filming, to record the part of the camera in the revised play *Procession to the Private Sector*, which was duly

21. David Gascoyne, 'Ivy'. MS signed 24 Aug. 1995, sent in a letter from Judy Gascoyne to Sophie Waterfield, n.d., Waterfield Papers, BL.
22. *The Poems of George Herbert*, ed. Helen Gardner (Oxford: Oxford World Classics, 1961), 156.
23. Judy Gascoyne to Robin and Sophie Waterfield, 9 Mar. 1998, Waterfield Papers, BL.

broadcast on Radio 3. There were live readings too, though less frequent now-adays and requiring a new level of practical assistance. Slowly David's eyesight was failing. 'Towards the end,' Hinton noted, 'Judy used to write out the poems he needed to read in extra-large handwriting. They even resorted in the end to what looked like flash cards.' At such gatherings Gascoyne stumbled and he mumbled, but the audiences stayed with him, 'willing him on'.

The falls continued with distressing results: there was a considerable alti-tude from which so tall a man might fall. In November 2001 he fell yet again in the night and, after consultation with doctors, he was moved to Inglefield, a council-funded nursing home in nearby Totland Bay. Judy drove across every day in her latest vehicle, a Ford Fiesta (a lorry had destroyed the Nissan) and, when she could not manage to be there, Hinton, who lived in Totland, took over, sitting with the poet as he dozed. The medical and nursing staff were oblivious of his reputation, and unimpressed by his efforts to enlighten them ('I'm a poet, you know'; 'What kind of books do you write then?'). Inglefield, Hinton recalled, had not always been a home for the elderly: in 1970 the house had been the headquarters of the Isle of Wight Rock Festival in the days when Judy had been a pop fan. Now she was locked in conflict with the Social Services Department, who would not let David go home, explaining that the necessary home help would certainly be too costly: 'I never admired her so much as then,' Hinton told me with evident feeling, 'She was fighting a losing battle on every front, especially with Social Services, but she simply would not give up.'

One day a present arrived. Appropriately enough, it was from Gerard Malanga, American poet, photographer, and former associate of Andy Warhol's who specialized in portraits of rock stars. Malanga wanted to come and do a photo shoot of David, and he had sent an album of his recent work, hoping to interest him in the project. Gascoyne lay in bed, slowly turning over the pages of images as Hinton attended to him in a chair to his side. At times Gascoyne seemed to rally, but at nine on the morn-ing of Sunday, 25 November, the telephone rang in the front room at Oxford Street. Bronchial pneumonia had set in and, after a very uncomfortable night, they were taking him into the Accident and Emergency Department in St Mary's hospital, the place of confinement he had learned to dread during his three months' incarceration there seven years previously. Judy's daughter Jenny drove her over to the hospital outside Newport and, Judy reported in her diary, 'He arrived almost as soon as we did. He looked very pale and his breathing was bad. He didn't wear the oxygen mask because without it he couldn't speak or drink... After two or three hours they decided to take him to the new Medical Centre. He was to be more fully examined before going to a ward.' At four the staff advised the two women to go home and rest. Not long after they opened the front door of 48 Oxford Street they were summoned to St Mary's again. From five until seven that evening Judy sat in the reception area holding David's hand: 'He talked of Paris and asked me to 'phone Christine Jordis.' At seven o'clock they were told he was being admitted to a bed in the cavernous Newport Ward on the top floor of the building: 'It was a long way to get to it, so Jenny pushed me in a wheelchair... David was given the end bed with curtains drawn round us. A nurse persuaded me to ask him to drink some chalky stuff, which he did reluctantly. Through the curtains I could hear husbands moaning to their patient wives. Poor David was breathing in such an exhausted manner. I realized he couldn't continue for long like that... I prayed that he would finally pass away into a peaceful state. While I was praying, his breathing gently became calm, and then all was silent. I gave him a kiss and called the nurse.'[24]

Early the following morning Judy rang Stuart-Smith at Enitharmon, and at six Gascoyne's death was announced on evening bulletins on BBC Radio 3 and 4. On Wednesday the obituaries began to appear, both in England and in France. In its notice *The Times* echoed Gascoyne's own rueful estimate of himself as 'a poet who wrote himself out when young and then went mad', before tracing enough of his personal history to suggest that this had not been the whole story of his long life. In *The Independent* Sebastian Barker declared that he had been 'first and foremost one of the great religious poets of the twentieth century'. In *Le Monde*, Christine Jordis observed that he had been that comparatively rare beast among twentieth-century British writers, 'a poet acquainted with Europe whose mind was impregnated with its culture'. In relating the history of his nervous collapses, she then reiterated an impression that was by now commonplace to the effect that he had endured 'ten years, or very nearly that' of confinement in a mental home, by which she meant Whitecroft. The exaggeration was only to be expected, since the lengthening of his spell there from three months to a decade had become an integral aspect of Gascoyne's personal myth and Judy, careful not to peer too closely into his early medical history, had always maintained that

24. *My Love Affair with Life*, 125.

this had been the case.[25] In his later years, Jordis continued, animadverting to her own visit to Northwood in 1976, Gascoyne had 'lived patiently and quietly by the side of Judy, in his little house on the Isle of Wight, the walls of which did not seem quite strong enough to contain him'. On the same day *Libération* recycled a slightly different version of a recurring half-truth: 'In the 1960s', it confidently summarized, 'Gascoyne stopped writing and sought refuge in an asylum.'

The twelfth-century Norman church of St John the Baptist lies about three-quarters of a mile to the south of suburban Northwood, down the Jane-Austenian-sounding Chawton Lane. At noon on Thursday 6 December, Gascoyne's long coffin was borne up the crowded nave his 'Lines': 'Can even Omega discount | The startling miracle of human song?' After an opening hymn, the Rector gave a short address of welcome from his stall. High in the pulpit, Stuart-Smith delivered a eulogy that opened with the words 'You couldn't possibly invent a life-story like David Gascoyne's. Not even the most fanciful of scriptwriters could devise such a heady mixture of drama, celebrity, romance and survival.' Judy's son Kevin then read the nineteen lines of David's 'Tenebrae'. Judy recited Tennyson's 'Crossing the Bar'. Jenny sang 'Fear no more the heat of the sun' from *Cymbeline* in her keening folk singer's voice. Prayers of deliverance and consolation were offered up. The granite organ sounded forth. Along the brown fields behind the old church, restless birds hovered, dipped, lingered on the bare soil, and again took flight.

25. When I enquired of Brian Hinton how long Gascoyne had been in Whitecroft, he unhesitatingly replied: 'Oh, years, *years.*'

Index

NOTE: Works by David Gascoyne (DG) appear directly under title; works by others under name of author or artist